ALWAYS A PATRICIA
A Veteran Remembers

Other works by Sydney Frost

Once a Patricia (Memoirs of a Junior Infantry Officer in World War II), Vanwell Publishing Limited, St. Catharines, Ontario, Canada, 1988.

A Life Worthwhile, Neptune Publishing Company Limited, Saint John, N.B., Canada, 1994.

ALWAYS A PATRICIA
A Veteran Remembers

by C. Sydney Frost

Borealis Press Ltd.
Ottawa, Canada
2004

Copyright © by C. Sydney Frost, 2004

Published by Borealis Press Ltd.
All rights reserved. No part of this book may
be used or reproduced in any manner whatsoever without
written permission except in the case of brief quotations
embodied in critical articles and reviews.

Canada

The Publishers acknowledge the financial support
of the Government of Canada through the Book Publishing
Industry Development Program (BPIDP)
for our publishing activities.

National Library of Canada Cataloguing in Publication Data

Frost, C. Sydney (Charles Sydney)
    Always a Patricia: a veteran remembers / C. Sydney Frost.

Sequel to Once a Patricia
Includes bibliographical references and index.
ISBN 0-88887-199-6 (bound).—ISBN 0-88887-221-6 (pbk.)

    1. Frost, C. Sydney (Charles Sydney). 2. World War, 1939-1945—Personal narratives, Canadian. 3. World War, 1939-1945—Campaigns—Italy. 4. World War, 1939-1945—Regimental histories—Canada. 5. Canada. Canadian Army—Officers—Biography. 6. Canada. Canadian Army. Princess Patricia's Canadian Light Infantry.
    I. Frost, C. Sydney (Charles Sydney). Once a Patricia. II. Title.

D811.F76 2004   940.54'215   C2003-905695-3

Cover design by Bull's Eye Design, Ottawa
Photographs by author and others

Printed and bound in Canada on acid-free paper

TABLE OF CONTENTS

DEDICATION viii
FOREWORD by the Right Honourable Countess Mountbatten
of Burma, CBE, CD, JP, DL. ix
AUTHOR'S PREFACE. x
INTRODUCTION by Dr. Desmond Morton, Professor
of History at McGill University xiv

SICILY

PREFACE TO THE PILGRIMAGES 1
MAP OF THE SICILIAN OPERATION. 2
CHAPTERS
    I   PILGRIMAGE, 1989. 3
    II   PILGRIMAGE, 1990. 10
    III   PILGRIMAGE, 1991. 27
    IV   PRINCESS LOUISE DRAGOON GUARDS—
           PILGRIMAGE, 1993. 54
    V   PILGRIMAGE, 1994. 59
    VI   PILGRIMAGE, 1997. 69
    VII   VETERANS AFFAIRS, CANADA—
           PILGRIMAGE, 1999. 85
    VIII   PILGRIMAGE, 2000. 100
POSTSCRIPT. 116
PHOTOS 118

TABLE OF CONTENTS

ITALY

PREFACE TO THE PILGRIMAGES 125
MAPS OF THE ITALIAN OPERATION 126
CHAPTERS
    IX   PILGRIMAGE, 1989 133
    X   PILGRIMAGE, 1991 154
    XI   PILGRIMAGE, 1994 169
    XII   PILGRIMAGE, 1997 205
    PHOTOS 216

HOLLAND

PREFACE TO THE PILGRIMAGES 231
MAP OF THE HOLLAND OPERATION 232
CHAPTERS
    XIII   GERMANY, HOLLAND, 1986.............. 253
    XIV   PILGRIMAGE, 1989 263
    XV   PILGRIMAGE, 1990 272
    XVI   APELDOORN, 1995 295
    XVII   PILGRIMAGE, 2000 328

Postscript to Chapter 17, 2000......................... 383

Epilogue I to Chapter 15: The Missing Germans, 1945 390

Epilogue II to Chapter 16: Texel and the Georgians (Russians) 1945 404

Epilogue III to Chapter 17: The Man with Two Hats
The Ottawa Monument May 11th, 2002 412

Epilogue IV to Chapter 17: Beekbergen, Oosterhuizen, Lieren
The Lieren Monument April 17th, 2002 418

PHOTOS 421

CYPRUS

PREFACE..446

CHAPTER

 XVIII   CYPRUS, 1971 448

Epilogue..472

PHOTOS 473

LIST OF MAPS....................................484

CHAPTER NOTES 485

LIST OF PHOTOGRAPHS..........................487

PHOTO CREDITS..................................490

ARMY RANKS 491

MUSICAL SCORES 492

THE ROLL OF HONOUR (with place of burial)..........502

INDEX..533

Dedication

*In memory of all those Patricias who
made the supreme sacrifice.*

FOREWORD

"Once a Patricia"—"Always a Patricia"

When Colonel Sydney Frost wrote the first remarkable story of his wartime experiences as a very young junior officer, "Once a Patricia," he never expected to write a sequel nearly 15 years later—"Always a Patricia"—thus completing the saying of our Regiment, Princess Patricia's Canadian Light Infantry.

He was encouraged to write his second book by the interest his first book evoked, especially among fellow veterans who realized the importance of remembering the valiant wartime endeavours of our soldiers, to ensure the peaceful lives of those at home in the future.

Syd Frost's recent pilgrimage to all the countries in Europe and places where he fought was to honour the memory of those of his fellow soldiers who did not survive and ensure that they are properly and suitably remembered, both in monuments and war cemeteries. A mammoth task undertaken with dedication and real affection.

In this way he is helping to ensure that the dogged determination and courage of those young men in wartime will always be recognised and honoured and never lost in the mist of peacetime.

For this endeavour we owe Sydney Frost a great debt of gratitude and I am proud to think he is one of my fine "Patricia" soldiers. I have learnt to admire them so much during the last nearly 30 years that I have had the honour and pleasure of being their Colonel-in-Chief.
Countess Mountbatten of Burma CBE CD JP DL
Colonel-in-Chief
                        Princess Patricia's Canadian Light Infantry

Mountbatten of Burma

AUTHOR'S PREFACE

This book is a sequel to my earlier book about the PPCLI in WWII—
Once A Patricia.

My new work is divided into four Volumes: Sicily, Italy, Holland and Cyprus, each with its own theme.

Sicily
How it has shaken off the yoke of fascism and is now a prosperous country. And how the citizens of a small town expressed their gratitude to their Canadian Liberators by erecting a Monument to The First Canadian Division.

Italy
How it too has emerged from the chaos of WWII with a strong economy. And how the sacrifice of Canada's soldiers is forever enshrined in War Cemeteries throughout the land that commemorate the almost 6,000 soldiers who gave their lives in the cause of freedom.

Holland
How the Dutch people were delivered from mass starvation by the timely arrival of the Canadian Army. And how Canada's Veterans are revered, remembered and loved by the people of Holland. They will never forget.

Cyprus
How it was my good fortune to visit a Battalion of the Patricias on peacekeeping duties in Cyprus. And how I was able to render a small service to the Battalion in connection with an important parade.

AUTHOR'S PREFACE

My story is told, I believe, from a new perspective—that of a Veteran returning to the battlefields and following the routes taken by the Patricias in Sicily, Italy and Holland during WWII. I made ten such journeys and visited not only the Fields of Honour but also the Fields of Remembrance—20 War Cemeteries, where 312 Patricias are buried.

For too many years the story of the First Division (The Red Patch Devils) in WWII has been shrouded in Canadian reticence, particularly the Italian Campaign. *Always a Patricia* gives that story new meaning.

It should be acknowledged, however, that in recent months the Patricias have become a household word. When I tell people I am (not was) a Patricia, they are impressed and want to know all about this Regiment. "How come they are so famous?" I believe that *Always a Patricia* shows how they got that way. The seeds were sown in WWI; the plant matured in WWII and Korea; the flower blossomed in Afghanistan.

But my tale is not only about war and solemn remembrance. It is also about peace, and embodies the profound changes that have occurred in the countries my fallen comrades helped to liberate. Thanks to their sacrifice and of many others, Sicily, Italy and Holland are free and have regained, and even surpassed, their former estate and influence in the Community of European Nations. Sicily, once a poor, almost barren country, is now the garden of Europe. Italy, despite its fondness for changing Governments, has an economy that at times is second only to Germany. Holland, is again a centre of world trade, commerce and finance.

None of this might ever have come to pass if Hitler's vision of world hegemony had not been challenged and finally overcome by the peoples of many nations, of whom 312 Patricias were a part.

My story also celebrates the deep respect, admiration and gratitude of the citizens of these countries for Canadian Veterans and indeed for Canada itself. Friendships forged in war have been strengthened in peace. These outpourings of affection once prompted a Minister of Veterans Affairs to observe that it was a love story. I would go even further to say it is the love story of the century, if not of all time.

To some, who have little understanding of military ethos, my writings in praise of my Regiment may seem chauvinistic, as if the Patricias were the best unit in the Division, if not the entire Army. While this may be true, I am not advocating such a premise. Every soldier thinks, indeed believes, his Regiment is the best. He is taught this at every stage of his career. It is called *esprit de corps* and is as necessary for morale as food is for the belly.

Likewise, it is not my intention to convey the impression that I was the only soldier who suffered serious wounds and fought long and hard

AUTHOR'S PREFACE

to rejoin my Regiment as soon as possible. It was not a custom peculiar only to the PPCLI. In Italy, every Unit was desperately short of reinforcements all the time.

Neither would I want my reader to conclude that all the accolades, medals and gifts that came my way were given because I had rendered some special service. Every Veteran can attest he received the same kind of recognition. However, perhaps my association with the City of Ispica, Sicily, is an exception, but my service there was due solely to the fortunes of war. It was my good luck to be given the duty of occupying the town and restoring it to some semblance of order. It may be true that I slightly exceeded my mandate by appointing myself Mayor as well as Town Major, but it seemed a necessary step in fulfilling my duties.

The case of Cyprus in 1971, is, of course, another exception. Again, it was a matter of being at the right place at the right time. And, I like to think my duties connected with the Cyprus tour exemplify the meaning of the title of this book—*Always a Patricia*.

To understand fully the significance of this maxim, I am obliged to refer to my prior work *Once a Patricia* published in 1988. The two titles taken together, *Once a Patricia–Always a Patricia*—have long been a saying among the members of the PPCLI, to the point that they are the unofficial motto of the Regiment.

In many ways, my present book is a sequel to my earlier one, but it presented me with a difficult problem. Unlike so many so-called sequels, it cannot stand on its own feet without background knowledge of my earlier book. I was thus faced with the dilemma of either forcing my reader to acquire a copy of *Once a Patricia*, or, supplying the necessary background in my present volume. I chose the latter course.

This does not mean that *Always a Patricia* is simply a rehash of old material with a new cast. The background is either supplied in a Preface, or woven into the main text.

I have stated that my new book is written from a perspective entirely different than other volumes about the War, including, I might add, *Once a Patricia*. In my writing I was not constrained by official records, histories and other books that cover the same material. There are none that apply. My only source of information was my own diaries and voluminous records of my ten Pilgrimages since the War. Four of these Pilgrimages, in 1956, 1975, 1980 and 1985, are described in *Once a Patricia* and are referred to, only incidentally, in my present book. The remaining six journeys are the subject of *Always a Patricia* and faithfully and accurately portray my experiences.

The only liberty I have taken, is to wander sometimes from my wartime trails to visit places not strictly associated with the Regiment's

AUTHOR'S PREFACE

advance, but which are, nevertheless, of interest, in the wider context of the War—places such as Dachau and Hitler's Eagle's Nest. Furthermore, on my many journeys throughout Sicily and Italy I could not pass by famous centres of historic or scenic interest without making a sojourn in each one: beautiful Taormina in Sicily and its neighbouring volcano, Mount Etna; the Island of Stromboli off the north coast of Sicily and its volcano; the picturesque Amalfi Drive and the charming villas of Positano, Ravello and Sorrento; the Bay of Naples with its volcano, Vesuvius, and Pompei; the Island of Elba and Napoleon's temporary palaces; Florence, Pisa and its tilted tower. These are but a few of the places I mention in my book.

In conclusion, I want to express my thanks to Florence Wilson, my legal secretary for many years, who came out of a well-earned retirement to decipher and type my original drafts.

If any errors have crept into my writing, I have only myself to blame.

C. Sydney Frost

INTRODUCTION
Dr. Desmond Morton, Professor of History at McGill University

As a military historian, I am often asked why some soldiers endure terrible harships, enter battle against stronger, better-armed enemies, fight, die and somehow prevail. It's a question that becomes both more theoretical and more poignant as the soldiers who fought Canada's battles, even in their teens, are now old and will soon be gone.

One of these veterans is Colonel Syd Frost. His answer is as good as anyone's and a lot better than I can give. It is bound up in a wonderful book called *Once a Patricia*, and it describes, in the lively, opinionated and highly independent style anyone associates with Syd Frost, how he became an officer in one of Canada's best-known Regiments, Princess Patricia's Canadian Light Infantry.

Always a Patricia not only completes a familiar Regimental slogan, but completes a unique aspect of postwar Canadian life. Like other veterans, Syd Frost swore that he would not forget his comrades who gambled their young lives for their country and their Regiment in Italy and North-west Europe. If he had the chance, his remembrance would be more than a minute's silence on November 11th or lifting an extra beer at the Legion. He would return, when he could, to their battle fields and to the beautiful cemeteries the Commonwealth War Graves Commission maintains for Canada and its allies all around the world.

As Syd Frost makes clear, he was by no means alone in this cause. Indeed, like veterans' organizations, Canada's Department of Veteran's Affairs has given steadily greater priority to commemoration as the number of its clients dwindles. Pilgrimages, which began with the Canadian-liberated Netherlands and the 1984 commemoration of the Allied landing in Normandy on June 6, 1944, eventually got around to including the apparently forgotten Italian campaign. By then, Colonel

INTRODUCTION

Frost had returned to Ispica, Sicily, where as a 21-year old subaltern, he had briefly been Town Major in 1943. Nowhere, on the beach between Ispica and Pachino, could he find even a trace of where the Canadians had begun the liberation of Europe by landing on Sicily on 10 July 1943. Wasn't the first successful assault on Nazi Europe a place to remember? No, said Ottawa, it had built two solid office buildings in Ottawa as its war memorial.

With the charm, shrewdness and steely determination of a true Patricia, Syd Frost led devoted Sicilian allies to cut red tape in Ottawa and Rome. They persuaded the senior citizens of Ispica on the Sicilian coast to locate, build and pay for a substantial monument to the Canadians who had charged ashore at dawn on the summer day in 1943, leaving many Canadians and Italians dead and local homes shattered. The heart-warming story of the first memorial to Canada's role in the liberation of Italy is surpassed only by the story of how a Canadian veteran became the Patron of a comparable monument to the Italians, civilian and military, who died on the same day.

If the centrepiece of this book is a Canadian veteran's long and successful struggle to give endurance to the ideals which took him and his comrades to Italy in 1943, *Always a Patricia* travels as far as his wartime Regiment, to Germany and the Netherlands, and even to Cyprus where Colonel Frost delivered the band of his postwar Regiment, Toronto's Royal Regiment of Canada, to the Patricias to celebrate Canada Day near a Green Line separating Turks and Greeks. The book also clarifies such fascinating historical footnotes as the Soviet Georgians who rose against the Germans on a little Dutch island and fought to the death until the Canadians came.

"Old soldiers fade away," claims a traditional army song, and Syd Frost would be the last to deny it. Syd Frost's latest book reminds us of how much honour, decency, and devotion to Canada we lose as our veterans slip away. Their service never stopped in 1945 but continues here and around the world.

(Desmond Morton is Hiram Mills Professor of History at McGill University, an ex-soldier, and the author of: *A Military History of Canada*, *Understanding Canadian Defence*, *A Short History of Canada*, and other books on Canadian military, political and social history.)

SICILY
Preface To The Pilgrimages

I am standing to attention as the Band plays "O Canada" and the Italian National Anthem. I am surrounded by Canadian and Italian soldiers and veterans of the First Canadian Division.

The date is September 22nd, 1991, and the place is Marza, Sicily, close to the beaches where the PPCLI, as part of the First Canadian Division, came ashore on July 10th, 1943. The citizens of Ispica and Pachino, small towns near the beaches, have erected a Monument to honour the men of the First Canadian Division.

On the monument are inscribed the following words:

> *July 10, 1943. On this day Canada's soldiers of the First Division landed on these shores. From little towns in a far-away land they came in the cause of freedom. Erected to their memory by the citizens of Pachino and Ispica.*

The occasion is the unveiling of the Monument in the presence of Canadian Veterans who are making a Pilgrimage to Italy and Sicily.

On behalf of the PPCLI, I thank the Mayors of Pachino and Ispica and present them with Regimental plaques.

Map Number 1

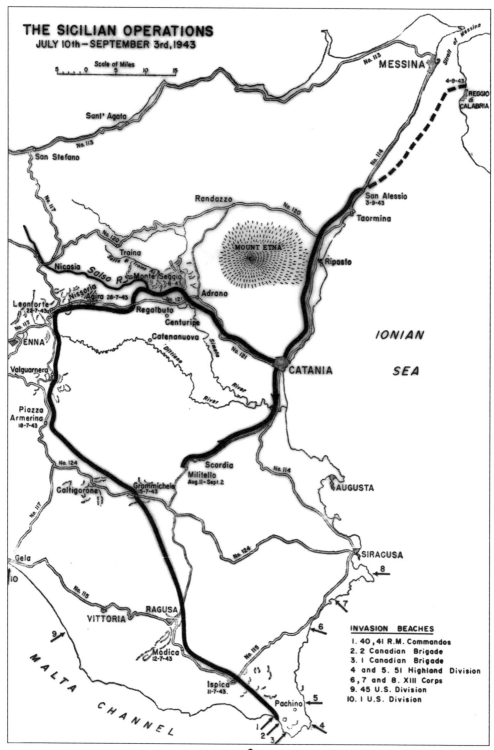

Chapter I

PILGRIMAGE—1989

The story of the building of this Monument begins with a Pilgrimage I made to Sicily in 1989. This Pilgrimage, in turn, had its own genesis in 1988 and that is where my story really begins.

In 1988, I published my book *Once a Patricia*, a memoir of my service with the Princess Patricia's Canadian Light Infantry during World War II. The book also described four Pilgrimages I made after the war to the battlefields and graves of my comrades. After six years of labour, I was quite certain I had written everything within my knowledge or competence about the war.

Then the letters and telephone calls from old comrades, veterans, friends, "arm chair" generals and a host of others began to arrive. Most, I am happy to say, were complimentary about the book; some gave slightly different versions than the stories I had told. But throughout all the correspondence, telephone calls, interviews and reviews, one common thread emerged—"We want more".

On reflection, I realized that there were many gaps in my story, particularly in connection with Sicily where I had served with the Patricias briefly at the end of that campaign. In my four earlier Pilgrimages only one took me to Sicily, in 1956, when my wife came with me. In my book, I frankly admit that this Pilgrimage, which covered some 7,000 miles visiting the battlefields of the Patricias in Italy and Holland, was more like a recce patrol than a full-scale attack. My purpose was to set the stage for subsequent visits and also, of course, to impress my wife with my wartime experiences.

And so I resolved to visit Sicily once more and spend some time examining the beaches where the Patricias came ashore on that memorable day, July 10th, 1943, when the Allies finally landed in Europe. I also felt a deep desire to re-visit the cemetery at Agira where 490

Canadians are buried and sign the Visitors' Register, as I had done in 1956. And, of course, I was keen to return to the little village of Ispica where in 1943, as a twenty-one year old lieutenant, I had been Mayor for nineteen days.

On May 18th, 1989, my plane touched down at the airport in Catania, Sicily. I picked up a car and drove to Taormina, a charming hillside resort on the Ionian Sea, near Mount Etna, where Hammie Gault, the Founder of the Regiment used to spend his holidays. This would be my headquarters while I visited Agira, Ispica and the beaches.

How long had I been away? My last visit was in 1956—33 years! Then, Sicily had not changed very much since the war. Many of the roads were still trails, winding up the sides of mountains to dirty villages perched precariously on top. It had taken me one-and-a-half hours to drive from Catania to Agira, along dusty roads blocked by farmers in Sicilian carts, while their wives plodded along in heavy black garments bearing huge jugs on their heads. They were worn out from the awful war years, and they seemed sullen and depressed. Much of the land was almost a desert.

Now, in 1989, all this had changed. The Sicilians had remembered the principles of irrigation which their ancient Roman forebears had used so effectively. Sicily was now a garden, an oasis, where agriculture flourished. It was known as the granary of Europe, as in ancient times.

Italy's economy was one of the best in Europe, second only to that of Germany. The people were proud, happy, industrious and rich. New construction replaced the hovels I was so familiar with. Autostrade crossed the land. To go from Catania to Agira took only half an hour along the A19. New Mercedes-Benz automobiles, not donkey carts, were now the main hazard.

Visiting the beautiful Cemetery at Agira is always, for me, a very moving experience. It is the only cemetery in World War II that is exclusively Canadian. The white marble headstones set among green foliage and flowers of every hue are carefully cared for by gardeners of the Commonwealth War Graves Commission. Every cemetery has a Visitors' Register and I always make a point of signing my name with, what I hope, is an appropriate comment.

I remembered that in 1956 I had found only a handful of names, and I was interested to see how many visitors had since been drawn to this cemetery, so far removed from the homes of those who lie here. I also wondered what I had written in the Visitors' Register.

Alas, after a careful inspection of the cemetery, I could not locate either caretaker or Register. Deeply disappointed, I drove away, determined to find the answer to the missing register and return as soon as possible. More disappointments awaited me as I continued my Pilgrimage.

The next objective of my mission was the little town of Ispica not far from the beaches where the Patricias landed in July, 1943. But, as always, time was running short. I was beginning to realize that this factor was never going to change. However, I could make a quick visit to nearby Mount Seggio, the scene of my first attack with the Regiment and Leonforte where the Patricias won their first Battle Honour and decorations for bravery. Ispica and the beaches would have to wait until the next day.

It had been 46 years since I first scaled Mount Seggio to the very top. Luck had been with us and my platoon had not suffered any casualties. Our only enemy had been the intense heat—a searing 110 degrees. During my 1956 Pilgrimage the heat seemed even more oppressive and I passed up the opportunity to climb the brute. Now, it was 1989 and I decided it was time to make the attempt—by car. I didn't get to the top, but I got high enough to appreciate the view of the surrounding country. Mount Etna was only six miles distant and between the two peaks lay the fertile Simeto Valley where some members of my platoon had "gone hunting" for Germans and chickens. The Germans had fled but the chickens had been easy prey.

Leonforte, like most Sicilian towns, clings to the side of a mountain and can only be reached by a switchback road. As my Fiat negotiated the numerous bends in the road and I finally reached the town, I marvelled at the bravery and sheer audacity of Capt. Rowan Coleman and his troops. They had raced up the hill in their vehicles under intense machine-gun fire and then cleared the town of enemy. Thirteen Patricias were killed and nine wounded that day. I was fortunate not to have been involved in the action.

Now, I was trying to drive my automobile through the same narrow, winding streets, clogged with pedestrians, motorbikes and other vehicles. Everyone was shouting and blowing their horns but nothing moved. Some of the occupants of the houses on either side threw open their shutters and added their insults. Bedlam! I thought of Capt. Coleman and how he might have handled this situation.

Next day, up bright and early, I took the coastal road from Taormina to Ispica and arrived about noon. I should have known better than to appear at siesta time in the blazing heat. But this was 1989 and I thought that the traditional siesta had gone the way of all such old-fashioned amenities. Not in Sicily where the temperature can reach 140 degrees at high noon. I sniffed around the town trying to find the Sindaco (Mayor) or any civic official who might have some record of my brief stint as Mayor in July 1943. All doors were *chiuse* and I was reminded by the few people in the streets that everything would remain closed until *ore quattro*. Now I had two problems. In addition to the frustration of the siesta, I realized that I had forgotten most of the Italian I had learned in the war. I had always prided myself in having a *dialetto siciliano* but apparently even that had departed and all that was left was a "dialetto Frosto" which no one understood but me.

I had counted on finding a guide in Ispica who would help me locate the exact place where the Patricias had landed on July 10th, 1943. Now I would have to rely on my maps and hope to find someone on the beaches who could help me.

I had a rough idea of the location from studying my maps but as any military person knows, it requires considerable skill to locate on the ground a specific area on a map, especially if you have a small-scale map that shows very few features. I tramped up and down those beaches for an hour or two trying to decide exactly where the Patricias had landed, but it was no use. I encountered a few fishermen and tried out my Italian on them. With blank stares they shook their shoulders and mumbled, "*Non capisco niente.*" Even recourse to my phrase book was no help.

The beaches themselves offered no clues. No long stretches of sparkling white sand. Only a bleak, forlorn area of sand and soil littered with driftwood, broken bottles, tin cans and other debris thrown up by the sea. In my frustration I kicked up the sand and dirt hoping to unearth some trophy from the war—a rusted tin hat, a can of spam, a piece of equipment, a mess tin. Nothing appeared. The passage of 46 years had effectively washed away all evidence of that great Armada that had landed on these barren, inhospitable shores on July 10th, 1943. I looked out to sea, half expecting that the Armada would suddenly appear, with its 3,000 ships bearing 180,000 men from England, United States, Egypt, Malta and North Africa. And where are all the enormous piles of equipment, rations and supplies?

I remembered experiencing the same kind of feeling in 1956 when I last visited these beaches. But now the feeling was more intense and a deep anger overcame me.

And where is a memorial marking this place where Canada's soldiers broke into Fortress Europe? Graves there are aplenty in Sicily and Italy but their message is one of sacrifice.

I knew instantly what I had to do. I resolved then and there to do everything in my power to erect on this beach a Memorial to the achievements of the First Canadian Division. For the next two years I would relentlessly pursue my goal.

I had no idea what such an undertaking would entail, but I realized there were at least two matters I had to deal with before I could accomplish my mission. The first was to improve my ability to speak, understand and write Italian so that I could cope with the local Italians as well as with the Italian government. The second requirement was to obtain large scale military maps of the area to establish the actual site of the landing and the best location for a memorial.

And so my tour of Sicily in 1989, which had begun with such anticipation and hope and which had soon turned into frustration and despair, finally ended on a note of high resolve.

I must now interrupt my story of the Monument in Sicily to refer briefly to the remaining parts of my 1989 Pilgrimage. It was, in fact, an ambitious (perhaps overly ambitious) tour of Italy, from Venice in the North to Reggio di Calabria at the Strait of Messina in the south. The trip also encompassed several days in London, five days in Holland and a long drive from Amsterdam to Vienna (visiting such places as Cologne, Bonn, Frankfurt, Nuremberg, Munich, Dachau, Salzburg and Berchtesgaden). From Vienna, I travelled by train to Venice, where my last conveyance was by gondola to my hotel.

Only my visits to Sicily, Italy and Holland can be considered as Pilgrimages. The remainder of my trip, while of considerable interest, especially places like Nuremberg, Dachau and Berchtesgaden, is not relevant to my tale.

I will, however, mention one event that occurred in Venice which has special significance for the PPCLI. May 8th is a proud day in the history of the Regiment. On that day, in World War I, the Patricias had withstood the fury of the Germans at Frezenberg, at tremendous cost— 10 officers and 392 other ranks. Each year the Regiment solemnly remembers this sacrifice.

I knew that on May 13th my comrades in Toronto would be celebrating Frezenberg Day at the annual meeting of the PPCLI Association. Seldom have I failed to honour this day since joining the Patricias and I did not intend to let a mere 5,000 miles separate me now from my comrades. But how to accomplish this feat? A simple telegram seemed to be the answer:

PILGRIMAGE—1989

Venice
May 13, 1989

Mr. James M. Reid
President
PPCLI Association
Carlton Inn Hotel
30 Carlton Street
Toronto, Ontario Canada, M5B 2E9

Greetings from Italy. Best wishes to the Regiment on the 74th anniversary of Frezenberg.
From a former member of the old spaghetti league,
Sydney Frost

I am constrained to mention one further item which had no significance for the PPCLI but was of great importance (at that time) to my grandchildren. After every trip I made to Europe, they always wanted to know how many miles I had travelled, presumably to impress their little friends at school. They had scant knowledge of how short the distance between cities is in Europe compared to Canada. So I always compared the miles I had travelled to the circumference of the earth, which they understood. With tongue in cheek and considerable reluctance, I now disclose the following memo from my top secret files.

Memo
Miles Travelled
Europe—May 1-27, 1989
By Sydney Frost

Car	Amsterdam — Vienna	1,140	
	Venice — Rome	575	
	Catania — Rome	1,072	2,787
Air	Toronto — London	5,000	
	London — Amsterdam	220	
	Rome — Catania	340	
	Rome — London	900	
	London — Toronto	5,000	11,460
Train	Vienna — Venice	400	
Ferry	Messina — Reggio	10	
Gondola		5	
		14,662	
Al Piede (on foot)		338	
Total Miles		15,000	
Earth's Circumference in Miles		24,900	

Chapter II

PILGRIMAGE—1990

On May 27th, I returned from my long Pilgrimage in 1989, tired in the extreme and terribly frustrated with the Sicilian part of the trip. None of the three tasks I had set for myself had been accomplished. Namely:

1. Locate the exact place on the beaches where the Patricias had landed on July 10th, 1943.
2. Visit the Agira Cemetery, sign the Visitors' Register and check the remarks I had written in 1956.
3. Visit Ispica and renew my relations with the Mayor and its citizens.

In my brief contact with the Sicilian people, I had found, much to my chagrin, that my supposed knowledge of the Italian language was only a chimera. I was thus saddled with another task:

4. Take an Italian language course.

The last task became my first priority. I enrolled in the Faculty of Continuing Education (Night Courses) at Seneca College, Newnham Campus, Toronto. It soon became a major undertaking. The other students were young and they were smart. And they were all Italian! I asked one of them why he bothered taking the course. *"No problema,"* he said. "It's an easy credit."

I soon found I had to start from the beginning. There was no way I could bluff my teacher by pounding the table and uttering Italian-sounding words like I did when I was Mayor of Ispica, or when I used to impress my fellow officers with my so-called expertise. One of my favourite words which I used to get attention, or when I was angry, was *cinquecentocinquantacinque*, accompanied by a scowl and much thumping on a table. My brother officers were duly impressed and even the Italians scurried about to comply with my demands. To this day I don't understand why. The word only means 555.

In any event, my serious study of Italian soon became a life-long hobby which I still pursue and enjoy. *Mille grazie, Collegio di Seneca, e la gente di Ispica.*

My next task was to obtain large-scale military maps of the landing area showing where the Patricias had come ashore on July 10th, 1943.

The first person I thought of was Dr. Bill McAndrew of the Directorate of History, National Defence Headquarters. He had been a great help to me in writing my first book and he did not disappoint me. He sent me the two maps I needed. One was an excellent topographical map he had obtained from that durable officer of The Royal Canadian Regiment and capable historian, Strome Galloway; the other was a large-scale map prepared by the Department's Cartographer showing the exact landing areas.

I shall always be indebted to Dr. McAndrew on at least two counts. He gave me the maps I so urgently needed and he sowed the seed that produced this book. When I told him about my deep resentment that there are no memorials in Sicily or anywhere else to commemorate the achievements of the First Division, and my plans to have such a Memorial erected in Sicily, he gave me his whole-hearted approval. And he added these words that I have never forgotten—"Perhaps it will result in a sequel to *Once a Patricia.*"

With my first two tasks in hand, I turned to my next undertaking—where were the gardeners at the Agira Cemetery and what happened to the Visitors' Register? Whom should I ask? It has long been a basic principle of mine that when you want to get an answer or something done, you go right to the top and not waste time climbing the ladder.

The Minister of Veterans Affairs was Gerry Merrithew. He had been appointed in September 1988, to succeed the popular George Hees. I had not yet met him, but I knew his credentials and they appealed to me. He had at least two things going for him: he had spent sixteen years in the Militia, rising to Commanding Officer, and he was a Maritimer. Anyone who knows my background will understand my reasoning.

The first thing I did on returning from my 1989 Pilgrimage was to write Gerry Merrithew a long letter reporting on the Pilgrimage and voicing the frustrations and concerns I have already mentioned.

The following extracts from my letter of June 19th, 1989, deal only with the Agira Cemetery.

> *All the cemeteries in Italy have been laid out with great care and are beautifully maintained. I am always moved by the stark setting of the Agira Cemetery atop a hill in the wastelands of central Sicily. Like an oasis, it beckons all within its sight. Its terraced slopes contain the bodies of 490 Canadians killed in Sicily, including many of my friends.*

PILGRIMAGE—1990

> *I had not visited the Agira Cemetery since 1956, when I was one of the first to pay my respects. On my trip just concluded, I went many miles out of my way to make a return visit. Once again I was deeply moved by the beauty of the place. But I was disappointed not to be able to find the caretaker and see the Visitors' Register. I suggest that a notice should be posted,* in English, *advising where the caretaker may be located.*

The Minister replied on September 21st as follows:

> *With regard to the absence of a caretaker at the Agira Canadian War Cemetery, it has been confirmed by the Commonwealth War Graves Commission (responsible for the Cemetery) that the Cemetery is maintained by mobile gardening teams from Catania, with no full-time gardener in attendance. The Cemetery register should have been there and it was no doubt replaced by the staff on their next visit. Too often, unfortunately, visitors will remove the visitors' book and keep it as a souvenir.*

This was not quite the answer I had expected but the Minister had obviously looked into the question and there was nothing further he could do. I let the issue drop for the time being and concerned myself with more pressing tasks.

The truth of the matter was that the tasks I have mentioned were all subordinate to my intense desire to have a Monument erected on the beaches of Sicily to honour the First Canadian Division. I felt saddened and betrayed that not a memorial of any kind in the whole of Sicily and Italy marked the achievements of the D-Day Dodgers, as we were called. In this chauvinistic mood, I fired off my letter of June 19th to the Minister:

> *I have just returned from another Pilgrimage to Italy. I stood on the beaches of Pachino and surveyed the peaceful harbour, once crammed with the ships and landing craft of the Canadian First Division. Not a memorial of any kind marked the place where Canada's soldiers first succeeded in entering Hitler's Fortress Europe.*
>
> *Later, I visited the battlefields. I could not find one marker indicating that Canadian soldiers had fought for Canada and Italy.*

Graves there are aplenty but their message is one of sacrifice. What I want to see is a memorial or memorials to the achievements of First Canadian Corps, erected on or near the main battlefields.

I am also prompted to speak on behalf of the surviving veterans of the Italian Campaign. There are not many of us left and unless our contribution to the winning of WWII soon receives the recognition it deserves, there will be no one left to appreciate the thanks of a grateful nation.

The Italian Campaign has always been overshadowed by the Second Front. After the invasion of Normandy, in the eyes of many, the troops in Italy became an irrelevant sideshow. We were called "D-Day Dodgers."

I can do no better than quote from my earlier book how many of us feel about the shoddy way we have been treated compared to the veterans of Normandy. In the Foreword I say:

> *This belittling of the Italian Campaign persists to the present day. Each year many veterans celebrate D-Day in Normandy, but deliberately ignore another D-Day which has a special significance that can never be claimed for the Normandy invasion.*
>
> *That 'other D-Day' was July 10, 1943, when the lst Canadian Division, as part of the famous 8th Army, and the Americans assaulted the beaches of Sicily. It was significant because it meant the Allies had finally landed in Europe, and it marked the beginning of the end of Hitler's Festung Europa (facts that most people, except the soldiers of the lst Division, attribute to Normandy).*
>
> *Why has there always been such a deafening silence in Canada about the lst Canadian Corps and the Italian Campaign—no memorial observances, no recognition? The irony of the matter is that there is still one group who will never forget the Canadians—their prime antagonists, the German paratroop and panzer divisions.*
>
> *I would like to see more recognition given to the D-Day Dodgers, whose contribution to Victory has so far been largely ignored, compared to the efforts of our brothers in the Normandy Campaign.*

PILGRIMAGE—1990

The die had been cast, but little did I realize what it would entail. Before my quest was over, I would be involved with friends and officials in Toronto, Ottawa, Rome, Ispica and Pachino. All were helpful, but heading the list was Gerry Merrithew and his fine Department of Veterans Affairs. Here are some of the other actors who played a significant part:

André Petelle—Director, Commemoration and Special Events, DVA
Peter Caissie—Commemoration and Special Events Officer, DVA
Canadian Embassy in Rome
The Italian Government
The Secretary-General of The Commonwealth War Graves Commission
The Director of the War Graves Commission in Rome
Mayors of Ispica—Giuseppe Monaco
      Quinto Bellisario
      Dr. Carmelo Tomasi
Mayor of Pachino—Prof. Lupo Sebastiano
Carmelo Nigro—School Teacher, Ispica
Associazione Centro d'Incontro Anziani (CIA)
  Mrs. Carmela Maucieri—President
  Sigr. Ferlisi Salvatore—President
Centro di Cultura Popolare UNLA
  Prof. Antonino Lauretta—Director
Frank Gennaro and family, Toronto
Sebastian Spataro and family, Toronto
Corriere Canadese, Italian Newspaper, Toronto
Radio CHIN—Toronto
Johnny Lombardi, Toronto
Paragon Travel Agency
Joe Maniscola, Toronto
And a cast of thousands (The citizens of Ispica and Pachino)

The Minister's reply to my letter regarding the lack of recognition of the D-Day Dodgers and the erection of a monument is contained in his letter of September 21st:

> *Thank you for your letter of June 19, 1989, concerning the treatment the Central Mediterranean Forces have received over the years.*
>
> *I regret that you feel disappointed and I can only reiterate what I have written to Professor Fraser on this matter. I do not feel the Department of Veterans Affairs has neglected the veterans of the Italian Campaign. Let me explain.*

> *My Department has been following a five-year commemoration plan aimed at drawing the attention of the Canadian public to important wartime achievements of our armed forces. In addition to important anniversaries such as D-Day and Dieppe, we also celebrate the liberation of Holland, Belgium, Italy, the Hong Kong prisoners of war, and the cease-fire in Korea.*
>
> *My Department took a large delegation to Italy in 1975 and again in 1985. We will be going back to Italy in 1991. We would have liked to celebrate the 45th anniversary of its liberation, but budgetary considerations make it necessary for us to delay our pilgrimage for one year.*
>
> *It has been a Canadian Government policy not to erect markers and memorials overseas in connection with the Second World War.*
>
> *Instead, two commemorative buildings were built on Wellington Street in Ottawa where the Department of Veterans Affairs has been located since 1947. All memorials in Europe erected during or after the Second World War have been the result of local and/or regimental initiatives. The same thing could have been or could still be done in Italy.*
>
> *In order to fulfill our mandate to maintain a public awareness of Canadian achievements in times of war, we always ensure that our pilgrimages are well covered by the Canadian information media. This is to ensure that the particular event we wish to emphasize is talked about through the testimonials and personal experiences of the veterans we bring with us.*
>
> *More publicity on the Italian Campaign by the veterans who return to Italy, or* through books such as yours, *will help in making this campaign better known to the Canadian People. We certainly do our part by publicizing our pilgrimages to Italy as they occur.*

Again, in typical fashion, the Minister had "done his homework" and answered some of my concerns about the lack of recognition of the First Canadian Division and its achievements, but the Government's decision to postpone the Pilgrimage to celebrate the 45th Anniversary from 1990 to 1991 because of "budgetary considerations" rankled. So did the stated policy not to erect memorials overseas. I had to respond and express my surprise and disappointment with such policies even though I realized Gerry Merrithew's hands were tied. This is my reply of October 16th:

Dear Colonel Merrithew:

Thank you very much for your letter of September 21st responding to mine of June 9th.

You have allayed some of my concerns. Until I received your letter and the two excellent brochures about the Pilgrimage in 1985, I had no idea of the extent of this visit to Italy. Indeed, I had no knowledge of it at all until some months after the event.

I am disappointed to hear that the scheduled 1990 visit has been put off to 1991 because of budget restrictions. After all, 1990 is the 45th Anniversary of the end of the war. To postpone the ceremonies of this event to the following year makes it almost a "non-event". I think that the Canadian Government will be censured by Veterans and Allied governments alike for treating the 45th Anniversary of the end of the War in such a cavalier fashion. I urge you to re-consider this matter at the earliest possible moment.

I am also surprised to learn that it is Canadian Government policy not to erect markers or memorials overseas in connection with WWII. To have erected two fine buildings in Canada to commemorate the First Division and other formations is certainly a very practical endeavour. But who in Canada or Italy knows about this?

The thrust of my letter of June 19th was not so much to urge that more official delegations be sent to Italy, but to plead for more recognition and awareness by the people in both Canada and Italy of the part played by the First Canadian Division in the liberation of Italy. Assuredly, visits to that country will help to foster recognition and awareness among some Italians for a short period of time. But what I want to see are memorials at the principal battle sites which will remind Italians in perpetuity of their debt to Canada.

Except for the Canadian cemetery at Agira, none of the cemeteries in Italy tell the visitor of the achievements of the First Canadian Division. As I said in my last letter, the message of these cemeteries is the terrible cost of war. Only at Agira could I find a plaque which explained in detail the battles fought by those who rest there.

I would not want to see a plethora of Regimental monuments, as their frequency and size would depend entirely upon the funds available within each Regiment, which in turn, would lead to inter-Regiment rivalry to erect the biggest memorial. I think what would be more appropriate would be a First Division Memorial erected on the beach of Pachino and at the sites of the main divisional battles— Ortona, Hitler Line, Gothic Line, San Fortunato, Savio River, Lamone River, Senio River, to name a few. In addition, a central memorial should be erected in Rome as an eternal reminder to the people of that Eternal City what Canada did for them.

If it is present Canadian Government policy not to erect memorials, (because of the cost, I assume), it seems to me that your Department could and should take the initiative in sounding out the Regiments of the First Division as to their views about having divisional memorials and sharing the cost of their erection. No one else is in the position, or indeed has the authority, to get this project started. All the commanders and most of the senior officers of the division are now dead.

Another reason why the government should take the lead in this matter, is because of the requirement to confer with the Italian Government about the location of such monuments. I understand it would be necessary to have the sites deeded to the Government of Canada in perpetuity and to set aside funds for maintenance.

In my view, these memorials would make a significant contribution toward fostering public recognition and awareness in Italy *of the fighting record of the First Division. They would also help develop closer ties between the people of both countries, with obvious benefits for each. I should think the Secretary of State would be only too happy to support the project.*

I do thank you again for taking the time and trouble to write me such a frank and informative letter. The pamphlets about the 1985 Pilgrimage have helped me to realize that your Department has not forgotten all about the D-Day Dodgers. Now let us do something to ensure that all Canadians and the people of Italy will also remember them.
With my warmest regards,
Sydney Frost

No immediate answer was forthcoming to my letter. Indeed, I didn't expect one. It was now up to me to get the game going again.

While I was working out my game plan, I received an unexpected assist right out of the blue from Peter Caissie, one of the actors listed above. On March 23rd, 1990, he telephoned and sent me a letter explaining the delay. The Department had its hands (and money) tied up with a Pilgrimage to Holland in 1990. But he sent me the address of the War Graves Commission in Rome and maps of Sicily and the beaches.

A Pilgrimage to Holland? I couldn't believe it. Peter didn't mention anything about including me in the Pilgrimage but he sent me a tentative program. I am certain that he was not aware of how incongruous the situation was. Once again the old D-Day Dodgers were being relegated to the status of second-class soldiers, just like it was during the war when all the new equipment, troops and supplies went to the Second Front in Normandy and we were left with the dregs! Now, there was money to send a delegation to Holland. But poor, old, suffering D-Day Dodgers would have to wait. I renewed my covenant with myself to get that Monument erected.

I now realized that if I was going to make any progress I would soon have to make a trip to Sicily, specifically Ispica and Pachino to establish personal contact and find out what kind of support they would give to the project. I immediately booked my hotel in Taormina for May 20 through May 23 and made the necessary flight arrangements.

I also wrote Mr. R. Simpson, the Director of the War Graves Commission in Rome, reporting on the missing caretaker and Visitors' Register at the Agira cemetery the previous year. I asked him to make both available during my visit in May. The following is his reply:

10 April 1990

Dear Mr. Frost,

1. I refer to your letter dated 27 March in which you mention that you will be visiting Sicily in May, and in particular Agira Canadian War Cemetery.

2. On the question of obtaining a photo copy of the page showing your signature in 1956, I am sure you will appreciate that our cemeteries have many visitors who sign the visitors book resulting in many visitors books being filled up. You can therefore imagine how many visitors books have been used in the past 34 years when you visited the cemetery in 1956, this then multiplied by the number of cemeteries in our care. Completed visitors books are only kept for a limited time then destroyed. I therefore regret that it is not possible to send you a photo copy of the page showing your signature in 1956.

3. There are no resident gardening staff at Agira as this cemetery is maintained by our gardening staff from Catania War Cemetery who normally visit Agira twice a week. I was most surprised to learn that there were no visitors book or register of burials when you visited the cemetery last year, these are normally kept in the register box in the building at the entrance.

4. If you can inform my office on the exact date when you will visit the cemetery we can perhaps arrange for our Head Gardener to visit the site on that day. This will also ensure that the books are available.
Yours sincerely,

Again, my plans were being frustrated by bureaucratic rules and regulations that the perpetrators believed were enshrined in stone, if not in marble. It made no sense to throw out these books. In my case, I had gone to a lot of trouble and driven many miles in 1956 to visit the Agira Cemetery with my wife whose cousin LCol. Ralph Crowe of the RCR, as well as 29 Patricias were buried there. We both signed the Register and made some appropriate remarks hoping that others would someday pass by and appreciate our thoughts.

I could not force myself to accept Mr. Simpson's reply without doing something. It seemed almost a desecration at the time and it still does. In this day of high technology, there should be no problem in keeping records indefinitely. So, once again, I called on Gerry Merrithew for help.

April 25, 1990

Dear Colonel Merrithew:
I enclose copy of a letter dated April 10th, which I have just received from Mr. R. Simpson, director of the Commonwealth War Graves Commission in Rome.

I expect that you are as shocked as I that the visitors' books are "only kept for a limited time, then destroyed."

One is tempted to ask what is the point of having a register at all! I acknowledge that my signature is not worth keeping, even for a limited time, but I would think that over the years a number of VIPs have visited the Cemetery and left their names and comments.

Even more important, however, are the signatures and remarks of parents of the deceased. Sicily is well off the beaten track and not many go to the effort and expense of visiting the Cemetery. But for the few who do make a Pilgrimage for the express purpose of leaving a final good-bye with their son, it would, I suggest, come as a deep shock to learn that a record of their visit, unlike their son's grave, will not be preserved in perpetuity.

PILGRIMAGE—1990

> *I hesitate to add to your burdens but I think, with respect, this is something that should be looked into. If there are no facilities for keeping the visitors' books in Italy, surely they could be shipped home and reside in the War Museum.*

This dreary saga ends with the Minister's reply. He had gone to a lot of effort to get to the bottom of the reason why visitors' books are destroyed. There was nothing more he could do and I appreciated his efforts. But I will never accept the decision of the Commonwealth War Graves Commission made 70 years ago (after WW1). Here is the Minister's informative letter.

> *July 5, 1990*
>
> *Thank you for your letters of April 25, 1990, concerning the visitors' books at cemeteries and memorials cared for by the Commonwealth War Graves Commission.*
>
> *To best serve you, I forwarded a copy of your letter to the Secretary-General of the Commonwealth War Graves Commission, Canadian Agency. I have now received the Commission's reply.*
>
> *Under the terms of its Charters, the Commission has no obligation to provide visitors' books at its cemeteries and memorials. The practice of doing so began soon after the First World War as people wished to have a book to sign when they visited a cemetery. The books were originally cloth-bound volumes but, in recent years, plastic ring binders with loose-leaf pages have been used. These are more economical and they allow vandalized and desecrated pages to be removed easily.*
>
> *The binders normally contain about 20 pages. As the pages fill up, the earliest ones are removed and blank ones inserted. In a rarely visited cemetery, a page may stay in the binder for several years, but in a well-visited site, the oldest pages might only be a few months old. When pages are removed, those with signatures of dignitaries are sent to the Commission's area office for safekeeping and all others are kept for a year before being destroyed.*
>
> *The act of signing a visitors' book is undoubtedly important to visitors and some of them possibly expect their signatures and remarks to remain at the cemetery forever. It would be unrealistic, however to store the thousands of pages accumulated each year. Your suggestion that the*

pages be shipped to the Canadian War Museum is not practical as the pages are signed by people from all over the world and it would be impossible to separate Canadian signatures from the others.

Once again, Mr. Frost, thank you for writing. I sincerely hope the information I have provided helps you understand the Commission's position on this matter.

With kind regards.
Yours sincerely

It was now time to make another Pilgrimage to Sicily. Unlike the others, I was well prepared for my mission. My tasks were:

1. Visit the Agira Cemetery.
2. Locate the area where the Patricias had landed on July 10th, 1943.
3. Visit Ispica and renew my relations with the Mayor and citizens of Ispica.
4. Seek their approval and help to erect a Monument.

I was also in better shape to take on my Italian friends in their own language. Over the winter I had been taking a course in Italian, and while I was far from fluent, I was confident I could make myself understood. I still had difficulty understanding them, especially when they talked fast (which is most of the time). But I had developed a little crutch to slow them down—*Per favore, parla lentemente. Ho difficulta di sentire.* (Please speak slowly. I have difficulty hearing.)

I arrived at the Catania Airport at 2:50 p.m. on May 19th and picked up my automobile. This time I eschewed renting my usual Fiat and instead chose an Alfa Romeo. Actually a Fiat is more comfortable, but I wanted to impress my Sicilian friends. There are two routes to Agira—one is via Autostrada A19 which I had taken on my last trip. The other is through mountainous country, via Highway 121, past Adrano, Regalbuto and Mount Seggio, names that are well remembered by Patricias who fought there.

I set off for my objective armed with maps, letters from the War Graves Commission in Rome, letters from Gerry Merrithew, and a water bottle. I should mention that I had taken the precaution of contacting Mr. Simpson, the Commission's Director in Rome and made an appointment to visit the cemetery.

A few miles to my right rose the snow-tipped peak of Mount Etna dominating the country to the north. Soon a smaller peak came into view—Mount Seggio where I had joined the Regiment in 1943 and fought my first engagement. In 1989, I had attempted to drive up the mountain in my automobile but it was not suited to the rough trails and I abandoned the attempt. Now, once again, I had the mountain in my grasp and I couldn't resist the challenge. In my fancy Alfa Romeo I shouldn't have any trouble. The car spurted forward and we were soon in Carcadi (formerly known as Carcaci) where the Regiment had started out on its midnight advance. I urged my beast forward and upward but the trail quickly petered out. By now the heat was intense and both automobile and driver had had enough. I wisely decided not to pursue my assault on Mount Seggio any further and I turned back to Highway 121.

As I drove away, I thought how lucky I was that my first action with the Regiment had not been a bloody affair. The Germans had decamped in haste and my company suffered no casualties. But the two follow-up companies were not so fortunate. They were heavily shelled and Lt. d'Arcy Horn was killed.

Agira Cemetery lies atop a hill about a mile from town. I had visited it in 1989 and been deeply moved by its beauty and the immaculate care being given to the graves. But I had been disappointed not to find a caretaker or Visitors' Register. This time, due to representations I had made to the Minister of Veterans Affairs and the Commonwealth War Graves Commission, my concerns were soon put to rest.

Two gardeners, smartly dressed in clean overalls, with name tags prominently displayed, greeted me. Their names were Sig. A. Galvagno and Sig. A. Quaececi. They escorted me to the Visitors' Register, which I signed, and with their help, I had the deep satisfaction of locating every one of the 29 Patricia graves. Before each one, I paused a moment or two and then moved on. Here was d'Arcy Horn, the tallest man in the Battalion; here was CQMS J. F. Stevens, one of my section commanders in England and the first to die on the beaches; and here was ...

I thanked the caretakers for their help and attention, and with a heavy heart slowly drove away. My mission had been fulfilled. On my return to Toronto, I wrote Mr. Simpson, the Director of the War Graves Commission in Rome, thanking him for his help and complimenting the two gardeners on the excellent state of maintenance of the cemetery—a noble resting place for Canada's dead.

Next day, my objective was the beaches where the Regiment came ashore, in the southeast tip of Sicily, about 3 miles southwest of Pachino. From my hotel in Taormina, the round trip would be about 250 miles, a good day's drive in heavy traffic along roads hugging the eastern coast: the A-18 Autostrada, and Highways 114 and 115.

Again, I was better prepared for my mission than the previous year. Now I could *parlare italiano* fairly well, both vocally and manually, and I had brought with me a set of large-scale military maps. I was confident I could locate the landing place of the Patricias without too much difficulty.

According to the maps, the landing place was located on the west side of Cape Passero in a bay, between Le Grotticelle on the east and Punta Castellazzo on the west. The beach was code-named "Sugar." This looked easy enough but as indicated earlier, the problem is to match the features shown on the map with those on the ground. As it turned out, I had no trouble, thanks to Dr. Bill McAndrew's and Peter Caissie's accurate maps and a couple of friendly fishermen. "*Scusi, signori,*" I said in my best Italian, "*Dove Le Grotticelle e Punta Castellazzo?*" They gave me a strange look as if to say "Everyone knows that." But I persisted and they said I was standing on Le Grotticelle and the Punta was just over there (about two miles away). I thanked them and explained who I was and why I needed the information. They became quite excited and offered to take me to the Punta in their boat. But I explained that this wasn't necessary as the PPCLI had landed just a few hundred yards from Le Grotticelle.

I then did a silly thing. I took off my shoes and socks, hoisted up my trousers, picked up a stick and waded into the water. "*Signore, Signore, che cosa fa. L'acqua è fredda*" the fishermen cried. I turned, and in imitation of an assault landing, charged the beach, waving my hat and stick and yelling terrible oaths about German soldiers. "*Morte ai soldati tedeschi. Sono figli di un cane.*"

The fishermen fled to their boat and two old ladies out for a quiet stroll headed for the protection of a nearby shack uttering, "*Il diavolo, il diavolo.*"

I am sure my friends cannot believe I would be capable of such nonsense, but I am. I have a picture to prove it.

It was time to leave this historic place where the Patricias had been one of the first regiments to break into Hitler's Festung Europa. I reached Taormina in time for a late dinner (as is the custom in Sicily) and to prepare for the morrow—a visit to Ispica.

Ispica is a typical Sicilian town perched on a steep cliff overlooking the country as far as the beaches, about six miles distant. After a heavy shelling from HMS Delhi, on July 11th, 1943, and a heavy aerial bombardment, the town had surrendered without a fight. The Patricias passed through the town on July 11th on their way north to their next objective, Modica.

As a reinforcement officer, I was ordered to occupy the town on July 16th and restore order. The story is told in Chapter VII of *Once a Patricia*. Suffice it to say, that for 19 days I thoroughly enjoyed my role as Town Major (or Mayor) and concluded that perhaps a benevolent dictatorship was not, after all, a bad thing. The people of Ispica soon shook off the terrible yoke of Fascism and made a fresh start on the road to democracy. They worked hard to rebuild their town and their Sicilian way of life; they found new confidence and hope for the future. I, in turn, received a unique education and soon fell in love with "my town" and its people, a feeling that matured over the years into a deep respect and admiration.

As I carefully drove my Alfa Romeo up the switchback road leading to Ispica, I wondered what kind of a reception awaited me. This time I had done my homework and read up on its ancient history. The site has been continuously inhabited since the Bronze Age. The Caves of Ispica are recognized internationally as an important archaeological site, including a long tunnel with steps dug into the rock and stretching below the level of a river. These caves were occupied until recent times and during the war served as bomb-proof shelters.

I remembered the fiasco of my last visit when I had arrived during siesta. This time I drove into town at a more civilized hour and parked my car near the Municipal offices. I noted with pleasure that these had been moved from rather dingy quarters in 1956 to the magnificent Palazzo Bruno. I also remembered, with a touch of irony, that I had occupied the Palazzo during my tenure as "Mayorz". *Plus ça change, plus c'est la même chose.*

I entered the Palazzo and was ushered into the presence of Mayor Giuseppe Monaco. A short, dignified man, he greeted me cordially in Italian and we spent a very pleasant hour reminiscing about my brief stint as Mayor of his town 47 years earlier. I thanked my foresight for having taken that Italian course, even though I had trouble with some of the words. The Mayor showed me around his palatial offices and suggested we go outside in the Piazza and meet some of the citizens. Soon quite a crowd gathered and seemed to be very happy to meet their "First Democratic Mayor." Some even claimed to remember me and one, Francesco Monaca, was in fact one of the civil servants I appointed to help me restore order. He followed me wherever I went and became known as my "shadow".

Pictures were duly taken and I was presented with a beautiful history of Ispica, with coloured pictures of all the wonderful buildings, churches, works of art and the famous Cava d'Ispica. It is a volume which I treasure to this day. The Mayor autographed it:

Al Sig. Col. C. Sydney Frost, QC
Con particolare fratitudine
Giuseppe Monaco
Sindaco Ispica
21 Maggio 1990

Fortunately, I had the foresight to bring with me a PPCLI plaque bearing the Regimental badge and the following inscription:

> *Presented by Colonel C. S. Frost of Princess Patricia's Canadian Light Infantry, who was Town Major of Ispica from July 6 to August 3, 1943*
>
> *May 21, 1990*

The inscription could not include the Mayor's name as I had no idea who he was or even if I would be so warmly received. But the Mayor accepted the plaque with obvious pleasure and I am happy to say it still hangs in his office, a tangible link between the citizens of Ispica and the PPCLI.

After more sightseeing and meeting people, we returned to the Mayor's office for coffee and exquisite Sicilian pastries. I thought the moment was propitious to broach the matter of a Memorial. Mr. Monaco immediately expressed his support for the project but felt that the Italian Government would have to be consulted. He suggested I contact the appropriate authorities in Rome.

It was time for me to leave, but the Mayor wanted me to stay a few days to see the town and especially the famous caves. Unfortunately, my plane left the next day and I could not accept.

We parted on the friendliest of terms and agreed to keep in touch. As I drove back to Taormina along the pleasant highway following the Ionian coast, I began to feel that at last there was some hope that my dream would be realized.

* * *

It will be recalled that on March 23rd, I had been informed by Peter Caissie of DVA that the Government was planning a Pilgrimage to Holland from May 2nd to May 10th, 1990. He sent me a program of the events but I was not asked to join the delegation, even though the Drum Band of the PPCLI would be present. However, the head of the Dutch Liberation Committee in Holland and the Burgemeester of the Municipality of Voorst, which the Patricias had liberated in 1945, had kindly sent me invitations to attend the Ceremonies on behalf of the PPCLI. I was happy to accept, but it meant that I would have two Pilgrimages in May: One at the start of the month to Holland and the other toward the end of the month to Sicily, at the southern extremity of Europe. What to do about the two weeks in the middle of the month. It seemed only sensible to visit the countries in between!

PILGRIMAGE—1990

Thus it was that on April 29th, I left Toronto and arrived in Amsterdam the next day to participate in the week-long ceremonies in Holland; then by car from Arnhem to Salzburg following the Rhine River past Cologne, Koblenz, Mainz and Mannheim; then to Heidelberg, Nuremberg, Munich and Salzburg. Instead of heading for Vienna, as I did on my last trip, I turned west to Zurich and from there to Interlaken, Montreux and Geneva. I turned in my car and flew to Catania, Sicily, arriving 2:50 p.m. May 19th as already described.

In a subsequent chapter, I will describe the Pilgrimage to Holland.

Chapter III

PILGRIMAGE—1991

I returned to Toronto on June 2nd well pleased with my 1990 visit to Sicily. Three of my four tasks had been completed and the Mayor of Ispica had been very supportive about the Monument. But, on reflection, I realized that he had raised a new obstacle I had not foreseen—obtaining the consent of the Italian Government. The more I thought about it the less I was satisfied with my mission. How does one get the Italian Government, or any government, to act on such a matter within a few months?

While I was considering my next move, lady luck again smiled at me in the person of Marie Gennaro of Toronto. Right out of the blue she phoned me on July 10th to say that her mother had just received a letter from one Carmelo Nigro in Ispica! She explained that Mr. Nigro was her mother's cousin and had sent her an article which he had written in the local newspaper *Il Coccodrillo*, about my visit to Ispica. He wanted her to get in touch with me and answer a number of questions regarding the landing of the First Division in Sicily on July 10th, 1943, and my subsequent stay in Ispica as Mayor of the town.

This was very exciting news and I invited the Gennaro family for dinner at a nice Italian restaurant (where else!). The father, Frank, the mother, Maria, and the daughter, Marie, were happy to attend. Frank came from Rosolini, a town close to Ispica, and emigrated in 1964. Maria was born in Ispica. All her family now live in Toronto. She was only 13 years old when I was the Mayor. Her cousin, Carmelo, was a school teacher and was thinking about writing a book about the landing of the First Division.

They gave me a copy of *Il Coccodrillo* and to my surprise and delight, there on the front page was a large picture of Mayor Giuseppe Monaco handing me the book on Ispica. Inside, a full page article by

PILGRIMAGE—1991

Carmelo described my recent visit to Ispica and my occupation of the town in July, 1943.

We spent the evening talking about Ispica and its liberation by the Canadians and I learned more about the fascinating history of this historic place; how it was occupied by many foreign powers—Normans, Turks, Spanish, French; in 1693, an earthquake levelled the town. The famous Caves of Ispica are still being explored by archaeologists who have found ancient tombs, churches, forts and dwellings all dug into the rock on which Ispica stands.

Some of this I had read about before and I boldly interjected that I had been told by the Mayor about the 100 steps cut into the rock leading down to the bed of a river. "Oh no," replied Frank, "there are, in fact, 280 steps but we call them the *Centoscale*." I understood enough Italian to know that *Centoscale* meant 100 steps and I was tempted to ask how 100 in Italian equals 280 in English, but I wisely held my tongue. I did, however, make a mental note to explore these caves on my next visit to Ispica.

It was not until 1997 that I was able to fulfill my desire. All that Frank had told me was true but he had only scratched the surface of the area, so to speak. After seeing the entrance to the *Centoscale* as they descended into the gloomy bowels of the earth, I decided to take Frank at his word about the 280 steps, and moved on to examine other wonders.

But I digress, something I find easy to do when describing the sights I have seen and the people I have met in my ten Pilgrimages to Italy and Holland over the past 50 years.

The Gennaros were truly proud of their town and I shared their enthusiasm. I mentioned how supportive Mayor Monaco had been of my "proposal" to erect a monument and I wondered what they thought about it. They warm-heartedly agreed with the Mayor and felt strongly that something should be done to recognize and honour the Canadian soldiers who had liberated them. They pointed out that there were many Ispicese and Pachinese in the Toronto area, as well as a large Italian population of over 500,000, who would be very interested in such a Memorial. Frank thought that the Toronto Italian newspaper, *Corriere Canadese*, would probably like to do a story on the project and interview me. He said he would see what he could do.

Frank also mentioned Johnny Lombardi of Radio Station CHIN who, he was certain, would also want an interview.

A few days later, I received a call from Franco Romano at *Corriere Canadese* asking if he could attend that very day to do an interview and take pictures. He and his photographer, Annamarie, spent an hour and a half listening to my stories of the landing. Here was a golden opportunity, not to be missed, to let the Italian community know about how Canadian soldiers played a significant part in the liberation of their country and how I felt about them. I would like to quote the whole article, but the following will suffice:

Corriere Canadese
Venerdi—Sabato 3-4 Agosto 1990
Friday—Saturday August 3-4, 1990

The Canadian Who Became A Sicilian Mayor
The 8th British Army landed at dawn somewhere between Marza and Portopallo on July 10, 1943. It entered Ispica in the afternoon as the Sicilian municipality surrendered.

Shortly after, the city's keys were given to Canadian Lieutenant C. Sydney Frost, who became the first mayor of free Ispica.

In 1943, Colonel Frost was just 21-years old. Despite his youth, in the 19 days he was mayor, he proved his competence and abilities.

Today, he is 68 and recalls with pride "his" Sicilian city.

"Right after we took the city, I became its mayor. I was confused at first, everything was in shambles. There was no water, no food, no electricity. They had many wounded.

The people, worn out by years of fascist domination and stricken by the war, received us as liberators, co-operating with us for the reconstruction.

When we landed in 1943, we didn't know what to expect. The only other time we had met Italians was in Africa, and they were our enemies.

When we met again, at first there was some tension, but after we 'smelled each other' we understood we would be friends.

We were fighting for a common cause, the freedom of the peninsula, the defeat of the Germans and victory over the Fascists.

I fought in Italy for two years and I learned to appreciate its people. When I think about them I am reminded of their positive disposition toward life and their hardworking nature, characteristics I have always admired.

During my following visits to Italy, I was amazed at the transformation. I left it poor, depressed, pessimistic, with

> *dusty roads and old hand-carts. Now we see an Italy among the top European Nations, crossed all over by modern and efficient highways, with a rich economy."*

The article was printed in both English and Italian.

While the interview was going on in my library, two of my young grandsons appeared at the door, Jason and Graham. I waved them away but the photographer insisted they come in, and took several photos of the three of us gathered around my desk. I am pleased to report that one of the photos appeared in the newspaper. It was so typical of that wonderful feeling Italians have for family, and added a nice personal touch to the article.

A few days later, I received a call from Johnny Lombardi himself, the well-known proprietor of Radio Station CHIN. He had seen the article in the *Corriere Canadese* and was keen to interview me. I duly attended the radio station and was interviewed by Alberto Mancha for about half an hour. Again it was a great opportunity to get my message across to the Italian community and arouse their interest in having a Monument erected to the First Division.

After the interview, Johnny Lombardi took me to his office and we had a very pleasant chat about Sicily and Italy and the war. I was surprised to find that this kindly gentleman, who was an icon in the Italian community, had served with the Canadian Army in Normandy and Holland. He wanted to join the fighting troops and loved the Army. But they put him in the band. I had no problem convincing him there should be a Memorial erected to Canada's soldiers on the beaches of Sicily where they were among the first to break into continental Europe. He was full of ideas. He felt the large Pachinese population in Toronto might well contribute to the cost of the project. Indeed, the Monument could be made here and shipped to Italy! He suggested I get in touch with his travel agent, Joe Maniscola, who operated Paragon Travel Agency and see if he could organize a trip to Sicily to attend a dedication ceremony. Johnny would be honoured to attend. Incidentally, Joe Maniscola happened to be from Pachino.

Johnny Lombardi's final suggestion was to have the cities of Ispica and Pachino twinned with Toronto's Little Italy. And I was not to forget the influence of local members of Parliament. What a man! No wonder he was so respected and so successful in his many undertakings. I am happy that I have had this opportunity to record his kindness to me which I am sure is not common knowledge.

As a footnote, it should also be recorded that Joe Maniscola did, in fact, try to organize a tour that would join the Official Pilgrimage to

Italy which the Government had planned for May, 1991. But when he wrote to the Government to get their approval, he was told it was a closed Pilgrimage insofar as it was restricted to invited guests. It was not open for other people wishing to travel with the Official group. But Joe Maniscola could organize his own tour.

As for the Government becoming financially involved in the construction of memorials, it was regretted that it would not be able to support the construction of a memorial in Sicily with a donation.

Shortly after my auspicious meeting with Johnny Lombardi, a letter arrived from Mayor Bellisario informing me he had succeeded Giuseppe Monaco and enclosing photos taken of my visit to Ispica. With regard to the Monument, he repeated what Mr. Monaco had told me: the problem was the sole responsibility of the Italian Government. However, he expressed his approval of the initiative.

I also received another letter from a citizen in Ispica I had not met during my visit. He was Antonino Lauretta, the Director of an organization known as the Centro di Cultura Popolare, Ispica. He regretted not meeting me and said he was making a video documentary of the landing of the Canadian Division in 1943, and of the time when I was Mayor of Ispica. He would be grateful if I could enlighten him with testimony about this important period in the long history of Ispica and send him photos and material.

He added a cultural note to broaden my knowledge of this history. The beaches where the Canadian had landed in 1943 have been known as Ulysses' Harbour since ancient times. There is still a Porto Ulisse there. The harbour is mentioned by Cicero, Pliny and Ptolemy. Several finds have been made in the sand including fragments of a Byzantine ship. Ulysses had landed there during his odyssey, before returning to Ithaca.

Well, this was certainly a welcome development and a request I could not refuse. I immediately sent Antonino extracts from my book and a copy of the article in *Corriere Canadese*. His reference to Ulysses I found intensely interesting. What an incredible coincidence that I had trod in his very footsteps or at least sailed in his waters. I could not remember whether the Staff Officers had given us this intriguing information when we were being briefed for the landing. It probably would not have inspired us to greater feats of valour but it would have made interesting reading in our letters home.

It was now time to knock on the door of Gerry Merrithew again, and advise him of the growing interest in the Monument by both the citizens of Ispica and the Italian community in Toronto. There was no use in flogging the issue of getting the Canadian Government to pay the cost. That was as *finito* as a dead Sicilian mule. The main issue now was to secure the approval of the Italian Government, as requested by the Mayors of Ispica. I asked Mr. Merrithew if he would be kind enough to obtain such approval. Though I made my request in pure innocence of the problems involved, I realized it would take some time. It was now November 7th and the proposed date for the Pilgrimage to Sicily was May 11/12, 1991.

I also realized that even if the Italian Government consented, they were not likely to pay for the project. This left only one source of financial support—me. Obviously I could not and should not pay the entire amount so I began sounding out my D-Day Dodger friends for financial support without yet having any idea of the cost. As I suspected, my friends were very enthusiastic but wanted an estimate of the cost before making a firm commitment.

Throughout all these developments, I reported to Carmelo Nigro, the author of the article in *Il Coccodrillo* the previous June, which had generated the remarkable enthusiasm for the project. I also kept in touch with Marie Gennaro who spent many hours translating letters and material to and from Ispica.

I didn't hear from Carmelo until late in December when I received some shattering news. There had been an earthquake in nearby Siracusa which had caused serious damage. As a result, he had noticed a certain lessening of enthusiasm for the project. Furthermore, the newspaper *Il Coccodrillo* had ceased publishing and he could no longer write any more articles.

No further communications from any of the actors in this drama arrived for the rest of December, all of January and into February, and I was beginning to feel the pangs of defeat.

A glimmer of light finally appeared on February 8th when I got a call from André Petelle giving me the news that, due to the Gulf War, the Official Pilgrimage had been postponed from May 11/12 to September 21/22. It wasn't much of a present but at least I had been given another four months to rally the troops and raise the money.

No further word arrived until Gerry Merrithew wrote on March 17th. This is his letter:

March 17, 1991

Dear Syd:

In your letter of November 7, 1990, you asked me to secure the consent of the Italian Government for the erection of a memorial on the beaches where 1st Canadian Division landed in July 1943.

> *An approach was made on our behalf by the Canadian Embassy in Rome and we have been informed that the Italian Government is not involved. In accordance with law No. 204 dated 9 January 1951 (Honours to the War Dead) the Department of Defence is only involved when dealing with memorials keeping, or destined to keep, the remains of Italian war dead.*
>
> *Memorials for others than Italians who died in war fall under local initiative (city halls, committees, private citizens).*
>
> *You are advised by the Canadian Embassy to submit a specific request to the City Hall administration of Ispica which, following the appropriate resolution, will make available to the group the piece of land required for the monument. Should the request be denied by the local administration, it is the opinion of the Canadian Embassy that the Italian Department of Defence would not be able to intervene.*
>
> *I trust this information will be useful. I wish you luck in your undertaking.*
>
> *Kindest personal regards.*

I appreciated very much Gerry Merrithew's support and interest but my simple request for the consent of the Italian Government had now burgeoned into a legal hassle or buck-passing exercise between two levels of the Italian Government, one in Rome and the other in Ispica. I thought of Ulysses. No doubt he had his problems when he landed in Sicily, but at least he returned home a hero. He didn't have to contend with the fine points of Italian law, the Gulf War, and earthquakes, that were frustrating my efforts. This was probably the low point in my own Odyssey.

In my extremity, I got in touch with Marie Gennaro. She suggested I write the new Vice-Mayor of Ispica and the Mayor of Pachino and tell them quite frankly that the Italian Government is only involved with memorials to Italian dead, in accordance with law No. 204, dated January 1951, and that a memorial to Canadian soldiers was the responsibility of the local governments.

With considerable foreboding, I wrote as suggested and sent the letters to Marie on April 3rd for translation and forwarding to Ispica and Pachino. She also sent copies to Carmelo.

On April 29th, Marie phoned to report that Carmelo had phoned her that the Mayors of Ispica and Pachino were looking for a plot of land. On May 2nd, she phoned again with further good news: The Mayors were getting prices for a stone or marble plaque.

Finally, on June 3rd, I received the following letter from Carmelo:

> *May 27, 1991*
>
> *Dear Mr. Frost:*
> *This is Carmelo Nigro from Ispica.*
> *The city administrations of Pachino and Ispica are willing to get the concrete base ready for the commemoration stone but you should send them a sketch, a design, of the monument you want to have built, as soon as possible.*
>
> *I should like to have this sketch, together with the words you wish to be inscribed on the marble stone. It shall be my concern to find a marble cutter provided that I get the expense money from you.*
>
> *I should also like to know whether you and I can get in touch by phone fax. If so, please send me your fax number.*
> *Truly yours,*
> *Carmelo Nigro*

I immediately phoned my intermediary par excellence, Marie, read Carmelo's letter and suggested that she ask Carmelo to clarify the following points:

Questions to ask Carmelo Nigro

1. Land and base for the monument.
Will this be donated by Ispica and Pachino, without any expense to me?
2. Where is the land?
I must know the location so that I can draft the words for the inscription. For example, if the land is not near the beaches, I can't say that the Canadian soldiers landed here on July 10th, 1943.
Also, the Honourable Minister of Veterans Affairs will be attending the Ceremony and he will want to know the exact location of the monument.
Also, the people I am asking to supply the money for the monument want to know where it is located.
3. Size of the monument.
I suggest a rectangular monument, 6 feet high, 3 feet wide, and 6 inches thick.

4. What material will the monument be made of?
Marble, brick, concrete, or some other material? The cost cannot be decided until the material has been chosen.
5. Cost of monument.
As I have to raise the money from a number of veterans, they will want to know the cost.
6. Ceremony to unveil the Monument—Sunday, September 22nd.
As I say, the Minister, as well as a group of veterans will be attending the Ceremony. Can you tell me who will likely be present from Ispica and Pachino, and how do you think the Ceremony should be conducted?
7. Letters from the Mayors of Ispica and Pachino.
The Minister of Veterans Affairs (Mr. Gerald S. Merrithew) and my contributors to the cost of the monument, will need letters from these Mayors confirming the above matters, particularly the location of the monument and the cost.

Two other matters concerned me. Carmelo had asked for a sketch or design of the monument and for the wording to be inscribed on the plaque. I was not an architect nor was I a Cicero or Pliny who could compose a wording that would be appropriate for a Monument to be erected on Ulysses Beach. But I decided to give it a try.

Marie phoned on June 11th. She had had long conversations with Carmelo and he had suggested that the three of us have a conference call to settle all outstanding points.

On July 12th, Marie attended my home and for the next hour we talked with Carmelo, with me speaking a mixture of Italian "dialetto" and English. In the end, all points were discussed and settled. *We Had Our Monument!* I felt like Ulysses after the siege of Troy.

The towns of Ispica and Pachino would pay the full cost of erecting the Monument and the inscription, including the Coat of Arms of the Canadian Forces. The land had been generously donated by the Gradanti-Fronte families of Ispica. The location would be about 200 yards from the beaches where the First Division had come ashore July 10th, 1943. The two Mayors would be present as well as a large gathering of Civilian, Military and Religious authorities, from the Provinces of Ragusa and Siracusa, and many others.

On June 13th, I sent Carmelo a fax along with a sketch of the Monument and the following inscription:

PILGRIMAGE—1991

> *July 10, 1943*
> *On This Day, Canada's Soldiers*
> *Of The First Division*
> *Landed On These Shores.*
> *From Little Towns In A Far-Away Land*
> *They Came In The Cause Of Freedom.*
> *Erected To Their Memory*
> *By The Citizens Of*
> *Pachino And Ispica*
> *September 22, 1991*

With the overall plans for the Monument approved, it was now just a matter of time. It was mid-June and the Ceremony was set for September 22nd. Would everything be completed?

I continued to receive letters and faxes from Carmelo reporting on the progress of the work including detailed drawings and specifications which I duly approved with my new-found expertise as an architect (unpaid). The Mayors of Ispica and Pachino sent me formal invitations and confirmed that all costs would be assumed by their Municipalities.

André Petelle and Peter Caisse sent me nice letters of congratulations for my part in the project. André kindly acknowledged that it was indeed an important accomplishment to have succeeded in having a Memorial erected in Sicily honouring the First Canadian Infantry Division. Peter invited me to attend their Ceremony at the Agira Cemetery on September 21st.

The Department also thanked Carmelo for his efforts in making the Monument a reality and said it would be an honour for the Honourable Gerald Merrithew, Minister of Veterans Affairs for Canada, to participate in the unveiling ceremony. His group would total 80 and would be accompanied by a Pipe Band of 12 musicians from the Canadian Armed Forces.

The Department would appreciate knowing what would be expected of the Minister: would he be asked to speak, lay a wreath, etc. A representative would be attending Ispica in advance of the official delegation to meet Carmelo and members of his committee to go over final details.

The project had suddenly taken on a life of its own and I could gracefully retire to the wings to await the big day. But unbeknown to me, there was one final actor in this drama to make his appearance on the stage. Without any prior warning, I received a telephone call one day from Sebastian Spataro of Toronto. His wife, Rosaria had just returned from Ispica and brought greetings from his cousin Carmelo. Sebastian had been born in Ispica and had immigrated to Canada in 1958. He was a brother of Maria Gennaro and an uncle of

Marie, with whom I had been working on the Monument for the past year. Moreover, Rosaria was a cousin of Antonino Lauretta, the Director of the Centro di Cultura Popolare in Ispica with whom I had had some correspondence and who also sent me greetings.

Are all Sicilians related?

From then on, the Spataros took over the parts formerly played so well by the Gennaros. In due course, I met the family and from that date to the present, have enjoyed the friendship of another fine Sicilian family. Besides Sebastian and Rosaria, there are two daughters, Rosanna and Josephine.

Rosanna was an Assistant Supervisor of a Bank and a professional translator. She generously gave her time to translate the steady stream of correspondence that still passes between Carmelo and me, as well as countless letters to and from officials and friends in Ispica and Pachino. As I am writing, she is busy translating another parcel of letters and material from Carmelo.

The following is just one of the many letters from Carmelo bearing timely and important information about the Unveiling Ceremony which she translated:

Comune Di Ispica

August 28, 1991

Dear Rosanna:
Please give Mr. Frost this information:
The Mayors of Pachino and Ispica, and other civil and military authorities of Ragusa and Siracusa's districts will be present at the Unveiling Ceremony, as I will specify later. As soon as possible, I would like to receive the stylized coat of arms that marks soldiers of the First Division to print on the memorial tablet.

The ceremony should take place on September 22, in the late hours of the morning, between 10:00 and 11:00 a.m. In the afternoon, few people would come for the very hot climate.

A religious function will be celebrated in the place where the monument rises. The President of "Centro Incontro Anziani", the Mayors of the two towns, Minister G. Merrithew and the undersigned will speak. Some wreaths will be laid.

Yours sincerely,
Carmelo Nigro

Right up to the date I left Toronto on September 11th, Rosanna translated last minute communications from Carmelo and Ispica and even helped me to compose and practise delivering my speech in Italian. A remarkable lady.

And so, on September 11th, I boarded Canadian Airlines Flight 44V for Rome where I picked up my car and drove to Sicily where I checked in at my favourite hotel in Taormina. I had the good sense to give myself a few days rest before attending the ceremonies at Agira and Ispica. I needed it.

My first priority was to get in touch with Carmelo Nigro and recce the site of the Monument. On September 19th, I drove to Ispica following the coastal road past Augusta, Siracusa and Avola, a distance of 188 kilometres. Carmelo and his family were waiting for me: Emanuela, his wife, Maria Luisa, a daughter, Angela, another daughter and her husband, Salvatore and their son, Leonardo. It was quite an emotional meeting with everyone talking at once, including me. (Again I silently thanked having spent all those evenings studying Italian at Seneca College.)

First order of business was lunch, which gave me a good opportunity to get to know this fine Sicilian family. Carmelo, short in stature but long in intellect and determination, was a school teacher; Emanuela, a gracious lady, plied me with gourmet food; Angela was a school teacher; Maria Luisa and Salvatore vied with Carmelo in admiring their young son. The only member of the family who was not present was the son, Giorgio, who lived in Sardegna.

Fortunately, I had the foresight to bring along some gifts: a PPCLI tie and plaque for Carmelo; Canada pins and PPCLI hat badges for mother and daughters; a book of photos of my earlier visits to Ispica for Salvatore. For young Leonardo I had a virtual treasure trove of souvenirs: my old campaign ribbons, division and PPCLI flashes from my uniform, several 10 lire notes from the war, and my whistle. Everyone was delighted with my souvenirs, except perhaps the whistle, which I was later told Leonardo blew continually to impress his little friends.

I was anxious to get going and see the Memorial for which Carmelo and I had laboured the past two years. We drove toward the sea and then along the coast and suddenly there it was—set on a white stone base with a shining marble plaque, and in rear, a large painted mural that extended on either side of the Monument—a magnificent memorial to the men of the First Canadian Infantry Division.

The Monument is located at Marza overlooking the beaches a few hundred yards distant. I asked Carmelo if the place had a special significance. "*Sì, Colonnello*," he replied. "Marza is an ancient Saracen term for 'port'. And, of course, the sea out there is Ulysses Harbour. Marza was, and still is, an important link to yesterday's and today's society. The Monument completes its centuries old history."

"*Bravo*," I said, "*tu sei un proprio professore, classico. Mille grazie.*"

As we drove away, I noticed several sailors in United States uniforms walking beside the road. "*Chi sono*?", I asked. Carmelo explained that the Monument was near a United States Naval Air facility. They had been very interested in the Monument and, in fact, had offered their dining facilities for a reception after the Unveiling Ceremony on September 22nd. "*Allora!*" I exclaimed. "*Questa sera una ceremonia internationale!*" Carmelo nodded gravely, "*D'accordo*".

A few miles further on, we came to a lovely wide sandy beach with modern hotels, swimming pools, tennis courts and all the amenities found in first-class tourist resorts. Again I had to query my friend. "What is this?" Carmelo was happy to tell me that the area is known as Villagio Marispica (Ispica By-the-Sea) and it is crowded with tourists from all over Europe, especially *tedeschi*.

"Germans," I cried, half in anguish, "I thought we had sent them packing to their own country in 1943." Carmelo laughed and quoted that old saying, "The more things change, the more they remain the same".

We turned into the complex, found a quiet bar and enjoyed a break from the boiling sun. I was quickly becoming acclimatized to the Sicilian way of life and would have enjoyed a little siesta. But we had more places to visit and people to meet. Carmelo relaxed his usual formal manner and told me some of the problems he had encountered in building the Monument. Money was the big obstacle. Several organizations reneged on their promises of support. He spent untold hours and many lire on telephone calls and trips to municipal offices arranging the details of the ceremonies. For some of these trips he borrowed a car but most were by his moped.

"You drove to Pachino and other places on your moped?" I asked. "*Si Colonnello, molte volte, e fa molto caldo.*" I had to suppress a smile as I imagined the dignified professor "putt-putting" along a busy highway, in his formal suit and sitting erect on his moped.

Carmelo continued. "Now we are going to meet one organization which did not let me down, Associazione Centro d'Incontro Anziani—CIA (Centre for Seniors). They were most supportive and donated a large sum to the project. The President is Mrs. Carmela Maucieri."

This was something that had bothered me right from the start. Where did Carmelo get the money. I was sorry to hear that my friend was out of pocket a substantial sum, but I knew he would be offended if I offered to share his loss. So, I suggested that I make a contribution to the Associazione. Carmelo was very pleased with the idea and suggested I tell Mrs. Maucieri when we met. And, he added, "Be prepared for a little surprise."

We arrived at the CIA and were met by Mrs. Maucieri and some of her staff. Carmelo did the introductions. *"Signora, ti presento il mio amico Colonnello Frost."* I hardly had time to shake hands before a little old man bounded forward and grabbed my hand. *"Colonnello, il mio Colonnello. È bello rivederti."* It was Monaca, my faithful civil servant when I was Mayor of Ispica.

I met many other senior citizens who had gathered to meet me; some even claimed to remember those days of 48 years earlier. It was wonderful to be among friends and be able to converse with them in Italian (provided they spoke *lentemente e fortemente*). In between conversations, I had a moment with Mrs. Maucierei and offered to make a modest donation to the Monument. She was very pleased to accept my gift. I also presented her with a PPCLI plaque, with the following inscription:

Presented
To Associazione Centro d'Incontro Anziani
In Appreciation of
the Monument erected
to the memory of the soldiers
of the First Canadian Division
September 22, 1991

It was time to go. Carmelo and I had accomplished a lot and I was satisfied that all was in readiness for the Dedication Ceremony on September 22nd. I promised to arrive in good time for the Ceremony which began at 11:00 a.m.

Meanwhile, the Official Pilgrimage of the Minister of Veterans Affairs had been following its own schedule of events. It had arrived in Rome on September 18th and had been visiting War Cemeteries in Rome, Cassino and Anzio. It was due to arrive in Catania on September 21st to take part in a Ceremony at Agira that afternoon. The Minister had kindly given me an invitation to join his delegation for this important event.

Delegation members are selected by the Regiments and Corps concerned. Navy and Air Force representatives are similarly selected by the associations representing these groups. All expenses of the members are paid by the Government, including air fare, accommodation and meals. The Department endeavours to have these Pilgrimages covered by the Canadian media, but sadly, through no fault of the Department, these events are often ignored by our newspapers, magazines, TV and radio. It is beyond the scope of this book to enumerate countless examples of this lack of interest but I can state unequivocally that my files contain ample evidence on which my assertion is based.

PILGRIMAGE—1991

Again, I have strayed from my main theme, but I feel strongly that our media have not in the past, properly recognized and honoured the sacrifice and achievements of Canada's Armed Forces. Although, I will admit, that in recent years this indifference is changing.

I have never had the honour and privilege of being a part of the Official Delegation in the many Pilgrimages I have made to Italy. Frankly, I am happy to pursue my own itinerary and not be subject to the necessary restraints of the Official Group, which must conform to a set timetable. Thus, in 1991, I was free to visit Ispica in advance of the Ceremony.

The members of the Official Delegation numbered 79 which consisted of the following groups:

Minister's Party	16
Veterans' Group	46
Project Team	10
Media	7
	79

Scanning the list, I was happy to see several Veterans I knew:

Smoky Smith, VC, of the Seaforth Highlanders of Canada. He was awarded the Victoria Cross for his incredible valour during the crossing of the Savio River on October 21st, 1944. The Seaforths were part of the Second Brigade which included the Patricias who also attacked across the Savio River. They suffered severe casualties and also won several decorations for bravery.

John Clarke, a member of the PPCLI and long time Secretary-Treasurer of the Toronto Branch of the PPCLI Association. He also took part in the crossing of the Savio River but was wounded in the next battle at Fossio Munio where Lt. Bill Roach won a DSO.

MGen. Pat Bogert, CBE, DSO. He had been our Brigade Commander during the secret move of the First Division from Italy to Holland, and for the remainder of the war. I relate only one incidental memory of the Brigadier. On March 9th, 1945, he called the PPCLI together and told us we were headed for Germany. One man called out, "We'll show 'em that the D-Day Dodgers know how to fight." Our soldierly, gentlemanly Brigadier immediately responded with some sage advise, "We'll show them by deeds rather than by words".

It also pleased me that the list of the members of the Project Team included a serving officer in the PPCLI—Capt. Kurt Fredrickson.

September 21st was the day set aside for a Service of Remembrance at the Agira War Cemetery. Again I took Autostrada

114 south to Catania, (which I now considered my private right-of-way) and then Autostrada 19 west to where a sideroad ran north to Agira. I have described earlier the magnificent location of the Cemetery where 490 soldiers of Canada rest, but perhaps I will be pardoned for making one last reference to this outpost of Canadian valour. As one approaches the site through a parched and barren land, the Cemetery arises like a desert mirage—verdant grass, beautiful hedges and flowers, shady trees, the whole watered by many unseen sprinklers. As you pass through the wrought-iron gates, you are immediately struck by the immaculate pathways and the freshly turned earth at every grave.

The Ceremony was performed with simple dignity. A beautiful program, bearing a coloured photo of the Cemetery was handed to each Veteran. I kept mine.

Veterans Affairs Canada
Pilgrimage To Italy—September 1991

Ceremony Of Remembrance
At Agira Canadian War Cemetery
On Saturday 21 September 1991 At 15:00 Hrs.

Order Of Ceremony
Addresses

Hon. Gerald Merrithew
Minister of Veterans Affairs of Canada
Dr. Giovanni Di Cara
Regional Commissioner in Agira

Prayers
Act Of Remembrance
Hymn
Last Post—Silence—Lament—Reveille
Wreath Laying
Blessing
The Pipes and Drums Band is from the 3rd Battalion,
Royal Canadian Regiment, stationed in Germany.

After the service, I signed the Visitors' Book and was gratified to find my signature from the year before. Perhaps the Commonwealth War Graves Commission had paid attention to my pleas not to destroy the books.

Once again, I strolled through the Cemetery paying a silent tribute at the foot of each of the 29 headstones marking the Patricias who fell in Sicily.

I slowly drove back to Taormina and prepared for the morrow—The dedication of the Monument.

* * *

September 22nd, 1991

I arose very early, almost with the sun, and dressed quickly. Then I went out to the balcony of my hotel, perched on a lofty terrace overhanging the meandering coastline far below. To the west, massive Mount Etna with its snowy peak dominated the lush countryside. A wisp of grey smoke issued from its volcanic core and lazily vanished into the clear blue sky. No earthquake today, *grazie Dio*.

To save time, I skipped breakfast, jumped into my Mercedes and carefully negotiated the switchback road down to Autostrada 18 leading to Catania. Traffic had not yet begun to build and I zipped along the coastal road enjoying the panorama.

Off to my left, the deep blue waters of the Ionian Sea; on my right, neatly terraced hillsides bearing trees and vines; and on both sides of the highway, flowers of every kind, some wild, some cultivated and others in baskets hanging from posts. Sometimes a high cliff would appear to block the road ahead, but tunnels, half a mile in length, allowed the road to continue on its course straight through the mountain.

I had driven this way many times before, but always in heavy traffic and I never had a chance to enjoy the magnificent scenery. I remembered the first time I had travelled an earlier version of the highway in 1943, going north to rejoin the Patricias after recovering from a malarial attack. Then, I had more pressing matters to think about than scenery but I remembered passing by Taormina where General Montgomery had his headquarters and thinking I might someday visit the place. I also remembered that the Founder of the PPCLI, Hammie Gault, used to spend his holidays in Taormina before WWII.

Now here I was speeding along the very route that Colonel Gault must have taken many times. This time I was not on a mission of War but on a mission of Remembrance of the soldiers of The First Canadian Division. I felt that Hammie Gault would have approved.

I checked my speedometer. 160 kilometers an hour was a little too fast even if I had the highway to myself. There are speed limits in Italy but they are irrelevant. Neither drivers nor police pay much attention to them.

This was not the time to tempt fate to deal me a blow. This was the day I had been looking forward to ever since my stroll on the barren beaches near Pachino two years earlier. How would it all turn out? I glanced at my watch. There was time to grab a quick breakfast at a roadside *Trattoria*. I would need it for the long day ahead.

I entered Ispica by the "back door," that is to say the road with the hairpin bends past the caves that I had first used when my platoon occupied the town in 1943. Carmelo was waiting for me outside his home and the two of us set off for Marza.

As we approached the site of the Monument, I could scarcely believe my eyes. The narrow coastal road was jammed with vehicles, soldiers (Italian and Canadian), sailors, airmen, Carabinieri, Boy Scouts, Church groups with large banners, citizens, members of the media and photographers (Italian and Canadian), policemen, bands (Military and Bag Pipes), Canadian Veterans, Senators and members of the House of Commons. It seemed as if half the population of Pachino, Ispica and adjoining municipalities had turned out for the occasion. I was totally unprepared for what was to follow.

A long wooden platform or stage had been erected in a field across from the Monument on which 30 or 40 dignitaries were assembled. Carmelo and I were escorted to the stage and deposited front and centre of this distinguished group. It is quite impossible to list all the names but I will mention a few.

- Mrs. Carmela Maucieri, President of Associazione d'Incontro Anziani, Ispica.
- Professore Lupo Sebastiano, Mayor of Pachino
- Dr. Carmelo Tomasi, Mayor of Ispica
- Assessore Ai Beni Culturali di Pachino
- Assessore Ai Servizi Sociali di Ispica
- Mr. Antonino Lauretta, Director of Centro di Cultura Popolare, Ispica
- The family Gradanti-Fronte (who donated the land)
- Minister of Veterans Affairs, The Honourable Gerald Merrithew
- MGen. Pat Bogert, CBE, DSO, CD
- Smoky Smith, VC
- Representatives from the Canadian Senate
- Representatives from the Canadian House of Commons
- Representatives from the Canadian Legion, Council of Veterans, Army, Navy and Air Force Veterans, War Museum
- Senior Officer of the U.S. Naval Air Facility
- Senior Officer of the Italian Army
- Senior Officer of the Carabiniere

- Senior Officer of the local Police Force
- Friar Pietro Iabichella, Order of Grey Friars

And many others, including representatives from the municipalities of Ragusa and Modica.

The Ceremony for the Unveiling of the Monument, on the 48th Anniversary of the landing of the First Canadian Division on July 10th, 1943, began sharply at ll:00 a.m. To my surprise and delight the "Master" of Ceremonies turned out to be two charming sisters, Enza and Rosy Scifo, of Pachino. They had spent many hours organizing the ceremonies, doing research and translating speeches. Their presence added a very warm touch to what otherwise might have been a very sombre occasion.

The first guest to speak was Mrs. Carmela Maucieri, the President of the CIA who had given so much support to the project.

Then the Mayors of Pachino and Ispica.

The next speaker was Gerald Merrithew who kindly mentioned my "campaign". The following is an extract:

> *My sincerest thanks to the Mayors and citizens of Pachino and Ispica for making this ceremony possible. On behalf of the Government of Canada and our veterans, thank you for your generosity.*
>
> *I know Colonel Frost also appreciates your thoughtfulness. He has long wanted to see a monument raised in honour of the lst Canadian Division. Again, the Colonel has led a successful campaign.*
>
> *Our landing in Sicily in July, 1943, was a special tonic for Canadians. I am sure that the memory of Dieppe haunted the minds of our military planners. They couldn't help but remember that less than a year before, other Canadians had landed in Dieppe on the French coast.*
>
> *The Dieppe raid, rooted in doubt, changing plans and faulty intelligence, was a disaster.*
>
> *The news from Sicily, in contrast, was a cause for relief and rejoicing. The invasion was well planned and decisive.*
>
> *This morning, we remember those of the lst Canadian Division who died securing such a firm foothold in Sicily and those who died carrying the fight deep into Italy.*
>
> *They died passing along a great tradition to future generations.*

Carmelo Nigro then came to the microphone and gave a powerful speech. He had done his homework and faultlessly described the landing of the First Division, right down to Brigades and Regiments, particularly the actions of the PPCLI and my brief stint as Mayor of Ispica. He then mentioned "my shadow," Monaca, who had been of such help to me in performing my duties. Whereupon Monaca bounded onto the stage and we embraced. Such a thoughtful gesture. "*Grazie, Carmelo.*"

The Mayors of Pachino and Ispica then advanced to the Monument for the Unveiling. After the blessing, the flags of Canada and Italy were flown and the Band played the National Anthems of both countries.

This impressive ceremony was followed by the laying of numerous wreaths, by the Canadian Delegation and the Italian authorities. One after the other they made their way through the crowd and reverently placed their wreaths beside the Monument. Another nice gesture was the laying of a huge wreath from Canada. It was borne by Italian Boy Scouts. Never before have I seen such beautiful wreaths. Some were at least three feet tall.

Returning to the stage, the Mayors of Pachino and Ispica presented medals to all the Canadian Veterans, inscribed as follows:

In Ricordo
Dello Sbarco
10 7 1943
11 9 1991
Ispica—Pachino

This was a welcome and much appreciated surprise. More was to come.

The Mayor of Ispica then called me to the microphone and after saying a few words of thanks for my service as Mayor of his town, presented me with a handsome plate. It is one of my most prized possessions and is before me as I write. It is inscribed as follows:

L'Amministrazione Communale
Al Primo Sindaco Democratico
Della Citta Di Ispica
10 Luglio 1943—22 Septembre 1991

Which translated reads:

From the Municipal Administration
(of Ispica) to the First
Democratic Mayor of The City of Ispica
July 10th, 1943—September 22nd, 1991

It was now my turn to respond to all this wonderful outpouring of respect, admiration and friendship from the citizens of Ispica and

Pachino to the soldiers of the First Division, and through them to Canada itself. How could one express our thanks in a meaningful way?

Fortunately, I had the foresight to bring with me PPCLI Regimental Plaques which I now presented to the Mayors of Ispica and Pachino. They were inscribed as follows:

Presented to
The Citizens of Ispica (Pachino)
By Col. C. S. Frost, PPCLI
In Appreciation of the
Monument erected to the
Memory of the soldiers
Of the First Canadian Division
September 22, 1991

It will be recalled that I had already presented similar plaques to Carmelo Nigro and Mrs. Maucieri of the CIA.

But I felt the occasion called for some special manifestation of my respect, admiration and friendship for the citizens of Ispica and Pachino. To this end I had prepared and practised *ad nauseam* a speech in Italian. Here it is in both languages:

Speech By Colonel C. S. Frost
To The Citizens Of
Pachino and Ispica, Sicily
September 22, 1991

Signor Presidente del Centro Incontro Anziani, Signori Sindaci di Pachino e Ispica, Onorevole Gerald Merrithew, Signore e Signori.

Vi ringrazio per questo magnifico Monumento, eretto dai cittadini di Pachino e Ispica. Questo Monumento rimane in memoria ai soldati canadesi che sbarcarono nelle spiaggi della Sicilia, il dieci Luglio, 1943. Questi eroici soldati, pagarano con la loro vita per la libertà di un paese non loro. È per questo atto daltruismo, che oggi, i nostri paesi si uniscono. Per dimostrarvi quanto questo gesto sia stato apprezzato da me e dal mio Reggimento, PPCLI, è mio piacere presentarvi, in omaggio, questo stemma che commemora questa occasione così grande e così memorabile. Grazie a tutti presenti.

> *President of the Old Peoples Meeting Centre, Mayors of Pachino and Ispica, The Honourable Gerald Merrithew, Ladies and Gentlemen.*
>
> *Thank you for this magnificent Monument erected by the citizens of Pachino and Ispica. This Monument stands in memory to the Canadian soldiers who landed on the beaches of Sicily on July 10, 1943.*
>
> *These heroic soldiers paid with their lives for the liberty of a country not their own. It is for this altruistic act that today our countries are united. To show how much this gesture has been appreciated by me and my Regiment, the PPCLI, it is my pleasure to present in honour, this Coat of Arms that commemorates this great and memorable occasion. Thanks to all who are present.*

The final scene in this incredible drama took place in the Messes of the US Naval Air Facility just around the corner from the Monument. The Minister and his party, the Veterans and the local Dignitaries were invited to a buffet lunch. What a splendid way to end a memorable day! It gave me a chance to meet some of the Veterans and the Minister's Party, and thank the members of the Project Team. First and foremost, was the Minister himself, Gerry Merrithew, who had expressed Canada's grateful acceptance of the honour bestowed upon the First Division; then, André Petelle and Peter Caissie who had supported me throughout the long ordeal and kept me informed.

I made a point of meeting Capt. Kurt Fredrickson, PPCLI, one of the conducting officers. He had played an important role in the Laying of Wreaths. During a lull in the reception, I whisked him and John Clarke, the Patricia representative, to the Monument and arranged to have a photo taken of the three of us standing in front of the wreaths.

At the same time, Capt. Fredrickson produced a name plate which he pinned to my blazer. It read "PPCLI Expert"! He wouldn't tell me where it came from or on whose authority, but it gave everyone a chuckle, not only that day, but many times since when I have had the nerve to wear it.

I also got hold of the Gradanti-Fronte family who had donated the land and had a photo taken of the family—all eleven of them!

Still more surprises arrived. Antonino Lauretta, of the Centro di Cultura Popolare, took me aside and presented me with five limited edition prints by a well-known Sicilian artist, Pietro Ricca. He also told me he had made a video of the Ceremony which he would send me as soon as it was edited. How to thank these wonderful generous people? It was impossible.

A little while later, a member of the Centro d'Incontro Anziani came up and handed me a dozen postcards showing a stylized drawing of the Monument. He was selling them for 1,000 lire each, (I assume to help pay for the Memorial), but refused any payment from me saying, "*Per i tuoi amici, Colonnello.*" (For your friends.)

The party began to breakup but I wanted to say hello to that durable soldier—Smoky Smith V.C. We've known each other a long time, and we talked of the Savio River where he won the highest military honour anyone can receive. Old soldiers can joke about anything, even a Victoria Cross. I pointed to his long row of medals and observed he wasn't wearing the new medal we had just received. "Well," he smiled, "I wasn't sure whether you put it in front of or after the V.C.". What a guy!

Another Veteran, whose name now escapes me, came up, shook my hand and said "Thanks, Syd. Perhaps this will inspire other Units to do the same thing".

The party was over but the memories of that day shall ever remain.

> *The tumult and the shouting dies,*
> *The captains and the kings depart,*
> *Still stands thine ancient sacrifice,*
> *An humble and a contrite heart.*
> *Lord God of Hosts be with us yet,*
> *Lest we forget, lest we forget.*

Before leaving Ispica, I was persuaded by Carmelo to join him and his family for a "light" supper. I couldn't resist, knowing there is no such thing in Italian culinary arts. In between courses of spaghetti, pesce, vitello parmigiano, frutta and dolce, we reviewed all that had happened. For me, it was the event of a lifetime and I think it was for Carmelo too. Everything had come together exactly as planned. In fact, it had exceeded everyone's expectations.

Over coffee and sambucca, I confessed that on several occasions in the past two years when the project seemed doomed, such as the earthquake, I had considered scaling it down to just a simple Monument to the PPCLI. I knew that was something I could handle with the support of the Regiment. Carmelo raised his hands in shock. "*Oh, no, caro Colonnello. Che peccato! Mi piace che lei ha deciso di rimanere con la Prima Divisione.*" (I am glad you decided to stay with the First Division.)

He was right. It would have been a great shame and I said so. "*D'accordo.*"

One other matter had bothered me. It was a touchy issue and I was not sure how Carmelo would react. I decided to come right to the point.

PILGRIMAGE—1991

"Dear Carmelo, do you mind if I bring up a rather delicate matter? Throughout the ceremonies today, there was nothing but friendship, goodwill and respect from all the people. It was very gratifying because I had thought there might be some objection to the very nature of the event—honouring Canadian soldiers."

Carmelo winced a bit and said that he had received a few complaints from Italian veterans that there should also have been erected a memorial to the Italian soldiers and civilians who perished in the bombing and assault.

I immediately agreed and told him I appreciated his frankness. In fact, that very idea of another Monument to the Italians had been growing in my mind for some time, and I added, "This time the cost should be paid by Canada."

It was a spontaneous remark which, for a moment, I regretted, but quickly realized it was the right thing to do. What a fitting way to thank our Italian friends who had done so much for us. I hadn't the foggiest notion where the money would come from, certainly not from the Canadian Government. But from the enthusiasm I had seen on this wonderful day, I was certain the D-Day Dodgers would support the new Monument.

Carmelo and I rose from the table, shook hands and embraced. We had just given ourselves a new cause to fight for and, as it turned out, a way of preserving the legitimacy and existence of the Canadian Monument for all time.

I said my last goodbyes to this wonderful Sicilian family I had come to love and respect. Little Leonardo gave me a shy look and asked if he could blow a few toots on his whistle. "*Sì, sì, mio caro ragazzo.*" I promised to return at the first opportunity. It was not an idle gesture. I knew I would soon be back again.

I left Taormina the next day by car, crossed the Strait of Messina to Reggio, then followed the route the Regiment had taken through the centre of the Aspromonte Range to Cittanova and Locri on the east coast, where I took the coastal road north to Catanzaro. From there, I turned inland, and instead of following the advance of the Regiment along the east coast, I traced the same route I had taken in 1943 on my dash to rejoin the Regiment—Soveria, Nicastro, Belvedere, Lagonegro, Corleto and Potenza where I had finally caught up with the Patricias. Then on to Foggia, Campobasso and Frosolone (where I had been wounded).

At Frosolone I drove east to the Adriatic Sea and followed the coastal road north to Rimini. On the way, I stopped off at Ortona to visit the Moro River Canadian War Cemetery where 1,375 Canadians are buried. Continuing north, I visited the following War Cemeteries.

(Numbers given are Canadian graves).
  Ancona (161)
  Montecchio (289) near Pesaro
  Gradara (369) near Cattolica
  Coriano Ridge (427) south of Rimini
  Cesena (307) north of Rimini

At Rimini, I turned west to Florence where there are 50 graves of Canadian soldiers.

As in Agira, the Cemeteries are gardens of greenery, hedges, beautiful flowers and thick verdant grass, immaculately cared for by professional gardeners. Each Cemetery has its own distinctive setting but all carry the same message—sacrifice and bravery.

These are not the only Cemeteries in Italy where Canada's soldiers rest. There are ten others including the one at Agira which I had visited earlier. Over 5,900 Canadian war dead are buried in Italy and Sicily.

After the war, I covenanted with myself to visit the graves of my comrades and friends as often as possible to keep their memory fresh in my mind. I am proud to say I have honoured my pledge many times over.

Thus my story of the building of a new Monument to Canada's soldiers ends. It now joins the thousands of marble headstones spread throughout Italy, recording the sacrifice of The First Canadian Infantry Division.

If any valedictory is needed, I can do no better than quote from a letter I wrote to the Minister of Veterans Affairs when I returned home, as well as his letter in reply.

November 7, 1991

Dear Gerry:
I am sure you will agree that the Monument is an enduring memorial to the soldiers of the First Canadian Division—the only one in the whole of Italy. It is also, of course, a lasting tribute to the cause of freedom and a symbol of the friendship that binds our two countries. It is my fondest hope that the Monument will inspire other formations and units who fought in Italy to erect their own memorials.

I thought that the Ceremony itself was impressive and inspiring, although some of the speeches were perhaps a trifle too long, (excluding, of course, yours and mine!). You can well imagine my feelings as I stood on the platform in the presence of so many distinguished guests and spoke to the citizens of Ispica and Pachino there assembled. Who would ever have imagined, forty-eight years ago, that such a Ceremony would take place on the very beaches where I landed in 1943.

Certainly the Monument itself is unique—planned, erected and paid for by our former enemies who even gave us medals to mark the occasion. I was also presented with a beautiful plaque as the "first democratic Mayor of Ispica"! Frankly, it strikes me as being somewhat ironic, that my own country has so far failed to honour not only these achievements but also the unique Re-enactment of the Crossing of the Ijssel River in Holland last May.

I have written letters of thanks to the Mayors of Ispica and Pachino, and the various Associations and people who sponsored the Project. In the case of the Associazione Centro d'Incontro Anziani, I have sent them a modest donation to help in their good works.

Thank you for your help in clearing the project with the Italian government, through your Embassy in Rome, and giving me your moral support. You were also very kind to attend the Ceremony with a strong contingent of Veterans, when Sunday had been set aside as a day of rest.

Sincerely,

December 18, 1991
Dear Mr. Frost:
I would like to take this opportunity to offer you my sincerest thanks for your kind letter and for enclosing photographs of the memorable unveiling of the monument to the 1st Division.

As you note, this monument is unique because it would not have been possible without the hard work and dedication of the good people of Pachino and Ispica. It was truly encouraging to see that so many of the local people still retain fond memories of Canadian soldiers. Our delegation of veterans were delighted by the positive reception they received.

Canada has many attributes, among them are the principles for which we stand and the lengths we will travel to defend them. The monument to the "1st Div." is fitting testimony to those Canadians committed to defending these principles. We can now state with some confidence that their efforts will never be forgotten.

I would like to commend you for all your efforts and wish you all the best.

Yours sincerely,
G. S. Merrithew
Gerald S. Merrithew, P.C., M.P.

Chapter IV

PRINCESS LOUISE DRAGOON GUARDS PILGRIMAGE—1993

After returning to Toronto on October 3rd, my first duty was to thank the people both in Italy and in Canada who had contributed their time, effort and money to the erection of the Monument. There were many, but I believe I wrote to most of them. I have already mentioned my letter to Gerry Merrithew; also, two members of his Department, André Petelle and Peter Caissie. The people of Ispica, too numerous to name, are referred to in my letter to the Minister.

For the next several months, I was overwhelmed by correspondence from Carmelo sending me photographs and countless articles in newspapers and magazines about the Ceremony, all in Italian. It seemed that each Sicilian newspaper tried to outdo the others in their graphic descriptions. Indeed, their accounts filled one of the many scrapbooks I keep of these events.

I received several lovely gifts. One was a photograph of the beaches, in a beautiful silver frame, which was delivered to me by two Pachinese gentlemen on behalf of Professor Sebastiano Lupo, Mayor of Pachino. Another was a video of the entire Ceremony, which I received from Antonino Lauretta of the Centro di Cultura Popolare.

Translating all the articles and letters and replying in Italian was a labour of love, but it was still a labour, as my courses in Italian at Seneca College had not yet prepared me for such a task. My teacher was helpful but even he could not keep up with the volume. So, once again, I called on Rosanna Spataro to be my official translator. She was very busy and in the midst of changing employment but she generously came to my aid. Without her help I would still be struggling with the Italian subjunctive which, incidentally, the Sicilians love to use.

Among the pleasant rewards of my journeys to Sicily was the privilege of getting to know so many members of the Toronto Italian community, especially the Spataro and Gennaro families whose connections with Ispica and Pachino I have already mentioned. One of my first acts on returning home, was to take them to an Italian Restaurant for dinner. I brought with me some of the photographs, articles and gifts I had received, including one of the huge posters (three and one-half feet by two feet) that the people of Ispica and Pachino had plastered all over their towns, giving the Program for the Ceremony. The last item was the presentation of a "plate" to Colonnello C. S. Frost. I wish I could have had the poster reduced in size and included in this book!

Then I received a letter from Carmelo that he was writing a book about the "Ups and Downs" of erecting a Monument to be called *La Storia di un Cippo*. He asked me to send him photos and articles from Canadian papers.

Articles from Canadian papers? Carmelo had no understanding of our Canadian media and their idea of what is news. Despite the fact that the Minister's Party to Ispica had included seven media representatives, nothing appeared in the Canadian newspapers about the event except an article in the Halifax Chronicle Herald by my friend Professor Duncan Fraser, which I had sent to him. I had also given reports to the following, which were duly published: The PPCLI, The Royal Military College, The Royal Canadian Military Institute, Doug Fisher of the Royal Canadian Legion and the The Garrison, a newspaper of the Army in Ontario.

Why did a unique event such as the erection of a Monument to the First Canadian Division, by the people of Ispica and Pachino, not receive any attention from the "civilian" media? I think I know part of the problem. By the time the Minister's Party returned to Canada and the Media representatives got around to thinking about what they would write, the event *was* history.

And who in Canada cares a damn about history? Precious few, but I do feel that thanks to the efforts of Jack Granatstein and others there is some hope for the future.

And with that volley, I think I have finished my account of my second Sicilian campaign.

* * *

PRINCESS LOUISE DRAGOON GUARDS PILGRIMAGE—1993

For the remainder of 1991 and into 1992, I was kept busy with the tag-ends of the Pilgrimage, many of which I have described. There were others but enough is enough. By mid-1992, I had pretty well cleared my desk and filed away all my material connected with the Pilgrimage, and I was beginning to think about what I would do in 1993. It would then be two years since the Dedication of the Monument and I wondered if it was being cared for like the Canadian War Cemeteries. I was filled with an almost irrepressible desire to make one more visit to Ispica in 1993.

As already related, I had sent to The Royal Canadian Military Institute, in Toronto, a copy of my report on my 1991 Pilgrimage, which they published, including a photo of the Monument. By chance, a classmate of mine at RMC, LCol. Jock McNeil, saw the article and was so impressed with the Monument that he resolved to organize a Pilgrimage of his own Regiment to Sicily in 1993. Jock was a distinguished officer who had fought throughout Italy with one of Canada's most famous Regiments, The Princess Louise Dragoon Guards (PLDG).

On June 23rd, 1992, I received a call from Jock. "Syd, that's a great thing you did in Sicily. I'm thinking of having the "Plugs" organize a Pilgrimage to see the Monument next May. Would you be interested in joining our group and helping to make the arrangements with the local people?" It was a request I couldn't resist. "Sure. I'll contact Carmelo and the others and send you some material from my last visit. But you'll have to send me your itinerary."

Jock and I are cut from much the same kind of cloth. When we say we're going to do something, we do it. He sent me the itinerary and I sent him the "bumph" on my visit in 1991. I also contacted my own travel agent to book reservations for another tour of Sicily and Italy in May 1993. True to my promise, I wrote Carmelo, the Centro d'Incontro Anziani, the Centro di Cultura Popolare and the Mayors of Ispica and Pachino, all in my brand of Italian (which was steadily improving thanks to my continuing study at Seneca College but I still had to call on Rosanna Spataro for help from time to time).

I kept in touch with Jock and his travel agent, Jim Hayes of Festival Travel, and gave them information on hotels in the area, routes to take and distances between various towns. Jim Hayes wrote me a nice note on October 6th:

PRINCESS LOUISE DRAGOON GUARDS PILGRIMAGE—1993

RE: Princess Louise Dragoon Guards—Sicily & Italy Tour—1993

Dear Mr. Frost,

I am pleased that you have "volunteered" to assist our Group in making the arrangements for a Civic Ceremony at the Canadian War Memorial in Sicily.

Your efforts were instrumental in creating this Memorial and I am pleased that you have taken the task to write to your contacts on our behalf.

The Princess Louise Dragoon Guards plan to leave the Taormina area enroute to the Pachino area on May 4. We expect to arrive around 11 a.m. Our Group size is expected to be approximately 80 people.

I will leave the type of reception to your discretion—I only suggest that we are not a great financial burden on these generous communities.

Once again, thank you for your assistance. Please feel free to contact me at any time.

Sincerely,

Plans were well advanced and everything seemed ready for the visit of Jock McNeil and his 80 Veterans of the PLDG. But, early in 1993, that Fickle Finger of Fate, which had lain dormant since the publication of *Once a Patricia* raised its ugly head and skewered my own plans. I became heavily involved with several legal matters as well as the publication of my second book and other personal problems that precluded my visiting Sicily in May. This was a body blow and I felt badly that I could not join Jock and his Regiment. However, he knew me well enough to appreciate that I had no choice in the matter and thanked me for my efforts.

Shortly after the Pilgrimage had returned, Jock and I met at the Military Institute for the annual D-Day Dodger Luncheon. It was a most appropriate venue to hear all about the tour. It had been a great success. Several members of the PLDG were present and all declared that the visit to the Monument had been the highlight of the trip. They were more impressed with it than with anything else. It was such an unexpected thrill to suddenly come upon this tribute to the First Division which had been erected where they had landed 50 years earlier!

Jock handed me some excellent photos of the Ceremony, including one of him speaking to the large gathering of Veterans and people of Ispica. It was a great relief for me to see that this outpost of Canada and memorial to our Division, at the southern tip of Europe, was still in good shape and had not been forgotten by the local citizens.

A touching epilogue to this story occurred two years later in June 1995. Once again I was at the Military Institute for lunch with Jock McNeil. This time he had brought along Reg Epp, a friend and fellow member of his Regiment, the PLDG, who had been on the Pilgrimage in 1993. To my great surprise, Reg presented me with a large replica of the PPCLI cap badge which he, himself, had carved in wood. He said it was in appreciation of the part I had played in having the Monument erected. A few days later, I wrote him a note:

June 11, 1995

Dear Reg:

I am so glad that at last we have met. Now I can understand why Jock holds you in such high regard. Your PPCLI crest or badge is truly magnificent and is prominently displayed in my library.

Some years ago, I gave all my PPCLI mementos to the Museum in Calgary. Ever since, I have regretted my decision because I have nothing left to remind me of the most important phase in my life. You have generously filled this void with your wonderful carving and I shall be forever grateful. Your work will be a family heirloom and will be carefully preserved for generations to come.

Thank you again for your kindness.

I am happy to say that this thoughtful emblem of my Regiment still graces the walls of my library and is a constant reminder of our motto:
Once a Patricia–Always a Patricia

Chapter V

PILGRIMAGE—1994

As 1993 drew to a close, I ruminated on events during the year and especially unfinished business. It had not been a very good year. Through circumstances beyond my control, I had reneged on my promise to help a classmate with his visit to the Monument and I had disappointed my friends in Ispica by not attending the Ceremony. This may not seem to be a matter of great moment, but it was to me.

How to restore my credibility with my friends? I was reluctant to burden them with yet another visit in 1994. But while I was pondering the problem, I received a telephone call from André Petelle of DVA on December 9th. At the request of the Italian Government, Canada would be sending a contingent of Veterans to Italy in May 1994 to attend ceremonies honouring all those soldiers who had fought in Italy during WWII, including the Germans! This was incredible news indeed.

André went on to say that troops from the Commonwealth (Canada, Britain, India, New Zealand) would be honoured at Cassino on May 15th; soldiers from France, Poland and Germany on other dates. The Canadian delegation would leave Canada on May 5th and return May 20th. The Pilgrimage would start at The First Canadian Division Monument at Ispica on May 7th. Further ceremonies would follow at Agira and other cemeteries in Italy. Could I join them? I would not, of course, be part of the Official Party, but they would appreciate my attendance.

It didn't take me long to make up my mind. I was delighted to accept the invitation to attend Ispica but I could not, at that stage, be certain that I would be able to attend the other events.

A further inducement to attend Ispica arrived at Christmas in the form of a beautiful, framed picture of the Convento e Chiesa di Santa Maria del Gesu which I had briefly occupied in 1943 when I was

Mayor of the town. The gift was from the present Mayor, Dr. Carmelo Tomasi. He extended a cordial invitation to visit him in 1994. On the back of the picture he had inscribed these words:

> *From these rocks, that fifty years ago saw you coming as foreigners, now as friends, we send you our best wishes of* Merry Christmas and a Happy 1994.

I immediately wrote Mayor Tomasi to accept his invitation, and inform him of the upcoming visit of DVA. I also advised the Mayor of Pachino, my friend Carmelo Nigro, and the Centro d'Incontro Anziani.

Through André Petelle, Peter Caissie of DVA and the Legion, I received further details of the 1994 Pilgrimage. I learned that Canada was preparing the biggest concentration of commemorative events in Canada's history. The national and international events would unfold in 1994 and 1995 as Canada commemorated the 50th Anniversary of the end of WWII from D-Day through VE-Day and VJ-Day.

The new Minister of Veterans Affairs (now called the Secretary of State for Veterans Affairs), Lawrence MacAulay, would head a 95 person delegation to Sicily and Italy, including 2 Senators, 3 members of Parliament, the media, administrative staff and one Veteran from each of the Regiments and Units (including Navy and Air Force) who had served in the Italian Campaign.

The Veteran who represented the PPCLI was Norm McCowan, a worthy soldier who had served with the Regiment throughout the entire war. He joined September 1st, 1939, and was discharged September 3rd, 1945—6 years! He rose from Private to Sergeant and served in the Anti-Tank Platoon. After the war, he remained active in the PPCLI Association, a prime example of our motto—*"Once a Patricia–Always a Patricia"*.

As I was not part of the Official Group, I had to make all the arrangements required to send an old soldier back to the battlefields on relatively short notice. I soon found that due to prior engagements, I could not conform to the Official itinerary. A further problem was my health. For some time I had been battling an insidious affliction known as Polymyalgia Rheumatica (PMR)—a fairly rare type of arthritis which attacks the muscles. The only treatment is large doses of Prednisone (a form of Cortisone) and plenty of rest. While I had the disease pretty well under control, I was concerned it might flare up again unless I set aside frequent rest periods. After juggling these factors around, I finally settled on an itinerary. I would fly to Rome on April 21st and drive to Taormina in easy stages. This would allow me a few days rest before I made a recce of the Monument to check it was in good condition for the Ceremony. As it turned out this was a wise precaution.

I also wanted to have time with Carmelo Nigro before the Ceremony to discuss another problem which had given us some concern a few years earlier—the reaction of the Italian Veterans to the Monument. Carmelo had written me that the President of the Association of Veterans had criticized the plaque on the Monument and posted a manifesto on the walls of Ispica. He felt there should be another plaque dedicated to the Italian fallen. It will be remembered, that from the outset, I had agreed that such a plaque or Monument should be erected and promised my support. I was anxious to have the matter settled before it became a serious issue.

So, saddled with these concerns, I became airborne on April 21st at 6:00 p.m., and after a flight of nine hours (with a short stop in Milan) arrived in Rome April 22nd 10:00 a.m. local time. Following a much needed rest, I drove south along the famous Strada del Sole (Autostrada) A2 to Naples, then the A3 to Reggio di Calabria where I crossed the Strait of Messina and finally came to rest in Taormina.

It had been three years since the Dedication in 1991 and I wondered how the Monument had withstood the ravages of time, tourists and the weather. As soon as I recovered from my long trip, I drove to Marza to make a personal recce. I was shocked by what I found. The base of the Monument was almost hidden by underbrush, small trees and weeds. The beautiful flowers had surrendered to the harsh elements. The Memorial was dirty and the colours in the mural had faded badly.

As soon as I returned to my hotel, I phoned Carmelo. I knew him well enough that I could express my concerns frankly. He told me not to worry. He would have a party of workmen start the next day to clean up the area. All would be in readiness for May 7th. He invited me for lunch to observe how the work was progressing.

A few days later, I returned to Ispica and received a joyous welcome from *la famiglia Carmelo*. Young Leonardo had grown six inches, so it seemed, but he still proudly carried my whistle and wore the PPCLI patches I had given him. We visited the Monument and found workmen busily restoring it to its former estate. Then on to City Hall where I met the new Sindaco, Dr. Giombattista Amore, the former Sindaco, Dr. Carmelo Tomasi and the members of the Town Council. I was particularly gratified to see hanging on the wall of the Mayor's office, the PPCLI plaque I had presented to Giuseppe Monaco in 1990.

The next port of call was the Centro d'Incontro Anziani which had been so supportive of the Monument. Mrs. Maucieri, the President, had died and been succeeded by Ferlisi Salvatore. I was saddened to learn that my right hand civil servant in 1943, Monaca, had also passed away.

Signor Ferlisi spoke English better than I spoke Italian and I heard all about his wartime service. He had fought in Algeria, been captured by the Americans and sent to the United States. He had a fine sense of humour and suggested that as I had been Mayor of Ispica, I should arrange for him to become Mayor of Toronto for a few days, or at least meet His Worship. I countered that perhaps a more lasting way to express reciprocity between the two cities would be to have them twinned! Indeed, Johnny Lombardi had once suggested that Little Italy and Ispica should tie the knot. So far as I know, the marriage has not yet been consummated. However, as a token of our friendship, he presented me with a large coloured photo of Carmelo Nigro and me at the Ceremony in 1991.

My recce was about completed. I had touched base with the main participants in the forthcoming ceremony and I was ready to leave. Carmelo, however, had one or two points to discuss and we retired to his home for a cool drink. Carmelo was concerned that I was expecting a grand ceremony similar to the memorable one in 1991 and he offered a Sicilian proverb. (Sicilians are very fond of proverbs and analogies.) He said, "Good things do not repeat themselves."

I told him I understood and agreed. In fact, the Canadian government was not expecting a big show this time because, frankly, it was overshadowed by the D-Day ceremonies in Normandy and France.

The other point Carmelo brought up, was one we had discussed before: the desire of the Italian Veterans to be recognized. He warned me that the Mayor of Ispica was going to mention this point in his speech and he hoped I would understand.

I replied, "Of course I do. Remember our last talk when I agreed, and gave you my full support. I even indicated that the project should be financed in Canada."

"*Sì, sì, d'accordo mio amico. Ricordo quello che hai detto.*"

Carmelo agreed to look into the matter and form a committee. He would keep me advised.

May 7th 1994

The ceremony was due to commence at 11:00 a.m., in the hope of avoiding the blistering noon-day heat. But there is really no way to avoid Sicilian heat, except at night and early morning. So I was happy to get up at 6:00 a.m. and be on my way, knowing that it would be a three hour drive from my hotel in Taormina. I planned to take breakfast at one of the numerous *trattoria* enroute and arrive well before the Official Party.

As my Mercedes careered along the Autostrada, I tried to relax, while the spectacular scenery floated by. I had not been too well and the sun felt good on my aching muscles. Surely, this was not a PMR attack. It was not an auspicious start to my mission.

Soon I began to feel uncomfortable from the heat and decided to pull into a roadside café near Catania for breakfast.

At Catania, you have a choice of routes: Continue south along the coast or turn inland and take a secondary road past Francofonte, Vizzini, Ragusa and Modica. I decided on the coastal road which I thought would be cooler than the inland route.

I arrived at Ispica well in advance of the Official Party of Veterans and was taken by Carmelo to Marza, the site of the Monument where the local dignitaries were assembling. I was relieved to see that the Monument had been cleaned and the area cleared of underbrush.

The Secretary of State for Veterans Affairs and the Veterans had been staying at a hotel in Catania. They arrived by bus and formed up facing the Monument. It was a large group, about 60 Veterans with the usual "ancillary troops": Senators, Members of Parliament, Project Team, Media, Photographers and Secretaries. I was happy to see two old friends with the Project Team who had been so helpful to me in the past, André Petelle and Peter Caissie. The Group also included a Flag Party bearing the flags of all the Provinces, a Piper and a Drummer.

The Italians were also well represented by members of the Military, Carabiniere and Police and by local Mayors and Officials. As in 1991, members of the U.S. Naval Base were also present. I was not asked to join the Official Group and attended as a spectator with my Italian friends.

Sindaco Giombattista Amore gave a very moving speech about how much the Monument meant to the citizens of Ispica. Then, as Carmelo had intimated, the Mayor brought up the matter of recognizing the Italian fallen.

After the Ceremony, I had a nice chat with the Mayor and Carmelo, and I assured them that it was my earnest desire to have the fallen Italians properly recognized and assured them of my support.

I also had an opportunity to mix with the Veterans and other members of their group. I was happy to see MGen. Bogert in fine form. He had been our Brigade Commander in Italy and during the move to Holland. Smoky Smith, V.C., whom I had last seen at the 1991 Ceremony, was also present with his wife. They are a fine couple—friendly and down to earth despite his heroic act on the Savio River and the many honours and publicity he has received. I am happy to record that a further, unique honour was recently bestowed upon Smoky Smith. On September 29th, 2001, he was made an Honorary Member of The Royal Military College Club.

Other Veterans I met were Norm McCowan, the PPCLI representative; Cliff Chadderton OC, O.Ont., DCL, LLD, the highly regarded advocate and friend of disabled Veterans; LCol. Mike George (48th Highlanders) with whom I had crossed swords about which Regiment was the first to cross the Ijssel River in Holland; Capt. Bill Graydon, MC (The Hastings and Prince Edward Regiment), a long time friend who subsequently became Honorary Colonel of his Regiment; and many, many others.

It was refreshing to meet the four members of a Youth Group who accompanied the Delegation. I could tell that they were deeply moved by the Ceremony and were very proud of the Veterans. Later Norm McCowan wrote about these young people in his report to the PPCLI:

> *They were astounded at the young age of many of the Canadian soldiers who were killed in action. They were great companions and were always helping us "old crocks" with any difficulties we encountered.*

Toward the end of the Ceremony, I was approached by a U.S. reporter from the nearby U.S. Naval Base. He saw me standing around with blazer, beret and medals and figured I might know something about the Monument. I was happy to oblige. His first question was, "Who erected and paid for this fine memorial? Canada?"

"No," I replied. "The citizens of Ispica and Pachino."

"You're kidding."

"Afraid not, the whole thing was done by the Italians in appreciation of the First Canadian Division who liberated them in 1943."

"Well, I'll be damned. This is quite a story. Tell me more."

So I did. He thanked me and said the interview would appear in the U.S. Navy Magazine. I am not holding my breath.

As the Group began to leave, André Petelle came up and invited me to join them for lunch at Ispica by the Sea. It was a thoughtful gesture but I had to refuse. I explained to André that during the Ceremony I had tried to climb the hill behind the Monument to get a better picture of the Veterans. By the time I reached the top, I was all in and my muscles had stiffened up. I was afraid it was the start of a PMR attack and I had better get back to my hotel and take some Prednisone pronto. André understood and wished me luck.

What I said about the PMR attack was quite true. As I mentioned earlier, the symptoms of the disease had begun to appear on my way to Ispica. I now realized that it was PMR and that I would be foolish to attend the luncheon.

However, I confess I had another reason which to some may seem picayune, but, to me, was important. The Canadian Government could find the money to pay for a fine luncheon for the Veterans and their hosts but it could not pay a cent toward the erection and upkeep of a Monument to Canada's soldiers. The more I thought about it, the more upset I became.

And I still am. And so are many other Veterans. Norm McCowan had this to say in his report to the Regiment:

> *The only sad part was that Syd Frost did not receive the recognition that he deserved. He was in Sicily prior to our arrival (two days) and found the monument to Canadians (the only one in Sicily or Italy and erected only through his efforts) was surrounded by weeds. Through his connections he rounded up some Sicilian volunteers who had the area cleaned up prior to our arrival. Our government can afford to put on a luncheon for our party and local officials, but have no money for our monument.*

John Moore, who fought with the Regiment throughout the war and is a dedicated Patricia, was kind enough to write me.

> *Dear Syd,*
> *I hope that this finds you in much better shape, health wise, than when you wrote last. So keep up with the medication and make plans for your next big pilgrimage back to Holland, as well as 'doing' Europe again.*
> *Many thanks for the photos that you had enclosed of the cairn at Ispica. I have shown them to numerous of the WWII fellows with whom we are still in touch. Everyone has shown a great deal of interest in your cairn photos, and I pass on a vote of thanks to you for getting this wonderful Monument built for us, and all other Canadians, who had passed on our route into Sicily, Italy, etc.*

When I returned home, I filed my usual report of the Pilgrimage with the PPCLI including MGen. Cammie Ware, and the Royal Canadian Military Institute in Toronto.

The R.C.M.I. published the following article in its edition of August, 1994:

Government Luncheon Deemed More Important Than Repair of Monument

I enclose comments on the Ceremony at the First Canadian Division Monument in Sicily, held May 7 last. The Monument was in a sad state of repair before the ceremony took place.

I thought this might happen so I arrived in Sicily a few days before the event. You can imagine my shock and disbelief. I contacted my good friend, school teacher Carmelo. He organized a work party of his family, citizens of Ispica and members of the seniors home who have always shown a great interest in the Monument. (Centro d'Incontro Anziani).

By May 7, the Monument was restored and in readiness for the Ceremony. The Canadian Official Party included about 60 veterans—senators, MPs, the press, photographers, veterans affairs liaison officers, etc. I was not part of the official party and attended the Ceremony as a spectator.

My only contribution to the event was an interview I gave to a U.S. reporter from a nearby U.S. naval base. He said the interview would appear in the U.S. Navy Magazine. Perhaps it will come to the attention of President Clinton and he may help to subsidize the repair of the Monument next year!

Despite the plethora of Canadian press and photographers, I did not see any reports in the newspapers in Toronto.

The attitude of the Canadian government to the only monument in the whole of Sicily and Italy to Canada's soldiers is shocking. The government is happy to "adopt" the Monument as its own and regularly send delegations to visit it, but it will not contribute one lira to its upkeep. This attitude was clearly expressed by one member of Veterans Affairs who said, "Well, that's the trouble with these monuments ... they are always causing trouble."

After the Ceremony, I was informed that the Canadian government was hosting a luncheon for a "select group" of veterans and local officials. I respectfully declined.

The government gave a luncheon but it can't find the money to repair a monument!

I didn't attend any other ceremonies planned by Veterans Affairs in Sicily and the rest of Italy. I headed for home.

To my great surprise and delight, even my "Militia Adversary" got into the fight. It will be recalled that in *Once a Patricia,* I described my battle with the famous 48th Highlanders of Canada, over which Regiment was the first to cross the Ijssel River in Holland toward the end of the war. After the publication of my book, they were kind enough to acknowledge it was the Patricias. We have been good friends ever since.

One of their distinguished Commanding Officers was LCol. Mike George who was a member of the Veterans group that had attended the Ceremony. He subsequently gave a talk to the Life Members Association of the 48th Highlanders which was published in their Newsletter. The following is an extract:

August 1994
Another Pilgrimage To Italy
During our meeting on June 6th, Colonel Mike George delivered a very fine talk on the Pilgrimage to Italy early in May. Colonel George reminded us of an event he described a few years ago involving Colonel Syd Frost, Honorary Colonel of the Royal Regiment of Canada. Colonel Frost who went through Sicily and Italy as a Junior Officer in "The Patricias" had visited the beaches at Pachino, on his own, back in 1991. He found to his dismay that while Normandy had swarms of memorials and monuments, there was not one thing to mark the place where the First Canadian Division landed in July 1943. Remember, it was at Pachino that Canadians made the first "successful" landing in any part of "Fortress Europe". Colonel Frost approached Ottawa about the matter and received encouragement but nothing else. Being a very determined man, he enlisted the support of the Mayors of Pachino and Ispica and in due course a suitable monument was erected, bearing the following inscription:

July 10, 1943
On This Day Canadian Soldiers Of The First Division Landed On These Shores. From Little Towns In A Far Away Land They Came In The Cause Of Freedom. Erected In Their Memory By The Citizens Of Pachino And Ispica, September 22, 1991.

For the second time Syd Frost arrived on the beaches at Pachino a few days ahead of the official group. He found to his dismay, that during the intervening three years, the monument had been neglected; it was overgrown with weeds and difficult to locate. Not being one to sit back and wait for others to do something, Syd dug in, recruited some help, the area was suitable for the Memorial Service. It just proves, you don't have to be "Dileas" as to do the right thing and his efforts are appreciated by all.

The Italians have a proverb (in latin) that would seem to be appropriate—*Quod erat faciendum.*

Chapter VI

PILGRIMAGE—1997

Following my Pilgrimage in 1994, I made an "appreciation of my situation" regarding further Pilgrimages and came to the tentative conclusion that enough is probably too much. I had made four Pilgrimages in the past six years and I was tired. I also suspected that my friends in Ispica needed a rest.

This is not to say I went into hibernation. Not at all. There were letters to write thanking all the people who had contributed to the 1994 Pilgrimage. And there was still the matter of recognizing the Italian fallen.

Even if I had decided to take a sabbatical for one or two years, it would have been rendered nugatory by a steady stream of correspondence, gifts, pictures and visitors from Ispica and Toronto. There is a large Ispicese and Pachinese population in Toronto and it seemed that everyone in the community was related, not only to each other, but also to the citizens of Ispica and Pachino. However, it was a great test for my Italian and I was grateful to have the chance to use it. I could almost hear Carmelo saying: "*Se non usi la lingua, la perdi.*" (If you don't use it you lose it.)

The first visitor was Sam Agosta, the son of Enza Spataro who was another cousin of Carmelo Nigro. Sam and his family lived in Toronto but were originally from Ispica. Sam had just returned from Ispica where he had been visiting Carmelo and other relatives. He brought with him a letter from Carmelo and photos of the recent Ceremony. Over the years, I have received many lovely letters from him and this was no exception. Let me quote from the English version which Sam Agosta kindly translated for me:

> *The Monument is always there, ready to remind future generations the beginning of a great event that changed the fate*

> *of Sicily, Italy and Europe, and that cost many lives of young soldiers on both sides. Thanks to the beautiful and historic photos, they will explain to our future descendants our commitments and our friendship.*
>
> *My dear Colonel, I finish this letter giving you all my affection. I'm glad to have helped you realize a big dream and to tell you that history passed by Ispica. Your friend Carmelo Nigro.*

Who would have suspected 51 years earlier, when I occupied the town, that one of its citizens would write such a tribute. Then, the people were our enemies; they were depressed, half starving and suspicious of the foreigners who had bombed and shelled their town. Since then, they had worked hard to restore their property and way of life. Ispica had emerged from the ashes of Fascism and was now a centre of culture and a modern, progressive town.

I felt very proud of my association with these fine people and I wrote Carmelo a letter of appreciation, using the best Italian I could muster, and ended with:

> Un affettuoso saluto a te, la tua famiglia e ai tutti I cittadini di Ispica. *(An affectionate greeting to you, your family and to all the citizens of Ispica.)*
>
> *Cordialmente.*

It will be observed that Carmelo and I were now addressing each other with the familiar, informal "tu," and not the very formal "lei". During the Mussolini era, he had insisted on using the formal except within the family. This excessive formality had pretty well been washed away along with other Fascist dogma. Just the same, it was an honour for me to be addressed in the friendly form.

I was still very concerned about the lack of recognition of the Italian Veterans who were killed in the war. The matter had surfaced once or twice and then faded away. I was certain it would erupt again, but my queries went unanswered. Then in 1995, my interest in Sicilian affairs were temporarily thwarted by events several thousand miles away. The people of Holland were organizing a Pilgrimage to mark the 50th Anniversary of the end of WWII. It will be recalled from my book, that I had ended the war in Holland and had made several Pilgrimages over the years. But, I had not been there since 1990. I thought it was only fair to devote my energies in 1995 to a return visit.

As is their wont, the Department of Veterans Affairs organized an Official Party which included a 100-member guard, a flag party and a band. In Holland and in Canada, committees were formed to offer tour packages to the Veterans, including accommodation and meals in Dutch homes. It would probably be the last great Pilgrimage and I was keen to attend.

Over the course of several weeks I made my travel arrangements which included a tour of France, Belgium, Germany, Austria and Switzerland. It seemed a shame not to take advantage of this opportunity to visit other countries I had not seen for many years. The aircraft was to leave Toronto on April 26, 1995.

Disaster struck April 6th. My wife became very ill and I had to cancel all my plans and reservations and notify my Dutch friends I would not be seeing them.

It was a nasty blow. However, after the tour, I was happy to learn that the Pilgrimage had been a great success, probably the most memorable of them all.

My Dutch friends were very kind and understanding. They sent me dozens of pictures, postcards, newspaper clippings and other material about the Pilgrimage. They even included a lovely medal and tie that each of the Veterans had received. But that is another story to be told in a later chapter of this book.

We now return to my first love (but not my only one), Sicily, and in particular Ispica.

As 1995 gave way to 1996, I began to wonder if my friends in Ispica had forsaken me. I had not heard from anyone for many months and, of course, I had been preoccupied with the Holland Pilgrimage and its aftermath. Then, on May 21st, 1996, without any warning, I received a call from one Giovanni Avveduto. He informed me that he had just arrived from Ispica where he worked at the Centro di Cultura Popolare and had some presents for me.

"*Che fortuna*," I almost shouted. "*Ho pensato che Ispica mi avesse dimenticato.*" (I thought that Ispica had forgotten me.)

He assured me they had not forgotten me and that his superior, Antonino Lauretta, sent his special regards.

On May 23rd, Giovanni and his wife, Carmela, joined me for lunch. He was another member of the Ispicese fraternity who had immigrated to Toronto many years ago. His family lived here but he divided his time between Toronto and Ispica.

I was beginning to think that Johnny Lombardi had been right. Toronto and Ispica should be twinned.

Giovanni brought me a letter from Antonino which he helped me to translate. Not for the first time I was impressed with the culture of Sicilians and the beautiful way they expressed themselves. Antonino closed his letter in the following way:

> *I remember you with grateful sentiments and for the merit with which you praise our City.*
> *Life is often cruel but more often, I am convinced generous. Because of this feeling. I believe that life will give us the occasion to meet each other again.*

Then Giovanni produced books, postcards, a brochure about Ispica and a huge wall map of the town showing every dwelling. I thought how fortunate I was that he didn't ask me for a similar map of Toronto.

How to thank these generous, friendly people? I can do no better than quote from my letter of appreciation.

May 26, 1996

Mio caro Antonino:

What a wonderful surprise I received this week when Giovanni Avveduto phoned to say he brought greetings from you and would be happy to meet me.

Two days later, I took Giovanni to lunch at my club—The Granite Club—and we spent a most enjoyable hour or two talking about Ispica and the great friendship that has developed between the citizens of your fine city and me over the past fifty-three years! I consider myself very fortunate and honoured.

In the course of our luncheon, further surprises came my way. Giovanni produced two beautiful books about Ragusa and The Iblei as well as several lovely postcards, a map of Ispica and an attractive brochure describing the Easter Celebrations in Ispica. As your first "democratic mayor", I thought I knew quite a bit about Ispica and the Province of Ragusa, but these wonderful mementos have further enlightened me about the deep historical significance of the area and its interesting architecture.

Having excited my curiosity about the intellectual wonders of Ispica, Giovanni then produced another surprise to arouse my appetite for fine food—a large box of delicious Sicilian pastries!

Antonino, you are a very thoughtful person and I do appreciate your kindness. My wife joins me in thanking you as well as the members of Centro di Cultura Popolare—Ispica.

As a gesture of my appreciation, I have handed a copy of my new book—A Life Worthwhile—to Giovanni, to be delivered to you.

A few weeks later, I received another letter from Antonino Lauretta inviting me to attend a week-long symposium in Ispica of writers and artists from the Mediterranean area, including Greece, Egypt, Jordan, Malta and Italy. This was not quite my line but it would have been a most interesting and challenging experience to have attended as an observer.

While I could not accept Antonino's invitation, it made me realize that it would soon be three years since my last visit to "my" city. On the spur of the moment, I decided it was time to return and wrote "Nino" that I would be visiting him in 1997. (Nino is the familiar form of Antonino.)

One should not undertake such missions without giving them a second, serious, sober thought. Aided by a few glasses of *vino rosso*, I gave the matter proper consideration, omitting, of course, the third requirement, and began planning my itinerary.

It soon evolved into a grand tour of Sicily and Italy by car. I would imagine I was once again a scout and sniper in my "scout car" (Fiat) and retrace the route of the Patricias from the beaches of Sicily to the Gothic Line, San Fortunato and Rimini.

Next day, I soberly reviewed my decision and concluded it made excellent sense. After all, I would be 75 years old and this might well be my last chance to career about Italy like a 21 year old.

I would fly direct to Rome and pick up a car. Heading south, I would pass through Frosinone, the Liri Valley and Cassino, cross the Strait of Messina and pause at Taormina, which would be my headquarters for the Sicilian part of the campaign. After chasing the enemy out of Sicily, I would follow the route I had taken in 1943 to catch up to the Regiment at Potenza, and from there, the trail my Scout Platoon had blazed to Campobasso and Frosolone where my service to the Regiment had been temporarily interrupted by a German bullet.

Then, a long drive following the Adriatic coast past the Moro River, Ortona, Pescara, Ancona, Pesaro, Rimini and San Fortunato where I had rejoined the Regiment. I would then turn west to Florence where the Regiment had taken part in a move to fool the Germans that would make them believe the 8th Army was going to attack in that area. (Whether the Germans were deceived or we wasted our time is still a matter of debate.)

From Florence, I would continue west to Pisa and Leghorn, where the Patricias had embarked for Marseilles. Finally, I would head for Rome and finish my journey in the Eternal City.

I reckoned the tour would cover 4,000 miles and take 38 days. I would stop over at all the War Cemeteries enroute to pay my respects. It was indeed the grandfather of all tours and I couldn't wait to get going. Best of all, I would be on my own and not part of any official tour.

After settling the route and making all the hotel reservations, my next task was to notify my friends in Ispica and Pachino. I emphasized that I was making a private visit to see them, untrammelled by government receptions and ceremonies in three languages. (French, English, Italian.) I felt they had graciously endured more than their share of such functions which always required much preparation and expense.

The first person I informed of my visit was, of course, Carmelo Nigro; others were:

Dr. Giombattista Amore—Mayor of Ispica
Prof. Sebastiano Lupo—Mayor of Pachino
Sig. Ferlisi Salvatore—Pres. Associazione Centro d'Incontro Anziani
Prof. Antonino Lauretta—Director Centro di Cultura Popolare

I received prompt replies from them all expressing delight at my visit and assuring me of a warm welcome. It would be my sixth visit to Ispica since the war and I was looking forward to seeing them.

I arrived in Rome on May 18th after a pleasant flight of eight hours from Toronto. Next day I picked up my "scout car" and headed south to Sicily on the first leg of my 4,000 mile journey. As explained earlier, the account which follows describes only my Sicilian Campaign; the story of the remainder of my trip will be told in later chapters.

This time I deliberately set aside a little "free time" to visit and explore areas of Sicily and Italy I had not seen before, and not confine myself to cemeteries and battlefields which were now so familiar to me. But I do not want to create the wrong impression. Long ago, I had covenanted with myself to visit these sacred places of sacrifice and honour at every opportunity. I am proud to say I have faithfully observed this covenant for the past 57 years and intend to continue doing so for as long as I am able.

Thus, shortly after arriving in Taormina, my first thought was to visit the beautiful Canadian War Cemetery at Agira which I have described so often in my story. It is not the largest, or best known, or most visited cemetery in Italy. But it is Canadian and it is the final resting place of the first Canadian soldiers who died in the Italian Campaign. It rises from the arid valley, like a Garden of Eden with foliage, flowers and neatly clipped hedges, all freshly watered as if by a sudden rainfall that has blessed only this cemetery and forsaken the surrounding countryside.

As on previous occasions, I wondered if the Guest Register was available and if it contained records of past visits. I soon found the book, but alas, the earlier pages had been removed, even though few visitors ever pass by this far-flung outpost of Canada.

My next mission can readily be surmised—Ispica. I was due to arrive at Carmelo's home at 10:30 a.m. on May 27th, a drive of about two and one-half hours. I was a little late leaving Taormina and decided to take the inland route which is faster than following the coast, but not as well marked. Trying to by-pass the congestion I got lost! My reader may find this hard to believe after all my previous trips to Ispica—but I did. In an effort to make up time, I turned on the "after burners".

For the first and only time, I got a ticket for speeding. Indeed, I have never before or since heard of anyone in Italy getting hauled over for such a minor misdemeanour. While the *polizia* was writing out the ticket, I sauntered over and tried out my Italian—"*Che cosa fa, Capitano?*" (He wasn't a captain but it sounded pretty good.) The startled officer looked at me as if I had just descended from the moon. "*Che cosa faccio? Mamma mia! Scrivo una multa. Chi è lei?*" (What am I doing? I am writing out a speeding ticket. Who are you?)

He had given me the opening I needed. I told him in firm tones, "*Sono un Colonnello, Canadese. Sto guidando a Ispica per una cerimonia importante.*" (I am driving to Ispica for an important ceremony.)

The officer nodded gravely and tore up the ticket. "*Scusa, Sig. Colonnello. My dispiace, buon viaggio.*"

I stepped on the gas and continued on my way.

Carmelo and family were waiting for me but were obviously a little annoyed that I was late. When I explained the reason for the delay, all was forgiven. Carmelo, always the learned professor, had an Italian proverb ready: "*Tutte le strade non sempre portano a Ispica.*" (All roads do not always lead to Ispica.)

* * *

May 27, 1997—Ispica

Of all the wonderful times I have spent visiting Ispica, this one ranks as one of the best because it was a personal visit with my friends and I had time to get to know them. I found too that my Italian had greatly improved so that I could join in the friendly banter that Sicilians enjoy.

While the day's activities were quite informal, Carmelo had arranged a pretty tight schedule of events.

10:30—Meet his Family

As I was late, there was only time for a quick 'hello'. I hardly recognized Leonardo who was now 11. He was only 6 when we first met. Such a fine, polite boy. I wondered what stories he would tell his friends in 10 or 20 years about the Canadian Colonel who appeared one day in 1991, and with his Grandfather, helped to build a monument for the Canadian soldiers who had liberated his town.

11:00—Arrive at City Hall

I was warmly greeted by the Mayor, Dr. Giombattista Amore, whom I had met in 1994. "*Buon giorno Titta,*" I said, as I offered my hand. I deliberately used the familiar version of his first name to emphasize the informal nature of our meeting. (These diminutive forms of first names are very popular in Sicily.)

I was then introduced to the members of his staff and City Councillors including a very fine gentleman, Dr. Michelangelo Aprile, who, later in the day, would do me a kind and thoughtful favour.

Dr. Amore made a nice little speech and pointed to the wall of his chamber where the two PPCLI plaques which I had presented in 1990 and 1991 were displayed. Turning to me he said, "And now I want to present you with a token of our appreciation for all you have done for our city both during the war and afterwards." He then handed me a lovely model in relief of the Basilica di Santa Maria Maggiore, set in an ebony frame. It is one of my most precious possessions. The work is signed by the artist and is inscribed on the back:

Argento 92.5%—Cesellato a mano con finitura oro
(Silver 92.5%—Engraved by hand and finished in gold)

11:30—Attend Centro d' Incontro Anziani (CIA)

It will be recalled that the CIA (Seniors' Club) was one of the main contributors to the Monument. I had met its President, Salvatore Ferlisi on my last visit when he told me all about his war service (mostly as a guest of the U.S. Army). He was genuinely pleased to see me again. "*È bello rivederti,*" he cried and I responded in like manner. Most of the members of the "Club" were on hand to greet me. Many remembered my previous visits and we talked about my faithful civil servant Monaca who had been my "shadow," but sadly was now deceased. I would have liked to spend an hour or two with these friendly people but Carmelo gave me a not too gentle nudge and pointed to the door. We had to leave for the ceremony at the Monument.

I submitted, but there was one question I needed to have answered. What was the Centro Geriatrico? In the course of my conversation with the members of the CIA, I had met a Director of the Centro Geriatrico. What connection did they have with the Monument? Carmelo started to explain but just then Salvatore Ferlisi called for silence and presented me with another exquisite gift—a framed Testimonial in remembrance of my visit, engraved in gold.

How can one express his appreciation for such generous, thoughtful acts? I can do no better than quote from the letter I sent Ferlisi on my return home:

> *I will never be able to thank you enough for what you have done for me and Canada's soldiers. The wonderful Cippo is a unique Memorial to my Division but it also stands as a lasting Monument to our friendship.*
>
> *Now you have done me further honour by presenting me with a beautiful framed Testimonial of my visit to Ispica. I have shown it to some Italian friends here in Toronto and they are very impressed with your Testimonial and, may I say, with me! Thank you so much for remembering my visit in such a gracious way.*
>
> *I enjoyed attending your Centro and meeting your officials, some of whom I remember seeing on my last visit. I cannot possibly recall all their names but I would ask you to give them my kindest regards.*

Later on, I learned that the Centro Geriatrico had also supported and contributed to the Monument. I should have known about them earlier, but somehow, they had been overlooked in my previous visits and I felt embarrassed about not properly thanking them earlier. However, I made partial amends by inviting their Director to a luncheon before I left.

12:00—Service at the Monument

This was a simple yet moving ceremony attended by just a few of the principal supporters of the Memorial, the Commandant of Police and an officer from the nearby U.S. Navy facility. A wreath was laid and a two minute silence observed. There were no speeches. None were required. The Monument spoke for itself.

1:00—Lunch at Ristorante Ippocampo

This was a delightful seafood restaurant by the beach at a place called Pozzallo. My last visit had been in 1943 when, accompanied by an American officer who was taking over my duties as Town Mayor of Ispica, we went swimming with a couple of signorinas. When I told Carmelo that it has been 54 years since my last visit to Pozzallo, he grinned and delivered another of his Italian proverbs. *"Meglio tardi che mai"*. (Better late than never.)

The luncheon was a small affair for a few of my friends and it gave me a chance to reciprocate in a very small way their kindness. Ferlisi Salvatore, the President of the Seniors Club, was his usual witty self and said a few words of thanks. He then proposed that I invite all nine guests to visit Toronto for a week! Thankfully my Italian had improved to the point where I could deliver an appropriate riposte. *"Grazie mio amico, ma credo che tu abbia un altro cattivo sogno."* (Thank you my friend but I do believe you are having another bad dream.)

It was time to leave and I handed out Canada pins I had scrounged from DVA.

2:30—Attend Centro di Cultura Popolare

Sicilians are very conscious of their cultural heritage and publish beautiful books and prints showing the many wonderful works of art, statues, palaces, churches and other edifices that abound throughout the land. On every visit, I am presented with a new volume which I treasure and I now have a fairly extensive and valuable collection. My current visit was no exception. Antonino (Nino) Lauretta gave me a book describing the journeys of famous visitors to Sicily over the ages and their impressions of what they saw. Again, I quote from my letter of appreciation:

> *Once again you have honoured me with splendid gifts. You make me feel like Caesar! I shall treasure the book* Il Viaggio in Sicilia. *It is a marvellous account of the history of Sicily and will be a very helpful guide for me when I visit Sicily again. It will also help me to improve my Italian!*
>
> *I also appreciated receiving the valuable Xilografia su Legno by Pietro Ricca, and the Map of Ispica. Your gifts will be constant reminders of our friendship and my pleasant visit to my favourite città—Ispica—in 1997. Already, I am looking forward to my next journey.*
>
> *I enjoyed visiting your offices and meeting your staff, as well as the kindly Monsignor who showed me around his beautiful church. I was glad I had a few Canada pins to hand out.*

3:30—Tour of Cava d'Ispica

It had been a busy day and I was surprised that Dr. Amore, the Mayor and his Councillor Dr. Aprile who had attended all the functions, now insisted that they give me a personally conducted tour of these fascinating caves. I was hot and tired and beginning to feel the effects of the sun, particularly on my exposed head. Dr. Aprile immediately noticed my discomfort and came up with an original remedy. He produced a large white handkerchief which he quickly fashioned into a kind of turban and plunked it on my head. I looked like a Bedouin camel driver but I didn't care. (I have a much prized photo which I exhibit only to my friends.) Clothed in my fancy headgear and refreshed with a cool drink, I was ready and eager to explore these caves.

While I knew something of their history and have mentioned them before, I was now in the company of two expert guides. The Cava d'Ispica is a deep gorge, 13 kilometres long that runs through the territories of Ispica and Modica. The rock walls on either side of the gorge are riddled with cave dwellings that were once inhabited but are now used for storage. Catacombs, palaces and rock churches also pierce the walls. Near the entrance to the Cava is a limestone monolith called Forza, on which ancient fortifications were built to protect the old Ispica, which was destroyed by an earthquake in 1693. Today, the area is preserved as a park.

Dr. Amore led me to the entrance to the famous Centoscale with its 280 steps descending into the bowels of the earth to an underground river. He invited me to follow him down the rock staircase, the steps of which were worn smooth by six centuries of plodding feet. I demurred, pleading the lateness of the hour and my desire to return to my hotel in Taormina before dark. Dr. Amore understood and agreed I should be on my way before the traffic became too heavy. He suggested I take the inland route and he gave me directions how to avoid the chaos around Catania.

* * *

I left my two "guides," Titta Amore and Michelangelo Aprile, with real regret. They wished me *buon viaggio* and expressed the hope I would soon return when we would visit the Cava once more and have dinner in a restaurant that was once a grotto occupied by ancient cave dwellers.

On the way, I stopped off to say goodbye to Carmelo Nigro and his family and thank him for all the time, energy and fortune he had devoted to what at times had seemed to be "mission impossible" but through his perseverance, had been such a success. I promised to keep in touch and return soon. Three years were to slide by before I honoured my pledge. Little did I know that in the interval, events would erupt that threatened the very existence of the Monument.

PILGRIMAGE—1997

When I returned home, I wrote my usual letters to Carmelo and Dr. Amore. It was becoming increasingly difficult to express my feelings of friendship and appreciation in a true and honest fashion.

Mio Caro Carmelo:
I arrived home safely on June 24th after another memorable trip to Italy. The highlight of my trip was, of course, my visit to Ispica and seeing you and your family again.

Leonardo is developing into a fine young man and I'm sure you are as proud of him as you are of your children. I enjoyed seeing some of the students of Maria Louisa and I was happy to have a few Canada pins to give them.

I was so glad to find that your wonderful Monument is still in good shape and well cared for. It is an enduring tribute to the friendship we feel for each other. You should be very proud of your accomplishment.

I was honoured to give a small luncheon for some of the distinguished citizens of Ispica. Unfortunately, I didn't keep a record of the names of those who attended. I wonder if you could send me their names and the office or position they hold.

Already I am looking forward to my next trip and I promise to spend more time in my favourite città—Ispica.

Dear Dottor Amore:
Thank you so much for the beautiful "regalo" you presented to me, depicting the Chiesa, S. Maria Maggiore. It is truly a work of art which will be a treasured family possession.

I enjoyed my visit to La Cava d'Ispica and hope I will have more time on my next visit to thoroughly investigate the Parco della Forza—a remarkable historic site. Please give my thanks and best wishes to your "consigliere" who accompanied us on our visit and was so kind to me, including making a special "bonnet" to protect my bald head from the sun!

I was interested to see your exciting new development by the sea—Mare d'Ispica? Next time I visit, perhaps I can rent a villa for a week or two and really have an opportunity to see you and my other kind friends in Ispica.

I am always deeply moved each time I visit the Cippo dedicated to the soldiers of my Division, and I was pleased to see that it is being cared for and is in good repair. It is a lasting memorial to the great esteem that we have for each other both as individuals and as two great nations.

* * *

As I drove back to Taormina, I thought about the day's activities and decided that everything had gone very well. I had visited all my old friends and met many new ones, and had received a new understanding and appreciation of their culture and fascinating history. I became philosophical and wondered what stroke of good fortune had brought me here in the first place. Thoughts drifted back to the beginning of the war, as I traced the route that had led me to Ispica.

Father had started me on the way by suggesting I enter RMC "to get a little discipline and learn to get up at a decent hour in the morning". What if I had chosen to go to the University of New Brunswick instead. Chances are I would have joined the Carleton and York Regiment and never seen Ispica.

When I graduated from RMC, I joined the PPCLI. Why? One of the reasons was Sam Potts, a friend from Saskatoon whose father had served in the Patricias in WWI and was a close friend of my own father when we lived in Saskatoon. But I might easily have joined The Royal Regiment of Canada in Toronto in which father was then serving in a Reserve Battalion. In that case, I would never have seen Sicily or Italy and would have ended up at Dieppe—perhaps forever.

After RMC, I was posted to Camp Shilo in Manitoba and took courses in Nanaimo and Vernon, B.C. I might well have spent a year instructing in Canada and missed the invasion of Sicily altogether. But by some stroke of fortune, I met Brig. Colquhoun in Vernon, who was the senior PPCLI officer in Canada, and persuaded him to send me on a draft to England to join my Regiment. Even then, I almost missed the chance to sail to Sicily.

The PPCLI was up to strength in officers and there were no vacancies for junior lieutenants. However, some unseen hand transferred me to a Battalion that would supply first line reinforcement officers to units of the First Division, and I sailed for Sicily and landed 3 days after the assault troops.

Normally I would have joined the PPCLI in a few days but again some guiding force arranged another assignment. The Regiment had few casualties in the initial stages and my services were not required up front. Instead, I was ordered to take my platoon to Ispica and restore order as a Town Major.

Why me? All along the way there were a hundred different routes I could have taken, some probably dead end. Throughout the war this strange force took charge of my life and directed me along paths I would not have chosen if I had had charge of my destiny. In my book, I called this force Field Marshal Fate and blamed all my disasters on him. Perhaps his long term view was, after all, better than mine and he had made all the right moves to bring me to Ispica, and all the happiness this had given me after the war.

My idle musings were brought to an abrupt conclusion as a long dark tunnel suddenly appeared before me. I frantically searched for the button to turn on the lights before my Fiat and I went to our separate Valhallas. Thank you Field Marshal Fate.

Having negotiated the half mile tunnel successfully, I relaxed and continued my thoughts about how lucky I had been to survive the war and to meet, quite by accident, the friendly people of Ispica. It also occurred to me that there is a word to describe my good fortune—"serendipity," allegedly coined by Horace Walpole, a Prime Minister of England. If he hadn't invented it, I think I would have.

Back safely in my hotel in Taormina, I had a late dinner (Sicilians are always late diners) and plotted my route for the next day. I had promised myself a relaxed holiday, within the holiday I was having, to visit parts of Sicily I had not had the opportunity to see before. First on the list was Mount Etna which I could see from my hotel. The first time I had set eyes on this active volcano was on August 6th, 1943, when my company attacked Mt. Seggio lying a scant 6 miles to the west of Mount Etna. The Germans had fled but laid down a heavy artillery barrage which caught the two follow-up companies and killed Lt. J. d'Arcy Horn. We were certain that the Germans had an artillery OP on the slopes of Mount Etna and I vowed to one day climb it to see for myself. That day was about to arrive.

Early next morning, I drove my Fiat to the base of the mountain where I took a bus that climbed the switchback trail leading to the top, but not the very top. On the way, I was surprised to see farmers working in their vineyards and orchards while a wispy cloud of smoke issued from the peak. I asked the guide if the mountain ever erupted. "*Sì, sì, Signor. Molti volte*—1958, 1971, 1983, 1991 and 1992." I asked him if some of these farmers ever lost their lives. He said, "Yes, but others quickly take their places. You know there are lots of Italians and the volcanic ash is very good for cultivation!"

I wryly commented that the mountain also made a very good observation post and told him about my attack on Mount Seggio in 1943. No wonder the Germans spotted us and brought down accurate artillery fire. The guide agreed and thanked me for liberating his country from the Nazis.

To get to the very top of Mount Etna, one has to take a cable-car from which you can peer into the boiling core of the volcano—an awesome sight. Our guide informed us that Etna is the highest volcano in Europe, 3,300 metres; its base perimeter forms a circle 212 km. In winter one can ski on its snowy peak in the morning and sunbathe and swim in the afternoon on the beach. No wonder, I thought, that

Hammie Gault loved this place so much. I would bet any money he not only skied and swam, but also flew his airplane around the crater.

* * *

Next on my list was another volcano, not quite as well known as Etna, but with a shady past. It was here that in 1950 the famous Italian director, Roberto Rossellini, seduced the equally famous Ingrid Bergman and persuaded her to leave her husband, Dr. Lindstrom, a Swedish surgeon. The two of them, director and actress, had gone to a small volcanic island off the north coast of Sicily called Stromboli, one of the Aeolian Islands, to shoot a film of the same name. It was not a great film, but the scandal it produced was.

I had never seen the film and knew nothing about Stromboli, but it seemed to me that the island must have some kind of special charm to cause such a sensation. Another inducement to visit it was the fact that Stromboli is the most active volcano on the planet.

So, in 1997, with a few days left on my tour, I climbed aboard a hydrofoil in the small port of Milazzo at the north east corner of Sicily, bound for Stromboli, (the accent is on the first syllable), about 70 kilometers distant. On the way, we passed some of the other Aeolian Islands including Salina which also had a connection with the movie industry but not quite so titillating. The 1995 Italian movie *Il Postino* was shot there.

As I approached Stromboli, the volcano belched and a cloud of dust and smoke erupted into the clear blue sky. Our guide told us not to worry. This happens every ten minutes. You can set your watch by it. We pulled into the pier and were met by a handful of "Apes." (No, this was not the *Planet of the Apes* although the barren landscape gave that impression.) An Ape is a small three-wheeled Italian truck. Aside from these and a few motorbikes, there is no motorized transport allowed on the island. The tourists threw their luggage into the open box-like compartment behind the driver and piled in themselves on top of the luggage. After a bumpy three mile ride, I was let off (dumped off) at my hotel. Welcome to Stromboli!

The few guests around were dressed in strange alpine clothes with heavy boots and sweaters. They were all German. I strolled down to the beach. It was covered with black volcanic sand and more Germans dressed the same way. It suddenly dawned on me that people come here to climb the volcano, not to lie around on the beach. I was clearly a fish out of water and had no inclination to stay there.

At dinner, my suspicions were confirmed. All the guests were ardent mountain climbers. They kindly invited me to join their party but I politely declined. Local guides lead these groups on a four hour climb at night to the top of the volcano. Here they watch red sparks flare up into fountains of fire from the crater. Some nights, chunks of debris are hurled toward the sea and lava flows down the slopes. Some climbers stay up there all night. Just good, clean fun. That night, I believe I had a few nightmares in which Stromboli and Etna were featured. It was wartime, and I had been ordered to attack Mount Etna but somehow I ended up scaling Stromboli which was held by German Alpine Troops. Just as we attacked, the mountain erupted and lava, Germans and ashes overwhelmed us. Stromboli is not my favourite volcano.

I am not a movie buff, but there was one other place with a movie connection I wanted to see—the ancestral home of the Godfather. To my surprise, I discovered there is actually a town in Sicily with the name Corleone and I decided to pay it a visit. I will confide with my reader that I had a personal interest in the matter as I, too, am an Honorary Godfather, as will be revealed, and wanted to pay my respects to the Capo di Capo.

Corleone is a pleasant agricultural centre 56 kilometres south of Palermo. Like most Sicilian towns, it has come under the influence of many foreign powers, including Byzantines, Arabs, Normans, Lombards and Spanish, which may account for some of the internecine warfare one sees in the movies and reads in the papers. My tourist guide described the town in rather euphemistic terms: "Its recent history has been disturbed by a number of grievous events involving only the protagonists and certainly not the entire population."

Undeterred by all these rumours, I boldly drove up to the main hotel for lunch in the hope of gleaning some information from one of the locals. Two burly guards refused me admission. There was a big wedding in progress and practically the whole town was invited. I would have to come back another day.

* * *

As I drove away, I had to indulge in a good chuckle. Whether there actually was a Godfather in Corleone I did not know but whoever was giving the wedding certainly had the Godfather's style.

Thus my 1997 trip to Sicily ended on a rather frivolous note. I make no apology. My comrades whom I honoured and remembered in the first part of my Pilgrimage would not have objected. They, too, enjoyed a little fun once in a while. Indeed, in the grim business of warfare, a sense of humour was often our only refuge.

Little more need be said. Next day I packed my bags and drove north to the Strait for the second part of my Pilgrimage—a tour of the battlefields and cemeteries of Italy, following the route of the PPCLI. An account of this journey will be found in a later chapter.

Chapter VII

PILGRIMAGE—1999 VETERANS AFFAIRS CANADA

On June 22nd, 1997, I finally came to rest in Rome after three strenuous weeks touring Italy from Reggio di Calabria in the very "toe" to Florence in the north. My faithful "scout car" had served me well and bested the challenges offered by the terrain, the elements and Italian drivers. I was not going to press my luck any further and attempt driving in Rome. I turned in my Fiat and took a taxi to my hotel.

Next day, at the Fiumicino Airport, while awaiting my flight, I received a pleasant surprise. A familiar face appeared in the line-up. It was Carmela Avveduto whom I had last seen with her husband Giovanni in Toronto the previous May. It will be remembered he brought me many lovely gifts from Nino Lauretta of Ispica. Carmela was returning to Toronto from visiting relatives in Ispica and had missed seeing me there by only a day or two. Her husband was now working in Toronto and would be meeting her. She was certain he would be happy to drop me off at my home. Talk about serendipity!

For the next few weeks I was kept busy writing letters to all my friends in Ispica. This could be a challenge. They all knew each other and would naturally compare notes to see if the Colonel favoured one over the other, or worse, sent out a form letter. Actually, it wasn't much of a problem if one took a little time and was sincere in his remarks.

One item of unfinished business concerned me; the proposed Monument to the Italian fallen. During my recent visit, I thought that someone would raise the issue but no one did. So I broached the matter with Carmelo and repeated my offer of financial support. He was very pleased to hear this and admitted he was worried too. There had been further rumblings in the press and he felt that sooner or later the matter would surface again. He would meet with his committee, draw up a design for the Memorial and prepare a list of the fallen.

On September 26th, 1997, I received a telephone call from Rosaria Spataro, the mother of Rosanna who had done so much translation for me. She said that her sister-in-law, Enza Agosta, had just returned from Ispica and brought with her a letter to me from Carmelo. I immediately phoned Enza to arrange a meeting later that day. Enza could not come but her husband Gaetano and daughter Eleonora could. I was beginning to think I had become a clearing house for visitors to and from Ispica.

Father and daughter duly appeared with Carmelo's letter, four Sicilian newspapers and a book from Mayor Giombattista Amore. As I had anticipated, the articles in the newspapers reported on my recent visit and asked when a memorial would be erected to the Italian dead. The papers mentioned that Carmelo was preparing a list and gave the names. I was relieved to see that some progress was being made.

The book from Dr. Amore was a special edition of the works of Salvo Monica, a well-known Sicilian sculptor and poet who had donated many of his sculptures to the City of Ispica. It was a valuable addition to my growing collection of books on Sicilian works of art.

The year 1998 was an uneventful one, so far as *cose Siciliane* were concerned. Work on the new monument was proceeding, albeit slowly. I decided to take a sabbatical from my Sicilian adventure and put my own house in order. Indeed, it was time to exchange living in a house, with all its attendant chores, for the simple life of a condo owner. After 40 years, it is not an easy matter to make such a drastic change in one's style of living, and it took many months before my wife and I were settled in our new abode. My advice to all septuagenarians and others who are contemplating such a move—do it sooner, rather than later!

Outside the usual exchange of greetings at Christmas and Easter and casual correspondence with Carmelo, the "Sicilian Front" remained quiet until September 11th, 1999, when I received a letter from Jim Reid, former President of the Toronto Branch of the PPCLI Association, with some startling news. DVA was organizing yet another Pilgrimage to Sicily and Italy, leaving September 30th and returning October 14th. The delegation would comprise 100 veterans of Indian descent who had fought in Italy in WWII. They would arrive in Ispica on October 2nd for a memorial service at the Monument to mark the 55th Anniversary of the landing of the First Division on July 10th, 1943.

I was stunned. DVA, without even giving me the courtesy of a notice, had organized this tour for 100 Indians? I immediately phoned Jim for confirmation. "What the hell is the Department doing now?" Jim's information was sketchy, but what he had said was what he had been told by DVA. Furthermore, he had been chosen as one of the delegates.

Jim, an Indian? Nothing wrong with that, but how come? Jim told me a fantastic story. "This trip is for Aboriginal Indian War Vets. I qualify because my great-great-grandfather, John Peter Pruden, a Chief Factor with the Hudson's Bay Company, married an Indian woman. She died in 1839 and he then married an English school teacher by the name of Ann Armstrong, but all the children's names appear in the genealogy of the Metis First Nations List."

"OK, Jim, but are you sure the Pilgrimage is just for Indians?"

"That is what I was told."

"Something else. You said this was the 55th Anniversary of the landing in Sicily—makes no sense—1943 plus 55 equals 1998, and this is 1999."

"Well, I didn't say the Department is good at math."

I wished Jim *buon viaggio*. Whatever his status, he deserved a place on this trip. He had joined the PPCLI on April 18th, 1941, and was badly wounded on May 24th, 1944, in the Hitler Line when the Regiment was all but wiped out. After the war, he had served as President of the Toronto Branch for many years. Jim was yet another example of that special breed who typify the Regimental Motto: Once a Patricia–Always a Patricia.

I immediately wrote Carmelo Nigro of this upcoming Pilgrimage but regretted that on such short notice I could not join the Delegation. Frankly, I had mixed feelings about DVA not informing me. On the one hand, my nose was slightly out of joint because of their neglect, whether by design or inadvertence. On the other hand, I was glad that DVA had overtly claimed the Monument as being in their area of responsibility and no longer required my assistance. There might even be a chance that the Government would now contribute to its maintenance.

However, I was very concerned that as there was now a new guard at DVA, they would not be aware of the long, involved background to the erection of the Monument, especially the vital part played by Carmelo Nigro, and the attitude of the Italian Veterans. As events transpired, my concerns were justified.

* * *

PILGRIMAGE—1999 VETERANS AFFAIRS CANADA

On October 25th, Jim Reid phoned to report on the Pilgrimage. He had been misinformed that the group was restricted to Veterans of Indian ancestry. He was the sole representative of all "Indian Veterans".

I was pleased to hear that my friend, Don Munro had represented the PPCLI. He had joined the Regiment as a Lieutenant on August 10th, 1943, a few days after me, at the end of the Sicilian Campaign. He had served throughout the Italian and Holland Campaigns and was twice wounded.

Heading the delegation was the Canadian Ambassador, Jeremy Kinsman, the Honourable George Baker, Minister of Veterans Affairs, and Vice-Admiral Larry Murray, the Deputy Minister. Accompanying the group was the usual assortment of Senators, Members of Parliament, members of the Legion, representatives from the media, photographers, secretaries and others.

Ceremonies were held at all the Canadian War Cemeteries in Sicily and in Italy in the presence of local Dignitaries, Bands and Colour Parties.

I could hardly wait to hear about the Ceremony near the beaches of Sicily. "Jim, tell me about Ispica and the Monument. How did it go?"

Jim hesitated, "Well—I'm afraid your friend Carmelo was not allowed to speak." I was dumbfounded. "What do you mean?"

"There were a number of speakers and the Ceremony dragged on and on and it was hot. Someone in the audience, I believe an Italian Veteran, started handing out a poem by Walt Whitman—*Hymn to the Glory of the Defeated*. Carmelo, through an interpreter, asked the Canadian Master of Ceremonies when he could deliver his speech. He was ignored and the Master of Ceremonies declared the proceedings over.

Carmelo then asked the Mayor of Ispica if he could speak and was told to go ahead but by this time the party was over and everyone began to disperse except me and most of the veterans.

After his speech, Carmelo came up, showed me the letter you had written to him and thanked me for staying. He was obviously very upset and I had trouble understanding him. I'm sorry to have to give you this news, Syd. I may not have got all the story but I expect you'll be hearing from him very soon."

A few days later, I received a call from Rosanna Spataro. She had just received a large package from Carmelo containing his letter, the Programme for the Ceremony, list of Guests, newspaper articles, his speech and the poem by Walt Whitman. Rosanna needed a few days to translate all this material so I suggested that she and her family join me for dinner at an Italian Restaurant when she was ready.

On November 13th, *la famiglia Spataro* met me at the well-known restaurant Il Giardino with a brief case full of material. The dinner and wine were fine and helped me "digest" all the papers.

In order to fully understand what happened at the Monument on October 2nd, it is imperative that I quote at length from the relevant documents I received from Carmelo.

Letter from Carmelo Nigro
Ispica, the eve of a very sad day—October 2, 1999

Dear Col. Charles Sydney Frost,

Today has been the saddest day since September 22, 1991, the day of the unveiling of ... your monument.

The ceremony, about which you informed me, occurred today. I met your Indian friend, Mr. Jim Reid. He was very kind, when I told him I was your friend. He gave me some Canadian badges/flags, which I distributed amongst my friends.

I wrote that this was a sad day for me. Well it was all due to the Canadian Speaker at the ceremony, who indicated the order of those who would speak. First, various Canadians spoke: Ambassador Jeremy Kinsman, the Honourable George Baker, Minister of Veterans Affairs, and others. Afterwards, the Town Major or shall I say 'Mayor' of Ispica, Doctor Rosario Gugliotta spoke. I was supposed to speak immediately following the mayor, reading my short speech, which I have also sent to you, but the 'speaker' did not want me to speak.

Then the priests, one from Canada and one from Ispica, blessed the monument. As you will probably see from the Canadian films or video, memorial wreaths were laid in front of the monument by veterans and the Mayor of Ispica.

The Italian interpreter approached the speaker many times to ask if I, (the elementary school teacher, Carmelo Nigro) could speak. But the speaker said it was not possible and he was quite inflexible. At the end of the ceremony he said (in both English and Italian), "For all of us, the ceremony is now over".

I was strong and I approached the Mayor and asked, "Who owns the microphone and the loudspeakers next to the monument?"

And he replied, "They are Ispica's".

And I continued, "Then I can go and read my speech without being introduced by the Canadian Speaker?"

And he replied, "Yes, absolutely".

I was angry and I began reading my speech in a raised voice. The bus drivers started up the buses and many of the veterans began to disperse. The spectators of Ispica and many officials present were visibly upset.

Many patient and kind veterans stayed to listen and at the end of my speech applauded. Even the kind Jim Reid was more polite than the others and shook my hand, but he seemed very upset. I introduced him to my grandson, Leonardo.

Now the Mayor, the City Councillors, the Aldermen and other officials await apologies from the Canadians.

Believe me Colonnello, I never thought I would be humiliated this way.

I would be very happy if you would write a letter or have a letter written to justify the "Speaker's behaviour". The speaker will say that my name was not on his outline, or that the veterans at the ceremony were tired, but these are not good excuses.

Returning to Ispica on the evening of October 2, I learned that some people from Modica had distributed copies of the Poem "Hymn to the Glory of the Vanquished by Walt Whitman". They had given copies to those present at the ceremony, but I did not know!

Giornale di Sicilia
October 1, 1999.
Ispica, One Hundred Veterans Remember The Allied Landing

A ceremony at Marina Marza to celebrate the anniversary of the allied landing in Sicily. Tomorrow at 12:30 pm, 56 years after the allied landing, a hundred veterans from the First Canadian Division accompanied by the Canadian ambassador Jeremy Kinsman and the Honourable George Baker, Canadian Minister of Veterans Affairs, will lay laurel wreaths at the foot of the memorial stone erected eight years ago in Marina Marza.

The enterprise was fostered by the ex-lieutenant, Charles Sydney Frost, one of the first to enter Ispica with his soldiers after the allied landing. The group was part of the Princess Patricia's Canadian Light Infantry contingent. Hosting the event will be the Mayor of Ispica, Rosario Gugliotta, the Police Chief, Capt. Vincenzo Piccitto and the entire Municipal Council.

Before the ceremony, Carmelo Nigro will speak briefly. He has always kept in touch with the Canadian veterans and has been an enthusiastic promoter for having the monument built, so much so, that in a wonderful letter to Carmelo Nigro, Charles Sydney Frost refers to it as "your monument".

Of particular interest, Jim Reid, whose great-great-grandfather married an Indian, will also be in attendance tomorrow.

Salvatore Puglisi

Giornale di Sicilia
October 3, 1999
Ispica, A Diplomatic Incident Takes Place With One Hundred Veterans Of The Allied Landing. Ceremony In Crisis Because Of A "Hymn To The Defeated"

A diplomatic incident almost occurred at the Marza during the patriotic ceremony in honour of the fallen Canadian soldiers during the allied landing in Sicily in 1943. A speech was cut from the program for fear of a poem dedicated not to the victors, but to the defeated.

Thanks to the initiative by Carmelo Nigro and Col. Charles Sydney Frost (the first allied official to set foot in Ispica immediately after the allied landing), on September 22, 1991, a marble memorial stone was constructed at the marza and paid for by the "Centro Anziani" (Community Centre for the Elderly) to commemorate the fallen Canadian soldiers.

After eight years, many Canadians returned to Ispica last Saturday. The ceremony was organized by the municipality of Ispica, with the Mayor, Rosario Gugliotta, regional director, Innocenzo Leontini, the entire municipal council, municipal law enforcement officials and many citizens of Ispica in attendance.

From Canada there were one hundred soldiers, veterans, ex-officials and petty officers, followed by the sound of bagpipes. Also present was the Canadian Ambassador, Jeremy Kinsman, the Hon. George Baker, Minister of Veterans Affairs.

Everything was proceeding as planned until the ceremony was interrupted by the Canadian speaker, who prevented an introduction of the official speaker, Carmelo Nigro. It happened that moments before an ex-second

> *lieutenant, Giovanni Caso from Modica, handed out copies of a poem from poet Walt Whitman entitled "Hymn to the Glory of the Defeated".*
>
> > *I come with loud music*
> > *With bugles and drums*
> > *Not to play the marches*
> > *Of the illustrious victors*
> > *But to sing the glory*
> > *Of the fallen and defeated*
>
> *The Canadian did not like this and it marked an abrupt end to the ceremony, eliminating Carmelo Nigro's speech even though he had nothing to do with this incident. Carmelo Nigro did not give up. In the end he managed to speak, all the while horns blared and buses started their engines.*
>
> *Salvatore Puglisi*

It was abundantly clear to me that Carmelo's letter and the two newspaper articles (one written before the event and the other after) showed beyond the shadow of a doubt what had happened. The question was—to whom should I turn for redress? Normally, one would seek out the Canadian Ambassador but, as he was present, he had at least passively acquiesced in the proceedings and was not likely to castigate his Government.

Likewise, the Minister and Deputy Minister were hardly disinterested parties. A further problem was that my quasi-political rank as Honorary Colonel of The Royal Regiment of Canada had lapsed and I had no excuse for marching into the Prime Minister's Office.

There was still one avenue open—the Colonel of the Regiment, PPCLI, MGen. Bill Hewson. If anyone could get things moving, I knew I could count on him.

This is my letter to him (with irrelevant matters deleted):

> *December 2, 1999*
>
> *Dear Bill:*
>
> *As you perhaps know, the Department of Veterans Affairs conducted a Pilgrimage to Italy and Sicily during the first two weeks of October to mark the 56th Anniversary of the Landing on Sicily, July 10, 1943. One hundred Veterans representing the Units of the First Division took part. The group visited all the Cemeteries and many of the Monuments, including the Monument near Ispica, Sicily.*

I knew nothing about the trip until mid-September when I received a form letter from Jim Reid, the former President of the Toronto Branch, advising that DVA had organized a trip to Italy for the Aboriginal War Veterans of Indian descent! He had been chosen because his great-great-grandfather, who was a Chief Factor with the Hudson Bay Company, had married an Indian woman.

It turned out that Jim's information was slightly exaggerated, as the group was not restricted to Veterans of Indian ancestry. Jim attended as the sole representative of all "Indian" veterans. I believe Don Munro represented the Regiment.

This farcical beginning of the trip set the stage for what was to follow during the Ceremony at the Monument in Ispica.

I am not sure that you are fully acquainted with the background leading up to its erection in 1991. It is a long story that has been written up in several Canadian military journals and in many Sicilian newspapers and magazines. I can do no better than enclose the following articles:

1. The Legion Magazine, March 1992—Article by Doug Fisher.
2. Newsletter of the RCMI, Toronto, December 1991.
3. The Garrison, Toronto, December 1991.
I also enclose the following photo taken at the dedication of the Monument in September 1991.
4. Photo showing me presenting a PPCLI plaque and a copy of Once a Patricia *to Carmelo Nigro.*

The purpose of this letter is to bring to your attention and seek your advice how to remedy, a terrible wrong that has been done to the person who organized the construction of the Monument and arranged for the entire cost of the project to be repaid by the citizens of Ispica. (The Canadian government paid not one cent). That person is my dear friend Carmelo Nigro, a school teacher, who gave generously of his time, money and energy to bring the project to fruition. Without his determination there would not have been a Monument at Ispica.

The terrible wrong was inflicted on him by a member of DVA or other Government Official who would not allow Carmelo Nigro to speak at the Ceremony last October. I enclose the following materials which tell the sad tale.

> 5. Article which appeared in the Giornale di Sicilia, together with translation into English.
> 6. Speech that Carmelo Nigro was not permitted to deliver during the Ceremony, but which he finally gave after the Ceremony was over (translated into English).
> 7. Letter from Carmelo Nigro to me, October 1, 1999, (translated into English).
>
> *I also enclose the following photos of the Ceremony taken by Jim Reid:*
>
> 8. Photo of the Monument showing the wreaths deposited by the Italian community and Canada.
> 9. Photo of the Veterans and Officials of Ispica and surrounding communities. Carmelo Nigro is in the front rank indicated by an arrow.
>
> *There is little more to say. You will notice in his letter that Carmelo Nigro, the Mayor and city officials of Ispica await an apology from Canada.*
>
> *I am sorry to saddle you with this problem, but I can think of no one else I can turn to who will give me the advice I so urgently need. It would be a tragedy if this unfortunate event were allowed to escalate and damage the friendly feelings and respect that the people of Ispica have for the Patricias, the soldiers of the First Division and for Canada itself.*
>
> *Sincerely,*

I realized that I was handing MGen. Hewson a hefty bill of goods and that it would be many months, if ever, before we received an apology. I took solace in an Italian proverb Carmelo had once quoted to me, *Chi non risica, non rosica.* (Nothing ventured, nothing gained.)

Bill Hewson kept me informed as he worked his way through the corridors of DVA and conferred with various officials. On February 22nd, I received electric news. He had spoken with Vice-Admiral Larry Murray and he had agreed to send letters of apology! All the material I had sent Bill Hewson was now duly filed in the Department, both in the records of the Pilgrimage and under my own name. It was highly unlikely that the same mistake would ever be made again.

How Bill Hewson was able to accomplish the impossible in less than three months, I don't know. He was much too modest to admit he had done anything special so I am saying it for him. He had created another unofficial motto for the Regiment: "The impossible just takes us a little longer."

Here is the letter Vice-Admiral Murray sent to MGen. Hewson (with a copy to me):

February 21, 2000

Dear Bill:

Thank you for your letter of February 8, 2000, concerning the Veterans Affairs Canada pilgrimage to Italy in October 1999, and specifically the commemorative ceremony which took place at the 1st Canadian Infantry Division Monument near Ispica, Sicily, on October 2, 1999.

Several days before the ceremony the Veterans Affairs advance team, including someone who speaks fluent Italian, held meetings with civic officials in Ispica and Pachino, the two communities most closely associated with the 1st Division Monument. This was done to review and finalize the formal ceremony program.

At Ispica, the advance team met with Mr. Rosario Gugliotta, the Mayor of Ispica and his officials. Mr. Gugliotta indicated that he wished to speak at the ceremony. It was also agreed that a local priest from Ispica would offer a brief prayer at the ceremony. It was also mentioned that Mr. Carmelo Nigro would attend the ceremony. However, the advance team was not advised of his desire to speak at the ceremony.

The actual ceremony at the 1st Division Monument commenced at 12:30 pm and was expected to take about 30 minutes to conduct. Given the high heat and humidity of mid-day, this is about all the time we would expect the veterans and the vigil party to stand in place without discomfort.

As it turned out, the ceremony took more than one hour to conduct, due, in large part, because local officials spent considerably more time at the speaker's dais than expected, and because the Mayor's speech was read by his English translator as well. I might add the local priest delivered a prayer which took about 15 minutes.

During the course of the ceremony our Master of Ceremonies was approached by the Mayor's translator who asked when Mr. Nigro would speak. This was, of course, all news to him. He was also not aware of the role Mr. Nigro had played in establishing the monument (nor was I until our lunch last week). Our Master of Ceremonies also noticed that our sentries were close to collapsing in the heat, and that some of our veterans were feeling some discomfort too. He advised the translator that Mr. Nigro was not scheduled to speak during the formal ceremony, but that he could do so after the ceremony, which would allow the sentries and vigil party to be dismissed and the veterans to move about. This is what took place.

Following the ceremony, our Master of Ceremonies was advised by the Mayor's translator that she, too, was not advised in advance that Mr. Nigro wished to speak until the ceremony had actually commenced. This was proven when she had difficulty translating his speech following the ceremony.

I was witness to the ceremony and I support the actions taken by our Master of Ceremonies. Indeed, many of the veterans in our delegation thanked him for trying to shorten the formal ceremony in the manner just described.

It is, indeed, unfortunate that this incident occurred, and that Mr. Nigro feels that he was slighted and insulted. I can assure you that there was no intention on our part, in any way, to offend Mr. Nigro or to not recognize him.

I have written letters of explanation and apology to Mr. Nigro and the Mayor of Ispica. Copies are attached for your information.

I am also sending a copy of this letter to Colonel Charles Sydney Frost and sincerely regret any inconvenience and concern that this unfortunate incident caused him.

Thank you, again, for your letter and for bringing this matter to my attention.

Yours sincerely,
Larry Murray

c.c. Colonel C. S. Frost

And the letter of apology to Carmelo Nigro:

February 21, 2000

Mr. Carmelo Nigro
c/o Mr. Rosario Gugliotta
Mayor of Ispica
Ispica, Sicily, Italy

Dear Mr. Nigro:
I am writing in response to a letter you sent to Colonel Charles Sydney Frost concerning the commemorative ceremony held at the lst Canadian Infantry Division Monument near Ispica, Sicily, on October 2, 1999, during the Veterans Affairs Canada pilgrimage to commemorate the 55th anniversary of the Italian Campaign. Colonel Frost passed your letter to Major General C. W. Hewson who, in turn, wrote to me.

I am very sorry to hear how distressed you are over not being able to speak during the formal ceremony. Please let me offer an explanation.

The Veterans Affairs advance team, including someone who spoke fluent Italian, met with the Mayor of Ispica, Mr. Rosario Gugliotta, and some of his officials several days before the ceremony to discuss and finalize the ceremony program. The Mayor advised our team that he wished to speak at the ceremony and that you would attend. However, we were not advised that you wished to speak during the ceremony.

While the ceremony was actually in progress the Mayor's translator approached our Master of Ceremonies and asked him when you would speak. This, of course, was all news to him. He advised her that you were not in the official program as a speaker, but that you could speak after the formal ceremony.

Due to the length of the ceremony and the extra time needed for speeches and translations, our Master of Ceremonies decided to try to shorten the official part of the ceremony as much as possible. He noticed that our sentries were close to collapsing and that some of our veterans were feeling uncomfortable. As you know, the day was very hot and humid and the ceremony took more than one hour to conduct.

It is, indeed, unfortunate that we were not advised beforehand that you wished to speak during the ceremony. I am certain that this was an oversight and that there may well have been some misunderstanding and miscommunication as well.

Your energy and dedication in being the driving force behind the construction of the 1st Canadian Infantry Division Monument is certainly recognized and appreciated by all of us in Veterans Affairs Canada. I feel, personally, very sad that this unfortunate incident occurred. I can assure you that there was never any intention on our part to deliberately embarrass you or prevent you from receiving the recognition you so richly deserve.

I formally apologize to you, on behalf of Canada and the Veterans Affairs Canada pilgrimage team, for the embarrassment you experienced on October 2, 1999.

When we conduct our next pilgrimage we will rectify this situation and ensure that you are included in any future ceremonial program.

Thank you very much for bringing this matter to my attention.

Yours sincerely,
Larry Murray
P.S. I have also sent a letter to the Mayor of Ispica (copy attached) along with a copy of this letter.

Thus ended the 1999 Pilgrimage which I had not been a part of or even given notice of. Yet, it had occupied much of my time and energy for the previous five months. Like a vacuum it had drawn in many other people who gave unstintingly of their time and energy. Rosanna had spent many days translating the correspondence and material to and from Ispica. The support of MGen. Bill Hewson was well beyond the call of duty and perhaps even exceeded his mandate as Colonel of the PPCLI. The humiliation suffered by Carmelo Nigro and the embarrassment felt by the Mayor and citizens of Ispica has been described.

But was all this necessary? Of course not.

Granted the new Minister of Veterans Affairs had probably never heard of Ispica, the Monument, Carmelo Nigro or Colonel Frost. But it was all in his files or the files of his officers who were arranging the Pilgrimage. It was also in the lengthy correspondence with Gerry Merrithew in 1991, some of which appears in this book, and in connection with the 1994 Pilgrimage to Ispica attended by the then Minister of Veterans Affairs, Lawrence MacAulay, as described earlier.

If I had been given a simple courtesy notice requesting advice and assistance, I would have enlightened the Department of the history of the Monument, the vital part played by Carmelo Nigro and the simmering desire of the Italian veterans to have their own memorial.

The claim of the Department that at the meeting of the DVA advance team with the Mayor, they were advised Carmelo would be present but not speak, is simply not credible. What was the point of even mentioning his name unless they were given the story of his part in the erection of the Monument. The Department claimed they had "someone who spoke fluent Italian," but they don't mention his fluency in English.

However, to his credit, Vice-Admiral Murray rose to the occasion, acknowledged there may have been a misunderstanding and made an unequivocal apology. It was a generous act and as a former Mayor of Ispica, I thank him from the bottom of my heart.

On that conciliatory note, I think this Chapter should end to make way for one more Pilgrimage to Ispica.

My final word to the Department of Veterans Affairs would be to express the hope that one learns by one's mistakes. Or, in Italian, *Sbagliando s'impara*.

Chapter VIII

PILGRIMAGE—2000

While I had been battling the Department to obtain an apology for the "Carmelo incident," the campaign in Ispica to erect a second Monument to the Italians was rapidly coming to a successful conclusion. On the very day I informed Rosanna (February 23rd) of the good news about the apology, she received an e-mail from Carmelo that the Italian Monument would definitely be erected. The ceremony was set for July 10th!

I immediately sent Carmelo a letter expressing my delight. At last our dream would be realized but there was still one hitch. Due to a prior commitment, I could not attend the ceremony on July 10th.

To understand my dilemma, a word of explanation is necessary. Very early in 1999, the people of Holland began planning a great celebration of the 55th Anniversary of the end of WWII, to be held during the month of May 2000. Every five years since 1980 the Dutch had organized similar ceremonies throughout Holland to honour the Canadian soldiers who had liberated their country. The citizens of Holland opened their hearts and homes to their Canadian liberators, and veterans came in their thousands to join in the celebrations, which came to be known as Pilgrimages. I had attended the Pilgrimages in 1980, 1985 and 1990 but missed the one in 1995 due to the illness of my wife. I was, therefore, very keen to attend the Pilgrimage in 2000.

By March 1999, I had made my hotel and travel arrangements for the period from April 26th to May 14th, 2000, which allowed me time to participate in all the main events. But I was not going to visit Europe without calling on my dear friends in Ispica. So, I also made reservations to visit Sicily for the last two weeks in May, hoping that the Monument to the Italians would be ready.

In subsequent chapters of my book, I will describe my 2000 Pilgrimage to Holland. In the meantime, let us return to my letter of February 23rd, 2000, to Carmelo, which, after my explanation, should now make some sense.

February 23, 2000

Mio Caro Carmelo:
I have great news for you. I have just been informed by my friend General Hewson that the Canadian Government is sending letters of apology to you and the Mayor of Ispica!

I phoned Rosanna this morning and told her the news. She informed me that she has received an e-mail from you advising that a Monument to Soldati, Caduti, Italiani will be erected, and that a Ceremony will be held on July 10th. I have already booked my flights and hotel reservations for May and I cannot change my schedule at this late date. First, I must visit Holland for important ceremonies there marking the 55th Anniversary of their Liberation, and then, of course, I am visiting you. I am flying from Holland directly to Rome and then to Catania and Taormina. I will be very happy to visit you between Tuesday, May 16th and Wednesday, May 24th. I am sorry I cannot change these dates.

It occurs to me that even though the Monument is not completed until July 10th, we could hold a little ceremony between those dates at the site where the Monument will be erected. This is often done in Canada.

I am very much looking forward to seeing you and your lovely family again.

Con affetto e rispetto. Tuo amico.

Now that the Monument had progressed this far, I wanted to ensure there would be no delays due to lack of financing. The time was ripe for me to make good on my offer to help. I phoned Rosanna and asked to whom I should make the cheque. On April 10th, I received, via Rosanna, a translation of Carmelo's reply.

My dear noble Col. C. S. Frost
On Thursday, March 23, I received a message from my niece Rosanna telling me about your generous offer to make a personal contribution towards the construction of the monument (in honour of the Italian soldiers killed the day of the allied landing July 10, 1943). You can make the

> *cheque payable to:* Presidente Comitato pro cippo marmoreol al caduti Italiani di Ispica.
>
> *At my suggestion, a committee is being nominated to deal with the details of the construction of the monument and the inaugural ceremony on July 10 of this year. I believe that when the Ispicesi find out that you have made a donation that they will also wish to contribute towards the monument.*
>
> *I met with the mayor, dott. Rosario Gugliotta, and he told me that perhaps when you are in Taormina we could meet on Saturday, May 20 at noon.*
>
> *Dear Col. more details will follow about the ceremony. I will say goodbye with the promise that we shall see each other soon. Everyone says hello, the mayor and my family.*
>
> Tuo amico Carmelo

It was now April 10th and my plane for Holland was due to leave April 26th. I had my work cut out to prepare for both Pilgrimages. I expected I would be asked to speak at the inaugural ceremony on May 20th, so I struggled to draft something appropriate. I soon realized that my text book Italian was not good enough to compose such an important speech in Italian and once again called on Rosanna to translate. This is what I sent her:

> *Dear Friends:*
>
> *On September 22nd, 1991, a splendid Monument was blessed and unveiled at this place to honour Canada's soldiers who landed on these shores on July 10, 1943. They came, not to subjugate this beautiful island, but as Liberators in the cause of Freedom. Many gave their lives.*
>
> *Today we stand on this same hallowed ground to honour the Italian soldiers, who, though vastly outnumbered, bravely remained at their posts and fought to the end.*
>
> *I have long wished that a Memorial be erected in honour of these heroic soldiers who now lie with their Canadian brothers-in-arms. Let us not think of them as Victors and Vanquished. What difference separates them now? Both died for a noble cause and now they sleep in peace.*
>
> *It is a great honour for me to be present at this Ceremony and be asked to be the Padrino of this fine Memorial. Thank you.*

Somehow, I managed to do all the things required to send me off on my Tenth Pilgrimage to Europe. I won't say I was ready, but I was keen.

After 17 exciting, strenuous days in Holland, I left Amsterdam on May 14th, via KLM, and arrived in Rome where I changed planes and took Air Alitalia to Catania, Sicily. It was raining heavily, probably the worst storm I had ever experienced in this hot, arid land. The Italians have a lovely name for a good rainstorm—*Piove a catinelle* (It's raining washbasins). With visibility reduced, I got lost trying to leave Catania during the rush hour and it took me two and one-half hours to reach my hotel in Taormina. Driving an unfamiliar Nubira Stationwagon with a gear shift didn't help. I was very tired and wondered how everything would turn out. It was not an auspicious beginning.

It is amazing how much punishment the human body can take if one's motives are strong. Next morning, I had pretty well recovered and was looking forward to a late breakfast in the hotel dining room. The Maitre d', who remembered me from earlier visits, gave me a warm welcome and said, "*È bello rivederti. Ho una sorpresa per lei.*" (It's nice to see you again. I have a surprise for you.)

He led me to the window and there, only a few miles distant, was Mount Etna—erupting! "*Mamma mia,*" I cried without thinking, and then added, "*Scusi ma ho pensato che la montagna era quasi morta.*" (Excuse me, I thought the mountain was almost dead.)

"*No, no, Colonnello. L'ultimo eruzione era alcuni anni fa, ma non si sa mai.*" (The last eruption occurred a few years ago, but one never knows.)

I remembered my guided tour of Mount Etna in 1997, when I asked the guide whether the mountain ever claimed any victims, and I remembered his frank but shocking reply. I was not going to repeat my query. I just hoped that the gods who look after Mount Etna realized I was not Italian.

According to plan, for the next few days I relaxed and prepared for my visit to Ispica. I could not have chosen a better place to unwind and enjoy the pleasures of a lovely Sicilian resort. Indeed, Taormina has been described as one of the most beautiful and impressive in the world. I cannot vouch for such high credentials but in my experience, it certainly ranks at the top. Indeed, the famous Guy de Maupassant, who visited the place in 1885, described it in these words:

> *If someone should spend just one day in Sicily and ask, 'What must one see?', I would answer without hesitation, Taormina. It is only a landscape, but a landscape in which you find everything that seems created on earth to seduce eyes, mind and fantasy.*

With that assessment, I would agree. Few places can equal its natural position, perched on a lofty terrace overhanging the blue waters of the Mediterranean with Mount Etna as its impressive background.

Every time I visit Taormina I think of Hammie Gault and his fondness for this place. With a touch of irony I also remember that the German Kaiser used to holiday here with his family before WWI. Pity the two didn't meet and settle the Kaiser's ambitions over a few glasses of red wine.

One of the wondrous sights of Taormina is the famous Teatro Greco-Romano which is still in use. From its restored seats one receives a spectacular view of Mount Etna, while enjoying plays, symphony orchestras, ballet and other entertainment from the ancient stage. The London Philharmonic has performed there, as well as many other international orchestras.

When I expressed surprise at the erupting Mount Etna, the Maitre d' suggested I attend the Greco-Romano theatre that evening to enjoy a Shakespearean play as well as the fireworks from Mount Etna. There was no extra charge for the latter!

Thus, I spent a very pleasant day or two attending the theatre in the evening and bathing in the Mediterranean during the day. The sandy beach lay at the foot of the precipice on which my hotel was perched and I was not too keen to clamber up and down the steep pathway. But the Maitre d' came to my rescue and directed me to a cable car.

It was now time to end these frivolous pursuits and get ready for my visit to Ispica. I had been in touch with Carmelo and we had agreed to meet at the City Hall at 11:00 a.m., May 20th. He suggested I take the coastal route, Siracusa, Avola, Noto, Rossolini. It would be about a three hour drive.

May 20th, 2000

At 11:00 a.m., I arrived at the City Hall and was promptly ushered into the office of the Mayor, Dr. Rosario Gugliotta, who greeted me warmly. Carmelo, of course, needed no introduction. Some of the others I met were the Police Chief, Capitano Piccitto Vincenzo, the President of the Centro d'Incontro Anziani, Prof. Giuseppa Peligra, Councillor Tony Blandizzi, two Police Officers, Zocco Biagio and Garaffa Giovanni.

I had previously told Carmelo that I was making a strictly personal visit and that everything should be as informal as possible. I was therefore surprised and not a little embarrassed when Carmelo called for silence and proceeded to give a five minute talk about Colonel Frost—going back to my time in 1943 when I was their "first democratic Mayor," and describing all my visits to Ispica and my part in erecting both the Monument and the Memorial to the fallen Italians.

Modesty prevents me from quoting the entire speech, but I can't resist giving his peroration:

Now we can certainly say that his name will never die. It is linked to the history of two commemorative stones and to that of the new Ispica and of its citizens.

I think that even Caesar would have blushed.

I was not ready for this encomium but fortunately had brought with me two plaques which I then presented. They were engraved as follows:

To Carmelo Nigro, through whose vision, energy and determination a Monument now stands at Marza in honour of Canada's soldiers of the First Division.
   Presented by his friend, Col. C. S. Frost, PPCLI.
                                                                May 20, 2000

To Mayor Gugliotta, in honour of the Italian soldiers who gave their lives in defence of their country.
   Presented by Col. C. S. Frost, the first democratic Mayor of Ispica, July 6 to August 3, 1943.
                                                                May 20, 2000

The Mayor responded by presenting me with five lovely books on Ispica, some with colour plates, describing the wonderful works of art, edifices and other treasures going back to antiquity. He also gave me a video about Sicily and an audio cassette of Sicilian folk music.

Again I was not ready for these generous gifts but I still had an ace, or actually a cheque, up my sleeve. I said a few words and then presented my cheque to the Mayor, who received it with obvious pleasure.

Then it was back to the Mayor who thanked me profusely and announced that I would be the Padrino (Godfather) of the new Memorial.

I believe I was speechless after all this and could only mumble "*Mille grazie.*"

But my day was not yet over. Capitano Vincenzo stepped forward and presented me with a magnificent embroidered Coat of Arms of the Police Force of Ispica and intimated that I was now an Honorary Police Officer.

At loss for something to say, I blurted out, in English, "I suppose I can now arrest the Mayor for speeding."

The Mayor understood English and immediately replied, "No, you can't arrest me, but you can now arrest yourself if you misbehave as a Godfather!" It was a clever rejoinder and I said so.

* * *

PILGRIMAGE—2000

May 20th, 2000

12:00 noon—Inaugural Ceremony

As the Memorial to the Italians had not yet been completed, only a brief ceremony was held at the site of the First Division Monument where the new Memorial would be erected. In keeping with my wishes, the participants limited to those who had attended the Mayor's Office and a few interested citizens.

I delivered the speech in Italian, which I have already quoted. The Mayor and Carmelo said a few words and the brief ceremony was over. Before leaving the site, several citizens came up to thank me for my contribution, including the mothers of two Italian soldiers who had been killed in the War. They said, "*Adesso i nostri figli possano restare in pace perche sanno che i lori nomi non saranno dimenticati mai.*" (Now our sons can rest in peace because they know their names will never be forgotten.)

Suddenly all the effort that Carmelo and I had devoted to the Memorial was worthwhile.

1:00 p.m.—Lunch at Cava d' Ispica

As mentioned in my account of the 1997 Pilgrimage, the Mayor at that time, Dr. Amore, and his Councillor, Dr. Aprile, had given me a "quickie" tour of these fascinating caves and invited me to descend the Centoscale to the bed of a river. When I demurred, they offered to treat me to a dinner at a restaurant located in one of the caves on my next visit.

Dr. Amore must have passed this on to the present Mayor because one of the first things he said to me was, "You'll be joining us for lunch in the Cava, of course."

We drove to the Cava area which has been set aside as a park (Parco Archeologico della Forza) and walked into the gorge past innumerable abandoned caves and catacombs until a sign declared that we had arrived at a restaurant. We entered. I didn't know what to expect. The place was fairly well lit with candles, some hanging from the roof of the cave. In the flickering light, I made out chairs and tables covered with white table cloths and adorned with the usual appurtenances of a fine restaurant.

Nine of us sat down, including the dignitaries I had met in the Mayor's office plus a charming young lady by the name of Angela Muriana who acted as my interpreter. I thought she was Italian but it turned out she was from Iowa, USA! She was studying foreign languages at the University and taking a year off in Ispica to improve her Italian. This was a very thoughtful act on the part of Dr. Gugliotta and

I thanked him. I can get along in Italian pretty well so long as they speak slowly. But there are only two speeds used in Italy—fast and faster. She was a great help in the rapid-fire conversation around the table and altogether it was a lot of fun in a very romantic setting.

I asked Angela if there was any way I could reciprocate her kindness. Yes, there was. She would love to receive a postcard from Toronto! This was certainly a modest request and I was happy to oblige.

I also wrote Mayor Gugliotta when I returned home. I am taking the liberty of quoting from my letter at length because it describes the events of that memorable day as I felt at the time:

June 18, 2000

Dear Dr. Gugliotta:

Thank you for the warm, friendly welcome you gave me, and for the five lovely books and video cassette. Each time I visit Ispica I come away with a new appreciation and respect for the wonderful works of art, imposing edifices and other treasures that go back to antiquity. From what I have read, Ispica is a city of tremendous historical importance far exceeding its modest size.

I was very interested in the writings of Pina Trigilia about Centoscale ad Ispica. I have asked an Italian friend to translate the book for me.

The audio cassette of folk music intrigues me but unfortunately it cannot be played on my machine. I am told, however, that the cassette can be converted and I will have this done.

I was pleased to meet your Chief of Police, Capitano Piccitto Vincenzo, the President of the Associazione Centro d'Incontro Anziani and the other citizens you had assembled in your chamber to meet me.

I was, of course, delighted to see my old friend Carmelo Nigro, who gave such a flattering speech about my career! I will be writing Capitano Vincenzo to thank him for the magnificent Standard of the Polizie he presented to me.

I am so happy that a Monument will at last be erected to honour the fallen Italian soldiers. Both Carmelo and I have long wished that such a Memorial be raised. It is gratifying to know that our desire will now be realized, and I am very honoured to be asked to become the Padrino. I trust my modest contribution will be of some help and that my short speech was appropriate. I enclose a copy for your records.

The luncheon in the Cave Restaurant was certainly a unique experience. I am sure it is the only such restaurant

> *to be found anywhere. The food was excellent, the service first class and the ambience, as I said, "out of this world"!*

My reference to the book about the Centoscale requires a little explanation. Dr. Gugliotta and I had talked about the 100 steps at lunch and I said they intrigued me but, because of my health, I felt I could not undertake to descend to the bottom and then climb back. He understood and presented me with a recent book on the Centoscale. I have not yet had the opportunity to have it fully translated, but it is a fascinating story. The stairway has been the subject of an ongoing archaeological study. There is evidence that the design, measurements and location of Centoscale, are, in many ways, related to the famous Cheops Pyramid in Egypt. Apparently, lunar and solar observations have revealed striking similarities between the two.

The luncheon in the Cave continued for two or three hours amid much carefree banter and good humour, although there were some serious matters to discuss, including the completion of the Memorial. It was obvious that my modest donation had given the project a good boost but the work would take several months, probably until December. The Mayor, Carmelo and others pleaded with me to come back then for the Dedication Ceremony. It was, of course, out of the question, and despite copious glasses of wine and friendly camaraderie, I was able to resist their entreaties.

I hated to leave but it was time to go. I made a "help me" gesture to Carmelo who nodded his head and delivered one of his Italian proverbs, "*Un bel gioco dura poco.*" (Fun doesn't last long.)

The party slowly broke up and we sauntered out into the bright sunshine for final farewells. When would we meet again? Soon? In a few years? Never? All three choices were on my mind but I quickly banished the last two from my thoughts and gave one and all the thumbs up sign and the Italian equivalent of "soon". "*Ciao, a presto.*"

On the way home to Taormina, I dropped Carmelo off at his house and said goodbye to his family. They were all there imploring me to stay for dinner, but again I had to force myself to say, "*Gratia, no. Non è possibile. Ritornerò presto.*"

I took the inland route along Highways 115 and 514 past Ragusa. I was in no rush to leave my friends and the country I had known since that day in 1943 when I came ashore on Ulysses' Beach, fifty-seven years earlier. I thought of all the good things that had happened to me since and I thought of some of the bad things. On balance, I had been very fortunate the way it had all worked out, at least so far as my Sicilian adventure was concerned. During the war, old Field Marshal Fate had dealt me some pretty bad cards but in the end he had given me a good hand, one that I would always treasure—my "Ispicese connection". In my long journey from being a Mayor to becoming a Godfather and Honorary Police Officer, there must have been a thousand times when my course might easily have gone in another direction. But some force had kept me on track. It had been a wonderful, exciting voyage. Thank you, Field Marshal Fate.

Only one matter troubled me. I had not been able to meet my good friend Antonino Lauretta, the head of the Centro di Cultura Popolare. For some reason he had not been informed of my visit beforehand. As soon as I arrived, I tried to contact him several times without success. Finally, on the day of leaving, I spoke to him. He had been very busy and could not break earlier appointments in order to see me. All I could do was express my regrets and leave a parcel for him with the Concierge. The parcel contained a Regimental Plaque, a CD of PPCLI songs and a small Canadian flag.

When I finally arrived home after my long Pilgrimage to Holland and Sicily, I wrote my usual letters to all the people who had been instrumental in having both Monuments erected. Heading the list was MGen. Bill Hewson, Colonel of the Regiment, PPCLI. It will be recalled that at the Ceremony on 2nd October, 1999, the Government Master of Ceremonies had humiliated Carmelo Nigro by not letting him speak. This quickly became an insult to the Mayor and to all the citizens of Ispica who demanded an apology. At the same time, some Italian Veterans had voiced their opposition to the Canadian Monument and demanded a Monument to recognize their own dead.

I sent a signal to Bill Hewson—help! He immediately went into action and soon obtained letters of apology from Vice-Admiral Larry Murray, Deputy Minister of Veterans Affairs, which greatly mollified Carmelo and the citizens of Ispica. Without Bill Hewson's timely intervention, the situation could well have escalated even further and jeopardized the security of the Monument as well as the plans to erect another one for the Italians.

Next to be thanked was the Spataro family, whose Rosanna had again faithfully translated all the letters and documents. She and her family deserved a special thank you so I took them to my old friend, Il Giardino Restaurant. I showed them all the gifts I had received—the five books from Mayor Gugliotta and the Police Banner. I left the book on Centoscale with Rosanna who said she wanted to read it and would send me a translation. I gave Sebastian a PPCLI hat badge and handed Rosaria and the two girls necklaces and medallions I had picked up in Holland.

I have almost finished my story. The only unfinished business, and probably the most important of all, was something beyond my control—the Monument to the Italians. I patiently awaited news from Carmelo.

Finally it came. The new Monument had been erected and the dedication would be December 8th. I immediately composed a speech and sent it to Rosanna to be translated into Italian and forwarded to Carmelo to be read by him or the Mayor.

Then I received coloured photos of the two new Memorials erected on either side of the Canadian Monument, of equal height and set back at a slight angle from the Monument. The three columns formed a sombre yet attractive trilogy in stone—worthy Memorials to the fallen of both sides.

A little later I received a large packet from Rosanna which she had received from Carmelo containing the following material which she had translated for me:

- Photo of the engraving on the two Memorial stones. On one, the names of the fallen Italian soldiers, on the other, the names of the civilians killed in the invasion.
- List of principal guests.
- Official engraved invitation of the Mayor.
- Programme of the Ceremony.
- List of contributors.

* * *

December 8th, 2000
Dedication Of The Memorials To Italian Soldiers
And Civilians
Marza, Sicily

The Memorials sparkled in the morning sun, their inscriptions shielded by Italian flags.

The Band of the famous Bersaglieri played quiet music while the invited guests arrived—44 in number from all the surrounding Municipalities and from every walk of life: Mayors, Prefects and Presidents; Commandants of the Carabinieri, Guardia di Finanza; the U.S. Navy Facility; representatives of Veterans Associations; General Tortorici; Carmelo Nigro; Professors and staff members from the University of Messina and local schools; former Mayors; Padre Pietro Iabichella of the Grey Friars; Senator Marisa Moltisanti; Centro d'Incontro Anziani, and many others.

Mayor Rosario Gugliotta opened the Ceremony with a speech describing the historical significance of the area, the landing of the Canadians, the bravery of the Italian defenders and the building of the Monuments. At the conclusion of his speech, he read an address prepared by Col. Frost who could not be present.

Carmelo Nigro also spoke on behalf of the Italian Veterans. He described, in some detail, the composition of the Canadian Forces and read out the names of the fallen.

The Memorials were dedicated and blessed and wreaths were laid. The Band played the Italian National Anthem.

Throughout the Ceremony, the Memorials were flanked by sentries from the Army, Navy, Airforce, Bersaglieri, local Police Force and the Guardia di Finanza which also supplied a Guard of Honour.

After the Ceremony, guests and spectators were served a buffet lunch in the nearby U.S. Naval Facility.

The above account of the dedication of the Memorial has been composed from material Carmelo sent me before and after the event. In addition to the material I have already mentioned, Carmelo sent me the following:

- A video cassette of the Ceremony.
- Newspaper clippings.
- Postcards commemorating the event.
- The Mayor's speech.
- Carmelo's speech.
- Letter from the Mayor to me.

The newspaper articles, letter and the speeches were all in Italian but I didn't have the heart to ask Rosanna to translate them word for word. Instead, we skimmed the material and I made notes of the parts I had difficulty translating. Thus, any errors or omissions in the above description of the Ceremony are mine alone.

Accompanying this mass of material was a letter from Carmelo which began as follows:

> *"Alea iacta est"* as they say in Latin. In our case, the Latin proverb would mean that after all our discussion and work, the Monuments we both wanted are finally blessed and unveiled.

How to reply to such a learned man? Italian was bad enough, but now Latin? I dug deep into my days at high school and remembered a phrase we used to put at the end of a geometry problem—Q.E.D., "We have done the work we were required to do." In my brief reply to Carmelo, I thanked him for his Latin expression and added one of my own—Q.E.D.

Perhaps the best way to sum up the beautiful and moving ceremony I have tried to describe is to quote from letters I sent Carmelo and the Mayor, Dr. Gugliotta.

Caro Carmelo:

Last evening I met with Rosanna and went through all the letters and documents you so kindly sent me.

Like me, she was deeply impressed with the beautiful Ceremony shown in the video and with the other materials included in your package.

May I offer my sincere compliments on the excellence of the program and the way in which it was carried out. The speeches were profound and the bearing of the officers and men on parade was exemplary.

I particularly enjoyed reading your own speech which, in your inimitable professorial way, described the events connected with the landing. You have captured a significant episode in the long history of Porto Ulisse.

And so your long, arduous labours on behalf of the fallen Italian and Canadian soldiers have come to an end. I cannot find words to express my gratitude and admiration for all that you have accomplished. You deserve a medal.

Last week, I was interviewed by a reporter from the Italian Newspaper, Corriere Canadese. They are very interested in the story of the erection of the two Monuments and they are going to publish an article. I told them to be sure to give you full credit for promoting the undertaking and seeing it through to completion. I will send you the article when it appears.

Dear Doctor Gugliotta:

Your letter and package of documents, memorabilia and the video cassette arrived safely, and I am overwhelmed.

It is very gratifying to know that my dream of a Monument to the Italian fallen has at last been realized, and in such a magnificent fashion. I am honoured and proud to have been associated with this noble undertaking.

May I take the liberty of complimenting you on your speech. I had no idea of the historical importance of Porto Ulisse, going back to ancient times. Now you have written a new chapter in that long history. I must also thank you for your kind and generous remarks about my modest contribution.

The video is a marvellous record of the event. I have shown it a number of times to my children and grandchildren and they are so impressed with the Ceremony and pleased that my name appears on the Monument.

I must not fail to mention your thoughtfulness in reading my own remarks, which I deeply appreciate.

My only regret is that illness prevented me from being with you. Nothing would have given me greater pleasure than to have participated in this great historic occasion. I join you now in expressing the hope you mentioned in your letter, that I may soon return to the land and people I helped set free.

* * *

And so we have completed our odyssey, both in time and in space. We have wandered for 11 years, from 1989 to 2000, surpassing Ulysses' record which spanned only 10 years. We have strolled on the very beach were he landed.

We have travelled to Ispica and returned to Toronto six times, plus numerous side trips to other Sicilian towns and places of interest. We have relaxed in Taormina, said to be the most beautiful resort in the world, and have enjoyed a Shakespearian play in the ancient Greco-Romano Theatre. We have bathed in the clear, warm waters of the Mediterranean.

We have called on the Godfather in Corleone but were repulsed. We have witnessed the eruption of two volcanoes. We have climbed to the very top of Mount Etna and peered into its fiery core. We were content to observe the erupting Stromboli from afar.

We have visited the Cava d'Ispica and seen the caves and catacombs where ancient people lived and died; we were invited to descend into the bowels of the earth at the Centoscale but had the good sense to demur. We have strolled along the beaches near Pachino where the Canadians landed in 1943. We have seen and done many other things.

But they are not the reason we have made this long, adventurous journey. The purpose of our voyage was to honour the men of the First Canadian Division who landed on those beaches almost 60 years ago. It is because of what they accomplished that we were able to do what we did.

What goes around comes around. As a result of our travels, there now stands a Monument to these men close by the beaches where they came ashore July 10th, 1943.

In conclusion, I can do no better than quote from the address I prepared but could not give at the dedication of the Monument on December 8th, 2000. Mayor Rosario Gugliotta delivered it for me.

PILGRIMAGE—2000

December 8, 2000

Dear Friends:

As many of you know, I am no stranger to this beautiful island or to the wonderful people of Ispica. On July 13th, 1943, I was part of a great Allied Armada that landed on these shores. We came not to occupy your land but as Liberators in the cause of Freedom. Many gave their lives.

A few days after the landing, I was ordered to take my platoon to Ispica to help restore order. The town had been shelled from the sea and bombarded from the air. Many civilians had been killed and wounded; some had taken refuge in the caves and were close to starvation. For three years they had been drained of their resources.

As a young Lieutenant in the Princess Patricia's Canadian Light Infantry, it was my task to help the people shake off the terrible yoke of dictatorship and make a fresh start on the road to democracy and prosperity.

Though I was Mayor for only a short time, I fell in love with Ispica and its people, and I learned to appreciate their aspirations and way of life. After the War, I was irresistibly drawn back, time and time again, to this fabled Amber Coast. It always gave me much happiness to see the spectacular progress you were making in every field since I was your first democratic Mayor. You have truly accomplished a miracle!

Then, in 1991, the people of Ispica and Pachino, in a most generous and memorable act, expressed their love and gratitude to Canada's soldiers who had liberated them. With the help, encouragement and inspiration of the distinguished Professor Carmelo Nigro, a magnificent Monument was erected in honour of the First Canadian Division.

The story might well have ended there had it not been for further initiative shown by Carmelo Nigro and other interested citizens of Ispica. They rightly felt that the Italian soldiers and civilians who had lost their lives in the war should also be remembered along with Canada's soldiers. I too, harboured the same feelings and expressed my firm support.

I was therefore pleased and gratified to learn early this year that the Mayor and Council of Ispica were going to erect Memorials to their fallen soldiers and civilians, and I was asked to be the Padrino. With humility and gratitude I accepted this distinct privilege and attended an Inaugural Ceremony on May 20th to launch the Memorials.

I have now received the further honour of being asked to attend this Dedication Ceremony on December 9th. With a heavy heart I must decline. For the past several months, and indeed at the Ceremony in May, I have not been well. On Doctor's orders I am not allowed to attend the present Ceremony.

I cannot tell you how disappointed I am not to be with you today. For these past fifty-seven years and more I have cherished my fraternal association with Ispica and its people. It grieves me that I cannot be present to witness the fulfilment of this noble dream I have shared with Carmelo Nigro.

Let me conclude by repeating what I said at the Ceremony on May 20th:

Today we stand on this hallowed ground to honour the Italian soldiers, who, though vastly outnumbered, bravely remained at their posts and fought to the end. I have long wished that a Memorial be erected in honour of these heroic soldiers who now lie with their Canadian brothers-in-arms. Let us not think of them as Victors and Vanquished. What difference separates them now? Both died for a noble cause and now they sleep in peace.

God bless you all.
Sydney Frost

POSTSCRIPT

Corriere Canadese

It will be recalled that in Chapter III, I referred to an article in the Toronto *Corriere Canadese* of August 3-4, 1990, about my "Ispicese connection" and how much I admired the people of Ispica.

In May, 2001, shortly after I received all the material from Carmelo describing the December 8th Ceremony, I got in touch with *Corriere Canadese* to see if they would be interested in the story. There were indeed, and sent Emanuele Oriano to interview me. They couldn't have sent a better man. He had served in the Italian Artillery in 1982/1983 and was keenly interested in military affairs.

Here is his article which appeared in the issue of July 10th, 2001, together with a photo showing the "trilogy" of Monuments taken on the day of the Ceremony.

So far as I know, it is the only account which appeared in Canadian newspapers.

Allied Landing—Italian-Canadian Memorial in Ispica

Who knows what the 21 year old Lieutenant Sydney Frost was thinking on that July 13th over 58 years ago as he lead his Platoon, named the Princess Patricias, onto the shores of Sicily?

The initial assault, which took place three days before, had been a success and the British troops of the Eighth Army, of which the first Canadian Division was a part, were advancing to the interior, conquering the springboard from which they would advance to the continent. The last thing the young officer expected was to have to act as the occupying military authority for a small Sicilian town: Ispica.

POSTSCRIPT

If the landing was painful for the troops, the civilian population suffered greatly as well under the constant attack of the naval artillery and air strikes. Ispica had four civilian casualties in addition to the artillery men and four officers (finanzieri) killed in battle, as well as two Italian military men wrongfully accused as deserters and executed.

During the 19 days he governed the town, helping it return to normal, the young Lieutenant Frost experienced the charm of the land and its people; the Canadian officer never forgot Ispica or its people in spite of the vicissitudes of the war, which took him all over the mainland where he was injured repeatedly.

Many years later, when he visited the cities of Pachino and Ispica, he was inspired with the idea of building a monument to the fallen Canadian soldiers (over 500). Thanks to the work of Carmelo Nigro, a school teacher in Ispica and to Sebastiano Spataro, an Ispicese who emigrated to Canada, the monument was unveiled on September 22, 1991.

Last December 8, at the monument commemorating the fallen Canadian forces, two additional memorial tablets were unveiled commemorating the fallen Italians. Col. Frost contributed financially to the Committee which made the monument a focal point of everyone's memory during the 58th Anniversary of the landing—the landing which inflicted the final blow to the unsteady regime of Mussolini.

1. Patrol enters Pachino, the first Sicilian town captured by the Canadians, 11 July 1943.

National Archives of Canada, PA-140204.

2. Mule struggles to keep in step with the troops near Modica, Sicily, 12 July 1943.

National Archives of Canada, PA-163669

3. Supplies are hauled up from the beach, 10 July 1943.

National Archives of Canada, PA-163668

4. A platoon advances from the beach, 10 July 1943.
National Archives of Canada, PA-163666.

5. Burnt-out German gun and vehicle on road to Nissoria, Sicily, July 1943.
National Archives of Canada, PA-163672.

6. PPCLI in action near Valguarnera, Sicily, 20 July 1943.
National Archives of Canada, PA-163670.

7. *On the road to Ispica, July 1942 — Capt. L. G. Beamish and Pte. M. Zabarylo, both PPCLI, inspect a German grave. In the background, an abandoned Italian gun from World War I.*
National Archives of Canada, PA-163670.

8. View of Mount Etna, 1997, from Grecian Theatre.

9. Agira Cemetery, 1989.

10. Agira Cemetery, 1990. Lt. J.S.C. de Balinhard.

11. Ispica Monument to the landing of the 1st Canadian Division in Sicily, 10 July 1943, unveiled 22 September 1991 on the beaches near Pachino and Ispica.
PMRC92-027

12. Author presents Carmelo Nigro with Regimental Plaque and a copy of Once A Patricia in the presence of an interpreter and Smoky Smith, V.C. (standing behind Carmelo) 22 Sept. 1991.

13. Carmelo and author after the Ceremony. 22 Sept. 1991.

14. Author with two Patricias — Capt. Kurt Fredrickson, John Clarke, 22 Sept. 1991.

15. Ispica Monuments to Canadians and Italians, Unveiled 8 December 2000.

ITALY
Preface to the Pilgrimages

The heading of this section of the book requires a word of explanation. Italy, it is generally agreed, includes Sicily, even though some members of that rugged isle would not agree. We are not, however, going to revisit Sicily. This section covers only my journeys in mainland Italy.

The reason for making this division is simply not to break the thread of the Sicilian adventure which was devoted to erecting two Memorials and spanned 11 years.

Map number 2

Map Number 3

Map Number 4

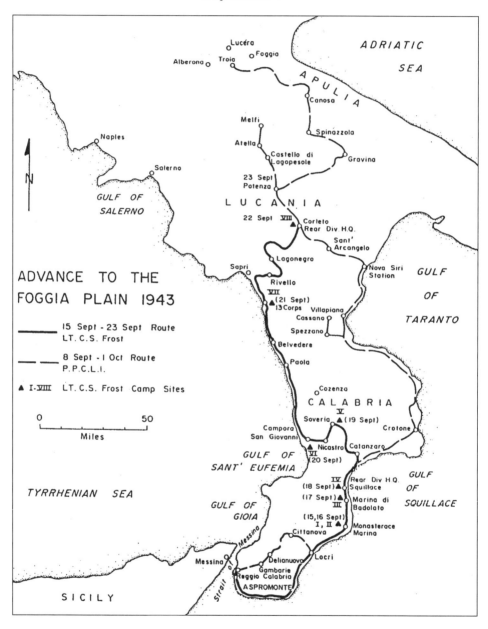

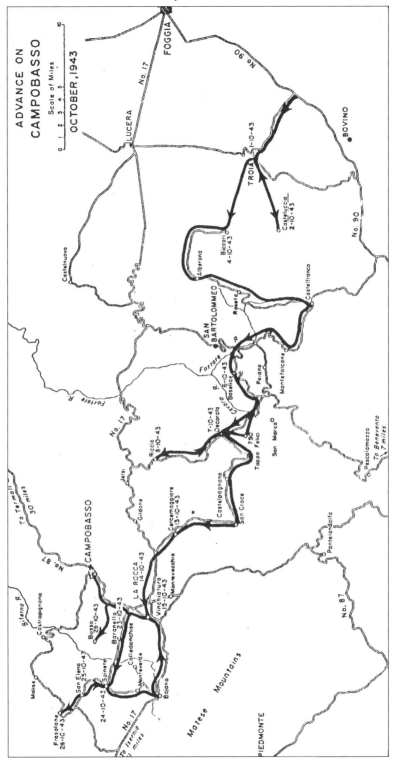

Map Number 6

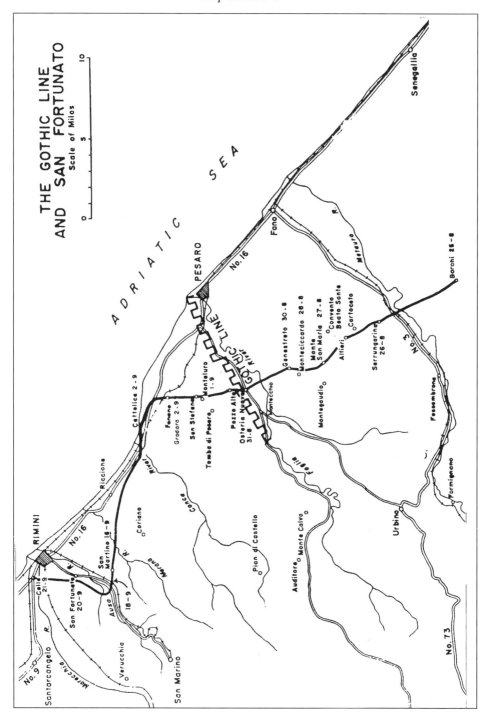

Map Number 7

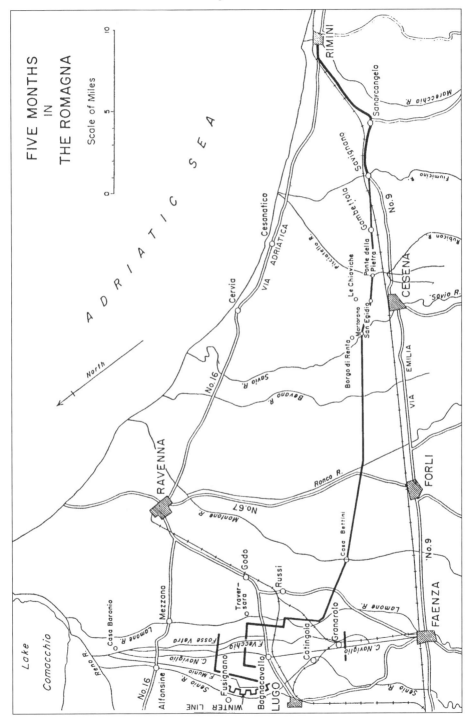

Map Number 8

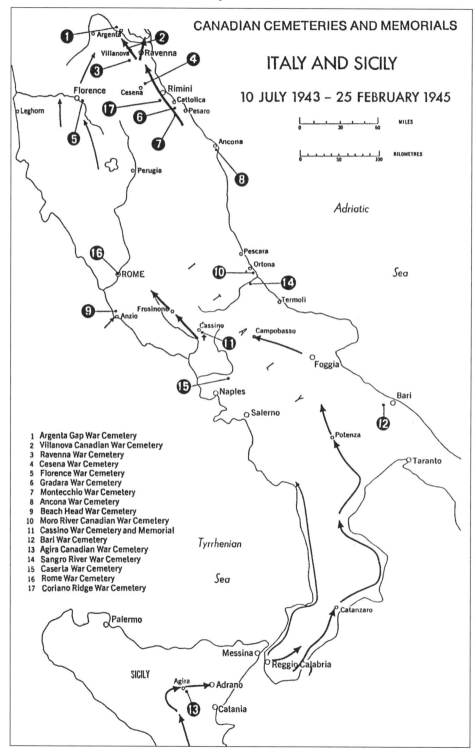

Chapter IX

PILGRIMAGE—1989

In Chapter I, I refer to this Pilgrimage, which covered 2,787 miles by car, as being "overly ambitious." On further consideration, thirteen years after the event, I wonder how I survived. I left Toronto May 1st, 1989, courtesy of British Airways and landed at Heathrow Airport, London, the next morning. Four days later I flew to Amsterdam to renew acquaintances in Holland. Then followed a long drive up the Rhine River into Austria where I came to rest in Vienna. From there a pleasant journey by train through the Alps took me to Venice where the Italian part of my Pilgrimage begins.

Whilst in London, I took advantage of the occasion to get in touch with the Countess Mountbatten of Burma, the Colonel-in-Chief of the PPCLI and known to members of the Regiment as Lady Patricia. She had kindly written the foreword to my book the previous year.

I learned that the Annual Dinner of the Overseas Branch of the PPCLI Association was to be held on May 6th and several of my friends would be present, including Rex Carey, M.C., whom I had not seen since our days in Sicily. Nothing would have made me happier than to attend the dinner, but my plane left that very day. I still regret having to miss that meeting as it was my last chance to see many comrades who have since passed on.

On May 12th, I left Venice by car, bound for Rimini and the venerable Grand Hotel. This would be my headquarters while I visited the battlefields where the Canadian soldiers in Italy suffered the worst casualties of the war, with the breaching of the Gothic and Rimini Lines. All signs of these battles have long since disappeared save one—the War Cemeteries, whose marble stones stand like sentries guarding the Adriatic coast, from Ancona in the south to Rimini in the north. In that short distance of only 60 miles, there are four cemeteries—

at Ancona, Montecchio, Gradara and Coriano Ridge. They contain the graves of 4,714 soldiers of whom 1,246 are Canadians. Just those bare numbers alone are mute testimony to the fierce fighting which raged in this area from August 25th to September 22nd, 1944.

I started my Pilgrimage at the little village of Barchi, five miles south of the Metauro River, where the Regiment had begun its advance on August 25th, 1944. I crossed the Metauro River without too much difficulty, just as the Regiment had done, and continued north through Serrungarina, to Ginestreto, two miles south of the Foglia River and the vaunted Gothic Line.

Here, the Regiment had paused before crossing that river and attacking the fortifications. The Patricias then assaulted Osteria Nuova, a strong point in the Gothic Line, and took 231 German prisoners. This success was marred by the death of Honorary Captain Ken Eaton, the very popular Padre who was fatally injured by a mine while helping to evacuate the wounded. He is buried in the Montecchio War Cemetery, just north of the Foglia River, which contains the graves of 289 Canadians, of whom 11 are Patricias.

The Patricias continued their advance north to Gradara, where their role in this phase of the operation ended and they moved into Cattolica, a resort area by the sea, for rest and recreation (R and R). Gradara is now the final resting place of 369 Canadian soldiers, of whom 5 are Patricias.

With the aid of my maps and occasional helpful advice from local inhabitants, I was able to follow faithfully the advance of the PPCLI from Barchi to Cattolica. Most of the route was by way of trails and side roads, but I was determined to complete my mission, as I had never before taken this route either during the War or on prior Pilgrimages.

I had been wounded on October 26th, 1943, at a hamlet called Frosolone, near Campobasso, in southern Italy, and evacuated to England for plastic surgery. After six months in hospitals and several more frustrating months in Reinforcement Depots I finally made it back to the Regiment in time for the next phase of the operation, the battle of San Fortunato and the crossing of the Marecchia River.

On September 15th, the Patricias marched out of Cattolica to join the battle. Almost immediately they were heavily shelled and Battalion Headquarters was struck. LCol. David Rosser was wounded and Major "Slug" Clark took over command. For the next seven days the intense shelling never ceased and the Regiment suffered severely, as it pressed forward to capture its objectives. By September 19th, the Ausa River had been crossed but Major Crofton and Lt. Dalquist had been wounded. In D Company, 14 men in one platoon had been killed or wounded by a single salvo. The tank commander had been killed. All the companies had been reduced to half strength. Into this cauldron I arrived at the Regiment on September 19th, and was posted to D Company.

The stage was now set for the final assault on San Fortunato and the crossing of the Marecchia River. The story of that attack has been told in *Once a Patricia* and need not be repeated. But the appalling casualties should never be forgotten. Command of C Company changed no less than five times during the course of the battle, with three officers killed and one wounded. Capt. L. G. Burton, a fellow ex-cadet of RMC, was killed on September 17th; Lt. J. W. MacNeill, one of my students on a course in Canada, on September 20th; and Capt. Corky Corkett, a fellow graduate of RMC and a close friend, on September 22nd. Lt. H. E. Dalquist was wounded on September 20th. Capt. Burton, Lt. MacNeill and Capt. Corkett are buried in the Coriano Ridge War Cemetery, where 427 graves belong to Canadians, of which 46 are Patricias.

Historian LCol. G.W.L. Nicholson had this to say about the battle:

> *Canadian losses were heavier than for any period of equal length, either before or after, during the Italian Campaign. From August 25th to September 22nd, the 1st Division suffered 2,511 battle casualties.*[1]

General Sir Oliver Leese, the 8th Army Commander, sent the following message to LGen. Burns, the Canadian Corps Commander:

> *You have won a great victory. By the bitterest fighting since El Alamein and Cassino you have beaten 11 German Divisions and broken through into the Po Valley. The greater part of the German armies in Italy were massed against us and they have been terribly mauled. I congratulate and thank you all. We must now hit hard day and night and force them back over the Po.*[2]

He also sent the PPCLI the following signal:

> *The Regiment may be proud of its part in a great and hard fought victory. Well done, Canada.*[3]

And yet, despite the bitter fighting, the heavy casualties and the strategic importance of the victory, historians give little respect or attention to the battles of the Gothic Line and San Fortunato. On the other hand, many books and articles have been written about the Liri Valley and Ortona.*

Why? There are several reasons. Without trying to take anything away from the hard fighting and the important victories won by these battles, it is a fact that they became international symbols of the fighting in Italy and exemplified the tenacity of the Germans and the sheer guts and determination of the Canadians. The battle for Ortona, while not on the scale of the Liri Valley conflict, became, according to the Associated Press, "A Miniature Stalingrad[4]."

Field Marshal Kesselring complained that "the English have made it [Ortona] appear as important as Rome.[5]"

Another factor in the case of Ortona was the publicity rightly accorded to the novel and imaginative methods the Canadian soldiers developed for "house clearing," notably, "mouse holing." By this technique a hole was blown in a wall by a demolition charge and the troops poured through to mop up the stunned defenders. In this way, a whole line of houses could be cleared without the troops having to expose themselves on the street.[6]

Again, in the case of the Liri Valley, a further consideration was the size and international character of the forces involved, and the possibility of making tactical manoeuvres. Although in the Hitler Line the PPCLI had no choice but to make a frontal attack.

In contrast to all these factors, the Gothic Line and San Fortunato battles were certainly not international symbols, nor was there any room for manoeuvre, and the number of troops engaged was much smaller than the Liri Valley operation.

For a Platoon Commander, as I was in the latter part of the San Fortunato battle, these considerations were of little importance, except for the inability to manoeuvre. The attacks on the San Fortunato and most of the earlier battles were frontal assaults. For a week we attacked while enduring the worst shelling of the entire campaign. There was no chance to make a flank attack and nowhere to go except straight ahead.

And that is exactly what we did, one day after another with no let-up, mostly against an unseen foe who poured a deadly hail of lead into our ranks. It takes a special kind of discipline to stand and take this kind of punishment because there is nothing you can do to stop it.

Medals are seldom, if ever, handed out to soldiers who simply stand fast and take a savage bombardment. Yet I have never heard any soldier complain about this lack of appreciation or recognition of his bravery under intense shelling. Apparently it just goes with the territory. To my mind, this stoic acceptance of one's fate only reinforces my argument that these kinds of soldiers are the unsung heroes of the war.

However, if they are never recognized individually, their steadfastness as a group has been recognized and honoured by the PPCLI. September 21st has been declared San Fortunato Day, on which Patricias honour all the battles of the war and those who died.

We now return to Cattolica, where I had rested during my 1989 Pilgrimage. I decided not to pursue any further the advance of the PPCLI to San Fortunato and the Marecchia River as I had already followed that route in my 1956, 1975 and 1985 Pilgrimages. Instead, I chose to visit the four War Cemeteries mentioned earlier: Ancona, Montecchio, Gradara and Coriano. Each one has its own distinctive setting, architecture and landscaping, and yet all bear the same message of sacrifice. One cannot help but feel saddened by the sight of so many headstones marking the graves of young Canadians struck down in the prime of life. For a Veteran who has lost a comrade, it can be a painful experience.

At each cemetery, I sought out the Visitors' Register and signed my name with a comment or two. Leafing through the pages, I found some beautiful remarks: "You shall always live in my heart"; "I will take you with me as I leave."

I sometimes find solace in the fact that my comrades' names will indeed live forevermore, enshrined in marble in a beautiful garden of flowers, hedges and greenery, all carefully tended and freshly watered. We who are left have done all we can to keep their memory alive forever.

Another reason for visiting this area was to renew the friendships I had made with two fine Italian families during my 1985 Pilgrimage, the Semprinis and the Festinos.

Gabriele Semprini and his wife, Renzi, lived in a magnificent home near the crest of San Fortunato Ridge. During the war our guns had done their best to demolish the place. It had been one of the objectives of our assault and had been given the code name of "Bovey." On my visits in 1956 and 1975, the building was in the same condition as it was in 1944. However, in 1985, I was surprised and delighted to find the house had not only been restored but had been enlarged and beautifully landscaped with an imposing entrance and two immense wrought-iron gates. Signor Semprini welcomed me with open arms and showed me around his *casa*. He bore not the slightest grudge that I and my fellow soldiers had tried to destroy it in 1944. He explained that he was not the original owner. He had bought the place in 1980,

---

* This lack of respect has recently been remedied by Mark Zuehlke, who has written a book entitled *The Gothic Line, Canada's Month of Hell in WWII, Italy.*

and, thanks to the damage we had caused, he got a good bargain. Ever since, he had devoted all his time to fixing it up.

He then led me to a small door off the kitchen which opened onto a spiral staircase descending into the depths of the earth. Down we went to the bottom. He switched on his flashlight and an immense cavern opened up around us.

He explained (or so I understood from my indifferent knowledge of Italian) that the cavern (he called it a grotto) had been carved out of the rock in 1944 by the owner of the property and his neighbours a few months before the battle for San Fortunato had begun. When the bombardment started, all the Italians in the area, some 300 of them, disappeared into the grotto taking with them food and water. There they remained until the Canadians passed on to their next objective.

I had always been a little leery about this story. How could such an immense cavern have been excavated under the very noses of the Germans? So in 1989 I told Signor Semprini about my concern in Italian—"È vero che questa grotta è stata costruita nel 1944?"

He shook his head. I was mistaken. The grotto was started during WWI when the Austrian Navy had shelled Rimini! The terrified civilians had fled to the hills and dug the cavern. In WWII it had only been enlarged.

I thanked my friend and apologized for my misunderstanding, which unfortunately had appeared in my book. He waved the matter aside and insisted I stay for dinner with his wife and children, which I accepted. We dined outside on his marble patio which overlooked vineyards and fields stretching to the Marecchia River and beyond. Off to the right, the lights of Rimini blinked in the gathering darkness. My thoughts wandered back to another night, 45 years earlier, when I had led the entire Canadian Corps down those slopes to the Marecchia River. I thought, too, of those soldiers who followed me and now rest in Coriano Ridge.

With mixed feelings, I bade my friends goodbye and promised to return. I am happy to say I was able to honour my pledge on each of my later Pilgrimages to Italy.

As I slowly drove back to Rimini and my hotel, I reflected on how the war had affected my own life. Here I was, carefully negotiating sunken roadways which had once been encumbered with German dead. Ahead lay a brightly lit city which had been reduced to a heap of rubble in 1944. For some inexplicable reason, I had been spared the fate of our soldiers on Coriano Ridge, so that I could enjoy the friendship of these people who had once been my enemies, and appreciate the beauty of their country. None of this would have been possible if I had not gone to war.

Next day, I drove along the Via Emilia to see another Italian family I had met on my Pilgrimage in 1985—Signor Mazzotti Festino and his wife, Paolina. During the war, their home on the Via Emilia was the final objective of my Platoon in D Company.

The Via Emilia (or Highway No. 9) is the ancient roadway running west from Rimini, north of the Marecchia River.

In September 1944, after enduring an almost continuous hail of shellfire and suffering many casualties, D Company took its objective and consolidated around the Festino home and an adjoining brickworks. All the Italians had fled the area. The Festino home, which my Platoon occupied, was reduced to rubble. Only one room was left, in which the remnants of my Platoon huddled together like sardines. After the battle, I resolved to return someday to meet the owners of the property and tell them how their *casa* had saved my men from certain death or dismemberment and express my regret that in the process their home had been destroyed.

In 1985, I had no difficulty finding the site, thanks to my maps and diary. But I could not recognize the home. It had, miraculously, been resurrected from a heap of bricks and mortar. I spent several happy hours with the Festinos reminiscing about the battle and marvelling how they had survived and restored their *casa*. Again I enjoyed the kind of dinner only Italians can prepare, and, aided by liberal potions of *vino rosso*, I promised to keep in touch and visit them on my next trip.

That was in May 1985. For the next few years, we exchanged Christmas cards but I really wondered whether I would ever see them again. Then, in January 1989, I received the following letter:

January 23, 1989

Dear Mr. C. Sydney Frost,

We are the M. Festino's grandchildren. Our names are Monica and Cinzia; as we attend the "school of tourism" and we study English, we would like correspond with an American person. We are 16 and 17 years old. Our grandfather asked us to write to you to give you some informations about his family because he doesn't speak American.

Festino and Paolina are well, and "anythink" is changed since your last visit except that the 29th December our great-grandmother Virginia is dead. Do you remember her?

Our grandparents want to return your wishes with theirs, they apologize for the delay and they greet you.

PILGRIMAGE—1989

> *If you want correspond with us or if you know somebody who want correspond with two Italian girls, we would be very "huppy" to have an American correspondent.*
> *To have some informations about our grandparents you can write to us!*
> See you
Monica and Cinzia
> *P.S.: Excuse us for the different mistakes.*

Who could resist answering such an endearing letter? I immediately responded, saying I would be happy to correspond with them. At that time I was still planning my Pilgrimage to Sicily. The letter helped me to decide that I should broaden my visit to include Rimini and San Fortunato.

And so I returned in 1989 and received a hero's welcome, as if I personally had evicted the Germans from the area. Not only the Festinos, but also all their relatives, going back several generations, were on hand to greet me. After a sumptuous meal and many toasts, including the PPCLI, I felt as though I had indeed bested the German Army, though not without the help of a few comrades! As usual, I was urged to stay a couple of days, but I had only begun my Pilgrimage and I had several thousand miles to travel.

That evening after dinner, I had an interesting conversation with the Manager of the Grand Hotel where I was staying. It is a magnificent edifice with a large, ornate foyer, high ceilings, bathrooms with heated tiles, beautiful gardens and fountains, a huge outdoor cage for exotic birds, and all the other adornments of a luxurious hotel built well before WWII. I complimented the Manager on his fine hostelry and asked if it pre-dated the war. "*Sì, sì,*" he replied, "*L'Albergo era costruito molti anni prima di Guerra.*"

This puzzled me. When the Patricias passed through Rimini, there was not one building or other structure left standing except the venerable Ponte di Tiberio. The Manager agreed that the hotel had been partially destroyed, but the plans had been saved and at great expense the hotel had been carefully restored to its former elegance. As for the Ponte di Tiberio, yes, it was still standing but, unlike the hotel, it no longer served its original purpose. The river had been diverted and waters no longer flowed under its ancient arches.

The following day, I headed for Rome via Florence and the A1 Autostrada. I had hoped to spend some time tracing the route of the PPCLI through the Romagna and across all those bloody rivers that had caused us so much trouble and so many casualties in late 1944—the Savio, the Bevano, the Ronco, the Montone, the Lamone, the

Naviglio Canal, the Fosso Vecchio, the Fosso Munio and finally the Senio, where our advance petered out due to the weather, the ground (actually lack thereof), and the Germans.

My study of these operations in the Romagna would have to wait for another time as I had to be in Rome that evening to catch a plane for Sicily the next day.

My Pilgrimage to Sicily has already been described in Chapter I. At the conclusion of that phase of my trip, I crossed the Strait of Messina bound for Cassino and the Hitler Line via Highway A3 (the Strada del Sole). At Salerno, I paused in honour of the soldiers of the American Fifth Army under General Mark Clark who had assaulted these beaches on September 9th, 1943. I remembered too that the Patricias and the rest of the First Canadian Infantry Division had crossed the Strait of Messina and landed at Reggio di Calabria on September 3rd. They had begun their long, arduous advance up the Italian Peninsula that, unbeknownst to them, was not to end until January 1945, when they came to rest along the banks of the Senio River.

Salerno is also noteworthy as the start of the spectacular Amalfi Drive. During the war, when I was fighting in northern Italy, I used to hear tall stories about the "goings on" of members of Base Units, Reinforcement Depots and Hospitals stationed in Avellino, only 60 miles from Salerno. I was told that officers, accompanied by nurses, spent all their free time in villas along the Amalfi Drive at such places as Positano, Ravello, Sorrento and even the Isle of Capri. I vowed, if I lived long enough, I would someday check out these romantic spots.

Now was my chance. I turned off Highway A3, made a hard left turn and found myself gliding along the Amalfi Drive with the deep blue waters of the Gulf of Salerno far below on my left, and a steep precipice on my right. The roadway had been carved out of the side of a cliff centuries before and there was barely room for two cars to pass. Every few miles the cliff hung over the roadway or it disappeared into a dark narrow tunnel. At one point, I almost ran into a bus which had got stuck under one of the over-hangs because the driver came too close to the wall of the cliff. I wondered how many passengers suffered whiplash injuries when the bus suddenly stopped.

The scenery and the driving were indeed breathtaking and I wished I had time to stop at one of the many villas and stroll along the white sandy beaches. Perhaps I would meet a nurse or two, or more likely someone bearing a striking resemblance to one. At one of the look-out points, the traffic had come to a stop and everyone was standing on the roadway pointing to the beach far below. I joined the onlookers and could hardly believe my eyes. A naked couple were making love and pausing every now and then to acknowledge the cheers of the crowd.

PILGRIMAGE—1989

I realized then that the wild stories I had been told 45 years earlier were probably true. The Amalfi Drive does have a special charm besides its spectacular scenery.

I completed my drive around the Sorrento Peninsula and turned north to Avellino to check whether the Base Depots or Hospitals had left any marks on the town or its citizens. None were apparent. Continuing north I passed through Caserta, another Base Depot area, and finally halted at Cassino and the entrance to the Liri Valley, which came to be known as "The Gateway to Hell."

Canadians were not directly involved in the battles that raged on the summit, on the slopes and around the base of Monte Cassino. This doubtful honour was shared by British, American, New Zealand, Indian and Polish troops. It was not until the fourth attempt, on May 18th, that Monte Cassino fell to the Polish Corps. In the meantime, the First Canadian Corps was engaged in the Liri Valley to the south of Cassino, culminating in the attack on the Hitler Line.

Much has been written and is still being written about Monte Cassino and the destruction of its famous Abbey. Time and time again, the troops were hurled against one of the strongest defensive positions in any theatre of WWII. It was a war of attrition in which both sides suffered enormous casualties. Adolf Hitler described the battle in these terms: "It was a First World War battle fought with Second World War weapons."

Many critics of the battle agree with that assessment. It was like the trench warfare waged in Flanders, Belgium.

On my last visit to Cassino in 1985, I had time only to pay my respects at the War Cemetery, not far from the base of the mountain. The Abbey would have to await my return. That time had now arrived and I joined a procession of tourists and other pilgrims wending their way along the Via Serpentina leading up to the Abbey. The road was well named. It wound itself around the steep slope like the coils of a serpent.

Once at the summit, I was rewarded with a spectacular view of the surrounding countryside. No wonder Field Marshal Kesselring had been ordered to defend Cassino to the last man, even after the Abbey had been reduced to a pile of rubble.

A guide informed us that the Abbey had been built in 529 A.D. by St. Benedict, the founder of the Order which bears his name. Benedictine monks preserved the heritage of Greece, Rome and Christianity through the Dark Ages and kept learning alive in Europe between the fall of Rome and the rise of universities many centuries later.

Then, in 1943, along came the Germans, who occupied and fortified Monte Cassino. The Allied bombers retaliated by obliterating the

Abbey in 1944. In the twinkling of an eye, they destroyed a beacon of Western Culture that had stood for fourteen centuries.

Fortunately, prior to the bombing by the Allied Air Force, the Germans had permitted the monks to remove from the Abbey all the precious artworks, books and even the plans of the building, and convey them to Rome for safekeeping. It was a singular, charitable act of the Germans, the guide solemnly intoned.

After the war, the Abbey was completely rebuilt and refurbished. Any artwork that had been part of the original building and impossible to remove had been faithfully restored.

Then the guide offered what I thought was a very insightful comment on the meaning of the destruction of the Abbey. He suggested that out of the tragedy some good did come because, later in the campaign, Rome was designated an open city and so was Florence.

The next and final objective in my 1989 Pilgrimage was the Hitler Line where the PPCLI suffered 247 casualties in one fateful day—May 23rd, 1944. Again, the battle has been written about in many books, the most recent being Mark Zuehlke's *The Liri Valley*, in which he quotes the words of LCol. Cammie Ware, who was the Commanding Officer of the Regiment during the battle: "Those were fine boys. They are gone. I haven't anybody left. They are all gone."[7]

Another book by David Bercuson, *The Patricias*, describes the casualties and Colonel Ware's assessment of the battle given many years later. His opinion had not changed. "A glorious failure if you want to call it that, because there wasn't anybody left."[8]

Still another graphic account of the fighting in the Hitler Line is given in a book by Colin McDougall, written in 1958, *Execution*. It is not a history. It is a novel about infantry soldiers at war in Italy, from Sicily to the Hitler Line and later. But I know of no other which rings so true about the horrors of battle. This is so because Colin served throughout the Italian Campaign as a Platoon and Company Commander with the PPCLI, and was awarded the DSO and mentioned in despatches. He received several awards for his writing, including the President's Medal from the University of Western Ontario. One extract from his book will convey the power of his narrative:

> *Captain Bill Begg was running. Heart pounding, lungs bursting, he ran with all his being. In the forest there was a woodpecker succession of hollow knocks as bullets struck the tree trunks. Tart sweat from under his helmet splashed in Captain Begg's eyes.*
>
> *Wherever his bobbing glance went Begg saw men falling – sliced down by shell fragments, bowled over by machine-*

gun slugs. Every few yards a tank seemed to be hit; dazed troopers bailed out into the stream of machine-gun fire. The German artillery D.F. was merciless; but the worst part was the blast of small-arms fire from the right flank where they were nakedly exposed to view.[9]

The official history of the PPCLI by G. R. Stevens, OBE, describes in eloquent terms the legacy of the Hitler Line Battle, and what he describes as "Gallantry beyond praise."

Out of such scattered and partial records, however, there emerge details which blend into a décor of courage and tenacity, of fine soldierly bearing and correct behaviour, of endurance, discipline and fidelity to duty in the face of all odds. Prominent in this gallery of gallant figures is the Commanding Officer, who that day so well captained his side. Lieut.-Colonel Ware constantly was on the move, striving to preserve cohesion between his companies, to maintain momentum in the attack and to keep Brigade and Division informed of the situation. He bore a charmed life; again and again men were struck down around him.

Of the same mould was Major W. deN. Watson, who led A Company to splendid failure. He wrote: "It was difficult to follow the barrage through dense woods, and we soon began to find the wounded of C Company in our path, whereas they should have been on our right. Under heavy fire we reached a large clearing running at right angles to our line of advance. We had not seen our supporting tanks but we knew we had reached the Hitler Line for we could see rows of barbed wire ahead. As soon as we came into the clearing a number of my men were hit. We located the enemy behind a house fifty yards on our left. We could not halt without losing the barrage and we could not advance until we had destroyed this enemy post. We had lost contact with Battalion Headquarters and also with our forward platoons.

"The intense shell fire had drastically reduced our numbers and crossing the two belts of wire took a further toll, as the wire was thickly studded with shrapnel mines. Beyond the wire we came to a tank. Thinking it derelict we paused beside it to gather together the few men who were left. We then discovered our error as the tank started firing the wrong way. The tank crew could not have been aware of our presence and as we had only small arms we could not destroy it. By that

time I only had four or five men left. Shortly after leaving the tank I lost all of them except L/Cpl. Amos.

"We stopped in a shell hole to take stock of the situation. Thereafter we set off for our objective—the Aquino-Pontecorvo road. Then L/Cpl. Amos was killed. The objective was quite close so I went on to it. I could find no trace of my men but the enemy was there. By that time I had been wounded twice and realized that the attack had failed."

Throughout the day Major Watson evaded capture and finally settled down in what he describes as a "large and quite comfortable shell hole." That night, thinking that the Patricias or the Loyal Edmontons might have come up, he went forward a second time to the Aquino-Pontecorvo road. He found the enemy still there. He lay doggo in his shell hole and on the following morning the war diarist recorded joyfully: "Major Watson was located in a shell hole near an 88 mm gun, suffering from a wound in one arm, a piece of his helmet and a Schmeisser bullet in his forehead (and a tremendous appetite)."

By the end of the day Capt. A. M. Campbell, who led B Company courageously and well, was the only officer of the rifle companies on his feet. As the officers went down or failed to return from their missions non-commissioned officers took over and bore themselves staunchly and well. CSM W. D. Davidson of B Company spent a full twelve hours in manifold duties under fire; in that time he searched for and found a lost platoon, stalked and killed a brace of snipers and went out again and again to bring in wounded. Sgt. E. D. Edkins of C Company, after being wounded twice in the initial advance, turned over command of his platoon to a corporal in order to stalk and capture a sniper in a camouflaged pit. Sgt. G. L. Dick, after a heavy shoot, found himself in command of D Company; he immediately reorganized it with resolution and skill. Sgt. F. Bentham of 14 Platoon, although wounded and with only two men left, continued to attack from shell hole to shell hole and was able to direct the accompanying tanks on to enemy machine-gun nests. Cpl. F. W. Snell fought a duel in the open in which he killed three snipers. When there were no non-commissioned officers left in 12 Platoon Pte. Ian Sangster took command, rallied the men and led an attack against an enemy tank. Thereafter for

> *eight hours he and his small group held their ground against heavy shellfire and repeated assaults.*[10]

With some hesitation, I mention my earlier book which describes the Hitler Line—*Once a Patricia*. I do this only because the book was instrumental in the production of a new account of that battle. It happened this way. A friend of mine in the United States read my book and sent it to a cousin of his wife, one Jim Simpson, in Australia, who had fought in the Hitler Line with the 6th British Armoured Division.

After reading the book, Jim wrote my friend a very vivid description of the carnage he found when his troop of tanks passed through the area where the Patricias had fought and died on May 23rd, 1944. My friend kindly passed the account on to me.

Jim Simpson praised the great courage and élan of the PPCLI and declared that one of our men deserved a Victoria Cross. I felt that the document was invaluable as it was an eye-witness record by one of the few survivors of the battle and gave an unbiased and independent account of the magnificent courage shown by the Patricias on that fateful day.

I was so impressed with the account that I sent a copy to MGen. Cammie Ware with the thought that it might be lodged in the Regimental Archives. I have no knowledge of whether this was in fact done.

In view of the importance of the document and the fact it has never been published, I now reproduce it in full, exactly as written.

> *February 12th, 1993.*
>
> *Dear Lowell,*
>
> *I've just finished reading "Once A Patricia" and found it to be very well written, minutely researched and most interesting.*
>
> *My personal contact with the PPCLI was very brief; shortly after the final overthrow of the German defences based on the remains of the town and Monastery of Monte Cassino, and on along the Garigliano River, to end in the mountains to the south west of the Monastery, effectively blocking the entire width of the Liri Valley, an attack was made on the second line of defence, the Hitler Line.*
>
> *The basic plan was a silent approach march in the dark, no artillery or aerial bombing ... it was hoped to surprise the wiley Hun, in this instance the Hermann Goering Paras supported by Mk V Panthers, MkVI Tigers and SP guns. At that stage the German Luftwaffe were, thankfully, getting pretty scarce.*

Our Division, the 6th Armoured, was to "pass-through" the Canadians and elements of another of our Arm'd Divs, the North Irish Horse, who were equipped with Churchill tanks, after they had achieved the initial break-through.

My troop, 3 Shermans and 2 Recce. Honeys, started out for the "sharp end" soon after midnight, May 23rd, 1944. After a fairly tedious trip with no lights and the minimum of noise, we finally arrived at what we were told was our start line, some seven to eight hundred yards to the rear of the leading troops; in our case the PPCLI were slightly to our right and the tanks of the NIH (North Irish Horse), slightly to our left, divided from the PPCLI by a narrow, unsealed country road.

The countryside was a typical valley bottom, with deserted farmlets, market gardens and an occasional hamlet. Not even a dog barked as we passed by. Generally, the lie of the land was flat, with an occasional low rise, some small wooded areas, creeks, ditches and, every so often, a small tributary running down from the mountains to join the Liri.

A clinging, cold mist filled the valley to a depth of some 30 to 40 feet; we had often experienced these mists in Italy, they filled the narrow bottoms and, as soon as the sun 'hit' them, rose and dissipated, often very rapidly.

The attack was timed for 6 a.m.

We waited in the eerie pre-dawn light; our tanks were parked about 20 or 30 feet apart; I climbed down from mine and went over to have a chat with my senior Sgt. There was the occasional thump of a distant mortar and some artillery away in the mountains. Ahead of us, just sporadic, scattered small arms rattling away. The mist lightened very gradually. I observed to Sgt. Brown, that I believed that I could just make out the dark, brooding bulk of Monte Cassino and then, as we watched, peering, the light began to touch the late snow, still adorning the peak of Monte Cairo, eastward and higher than Monte Cassino.

Quite quickly the sun came up, the craggy profiles of the mountains flared, the grey mist became bright white and lifted like a blind.

Up front everything happened. The flat, harsh, crash of the high velocity tank cannons, the ripping sound of the Spandaus, the slower Brownings and Besas firing from our side, all blended into one enormous cacophony of frightful, yet, somehow, stimulating sound.

Ricocheting AP projectiles came screaming and whirring overhead. One came close by, lower down, crashing into, but not penetrating, a tank behind me. I thought that standing out there in the open was no place for James. I was back in my tank in a trice.

The radio messages gradually advised what had happened. Apparently the leading troop had advanced beyond their intended start lines, so that, when the mist went up, instead of being able to form up and commence their attack from more or less concealed positions, they had in fact, advanced to the very edge of the area that the Germans had cleared in front of their extremely well prepared defences; dug in Mk Vs, an occasional Mk VI, all in trenches so that they were "hull-down". Concrete pill-boxes", almost completely buried, each containing a Spandau 7.92 MG (1,100 rounds per min.) and crew and minefields, both anti personnel and anti vehicle right across the cleared field of fire area.

The initial heavy firing did not last too long, maybe 45 to 50 minutes; then, as it eased off, we were ordered to advance and pursue the now retreating enemy.

We followed the country road that had roughly divided the PPCLI and the NIH.

As we debouched into the cleared area in front of the now battered German defences, we passed a troop of the NIH, 3 tanks, parked side by side, so that the crews could step from one tank to the other. They were still burning, all knocked out without firing a shot. When the mist went up, there was this Mk V dug in, directly in front of them, about 300 to 400 yards away. The poor sods didn't have a chance.

To the right of the road, the equally unfortunate PPCLI found themselves in a similar situation when the mist lifted. They acted with great courage, desperation and élan and just threw themselves at the pill-boxes.

Col. Frost did not take part in this battle, as he still had not fully recovered from a wound sustained in an earlier action. However, he does refer to it in his book, calling it a tragic day for the Brigade as they suffered a total of 543 casualties, including 162 dead.

The firing once again became scattered and sporadic. Suddenly it would flare up and then ease off again. The long columns of Medic jeeps, ambulances, etc., had carried their pain racked cargoes to the rear as I led my troop across the field of fire area. The dead PPCLI lay everywhere, particularly thickly, in a broken triangle in front of the pill-box nearest to the road. I remember we were just passing under the widespread boughs of a very large tree, an oak of some sort. I noted a Honey blown up about 30 yards up the road ahead of us. There was a body lying beside it, loosely covered with a gas cape. One of the other troops from my Squadron had lost someone. I was wondering who the dead man was then there was a gigantic explosion, a blinding flash of light. The tank seemed to lift and rock under my feet, my teeth were gritty. There was dust everywhere and the pungent smell of cordite or whatever it was that the mine we had driven onto was made of.

In the turret, the gunner and wireless/op loader were very shaken but OK; not so the driver and co-driver who were both unconscious. We hauled them out and lay them by the roadside, after carefully checking the verge for disturbed earth (schu or anti personnel mines) together with two unlucky infantry who had been passing by when we hit the mine.

One chap had compound fractures of his jaw and the other of his ribs. We did what we could for them and radioed for Medics.

I had a stinker of a headache.

Traditionally, if the troop leader loses his tank, he takes over his senior Sgt's. Sgt. Brown was getting his gear out so I could get mine in. We had to wait for the engineers to re-sweep for mines. I looked at all the dead PPCLI. My head throbbed. I took another aspirin. I very carefully made my way over toward the pill-box with all the dead apexing in a sort of triangle in front of it. Each step was carefully taken. Each foot was placed in clearly unbroken bare ground. I reached the pill-box The last PPCLI to die lay on the protruding muzzle of the Spandau. I raised his body slightly; about 20 or 21; his battle dress jacket was scorched; his right hand dangled limply into the narrow gun embrasure. I crossed over to the rear of the pill-box. There were three dead Paras inside. One probably died before his comrades, was almost buried in empty cartridge cases, the other two had obviously been killed by a grenade. Had it been pushed through the embrasure by the PPCLI lying out there on the gun muzzle? If so, he deserved a VC.

I returned to my troop. The medics had been and gone. I checked the identity of the dead man by the Honey, Tpr. Jake Fieldhouse. He had been in my troop in Tunisia.

A Padre came by in a jeep. He wanted to go and look at the dead PPCLI. I didn't know why, he didn't seem to be a

> *Canadian. I warned him about the mines, he just waved and ambled off with a far away happy look of anticipation (?) on his face.*
>
> *I was just about to resume our advance, now as commander of Sgt. Brown's tank, when I heard a muffled sort of a "POP" followed almost immediately by a second, much louder explosion. The Padre had stepped on a S mine and had collected a fair share of the three hundred or so ball bearings which they contained. I examined him with my binoculars. He appeared to be dead. His driver and another soldier went, hesitantly, tippy toeing out toward him. I gave the order to advance.*
>
> *Late that afternoon I lost Sgt. Brown's tank too, but that is another story.*
>
> *Thanks again for the book Lowell, maybe we will make it back to the States again someday.*
>
> *Your cousin-in-law,*
>
> *Jim Simpson*

It will be observed that Jim Simpson refers to the fact that I took no part in the battle because I had not fully recovered from a wound sustained in an earlier action. This is substantially true but, in fact, I had pretty well recovered from being wounded in the face on October 26th, 1943, while on a scout patrol to Frosolone, near Campobasso. I had been sent back to England for plastic surgery and on May 23rd, 1944, I was cooling my heels in a Reinforcement Depot trying desperately to get back to the Regiment.

When I first heard the news of the battle, I was devastated. The early reports claimed that the Battalion had been wiped out. Here I was, in a lousy Reinforcement Depot in England when I should have been with my Regiment. I was overcome by a deep feeling of remorse that has really never left me. I redoubled my efforts to return to the Regiment and was finally successful. I left England by troop ship on August 21st, 1944, with Capt. George (Corky) Corkett and arrived in Italy in time for the Battle of San Fortunato, which, sadly, claimed his life.

Over the years, I have often thought about the quirk of fate which removed me from the battle, sent me back to England, thereby causing me to miss not only the slaughter of the Hitler Line but the bloody battles south of Ortona—the Moro River, Villa Rogatti and the Gully. My odds of surviving them as a Platoon Commander would have been very slim.

There are many ways to express this element of fate—good luck, charmed life, "someone looking after me," and so forth. In my book I called this power Field Marshal Fate. While he dealt me some rotten blows, the fact remains that he brought me home more or less intact.

I have also thought about how fate gave my father a break. He was a member of the famous "Fighting Newfoundlanders." At the Battle of Beaumont Hamel, on July 1st, 1916, he was one of the 10 percent left out of battle (LOB) to form a nucleus for rebuilding the Regiment if it was decimated. That is precisely what happened. When the battle was over only 68 had survived; 233 had been killed, 386 wounded and 91 were missing. The people of Newfoundland have never forgotten the slaughter. Each year, on July 1st, while the rest of the country celebrate Canada Day, Newfoundlanders solemnly remember Beaumont Hamel Day.

I am one of them. I was born in Newfoundland.

After surviving Beaumont Hamel, Father was grievously wounded at the battle of Gueudecourt on October 10th, 1916. He was invalided first to England and then to Canada. But through pluck and determination he recovered, made his way back to his beloved Newfoundlanders and went into action with them in August 1917. He had been away almost eleven months.

It is interesting to compare Father's record with mine. I was wounded October 26th, 1943, 27 years to the month after my father's injury. We both spent six months in hospital or convalescing. I re-joined the PPCLI in the middle of the battle for San Fortunato. I had also been away for eleven months.

One other comparison should be recorded. In the two great battles of our respective Regiments which Father and I missed, the number of survivors was almost the same:

PPCLI – 77

Royal Newfoundland Regiment – 68

I would think that the chances of both of us surviving our respective wars were close to nil. In the circumstances, I suppose I should be doubly grateful to Field Marshal Fate.

Indeed, I would be remiss if I failed to thank the kindly Field Marshal for also taking care of my brother Bob. He served in Korea with the Patricias and came home without a scratch.

Let us now return to my account of my Pilgrimage of 1989 and the Hitler Line. In 1985, I had carefully explored the area where the Patricias made their attack, south of the little village of Aquino. Not a trace did I find of the German fortifications or any other evidence that a bloody battle had ever been fought there. The busy A1 Highway, also known as the Strada del Sole, thundered through the area and farmers still ploughed their fields as their forefathers had done for generations.

In 1989, the scene had not changed and I was glad. Through the efforts of my Regiment, peace and prosperity had been brought to this land—but at what a terrible price.

I turned my car around and headed back to Cassino to visit my friends who had paid that price.

The Cassino War Cemetery is the largest WWII Cemetery in Italy. Among the 4,266 headstones, 855 are for Canadians who died during the battles of the Hitler Line and the subsequent advance toward Rome. The Cemetery also has a Memorial which commemorates 4,054 men who died in the Sicilian and Italian campaigns and have no known grave, and includes 192 Canadians. In all, 8,320 Commonwealth soldiers are buried or commemorated here.

But bare numbers do not convey a true sense of their meaning. The dead soldiers and airmen commemorated here could have populated a city about the size of Fredericton, New Brunswick, in 1944. Even that comparison is difficult to grasp until one actually visits the Cemetery, as I have done many times. The mere sight of so many shiny marble headstones lined up in orderly ranks, like soldiers on parade, with their uniforms pressed and shoes gleaming, has reduced many a visitor to tears.

The Cemetery lies in the Liri Valley not far from the foot of Monte Cassino whose mass now seems to shelter and protect the soldiers who lie here, to atone for all the misery it had caused them during the war.

I walked down the ranks to locate the graves of the 75 Patricias who fell in the Hitler Line. Here was the grave of LCpl. George Amos, the last man left in Maj. Watson's A Company, who died on the objective; and there was my friend, Lt. Cecil Shea, who was one of my students in Camp Shilo, Manitoba. He accompanied me to England and then to Sicily and was wounded at La Rocca in southern Italy. Cecil had been a Private in the pre-war Patricias. He went to England with the Regiment in 1939 and returned to Canada in 1942, to gain his commission on the course at Shilo.

Another grave I visited was that of Lt. J. C. Crabtree, also a Patricia other rank in the Permanent Force, who returned to Canada to be commissioned.

And here was another Permanent Force Patricia who had returned to Canada to take his commission—Lt. J. R. Heppell, who had won the MID.

These three officers, Shea, Crabtree and Heppell, were all dedicated, professional soldiers who would have achieved higher rank had they lived. All their training experience and future careers were snuffed out in an instant by a German shell.

Four other Patricias whom I did not know but whose lives were similarly shattered were: CSM G. S. Moore, who had been twice wounded, Private L. G. Pearson, Cpl. L. C. Manness and Sgt. W. Grimshaw.

Sadly, I signed the Visitors' Register and slowly drove away.

As one might expect from the prolonged fighting in this valley of death, there are cemeteries for the soldiers of other nations who fought there. High up on the Monte Cassino itself, the Polish cemetery holds 1,000 graves. It is fitting that these soldiers are the only ones given the honour of lying close to the Abbey they finally captured.

The other cemetery is German, lying atop a nearby hill but lower than the Poles. Like the other cemeteries, it is immaculately cared for and adorned with green foliage, but there are striking differences. The headstones are not set in serried ranks like soldiers on parade, as one would expect of the German Army. Instead, small stone markers are set in irregular patterns in circles around the hill with five or six feet between each one. The markers are set so low that one has to bend down to read the inscriptions.

On my first visit in 1985, I had expected to find that the markers had been arranged according to seniority, with Generals at the top of the hill and Privates at the bottom, in true German fashion. To my surprise the first marker bore the following inscription:

Ein Deutcher Soldat
Ein Deutcher Soldat
Ein Deutcher Soldat

On the back of the marker the same inscription appeared. The stone represented the unidentified remains of six German soldiers and there were hundreds of them. Some stones bore the names and ranks of the soldiers but most did not. What greater testimony could there be to the terrible bombardment the Germans suffered. I had no idea how many dead were interred and there was no caretaker to ask.

In 1989, I did locate a caretaker, dressed in uniform. He had served in the German Army as a paratrooper and had fought at Cassino. He had been a Company Sergeant Major in the elite 1st Parachute Regiment. Yes, he knew exactly how many Germans were buried here—20,057—and gave me a snappy salute. In the end, true German efficiency prevailed.

I returned to my car and headed toward my final destination—Rome and home.

It had been a long, arduous journey of 2,787 miles by car alone, to say nothing of air flights from Toronto to London to Amsterdam, then from Rome to Catania, and finally from Rome to London and home. The gaps in between had been covered by car and by train from Vienna to Venice.

In Sicily and Italy I had tried to follow the long trail of the PPCLI and visit all the cemeteries. Time, however, was my enemy on this occasion and not the German Army. I was not able to visit some of the cemeteries and several battle sites, such as the Moro River, the Rivers in the Romagna in northern Italy, and the advance to Campobasso. These would have to await my next Pilgrimage.

Chapter X

PILGRIMAGE—1991

After my successful "campaign" in Sicily, I was in a fine mood to cross the Strait of Messina and follow the route of the PPCLI up the toe of Italy. In my prior journeys from Sicily to Rome, I had always taken the A3—Strada del Sole, and avoided the tortuous trail the PPCLI took during the war through the centre of the Aspromonte Range. The peaks in this range rise to 6,400 feet and the gradients of the roads are stiffer and the turnings more frequent that in any other part of Italy except the Alps.

It had taken the Regiment four days to reach the little town of Cittanova in the middle of the mountains, about 40 miles from Reggio as the crow flies but at least twice that distance by road. In my high-powered Mercedes-Benz, I reckoned that this short distance should not take more than an hour or two. I spent all day winding around trails that sometimes ended in a farmer's pasture. I got lost and needed a guide to lead me into Cittanova. No four star hotels there so I limped my way along the coast, where I found a pleasant seaside resort at Siderno. I thought of the troops slugging it out, on foot, over these rough mountain trails. No wonder they were dog-tired, as the Regimental Historian aptly described their condition.

I remembered that in September 1943, after recovering from a bout of malaria, I had been ordered to take a draft of men from Reggio to Potenza, where the Regiment was at rest after their long advance up the toe of Italy. At that time, I shunned the route through the mountains taken by the PPCLI and followed the much easier and faster road along the eastern coast.

However, when I reached Catanzaro with my draft of 22 men, I found this coastal road so congested with traffic that it would take several days to reach Potenza by that route. Being a young officer of independent mind, I converted myself into a Corps Commander and asked myself what I would do to ensure that this vital draft of PPCLI soldiers arrived without delay. The answer was not difficult. The 5th British Division had been rolling along the west coast of Italy without any trouble. I decided to cross the mountains and follow that road to Potenza.

My appreciation of the situation had not taken into account the doubtful skills of our driver, a former member of the Italian Army, and trouble with our Italian truck.

The driver almost got us all killed by taking a bend in the road much too fast, and later the truck itself broke down. Despite these and other setbacks, I finally arrived at the PPCLI, after my "unguided" tour of southern Italy of 500 miles, on all manner of roads, trails, diversions, donkey tracks and makeshift bridges. I reported to the Adjutant, who gave me the worst dressing down I had ever experienced. In his view, I had been AWL for eight days and but for the war, I should have been court martialled.

I have only one regret. At the start of my 1991 Pilgrimage, I had vowed to faithfully follow the route of the PPCLI from Reggio to Potenza. But when I reached Catanzaro, I couldn't resist playing the role of Corps Commander again. I took the route along the west coast to Potenza and eschewed the coastal road along the east coast which the Regiment had taken. The reason for my regret is that this is the only part of the long and hazardous route of the PPCLI in southern Italy I have not yet covered—a small point, maybe, but not for me. Still, there may yet be time to complete this gap. As the Italians say: *Meglio tardi che mai*—(Better late than never).

At Potenza, I had returned to my old job as head of the scouts and snipers. (The Adjutant had forgiven my little frolic in southern Italy.) My first task was to report to Maj. Brain at Castello di Lagopesole, an immense castle built in 1242 by a German, Frederick II. The present owner, an Italian, Prince Doria Pamphyli, had been interned by the Germans, a perfect example of the maxim—"What goes around comes around."

In 1991, I spent some time inspecting this great thirteenth-century fortification. From its ancient battlements, on a high hill, I had a clear 360-degree view of the surrounding countryside for many miles. What a perfect observation post, I thought, but quite useless as a modern fortification. A squadron of bombers could level the place and any defenders who survived would have nowhere to go.

In 1991, I found that the castle had been fully restored (not that it needed extensive repairs as its massive foundation blocks would resist deterioration by time or weather forever). I visited the bedroom of the

Prince which I had occupied in 1943, and wandered around the inner courtyard where my scouts and snipers had set up shop and rested before moving on to the next objective. The only thing that had changed was the inevitable souvenir shop where I spent a few thousand lire purchasing attractive books and postcards. But I wanted something more substantial from this fortress which had been my home. On the way out, I spied a piece of rock on the cobblestone. It looked like a chip from the massive foundation walls and had obviously lain there, unwanted, for centuries. I scooped it up and put it in my pocket. It now rests in my library, a tangible reminder of those incredible days.

My next objective in 1991 was Campobasso, where the Regiment had ended its long advance up to the centre of southern Italy. In my Mercedes-Benz, I was once more the Scout Officer leading the Battalion, albeit in a more commodious vehicle. I passed through towns I still remembered—Gravina, Spinazzola, Canosa, and Troia, 15 miles southwest of Foggia which became an important base for the Strategic Air Force.

I continued northwest on trails through the mountainous terrain and across deep ravines and rivers that had reduced the Regiment's advance to a snail's pace. At Casteluccio, I had bagged a sick German paratrooper the enemy had thoughtlessly left behind, and sent him to the rear for interrogation. He had had enough of the Nazis and "spilled the beans" to the Intelligence Officer. All he wanted was to get to a hospital.

At Alberona, I had just missed seeing the famous Popski who commanded the only private army in the Allied Forces. It had been formed in North Africa and was an elite band of bold adventurers who made deep patrols behind German lines. General Montgomery became very fond of this irregular group and took them with him to Italy, where they continued to run amok behind enemy lines, spreading fear and despondency among the confused Germans. Such was the case at Alberona, where Popski had worked his way behind the enemy, forcing them to flee to the hills and leave 15 dead comrades behind.

My route in 1991 continued through the heart of the Apennines past Castelfranco, Montefalcone and Baselice to an important crossroads at Decorata. During the war, the Germans had ransacked the place and taken away anything of value. I stopped for a cappuccino at a roadside *trattoria*, hoping I could find someone who remembered the war. No one I spoke to had any knowledge of the war except one old man who accused me of looting his village. (He had seen my Mercedes-Benz.) When I explained I was *canadese*, not *tedeschi*, he apologized and bought me another cappuccino.

My next objective in 1991 was Cercemaggiore, a small village about 9 miles from Decorata along a winding trail which my scouts had taken in 1943. Beyond that lay La Rocca, a feature 3,000 feet high, about 6 miles to the northwest. I was glad to have a decent map compared to some of the ones we had been issued in 1943. I remembered one instance when our maps had shown a hamlet, with the name of Monteverde, at a crossroads near the foot of La Rocca. In fact, no such hamlet, or any hamlet, existed at these crossroads.

As I approached La Rocca, I wondered if my memory had perhaps lapsed after 48 years, but to my relief there was still no sign of Monteverde. By chance, I scanned the surrounding area on the map and there was the missing village, some 8 miles distant!

I had no such trouble locating La Rocca. There it stood, where it should be—its commanding presence dominating the countryside for miles around. The Germans had been quick to appreciate its value and, according to our Intelligence, had established an Observation Post on its peak. My job, as Scout Officer, was to confirm this information.

I had set out with my platoon in broad daylight and scaled the heights which offered very little cover. As suspected, the O.P. was occupied. A fire fight developed and we chased the Germans off the summit, leaving their partly-eaten dinner for us to consume. I spurned their hospitality. I don't care for sauerkraut and the food was cold.

Our pursuit of the enemy was abruptly halted when we were met by a troop of German tanks and a Mortar Platoon on the reverse slopes. This vital information was quickly sent back by wireless to our own artillery who promptly gave the enemy a solid pasting.

In 1985, I had returned to La Rocca for another view of the countryside from its summit, unimpeded by any hostile forces. But there was no way I was going to climb that mountain again *al piede*. So I circled around the base in my car trying to find a trail leading to the top. How did those tanks get there? Finally, I gave up and drove west to the crossroads at Vinchiatura, hoping to find a *buon ristorante* for lunch.

At the Hotel Le Cupolette, I had a fine meal and met the owner, Signor Biaggio Fazzino. I told him about my little patrol to La Rocca during the war and my desire to climb it again, but *alla machina* not *al piede*. He understood and offered to drive me there in his car. We took off and were soon at the summit. The view was just as spectacular as I had imagined. Then I remembered there had been a cross near the top which had guided my patrol as we struggled up the mountainside. What had happened to it?

Signor Fazzino explained that it was now hidden by trees but he would take me there. We walked through the woods and soon found the cross atop a pile of rocks. Nearby was an ancient-looking church with a high tower. I could not remember seeing these structures in 1943. Signor Fazzino sensed my disbelief and told me an amazing story.

The Germans had destroyed the original church and tower but they were rebuilt after the war. Many centuries past, a large monastery had stood on this very site, but it too had been destroyed and the monks had disappeared. They had been skilled stone cutters and carved many beautiful statues. They had erected an enormous cairn and cross where the rock pile now stood. All that was left was rubble and stones scattered about the site, from which the present church was built. It was all a great mystery but the mountain had been known as La Rocca from the earliest of times.

I couldn't help thinking of Cassino and its Abbey, which had been so utterly destroyed in the war, but had risen again to its former glory. I was pressed for time and had to leave but I promised Signor Fazzino that I would return as soon as I could, to see him and visit this fascinating place.

In September 1991, I honoured my promise and spent a wonderful afternoon with Signor Fazzino exploring the mountain, the church and the cross and the remains of the Abbey that had once stood watch over the countryside.

My long Pilgrimage from Reggio to Campobasso was nearing its end and I was depressed because I remembered how that journey had prematurely ended for me at Frosolone on October 26th, 1943, a few miles north of Campobasso.

Shortly after my patrol to La Rocca, the Battalion had put in an attack and seized the feature without incurring any casualties. The enemy with their tanks and mortars had decamped after our artillery barrage.

But Germans never give up, even when they retreat. They retaliated with heavy shell fire and killed Sgt. Robert Carter who had been my first Platoon Sergeant in England. Later in my Pilgrimage, I visited his grave in the Moro River Cemetery. He was a fine soldier and had been a great help to me when I joined the Regiment as a very green, 20-year-old lieutenant. He seemed much older than me and was certainly more knowledgeable. As I stood at the foot of his grave and read the inscription on his headstone, I found he was only 23 when he was killed at La Rocca by an enemy shell. The irony of it all was hard to bear. I had survived my encounter with the enemy but he had been struck down by a lousy shell after the attack was over. My sorrow was, however, tempered by the satisfaction of being able to honour my brave comrade 48 years after his death.

Another comrade and close friend, Lt. Cecil Shea, was wounded by the same shellfire which killed Sgt. Carter. He returned to the Battalion only to be killed in the Hitler Line, as already mentioned. The ranks of the veterans were beginning to thin out and I wondered when my turn would come. I had not long to wait.

After La Rocca, my next patrol was to recce a route for the Battalion to cross the Biferno River, from Baranello, on the east side, to Spinete on the west. It would be a night patrol over difficult mountain terrain. From Baranello the ground fell away sharply to the Biferno River. Down into the deep valley we went, over rocks and across gullies, relying on my compass for direction. Finally, we saw through the trees a broad silver streak—the Biferno River. By sheer luck we had arrived at the exact spot where the Patricias would cross. We had found a route for troops and mules, difficult though it was, but it was certainly not a passage for tanks or heavy vehicles. The Battalion would have to attack without tank support.

In the darkness, I observed a small wooden bridge. We silently crawled to the water's edge. Just as I was deciding whether to cross the bridge, I heard the unmistakeable tramp of German jack boots. In a moment the sentries appeared only yards away. One of my men, a new member of the Platoon, cocked his rifle to shoot the sentries but slipped and fell into the water with a crash. The sentries let out a howl and hightailed it back across the bridge.

It was clearly foolhardy to attempt to cross the river but we still had work to do—locate enemy positions and strength. I decided to withdraw to a hill in rear of our position and wait until daylight. As the first streaks of dawn appeared, I scanned the other side of the river and saw a farmhouse and a haystack near the bridge. Two figures emerged from the haystack and ran toward a barn. Was it a German position covering the bridge?

We waited for half an hour to see if the enemy would show himself. Nothing moved. Time was running out. Something had to be done to make the enemy disclose his positions and draw his fire.

Indicating to my Platoon to give me covering fire, I spurted along the river bank in full view of the enemy as if I were running the 100-yard dash. No reaction. I repeated the exercise but not at full speed. An MG42 immediately opened up from the haystack, another from the barn; bullets cracked about as I accelerated to take cover behind some rocks. I made it with only two nicks from the bullets that had grazed my arm and leg. In accordance with the unwritten code of the Patricias, superficial wounds don't count as wounds and are never reported. It made sense. If every scratch was reason to be evacuated, there would soon be no one left to fight.

I duly observed this rule, patched up the wounds and carried on.

On the next patrol I was severely wounded and sent down the line. The scratches I had received at the Biferno River were ignored as the surgeons had their hands full looking after the new wound. When they finally had time to give me a thorough check-up, they found that the nick in my leg had become badly infected and required plastic surgery.

To return to my patrol to the Biferno River, we completed our mission to locate the enemy and headed for home to give LCol. Ware a full report. Early next day the Battalion put in its attack across the Biferno River and occupied Spinete. It was a bloodless attack as the enemy had decamped, probably stupefied by this crazy Battalion whose officers ran foot races in front of the enemy. The only casualties were two mules which had neglected to keep their heads down.

The following day I was again sent out with my scouts to investigate a small village named San Elena, three miles northwest of Spinete. Germans had been observed in the area. Travelling cross-country (to avoid mined roads and save time) we soon got into San Elena. As soon as the citizens realized we were *soldati canadesi*, they flocked into the narrow streets, waving Italian flags and offering us the usual gifts we now expected as our rightful reward. I received a special present from a former Italian major: a beautiful Beretta pistol and a supply of ammunition. The weapon was quite small and could easily be carried in my pocket as an emergency weapon for close-quarter action.

Large flags were now unfurled from some of the taller buildings, and church bells started to ring, supposedly in our honour. Immediately German artillery began to shell the town with some pretty heavy stuff, sending the people inside their sturdy dwellings. I was not at all convinced that the flags and bells had been for our benefit. Despite the outward showing of enthusiasm our troops received from the Italians, occasionally Fascist sympathizers lingered behind in the towns evacuated by the enemy and sent information back to the Germans by waving flags and ringing bells.

Keeping a careful lookout for Germans and fellow travellers, we completed our patrol of the town and found no enemy, at least none dressed in German uniforms. We passed this information back to BHQ by wireless and scouted the area ahead, in the direction of Frosolone, again without encountering the enemy.

The occupation of Spinete by the Patricias marked the end of their drive up the boot of Italy. The advance had been mainly through the mountainous spine of central Italy, along rough trails with hairpin bends, over deep gorges and across makeshift bridges. The main enemy was the terrain, not the Germans, although they did their best to blow up every bridge, mine every road and intimidate us at every obstacle with heavy shellfire.

Personally, I detested the shellfire but I feared the mines more. The Germans had a nasty habit of setting mines so they would not explode until a certain number of vehicles had passed over them. The closest I came to going to my Valhalla was on the patrol to Decorata. Not once but twice my carrier went over a mine without mishap. But a little later, Lt. Gerry Richards in his carrier was blown up. He survived but his driver Pte. C. A. Calder was killed.

While on the subject of mines, I feel constrained to comment on the well-intentioned but sadly misinformed parties who campaign to have mines "outlawed." They rightly claim that thousands of civilians are killed or maimed each year but they don't mention that hundreds of thousands of soldiers have lost their lives or been injured by mines in wartime. The fact which is overlooked is that mines are one of the most effective means of defence. Witness the expert way they were employed by the Germans in our advance up the Italian Peninsula; witness the United States, which will not sign the Anti-mine Treaty. Furthermore, of what value is a piece of paper? Will a determined aggressor abide by its terms in war? Will a nation whose very existence is threatened by such an aggressor eschew the use of mines? Surely we have learned something from Munich. Is it possible to distinguish between "aggressive" mining and "passive" or "defensive mining"? The whole subject is an exercise in futility as long as nations resort to war.

But I digress from my reflections on the drive up Italy by the Patricias during September and October 1943. I have mentioned that the main adversary was the terrain which the Germans skilfully used to delay our advance. They mined the roads and demolished the bridges—forcing interminable delays until our engineers repaired the damage. As soon as we mounted an attack, the Germans withdrew to the next obstacle. Their tactics could be described as "hit and run."

Still another enemy was the cold and heavy rain we endured in the mountains during October. We were still wearing tropical kit—bush jacket, shorts and puttees—issued aboard ship before we landed in Sicily. Our winter battle dress did not come forward until late October, leaving us with no alternative but to "liberate" clothing from the Germans and Italians.

Sickness also took its toll, mainly yellow jaundice and malaria. I had my attack in Sicily and was hospitalized in Catania for the regulation three weeks. But, like most Patricia Officers, I skipped the usual one-week convalescence and went straight to the Reinforcement Depot and then joined the Regiment for its long drive up Italy.

After the occupation of Spinete, the Battalion readied itself to move to a rest area in Busso not far from Campobasso, where a Divisional Leave Centre was to be established.

However, before we handed over the area to the 5th British Division, our Brigadier wanted us to "tidy up" our front. About eight miles from Spinete stood the little village of Frosolone which the Brigadier believed was held by German troops. What platoon should be sent to oust these uninvited guests from our area? The scouts and snipers, of course. The Adjutant called me in and I received orders to take a strong fighting patrol to Frosolone to deal with these interlopers.

The story has been told in *Once a Patricia*. I received a bullet in the jaw but the rest of my platoon returned safely with the required information. Perhaps an excerpt from the War Diary will suffice:

> *The patrol commanded by Lt. C. S. Frost returned at 2130 hours. The patrol had reached the outskirts of Frosolone shortly before 1700 hours. Lt. Frost decided to converge on the town from three directions. One section commanded by LCpl. Brautigan to go in from the west, one section commanded by Lt. Frost to go in from the south and the remaining section commanded by LCpl Slimkowitch to go in from the southwest. All sections came under heavy MG and rifle fire at approximately 1700 hours. LCpl Slimkowitch's section knocked out one MG position, killing two enemy and a further one when assaulting a second MG post. LCpl. Brautigan's section killed one enemy and these two sections claimed a possible three more enemy killed and an unestimated number wounded.*
>
> *Lt. Frost's section, which came under heavy fire, was pinned down and had difficulty in getting out. In so doing, Lt. Frost was wounded by a bullet through the jaw. However, in such a condition he succeeded in regrouping his patrol and returning to D Company with himself as the only casualty. The patrol estimated Frosolone held by one company of enemy with at least 5 MGs.*

Thus ended my brief service with the Patricias, or so I believed at the time. Ahead lay six months of hospitals and plastic surgery in Italy, Africa and England before I was fit to return. Then followed more months of frustration in Holding Units in England until September 1944, when I rejoined the Patricias in the battle for San Fortunato, as already described.

On previous Pilgrimages, I had always been drawn to Frosolone like a Bedouin to water. I wanted to check the mileage from Spinete. Was it really eight miles as the patrol report stated? It was. I wanted to check the ground from the German position. Did they have a clear, unrestricted view of my patrol as we advanced toward the village? They did. Was there a covered route available? No, there was not. And finally, I wondered if I might find the fancy Beretta pistol given to me by an Italian Major in San Elena which I lost in the engagement. No such luck.

Now it was 1991 and I had returned once more despite my firm resolve in 1985 never to visit the place again. It was a silly obsession, but I poked around the brush where I had lain wounded for several hours, hoping, finally, to pick up a rusted old pistol. Suddenly, a snake slithered toward me. I withdrew in haste, not wanting to tangle with this new enemy.

Some years earlier, whilst in London, I had called on LCol. Jeffery Williams, a distinguished officer of the PPCLI and an author of several books about World Wars I and II, including a short history of the Regiment. We discussed his book and my *Once a Patricia* to check on any inconsistencies. There were none, but Jeffery made an interesting comment: "When I was researching my book, I read about this young officer who foolishly got himself shot up at Frosolone and I always wondered what happened to him. Now I know."

Jeffery continued, "Another thing about your book that puzzled me was your obsession with finding that old Itie pistol, then I realized that returning to the place where you received such a terrible wound probably acted as a catharsis without your knowing it."

It was a profound remark and I thanked Jeffery for it.

One last tale should be told and we can truly banish Frosolone forever. After I was wounded on October 26th, 1943, my parents tried to keep track of my whereabouts as I was shunted from one hospital to another and from Italy to North Africa to England and then back again to Italy. Sometimes, for many weeks, my parents hadn't a clue where I was.

In late May, 1944, they suddenly heard on the news that the Canadians were fighting around Frosinone. They couldn't understand this as they thought this was the name of the village where I had been wounded in October the previous year. Had the Patricias not made any progress since I left them?

The reason they were confused was quite apparent. Frosinone, on Highway 6, north of Cassino and south of Rome, sounds and looks very much like Frosolone, near Campobasso, where I was wounded. On a map, the two places are only about 60 miles apart.

For the rest of the War and many years afterwards, my parents used the two names interchangeably to refer to where I was wounded. In desperation, I made up a little rhyme to help them, because I too was becoming confused.

      Lieutenant Frost was sick and lonely
      When he was hit at Fro-so-lone

On that low note, the story of Frosolone should come to an end.

We now continue to follow the advance of the Patricias from Busso where we left them at rest, to Ortona. Missing, of course, was one Lt. Frost nursing his wounds in a hospital in Algiers. On November 30th, 1943, the Battalion embussed and drove east to Termoli on the coast. By December 4th, the Patricias were in position on the southern tip of the Moro Valley, ready to cross the river.

It is not my intention to describe in any detail the Battle of Ortona, or the fighting leading up to its final capture. I have various reasons. In the first place, I wasn't there. That should be reason enough, but it hasn't deterred others from writing excellent accounts. Mark Zuehlke's *Ortona*, published in 1999, is a monumental work. It, together with his later book, *The Liri Valley*, are the definitive works on those battles.

From the perspective of the PPCLI, *The Official History* by G. R. Stevens describes the operations of the Regiment in clear and concise terms.

The Official History of the Canadian Army, *The Canadians in Italy*, by LCol. G.W.L. Nicholson, gives an accurate overall picture of the First Division's operations.

For an insight into the minds of the men who endured the horrors of these battles, *Execution*, by Colin McDougall, already referred to, gives a vivid description of what they went through.

From these sources, it is clear that the PPCLI was not directly engaged in the clearing of Ortona. They paid their blood dues in the battles leading up to the fighting in that city. Indeed, some of the fiercest fighting took place north of the Moro River at San Leonardo, Villa Rogatti and Vino Ridge, in the approaches to Ortona. MGen. Chris Vokes threw in every battalion in his division. At one point, all nine battalions were committed at once and he had no reserves. One observer has claimed that it was fortunate he had no more reserves as the General would also have thrown them into the slaughter.

But the most striking evidence of these savage battles north of the Moro River is the heroic action of Capt. Paul Triquet of the Royal 22nd Regiment, at Casa Berardi. On December 14th, his company broke through the tough German defences which had so frustrated General Vokes, and captured Casa Berardi. Capt. Triquet and 15 soldiers were the only survivors of this gallant company. But their day was not yet done. They dug in on the objective and repelled desperate German counter-attacks while Capt. Triquet encouraged his defenders with the famous battle cry of General Henri Philippe Petain at Verdun in WWI—"*Ils ne passeront pas*," and they did not. For his gallant action, beyond all praise, Paul Triquet was awarded the Victoria Cross.

Prior to the war, Ortona had been noted for its beaches and fine *Trattorias* and *Pensiones*, as well as being an important fishing village. It was known as the Pearl of the Adriatic. It was hardly a fortress town that would be denied to its attackers at all costs. Yet that is what it became in December 1943. From the plethora of writings on the battles of and for Ortona, one fact clearly emerges. Neither the Germans nor the Allies wanted the war to get bogged down in Ortona.

The Germans, in particular, had learned from Stalingrad how costly, in lives, morale and resources, fighting in built-up areas could become. The Canadians likewise had no desire to be committed to a long-drawn-out battle in the streets of Ortona.

In the opinion of many observers, it was the power of the press which gave such prominence to Ortona that it "turned a limited tactical operation into a long and costly prestige battle."[1] As already mentioned, in comparing Ortona with San Fortunato, the Associated Press reported that "for some unknown reason, the Germans are staging a miniature Stalingrad in hapless Ortona."[2]

Field Marshal Kesselring stated, "It is clear we do not want to defend Ortona decisively, but the English have made it appear as important as Rome."[3]

In an article in *The Press in the Ortona Battle*, an analysis of the role of reporters in the December battle, concluded that the press "is a power for evil as well as good ... It played a large part in turning a tactical fight into a prestige battle with the consequent unnecessary loss of many lives."[4]

There is little more to say about Ortona except for the casualties. In the fighting for Villa Rogatti, Lt. Knobby Clark fell with a bullet through his throat. He was evacuated to hospitals in England where I met him at a March 17th Reunion. As he couldn't talk and I had my jaws wired due to plastic surgery, we made quite a pair sputtering over our drinks. The Battle of Villa Rogatti claimed 8 Patricias. Fifty-two more were wounded.

During the Battle of Vino Ridge (also known as the Battle of the Gully), LCol. Ware, Maj. Watson and Maj. Brain were in consultation in the lee of a tank. A shell struck the vehicle; Maj. Watson was wounded for the second time in four days and Maj. Brain was killed instantly. He had just returned to duty. As D Company led off the advance, Capt. Crofton was wounded—the third Company Commander lost that day.

On December 14th, the very day that Capt. Paul Triquet was gallantly earning his Victoria Cross in another action, Capt. J. B. Hunt was struck down. He had been loaned to the Patricias by The Royal

Canadian Regiment two days before as the Battalion had run out of Company Commanders.

In ten days' fighting every Canadian battalion had suffered severely. On the morning of December 15th, B Company of the Patricias absorbed the remaining 30 men of C Company and the Battalion thereafter operated on a three-company basis. In spite of losses morale was high and the spirit of the offensive prevailed. On being asked by the Brigadier if he wished to wire and mine his front, LCol. Ware declined such protection. He did not need wire, he said, and as for mines, the enemy already had laid them.

The Patricias had indeed paid their dues in the fighting before Ortona.

In my 1991 Pilgrimage, I crossed the Moro River, visited the little village of Villa Rogatti, and explored Vino Ridge and its gully. Not a trace could I find of the battles fought by the Regiment almost 48 years earlier. The village and the countryside had returned to their peaceful existence, and quiet reigned along the Moro River.

If you want to see the true cost of war, you have only to visit the War Cemeteries that are spread throughout the land.

On a cool autumn day toward the end of September 1991, I visited the Moro River Canadian War Cemetery, sited on high ground near the Adriatic, 5 kilometres south of Ortona. Like all Commonwealth War Cemeteries, the land was generously provided by the Italian Government. The Cemetery has 1,615 graves, including 1,375 for Canadians of whom 65 are Patricias. This is the largest number of Canadian burials in Italy. As I slowly walked through the neat lines of marble headstones, each set in its own patch of freshly watered earth, I realized, once more, how lucky I was not to be there, with my brave comrades. Here was the grave of Don Brain, a promising young officer who taught me some useful lessons in tactics when I first joined the Regiment in England; and here, Pte. Vernon Anderson, age 19; and there, Lt. Campbell Munro; and there, Pte. William Saunders, age 20; and Cpl. Robert Turcotte and Pte. Mike Bazzlo and Pte. William McIvor, and ... and ... endless headstones marking the son or husband of a parent or wife who lost their loved one 48 years ago.

Night was falling and an autumn chill rolled in from the Adriatic. It was time for me to leave my friends and bring my Pilgrimage to an end. I headed north along the Adriatic coast past Pesaro, Cattolica and Riccione to Rimini and my Grand Hotel, where I luxuriated for a night. Ahead lay the Romagna and all those rivers to cross: Marecchia, Uso Rubicon, Pisciatello, Savio Bevano, Montone, Lamone, Naviglio Canal and finally the Senio where our advance ended.

I had planned to visit each river and re-fight all the battles but again I had run out of time. They would have to wait for another day.

Next day I took the A14 to Forli and then south west on Highway 67 to Florence, where the Regiment had taken up positions after the Hitler Line pursuant to a grandiose scheme to fool the Hun. The plan was to concentrate the Eighth Army on the Adriatic coast and make a surprise attack. To accomplish this plan, the bulk of the Eighth Army would be temporarily moved to the west side of the country, in the vicinity of Florence. After making its presence known to the enemy in this sector, the Army would then return to the Adriatic coast and overrun the surprised Germans.

Whether the plan worked or not is still a matter of conjecture, but at least it gave the Patricias a pleasant change of venue, a thousand yards south of the banks of the Arno River. Here, the Regiment was faced by the tough 4th Parachute Division, who had destroyed all the bridges except the venerable Ponte Vecchio. They were in a surly mood and resisted every effort to penetrate their lines.

In September 1991, I paused briefly in my journey to survey the area occupied by the Patricias. I also checked to see if the Ponte Vecchio was still in its position. It was.

My long trip was almost over. All that remained was a short drive down the west coast to Rome and home. But as I was checking my map, a familiar name of an island in the Tyrrhenian Sea popped up, Isola d'Elba, where Napoleon sojourned for 10 months in 1814. Although pressed for time, I had to visit this famous "prison isle." I caught the car ferry at Piombino and landed at Porto Ferraio at dusk. It was too late to view Bonaparte's mansion so I checked in at the Fabricia Hotel and relaxed beside the pool amid the palm trees.

Elba is a beautiful island with lush vegetation, sandy beaches, rocky shorelines, rugged mountains and luxurious resorts. The standard joke among the people is: Why did Napoleon want to leave this Island paradise? He had it made.

The following day I spent examining Napoleon's "prison." Actually there are two of them: one in the city of Porto Ferraio, Palazzina del Mulini, and the other Villa di San Martino, hidden away in the forests. The Palazzina is a small palace, with elevated gardens and a spectacular view of the blue Tyrrhenian Sea. The main bedroom contains an immense, gold-leafed, four-poster bed adorned with birds and beasts.

The "little" retreat in the woods, about 4 kilometres away, is hardly less ostentatious. Standing on a rise, the Villa overlooks the harbour. The bed is admittedly not as large, but is built in the form of a sleigh, perhaps to remind the Emperor of his "gallant" retreat from Moscow. Hitler would have been impressed with his style, I thought.

Another reminder of past glories was the Egyptian Room with a pool and fountain sunk in the marble floor. It had hieroglyphics and frescoed scenes of the Emperor's campaigns.

But 10 months of blissful idleness in this paradise had been too much for Bonaparte. He took off and lost it all at Waterloo. As the locals say, "He blew it."

On October 3rd, I boarded Flight 41, Canadian Airlines, at the Rome Fiumicino Airport for a direct flight to Toronto. It would take $9^1/_2$ hours—lots of time to reflect on my Pilgrimage. I had travelled 3,088 miles and I had now faithfully followed the wartime route of the Patricia's from the beaches of Sicily to Rimini. Only the rivers in the Romagna had escaped my view. Their turn would come on my next Pilgrimage.

As my aircraft climbed to its height over the Tyrrhenian Sea, I said *arrivederci* to this beautiful land where Canadian soldiers had fought and died that it might be free.

Chapter XI

PILGRIMAGE—1994

My Pilgrimage in 1994 comprised two quite separate missions. The first was to Sicily to ensure that the Monument was in good shape for an official visit by the Minister of Veterans Affairs and a 95-person delegation including one Veteran from each Unit that had served in Italy. A further concern was that a few Italian Veterans had voiced their opposition to the Monument.

My second mission was to the mainland of Italy to complete my avowed intention of visiting the cemeteries and following the wartime route of the PPCLI from Reggio in the south to the Romagna and the Senio River winter line in the north. On prior quests, I had pretty well covered this route except for the final battles in the Romagna and the Cemeteries in that area.

The story of the Sicilian portion of my journey has been told in Chapter V. We now pick up my trail in southern Italy after crossing the Strait of Messina. My objective was Rimini with a stopover in Potenza to examine my favourite castle in Italy, the Castello di Lagopesole.

I took my usual route north along the A3, Strada del Sole, despite hordes of Fiats going north, going south, and darting across my path. My fears were slightly allayed by the fact that I was driving a Mercedes-Benz which the Head Office in Stuttgart had kindly placed at my disposal.

After the War, and my call to the Bar, I had the privilege of incorporating the Canadian Mercedes-Benz Company and acting as one of its first Directors. It was an interesting experience. I was serving my once-hated enemies. Most of the German personnel had, of course, served in their Armed Forces. But very quickly we put aside our past differences and learned to respect each other. Indeed, in many cases, we became good friends and I am happy to say this friendship has endured. Strangely enough, the fact we had all been soldiers had a beneficial effect. We missed the camaraderie we had enjoyed in wartime and welcomed the opportunity to renew this bond with soldiers from the other side.

I reflected on these things as my automobile sped along the A3. South of Salerno, I turned off the Autostrada onto a sideroad that led to Potenza. It was now almost dark and the traffic had thinned out to a few trucks. The road steadily climbed into the mountain range. It began to rain. I thought how typical! Fifty-one years ago I was chugging along this very road, at night, in pouring rain in an Army 30 cwt lorry, trying to locate my Regiment near Potenza. Then, my only fear had been meeting a German patrol. Now, I was safe and secure in my German automobile negotiating hills that would have been a challenge to my Army vehicle.

Bam! Rattle! Clunk! My automobile ground to a halt and refused to move. I struggled with the gearshift and finally got it into neutral and there it stuck again. For a horrible moment the fear of 51 years ago was in me. Here I was, all alone, in the dead of night, in a mountain range, umpteen miles from the nearest habitation. Gradually, my fear gave way to a feeling of exhilaration that I had often experienced in the Army when faced with an unexpected challenge. There must be an answer. I had certainly been in worse situations before.

Then I remembered noticing a road assistance telephone booth at the side of the road perhaps half a mile downhill. These booths are a feature of Italian roadways. You pick up the phone and are connected to a nearby service station operator who is supposed to immediately come to your aid. Whether the phone that I had observed was working on Sunday at this time of night was doubtful, but it was worth a try.

Backing a car down a winding mountain trail, in the dark, with the possibility of meeting an oncoming Fiat is not my favourite motor sport. Thankfully, my brakes worked, and by inching the car back very slowly I arrived at the booth. Would the thing work?

I picked up the receiver and in a breathless moment heard a voice: "*Pronto?*"

What to say and how to say it? I tentatively tried, "*La mia machina è finito. Puoi aiutarmi?*" (Can you help me?)

"*Sì, sì, Signor.*"

"*Quando arriverai?*"

"*Fra venti minuti. Ciao.*" (In 20 minutes.)

"*Mille grazie.*"

Not for the first time I thanked those Italian courses at Seneca.

A tow truck arrived within the hour. The driver jumped out and with a big smile announced, "*Buona notta. Mi chiamo Felice. Che cosa è il problema?*"

I told him I wasn't sure but the trouble was perhaps with the *frizione* (clutch) or the *cambio* (gears). He quickly hitched my car to his truck and we drove to his garage in a little hamlet called Sicignano degli Alburni.

Felice unhitched my car and saluted. (I had informed him during our drive that I was a Colonnello Canadese, hoping I might get a little respect.) It was Sunday, late at night, and everything was closed tighter than that lousy gearbox. Where was I going to stay the evening?

"*Dove un albergo?*" I asked.

"*Non ci sono alberghi qui, Signor Colonnello.*" (There are no hotels here.)

"*Dove dormo stasera? A casa tua?*" (Where am I going to sleep? At your house?)

"*No, no, Colonnello mio. È impossibile. C'è solo un letto per me e mia moglie.*" (There is only one bed—for me and my wife.)

Presumably three was a crowd. A ménage à trois was not acceptable.

My exhilaration with this little caper was beginning to evaporate. Here I was stuck in a mountain village, with no hotel and no place to sleep. While Felice seemed like a nice Italian boy, who knew what he might do. I missed having that handy Beretta pistol I had lost in these hills so long ago. My concern was not just for myself but for the automobile. If it and I disappeared, no one would ever know. The police report on my disappearance would simply state I had a reservation at a hotel in Potenza, but for reasons unknown, I never checked in. Just another case of a mysterious disappearance.

When in doubt, shout, was one of my not-too-popular methods of getting co-operation from an indifferent Italian during the War. It was time to try it again.

I repeated my request to Felice. "*Dove dormo stasera?*" He just shrugged his shoulders.

Then I let him have it. "*Chiama la polizia, presto*" (call the police), I yelled, as I banged the hood of my car.

That seemed to work. He entered the garage, turned on a light and motioned to me to come in. "*Per favore, Signor, Colonnello. Ecco il telefono.*"

He gave me a number and I phoned the local police. Just in case they didn't get the message, I also phoned the closest Carabiniere station. They are the National Police Force and carry considerable weight with the citizens.

Within half an hour, both policemen arrived and I explained the situation. I was stranded in this place; my car was broken; there was no hotel; I was tired and I was damn hungry. Furthermore, I wished to telephone the Canadian Embassy in Rome to let them know my whereabouts. I also wanted to contact the Head of the Mercedes-Benz organization in Rome. And I had to cancel my reservation at my hotel in Potenza and find a place to sleep. Finally, I was a Colonnello Canadese and I expected their immediate co-operation. *"Capisce?"* I roared.

Even though it was Sunday, the Carabiniere Officer got through to the Canadian Embassy in Rome and I talked to one of the duty secretaries. She in turn gave me the number of the President of Mercedes-Benz in Rome. I phoned his home but he was away for the weekend.

The Officer then phoned my hotel in Potenza and cancelled my reservation.

The next problem was where to stay until my car was repaired. The Officer suggested that he try to find me a room in the Jolly Hotel in Salerno, even though at this late hour they might be fully booked. "Why Salerno?" I asked. The Officer explained that my car was obviously beyond local repair and the work would have to be done by a Mercedes-Benz garage in Salerno. This made sense and I told him to make the reservation. One problem remained—how would I get to Salerno, a mere matter of 70 miles? No trouble. The Officer would order up a taxi from nearby Buccino.

The rest of the story can be quickly told. The taxi arrived and I transferred my baggage from the Mercedes, making a note of the mileage on my car. I got a receipt from Felice stating that the car appeared to be in good order, except it wouldn't go, and undertaking to look after it until he received instructions from Mercedes-Benz in Rome, likely the next morning.

I thanked the two police officers for their help and presented them with Canada pins left over from my Sicilian visit. Felice and his wife (who had just appeared on the scene) were likewise rewarded. As I was getting into the taxi, Felice said, *"Scusi Signor, Colonnello, ma il telefono costa 37,000 lire"* (37 dollars). I forked over the money.

I was safely delivered to my hotel in Salerno and paid the driver 160,000 lire (160 dollars). The room was really a large closet but I didn't care. I was back in civilization and I was going to devour the largest plate of spaghetti the ristorante could produce.

Early next morning, I got in touch with the President of Mercedes-Benz, Rome. He had already heard of my difficulties from the Canadian Embassy and was full of apologies. He would immediately supply me with a brand new automobile and send out a tow truck.

The new car arrived early that afternoon. I had lost a day due to the breakdown so I would have to bypass Potenza and Castello di Lagopesole and head straight for Rimini and my Grand Hotel, a distance of 310 miles.

Two points, and my story will be finished. I have deliberately given it at some length and in great detail, the reason being I felt it might serve as a guideline for a traveller in Italy who is confronted with a similar problem. The first lesson is not to drive around the country on your own, but if you do, you should acquire some knowledge of the Italian language, or have an Italian driver. Of the two, I would prefer the former. I was lucky to have secured the services of two policemen, without which I might have been in serious trouble.

I would also emphasize that if you are alone, or perhaps even when you are with another person, it is wise to let someone know where you are if you become involved in a situation similar to mine.

The other point is a rather personal one but I will mention it anyway. As a former Director of Mercedes-Benz Canada, I would not want anyone to think I am blaming the Italian company for my troubles. There was nothing inherently wrong with the automobile. It subsequently became clear that the vehicle, through the fault of the prior owner, had not been properly serviced, or had been serviced at an unauthorized garage. In any event, the President of Mercedes-Benz in Rome immediately went into action and within a few hours I received a new machine. I suspect he may have been an officer in the German Army, which had a reputation for super efficiency.

I arrived in Rimini late that night, exhausted but looking forward to returning to the battlefields in the Romagna, in my spanking new Mercedes-Benz.

It will be recalled from Chapter IX that in 1989 I had followed the advance of the Patricias along the eastern coast of Italy from the Metauro River through the Gothic Line to Gradara, San Fortunato, the Marecchia River and Rimini. Due to pressure of time, I was not able to continue my journey north into the Romagna where the Regiment had spent the last five months of the Italian Campaign battling its way across endless rivers, through sodden plains, against a defiant and ugly foe.

After the San Fortunato Battle, I had been transferred to command the Machine Gun Platoon. Like the Scout and Sniper Platoon that I had led in southern Italy, the Machine Gun Platoon was unofficial and carried the brand name "Made in Italy." From the earlier fighting in Sicily and southern Italy, it was found that we needed more firepower in the front lines to neutralize the tremendous fire the Germans were pouring at us with their quick-firing weapons. The fact that our machine guns had been made in 1914, for WWI, was regrettable but couldn't be helped (so we were assured by the staff). At least our guns would be a great morale builder for the front-line troops.

So, in October 1944, I was keenly looking forward to leading my machine guns into the Romagna and, hopefully, finishing off the war in Venice. Another factor that made my new appointment quite attractive was the likelihood of coming through the war without absorbing any more enemy lead. The odds of avoiding death or injury in the Machine Gun Platoon were supposed to be much better than those in an Infantry Platoon. In the event, my fond hopes turned out to be wishful thinking.

At least I had survived, or obviously this tale would have been stillborn (or still-dead). As I drove along Highway No. 9, the famous Via Emilia, in May 1994, I experienced the same feeling of excitement I had felt in October 1944. At Savignano, I turned off the main highway, as the Regiment had done, and crossed the first of the many rivers that lay ahead—the Fiumicino, said to be the Rubicon which Caesar himself had crossed 2,000 years earlier, but going the other way. Like Caesar, the Regiment had made an unopposed crossing.

Continuing along country roads north of the main Highway, I reached the small village of Martorano, on the Savio River, where I halted. Rain, which had begun earlier, now came down in wash basins (as the Italians say), and the trail I was following became a quagmire. Old Field Marshal Fate, whom I had thought long deceased, was giving me a reminder of what the troops had to contend with in 1944—a low-lying plain and continuous swamp, criss-crossed with rivers and canals.

Another Field Marshal, Harold Alexander, had long ago warned us of the morass we would have to flounder through in the battlefields ahead:

> *The whole area is nothing but a great reclaimed swamp—and not wholly reclaimed in some parts—formed by the lower courses of numerous rivers flowing down from the Apennines. In addition there are hundreds of smaller streams with canals and irrigation ditches between them. By canalization of the main rivers the primitive swamp had been drained after centuries of patient effort; as the water flowed off so the level of the ground sank. The river beds were left thereafter higher than the surrounding country. As soon as they descend to the plain all these rivers need high banks on each side to keep them in their courses and to guide them against sudden rises of level which heavy rainfall or snow melting in the mountains invariably cause. Even in the best drained areas the soil remembers its marshy origin. When rained on it yields the richest mud known to the Italian Theatre.*[1]

On October 20th, 1944, the Patricia's made the first of several attempts by Second Brigade to cross the Savio River, swollen by the storm waters from the mountains and the recent rain. By now it was three times its normal size and the current was swift. The soft banks of the river dykes were steep and had turned into walls of mud.

As if these obstacles were not enough, the Germans had cleared the fields of all trees and vegetation to give their machine gunners unrestricted fields of fire. Despite all these obstacles—the adverse weather, the impossibility of tank support, the likelihood of mines and the fact that the attack would be made in broad daylight—the Patricias had been ordered to attack.

No battalion, not even the Patricias, had the slightest chance of success. But they bravely tried and were brutally beaten back, all except Maj. Ted Cutbill and 16 of his A Company. They had crossed 600 yards of minefield, plunged into the river, swum across and gained the shelter of the opposite bank. Despite repeated counter-attacks they clung to their toehold until some reinforcements struggled forward with more ammunition.

Later, D Company under Capt. A.G. Robinson fought its way across the river and dug in on the far side. Then a group of enemy tanks charged right through the position. Some of the Patricias made it back across the river, but a whole platoon was cut off. Miraculously, they too were able to withdraw later in the day.

As LCol. Clark prepared to send the rest of his battalion into the battle, he was ordered by the Brigade Commander to stand fast. The other two battalions of the Brigade, the Seaforth Highlanders and the Loyal Edmonton Regiment, would make a combined attack. This time the chance of success is marginally improved. The strength and position of the enemy is known. There is time to make a detailed plan and lay on an overwhelming artillery barrage. The weather has improved. Two battalions are making the attack instead of one and it will be made at night.

But even then, the gallant attack by the Seaforths and Loyal Eddies was a bitter fight that succeeded only because of incredible heroism. At Pieve Sestina, 1,000 yards from the river, a singular act of high valour took place. Charlie Company of the Seaforths was attacked by three Panther tanks, two self-propelled guns and about 30 infantry. Pte. E. A. Smith, a member of the tank-hunting platoon, single-handedly took on this formidable foe; when the smoke cleared away one tank had been disabled and the others and their supporting infantry had withdrawn in disarray, leaving the field strewn with dead and wounded Germans. Pte. Smith was awarded the Victoria Cross.

The bitter fighting at the Savio brought the three units of Second Brigade—the Patricias, the Seaforths and the Loyal Eddies—one VC, four DCMs and four Military Medals.

It will be recalled that we first met Smoky Smith in 1991 in Chapter III of this narrative. He was still the same durable soldier I had known in wartime.

LGen. McCreery, the Corps Commander, wrote the Brigade Commander: "The way your Brigade secured a big bridgehead, smashed an enemy counter-attack, and surmounted all the difficulties of having no bridge behind was magnificent."[2]

We now leave the Battle of the Savio River to the annals of history. It will never be forgotten by the Patricias. It is one of its proud battle honours.

* * *

By October 23rd, the Germans knew the game was up and rapidly departed to their next line of defence, hotly pursued by the Scout and Sniper Platoon. At the Bevano River, the enemy had no chance to dig in and could only blow the bridge before continuing their withdrawal.

The next river, the Ronco River, would likely have been a serious obstacle but luck was with us. The Patricias had completed their tasks for this phase of the operation and were withdrawn to Riccione, for a well-earned rest.

However, before the Battalion was relieved, LCol. Clark had a small mission for my Machine Gun Platoon. He wanted us to check out a village at a crossroads about 2,000 yards distant on the right flank. There were reports of enemy in that area.

As we approached the crossroads in our carriers, a warning from earlier days burst in my mind—mines! As I have indicated earlier in this story, my greatest fear was to be blown to bits by a mine.

We dismounted from the carriers and advanced along the road on foot. As we approached the outskirts of the village, we left the road and moved forward through the backyards of the first houses. I halted for a moment. Then I took a step and felt the ground give way. My other foot came forward; it too started to sink into the earth. Now both feet were together and my whole body was slowly disappearing into the ground. I did not utter a sound but I was going to if I sank much farther. Then my feet hit solid ground. A pleasant warmth embraced my body; an overpowering stench filled my nostrils; sulphur fumes ate my eyes. I was up to my armpits in a farmyard cesspool!

I looked back and saw the rest of my section, one by one, silently follow me into the stinking sump hole.

We ploughed through the sewage in single file and climbed out the far side of the pool, saturated with excrement and gasping for air.

Whether the house was full of Jerries hardly entered our minds. We burst into the place looking for something to wipe away some of the foul mess. An Italian family emerged from a cellar. An old man squeeked, "*Madonna, il diavolo!*" I felt like the devil and smelt worse.

The village was not occupied by the Germans. They had left a few hours before, after thoroughly mining all the roads.

News of our encounter with the cesspool rapidly spread throughout the Battalion and the Brigade. LCol. Clark immediately moved forward to an unmarked intersection and refused to see me. It was rumoured that the Brigade Commander wanted to send us forward at once as a secret weapon, straight through the German lines to Bologna. The Brigade Major vetoed the idea as the enemy might consider it was the start of a gas attack and retaliate. Our gas masks were somewhere back in Sicily.

Thus ends my little "cesspool caper." I rejoined the rest of the Battalion and we withdrew to Riccione where a Mobile Bath Unit cleansed our stinking bodies. I stripped off my rotten clothes and gave my lice-ridden body its first bath in weeks.

* * *

Fifty years later, in 1994, I revisited the little village and the scene of my "caper" in 1944. Time had changed the area considerably, but my memory of the event remained crystal clear, and so did the smells. I urged my car forward to the next river obstacle, the Montone River.

Before proceeding any further in my journey, it might be helpful to review the overall plan of the forthcoming Canadian Operation. It carried the code name "Chuckle" but, as the Regimental Historian so aptly observes, it was to be no laughing matter.

The general intention was to capture Bologna by a general offensive involving four corps of Eighth Army. The task of the Canadian Corps was the capture of the Montone and Lamone river lines and an advance to the Senio, whose high flood banks held the most formidable of all the enemy's prepared positions. This operation envisaged a gain of 12 miles across a countryside with more canals than Venice, and whose narrow built-up roadways offered the only feasible routes of approach for either tracks or wheels. On return from a Montone reconnaissance a Patricia officer wrote:

> *The ground is monotonously flat, intersected by a network of drainage ditches, with heavily cultivated fields oozing with sticky mud. All bridges have been blown, the roads cratered and the paths mined. The Montone, a sludgy stream, is no great obstacle, but inside the flood walls a soft mud bottom extends on either side of the watercourse. The distance between the flood banks is about three hundred*

feet. The enemy has breached the banks in places and for a thousand yards the approaches are under water. The built-up roadways leading to the river are well ranged by artillery and machine guns.[3]

By the luck of the draw, the Patricias were not called upon to attack across either the Montone or the Lamone River. The Regiment had already paid its dues at the Savio River.

On December 1st, 1944, the Battalion left Riccione for the front. Crossing the Montone, after the successful fight of the Third Brigade, the Patricias moved up to the Lamone River, to await the outcome of the assault on that obstacle by the First Brigade.

The attack was an unmitigated disaster. It was the Savio River crossing all over again, only much worse. Two fine regiments, The Royal Canadian Regiment and The Hastings and Prince Edward Regiment, were all but decimated. Of a total of 205 all ranks of the RCR who crossed the river, 3 officers and 26 other ranks were killed, 3 officers and 43 other ranks were wounded, and 2 officers and 29 other ranks were missing. Total casualties 106. And, but for the grace of God, the Patricias would have been involved.

Five days later, the Third Brigade renewed the attack. This time there had been ample opportunity for recce, the artillery had a superior fire plan, and three battalions made the assault instead of two, as in the previous attack. Two of the battalions achieved success, but the third ran into an inferno of mortar and machine gun fire, and was momentarily repulsed when its Olafson bridge capsized in the swift current. However, the battalion soon renewed its attack through the bridgeheads of the other two battalions and was ultimately successful. The strength of the German defences in the area was then revealed. The attacking troops "discovered on the reverse side of the embankment numerous weapon-pits near the crest and a series of deep and strongly timbered dug-outs spaced at intervals of 20 feet, impervious to artillery fire, and equipped with every possible device, including electric lights."[4]

Upon the success of Third Brigade, the Patricias closed up to the Lamone River and crossed it at Traversara by a raft bridge. My Machine Gun Platoon set up in an enormous structure beside the east bank (on our side) of the Lamone. The ancient building had once been a magnificent palace, Palazzo San Giacomo, but now appeared to serve as a convent and a temporary hospital for civilians and soldiers. The Germans gave not a hoot what the building was used for and clearly resented the fact that the place was still standing; they continued to blast it with everything in their arsenal. Occasionally, a shell dropped cleanly through the remains of the roof and exploded with a terrific crash. A large number of civilians from the surrounding countryside had foolishly taken refuge in the convent and could not seem to comprehend why the Germans were trying to destroy it. They milled around, wailing and sobbing, imploring the help of their Protector, as well as ours. We rounded up these poor farmers, and the nuns who were bravely tending sick and wounded, and got them into strong rooms forming part of the outside walls.

Some of the rooms still showed evidence of the casualties that First and later Third Brigade had suffered in the recent fighting—broken stretchers, bloodied bandages, empty plasma bottles and torn equipment. The smell of death was still there.

* * *

As I tried to follow the route of the Patricias in my new Mercedes-Benz, I realized that it was impossible to faithfully retrace every step. After all, I was not driving a beaten-up tracked carrier as I had been in 1944. The raft bridge over the Lamone had long ago given way to a fine concrete bridge. But I was still keen to visit once more the Palazzo San Giacomo.

In 1985, I had returned to the Palace hoping to see it restored to its former magnificence. I was sadly disappointed. The structure had been converted to a junk yard. The Italian Government had tried to repair the damage caused by the war and the elements but soon discovered that due to the low-lying land and constant flooding, the foundations had started to give way. It would cost billions of lire to restore the place. So the Government rented out rooms in the Palace to anyone who was crazy enough to risk having the whole structure collapse on them at any moment. One of these brave tenants had turned the former gardens into a junk yard.

After receiving dire warnings about the perilous state of the foundation, I was allowed inside and prowled around some of the rooms I had occupied in 1944. It was not a pretty sight. Beautiful old frescoes, balustrades, altars, statues, leaded panes of glass, all lay in pieces on the once beautifully tiled floors. Gaping holes in the roof that went through six or seven stories to the basement, caused by German and Canadian bombs, let in the elements. Rats scurried among piles of refuse and debris.

That was in 1985. Now, nine years later, the magnificent old Palace was just a shell, a sad reminder of its former glory. I thought of a favourite saying of my dear friend, Professor Carmelo Nigro in Ispica—"*Sic transit gloria mundi*" (So passes away the glory of the world).

PILGRIMAGE—1994

Ahead lay the Naviglio Canal, 400 yards distant. Unbeknownst to me in 1944, I was about to end my personal contribution to the advance. On December 14th, I was driving my jeep along a road jammed with tanks and other vehicles heading for the canal. The Germans were paving the road with lead from their artillery shells and mortars. Crash! A heavy shell slammed into the tank in front. A red sheet of flame shot into the sky. It blew up.

I pressed the accelerator to the floor and shot past the burning tank. My passenger yelled, "Watch out ... Here comes a ...."

The bomb exploded in a blast of heat and dirt and I was thrown into a ditch. I climbed back to the road. Two men lay there: one, a shattered form of a man lying in a grotesque pattern; the other, still alive but badly wounded. Someone yelled at me, "You've got a hell of a hole in the seat of your pants." I felt something warm and sticky covering my right buttock. They helped me back to the road and the MO, Capt. Steve Worobetz, had a good "look see."

"Yeah, you've got a slug in there—deep, probably right to the bone, but you're lucky. Anywhere else in the back and you'd be a dead man."

Thus my services to the Regiment had been terminated again. I was evacuated through a series of hospitals to Cesenatico, Cattolica, Jesi and finally to Perugia high in the midst of the snow-covered Apennines. By January 30th my wound was sufficiently healed that I was able to convince the doctors that I should be discharged. I left Perugia with orders to report to a Transit Camp to be posted to Avellino for convalescence.

Avellino is a familiar name in these pages. It was where Staff Officers, Reinforcement Officers and Nurses played games and near Sorrento and Capri, where they spent weekends. While it may stretch my credibility to say so, this idyllic life was not, at that point, for me. It was an unwritten rule that PPCLI officers always returned to the Regiment as soon as possible and eschewed any convalescence. The Battalion was always desperately short of officers, and especially at this stage in the war.

So, I managed to "escape" from the hospital at Perugia on January 30th and bummed a lift with some Seaforth officers who were returning to their Unit. The next day I arrived at the PPCLI main Headquarters outside Ravenna. I had only been away 7 weeks but in that short time the Regiment had been engaged in savage fighting on the Naviglio Canal and Fosso Munio.

In one 24-hour period (December 14th/15th), all four members of my class at RMC who were fighting with 2nd Brigade became casualties. From the PPCLI, Lt. R. S. (Bob) Huestis came down with fever and had to be evacuated; Lt. V. S. (Vaughan) Allan was killed; I was wounded. From The Loyal Edmonton Regiment, Capt. G. G. (George) Brown was also wounded.

George went on to have a distinguished military career. He remained in the Army after the War, as a Patricia, rose to the rank of Major General and served as Colonel of the Regiment.

My classmate Vaughan Allan met a brave death. The Regimental History gives this account of his last attack on December 15th:

> *When Lt. V. S. Allan and his men approached a group of buildings they were fired upon; whereupon the officer told off two sections to give covering fire while with the remainder of his men he charged the enemy nest. Resistance was too strong; when the platoon withdrew Lt. Allan and three of his men were missing. Their graves were found afterwards.*[5]

The bearer of these sad tidings of my friends was George Brown himself. He arrived at the hospital at Jesi on December 16th and was in the same ward as I. Other news of the heavy fighting in the Naviglio Bridgehead continued to arrive. On the day I was wounded, Lt. W. E. Harrington knocked out a Panther tank, killed a number of the enemy and brought back 16 prisoners. For this and other sterling acts of leadership, he was awarded the Military Cross.

On December 19th, my senior from RMC, Maj. R. W. (Sam) Potts, in command of C Company, finally ran out of luck. He had landed on the beaches in Sicily as a Platoon Commander and had served the Regiment with distinction ever since, including a stint as Adjutant. In the evening of December 19th, his company attacked a house which commanded a road junction. On capturing it, Maj. Potts entered the house and flicked on his flashlight to scan his map:

> *Apparently one or more enemy tanks or self-propelled guns had crept up to point-blank range; on the flicker of light a series of shells crashed through the building. Its upper floor collapsed; Maj. Potts, painfully wounded, was dug out from under the rubble.*
>
> *Maj. Potts comments: "I hit the deck and I recall having one shell go through the wall so close to my head that I saw the gun flash of the next round through the hole, without taking my chin off the floor."* [6]

Command of the company then passed to Lt. W. D. L. (Bill) Roach, whose platoon had led C Company's attack on the house and silenced the defenders. His subsequent act of bravery on that day is also recorded:

> *Lt. Roach could smell counter-attack in the air. Out of the night groups of Germans dashed to the close, seeking to overwhelm the small garrison. The young officer took charge in magnificent fashion, rushing from post to post to encourage and to direct the defence. Inspired by his example, his men gave no ground and beat off two successive assaults. The enveloping force was estimated at company strength; against it stood no more than a dozen Patricia riflemen.*[7]

For his gallant leadership, Lt. Roach was awarded the DSO, a very rare distinction for a junior officer. Indeed, such an honour was considered the next thing to a Victoria Cross. It was usually awarded where a junior officer's valour merited a VC, but the overall nature of the operation was not of sufficient importance (in the opinion of Higher Command, of course) to warrant a VC.

Whatever the Higher Command thought of the battle at the time, the committee that awarded Battle Honours after the War held a very clear view of the significance of the operation in which Lt. Roach won his DSO. The name of the battle, Fosso Munio, is emblazoned on the Regimental Colours of the PPCLI.

Patricia casualties in the Naviglio operations were 2 officers and 23 other ranks killed or died of wounds; 2 officers and 57 other ranks wounded; 3 other ranks missing; 108 prisoners had been taken. The battalion game book was augmented by a Panther tank, two self-propelled guns and a German staff car.

The bitter fighting had not been confined just to the PPCLI. In the 20 days of the offensive that began at the Montone River on December 2nd, the Canadian Corps (1st and 5th Divisions) had suffered casualties of 548 officers and men killed, 1,796 wounded, and 212 taken prisoner—a staggering total of 2,646.

These figures do not take into account the large numbers that had been evacuated because of fever, jaundice, hepatitis and other illnesses caused in part by the appalling weather conditions. One brigade had even suffered from trench foot, brought on by long periods in water-soaked slit trenches.

These figures give the casualties to December 22nd, but the Patricias were engaged in more bitter fighting after that date.

The ambitious plans of the Generals to reach Bologna or even Venice in 1944 had foundered in the morass of the mud flats of the Romagna, on the greasy banks of its swollen rivers and on the tenacious stand of the German defenders.

Field Marshal Alexander sensibly realized the impossibility of advancing any farther and decided to go on the defensive for the remainder of the winter. There was, however, one pocket of enemy in and around Granarolo which had to be cleared before the Canadians could settle into a winter line along the Senio River.

On January 3rd, the Patricias assaulted across the Naviglio Canal, half a mile south of Granarolo, under a heavy artillery and mortar barrage, and quickly gained their objectives, taking 60 prisoners and capturing intact a self-propelled gun and a fancy staff car. The Germans counter-attacked with SP guns and infantry and were driven off, but only after the inevitable casualties, including Lt. W. A. Groomes killed (he had been with the Regiment less than a month) and Lt. G.D.M. Nicholson wounded.

Two officers in particular distinguished themselves in the battle and contributed greatly to its success. At the point where the Patricias had crossed the canal there was no bridge, but there was a built-up road leading to the canal through the marshy fields—the only possible route for tanks and support weapons. It was vital to clear this road of mines and build a bridge as soon as the battalion crossed the canal so that the armour and anti-tank guns could be pushed across to meet the inevitable counter-attack. The building of that bridge is the story of the coolness under fire of Lt. J. H. Horton, the Pioneer Officer.

As soon as the attack opened, Lt. Horton hurried to inspect the road which had been allotted to the Patricias. It was under fire; in addition, the enemy had cratered it. An armoured bulldozer and an Ark bridge were sent forward, but before these heavy pieces could be moved, the road had to be swept for mines. A number of Teller mines were discovered so firmly embedded in the surface of the roadway that all attempts to remove them by hand failed. A tow was attached to individual mines; the tow-bar bent, the mines did not give.

Lt. Horton set charges to explode them but only one mine obliged. Heavier charges were prepared, and the mines blew up with a resounding blast. The Naviglio dykes rose about six feet above ground level; they were impassable to tracks or wheels. Lt. Horton brought up more charges, blew the dykes inward and used the rubble as filling for his crossing. All this was done at great speed, working against time and under fire.

The building of the bridge, however, was only one of many feats of daring that saved the day and brought distinction to the Regiment. Unless immediate anti-tank support could be sent forward, the bridge would be of no avail; by the time it was completed and ready for tanks, the enemy counter-attacks might throw the battalion back to the canal. Into the breach stepped Lt. A. B. McKinnon of D Company. He was given a two-pounder gun and told to use his native wits in getting it forward. He and his men manhandled the piece for 1,000 yards across fields, surmounting en route three drainage ditches and a railway embankment. Shortly after midnight they reached the canal. In two hours they built their own crossing; they were constantly under fire. Having dragged the weapon to the far bank, they were given the location of the forward companies and were told that the available road was mined. Lt. McKinnon walked ahead and tested the road; the gun followed in tow of a jeep. At 0845 hours it was delivered to B Company.

Lt. McKinnon's day was not yet over. As he and his men retraced their steps, a British fighter plane crashed in a nearby field and burst into flames. Ordering his men to stand back because of exploding ammunition, the officer climbed into the cockpit and dragged out the badly-burned pilot.

For his spirited leadership and determination to succeed despite the odds Lt. McKinnon was awarded a well-earned Military Cross.

Once again, the Regiment had added another name to its long list of Battle Honours—Granarolo.

This was to be the last major offensive action of the Regiment in Italy. During the next six weeks they would hold a series of defensive positions along the Senio and to the east of that barrier, until they and their comrades in the First Canadian Corps were called back to join the fold of First Canadian Army in Northwest Europe.

Lt. Allan McKinnon's service to his country did not cease with the end of the War. He became a school teacher, a Member of Parliament and finally Minister of Defence. We kept in touch over the years and I often kidded him that the reason he attained such high office was the training he received from me in D Company during the fighting in Holland. I also chided him for allowing the peacetime Army to wither away until it was smaller than the First Canadian Corps had been in Italy when he was only a Lieutenant. He took it all in good humour.

Allan McKinnon's career after the war is typical of many Patricia officers and men who endured the fear and fatigue of prolonged combat and yet had the strength and fortitude to put it all behind them and pursue outstanding careers in peacetime. At the risk of offending a great number of Patricias who distinguished themselves in war and in peace, I am going to mention only a few whose names appear in these pages.

Capt. Steve Worobetz, MC
Our popular Medical Officer who tended my wounds near the Naviglio Canal and was himself wounded later the same day. After returning to his medical practice, he became Lieutenant-Governor of Saskatchewan, and Honorary Colonel of the North Saskatchewan Regiment.

Lt. Bill Roach, DSO
Joined the PPCLI on September 1st, 1939, as a Private and was commissioned. He won his DSO as a Lieutenant, a very rare distinction for a junior officer. It is considered the next thing to a Victoria Cross. After the War, he studied law and practised in Kitchener and Vancouver.

Capt. Egan Chambers, MC
Was wounded but remained on duty. After the War, he was elected to the House of Commons and became head of the Progressive Conservative Party and Parliamentary Secretary to the Minister of Defence.

BGen. Rowan Coleman, DSO, MC, MID
Was wounded in the battle of the Hitler Line while commanding the Loyal Edmonton Regiment. After the war, he commanded the 18th Infantry Brigade (Reserve) in Calgary, and became a Registrar at McGill University.

Capt. Grant Robinson, MC
Joined the PPCLI as a private on September 1st, 1939, and rose to Captain and Company Commander. After the war, he went to university and ultimately became Professor Emeritus of Entomology at the University of Manitoba.

Major Colin McDougall, DSO, MID
Served continuously in action from July 10th, 1943, until January 9th, 1945, when he was invalided home with recurrent jaundice and malaria. After the war, he became Registrar of McGill University and wrote numerous short stories, including "The Firing Squad" for which he was awarded first prize by *Maclean's Magazine* and the President's Medal, University of Western Ontario. He was also the author of a novel, *Execution*, mentioned frequently in these pages.

Pte. Mel Murdy
Was one of the first to be wounded, on D-Day, July 10th, 1943. He was severely wounded on January 7th, 1945, and after many months in hospital, returned home. His back had been broken. He had lost 2 vertebrae, and one foot was $2^1/_2$" shorter than the other. Despite these disabilities, he was gainfully employed for 27 years. His story appears later in this chapter. Murdy was my batman.

Dr. Jerry Richards
Joined the Regiment in Sicily. He was twice wounded: at Decorata, in southern Italy, when his carrier was blown up on a mine (I had earlier

travelled the same road on foot, having decided to leave my carrier behind); at the Moro River, where he was severely wounded, evacuated to England and Canada and eventually discharged after many months in hospital. He returned to England on the Hospital Ship, *Lady Nelson* (I too was a passenger). Despite a long and painful series of surgical operations, or perhaps because of them, he studied medicine and became a specialist in nuclear medicine. We lost touch with each other until the publication of my book, when he sent me a generous letter of congratulations. I responded:

> *November 3, 1988*
>
> *Dear Jerry:*
>
> *What a wonderful surprise to receive your letter!*
>
> *I vividly remember both you and George Garbutt aboard the Lady Nelson, lying terribly wounded in your bed, but still able to make light of your injuries. As mentioned in my book, it saddened me to see you struck down and sent home without recognition or remembrance. Indeed, I gave serious thought to dedicating my book to that forgotten legion who gave so much without any thought of return.*
>
> *You are certainly to be lauded for making such a success of your career after the hardships you suffered during the War. Perhaps the discipline we learned in the Army helped. Next to being shot at by Germans, I found that going back to school was the greatest challenge I ever endured!*
>
> *I enjoyed very much reading your Article in the Canadian Doctor. I heartily agree with your assessment of Quinine—the most bitter substance known to man. But I don't share your enthusiasm for ether.*
>
> *Sincerely,*

These are but nine examples of men who endured the harrowing experience of prolonged battle, but yet had the will, the determination, and yes, the guts, to shake it off and get on with their lives. They didn't complain and say, "Oh my God, I'm a goner. I can't face the real world again." Instead, they braced their shoulders and proclaimed to the world, "I'm lucky to have survived and I'm going to make the most of it. Sure it will be tough, but not as tough as the Germans."

Some took the pragmatic approach. "I'm damn well going to put to good use all the experience and training I have had in the Army. Hell, I've led one hundred men in battle; I've cared for them like a father. Am I going to be intimidated by one lousy Professor, by one stay-at-home job interviewer, by one slick psychiatrist, or by anyone? Not bloody likely. And furthermore, I'd be a fool not to take advantage of the Government's offer of free tuition. To hell with the wounds. Let them take care of themselves."

There are three glaring omissions in my short list of peacetime heroes. I have, with only one exception, given the names of officers only. Secondly, I do not mention those officers and men who stayed in the Army. The third omission will be revealed shortly

The reason for the second omission is obvious. The thrust of my submission is to show how those members of the Regiment who returned to civvy street after experiencing the horror of war made an outstanding success of their chosen careers. Those who remained in the Army also achieved distinction: MGen. Cammie Ware, DSO, MID; BGen. Stu Graham, MID; Colonel Bucko Watson, DSO, MC; Colonel Sam Potts, DSO; LCol. Willie Mulherin, GM, MID; LCol. P. D. Crofton, MID, to name a few. They too had to put their own hell behind them and soldier on as they had done in wartime. Both groups richly deserve all the success they achieved.

The omission of the names of Other Ranks who pursued brilliant civilian careers is deeply regretted, but is beyond the scope of this book. After the war, the members of the Regiment were scattered, not only throughout Canada, but literally around the world. It was impossible to keep in touch just with all your fellow officers, let alone the 120 men in your Company or 800 men in the Battalion. The few names of officers I have mentioned were personal friends whose careers I followed with great interest and admiration.

The third omission is the failure to mention the Canadian Nursing Sisters, whose tender loving care, even on the battlefield, restored to full health many a soldier who suffered grievous wounds. I was one of them. In my *Once a Patricia*, I frequently mention the dedication and skill of our nursing sisters whom I describe as "my 'angels,' so pertly dressed in their blue and white uniforms, with white veils and starched cuffs."

Of the many sisters who gave me a chance to return to action and later lead a normal life, I mention only one, Eva Wannop, for reasons which will appear. After I was wounded in Italy, I spent six months in hospitals in Italy, Africa and England, where I received plastic surgery to restore my shattered jaw. Sister Wannop was one of the "angels" in my ward. According to my diary, "Sister Wannop is taking excellent care of me and gives me all sorts of drinks. Very conscientious."

That was written in 1944. Forty-four years later, in 1988, in the course of doing research for my book, I established contact with Dr. Hoyle Campbell, a distinguished plastic surgeon in Toronto who had operated on me at Basingstoke Plastic Surgery Hospital in England. He still had many of his old records and allowed me to browse through them. As I was leaving he said, "By the way, did you know that your favourite nursing sister, Eva Wannop, lives in Toronto?"

I lost no time meeting her and found she was now retired after a full and rewarding life dedicated to caring for others. A few months later my book was published and Eva Wannop was my very special guest at the launching ceremony.

Regrettably, I lost touch with her until January 2001, when my dentist gave me the incredible news that Eva Wannop was one of his patients and had recently asked about my health! For the second time in 13 years, I made haste to see her and found she was about to celebrate her 90th birthday. It gave me much happiness to invite her for dinner to mark the occasion.

Since then, I have kept in touch and learned more about this remarkable lady. There is no doubt that she deserves a place in my short list of heroes who served their country in war and in peace.

The following are some of the highlights of her career. Eva was born January 27th, 1911, in Carmangay, Alberta. She took her training as a nurse in Calgary and served with the Royal Canadian Medical Corps from 1940 to 1945. She became a member of the plastic surgery team at Basingstoke Hospital, England, in 1942. (I was one of her patients in February, March and April 1944.)

Following WWII she returned to Canada and enrolled at the University of Toronto, where she studied Administration and Supervision. In the course of her career she attended two World Congresses on Occupational Health, in Vienna and Tokyo.

She also served as a volunteer worker in Palliative Care at Grace Hospital in Toronto for eight years, and in 1985 received a Certificate for adding to the quality of life in the community.

Now in her ninety-third year, Eva remains active. She tells me it doesn't seem possible but the calendar tells her it is true. She recently gave a talk to a group of "young" ladies in their forties and fifties. She spoke of her days at Basingstoke Plastic Hospital and was kind enough to read from my book.

In December 2002, Eva Wannop was awarded the Queen's Golden Jubilee Medal.

One last word on the vexing question of why some men were able to withstand the rigours of combat and not give in to the fear that everyone felt, whereas others could not cope with what a famous author, Farley Mowat, has called "the worm."

The subject is complex and many books have been written about stress, trauma and battle exhaustion. I do not intend to add to that list. In fact, you will observe that, in the foregoing pages, not once do I use the "S" word.

In an excellent article in the *Toronto Globe and Mail* (January 2002), MGen. Lewis MacKenzie, Canada's Peacekeeper nonpareil, and incidentally a Patricia, gave an insight into why Canadian Peacekeepers in Croatia suffered stress casualties when those in Sarajevo did not. I wrote a letter congratulating him on his frank opinion. I quote from my letter, not because it offers any intellectual treatise or academic theory on the subject, but because it is based on the best approach of all—experience.

February 4, 2000
Dear Lew:
Bravo! Your article in the Globe & Mail was right on the money.

There's altogether too much emphasis on "stress" today, not only in the Army, but at home, in the workplace, in sports and in just about every other activity.

I can't remember ever hearing the word used in WWII, although we no doubt suffered from it. When you've spent weeks and even months seeing your comrades blown to bits, enduring painful wounds, extremes of heat and cold, suffering from lack of sleep and food—when you've survived all these and other challenges, then I think the "S" word might be appropriate.

A few years ago I gave a lecture at the Staff College in Kingston on the Realities of Combat. At the end of my talk, the first question was, "How stressful was combat and how did I deal with it?" I bit my tongue and said we never used the word. Yes, we had some cases of battle fatigue, but it was not a big issue. We all suffered it to some extent and most of us learned to cope. The few who couldn't were sent down the line to "A" or "B" Echelon for a few days rest before returning to the fray.

The "S" word came up again at a PPCLI reunion in Calgary. I was on a panel and the new officers fired questions at us. The first one to me was, "What was the most stressful thing for you?" Without a moment's hesitation I replied, "The Adjutant."

It brought down the house. I explained that when I was the Scout Officer, the Adjutant didn't suffer fools gladly (including me!).

You're absolutely right that the thing which keeps a soldier from going round the bend is the support of his comrades as well as a determination not to let them down, and

> *pride of Regiment. As you know, I considered the Regiment my home and I always fought long and hard to return after my various "A.W.L. escapades."*
>
> *In line with your theory, I can relate a personal experience. The only time the "S" word almost got to me was when I retired from the Patricias and returned home after an absence of six years. It took a long time to learn how to cope with this strange milieu without the support of my men and the camaraderie of my brother officers.*
>
> *Thanks for your wise words. Every soldier returning home should read them.*
>
> *Sincerely,*

* * *

We now return to my 1994 Pilgrimage, where I was left surveying the ruins of the Palazzo San Giacomo, on the Lamone River. The next obstacle would be the Naviglio Canal, where I had a contretemps with a mortar bomb in 1944, as already described. I realized I could not possibly locate the exact spot where I had been wounded, but I wanted to make one more advance along that road to satisfy myself that I was the ultimate victor in that engagement.

Against all odds, I did actually find the approximate place where I had absorbed some Jerry lead. The farmhouse where the RAP had been set up and where Capt. Steve Worobetz had bandaged my wound was still there, where it should be. I thought that I might even see a bronze plaque, commemorating the great event! But no such memento did I find. Indeed, the farmer had not even known that Canadians had one time passed this way.

And so it was at each of the rivers I crossed. None of the people I spoke to had any knowledge about the terrible casualties the Canadians had suffered in driving the hated *tedeschi* from their lands. A few old timers remembered there had been a war but it was so long ago they had forgotten the details. However, when I reached the Senio River where the Regiment had established its Winter Line, the memory of the Patricias was still alive and well, as will be described.

Another curious thing about all the bitter fighting in the Romagna is that it has received little interest or respect from historians—much the same situation as one finds with the battles of San Fortunato. On the other hand, the Liri Valley, the Hitler Line and Ortona have been the subjects of books, articles and staff studies. The reason is obvious. The battles of the Savio, Lamone, Naviglio and the other river crossings in late 1944 were of no interest to the press.

After D-Day, all the attention of the war correspondents was focused on the campaign in northwest Europe, where the action was.

The battles of the isolated, under-strength Canadian Corps in Italy, through the Romagna mud and over countless rivers, lacked the glamour of large armies scoring great victories by brilliant tactical manoeuvres in Northwest Europe. The fact that the Canadians in Italy had crossed another river and suffered casualties was of no interest to anyone, except, of course, to the casualties themselves and their next-of-kin. Even the fact that almost 6,000 Canadians were being killed in Italy was generally overlooked during the war and afterwards, compared to the heavier casualties of the Second Front.

On January 31st, 1945, I returned to the Regiment as previously related, and was posted to D Company as Second-in-Command. Two weeks later the Battalion moved from its rest area in Russi to occupy positions in fortified houses on the flats just below the high flood banks of the Senio River.

The Germans occupied the near bank of the river, which rose 35 feet above the plain and gave the enemy a commanding view of our position. Movement was restricted to night-time when supplies, food and ammunition were brought forward, along carefully-marked lines, through the heavily mined and booby-trapped positions.

It was exhilarating to be so close to the foe that when they were hit by our fire I could hear their shouts and screams. Our lives were also enlivened by a platoon of Italians attached to our company. These irregular Partigiani loved to wander around the front at night and pick up the odd prisoner from the other side.

German snipers were very active, but apparently not too well trained in their deadly art. Few of our troops were felled by these supposed sharpshooters, though we gave them not a few fleeting opportunities in an effort to locate their positions.

Of more concern were the MG42s firing on fixed lines. One corner of my *casa* was a favourite target for these machine gunners; each night it was hotter than the action in Piccadilly Circus on a Saturday evening.

Another favourite pastime of the Germans was to roll Teller mines down the river embankment into our heavily-sandbagged houses. Usually the mines became ensnarled in obstacles placed in front of our strongholds, or the mines simply didn't explode on contact. But when they did, they gave our *casas* a severe test.

Then, on February 12th, 1945, after 2 years as a Patricia Lieutenant, I was finally promoted to Captain. I can't think of anything before or since that has given me such a feeling of satisfaction. Instantly, I knew I would survive the war.

My good mood was cut short by a tragic accident. Sgt. Goodburn, of the Machine Gun Platoon, and five other men were wounded when several of our 3-inch mortar bombs fell short. Sgt. Goodburn died the next day. The fault lay not with our expert mortar crew, but with the ammunition, which was defective. I tried to see him before he died, but I was too late. I was told that even in his extremity he was able to cast a parting shaft of wit at the Mortar Platoon: "First time they've ever been on target."

Forty-three years later, in January 1998, I noticed the following request in the *Legion Magazine*:

> *Book wanted*—Once A Patricia *by Col. Charles Sydney Frost. Muriel Hutchins, Box 98, Napinka, Manitoba, R0M 1N0*

I promptly wrote Muriel Hutchins saying I had a few copies left, gave her the price and forgot about the matter. About a month later, I received the following letter which shook me to the core.

> *Dear Mr. Sydney Frost:*
>
> *Thank you very much for answering my subscription in the Legion Magazine for a copy of* Once A Patricia. *Apparently you were a very close friend of my brother Wilfred. He was 23 years old when shot by his own men (practice shooting) on 15th Feb. and died on 16th Feb.*
>
> *I understand you were going to visit him in hospital but unfortunately you were called away on some other business and Wilfred died before you got to see him. I have at least 10 Legion members, also veterans, trying to locate the book for me, with no luck.*
>
> *Please oblige me and send me a copy. I will always be very grateful to you.*
>
> *Sincerely,*
Mrs. Muriel Hutchins

It will be quite apparent why I was so overwhelmed by this letter from a sister of my comrade. For all these years she had harboured the thought that her dear brother had somehow been "shot by his own men." I hastened to reply but it was not an easy letter to write. The task saddened me but I was gratified that I had been given this opportunity to set the record straight and let her know what a fine soldier Wilfred had been and how much I thought of him. I am taking the liberty of quoting my letter in full, not because it has any particular merit, but because it will stand as an enduring tribute to H17155 Sgt. W. Goodburn, my friend and comrade.

February 16, 1998

Dear Muriel:

I received your letter with considerable surprise and rather mixed emotions. I was happy to hear from the sister of a close comrade of mine during the War, but it brought back sad memories of the terrible cost of that War in terms of human suffering and the loss of so many friends, particularly your brother Wilfred.

Wilfred joined the Regiment in Sicily on August 16th, 1943, when we were at rest at a little village called Militello. He was with the Regiment when it crossed the Strait of Messina and landed on the shores of Italy—one of the first soldiers to set foot on the continent of Europe. He fought all the way up the Italian Peninsula, including some of the worst battles at Ortona. He soon made his mark as a fine soldier and eventually won his sergeant's stripes. We knew each other in Sicily and southern Italy, when I was in charge of the Scout Platoon, but unfortunately I was seriously wounded in October 1943 and sent back to England to recover. I rejoined the Regiment a year later and took over command of the MMG (Medium Machine Gun) Platoon in October, 1944, when we were out of the line at a little fishing village on the Adriatic coast, named Cattolica, a few miles south of Rimini.

I was happy to find that Wilfred was now a sergeant and in charge of No. 1 Section of the MMG Platoon. We became good friends and he taught me a lot about machine guns. Even though I was an officer and supposed to know something about machine guns, I had never fired them in action and I appreciated his knowledge and help.

He continued to command No. 1 Section until his tragic death on February 16th, 1945. In the meantime, I had been wounded again but returned once more to the Regiment in January 1945. Another officer had taken over the MMG Platoon, so I was made a captain and became Second-in-Command of D Company. The Regiment was now in its Winter Line along the Senio River, preparing for the last great attack to push the Germans out of Italy and end the War. Except for shelling and night patrols, there was little action on either side. Whenever I could, I visited my old comrades in the MMG Platoon and reminisced with your brother about our shared experiences. Things were pretty relaxed and we all looked forward to the end of the War and coming home. Sadly, for some of us it was not to be.

In your letter you mention that Wilfred was shot by his own men (practice shooting). While I understand what you meant, it did not happen the way you describe it. What happened was that during the day both sides would fire a few shells or mortar bombs against the other side to see if the rounds were on target. If not, corrections would be made and then later, when you least expected it, the other side would plaster your area with bombs.

In Wilfred's case, our own Mortar Platoon was firing their mortars in preparation for a shoot early the next morning. Unfortunately, some of the bombs were defective and one landed on the MMG Platoon. Six men were wounded including Wilfred who died the next day. Such a terrible tragedy. By the time I heard of it, it was too late and I have always regretted the fact I was unable to be with him when he died. I can do no better than quote from my book at page 396:

"This was a sad blow to me. Sgt. Goodburn and I had been through good times and bad and had always got along well together. He was undoubtedly one of the mainstays of the MMG Platoon and was much liked and admired for his ready wit and soldierly qualities."

You will find other references to Wilfred at pages 311, 312, 313 and 320. They are much too short. He deserves much more.

I enclose a copy of my book which I have inscribed to you in memory of your brother. I also enclose a few of the Book Reviews I received. I thank you for your cheque but I am sure you will understand that I could not possibly accept any payment. I return the cheque herewith, which I have cancelled.

I should mention that I had the honour, in 1989, of sponsoring your brother's name in the PPCLI Memorial Hall of Honour. The following plaque appears among the names of our fallen comrades:

H17155 Sgt. W. Goodburn
16 February 1945

I enclose a copy of a letter from the President of the Association, dated February 14th, 1989 describing the PPCLI Memorial Hall of Honour.

> *As I said at the outset, this has been a very emotional experience for me. Sadness to be sure, but I am very gratified to have this chance to tell you something about your brother's fine record with the Regiment.*
>
> *I cannot resist observing that I am writing this letter fifty-three years, to the day, since the death of my comrade and friend. In a way, it helps to atone for my not being at his side on February 15th, 1945. His sacrifice will never be forgotten.*
>
> *Sincerely,*

The story of Sgt. Goodburn is not finished and, in fact, will never end. Muriel Hutchins and I have become "pen pals" and keep in touch regularly. She has sent me several photos of Wilfred as well as a copy of a Certificate issued by the Manitoba Government in 1995. It states that a lake has been named in his honour—Goodburn Lake.

Shortly after I returned to the Regiment, on January 31st, 1945, I received word that another comrade and friend had been wounded, my batman Private Mel Murdy. It is perhaps difficult for someone who has not served in the Army in WWII to understand why an officer needed a "servant," or a "go for," which the name might imply.

Batmen were, in fact, a special breed whose services went far beyond the master-servant relationship. Besides looking after and cleaning an officer's kit and equipment, thus freeing him to look after his men, a batman was an invaluable, unofficial link between the officer and the rest of the platoon.

Whenever I was upset about some action, or lack of action, by the platoon, and was considering drastic steps to rectify the matter, Murdy would pass the word that "the lieutenant was going to raise hell if the mess wasn't cleaned up pronto." Likewise, if the platoon had some legitimate beef about me, about something I had done or not done, Murdy would discreetly (and sometimes not so discreetly) suggest that I smarten up.

These underground messages, via Murdy, saved everyone a lot of unnecessary confrontation and grief, and made for a happy platoon. No one considered Murdy to be an "informer," and he was, in fact, shown a lot of respect by the men.

Another service Murdy rendered was to offer suggestions on how to improve the welfare of the platoon. "We're getting low on cigarettes; haven't had a mobile bath in a month; all the other platoons are going on leave; when's our next smoker?" On the other hand, he also acted as a good sounding board on which to bounce off my own ideas on how to keep the platoon in good humour.

Murdy, however, was not just a service type; he also had an important role in action: carrying and operating the 38 wireless set, and acting as my personal bodyguard. In an emergency, he could also man the Vickers guns and drive a carrier.

Mel Murdy had joined the Battalion in 1942 and was one of the first to be wounded in Sicily. A tough little guy, he was somewhat older and had seen much more action than I had. In his mind this allowed him to bully, or "mother" me to death, depending on his mood. He would sometimes go to great lengths to do some little act he thought would please me. For example, early in the morning, he would wake me up with a cup of tea, which he would place beside my inert form curled up in a bed roll or blanket. It became a ritual that he was determined should continue, even in action, when I needed all the sleep I could get.

I tried to explain to Murdy that while I appreciated his fine service, I needed my sleep more than the tea. Still the brew appeared each morning before dawn. Finally, I had to tell him the tea was cold and not fit for a mule to drink. He was to cease and desist forthwith.

"Sir," smiled Murdy with a sly wink, "you're not supposed to drink the stuff. Just stick your finger in the cup. When it's cold, you know it's time to get up."

Perhaps this short digression in praise of batmen, and Murdy in particular, will help my reader understand the bond which had grown between us. I was devastated when I learned that he had been badly wounded. He was evacuated to England but I never knew what finally happened to him—until 44 years later, October 6, 1989.

On that day, out of the blue, I received a telephone call. "Hello, this is Cathy Murdy from Manitou, Manitoba. My father was your batman in the war. He's with me now and would like to speak with you."

I was slightly stunned but managed to stammer, "That's great, but what took him so long?"

Murdy came on the line and told me the incredible story of his life after he was wounded in January 1945. I am going to repeat it at length because it is a tale of pluck, determination and will to survive that might encourage others.

He was severely wounded in Bagnacavallo by a shell. His back was broken and he spent a long period in hospitals in Italy, England and Canada. The doctors told him he would never walk again. How wrong they were. He worked for Beaver Lumber for 17 years and then with the Municipality for 10 years more. He learned to play golf. He married an English girl, and had five children, fourteen grandchildren and four great grandchildren. Not bad for a man who was not supposed to walk.

We talked for a long time and he promised to visit me as soon as he could arrange for one of his children to do the driving. His wife had recently passed away. Over the next few days, I spoke with his two daughters. They confirmed that he was indeed a tough little guy and told me how badly he had been wounded. He was really keen to see me again and one of them would drive the car.

In the meantime, I sent him a copy of *Once a Patricia* and a letter, from which I quote:

> *Dear Murdy:*
>
> *It was quite a thrill to speak with you. At the PPCLI Reunion in Calgary I was told by several people that you had either died from your wounds or passed away a few years after the war. So you can imagine my surprise when your daughter announced that my batman was on the line!*
>
> *I have sent you an autographed copy of* Once a Patricia *by separate mail. You will notice that you have the honour (I hope you will consider it as such) to be mentioned on 14 pages of my book and in many cases the entire page is about you. In fact, there are more references to you than there are to my first Commanding Officer, Lieut Colonel Ware.*
>
> *So obviously you were a very important part of my life in those days. I only hope I have given you adequate recognition for the support and advice you gave me while I commanded the MMG platoon. If not, knowing you, you will probably tell me!*
>
> *I congratulate you on surviving a serious wound that would have incapacitated most men, and on leading a full and active life. I am surprised you are only 71 as I always thought you were so much older (and wiser) than me. But, of course, you saw much more action and joined the PPCLI long before I appeared on the scene.*
>
> *According to my records, you were TOS the Regiment on March 12th, 1942. You were wounded on July 10th, 1943, and again on January 7th, 1944, when you were SOS.*
>
> *Since writing my book I have heard from a great number of Patricias, including several from our MMG platoon. You may remember Sgt. Russ Mableson. He was the platoon sergeant. His daughter phoned to order a copy of my book for Christmas.*
>
> *Also, a Pte. Lawrence Sexsmith phoned me about the book. He joined the MMG platoon in Cattolica and was a good friend of Cpl. Kilborn and Sgt. Goodburn (who was later killed).*

> *Another member of the MMG platoon was Pte. Roy (Bud) Drury. He was my dispatch rider. I saw him at the Reunion in Calgary and at the Reception in Ottawa when the new postage stamp commemorating the Regiment was issued.*
>
> *One of the wonderful things about having the book published is hearing from so many old friends, including yourself. I answer all the letters even though I am still practising law and leading a pretty active life including a fair amount of travelling. (I've been back to Italy and Holland five or six times, most recently last May.)*
>
> *If you are ever passing through Toronto, please get in touch with me. We have lots to talk about. I will certainly set aside an evening for us to re-fight the battles in the Italian Romagna. How is your Italian lingo?*
>
> *Sincerely,*

We kept in touch, but for various reasons Murdy was not able to make travel arrangements to drive east until the spring of 1992. On April 26th, he phoned to say that he and daughter Laura, accompanied by two of his Legion friends, would arrive in Toronto on May 19th and be staying at a local motel. I suggested that I should lay in a good supply of his favourite "heart starter" (as LCol. Clark used to call strong drink).

Murdy replied, "Not to worry. I've given up drinking and smoking, and anyway, I don't need to worry about money. Besides my pension, I just won a lottery."

I couldn't think of a person more deserving.

On May 20th, 1992, I was in the lobby of the Radisson Hotel waiting for Murdy to appear and wondering if I would recognize him after 48 years. The elevator doors opened and a short, solid, distinguished-looking Murdy emerged in a smart Legion blazer. He greeted me warmly enough but with a touch of respect. "Sir, it's been a long time."

It didn't take long for all those years to melt away as we talked about our past deeds and misdeeds in typical "soldier-speak" but tempered with the passage of time. After all, we were both fathers and grandfathers. The presence of his daughter Laura was a welcome aid to our failing memories and kept us on track.

Both Murdy and Laura had one request. They wanted to visit Hornings Mills, where Murdy's parents lived before making the long trek out west at the turn of the century. Laura, as well as having a degree in social work, was very interested in genealogy. So we made a short trek to the town and Laura was able to establish contact with some descendants of pioneers who knew the Murdy family. It was a wonderful day but we parted with regret, knowing it would not happen again. I presented Murdy with photos of the Monument in Sicily which had been erected during my Pilgrimage the year before. This almost brought tears to his eyes as he said, "Sir, I was first wounded on the beaches within sight of that Monument."

Then it was my turn to be surprised. Laura handed me a photo of her son Pat LeBlanc, who had recently joined the PPCLI. It was an inspiring finish to a remarkable day.

One further episode in the Murdy story remains. He was so impressed with the Monument in Sicily that he had the pictures framed in a large plaque with a French grey backing. Included in the frame is an account of the building of the Monument. He then presented the plaque to the Regimental Museum in Calgary on behalf of himself and his old Platoon Commander. And there it rests today.

We continued to keep in touch until May 4th, 1997, when he phoned to say he had just been in a car accident and his car had been a complete write-off but he was okay.

On May 12th, his son Marvin and daughter Laura phoned. Murdy was dead.

He had fought the good fight right up to the end.
Rest in Peace, Dear Comrade.

* * *

We now return to the Senio River in February 1945, when I finally received my captaincy. Within two weeks, the Battalion was secretly withdrawn from the line and embussed south along the Adriatic coast to a seaside resort at San Benedetto. The move, according to Orders, was a new training ground, but the troops knew that something big was in the air. Rumours floated around. We were going to Yugoslavia or even to Greece.

After a short rest, we were on the move again, westward to Foligno in the heart of the Apennines, where the Battalion had paused on its way to the Gothic Line in August. Then northwest through the centre of the mountains, past Perugia (where I had been in hospital only 5 weeks earlier) and along the east side of Lake Trasimene to Arezza. This was the route the Regiment had taken in August, but going in the opposite direction to a new battlefield. Now things really were not kosher and the troops knew that we were not on a training exercise. But where were we going, and why?

Next evening, we arrived at Pontesieve, about 15 miles east of Florence. In the morning, we were away before daybreak, and entered the Tuscany Plains. In the distance we spotted the most famous tilted

PILGRIMAGE—1994

tower in the world and camped in a forest not far from Pisa. The troops could not be kept in suspense any longer. On March 9th, we were given the big secret—we were on our way to France and then Germany to join First Canadian Army in the final battles to end the war.

As it turned out, we would actually end up in Holland and be given a major role in defeating the Germans in that country and saving the Dutch from starvation. But that is another story, to be found in later chapters of this book.

The final part of my 1994 Pilgrimage has still to be told. After my visit to the miserable remains of the Palazzo San Giacomo on the Lamone River, I drove toward the Winter Line along the Senio River, north of Bagnacavallo.

Here, the Patricias had spent the better part of January and February, 1945, before being withdrawn and moved to Holland. My D Company had occupied fortified houses in the flats, only a few yards from the German positions on the high flood banks. Company H.Q. was set up in a house in a small village near the dykes.

In 1985, I had visited the village and been given a warm welcome. Of course they remembered the *soldati canadese*. One of the villagers had been attached to my company as a *Partigiani*. He insisted that he show me their position—in a cemetery! I remembered where it was but let him lead me to it. To some, a cemetery may seem to be an unlucky place for a soldier, but cemeteries were highly desired positions because of the strong vaults and high walls. We then visited my company H.Q. which was not difficult to find. It was in the same condition as when I had left it in 1945—pockmarked with shell holes and abandoned.

Now it was 1994 and again I was welcomed with open arms by the villagers. Some even remembered my last visit in 1985, and my name. We made the "grand tour" of my company positions and stood on the river banks where the Germans had been so close to my platoon positions we could smell their cooking from our houses nestled into the river bank. Why we hadn't been blown to our Valhalla and the Germans to theirs remained a mystery. Then I was shown my company H.Q., still in the same condition. I muttered my favourite proverb. "The more things change, the more they remain the same," but it was lost on my Italian guide. I had said it in French, not knowing the Italian equivalent.

Thus ended my 1994 Pilgrimage to the rivers and battlefields of the Romagna. There remained but one mission yet to be fulfilled—the cemeteries.

The bloody battles of the rivers in the Romagna yielded the dead who are buried mainly in these War Cemeteries. The figures shown are the numbers of Canadians in each. The figures in brackets are the numbers of Patricias.

Villanova — 206 (none)
Ravenna — 438 (37)
Cesena — 307 (11)

In addition, there is the Argenta Gap War Cemetery, north of Ravenna, which contains the graves of 75 Canadian soldiers and airmen, including 2 Patricias. These Canadians did not fight in this area, but were brought there from battlefield graves to the south.

Altogether more than 1,000 Canadians died fighting in the mud and rivers of the Romagna.

From the Senio River, I retraced my steps south to the infamous Savio River in order to visit the Cemetery at Cesena, on Highway No. 9 about 12 miles from the coast. Of the eleven Patricias buried there, I mention only four, chosen at random:

> *Cpl. Alastair Duncan McLeod — Age 21, killed October 20th, 1944*
> *Pte. Julius Allan Youngren — killed October 20th, 1944*
> *Sgt. Jack Nile — killed October 22nd, 1944*
> *Pte. Harvey Robinson — Age 23, killed November 6th, 1944*

The Ravenna Cemetery is near Highway No. 16, only a few miles from the coast. I paid my respects at each of the 37 Patricia graves, including the following, again chosen at random, except the three officers who were personal friends:

> *Lt. Vaughan Stuart Allan — Age 22, killed December 15th, 1944.* Vaughan was a classmate of mine at RMC
> *Lt. Mervin Edward Garrity — killed December 20th, 1944*
> *Lt. William Anthony Groomes — killed January 4th, 1945*
> *Pte. William H. Charry — Age 20, killed December 10th, 1944*
> *Pte. Reginald Roy Blair — Age 20, killed December 20th, 1944*
> *Sgt. William Ross Howard — Age 22, killed January 4th, 1945*
> *Pte. Gisli Sigurdur Stefanson — killed February 23rd, 1945*
> *Cpl. John Gates — killed December 22nd, 1944*

PILGRIMAGE—1994

The Cemetery at Villanova has been described as a memorial to the fallen of the 5th Division, as 85 members of two battalions of this division are buried there.

The last cemetery in this area, the one at the Argenta Gap, had a special significance for me. My friend and comrade, Sgt. Wilfred Goodburn, mentioned several times in this narrative, is buried there. I had searched for his grave at the three other cemeteries without success. Then I decided to visit Argenta Gap on Highway 16, about 30 miles north of Ravenna, west of Lake Comacchio. This area is far removed from the Winter Line along the Senio River where Sgt. Goodburn was killed. My feelings can perhaps be imagined when I finally found his grave. With almost overwhelming grief I stood to attention and let all those lost years roll away until we were together in our platoon advancing to our next objective. I left with heavy heart but satisfied my quest had not been in vain.

With my visit to Argenta Gap Cemetery concluded, I had at last honoured the covenant I had long ago made with myself to visit the graves of my comrades and friends throughout Italy and Sicily. It had been a sad but revealing experience that would stay with me for the rest of my life. Sad, because so many fine men had been struck down in the prime of life, and yet, revealing, because of the knowledge that their sacrifice was being honoured and would be remembered for all time in these beautiful gardens.

Lugo, on the far side of the Senio River, had always exerted a strange fascination for me. During the war, it was held by the Germans, who used it as a supply depot and rest centre for their troops manning the Senio River, just as we used Bagnacavallo on our side of the river for the same purposes.

Lugo was so close to our position that every night we could hear lorries and tanks milling about its streets with impunity. I could never understand why our heavy artillery hardly ever shelled the place. A good, solid barrage would have flattened it and the German soldiers.

For some reason, the Staff issued us aerial photos of Lugo that clearly showed vehicles and tanks harboured there; also large buildings, a sports stadium, oil tanks and other sensitive targets. It was maddening not to be able to do something about it.

The time at last arrived, in 1994, when I could do something about it. I had brought with me the aerial photos from 1944 and I intended to occupy the town, in particular the football field which had so annoyed me 50 years earlier.

I drove south from Argenta to Ravenna, then west to Bagnacavallo, the Senio River and Lugo on the other side. For a moment I wondered whether the old bridge had been rebuilt but I didn't slow down to look for it. Across a fine, new bridge I sailed in my Mercedes-Benz and landed in Lugo. I whipped out my aerial photo for direction and was soon at the entrance to the sports stadium. I felt like getting out and running a few laps to consolidate my capture of the place, but the passage of half a century proved as tough an obstacle to my body as the German Army had been 50 years earlier. I was content to sit in the bleachers and have a good laugh. But as I looked around the place I imagined it filled with 10,000 German soldiers. I felt like yelling to our artillery, "For God's sake bring down a Mike target now and flatten the SOBs."

My command was 50 years too late. Anyway, my war-like mood was quickly dampened when I saw my German automobile waiting for me to depart.

From Lugo, I took the Autostrada E45 to Bologna. I remembered how our Generals had made grandiose plans for us to capture the place in 1944 and even advance to Venice. Unfortunately, they had overlooked several factors that nullified their schemes—the lousy weather, the fortified rivers and the desperate Germans.

As I lounged in a fashionable restaurant in Bologna, enjoying my spaghetti Bolognese, I regretted that we had not tried a little harder to capture Bologna. It is renowned for its fine *ristoranti* and *trattorie*.

I longed to sojourn in this fine old city known as *La Dotta* (the learned one) where the first university was founded in 1158. But I had a date with a plane leaving Rome the next day.

As I pondered my route, I remembered one of Professor Carmelo Nigro's sayings, "*Tutte le strade portano a Roma*" (All roads lead to Rome.) True enough, but in my case I first wanted to follow the route the Patricias had taken to Florence after the Hitler Line, but going in reverse.

From Florence, I passed through Siena, then travelled south-west to meet the A1 and follow it south past the west side of Lake Trasimeno where the Patricias had bivouacked on their way north. Continuing south, the highway by-passed Orvieto and soon the Eternal City was within my grasp.

I had planned to allow myself a few days in Rome to relax and do some sight-seeing. I felt I had earned a rest after a gruelling 2,443 miles and switching automobiles in the middle of the night due to a breakdown in the mountains near Salerno.

With the completion of this Pilgrimage and all the prior ones, I had now faithfully followed the entire route of the Patricias from Pachino in Sicily to Florence and the Senio River in northern Italy, except for a small section in southern Italy along the Ionian coast, from Catanzaro to Potenza. In addition, I had now visited all the battlefields and all the main War Cemeteries (some more than once) where Canadian soldiers are buried. A few points of interest not directly connected with the battles of the Regiment had not been explored, such as Pisa and Leghorn (where the Regiment left Italy for France), San Benedetto on the Adriatic coast (where the Regiment paused on its trek to Leghorn from the Romagna), and beautiful San Marino, an ancient republic perched on a precipice overlooking Rimini.

As my plane headed for home, I knew I had to return some day to this land where I suffered so much pain and misery, and yet gained knowledge and experience that stood me in good stead for the rest of my life; where I matured from youth to man and learned to appreciate and enjoy the culture and traditions of another people—*Arrivederci Roma.*

Chapter XII

PILGRIMAGE—1997

It will be remembered that my decision to make a Pilgrimage in 1997 was the result of an invitation I received in 1996 from my Sicilian friend, Antonino Lauretta. He invited me to attend a symposium of writers and artists to be held later that year in Ispica. This was not quite my line but it incited me to make one more Pilgrimage to Sicily the following year.

As my plans developed, my proposed trip to Sicily became a grand tour of the whole of Italy. I would hire a Fiat and imagine I was once again leading the Regiment in my scout car from the beaches of Sicily to Florence in northern Italy. And that is exactly what I did in 1997. But this time, I would also visit the points of interest that I had missed on earlier trips.

I landed in Rome on May 18th after an $8^1/_2$ hour direct flight from Toronto. Next day I was away smartly at first light in my scout car (the Fiat) heading south along the A1 Autostrada toward Frosinone, where the Patricias had come to rest in June 1944, after the tragic Hitler Line. At Frosinone, I turned off the A1 onto the venerable Highway 6 and soon arrived at Aquino, where the Regiment had suffered so grievously on May 23rd. The formidable mass of Monte Cassino loomed on my left, topped by its famous Abbey, faithfully and lovingly restored to its original estate after its destruction by Allied bombers.

At the Cassino War Cemetery, I stopped once more to pay my respects at the graves of the 75 Patricias who fell in the Hitler Line.

Then back to the Autostrada for a speedy trip to Naples and Monte Vesuvio, with a mandatory halt at Pompei. On past occasions I had joined the hordes of tourists milling about, but this time I found a knowledgeable guide who spoke fair English. She explained how an earthquake in A.D. 63 did much damage before the eruption of

Vesuvius in A.D. 79 buried the city under cinders and ashes. So completely were the ruins preserved that the colours of the wall paintings were as fresh as they had been when disaster struck. Then, with a shy smile, she announced that a recent excavation had unearthed a rather pornographic painting of the Roman God Priapus, but the tourists would have to pay a special fee of only 2,000 lire ($2.00) to see it. The first to step forward were two old ladies, followed by a few men, including myself. We were escorted to a small darkened room, the lights were turned on, and lo and behold, we were greeted by a painting of the naked form of the god in the act of weighing his gigantic penis—at least two feet long. Above the gasps and grunts of the tourists the voice of one of the old ladies rang out, "Blimey, me 'usband never 'ad one that big." Unfortunately, we were not allowed to take pictures.

Refreshed by this change of scenery, I vaulted into my Fiat and headed for Sorrento and the Amalfi Drive. It will be recalled that on a prior trip I had driven around the rocky peninsula, taking the inside lane as the narrow road skirted cliffs, crossed gullies and viaducts, and disappeared into long, dark tunnels. I pitied the drivers coming the other way, on the outside lane with nothing but a small strip of grass between them and a 500-foot drop to the sea below.

Emboldened by the old Roman god, I decided to tackle the Amalfi Drive by way of the outside lane, hoping that I might get a better view of the couple making love on the beach that I had seen on my last trip around the peninsula. Alas, it was cold and the beach deserted.

At the base of the Sorrento Peninsula lies the city of Salerno, the site of the landing in September 1943 of the U.S. Fifth Army under General Mark Clark. After meeting stiff opposition from the Germans, the Fifth Army consolidated its beachhead and linked up with the Eighth Army pressing north.

Salerno and the Amalfi Drive, it will be recalled, were popular leave centres after the Germans withdrew, especially for Canadian doctors and nurses stationed at nearby Avellino. It was an appropriate venue for the medical profession. In the eleventh century, Salerno was the medical centre of the western world and boasted the first University of Medicine. It is doubtful, however, that the doctors and nurses availed themselves of such knowledge. They likely followed other pursuits only remotely connected to medicine.

It was time to move on and head for Sicily, where friends in Ispica awaited my arrival. Following the popular A3 Strada del Sole, I soon reached Reggio di Calabria, crossed the Strait of Messina, and came to rest in Taormina. My stay in Sicily has been described in Chapter VI and will not be repeated.

On June 1st, I left Taormina in my sturdy "scout car" and, following the A3 again, arrived at Potenza, a respectable drive of 300 miles plus the trip by ferry across the Strait. In the interest of saving time, I avoided the tortuous route the Regiment had taken (and which I had followed previously) through the mountains and across chasms of the Aspromonte Range. In 1943, the Battalion had rested at Potenza after their arduous advance. Ahead lay more of the same kind of terrain and circuitous routes. The Germans had taken advantage of every obstacle and mined every approach. With a fine touch of humour coupled with irony, General Alexander had summed up what the Patricias faced. "All roads lead to Rome," said the General, "but all the roads are mined." It was a clever switch of the proverb Professor Carmelo Nigro had often quoted.

From Potenza, I could not resist making one more visit to Castello di Lagopesole and marvelling at the skill of the thirteenth-century engineers who had erected this immense fortress for a German, Frederick II. But it also reminded me that WWII was not the first time this beautiful country had been occupied by the Germans.

I continued north in my scout car to Troia and then to Alberona, Baselice, Decorata, Cercemaggiore, La Rocca and finally Campobasso, names that have often appeared in this narrative, but names that will always have special meaning for me and all Patricias.

At Campobasso, I had an important decision to make. Would I, or would I not, make one last visit to Frosolone, where my advance in 1943 had been terminated by a German bullet? I am happy to say that I firmly rejected any further visits to that place. The catharsis that my friend LCol. Jeff. Williams had predicted had occurred. No longer did I feel compelled to return and find my long-lost Beretta pistol. The memory of that fateful day had been erased from my mind.

Next morning, I drove east to Termoli on the Adriatic coast and then north to Ortona.

En route, I paused at the Moro River Cemetery, where 65 Patricias, who died in the bitter fighting at the Moro River, Villa Rogatti, Vino Ridge and the Gully, are buried. I remembered how I had been spared that fate. While the Regiment was fighting these battles and enduring a cold and miserable winter in positions north of Ortona, I was comfortably ensconced in a warm hospital ward in Algiers.

My next objective was San Benedetto, a seaside resort on the Adriatic coast roughly 60 miles north of Ortona. I have seldom referred to San Benedetto because it was not a battlefield. After Ortona, the Patricias were moved in May 1944, in great secrecy, to the Liri Valley south of Rome, to take part in the battle of the Hitler Line. Their next battleground was the Gothic Line and Rimini, and then the Romagna where they fought their way over countless rivers to the Senio Winter Line. It was not until March 1945, that the Regiment left the Senio River and rested at San Benedetto on its way to Leghorn, where it embarked for Marseilles to take part in the final battles in northwest Europe.

These interludes between battles were euphemistically called "rest and recreation" periods, but in reality there was little rest. Whether the pursuits of the soldiers could be termed "recreation" was a matter of semantics. As for the officers, it was mandatory, in rest areas, to convene at least one mess dinner. As I recall, the one at San Benedetto was memorable. After a six-course meal with six different wines, brandy and cigars, the officers engaged in a little indoor wrestling. Across the street from the restaurant, the waters of the Adriatic beckoned to cool down the participants. They madly dashed out the door, crossed the road, and made beautiful swan dives over the high seawall. At the last instant, they realized the tide was out. Such was their athletic ability that they converted the dive into a harmless headroll and tumbled down to the water's edge, thus saving the Regiment countless hours practising the slow march with muffled drums.

Forty years later, during my 1985 Pilgrimage, I stopped for lunch at San Benedetto and went looking for the restaurant where the officers had convened their historic mess dinner. With the help of a member of the Carabinieri, I soon found it—the Hotel Progresso. The place had not yet opened for the season but I banged on the door and the owner appeared. In a few words I introduced myself and asked if he remembered the mess dinner.

Of course he did. How could he forget it. He described the event with obvious delight.

"The tables were arranged so—" he described a U shape. "The Colonel sat at the head with his senior officers on each side. You were there too as the ... chairman?"

"No, the Mess President."

"Yes, that's it. The Mess President. You proposed so many toasts that I believe we ran out of wine. Then you started on the liqueurs. Same thing happened."

"What then?" I asked, innocently.

"Well, a most incredible thing happened. Those officers who could still walk decided they should go for a swim, in their uniforms. So they staggered out the door, crossed the road and dove over the seawall."

"Yes?"

"Signor, there was no sea on the other side of the wall. The tide was out. But by the Grace of the Virgin Mary, no one was seriously hurt. A few sore heads maybe, but that could have been from the wine."

The friendly proprietor pleaded with me to stay a few days. The hotel opened for the season the following week. It was, of course, impossible. I was on a strict schedule and running out of time. He made me promise to come back and I agreed to return.

As I drove away past the resort hotels, I suddenly saw a very familiar name on one of them. "Hotel Sydney." My mind shot back 40 years to the mess dinner at the Hotel Progresso. What else happened on that memorable evening? I decided I had nothing to worry about but I didn't stop at the Sydney to check.

It will now be apparent why I decided to visit San Benedetto in 1997. I don't make idle promises and I had a long-standing date at the Hotel Progresso. I soon found it, but my heart sank. It was beginning to show its age (something I could personally understand). I entered the lobby and rang the bell at the desk. A pleasant young man appeared and asked, "*Che cosa desidera.*"

I explained my mission, but I realized it was in vain. The hotel had changed hands and the former owner had retired to the country. However, the new proprietor would be delighted if I stayed for lunch courtesy of the hotel and told him more about the PPCLI.

This time I accepted his hospitality with pleasure and reminisced about those happy days in San Benedetto. I said goodbye with real regret, but I did not promise to return.

I thought of a favourite saying of Professor Carmelo Nigro: "*Le cose belle, non si repetono due volte.*" (Nice things do not repeat twice.)

Neither did I spend time looking for the Hotel Sydney. It was another memory of those carefree days that I wanted to remember, untrammelled by the sands of time.

San Marino, lying southwest of Rimini, was my next destination. On the way I would pass by a War Cemetery at Ancona which I had not visited for some time. This cemetery was begun during the fighting to breach the Gothic Line in August, 1944. It is a small cemetery and contains the graves of 161 Canadians, of which 5 are Patricias. The majority of their dead comrades lie in cemeteries farther north, Montecchio, Gradara and Coriano Ridge. I felt somewhat ashamed that I had neglected this cemetery over the years, as even a cemetery with only five Patricia headstones is five too many for their loved ones at home. So I made a point of pausing at each of these lonely graves in solemn remembrance. I now list their names:

> *Pte. John D. Cousens, killed September 4th, 1944*
> *Pte. Kenneth Reginald Ray, killed September 11th, 1944*
> *Pte. James Howard Reid, killed September 17th, 1944*
> *Pte. Ronald Birch, killed September 27th, 1944*
> *LCpl. Hubert Clayton Weidenhamer, killed November 23rd, 1944*

PILGRIMAGE—1997

Continuing north on the old Highway 16, I passed by the three cemeteries just mentioned and the rivers, towns and features associated with the Patricias' advance to Rimini, already described—Metauro River, Foglia River, Pesaro (on which the eastern end of the Gothic Line was hinged), Montecchio, Gradara, Cattolica, Coriano, Riccione, Ausa River, Rimini, San Fortunato and the Marecchia River, where I had the unpleasant experience of being almost bombed out of my *casa* in 1944.

During the latter part of this advance to the Marecchia River in September 1944, the fortress-like height of San Marino, on our left flank, seemed to watch our every move. Whenever we were caught by German shellfire in the open plain, we blamed San Marino, particularly after San Fortunato had fallen. The staff, as always, had a fine legal answer to our paranoia. San Marino, as everyone knew, was a neutral state and the Germans would never occupy a non-belligerent country. I didn't believe it and resolved to find the answer after the War.

Find the answer I did during a Pilgrimage I made with my wife in 1956. In those days the tourist traffic was nothing like it is today and San Marino could afford to exert its independence by stopping each car at a barrier and demanding production of a passport. I think I was one of the first Canadians to try to enter this fortress in peacetime. The Customs Guards in full military uniform questioned my Canadian passport, but when they realized I was driving a Mercedes-Benz, they smiled and waved me through. I was soon settled in an open air café clinging to the side of a cliff, with a view of the countryside for miles around—the Ausa River, San Fortunato, the Marecchia River all lay at my feet. A waiter approached and I ordered a *caraffa* of the local wine. In Italian, I told him I was a Canadian soldier who had fought in the plains below in September 1944. We had trouble with German shellfire and some of us suspected that it was directed by Germans in San Marino. However, our staff officers assured us that this could not be the case as, after all, San Marino was neutral and the Germans would respect this.

The waiter nearly fell over the cliff laughing. He wished he could have had ten lire for every German officer he served at this very *ristorante* during the war. There were hundreds of them. Several of their powerful "spy glasses" were left behind (stolen by the Ities) and were available for the tourists, for a small fee, of course.

All that occurred in 1956. Now it is 1997, 41 years later, and again I am approaching this natural fortress, but not in a Mercedes-Benz. Not that it made the slightest difference in my status. There are no Custom Guards, no barriers and no passport control. The old single lane road has given way to a four lane highway, clogged with tourists of all types and nationalities (with Germans and Japanese in the majority), driving Mercedes-Benz, BMW, Fiat, Alfa Romeo, Ferrari, Lamborghini and other makes of automobiles.

I squeeze my little "scout car" into the last parking space in the town and collapse in a crowded *Trattoria*. My war-like attitude of 41 years ago has been replaced by the acceptance that WWII has no meaning here. I am more interested in learning about the history of this place, and I engage an Italian tourist in conversation. By luck, he is a Professor of History and is happy to contribute to my knowledge.

San Marino is the world's oldest Republic. The town itself is perched on Mount Titano and has only 5,000 inhabitants. The fortress was built in the twelfth century, or maybe even earlier. The tiny state is only 24 miles square and has been independent from Italy since 885. It has its own stamps which are almost its most valuable export.

San Marino has a sixty-member Parliament and a General Council. A bust of Abraham Lincoln looks down on members of the Council. He was named an honorary citizen in 1861. The President of the United States acknowledged the gesture with a letter declaring, "Although your dominion is small, your State is nevertheless one of the most honoured in all history."

As I drive away from this unique State within a State, I once again thank the gods of war who spared me that I might appreciate and enjoy my journeys through this land, which I helped to preserve and set free. I think, too, how tragic it is that so many of my comrades who made it possible are not with me.

My grand tour was nearing its end. Florence and Pisa beckoned. It is not my intention to attempt to describe the beautiful city of Florence. During the war, the Patricias briefly occupied a position one mile to the south and two miles to the west of the centre of the city. As mentioned earlier, it had been declared an open city, like Rome, and its treasures spared, unlike Monte Cassino which Allied bombers reduced to rubble. However, the Germans had blown up all the bridges except the famous Ponte Vecchio.

Even though the Regiment had been in static positions only a short time, they still suffered casualties from patrolling across the Arno River and from shelling. It always annoyed me, and still does, to read in the papers that "it has been a quiet night at the front and there have been only a few casualties." For the soldiers involved and their next-of-kin, just one casualty is one too many.

The War Cemetery at Florence, like the one at Ancona, is not large. It contains the graves of 50 Canadians, including the following Patricias:

PILGRIMAGE—1997

> *Pte. Augustus Proulx, killed August 7th, 1944*
> *Pte. Lindsay Francis, killed August 7th, 1944*
> *Pte. Omer Cormier, killed August 8th, 1944*
> *Pte. Douglas Alexander Black, killed August 8th, 1944*

Each time I visit Florence, I always check that the durable Ponte Vecchio is, in fact, still intact. In 1997, I was standing in the middle of the bridge contemplating the purchase of some article from the wall-to-wall stores lining both sides of the bridge. (Apparently, even in ancient times real estate was so scarce they had to build their stores on the bridge.) An elderly couple, obviously lost, inquired where the Ponte Vecchio was. I nonchalantly replied, "You're standing on it." When they shook their heads in disbelief, I guided them to a narrow break in the walls and pointed to the river below. "*Mamma mia,*" the old girl cried. "*C'è un ponte di case.*" (It's a bridge of houses.) I believe I would make an excellent guide but I don't think I will apply to the Florence Tourist Board any time soon.

Pisa lies due west of Florence, about 70 miles distant as the crow flies but probably twice that distance along the winding road through the mountains. A quicker route is via the A-11 Autostrada, northwest to Pistoia and Lucca and then south to Pisa. I chose this route because I had been told that Lucca is probably the only walled city in Europe whose ramparts, bastions and moats are still intact after 400 years. The city itself is not relevant to my tale but I couldn't resist exploring the massive fortifications.

I entered one of the towering gates and found a quiet café nestled against the inner walls. As is my wont, I soon engaged an obliging citizen in conversation and learned something of the history of the place.

Lucca's walls are 2.6 miles in circumference and rise to 30 feet at some points. The fortifications were equipped with hundreds of guns and no enemy has ever challenged these ramparts. I thought how lucky we were during the war that the Patricias were not required to assault the city. The battle would have made Ortona look like a sideshow.

Lucca was a tiny Republic until 1799, when Napoleon invaded Tuscany and installed his sister Elisa as a Duchess. There is still a Piazza Napoleone in the city.

I asked my knowledgeable informant if it were true that the walls are so wide that a car can be driven along the top. Indeed it could. There is an avenue on top of the walls, shaded by chestnut and beech trees. Would I care to take a stroll? It would only take an hour and a half to circle the entire city.

I politely declined, with regret. This was a city that deserved a week to explore. It is at the top of my list for my next journey to this country which never ceases to fascinate me.

Pisa with its Leaning Tower is only 30 miles southwest of Lucca. It had a close connection with the Patricias during WWII that fortunately did not involve fighting. On February 27th, 1945, the Battalion was withdrawn from the Senio River Winter Line and moved across the boot of Italy to a camp near Pisa, as already described. From our tents the leaning tower was clearly visible and the troops clamoured to be allowed one last fling in Italy before joining the Canadian Army in Northwest Europe. LCol. Slug Clark was a strict disciplinarian and knew his troops. Our move had been made in the greatest secrecy and he didn't want it blown by some soldier spilling the beans to any of the local Italians. At first he refused to allow any visits outside the camp, but finally relented and allowed a few short tours to Pisa under the strict control of officers. I was one of the officers chosen.

I am about to relate my only breach of duty (so far as I can remember) in my long service. I believe at this stage I am free from prosecution due to the Statute of Limitations. After all, after 57 years I deserve a break. It happened this way.

My little party of "sight-seers" were transported to Pisa and given one hour to visit the Tower. I was given instructions to allow the men to climb the tower, but I was to remain on the ground to ensure that no one "bugged-off" into the town. The pull of the tower proved too much and I allowed myself to climb it. Unfortunately, the 294 steps took longer than I had anticipated. When I reached the top, quite out of breath, I looked down and to my horror saw two soldiers "bugging-off" at the highport with two signorinas. I didn't know whether to jump or shout. But I did the latter, to no avail. By the time I descended, the two soldiers had disappeared into town and it was time to leave.

Eventually, the culprits showed up, an hour late, and we returned to camp. LCol. Clark was waiting for us, or I should say for me, at the gate. His well-known temper exploded and I was sure I had seen my last days as a Patricia. I had only recently been promoted to Captain and held only an acting rank. At the very least I would be demoted to Lieutenant.

That was exactly what Col. Clark had in mind, plus Orderly Officer till the end of the War, severe reprimand and other punishments. I can still feel the sting of his wrath.

I am happy to report that none of the above sentence was carried out. The good Colonel relented, but not without giving me the finest tongue lashing I had ever experienced. Whether some of the senior officers interceded on my behalf, I do not know to this day. In any event, Col. Clark gave me command of D Company for our first action in Holland—the attack across the Ijssel River.

Whatever became of the two culprits I do not know. I never saw them again.

As it turned out, my thoughtless ascent of the tower in 1945 proved to be a propitious act. I climbed it once more, in the company of my wife, in 1956. But it was closed in 1990. The Government deemed it too dangerous to climb because it was about to collapse. I must, therefore, be one of a select group who has bragging rights to say he climbed the tower 57 years ago and again in 1956 and is still living to boast about it.

An interesting postscript to the story is that the tower did not collapse, but its future was very much in doubt. For many years the experts tried to arrest the increasing tilt by pouring tons of concrete under the foundation on the south side (the tower tilts south). This had only a marginal effect and the tower continued to sink.

Then, in 1998, the engineers came up with an idea that rivalled the genius of Galileo himself, who loved to drop things from the top of the tower to prove his theory of gravity.

What the engineers are now doing is called "controlled subsidence," meaning that the ground below the north side (the higher side) will be lowered to provide a more secure base. The tower will continue to lean but it will be stabilized.

It makes sense to me, but of course, I am not an engineer. I just wonder why it has taken so long to come up with such a simple answer.

But some Pisans are not convinced that the new method will work. They point out that over the years the tower has shown greater stability than Italy's governments. There have been more than fifty since the end of WWII.

The final word belongs to Professor Carmelo Nigro. I am almost certain that his pronouncement on the subject would be *"Sbagliando s'impara."* (By making mistakes one learns, or ought to learn.)

To which I feel compelled to add: *Viva la torre pendente.* (Long live the Leaning Tower.)

Livorno (Leghorn) on the Mare Ligure (Ligurian Sea) is only 25 miles southwest of Pisa. At 0600 hours on March 13th, 1944, the Patricias left Leghorn in Landing Ships (Tank) bound for Marseilles, France. I was on deck even earlier to say goodbye to this beautiful, strange land of so many contrasts which had been my adopted home for so many months. The shores of Italy slowly dipped below the horizon. Suddenly I felt overcome by a wave of sadness and regret that surprised me. Was this any way to say goodbye to the land so many Canadians had fought so hard to set free? No ceremonies, no special orders of the day, nothing to mark the passing of the most important period in my life.

And what about the casualties? All that Canadian blood that had been shed and would forever remain in the mountains, valleys and plains. I had left a little myself. Would these sacrifices ever be recognized, or appreciated, or remembered? Whether they would be or not, I knew what I had to do. I entered into a covenant with myself to return to the battlefields of my Regiment and the graves of my comrades at the earliest opportunity. I realized, too, it was not just the battlefields and the casualties that were pulling me back. Despite all the dirt, blistering heat, bitter cold, rain, mud, rugged mountains and treacherous torrents, I knew I loved this land and its people.

Those words were written in 1988 when I published *Once A Patricia*. I believe they accurately and sincerely express my feelings in 1944 when LST 692 pulled out of Leghorn. I cannot say it any better.

Throughout these pages, I have often referred to my covenant, which was the genesis of all my Pilgrimages and the reason for writing this book.

I stood on the quay at Livorno in June 1997, and looked out to sea. In the distance a flotilla of Landing Ships gradually faded into the deep blue of the Ligurian Sea. I cried out to them, "Stop. Turn about. Take me with you," but it was too late. Their mission to Italy was over and done. They had other duties to perform in a new land.

I slowly returned to my little scout car that had faithfully served me on my long journey of 4,000 miles. It was time for me to leave too. My covenant entered into so long ago had been fulfilled many times over. My mission had been accomplished. I could now join my comrades.

> Arrivederci, Italia
> My ship's far out to sea
> Farewell to Lombardy's Plain
> Rivers, dykes and mud and rain
> Will I ere come back again?
> Who can foresee
>
> Arrivederci, italiani
> My heart goes out to thee
> Goodbye sturdy peasant folk
> Who suffered under Fascist yoke
> For you we cleft a mighty stroke
> And set you free

16. "Death by a mine was a rotten way to go." Here, a detector has located a mine and it is about to be marked with a "Hot Cross Bun". Italy, 1943.
Canadian Army Overseas Photo 28601

17. Castello di Lagopesole, where the author rejoined his Scouts and Snipers after Lt Jones was wounded. Note camouflaged vehicle in foreground.

18. White house on the summmit of San Fortunato viewed from the west. Author, with his German binoculars surveys the ground over which his platoon advanced into the Italian plain—1956.

19. Same View, 1975. The white house is now a discothèque.

20. White house viewed from the east is still badly marked by shellfire and is barely inhabitable—1956.

21. Same View, 1985. White house is now a first class restaurant. Author with proprietor and friends after a fine meal on the house.

22. "Bovey"—From here the author led his Regiment into the plains, without a weapon. House still abandoned—1975.

23. Same view of "Bovey"—1985. The house has been completely rebuilt. A huge grotto under the house sheltered 300 Italians during the War.

24. Marecchia River—crossed September 1943. Photo taken 1985.

25. Savio River and the open "killing ground" over which the Patricias advanced in October 1944, from a start line in the village of Martorano in the background—1985.

26. Lamone River—crossed December 1944. Photo taken 1985.

27. Lamone River from the German side, Palazzo san Giacomo on the other side of the river and the railway bridge where a platoon of the RCR were annihilated by mortar fire—1985.

28. Palazzo San Giacomo where the author set up his Platoon HQ prior to crossing the Lamone River and advancing to the Naviglio Canal. Note that only part of the Palazzo has been restored—1985.

29. One of the many beautiful rooms in the Palazzo which were destroyed by Allied and German shells—1985.

30. Senio River Winter Line, January-February 1945. Germans occupied both banks of the river and overlooked D Company's positions in houses close to the left dyke—1956.

31. Same view of Senio River, taken 1985. Platoon position in houses beside dyke is now almost hidden by trees.

32. *Senio River Winter Line. View from German positions on dyke shows houses that were occupied by two remaining platoons and D Company HQ—only a No. 9 iron shot from the dyke—1985.*

33. *Rimini Grand Hotel, 1997.*
Foto di Frederico Compatangelo.

34. *The Republic of San Marino whose supposed neutrality was naturally ignored by the Germans who maintained observation posts there. Photo taken in 1956.*

35. *Cassino Commonwealth War Cemetery still in the process of construction. The abbey is clearly visible through the scafffolding for the Cross of Sacrifice—1956.*

36. The unfinished cemetery looks barren and forlorn—1956.

37. Same view taken in 1975. The completed cemetery with its greenery and careful landscaping now makes an attractive contrast with the sombre mass of the mountain.

38. *Author beside the graves of Patricia fallen, Moro River Cemetery—1975.*

39. *September 25, 1991. Gradara War Cemetery. Canadian Veterans' Commemorative Service.*

40. *September 25, 1991. Gradara War Cemetery. One of the views of the terraced cemetery overlooking the Adriatic Sea in the distance. Canadian burials are in the top row.*

41. Coriano Ridge Cemetery. Photo taken 1956.

42. Same view 1945.

43. *Coriano Ridge Cemetery. Jim Reid pauses at the grave of his Company Commander, Capt. George Corkett— 12 October 1999.*

HOLLAND
Preface to the Pilgrimages
1945, 1985

My Pilgrimages to Holland were not separate journeys but only the first phase of my many trips to Europe. My visits to Italy and Sicily have been described in earlier chapters and need not be referred to again except to explain why the Patricias ended their war in Holland and how they got there.

It had always been the intention of the Canadian Government that the First Canadian Corps in Italy (of which the First Division was a part) should join the First Canadian Army in Northwest Europe. At the Malta Conference in January 1945, it was finally decided to repatriate the Canadians to their alma mater.

On February 27th, 1945, the Patricias were withdrawn from their Winter Line along the Senio River and began their long trek across northern Italy to Leghorn. There, they embarked in Landing Ships, on March 15th, 1945, and landed in Marseilles the following day.

The immense task of transporting approximately 60,000 officers and men and their equipment, code named "Goldflake," began in mid-February and was completed by the end of March. During the whole of that time, the enemy had not a clue as to the whereabouts of the Canadian Corps.

The Patricias left Marseilles on March 16th in troop-carrying vehicles and proceeded north by way of the Rhone Valley, past Lyon, Macon, Dijon, Compiegne and Cambrai, to a rest area at Boisschot, in Belgium, mid-way between Molines and Antwerp—a total distance of 800 miles from Marseilles. This journey had special significance for

Map Number 9

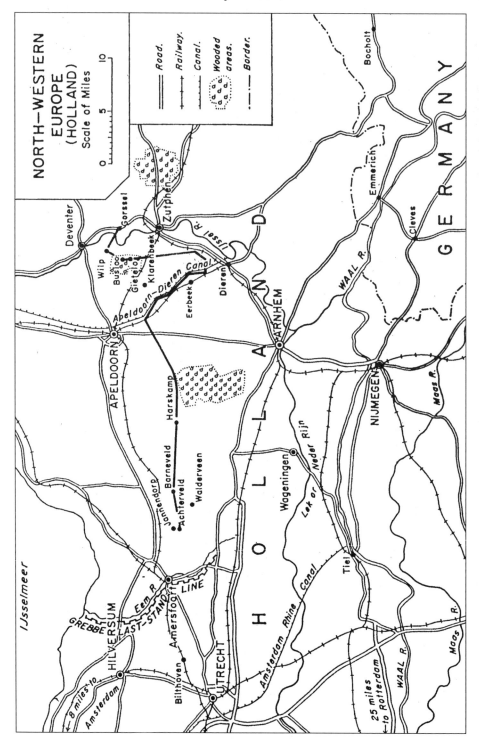

me because my father's Regiment, the Royal Newfoundlanders, had taken this same route through France in March 1916, on their way to the battles of the Somme, after the disastrous Gallipoli Campaign.

After a pleasant two weeks billeted in private homes in Boisschot, the Regiment embussed on April 3rd, entered Germany and bivouacked in a desolate area of the once mighty Reichwald Forest, 15 miles southeast of the Dutch city of Nijmegen and just a few miles south of the German city of Cleve. The forest had been heavily shelled by both sides and was a jungle of shattered trees and uprooted trunks.

It was a depressing but appropriate introduction to the country that had sown so much evil and was now reaping such dreadful retribution. More scenes of destruction were to follow.

My feeling of depression was soon lightened by the Adjutant, who informed me that I would be leading D Company in our first attack in Holland, across the Ijssel River. This was the best news I had received since my promotion to Acting Captain two months earlier. Apparently, my little frolic at Pisa had been forgiven.

On April 7th, we embussed in our TCVs and moved off to a concentration area in Holland. En route, we passed through what had once been the ancient city of Cleve, now completely flattened by the Allied bombing and shellfire. A few sullen civilians crawled out of their holes and half-looked at us, with dull, expressionless eyes. The same scene of utter devastation was repeated at Emmerich, where we crossed the Rhine on a long pontoon bridge. The horror of seeing these dead cities and cities of the dead is hard to describe. Fifty-nine years later, it is impossible to believe.

How, I wondered, could the Germans go on fighting us when their homeland had practically ceased to exist? I must confess I felt no mercy or pity toward them at all.

We crossed into Holland and came to rest at Baak, on the Ijssel River, in a pleasant wooded area, six miles southeast of Zutphen.

The sector chosen for crossing the Ijssel River was about eight miles north of Baak at a point where the river looped to the west. On the morning of April 9th, the Patricias moved to their Assembly Area in a forest, two miles east of the crossing area and the same distance west of Gorssel. That afternoon, the Commanding Officer, LCol. Clark, led a recce party to the exact site where we would cross the Ijssel River.

With my glasses, I easily picked out my D Company objective, a group of houses about 1,000 yards from the crossing place. The river itself seemed about 100 yards wide, muddy and sluggish. From our vantage point, the area was as flat as a billiard table and no cover was available.

The CO gives his orders for crossing the Ijssel, code named "Cannonshot":

> *Second Brigade will cross the river with two Battalions, the PPCLI on the right and the Seaforth Highlanders on the left.*
>
> *The Patricias will assault with Dog Company right and Charlie Company left. Dog Company's objective is the house and orchard code-named "Ness."*
>
> *On success of Charlie and Dog Companies, Able and Baker will cross the river; Able to Dog Company area, Baker to Charlie Company area. Able Company will then pass through Dog Company and occupy crossroads, code-named "Watrous." Baker Company will then pass through Charlie Company and capture a group of houses at road junction, code-named "Byron."*
>
> *On Baker Company reporting "Snug," Dog Company will pass through "Byron" and capture a group of houses on the outskirts of the village of Wilp, code-named "Winchester." On success of Dog Company, Baker Company will move forward and occupy the village, code-named "Champlain."*
>
> *Further advances will be ordered after the bridgehead is secure. H-Hour is 1630 hours, April 11th.*

It is now time to take a break in this long prelude to the Patricias' first attack in Holland. In the foregoing pages of this chapter, we have travelled from the banks of the Senio River in northern Italy to the banks of the Ijssel River in western Holland, a distance of about 1,500 miles by road, plus the sea voyage from Leghorn to Marseilles. Not bad for a bunch of footsloggers!

We will now accompany the soldiers of D Company, as they assault across the Ijssel River in their Buffaloes (a tracked vehicle that can also swim). The narrative is taken from my diary, as recorded in *Once a Patricia*.

April 11—1000 hours
Cannonshot is on! All companies report to their Buffaloes at 1430 hours. Smoke will begin at 1600 hours for 20 minutes. High explosive fire will start at 1620 hours, right up to H-Hour. H-Hour is 1630 hours.

April 11—1430 hours

Dog Company quickly loads on the Buffaloes. We've practised this so many times we can do it blindfolded. I speak briefly to the platoon commanders and wish them luck.

The Buffaloes roar into life and fill the woods with their heavy fumes. I run back to my vehicle and hop on the ramp just as it is pulled up. All are present and raring to go.

The beasts snort and lurch forward to the river. God, it feels good to be leading my company into action at last!

I look at my watch—1530 hours. In 30 minutes the smoke screen will start. It's a fine day for smoke, just a light breeze.

Ten minutes to smoke—five minutes. We emerge from the woods. The artillery opens up. Shells whine over our heads and land on the far bank of the river. Smoke drifts across the whole front, completely shielding us from enemy observation.

Now we are churning along the flats. The river is about 1,000 yards away. The artillery starts to fire HE. We can't see the targets, but the tremendous explosions tell us Jerry is getting a pasting.

April 11—1630 hours

My Buffalo hits the water and dives in without missing a stroke. The nose dips down and then bobs up again. The thing actually floats! More important, it also swims. In minutes we are across the river.

The Buffalo nudges into the far bank. We rush over the nose of the vehicle, fan out, and hit the ground. Now the smoke starts to thin out. We have to get our tails up. CSM Milko charges over from his Buffalo and urges the men forward. They don't really need any urging as now we are getting small arms fire from Ness. But sergeant majors are supposed to give men hell—"Come on, Dog Company, move it, move it," he yells. "Now's the time you earn your King's shilling."

Lt. McKinnon and his 17 Platoon are in fact earning their King's shilling and several months' pay besides. The houses at Ness are full of Jerries and they are supported by a tank. They pour fire on 17 Platoon. What happens next is best told by the Regimental Historian.

D Company on the right encountered a dyke which
  fortunately was unmanned; as it crossed this ramp fire

opened from a group of houses 150 yards ahead. A German tank was spotted; the 17 Platoon Piat missed with its first three bombs. Further ammunition was being brought forward when LSgt. T. Hanberry discovered another bomb in hand. He crept forward, boldly stepped into the open for his shot and scored a bullseye. Thereafter the advance continued without opposition and at 1720 hours Capt. C. S. Frost reported his situation as "Snug," although his men were under harassing fire from the right flank. For his brave action that allowed the advance to continue, LSgt Hanberry was awarded a well-deserved Military Medal.[1]

April 11—2100 hours
Pte. Favel, my signaller on the 18 set, has messages for me. Able Company have reported they are firm on their objective, Watrous. Baker Company are snug on Byron. The CO wants me to start moving immediately to Winchester, via Baker Company. We can't expect any tank or anti-tank support tonight. The Germans have finally wakened up and are shelling the hell out of the crossing where the sappers are trying to build a bridge.

I hold a quick O Group with my platoon commanders. "The attack has gone well. All the objectives in the second phase are secure. It is now vital to the whole operation that we reach the third and final objective, Winchester, before the enemy has a chance to organize a new defensive position."

April 11—2330 hours
It takes us longer than I had planned to reach Baker Company at Byron. Capt. Egan Chambers reports no recent enemy activity in his area, but is concerned that Jerry will soon move into Wilp if we don't get there first. I agree. We pore over our maps and discuss routes to our objectives.

I decide to send Lt. Beardmore and his 18 Platoon immediately to Winchester, about 1,000 yards ahead. With any luck, if they move quickly, they can occupy the place before the enemy has brought in reinforcements.

As soon as the platoon is snug they are to send back a runner and the rest of the company will join them.

April 12—0100 hours
Not a word has come back from 18 Platoon, nor has there been any sound of firing up ahead. The runner has probably got lost. The night is as dark as the insides of that dead cow we passed on the way here. Egan Chambers is fretting to get moving and dig in before first light. So am I.

Still no runner appears. We'll have to get going and take a chance that 18 Platoon is safely on the objective and has not strayed.

I move off across the fields and immediately realize it would not be difficult for a runner to get lost. While the map shows the country to be flat, there are innumerable streams, hedges and orchards to negotiate and I am glad I have a compass. We continue our silent approach along the ditches and through hedges. Any moment I expect a challenge or the burst of a Schmeisser. Our single file, tightly closed up to maintain contact, would be cut to pieces by a well-sited MG42. Can't do a damn thing about it. We've got to get there before the Germans do. Where is 18 Platoon?

Sooner than I had expected, I see the outlines of a barn and a small house. Whether this is Winchester, I am not at all certain. Lt. Bolton goes forward to investigate. In minutes two figures appear out of the darkness. One is Bolton and the other has to be Beardmore. I can tell by his relaxed, rolling gait. He comes up close to me so that I can see his grin and a finger at his lips. "We sneaked right into those buildings without any trouble," he whispers, "but I can't believe there aren't Jerries in the village. Just a few moments ago we heard rumbles coming from that direction. Sounded to me like tanks."

I hurriedly give orders to the platoon commanders to take up positions in all-around defence.

I get off a signal to BHQ that we are snug at Winchester. But for how long, only time will tell. Sounds of tracked vehicles on our left are getting louder and closer. It is now 0200 hours.

April 12—0300 hours
Beardmore reports that tanks are definitely entering the village. He has two good Piat men ready to greet them if they come along the road in front of our position.

I try to send off a signal to BHQ that a counter-attack is coming in with tanks and probably infantry—how many we don't yet know. I make an urgent appeal for anti-tank guns. As usual the lousy 18 set is acting up, despite the efforts of my best signaller. He can't get any response to the message. He keeps trying.

Then all hell breaks loose in the village. Thuds and explosions of guns are mingled with rapid bursts of Schmeissers and the steady beat of our Bren guns. Good old Baker must have got into the village and is intercepting the Jerry tanks.

I keep huddled over the 18 set trying desperately to get through to BHQ to send anti-tank guns. Still no response to our messages. Then a small chill goes down my spine. I suddenly remember the earlier message from the CO—"The crossing is being heavily shelled. The sappers are having trouble erecting a bridge. No anti-tank guns can be expected before first light."

Everything now depends on our Piat gunners with Harvey Beardmore's 18 Platoon on the road in front.

A runner from 18 Platoon bursts into the house. "Three tanks are coming down the road in front with a bunch of German infantry. They're travelling fast and seem to be heading for Able Company's area, 600 yards to our right. They haven't yet spotted 18 Platoon."

Clang—swoosh—crash! A shell hits the lean-to outside. It disintegrates. Then another explodes in the front yard. I wish I were back in a strong casa in Italy.

Then a Piat bomb explodes outside. Bren guns open up. A shell crashes into the front of the house. A look-out at the window yells: "They're coming at us." I jump up from the 18 set and pull out my pistol.

Norton is at my side. Favel the signaller grabs his Sten gun and heads for the door. He doesn't quite make it. The door bursts open and four or five Germans rush in. Favel lets off a deadly burst, then another. I lift my pistol to fire and then lower the weapon. Favel has cut down the entire party. Five Germans are writhing on the floor in agony.

The RAP man comes up to help the wounded. Favel goes outside. The tanks and infantry have passed our position and are heading for Able Company. The battle is not yet over.

I look briefly at the Germans. All are wounded quite badly. I ask if anyone speaks English. One says he can. I tell him I want to know how many infantry are with those three tanks. He says a company—about 120.

I rush back to the 18 set. The other signaller has stayed with the set trying to establish contact. He finally gets a message through—we are being counter-attacked by three tanks and a company of infantry. There is no point in asking for anti-tank guns. The need is obvious. Anyway, they can't get across the river.

I go outside to check the platoons. They have had a hot time of it beating off the tanks and infantry. McKinnon comes up. "I don't think we're finished with them yet. Able Company will give them a warm reception. Then they'll turn tail, and head back. We're ready for them."

McKinnon is right; flares go up in Able Company's area. The night explodes in a fearful roar of shells, Piat bombs, Schmeissers, mortars, Brens and Stens. I can't tell who's getting the best of it, but I'm putting my money on "Bunchy" Newlands and his Able Company.

McKinnon returns to his platoon and I hurry over to Beardmore. "We'll get the SOB this time, Sir. Pte. Sykes is ready and waiting."

A shell whistles overhead. The tanks are returning and firing wildly in all directions. A great explosion rends the night air and red flames shoot into the sky in front of Beardmore's platoon. Pte. Sykes has got his tank! (He received a Military Medal for his determination and skill in helping to break up the German counter-attacks, the second MM earned by Dog Company in the river crossing.)

* * *

Later that day (April 12th) the 48th Highlanders of Canada of lst Brigade pushed through our position to expand the bridgehead westward to Apeldoorn. In the course of the fighting, they lost their fine, young commanding officer, LCol. D. A. MacKenzie, who was killed by a shell.

Thus ended the battle known as the Crossing of the Ijssel River and the Liberation of Wilp. The battle has been given at some length because it was the most significant engagement fought by the Regiment in Holland. It marked the beginning of the drive of the Canadian Army into western Holland to help liberate the starving Dutch and end the war.

A further reason for such a detailed narrative, hour by hour, is that the role of the Patricias has been challenged by another Regiment which claimed it, not the Patricias, made the attack.

HOLLAND 1945, 1985

The story begins January 1985, when I heard that ceremonies were being planned by the Dutch to mark the 40th Anniversary of their liberation in May 1945. The arrangements were in the hands of two committees, one in Holland, the Liberation '45 Committee, and the other in Toronto, the We Do Remember Committee.

Having participated in the exciting but exhausting 1980 Return to Amsterdam, I felt I did not have the stamina to make a repeat performance. Furthermore, I thought that the wonderful people of Holland deserved more than five years of peace before another contingent of Canadian veterans invaded their country once again. Yet something moved me to make enquiries about the trip. At a Dutch travel agency in Toronto, I found that this time the ceremonies would be held in a number of smaller towns including Apeldoorn, where the Dutch citizens had offered to billet the veterans for a week to ten days.

I told the travel agent this was an offer I found difficult to refuse, as I had always wanted to return to the nearby village of Wilp, which the PPCLI had liberated on April 11th, 1945, after crossing the Ijssel River.

"PPCLI?" enquired the Dutch travel agent. "Who are they?"

"Princess Patricia's Canadian Light Infantry," I declared, with more than a hint of annoyance and disbelief. "It so happens that I commanded D Company of the PPCLI in that battle."

"Well, I don't understand that. Have you ever heard of the 48th Highlanders?"

"The 48th Highlanders? What have they got to do with that battle?"

"Well, they are the ones who attacked across the Ijssel River and liberated Wilp. Their Commanding Officer was killed there. In 1982 a group of their veterans returned and the citizens of Wilp held a great celebration to honour them. Prince Bernhard and a number of other dignitaries were present. A plaque was unveiled in honour of their CO and a street was named after him.

"By the way, what did you say PPCLI stands for?"

"Peanuts, popcorn, candy, lemonade and ice-cream! And please put my name on your list for billets in Apeldoorn. This is one pilgrimage I don't want to miss."

A few days later a representative of the Liberation '45 Committee from Holland appeared in Toronto to make final arrangements for the visit. The travel agent was kind enough to suggest that I should meet him and tell my story about the PPCLI at the Ijssel River and Wilp.

Armed with extracts from the PPCLI Regimental History, the War Diary and my personal diaries, I had lunch with the Dutch representative, Mr. Jan Koorenhof. Little did I realize that this was the start of a life-long friendship. He patiently heard me out and then responded by handing me materials the 48th Highlanders had distributed to the citizens of Wilp in 1982. He added words to the effect that Wilp belongs to the 48th Highlanders and I would have one hell of a time convincing the Dutch that the PPCLI had anything to do with it.

It was a challenge I could not resist. My casual enquiry about a return visit to Holland had exploded into a burning mission to fight once again the crossing of the Ijssel and the liberation of Wilp; and to restore the names of these battles to their rightful owners—the Patricias.

How could such an incredible mistake have been made? Who was responsible? How could the error be rectified? To find the answers to these and other questions I boarded KLM flight 692 at Toronto on May 2nd, 1985, and arrived in Amsterdam the next morning. At the Schiphol Airport we were given a warm welcome by the Dutch Liberation Committee; then placed in buses and driven to Apeldoorn.

At Apeldoorn, our tired but happy group was taken to a club built especially as a centre or rendezvous for the veterans and named the Canadian Club. There, we "married up" with our hosts and were whisked away to their homes.

It was my good fortune to be billeted with a retired dentist and his wife, two of the most charming and delightful people I have ever known. They gave me the run of their lovely home, pampered me with gourmet meals, and drove me around the battlefields that I so desperately wanted to see.

In the course of a late evening's discussion following my first night in the club, I learned that my hosts were Jewish and had lived in Apeldoorn before the War. When the Germans came in May 1940, they had narrowly missed becoming inmates of a concentration camp by taking refuge in the embassy of a friendly Central American country. There, they were given new passports and escaped to Spain. After many dangers and delays they finally made their way to England, where the doctor took a commission with the British Navy as a Dental Officer. After the War, they returned to Apeldoorn to rebuild their lives and his career. Nearly all their relatives and friends had perished in the Holocaust.

That same night, I told the doctor a little bit about myself and explained my real reason for returning to Holland—to rectify the calumny perpetrated by persons unknown on the PPCLI's battle record. My host was most sympathetic and eager to help me in my good work, but there were other duties and engagements more pressing.

"It's very late," he said, "and we have a heavy day coming up, as well as a very busy week of parades, receptions, parties and so forth. As soon as these functions are over we'll take my car and visit the Ijssel River and Wilp and straighten out the terrible wrong that has been done to your Regiment."

I couldn't ask for more.

For the next five days the wonderful people of Apeldoorn opened up their hearts to their Canadian liberators. The ceremonies began with a moving address of welcome by the Burgemeester of Apeldoorn, Mr. Beelaerts van Blokland. Urbane, knowledgeable and kind, he presided over the festivities with great wit and charm, ably assisted by various committees of local citizens.

While these official and extra-curricular activities were going on, I was laying plans to set the record straight about the PPCLI and the crossing of the Ijssel. With the help of a member of the Liberation Committee, I obtained an appointment to visit the Mayor of Voorst, in whose municipality the Ijssel River and Wilp are situated.

My host, the dentist, was all geared up to provide a naval escort for the venture. He suggested we recce the area in his destroyer (car) before we attended the Mayor of Voorst.

On a fine morning in May, we set off together, my host armed with a set of high-powered naval binoculars, camera, rations (both dry and wet); I, with my old maps from the War still bearing the exact routes taken by the PPCLI during the battles. Like two young officers, we scouted the area east of the Ijssel River and soon found the assembly area where the Patricias had formed up for the attack. From there, we followed the route the Buffaloes had taken to the river. As we approached the eastern bank, my escort, the dentist, pointed out that the high dykes ahead would certainly bar our way in the car.

"How did the Buffaloes manage to navigate those obstacles?" he demanded.

"Wait and see, Henk. At the end of this trail, make a left incline and you'll find a nice fat opening in the dykes you can drive a tank or your car through."

"I don't believe it."

But in a moment Henk became a believer. The crossing site had not changed and there was the promised gap in the dyke.

"Fantastic," yelled a relieved Henk. "What a memory."

"Yeah, but also a damn good map."

We drove through the gap, stopped the car and got out to survey the situation. Now it was my turn to be the unbeliever. Nothing had changed in 40 years—ahead, the same barren flats, and beyond them the river, about 100 yards wide. On the other side, more mud flats and dykes and the top of a house hidden behind one of them.

"This is incredible, Henk. Let's leave the car here and go back to that wooded area near the river and plan our attack. It was in that wood that I made my final recce on April 11th, 1945."

After making our recce in the wood, Henk and I returned to his car at the dyke. As I checked the area to the right I saw, 50 yards distant, what looked like a cairn, surrounded by flags and fresh flowers.

"What the devil's that, Henk?"

"I don't know. We'd better investigate."

The object was indeed a memorial cairn erected by the Municipalities of Gorssel and Voorst to honour the Canadian troops who had crossed the Ijssel River at this place on April 11th, 1945. Henk suggested I put on my PPCLI beret and medals and he would take a snap of me standing beside the cairn, flanked by the flags of Canada and the Netherlands. He had no sooner taken the picture than a dozen or more people suddenly appeared and excitedly gathered around us at the cairn. In moments they were joined by about 50 others on bicycles.

Then a reporter and cameraman from a local newspaper appeared and asked me to describe the events of April 1945, when the gallant Canadians stormed across the Ijssel River and captured Wilp. What a splendid opportunity to place on the record that it was the PPCLI and not the 48th Highlanders who did the job!

To an incredulous reporter, I described how the Patricias, conveyed by the ubiquitous Buffaloes, launched the attack across the Ijssel River at 4:30 p.m. on April 11th, 1945, and occupied Wilp by 1:00 a.m. on April 12th. The 48th didn't arrive in their Assembly Area on the east bank of the Ijssel until noon on April 12th. By that time, B Company and my D Company had been in Wilp at least ten hours and had repulsed a strong enemy counter-attack by 120 German infantry, three tanks, an SP gun and supporting vehicles. The 48th Highlanders had a strictly break-out role in the operation once the PPCLI had won the bridgehead. The 48th did not assault across the river; they were simply ferried across in the afternoon of April 12th.

It was true that the 48th Commanding Officer, LCol. D.A. MacKenzie, was killed by shellfire late in the afternoon of that day, about 1,200 yards north of my position in Wilp. I remembered him coming through my position and getting briefed on the situation. The 48th rifle companies actually by-passed Wilp and headed for another town, Twello, to the northwest of Wilp. In short, the 48th Highlanders had nothing whatsoever to do with the crossing of the Ijssel or the capture of Wilp.

At the end of the interview the reporter asked me why I wasn't present at the cairn earlier that day.

"What happened?" I queried.

"Well, the Municipalities of Gorssel and Voorst dedicated this cairn in the presence of the 48th Highlanders, its band and other dignitaries. No PPCLI veterans were present."

I was stunned and could barely reply. "The PPCLI were not asked and knew nothing about the ceremony."

"That's too bad. There was also a re-enactment of the crossing of the river. Representatives from Gorssel, Voorst, Wilp and the 48th Highlanders were ferried across the river in a pilot boat and another cairn was dedicated on the far side of the river."

Now I was speechless. I looked at Henk. He put a finger to his lips, indicating I should remain in that state.

When the smoke (from my nostrils) cleared, and my power of speech returned, I asked the reporter if there were any other ceremonies involving the 48th.

"Oh yes, their pipes and drums are putting on a tattoo in the village of Bussloo."

"That figures."

"Beg your pardon?"

"I'm not surprised—the PPCLI captured Bussloo shortly after taking Wilp."

This time Henk was speechless too. He pointed to the car and we slowly made our way through the throng who had been listening to my remarks with some astonishment, but also, I sensed, with some concern about the way my Regiment had been ignored.

Henk was the first to speak. "You certainly have a job of work ahead of you to put the PPCLI back on the map."

"Never fear. We'll put the record straight tomorrow when we call on the Mayor of Voorst."

But Henk was right; there was a lot of work to do and very little time to do it before our meeting with the mayor. First, I had to get in touch with any PPCLI members who had returned to Holland for the Anniversary celebrations. None were billeted in Apeldoorn, but I found two who had chosen to stay in a nearby village—Barneveld. They were Lt. Bert Bolton, who had commanded No. 16 Platoon in my D Company in the battles just described, and Cpl. John Moore, a member of the Mortar Platoon. I got in touch with them and they enthusiastically agreed to join me in the town hall at Twello, the seat of the Municipality of Voorst.

Next day, accompanied by Lt. Bolton, Cpl. Moore, Henk and his wife, I attended Dr. J.H.J. van Blommestein, the Burgemeester of Voorst, wondering how he would receive my little band and how he would react to my plea to give the PPCLI their due.

I need not have worried. Dr. van Blommestein was cast in much the same mould as the Mayor of Apeldoorn—a kind, gracious man and a professional, who was very much aware of the responsibilities of his office. He had also done his homework.

With genuine warmth he welcomed our delegation and ushered us into his chambers to meet some members of his Council, including LCol. Ritse R. Reitsma. After a few words over coffee and cakes, I realized that Dr. Blommestein had been made very much aware of the reason for my visit. He could not have been more understanding and sympathetic. I brought out my old battle maps and traced the route taken by the Patricias before and during the battle for Wilp.

"Yes," he said, "we always knew the PPCLI had taken some part in the action but, regrettably, I was not informed that there were any representatives from the PPCLI in Holland. Otherwise, of course, they would have been included in all the ceremonies connected with this important Anniversary. We are so happy that we can at last give the PPCLI its proper recognition."

Whereupon he glanced at his protocol officer, who produced a scroll under the seal of the Municipality of Voorst acknowledging their gratitude to our deputation on the occasion of our visit to the town hall. The mayor then handed me a detailed map of Voorst and presented each member of our group with appropriate gifts, including a tin of cookies, made in Wilp in honour of the 40th Anniversary of their liberation, and a bottle of fine liqueur.

Then it was my turn to reciprocate his kindness. I thanked my hunch in Toronto that I would need a PPCLI plaque for such an occasion. With a few words of appreciation to the mayor and his council, I presented the plaque. It was inscribed as follows:

Presented to the Municipality of Voorst by Colonel C. S. Frost to commemorate the 40th Anniversary of the Liberation of Wilp on April 12th, 1945, by Princess Patricia's Canadian Light Infantry.

May 8th, 1985

But the occasion demanded some further token of our appreciation to the mayor himself. I dug into my pocket and produced a PPCLI cap badge which I presented to him personally. At the same time I filed with the clerk extracts from the PPCLI Regimental History giving the correct account of the battles.

The mayor suggested we all attend the cairn erected on the west bank of the Ijssel, and honour the men of the PPCLI who fought and fell in the battle. It was a gracious gesture and I happily agreed.

And so it was that 40 years to the day after the end of the War, three old comrades, Bolton, Moore and Frost, quietly stood, proud and erect, beside a cairn on the bank of the river they had assaulted so long ago. In the presence of the Burgemeester of Voorst and other members of his Council, a minute's silence was observed in honour of the PPCLI. My mission had been completed.

It was now time to return to Apeldoorn for other ceremonies. LCol. Reitsma of the municipality insisted, however, that we adjourn to the best pub in Wilp and exchange mutual toasts in honour of the occasion. On the way we could follow the route my D Company had taken from the river to the first objective, a group of houses behind a dyke code-named Ness; then we could carry on to the second objective, a farmhouse in Wilp, code-named Winchester, where we had been counter-attacked by German tanks and infantry.

We quickly piled in our cars and in minutes we had "captured" the first objective, Ness. But instead of 40-year-old buildings, a handsome new farmhouse was in the final stages of construction. A workman approached our party.

Through our naval escort and interpreter, Henk, I explained that we were looking for some old farm buildings that we had captured from the Germans in 1945. Possibly we were in the wrong place.

"No, you're not," declared the workman. "This is where several farm buildings stood in 1945. But after your artillery and infantry had finished with them, and with the Germans inside, there wasn't much of anything left. The place was abandoned until recently when this new house was erected."

I looked at Bolton and Moore, not having a clue what to say, but feeling we should never have come here and stirred up old memories. The workman instantly surmised what was going through my head. "Please don't feel like that. The loss of a farmhouse and barn was a small price to pay for our freedom. Thank you, thank you, Canada." He ran forward and put his arms around me.

At the second and final objective, the farmhouse code-named Winchester, on the outskirts of Wilp, more surprises awaited us. The farmhouse looked pretty much the same as it did in 1945, although a number of fine buildings had been added to it. The farmer who had occupied the place in 1945 had, however, left many years ago and moved into town. But the Protocol Officer of Voorst, accompanying us, had done his research and took us to the farmer's present home. There, we had a joyful reunion with him, now retired and in his eighties, his wife, and his daughter, who was only 15 when we fought off the German counter-attacks against her home.

At least we didn't destroy her home, I thought, with some relief, as I waited for her reaction to our visit.

"There were about 17 of us," she began. "We were so afraid that terrible night, when the Germans came back with their tanks. We thought we would all be killed."

"Seventeen of you?" I queried.

"Yes, we were all in the basement of the house, but didn't dare come out until a day or two after the attack, as we thought the Germans had driven you back. By that time, of course, you had moved on. We are so thankful to you for saving us. Words cannot express our gratitude."

Then the old man perked up. "You know, I lost two horses and 35 cattle that night."

Unfortunately, we had to leave or we would be late for the ceremonies in Apeldoorn. Henk took pictures and we stepped out into the street.

News of our presence had spread and a crowd had gathered, including people we had met on our recce of the east bank of the river the day before. A lady who had given me her orange pin was there; also the family who wanted us to come for lunch and dinner. They now insisted we join them. So did half a dozen others.

Again I was overwhelmed. What to do? LCol. Reitsma pushed through the crowd. "Let's make a graceful retreat to the pub down the street, opposite the church. It's our only chance."

As we moved down the street toward the church, a German 88 suddenly exploded in my mind. This was the very route those tanks and Germans had taken as they churned along the road to my company position.

We were nearly at the pub. "My God," I exclaimed, "This is the place where Egan Chambers and his B Company opened fire on the German column and mowed down half a company of them."

Bolton laughed. "Trust good old B Company to find the only pub in town."

Our "happy hour" in the pub had to be cut short because of the other events in Apeldoorn. There was, however, time for mutual toasts and expressions of our deep friendship for one another. Finally, LCol. Reitsma (who was a retired Dutch Engineer Colonel) got up on a chair, smiled at me and said, "Colonel, there is one final act we must do to express the close ties that exist between your Regiment and Wilp. We shall exchange our Regimental ties." In a moment the deed was done, amid much cheering and laughter.

My mission had not only been accomplished, it had been done with panache, in the best Patricia tradition.

On the way back to Apeldoorn, with Henk at the wheel of his "destroyer," neither of us said a word for several miles. Finally, Henk broke the awkward silence. "Syd, you're being awfully quiet. But I think I know the trouble. It bothers me too. You really haven't completed your so-called mission. You swore to find out how such an incredible mistake about the Patricias could have happened. You vowed to find out who was responsible. What about it?"

"You're right. But the most important part of my mission has been achieved. There's not a person in Wilp, or the whole Municipality of Voorst, for that matter, who doesn't know all about the PPCLI."

"Yes, I suppose you're right. What are you going to do about how the error was made and by whom?"

"Nothing. It doesn't matter anymore. Whoever was responsible can worry about it, not me. The 48th may never speak to me again; but I really don't think that will happen. Perhaps some of the blame lies with my own Regiment. After all, they haven't shown much interest in this Anniversary."

"Why's that?"

"Well, as battles go, it wasn't by any means the biggest, and certainly not the bloodiest when you think of the terrible slaughter in Italy."

"Yet it had a great significance, both for you and the Dutch. It was really your last battle and it helped save the starving Dutch."

"I appreciate your saying that, Henk."

When we arrived home a message was waiting for me from the Mayor of Apeldoorn. Would I be kind enough to join him and the City Council for dinner that evening? How Mr. Beelaerts van Blokland found out about the PPCLI and what I had been up to, I never did ascertain. But it didn't surprise me. At dinner that evening, I had the honour of sitting beside him and enjoying his wit and charm. There was no need for me to elaborate on the PPCLI—he knew all about the Patricias. He was only sorry the full story had not been known by him earlier. After dinner I presented him with my Patricia blazer crest and my cap badge, as well as extracts from our Regimental History.

An interesting sequel to these events occurred when I returned to Toronto and was invited to attend the change of command of the Commanding Officer of the 48th Highlanders. I was pleased to accept. I have known the 48th since the War. Their officers are gentlemen and I count many friends among them. Still, I wondered what kind of a hornet's nest I was getting into.

I need not have worried. I was seated in the front row for the parade and shown the greatest respect. Indeed, the officers could not have been friendlier, all except one ex-officer who came up and quietly suggested I read the history of The Royal Canadian Regiment as it agreed with his version of the crossing of the Ijssel River and the capture of Wilp.

Well, one unbeliever out of thousands is not so bad.

And so, the "Second Battle" of the crossing of the Ijssel River and the liberation of Wilp ended in another victory for the Patricias. The evidence was overwhelming and conclusive. The case was closed— so I thought in 1985. But I had not counted on the desire of the Dutch people themselves to make amends for the way the PPCLI had been overlooked, even though they were quite blameless. Unbeknownst to me, shortly after the 1985 Pilgrimage, Dr. Johannes van Blommestein, the Mayor of Voorst, began making plans to demonstrate their respect and affection for the PPCLI in a way that would never be forgotten. This unsullied act will be revealed in the following chapters.

However, before joining the 1989 Pilgrimage we should briefly follow the route taken by the PPCLI in Holland after the crossing of the Ijssel River, and record the names of the towns and villages the Regiment liberated.

On April 13th, the Regiment seized Bussloo and Gietelo—twin hamlets on the eastern fringes of the Appensche Veld, a triangle of dense woodland. Then the Battalion scouts reported enemy lurking in the woods. LCol. Clark organized a forest force consisting of three groups. Each group had a flamethrower, medium machine guns (Vickers) and Bren guns. When the Germans fled from the flamethrowers the Vickers' Gunners mowed them down. Ten were killed and fifteen taken prisoner.

The Patricias were then directed south toward the village of Dieren to link up with the 49th British Division coming up from the south. I am proud to say that a D Company patrol made the first contact. Let the Regimental History tell the tale.

> *A D Company patrol under Lt. H. E. Beardmore, wearying of footslogging, borrowed bicycles from the Dutch Resistance and rode in carefree fashion into the south. Out of the ditch beside the road a balaclavaed head rose and in broad East Anglian shouted "CLOSE." As one man the Patricias replied "SHAVE." It was the joint code-word and the gap between 1st Canadian and 49th British Division had been closed.*[2]

* * *

On April 16th, the line of advance of the Regiment was again changed to a northwest direction toward Klarenbeek and then due west. The three villages of Oosterhuizen, Lieren and Beekbergen were soon liberated and the sweep continued into the west without encountering any opposition, but gathering in large numbers of prisoners (who surrendered without even a show of resistance) and acquiring much loot from the beaten Hun.

The War Diarist of The Loyal Edmonton Regiment could not restrain his envy of the staff cars, vehicles, household wares, food and other loot left by the Germans for the Patricias:

> —the PPCLI—had been busy on our right, capturing hundreds of wandering enemy with so much loot that most of the Patricias were offering to resign their position as privates and go home to live in a manner befitting their status as millionaires.[3]

In the morning of April 17th, the rapid advance continued without pause, first in troop carriers, then a few miles on foot, and then on the backs of tanks to the village of Harskamp, where we made contact with the Canadian 5th Armoured Division coming up from the south.

Prisoners continued to surrender in droves; loot continued to pile up; the Dutch Underground continued to round up their chastened overseers, and the civilians welcomed us with open arms and tears in their eyes. Infantry regiments became intermingled with tank regiments, artillery regiments and units from 5th Armoured Division. And the whole, happy, confused array madly pursued the scattered remnants of the retreating Hun. It was an exciting, glorious time to be with the Regiment and I silently thanked old Field Marshal Fate.

The next move of the Battalion was to Barneveld where the Patricias were destined to end their war. Patrols were set out to the neighbouring villages, one of which will be mentioned frequently in this narrative—Achterveld. On April 19th, a patrol ran into a pocket of Germans in Achterveld who put up a fight but soon withdrew, leaving a number of prisoners. They had been occupying the church tower, which offered a commanding view of the countryside for miles around. When a Patricia officer was about to enter the tower a Dutch civilian presented him with 25 pounds of dynamite and several feet of fuse he had found in the church.

Other patrols to surrounding villages engaged in similar firefights and gathered up more prisoners. On April 21st, D Company ambushed two German patrols near Achterveld, and the next day moved into the village. On April 17th, a further ambush was laid which the enemy walked into—and left several killed and five prisoners. In this ambush, the Patricias fired their last shots of WWII. Approximately 700 Germans had been captured in the advance from the Ijssel River.

The Germans were on their last legs and they knew it. Their only concern was how to surrender without losing their much-prized honour. Of greater concern to the Allies was the near starvation of the Dutch population, especially in the larger cities still occupied by the Germans.

As soon as the line of the Ijssel had been forced, Seyss-Inquart, Reichskommissar of Holland, had opened negotiations with the Allied High Command. He was ready, he said, to carry out Hitler's orders and to fight to the last man; if necessary, he would breach the dykes and flood much of western Holland. On the other hand, he knew that the game was up and he was willing to negotiate if he could avoid the appearance of treason. If the Allies would halt their forces, he would refrain from destruction of the dykes and would allow food supplies for Dutch civilians to enter German-controlled territory. As a result of such undertaking, a truce was arranged and a conference was held on April 30th between representatives of the Allies and the Germans. The Allied representatives were headed by LGen. Bedell Smith, General Eisenhower's Chief of Staff, and included MGen. Freddy de Guingand, Montgomery's Chief of Staff, and LGen. Charles Foulkes. Prince Bernhard was also present. The German emissaries included Seyss-Inquart and General Blaskowitz's Chief of Staff. Even a Russian Colonel was in attendance. According to some reports he drank the rest of them under the table. After putting away four quick vodkas he refused a fifth, saying he never drank before dinner!

The conference was held in the Achterveld schoolhouse, in the middle of D Company's area. The Patricias' Medical Officer, Major G. D. Fairfield, supplied the typewriter on which the agreement was copied; the Battalion loaned the Russian representative an electric generator to provide power for his radio transmitter. The Battalion also supplied pickets, checkposts and guards in the village and refreshments in the messes.

As a result of this conference, food and supplies immediately started to flow into stricken Holland by road, rail and barges, in accordance with plans previously made to deal with the emergency. 1st Canadian Army was ready to move 1,600 tons daily into the distressed area. In addition, food packages were dropped by RAF Bomber Command and the U.S. 8th Air Force. This relief continued on a rising scale and, during the period ending on May 8th, over 11 million British and American rations were dropped.[4]

After the War, it was found "that there were between 100,000 and 150,000 cases of starvation oedema, with a death rate of 10 per cent in the larger cities."[5]

It was clear that a major disaster had been narrowly averted. Queen Wilhelmina herself had foreseen the mounting crisis some months earlier and had written to King George, Roosevelt and Churchill. She declared "conditions ... have at present become so desperate that it is abundantly clear that, if a major catastrophe, the like of which has not been seen in Western Europe since the Middle Ages, is to be avoided in Holland, something drastic has to be done now, that is to say, before and not after the liberation of the rest of the country."[6]

It has always been a source of immense pride to me that the negotiations which led to the relief of the starving Dutch people were held right in my company area, and that the PPCLI played a part in making the arrangements. As one of the reporters wrote, "The modest school building deserves to go down in history as the place where Britons, Dutch and Germans discussed the chances of giving humanity a break."[7]

The little schoolhouse is now a museum. On each of my Pilgrimages, I never fail to visit this enduring memorial to the liberation of the Dutch people.

Five days after the Achterveld conference, the War was over for the Patricias. On May 5th, at a shell-scarred hotel in Wageningen, the German Commander, General Blaskowitz, surrendered his defeated Twenty-fifth Army to LGen. Foulkes in the presence of Prince Bernhard. Thus, May 5th is celebrated as Liberation Day in the Netherlands.

The formal surrender of all German Forces was signed at General Eisenhower's Headquarters at Rheims, on May 7th, and May 8th was declared the "official" VE Day.

This Preface has also reached its end. It will probably establish a record for the longest preamble ever written. One must wonder if there is anything left to say in the chapters that follow.

However, I can assure my reader that a review of the crossing of the Ijssel River, the subsequent advance of the PPCLI into western Holland, and the timely liberation of the starving Dutch are all germane to what follows.

To my Dutch friends, I must offer my apologies for two apparent errors that occur throughout my story. The first is using the word *Holland* when I am referring to the *Netherlands*; the other is the spelling of the word Ijssel.

I am aware that Holland is only a part of the Netherlands. Indeed, some of my Dutch friends have made this quite clear. They claim that using the word *Holland*, as I have done, is like telling a Glaswegian that he lives in England! However, many Canadian historians, including LCol. G.R. Stevens, the author of the Official History of the PPCLI, use the two words interchangeably.

I also know that "IJ" is one vowel in Dutch and is printed in capital letters at the commencement of a word. But again, most Canadian historians capitalize only the I in referring to the *Ijssel River*. These historians include the respected Col. C. P. Stacey, author of *The Victory Campaign* and *The Canadian Army*, and LCol. G.W.L. Nicholson the author of *The Canadians in Italy*.

With these solid precedents before me, my legal training will not allow me to ignore their authority. I trust my friends in the *Netherlands* will forgive me.

Chapter XIII

GERMANY—HOLLAND—1986

This visit to Holland arose out of a business meeting I attended in Germany. In 1986, Daimler Benz AG, the makers of Mercedes-Benz automobiles, celebrated "100 years of the Automobile." A number of important receptions and celebrations were held throughout the world, including the Head Office in Stuttgart. As a Director of the Canadian company, I was invited to attend. The various functions were held over a three-day period, January 28, 29, 30. Among the distinguished guests was the German Chancellor, Dr. Helmut Kohl.

Always eager to take advantage of every opportunity to see my Dutch friends, I left Stuttgart as soon as the ceremonies concluded and caught a flight to Amsterdam where I checked in at the Amsterdam Hilton. For the next five days, I retraced the advance of the PPCLI in Holland from the Ijssel River to Wilp, Gietelo, Bussloo, Beekbergen, Lieren, Oosterhuizen, Haarskamp, Barneveld and Achterveld, where my D Company finished the War.

I will frankly admit I had a further reason for visiting Holland in 1986. My book was in its final stages, but before it was published I wanted to check a number of facts, especially in connection with the crossing of the Ijssel River and the capture of Wilp. It still rankled that a person or persons unknown had put about that the 48th Highlanders had made the attack. In 1985, I had done my best to convince the Dutch that this was a grave mistake that had to be rectified.

Toward this end, I wrote a very detailed account of the operation for my Dutch friends to read. I wanted to ensure it was not only accurate but also fairly described the battle. The first person I consulted was Dr. Johannes van Blommestein, Mayor of the Municipality of Voorst, within which Wilp is located. It will be remembered how understanding and sympathetic he was in 1985 to my pleas to recognize the Patricias. I can do no better than quote his response once more.

> *Yes, we always knew the PPCLI had taken some part in the action but, regrettably, I was not informed that there were any representatives from the PPCLI in Holland. Otherwise, of course, they would have been included in all the ceremonies connected with this important Anniversary. We are so happy that we can at last give the PPCLI its proper recognition.*

I couldn't have asked for more. Little did I know that he was already making plans to recognize the PPCLI in a most generous and spectacular fashion.

I also met LCol. Ritse Reitsma with whom I had exchanged ties in Wilp during the 1985 Pilgrimage. He read my draft chapters of the book and made some valuable changes and additions. For many years he had served as the Head of the Liberation Committee for Voorst. He had been responsible for the celebrations in 1980 and 1985 and would continue in this capacity in 1990 and 1995. He was also very active in the Canadian Legion. In his opening speech to the Veterans he always apologized for having such a difficult name to pronounce. "Just call me Bill," he said, and that is the name he will always be known by.

Both Johannes van Blommestein and Bill Reitsma became great friends of the Veterans, as did many, many other citizens of Voorst. Both received the highly prized Order of Orange Nassau in recognition of their service to their country and to Canadian Veterans.

The next stop in my 1986 quest was the beautiful city of Apeldoorn where the 1985 Pilgrimage had been concentrated. I was especially keen to meet Jan Koorenhof, who was the first Dutch person to tell me of the perceived attempt of the 48th Highlanders to lay claim to the PPCLI Battle Honour of the crossing of the Ijssel River and the liberation of Wilp. He had attended a meeting in Toronto in March 1985, to co-ordinate plans for the 1985 Pilgrimage to Apeldoorn and forewarned me of the claim. He is another example of a Dutch citizen who has devoted a major part of his life during the past 15 years, and more, to organizing and participating in the Liberation Ceremonies. Jan Koorenhof acted as liaison officer and personal advisor to every Mayor of Apeldoorn during that time. Whenever I needed advice or assistance in my visits to Apeldoorn, he was always available. He seemed to have the knack of being everywhere at once and kept the show rolling. I told him his middle name should be "ubiquitous."

During my visit to Apeldoorn in 1986, he introduced me to two Dutch gentlemen who would also become fast friends—Klaas Huisman and Evert Gerritsen.

Klaas Huisman was Chief of Cabinet to successive mayors of Apeldoorn over many years. He made an outstanding contribution to all the Liberation Ceremonies as one of the principal organizers of the Apeldoorn events. He and his wife Ellen were always there, behind the scenes, giving aid and assistance to the Veterans. On one occasion when I was quite ill, they took me to my hotel and brought in the food I required for my diet. A remarkable couple.

Evert Gerritsen, a well-known citizen of Apeldoorn, was highly respected for his interest in the Veterans and for service to his community. He was the proprietor of the largest taxi cab company in Apeldoorn and many a time gave generously to Veteran activities. He often visited Toronto and I had the pleasure of reciprocating his generosity by hosting lunches and dinners in his honour. He too was decorated with the Order of Orange Nassau.

Two people I failed to meet in 1986 were Pieter Beelaerts van Blokland and Dr. Henk Hannivort.

Pieter Beelaerts, it will be recalled, was the gracious Mayor of Apeldoorn in 1985 who presided over the festivities. Unfortunately, he was not available during my brief visit in 1986 due to my not giving him notice of my coming. I resolved to make amends in the forthcoming Pilgrimages. I am happy to say I honoured my pledge to the "Queen's taste." He subsequently became Queen's Commissioner for the Province of Utrecht (a post similar to our Lieutenant Governor, but with real authority). Later, he agreed to become Mayor of another city to help a troubled administration. He also served on various National Liberation Committees and received the Order of Orange Nassau. His interests took him and his wife, Dieuwke, abroad to the Far East, the United States and Canada. Whenever he was in Toronto, he would give me a call and I had the pleasure of meeting with him and his wife over dinner.

The last person I intend to mention is Dr. Henk Hannivort. It will be recalled I was billeted in his home in 1985. I had brought with me the first proofs of my book which I had asked him if he would read and give me his frank comments. That he did with obvious pleasure and endorsed my sometimes uncomplimentary references to German officers and soldiers. He was Jewish. All his relatives had perished in the Holocaust. Sadly, he was not at home in 1986. When I returned in 1989, he had passed away.

One community remained to be visited during my 1986 "unofficial" visit—the towns of Achterveld and Barneveld, where the PPCLI ended their War. Achterveld was also the place where the Food Truce was signed on April 30th, 1945.

The most hated German in Holland was Reichskommissar Seyss-Inquart, known as the Head Hun in Holland. He flooded the country, cut off food, coal, supplies, and sent tens of thousands to labour camps. His favourite automobile was a grand Mercedes-Benz, hated almost as much as the ugly little man in the back seat. The Dutch had captured the automobile (sans Seyss-Inquart) and presented it to Prince Bernhard. At the Food Conference, he parked it right in front of its former owner, who had to hobble around it. I was well aware of the Dutch aversion to large Mercedes-Benz automobiles and thus eschewed driving one during my brief visit in 1986. I was quite content to drive a modest Orion Escort.

As I crept along the A1 Superhighway from Apeldoorn to Achterveld, it was hard to believe the immense change that had taken place since 1945. Then, the narrow, pock-marked, heavily shelled road was shorn of all traffic except tanks and lorries. All the magnificent tall trees bordering the highway had been cut down by the desperate Hun.

Now, a four-lane highway, clogged with shiny, new automobiles, polluted the tulip-laced countryside. My advance was slowed to a snail's pace. After Achterveld, I had hoped to reach Amsterdam by early evening, but it was impossible. I had unthinkingly left Apeldoorn late in the afternoon and now I was in the middle of the rush-hour traffic. The distance from Apeldoorn to Amsterdam is less than 80 miles. I had been told that at rush-hour cars are nose to bumper all along the A1, and I was in the middle of it. I would be lucky to reach Achterveld by last light.

Nothing I can do about it. So I let my mind wander and think about my present situation. Here I am in Holland visiting old battlefields where the Hun and I were engaged in mortal combat 41 years ago. And how did I get here? Well, my former hated enemies invited me (and paid the airfare) to visit them in Stuttgart. How nice—so now the Germans are in effect subsidizing my trip to Holland on a mission to visit the battlefields where the PPCLI beat the hell out of the Germans. Well, I'll be damned. I allowed myself a large smile of ironic pleasure.

At last the Achterveld turn-off appeared and I was soon in the village. This was one place which I knew intimately and did not require any directions. My D Company had occupied the village in 1945. I drove directly to the house where my Headquarters had been located and knocked on the door. Mr. Jan Schouten greeted me warmly and I went inside.

Jan Schouten is the Archivist of Achterveld and has amassed an incredible collection of books, papers, articles, photos and memorabilia from the beginning of the War to date. His records include accounts of the bitter fighting around Achterveld in 1940 when the Dutch Forces killed 300 Germans. He has copies of the Truce Agreement in 1945, War diaries of the Canadian Forces and much to my surprise, a large collection about the PPCLI, including pictures of members of D Company in 1945 and a diary of B Company in August 1967, when it re-enacted the crossing of the Ijssel River.

I first met Jan Schouten, quite by chance, during my Pilgrimage in 1985, and spent many hours going through his PPCLI material and making notes for my book. What a crushing dénouement to the wild stories of the 48th Highlanders that they had attacked across the Ijssel River and captured Wilp.

Jan Schouten's records are a veritable mine of information about the Patricias that rivals the material of the Archives in Calgary. Over the years I have sent the museum extracts from some of these valuable records. It should be noted that quite recently Mr. Schouten sent all his archives to the Municipal Offices in Barneveld where they are secure from fire, theft and humidity and will be available for examination and research for years to come.

In February 1986, I again reviewed Jan Schouten's material on the PPCLI and discussed with him several draft chapters of my book. He gave me some new insights into the Truce negotiations and Agreement that were concluded in the schoolhouse only a few steps from his home. He also handed me a copy of the Agreement itself and other valuable documents, articles and photos. I was also interested in the re-enactment of the crossing of the Ijssel River by B Company in 1967. He gave me a copy of the complete journal kept by the Company Commander, some of which appears in my book. In my opinion, Mr. J. M. Schouten deserves official recognition by the Regiment for obtaining and preserving these invaluable records of the PPCLI.

My final destination in February 1986 was the nearby town of Barneveld where the headquarters of the Battalion was located in 1945. In prior Pilgrimages, I had neglected visiting the place because my main interest was, quite naturally, the village of Achterveld, where my D Company had been located. But as I entered the town I felt a twinge of guilt for not visiting it sooner, until I suddenly realized that my conscience was playing tricks on me. It wasn't disinterest that was keeping me away from Barneveld, but a deep-rooted aversion left over from the war to visiting Battalion Headquarters. You were always liable to become enmeshed in their paperwork!

Putting these wild thoughts aside, I soon found the Town Hall, entered the building and asked to see the Mayor. He was away but Mr. Dick Veldhuizen would be pleased to see me. Once again in my travels fortune smiled on me. Dick Veldhuizen was the historian and Assistant Archivist of Barneveld. I quickly introduced myself and mentioned I was writing a book about the PPCLI. Could he help me.

He certainly could. He was very interested in learning more about the Canadians who had liberated his country and saved his family from starvation.

He then produced two books about the war in Holland by Evert van de Weerd and others, which included material and pictures of the crossing of the Ijssel River and the Truce negotiations in Achterveld. Dick had drawn maps for the book and was well aware of the part played by the Patricias. He generously gave me the books as well as photos and maps of the operations. I thanked him and said, "Dick, this is wonderful. I only wish I had all this interesting material when I started to write my own book. Now I'll have to start all over again." I then produced some of my draft chapters which we discussed, amended and enlarged. I am sure my book is the better for having had Dick's helpful advice.

It was now quite late and I had to leave my new friend if I had any hope of reaching Amsterdam at a reasonable hour. Dick understood and made me promise to come back soon with a copy of my book, which he insisted I autograph. I am happy to say I have honoured both promises.

So far, I have mentioned only my visits to the towns and villages the Patricias liberated during the War, except Apeldoorn, which I will surrender to the 48th Highlanders! There was neither time nor occasion to get acquainted with the Dutch people on a personal basis during the War, except for a few fleeting opportunities.

Following VE Day, May 8th, 1945, all this drastically changed. Canadian soldiers instantly became heroes and friends with millions of Dutch citizens. On May 8th, 1945, the Regiment began its triumphal entry into western Holland by way of Amersfort, Hilversum, Amsterdam and Haarlem to Bloemendaal, where we were billeted in private homes. For a Patricia who had the good fortune to be there at that time, the memory of that experience would last a lifetime. For me, the reason I went to war was justified a thousand times. It had all been worthwhile.

Let another officer describe the scene as we pushed our way through the crowds of delirious Dutch citizens.

> *Every village, street and house was bedecked with the red, white and blue Dutch flags and orange streamers. The Dutch people lined the roads and streets in thousands to give us a great welcome. Wherever the convoy had to slow*

up for a road block or a bridge, hundreds of people waved, shouted and even fondled the vehicles. When the convoy reached the outskirts of Amsterdam it lost all semblance of a military column. A vehicle would be unable to move because of civilians surrounding it, climbing on it, throwing flowers, bestowing handshakes, hugs and kisses. One could not see the vehicle or trailer for legs, arms, heads and bodies draped all over it.[1]

Thus began the love story of the century, if not for all time. During the 1985 Pilgrimage more than 2,000 Veterans paraded through the streets of Apeldoorn and marched past Princess Margriet and our Minister of Defence, the popular George Hees. Most of the 140,000 inhabitants of the city lined the streets, waving more maple leaf flags than could be seen at any parade in Canada. The crowd broke through our ranks, hugging us, kissing us, pressing flowers into our hands, crying, shouting, cheering us in one continuous roar. Our fine parade melted away into the arms of our admirers.

Later, George Hees, in typical fashion, expressed our feelings to Princess Margriet. "This is really a love story. The Dutch people make us feel like delivering angels." The Princess replied, "The Canadians have brought Apeldoorn alive. People are talking to each other who never met before. The feeling is like it must have been at liberation."[2]

Canada's Veterans have been given the same overwhelming reception ever since. Is it any wonder that we return in our thousands to share these feelings with the people we helped to set free.

Now, back to the events following our arrival at Bloemendaal on May 8th, 1945. Our task was to round up 100,000 Germans and send them packing to the Fatherland. At the same time, the Dutch, starved for excitement and friendship, showered us with receptions and parties. At nearby Overveen, the Mayor presented the Patricias with a beautiful Charter of Thanks for their Liberation, which declared, among other things, that the officers and men of the PPCLI would always be welcomed into their midst and would find every door wide open.

On May 11th, my D Company moved to Noordwijkerhout to take over a Luftwaffe Battalion and a Field Hospital in nearby Noordwijk. It had formerly been a Mental Hospital, but the Germans had simply opened the gates and let the inmates run free. We helped the former head of the Hospital, Dr. de Witt Hamer, move back to his hospital and met his family, including two lovely daughters.

And so we passed the time—gathering in Germans and restoring the Dutch to their rightful possessions. Other towns were "liberated"—

GERMANY—HOLLAND—1986

Noordwijk-on-the-Sea, Zandvoort, Lisse and Sassenheim. At each place we were welcomed effusively by the Burgemeester in the presence of the entire populace and afterwards attended receptions, parties, dinners and dances. In Sassenheim, I met an exceptional family, the Boots. The father, Phil, had been a prosperous bulb grower, had travelled extensively in Canada and had established a company in the United States. Like the de Witt Hamers, he had hidden Allied airmen, and his son was active in the Underground. He also had two charming daughters.

The friendships I formed with these fine Dutch families, the de Witt Hamers in Noordwijkerout and the Boots in Sassenheim, were to last a lifetime.

Following our rigorous but happy times in these towns, the Battalion moved to Bilthoven, mid-way between Amersfoort and Utrecht, to prepare for the return to Canada. Finally, on September 4th, 1945, the Regiment moved to a camp at Nijmegen, then by train to Ostend and across the Channel to Dover and a camp at Esher.

On September 26th, we embarked at Southampton on the *Isle de France* and arrived in Halifax on October 1st. But that is another story.

* * *

We must now pick up the main thread of my story where I said goodbye to Dick Veldhuizen at Barneveld, toward the end of my journey to Holland in February 1986. I was about to round out my visit by calling on friends I had made in 1945 after the war was over. Now that we are acquainted with them, I can briefly record the thrill of seeing them again.

Dr. de Witt Hamer had passed on, but I located one of his daughters, Mimi, in Noordwijkerout. Her sister Jetti was in the United States and her brother Jim, a doctor, had served in Indonesia. Mimi, herself, held an executive position with the Netherlands Universities Foundation. She had married and had a son. I suggested we visit her old home, the Mental Hospital at Noordwijk, to see if I could find a secret room where they had hidden Allied Airmen.

"Fine idea," said Mimi. "Haven't been back for years. The new head is Mr. van der Zanden."

With her as co-pilot, we soon found the hospital and met Mr. van der Zanden and his wife. They knew all about the entrance to the secret room leading off one of the bedrooms up to the attic. But the room had just been redecorated and they weren't about to bash in the wall where the stairway was located.

I queried Mimi, "What if the Germans had discovered that room and found an Airman? You all would have been taken out in the street and shot."

"Well, in that case," Mimi nonchalantly replied, "we had no more worries, had we?"

I had nothing but admiration for such a cool and determined lady.

I had no trouble finding Jean Boot as we had kept in touch over the years. Her parents were deceased but she had married, and now lived in Muiden with her husband, daughter and son who was a lawyer. I was lucky to catch her as the family usually wintered in Greece. Like many Dutch people she had put behind her the terrible years of suffering and starvation and had led a happy and rewarding life. Her brother and sister had likewise enjoyed successful careers.

For old times' sake, we visited her former home in Sassenheim where I had enjoyed the friendship and hospitality of her father and mother. Sassenheim is in the centre of the tulip country. Not far away, the famous Keukenhof Gardens beckoned. Though I have visited these gardens many times, their beauty never ceases to enthral me. Bed upon bed of tulips of every kind and hue—soft, pastel shades; bright, vivid colours; the whole set amid forest greenery and winding brooks. Truly an unforgettable sight.

One final act remained outstanding in this "unofficial" visit in 1986 to Holland, which had really developed into a full-fledged Pilgrimage. I was keen to test the Charter which the town of Overveen had given to LCol. Clark and all Patricias—every door would be open wide. I thought a good place to start would be City Hall. Wearing PPCLI blazer, beret and medals, I presented myself to the Town Clerk and started to explain my mission.

No need for any explanation. I was immediately shown into the Mayor's Chamber where I was warmly greeted by three Aldermen—Drs. O. F. Staleman, (who was also Vice-Mayor), Drs. W. van der Ham, and Miss G. D. Bredius-Gockinga.

I had taken the precaution of bringing a copy of the Charter with me and the Aldermen had a good laugh at my ingenuity. Of course every door would be open. Where would I care to start? Or would I settle for a few gifts?

I quickly accepted the latter suggestion and I was promptly presented with a silk tie, a silk scarf for my wife, a beautiful book on Bloemendaal (Overveen is a suburb) and several magazines including a coloured reproduction of the Charter. In thanking them I said, "I suppose I had better not inform the PPCLI of your generous gifts, as there are still many Veterans around who would certainly take advantage of your offer, and that might well bankrupt the town."

One of the Aldermen replied, "That's fine. We are happy to make this small gesture to the soldiers who gave us back our Liberty.

GERMANY—HOLLAND—1986

And, by the way, don't worry about the cost. Overveen has more millionaires than any other town in Holland!"

Thus ended a very emotional but very productive visit to Holland. I had been given enough material to write two or three books on the PPCLI and the part they played in the Liberation of Holland. But most of all, I was inspired to tell the story of the deep respect, friendship and goodwill the people of Holland have for Canada and its soldiers. It is a marvellous thing that cannot be fully described but it can be felt and it is overwhelming.

Each time I visit the Dutch people, I experience this special feeling, and I am thankful and proud to have taken part in their Liberation. George Hees said it is a love story and I would agree.

Chapter XIV

PILGRIMAGE—1989

The prime reason for my Pilgrimage in 1989 was to visit Sicily, in particular the beaches where the PPCLI had landed on July 10th, 1943. In my book *Once a Patricia*, which was now published, I had given scant coverage to the landing as I had not been part of the assaulting force. I came ashore on July 13th as a Reinforcement Officer and didn't join the Patricias until their last battle in Sicily at Mount Seggio. Some of my readers and one reviewer were at pains to bring these omissions to my attention. Others suggested I write a sequel, not only for Sicily but for Italy and Holland as well.

And so, after another gap of some 14 years, I am now, finally, putting pen to paper to satisfy both my critics and admirers.

While planning my 1989 trip to Sicily, I felt I could not come all this long way without spending some time with my friends in Holland. As a result, my itinerary escalated to 2,787 miles by car, as I have already intimated.

On May 6th, 1989, I arrived at the Schiphol Airport, Amsterdam, after a two-hour flight from London, and checked in at the Hilton Apollolaan, a pleasant hotel overlooking a canal. It would be my headquarters for the Holland phase of my journey. This time my mission was not to gather material for my book, but to thank all the people who had so generously given me the information I needed.

My first objective was Barneveld and its Mayor, Mr. C. W. Labree, whom I had missed in 1986. Mindful of the rush-hour congestion I experienced along Highway A1 on my last trip, I left Amsterdam at an early hour and arrived in Barneveld in time for a hearty Dutch breakfast with my friend, Dick Veldhuizen. My intent was to present a copy of my book to all my friends in Holland, but I realized that I would require a cargo plane. I explained this to Dick and said I had only one book for him and the Mayor. Would he mind if I presented it to the Mayor and I would see that he received a copy later. Dick understood and accompanied me to the Mayor's office.

Mr. Labree had of course been thoroughly briefed on my last visit and gave me a warm welcome. He knew all about the PPCLI, their occupation of Barneveld and the Food Truce. Again and again he thanked the Regiment for liberating his country and for their kindness to the citizens of Barneveld during the critical days at the end of the war.

Mr. Labree was cast in much the same mould as all the other Mayors I had met over a span of 20 years or more. They seemed to be a special breed. They are all fine gentlemen, knowledgeable, erudite, polished, kind, fluent in many languages and sincere. Later I commented to Dick Veldhuizen, "I wish our Mayors were more like yours. How do they get that way? Is there a school for Mayors?"

Dick laughed. "It's very simple. They are all appointed by the Queen."

I thought it interesting that he didn't go on to say that the citizens trusted their Queen to choose wisely, above and beyond the call of politicians. He didn't need to. It was implied.

Mr. Labree was genuinely pleased to see me and disappointed that I had to leave. I reached into my briefcase and produced a copy of *Once a Patricia* which I presented to him. On the flyleaf I had inscribed:

> *For the citizens of Barneveld, in appreciation of their kindness to the Canadian Soldiers and Veterans, and in memory of all who gave their lives in Holland, that we may be free.*

Shortly after I arrived home in Toronto, I received a letter from Mr. Labree:

> *Dear Mr. Frost,*
>
> *Thank you very much for the copy of your book "Once a Patricia"—a title which is not entirely according to the facts, as you are still a Patricia at heart! That is the conclusion I had to make after reading this wonderful story about your adventures as a cadet and as an officer of the Canadian Army during the Second World War.*
>
> *May I begin this letter with my congratulations because of your authorship, your fine style of writing,—but most of all because of your telling the (for Dutchmen generally quite unknown) history of Canadian fighting in Italy. Those battles you went through in that difficult country, those suf-*

ferings, the death of so many of your friends, the misery of those who got wounded or died in mud and cold—I read it all with fascination. Thank you for having given me the chance to read your book.

At the time you came to Holland and crossed the Ijssel, March/April 1945, I was at the age of seventeen, just old enough to be taken by the Germans to dig trenches for them outside Amersfoort, where I lived. So I had to stay at home and hide at some secret place below the floor of the drawing-room. Very cold during that (hunger) winter.

*They didn't find me, fortunately; they didn't search for us all the time—but especially during autumn 1944 a good many men had been caught and transported to the east (around the city of Doetinchem) where they had to work hard to make those trenches—and got hardly any food....
That's why we will always be so grateful to you and your fellow-Canadians: We were liberated just in time!*

Well, I thank you again for your letter, and for the fine history of your life as an officer—but not less for the friendship we have enjoyed from all our Canadian friends, especially when hundreds of them were our guests in Barneveld in 1985.

Such a fine, sincere letter. It helps to show why the people of Holland are so grateful to the Canadians.

I saw Mr. Labree once more during the 1990 Pilgrimage and presented him with a PPCLI cap badge which I know gave him much pleasure.

Eighteen months later he died from a cerebral haemorrhage on his 64th birthday.

I received a note from the new Mayor.

As you may understand we are mourning because of the death of a respected and beloved mayor.

On Saturday, the 18th of January, during a memorial service in the Old Church of Barneveld, many people were present and paid the burgomaster their last respects.

Grateful for the good contacts we had with you in the past, we do hope these contacts will continue in the future.

* * *

PILGRIMAGE—1989

Achterveld was supposed to be my next stop, but I received news that Mr. Jan Schouten was not at home. So I deferred my visit to the following year.

Likewise, most of my friends in Apeldoorn were busy or out of town. Pieter Beelaerts van Blokland, The Queen's Commissioner for Utrecht, was in Japan. The Dutch are great travellers! Compressed into such an interesting but tiny country, they seem compelled to fly away whenever they can.

The new Mayor of Apeldoorn, Mr. Ton Hubers, and Evert Gerritsen were away but they kindly visited me in Toronto the following September. We had dinner together, and I presented each of them with a copy of my book, suitably autographed. It may stretch my credibility to say that my third guest was none other than a member of the 48th Highlanders! I had decided there was no point to prolonging the controversy about who attacked across the Ijssel River and captured Wilp. In fact, there was no longer any controversy. Most members of the 48th Highlanders acknowledged that a terrible mistake had been made. At dinner we briefly discussed the matter. My guest did not know how the slander was started or by whom. Probably one or two old Veterans, whose memories of events 40 years earlier were at best shaky, had started the story, and unlike the proverbial rolling stone, it had gathered moss. Soon everyone believed it.

I couldn't help interjecting, "more like a loose cannon on a ship. It does more damage than a rolling stone."

With that we agreed to bury the matter, and there it has lain ever since. Peace and quiet now reign along the Ijssel River. I have visited the 48th Highlanders Officers' Mess and attended their parades. After I had been successful in having a Monument erected in Sicily, LCol. Mike George of the 48th gave a talk about it to his Association and said some kind words about me.

Before our little party broke up, I learned that plans were being made for another big Liberation Anniversary in 1990. Apeldoorn would be the centre of the celebrations. I was asked if I would attend.

Even though I had visited Holland five times since the War, I replied without any hesitation, "I'll keep coming as long as you can put up with me." Next day I got in touch with my travel agent. As events turned out, I should have added "barring sickness," but that problem could not have been foreseen.

* * *

We now return once more to my Pilgrimage to Holland in May 1989. After my visit to Barneveld there remained one final objective—

Wilp and the municipality of Voorst. It will be remembered that this was actually my first objective in 1945. As soon as my book had been published in September 1988, I arranged to have a copy delivered to Johannes van Blommestein, the Mayor of Voorst, and I told him I would probably visit him in May 1989. He wrote back a kind, generous letter from which I quote:

> Twello, December 22, 1988
>
> Dear Colonel Frost,
>
> First of all a very good and happy New Year for you personally and yours. I hope to see you this year again. Your PPCLI cap badge is still on my office desk table lamp in remembrance of those memorable days in 1985.
>
> It was a big surprise to receive your greetings via Mr. and Mrs. Kooter of Nymegen who rang me up a month ago. I headed directly to the south to meet him. And what a gift of you he handed over to me! "Once a Patricia" is really a monumental work you have finished and wonderfully published. Your personal note on the front page is a golden souvenir of a friend of our municipality. I carefully read the chapter of the 4th pilgrimage. I recognize forever the contribution of the PPCLI to the liberation of our community and Wilp by the D Company, as the very first of all Canadian troops. Your work in this book is the very best monument to April 11, 1945. I am very grateful to you for receiving this.
>
> With my warmest personal regards and best wishes to you.
>
> Sincerely,
> Johannes van Blommestein

Another remarkable letter from a fine Dutch gentleman. Perhaps my reader is beginning to appreciate the depth of feeling the people of Holland have for their Canadian Liberators. More is to come.

On May 9th, 1989, I attended the Municipal Offices of Voorst to greet my dear friend and thank him for his kind note. I said how gratified I was that he had acknowledged the role of the PPCLI in the Ijssel River crossing and the Liberation of Wilp. The fight was over and the matter could now be laid to rest.

Johannes shook his head, "Not yet, my dear Colonel. The fight may be over but the matter is not yet laid to rest. You must come next year to see the final act."

"The final act," I queried, "tell me more."

Johannes gave me that charming smile of his and said, "you'll see next year. Come now, let's visit some book stores to see if they are interested in selling your fine book."

We set off in his car and called on several book stores in Twello and the surrounding villages. After lunch in a restaurant that served only asparagus (but in 20 different ways), he had to get back to the office and I to Amsterdam. As we clasped hands he said, "Oh, by the way, I have a few little souvenirs for you to take home."

Whereupon he handed me an illustrated book about the city of Deventer, a beautiful Delft candy jar and a bottle of fine liqueur. His parting words were, "See you next year, in May."

How does one respond to such generosity? The education of my reader about the kindness of the Dutch people is continuing.

I was intrigued by Johannes' invitation to come back next year to witness the "final act." I had to wait twelve months. My reader will find out in the next chapter.

I returned to Amsterdam and prepared for my long trip by car to Vienna.

My itinerary was the following: Amsterdam, Utrecht, Arnhem, Rhine River, Cologne, Bonn, Mainz, Frankfurt, Nuremberg, Dachau, Munich, Salzburg, Berchtesgaden, Vienna—a total distance of 1,140 miles. Each place has a claim to fame or notoriety. We have only time to pause and examine those that fall in the latter category.

Nuremberg

After Hitler came to power in 1933, Nuremberg was made a national shrine by the National Socialists, who held their annual party congresses there. It was the home of the notorious Julius Streicher and became the centre of the anti-Semitic propaganda. In 1935, the Nuremberg laws were passed, depriving Jews of civic rights. After the War, Nuremberg was the seat of the War Crimes trials.

I was fully aware of these facts taken from a tourist guide book, but what I wanted to see was the immense stadium where Hitler brazenly paraded his military might for all the world to see (and to tremble). None of my maps showed the stadium. Several passers-by shook their heads when I asked dircctions. Policemen were no help, some of whom acted as though they had received their basic training in an SS Regiment. Finally, in frustration, I said "To hell with it" and drove on. Perhaps it was just as well, because I had contemplated doing an obscene act right in the middle of the stadium. I was relying on solid precedent. Churchill himself had done the same thing in the Rhine River when the Allies completed their successful crossing.

Dachau

Dachau is about nine miles northwest of Munich. It enjoyed a notable history for a thousand years until March 21st, 1933, when Heinrich Himmler opened the first concentration camp.

It is not my intention to describe the atrocities that were committed, but perhaps a few facts bear repeating. The number of prisoners who went through Dachau was 206,206 including 2,720 Clergymen. The number of "certified" deaths was 31,951. Inmates were murdered by gas, by cremation, by hanging, by torture, by starvation, by medical experiments and by other diabolical means.

Only one thing can be said in favour of the Nazis: They kept accurate records of their crimes, including complete dossiers on all their victims.

As I walked through the perfectly preserved camp and observed the awful instruments of death, the medical records, the horrible photographs of human beings near death from starvation and the savage looks of the SS guards, I felt revulsion beyond measure. Not for the first time I was thankful and proud that I had played some small part in bringing to an end these obscenities against law and nature.

I thought too of the weaknesses in our own legal system that allow people to tie up our courts with claims that the Holocaust never happened, or if it did, only a few million Jews were massacred. I have a suggestion, which I make as a lawyer and with the utmost sincerity. Let all those people involved in litigation about the Holocaust—the judges, jurors, lawyers and particularly the complainants—visit Dachau, and all the hundreds of similar camps, although I believe that just Dachau will serve my purpose. Let them see, read, hear and feel what went on in these camps. The expense of sending these people will be far less than the cost and time spent in a long trial. But saving money is not the main purpose of my suggestion. It is a matter of educating the judiciary and lawmakers of our country, and possibly amending the Bill of Rights. In my view, the scales of justice are too heavily weighted in favour of the accused, the guilty, the crackpots, the pornographers, the child molesters, the eccentrics of this country. The concept that "everyone must have his day in court" is overworked and abused.

What we need is a Bill of Duties and Responsibilities. A lawyer friend of mine once sponsored such a Bill in Parliament. What happened to it? Nothing. Perhaps we should send the entire House of Commons to Dachau. The idea is not to imprison them (although some might think that not a bad thing), but to educate them about the Holocaust. The Senate should also attend, but pay their own way.

I apologize for this digression. The latter part about our Parliament is said with tongue in cheek and not in derogation of my earlier remarks about the horrors of Dachau and the indisputable evidence of the Holocaust. But if further proof is required, a small book by Dr. Johannes Neuhausler, Auxiliary Bishop of Munich, entitled *What Was It Like in the Concentration Camp at Dachau*, will give the answers.

Allow me to conclude this "sidebar" on Dachau with a reference to Dante Alighieri. It may be remembered that I last mentioned his *Divine Comedy* in connection with a briefing given in the Teatro Dante on a forthcoming operation in northern Italy which the staff had named Operation Chuckle. It turned out to be a tragedy equal to Dante's work.

Bishop Neuhausler, in his book, also called on Dante to provide an inscription for the entrance to Dachau. His *Divine Comedy* supplied the answer in describing the entrance to hell, "All hope abandon, ye who enter here."

Berchtesgaden—The Eagle's Nest

Berchtesgaden is a village in the mountains about 11 miles south of Salzburg. The Eagle's Nest is 2 miles southeast of Berchtesgaden and sits atop the 6,017 foot Kehlstein mountain.

Martin Bormann gave the Eagle's Nest (also known as the Tea House) to Hitler on his 50th birthday in 1939, as a gift on behalf of the National Socialist Party. Work on the project started in 1937, involved 3,000 workers and cost 90 million U.S. dollars (1981).

The road up the mountain is a masterpiece of engineering. It is 4.2 miles long, winds through five tunnels and has a series of dangerous turns. At the top, the road ends in a large parking lot. From there a 136-yard-long tunnel for pedestrians leads to an elevator cut into the middle of the mountain. The elevator is fitted with highly polished brass, Venetian mirrors and green leather seats designed to soothe Hitler, who suffered from claustrophobia.

Hitler's valet reported that Hitler disliked the house from the very beginning. He forced himself to go up there occasionally just to please his mistress, Eva Braun, and Martin Bormann. Hitler suffered shortness of breath and palpitation due to the sudden change in altitude. He was also afraid that the elevator cable would be struck by lightning while he was going up to the house.

Hitler seldom visited the Eagle's Nest, because of these phobias and medical problems. Some say he went up only five or six times. On the other hand, he was very fond of his Berghof, or mountain home, in a community known as Obersalzberg at the foot of another mountain, the Hohe Goell. It was here that he received Heads of State and other dignitaries—The Duke of Windsor and his wife, Mussolini, Count Ciano, Francis Poncet of France and many others.

It all came to an end on April 25, 1945, when 318 Lancaster bombers dropped 1,232 tons of bombs. Obersalzberg was badly damaged but the Eagle's Nest escaped (Hitler was in his bunker in Berlin).

Today, Hitler's Berghof and those of his henchmen on the Obersalzberg have all followed the same fate as their owners— Goering, Bormann and the others—all have been destroyed.

Tourists may wander freely through the ruins of Obersalzberg and, if willing to assume the risks, ascend the 4.2 miles of the Kehlstein Road to the Eagle's Nest and admire the unequalled view.

For me, it was an eerie sensation to be driven up the mountain and then to take the elevator to the top. I think the ascent in the elevator was the weirdest feeling of all, not because I felt claustrophobic, but because I was surrounded by the ghosts of Hitler and his jack-booted henchmen who had been there before. It was a relief to arrive at the top and not find a party of SS men waiting for me! My nerves were somewhat calmed by some fine Bavarian beer and a schnitzel served in the elegant restaurant that now occupies Hitler's conference room.

After lunch, I went outside to admire the view. There, in the middle distance, Salzberg; just below my perch, Obersalzberg; and in between, quaint little villages, green pastures, forests, mountain streams. In all my travels I cannot think of a more breathtaking panorama, except possibly San Marino, in Italy, but that did not have the imprimatur of der Fuehrer himself.

I left Obersalzberg with unsettled feelings. For years I had wanted to visit the Eagle's Nest and see for myself this pinnacle of Hitler's folly. As he gazed over the countryside, as I had just done, what were his thoughts and his plans for world domination? Like Napoleon before him, he had it made on his 50th birthday in 1939.

Then, later, as his plans went awry, what were his feelings? Did he have any remorse at all for the millions who had perished? Did he, like the Colonel in *The Bridge Over the River Quai*, ever say to himself, "My God, what have I done? What have I done?" Did he ever think of stopping the killing? No. The demons inside this architect of destruction urged him on until he had almost destroyed civilization and suffered an ignominious end himself, far removed from his cherished Obersalzberg and the Eagle's Nest.

I pressed down the accelerator on my automobile as if to rid myself of the evil spirits that still lingered around this place, and headed for Vienna.

The remainder of my 1989 Pilgrimage to Italy and Sicily has already been told in earlier chapters.

Chapter XV

PILGRIMAGE—1990

During my visits in 1986 and 1989, I had received strong hints from many people that a grand celebration would be held all over Holland in 1990 to commemorate the 45th Anniversary of the Liberation.

On September 22nd, 1989, Evert Gerritsen, the well-known owner of Apeldoorn Taxi, and Ton Hubers, the Mayor of Apeldoorn, called on me in Toronto to give me a list of the proposed events and formally invite me to attend. Then, on October 10th, Evert phoned to confirm the tentative schedule and supply more details. Again, on March 22nd, 1990, he gave me the final program. The next day Klaas Huismann, Apeldoorn's Chief of Cabinet, phoned to confirm all the events. I had the distinct feeling that I would be a welcome guest.

Invitations also poured in from other municipalities. On November 6th, I received a long letter from Johannes van Blommestein, Mayor of Voorst, inviting me to participate in the festivities being held in his Municipality and to stay at the home of one of the citizens. I quote from his letter to show the close relationship that had grown up between Voorst and the Patricias.

> *With much pleasure we remember the contacts we had with you in the past. These contacts, together with the extremely important part your Regiment (Princess Patricia's Canadian Light Infantry) played at the time, have greatly contributed to keeping alive among us the memory of the liberation in April 1945.*
>
> *In Holland there are going to be organised various manifestations and festivities to celebrate the liberation on a*

large scale in 1990. Many World War II veterans will participate in these celebrations.

The local committee in our municipality of Voorst—has the intention to find ways and means to offer home-hospitality to a certain number of Canadian veterans in the period from April 28/29 to May 8, 1990.

It will be remembered that Johannes had dropped a thinly veiled hint the previous May that his Municipality had lined up something very big to confirm for all time that the Patricias were the first Regiment to liberate its citizens. I still had not the faintest idea what it was.

From Pieter Beelaerts van Blokland, former Mayor of Apeldoorn, but now the Queen's Commissioner for the Province of Utrecht, I received a note from Japan, of all places, inviting me to visit him in Utrecht.

Jan Schouten, my archivist friend in Achterveld, sent me a letter inviting me to speak at the Ceremonies to be held in his town and requesting photos for the local newspaper.

In the meantime, I heard from my friend who was helping me in my Sicilian adventure, the Honourable Gerry Merrithew, Minister of Veterans Affairs. The Canadian Government was participating in this Anniversary and would be sending an official delegation of Veterans and the Band of the PPCLI to Holland. It was understood, of course, that I would not be a part of the Official Party, but I was invited to attend some of the main events.

I also received a telephone call and a letter from a member of the Minister's Department, Peter Caissie, about the Anniversary. Later he sent me the program for the Official Group. It was an ambitious undertaking and I was glad I had not been invited to participate. Among the cities to be visited were The Hague, Amersfort, Nijverdal, Holten, Amsterdam, Wageningen, Groesbeek, Groningen, Bergen op Zoom and Westerbork.

Peter Caissie had a lot on his plate organizing not only this Pilgrimage but others to Vimy and Hong Kong. Yet he found time to give me valuable help and material not only for Holland but for Sicily as well.

A month later, I received a call from another dedicated public servant, André Petelle, who has also been mentioned in these pages. He warned me that the Dutch Army were preparing to erect a pontoon bridge across the Ijssel River. It would be a pretty impressive operation. Canadian troops were coming down from Lahr, Germany, to participate in the ceremonies, including a guard from 1 RCHA and the bagpipes of the RCR. I had better be ready to explain to the large crowd of spectators how the PPCLI had crossed the river at that very spot on April 11th, 1945! "My God," I thought, "what have I got myself into this time?"

Further invitations and information continued to arrive until my library looked more like a Tourist Office. I wondered how I would ever fit all the events into my schedule. It should not be forgotten that at the same time, I was heavily involved in planning my Pilgrimage to Sicily. How I found time to pursue my other profession I have no idea.

The time finally arrived to board KLM Flight 692 for Amsterdam. I left Toronto at 5:45 p.m. April 29th, and arrived at Amsterdam at 9:25 a.m. the next day. A short drive (in distance, but not in time) along the A1, clogged with the usual rush-hour traffic, took me to Apeldoorn and the Hotel Keizerskroon where I crashed (not the car but myself into bed). Fortunately, I had allowed myself the rest of the day to rest and prepare for a strenuous and emotional Pilgrimage over the coming week.

From past Pilgrimages I knew that I would be required to speak on several occasions and I had prepared for this. But I was concerned about how I could ever thank our Dutch hosts for their kindness and hospitality. The best I could do was to stuff into my already bulging luggage Regimental ties, badges, plaques and a few copies of my book. I also brought with me a supply of blank inscription plates which I hoped my friend Evert Gerritsen, who had helped me in the past, could have engraved.

I believe there is only one way to properly describe the events which follow. I kept a day-to-day diary of these events and filed a full report with the Colonel of the Regiment, MGen. H.C. Pitts, MC, CD. The following account is based on these records.

May 1st, Tuesday

Mr. Pieter Beelaerts van Blokland, who had been the Burgemeester of Apeldoorn during the 1985 Pilgrimage to that city, was now the Queen's Commissioner in the Province of Utrecht. On May 1st, he held a dinner in his "Palace" in Utrecht to honour the 45th Anniversary of the Liberation and invited the present Burgemeester of Apeldoorn and many city officials, including General A.W.T. Gijsbers, Chairman of the Liberation Committee, and Klaas Huisman, the Chief of Cabinet to the Mayor, who kindly drove me to Utrecht. I had the honour of attending the dinner on behalf of the Patricias, one of the few Regiments represented. Fortunately, I had brought with me a Regimental plaque and a blank inscription plate. I was able to have the plate suitably engraved and affixed to the plaque which I presented to Mr. Beelaerts van Blokland, together with a tie.

Pieter Beelaerts, as he is known to his friends, is renowned for his ready wit and charm. The menu for this memorable dinner was a celebration of the art of food. He had thoughtfully laid in a generous supply of wines from each country the First Division had traversed on the long road from Ispica to Wilp—Sicily, Italy, France, Belgium, Germany, and I believe Holland, but I don't remember for certain.

Of course, the 48th Highlanders were present and had a piper play in the head table guests. Unfortunately, the piper slipped on the wet floor and fell down quite heavily. For a moment we thought he had injured himself, but he gamely picked himself up and resumed his duties with fine soldierly bearing. I shamefully took advantage of this little accident by throwing a shaft of humour at the 48th in my remarks at the conclusion of the dinner.

> *Your Commissioner is a man of many parts. He has a fine appreciation of wine. He speaks first and has me speak last—after all that wine. He can recite all the Battle Honours of the 48th, but he omitted an honour that has just been won—the Battle of Utrecht.*

The remainder of my speech was in a more serious vein:

> *Year after year you keep asking us back and year after year we gladly accept your hospitality. How do you have the patience and stamina to put up with so many old men? And how do we survive? As one veteran said the other night: "The Dutch are doing their best to do what the Germans didn't—kill the survivors."*
>
> *One of the few good things to come out of that terrible War was the tremendous respect and goodwill we have developed for each other. And these feelings are not just confined to the war generation but are passed down, as part of the Dutch heritage, to each new generation. I can't express how proud and thrilled I am to march in your streets and see so many young children lining our route and waving Canadian flags. Their enthusiasm and warmth far exceeds anything we have ever experienced in Canada.*
>
> *These Pilgrimages are indeed a wonderful bond between our people and our countries. I, for one, shall never tire of them and I look forward to the next one, which I assume will be in 1995, the 50th Anniversary of the Liberation. That is only five years from now, and you really deserve more than five years of peace before you are invaded once more by a*

PILGRIMAGE—1990

> *horde of Canadian Veterans! But if I am still around, and you ask me, I shall come.*

May 2nd, Wednesday

This was the day of the Re-enactment of the crossing of the Ijssel River at the exact point where the Patricias had crossed on April 11th, 1945. The genesis of this event was many years earlier when certain members of another unit had circulated the myth that they, not the Patricias, had assaulted across the river and captured Wilp. The Dutch people, not knowing the true story, had gone along with it.

During the 1985 Pilgrimage this mistake came to light. The Burgemeesters of Apeldoorn and Voorst (in which Wilp is situated) were most apologetic and promised to put the matter right at the 45th Anniversary in 1990. The Burgemeester of Voorst, Dr. Johannes van Blommestein, immediately started planning a Re-enactment of the Crossing of the Ijssel River.

It was an enormous undertaking and required the co-operation of the Municipality of Gorssel on the east bank of the river. Permission also had to be obtained from half a dozen government agencies, including the Waterways Authority, the Environmental Authority, the Department of Municipal Affairs and the Dutch Army. The result was that on May 2nd, the Dutch Engineers erected a pontoon bridge. It only took them thirty minutes to do a job that in 1945 had taken our Engineers a full day to complete. Of course, there were no Jerries present on May 2nd, 1990.

The Dutch are much like the Patricias. They do everything with panache and with class. Early on the morning of May 2nd, I was picked up at my hotel and driven to the home of Mr. Anton aan de Stegge in Wilp. This was not an ordinary home. It was a large mansion with a history. During the filming of *A Bridge Too Far* it became the headquarters of the German General. Mr. de Stegge showed me mementoes, uniforms and equipment used in the film and gave me many photos of the actual scenes, as well as informal shots of the actors.

Sharp at 10:30, Mr. de Stegge announced he was going to drive me in a Rolls Royce convertible to the Ijssel River where the Dutch Engineers were in the process of completing the bridge. On either side of the river, bleachers had been erected and several thousand people lined the banks, including many Veterans. I had some inkling about the building of the bridge but no idea of what was to follow. First, I was introduced to the spectators by the Burgemeester of Gorssel, Mr. Jim van Notten, and then asked to come forward and tell the true story of the crossing of the Ijssel by the Patricias. It was an invitation I had been waiting for these past five years!

After my speech, I innocently asked Dr. van Blommestein, "Who's going to be the first person to test whether the thing really works?" He said, "You." A jeep appeared and I was loaded into it. Just as we were about to drive off, some official ran up and asked if it would be all right if a representative of the 48th Highlanders joined me. For an instant a bolt of disbelief and anger shot through me, but quickly my better nature emerged and I agreed. The battle was truly over and, thanks to Johannes van Blommestein, could at last be laid to rest. We set off across the pontoon bridge, followed by the pipes and drums of the RCR, the Band of the R22ndR in full scarlet and a Guard of Honour from the RCR. On arrival at the other side of the river the guard fired a "feu de joie." The honour of the Patricias had been fully redeemed!

Later the Municipality of Voorst provided a lunch for the Veterans at Bussloo. This place was familiar to the PPCLI. We had captured it after Wilp. I was happy to meet four of those Patricias: Bill Roach, DSO; Wally Smith; Lloyd Kramer, MM; and Charlie King. We all agreed that this crossing was more enjoyable than the original version which had neglected to supply us with lunch.

An interesting footnote to this great undertaking occurred a little later when I was chatting with Dr. van Blommestein and Mr. van Notten, the Burgemeester of Gorssel (on the east bank of the river), who had been a keen supporter of the project. One of them said words to the effect that prior to this event the citizens of the two municipalities of Voorst and Gorssel had little in common and seldom spoke with each other. The river seemed to create a barrier between them. Now, after the Re-enactment of the Crossing, the people on both sides of the Ijssel had come together. The river was no longer a barrier, but a means of communication with each other.

Throughout this drama, a large corps of photographers (including aerial photographers), TV, radio and the press recorded the event. All the Dutch newspapers carried the story on the front page. The following is an example:

DEVENTER JOURNAL
May 2, 1990

THOUSANDS TASTE ATMOSPHERE OF APRIL, 1945

Wilp—Gorssel
  Viewed by hundreds of Canadian veterans, hundreds of invited and other interested citizens on both sides of the Ijssel, the Dutch Engineer Unit installed a bridge between Wilp and Gorssel early this afternoon.

> *At the liberation of Holland 45 years ago, advanced units of the Canadian Army did the same thing on April 11, 1945. Today, in brilliant sunshine, the river crossing was an impressive event in the series of events during May in the Provinces of Overijssel and Gelderland. With heavy army equipment, boats and pontoons were manoeuvred into position and Colonel C. Sydney Frost, a former officer of the Princess Patricia's Canadian Light Infantry, drove over the bridge.*

Another interesting sequel to this memorable day, was the magnanimous act of a Dutch citizen, Mr. Gerard Burgers, who had helped in the planning of the event. He was so moved by the significance of the occasion that on the spur of the moment he arranged for 1,000 aerial photos of the bridge to be hurriedly printed and distributed to the Veterans and Dutch spectators without charge. He had been the manager of the nearby Teuge Airport and knew the aerial photographers who had taken the pictures.

But that was not all. Again, on his own initiative, he borrowed from another friend the coloured snaps he had taken of me crossing the bridge in the jeep. He then had 200 large prints made, which I was happy to autograph, and sold them for 5 guilders each. From the proceeds of the sale, he realized $263 which he sent to the PPCLI Headquarters in Calgary to be placed in the Regimental Fund. He should have received a medal.

May 3rd, Thursday

On this day, the City of Apeldoorn held a reception for all the Veterans lodged in the area. In our hundreds, we gathered at the Canadian Club. For many of us it was the first time we had met since 1985, and for some, since the war—45 years earlier. The emotions generated by these happy meetings can easily be imagined.

The venue of our celebrations, The Canadian Club, requires a word of explanation. In 1985, when the Apeldoorn citizens were planning that Pilgrimage, they realized there was no facility large enough to accommodate a meeting of all the Veterans. Furthermore, they wanted to provide a central place for Veterans to "meet and greet" during the week-long celebrations. What to do? No problem for the generous, thoughtful Dutch people—build a facility. And that is exactly what they did—with restaurant, bars and even a stage to accommodate dance bands and other forms of entertainment.

In 1985 and again in 1990, The Canadian Club served its purpose admirably and helped to establish Apeldoorn as the centre of these and all the other anniversaries.

The reception on May 3rd also afforded the Mayor and the members of his Liberation Committee an opportunity to meet the Veterans, and for the Veterans to thank them for their wonderful hospitality and friendship. In truth, there was no way we could adequately express our appreciation, but the Dutch people understood this and did not want or expect any *quid pro quo*. They were overjoyed they could do something for us to demonstrate how much they appreciated the liberty we had given them.

Nevertheless, I had packed my bags with various small gifts that I wanted to present as a token of our appreciation. Now was the time to do it. After a warm welcome by Ton Hubers, the Mayor, and after several Veterans had responded, I made the following comments:

> *Here we are together once again enjoying the hospitality of our wonderful Dutch friends. Your friendship, warmth and kindness are really overwhelming and I've run out of words to adequately express our thanks. The best I can do is present, on behalf of my Regiment, a few tokens of our appreciation.*
>
> *First—To Mr. Hubers, to signify the close ties that exist between us—a PPCLI Regimental tie.*
>
> *Second—To the people of Apeldoorn, who have been so generous, a Regimental Plaque commemorating the 45th Anniversary of the Liberation.*
>
> *Third—To the Canadian Club, where we had such fun in 1985, which I am certain is about to be repeated—a copy of a book that describes those good times, and incidentally gives a history of my Regiment.*

Later that evening, I quietly handed the members of the Liberation Committee, who had become personal friends, gifts of ties, badges and plaques: General Andrew Gijsbers; Head of the Committee, Klaas Huisman, long-time Chief of Cabinet; Evert Gerritsen, Benefactor of the Veterans; Jan Koorenhof, Senior Advisor to every Liberation Committee over a period of 15 years; and several others.

May 4th, Friday

This was National Memorial Day and was observed at the Holten Canadian War Cemetery, just north of the city of Holten, and 20 kilometres east of the town of Deventer. Here lie 1,355 Canadians of whom 8 are Patricias. All cemeteries are objects of grief and sadness but the one at Holten is especially poignant. These young Patricias died in the last weeks of the war, some after surviving many battles and wounds. Sgt. James Duncan Wright is one of them. He joined the

Regiment on May 23rd, 1941; was twice wounded, once on September 16th, 1944; when he remained on duty, and again the next day. He returned to the Regiment and fought all through northern Italy and into Holland. He died of injuries after the war on June 15th, 1945.

And there are a few who joined the Regiment a few weeks before the end of the war and were killed in their first action. Pte. J. W. Purvis is one of them. He joined the Battalion on March 28th, 1945, and was killed two weeks later on April 11th at the Ijssel River.

In my long odyssey retracing the route of the PPCLI from the beaches near Ispica to the crossing of the Ijssel River, we have visited the graves of all the Patricias who fell in WWII. It is not possible to list them all, but I would like to record the names of those who fell at the last, even as the guns ceased their dreadful toll.

HOLTEN CANADIAN WAR CEMETERY

Brown, Private, Edward Hector H/60603, 22nd April 1945. Age 22. Son of William E. and Alice M. Brown, of Petersfield, Manitoba.
Gosselin, Private, Romeo, H/2691, 12th April 1945. Age 24. Son of Philippe and Cora Gosselin, of Winnipeg, Manitoba.
Graham, Private, John James, L/107406, 15th July 1945. Age 31. Son of James and Sarah Ann Graham, of Leroy, Saskatchewan; husband of Gwendolyne Graham, of Leroy.
Hudson, Private, Mitchell, H/204125, 22nd April 1945.
Ilasevich, Corporal, Harry, H/17855, 12th April 1945. Age 21. Son of Michael and Lena Ilasevich, of Sadlow, Manitoba.
Purvis, Private, Jack William, H/18598, 11th April 1945. Age 19. Son of Louise C. Purvis, of St. James, Manitoba.
Slyzuk, Private, John, H/204139, 11th April 1945. Age 30. Son of Nicholas and Pearl Slyzuk, of Ashville, Manitoba.
Wright, Sergeant, James Duncan, H/16782, 15th June 1945.

BLOEMENDAAL (ST. ADELBERTUS) ROMAN CATHOLIC CHURCH—NOORD-HOLLAND

Donohue, Private, Alex Joseph, F/4007, 11th May 1945, Grave 17.

At the Ceremony on May 4th, wreaths were laid by the following:
- Children of the 7 primary schools of Holten
- The Minister of Veterans Affairs of Canada, The Honourable Gerald S. Merrithew

- The Provincial Governor, Mr. J. Hendrikx
- The Dutch Veterans' Branch, Holten
- Mr. Gaston Garceau, President Royal Canadian Legion
- Mr. H. C. Chadderton, Chairman National Council of Veterans' Associations in Canada

A touching note was the recitation of a poem, "The Brave Sons of Canada," by a young Dutch boy. This was followed by community singing by a large choir of school children, who then laid floral tributes on the graves.

The program indicates how the Dutch involve their children in the Remembrance Ceremonies. It is wonderful to see how the memory of the Liberation is passed on from generation to generation. Each year, on Christmas Eve, school children place a candle on each grave in Holten Cemetery and gradually the whole cemetery is flooded with candlelight.

After the Ceremony at Holten, I was due to attend a reception at Barneveld, about 60 miles away. Luckily, the A1 was free of heavy traffic and I arrived at Barneveld at 3:00 p.m. I was pleased to see three Patricias who were billeted there, Bert Bolton, John Moore and Rudy Deutsch. We were warmly received by the Mayor, C. W. Labree, and I presented him with a cap badge.

* * *

Later, that same day, the village of Achterveld held a Memorial Service to honour 25 of their citizens who were killed during the War. It will be remembered that Achterveld was occupied by D Company in April/May 1945. It was here, in a little schoolhouse, that conferences with the Germans were held on April 28th and 30th to arrange a truce to send food and supplies into western Holland.

Through my good friend Jan Schouten, the Archivist of Achterveld, I had been asked to attend the service, make a speech and lay a wreath on behalf of the PPCLI. The ceremony was held in the churchyard just opposite to the house where my Company Headquarters had been located in 1945.

This is my speech, which was translated as I spoke by Mr. Aart van den End.

> *Citizens of Achterveld:*
> *I am greatly honoured to be asked to say a few words on this memorable occasion, on behalf of my Regiment, the Princess Patricia's Canadian Light Infantry.*
>
> *Exactly forty-five years ago, to the very day, to the very hour, almost to the very minute, I was listening to my wire-*

less set, in my Company Headquarters, in a house only a few paces from here, when I received word that the Germans had laid down their arms—the War was over.

Some of you here this evening will remember that great event. The streets of Achterveld came alive with people as they cheered, sang and embraced each other and the Canadian soldiers who had fought to restore their liberty. This was the end of five years of brutal oppression and they had every right to be happy.

And so, tonight we come together once more, this time not in a cheerful, happy mood, but in a spirit of commemoration and remembrance of those who did not survive the War, in particular 25 citizens of Achterveld who died as a result of the fighting in this village, or were killed by shellfire and landmines (including little children who lost their lives while playing with these mines), and those people who died in concentration camps.

On this solemn occasion, I would also ask you to remember the more than 7,000 Canadians who gave their lives in the Liberation of the Netherlands during the last nine months of the War. They lie buried in nine cemeteries in Belgium, Holland and Germany. I have visited many of these cemeteries, some more than once, and I am always moved by their setting and beauty. But it is the 7,000 names of the young Canadians that move me most of all. They could have populated a good sized town in Canada or in Holland.

Let us never forget the suffering endured by both Canadian soldiers and the people of Holland, and the sacrifices they made in the struggle for freedom.

It has been a great privilege to share these few thoughts with you this evening. I thank you for asking me to participate in the unveiling of this fine memorial.

At the conclusion of my remarks, I presented the village with a Regimental Plaque, suitably inscribed.

When I returned to Toronto, I received the following letter from Aaart van den End:

Dear Mr. Frost:
I am writing to you on behalf of Mr. Schouten from Achterveld. He asked me to let you know the following:
It was for us a great honour to have you present at the unveiling ceremony. We still owe much gratitude to the

PILGRIMAGE—1990

Canadians, young boys from another country, who fell for the sake of others, unknown to them. I am now working on having the school furnished with, among other things, photos from 1945, and, of course, your plaque.

We hope that the official conversion of one classroom into an exposition room can take place in 1995. It is our wish to have you and Rudy Deutsch as our guests of honour during the opening ceremony.

I would like to add that it was a very pleasant experience for me to act as an interpreter during your speech.

May 5th, Saturday

This was National Liberation Day. Again, I was asked to speak at a Remembrance Service held in the church in the little village of Wilp which the Regiment had occupied on the night of April 11/12, 1945.

This is my address:

Dr. van Blommestein, Mr. van Notten, Citizens of the Municipality of Voorst (especially the people of Wilp), Distinguished Guests, Fellow Veterans.

I am deeply honoured to be asked to say a few words on this memorable occasion, on behalf of my Regiment, The Princess Patricia's Canadian Light Infantry.

Forty-five years have passed since German tanks and infantry roared down the road beside this very church and counter-attacked my Regiment which had crossed the Ijssel River a few hours earlier. The date—April 12th, 1945; the time—three o'clock in the morning. You all know the outcome. By first light, all the tanks had been knocked out and 120 Germans had been killed, wounded or taken prisoner. The bridgehead over the Ijssel River was secure.

Little did I think 45 years ago that I would be standing here, in this church, making a speech on the occasion of your National Liberation Day. And yet, despite the passage of all those years, my memory of the Liberation of Wilp by the PPCLI is as fresh as though it happened yesterday. I think of the battle that swirled about this church; I hear the clanking of the tanks and the blasts of their guns; I see the terrified civilians, dazed by our bombardment and fearful that the enemy will throw us back into the Ijssel. I think too, of the casualties and the suffering endured by the Dutch, as well as by ourselves. And I feel very humble when I realize that I had the good fortune to survive, when so many better men and women were struck down in the prime of life.

But today is not the time to dwell on the sacrifices and hard times of the past. Let us be happy and thank God that our struggles were not in vain, and that we are together once again to celebrate the glorious Liberation.

Let us rejoice too, in the strong ties that have developed between the Canadian Veterans and the people of Holland. Beginning in 1956, I have now visited Wilp six times, and on each occasion I am overwhelmed by your friendship, warmth and kindness. Indeed, our feelings of respect and goodwill for each other seem to grow on each visit. And for that I shall be forever grateful.

I am indebted to many people who have made my visits to Holland, and particularly to Voorst, Twello and Wilp, so memorable. I cannot find words to adequately express my thanks to Dr. Johannes van Blommestein and his staff, particularly Col. Reitsma. Since 1985, they have graciously welcomed me year after year, as if each occasion was the first time they had met me. I am sure they must have thought—here is that man again! But if so, they never showed it.

I tried to repay their kindness, in a very small way, by writing an account about my visit to Twello in 1985 and telling how helpful Dr. van Blommestein was, in setting the record straight about which Canadian Regiment attacked across the Ijssel River and liberated Wilp. As a result of his efforts, I don't think there is one person in the whole Municipality of Voorst, or the whole of Holland, for that matter, who doesn't know it was the PPCLI.

What a spectacular way he chose to prove his point. Re-enact the crossing of the River!

I can tell you, quite frankly, that I had no prior knowledge of his scheme, until I sat on the river bank and saw those capable young Dutch Engineers erect a pontoon bridge. As the bridge was nearing completion, I innocently asked Dr. van Blommestein, "Who's going to be the first person to test whether the thing really works?" He gave me that engaging smile of his and said, "You."

You can imagine my complete surprise, disbelief and concern when a jeep pulled up and I was invited, or rather ordered, to get in, and we headed for the bridge.

The rest is history. To say I was thrilled would be an understatement. It was the most emotional, memorable thing that has happened to me since the War. For a wonderful moment it was April 11th, 1945, and I was a young soldier again leading my men across the river. I only wished they could have been with me—all of them—those who are still living and those who have passed away. And particularly those who gave their lives, that we all may be free. I know they would have been just as proud and thrilled as I was.

Thank you Dr. Johannes van Blommestein, Mr. Jim van Notten, your hard working staffs and all others who organized this great tribute to the soldiers who crossed the Ijssel in 1945.

And so, on that happy note, I would like to conclude my remarks this morning. I have only one thought to leave with you and it is this. Let us all be ever vigilant that the peace and freedom we now enjoy, and which was bought so dearly by the sacrifices of our people, will never again be taken from us.

At the conclusion of the service, I presented Regimental plaques to the village of Wilp, the Municipality of Voorst (of which Wilp is a part) and the Municipality of Gorssel.

Another excellent lunch was then provided by the Municipality of Voorst for the Veterans and civil leaders, at the Recreational Centre, de Lathmer. It was here that Gerard Burgers sold 200 photos of the Crossing of the Ijssel River, the proceeds of which he sent to the PPCLI.

In the evening, the City of Apeldoorn held a Tattoo (or 'Taptoe,' as it is called by the Dutch) in the grounds of the Het Loo Palace. Five bands participated—our own Regimental Band, the United States Army Europe Band and three Dutch bands. The PPCLI Band, under the Command of the Director of Music, Capt. Don Embree, had been flown over from Calgary. As a disinterested observer, I would say that our Band, in their scarlet uniforms, stole the show.

May 6th, Sunday

On this day, all the Canadian Veterans in Holland gathered in Apeldoorn for the National Liberation Parade. Four days earlier, General Andrew Gijsbers, Head of the Liberation Committee, had asked me if I would act as Deputy Commander of the Parade. He could not at that point make a firm offer as the appointment had to be cleared by his Committee as well as by the Department of Veterans Affairs. I was greatly honoured, to say nothing of being completely surprised, and of course assented. Next day I received this letter:

PILGRIMAGE—1990

> *Dear Colonel Frost,*
> *Confirming last night's conversation, I invite you to act as deputy commander of the Veterans Parade on Sunday May 6th.*
> *You will be met in your hotel at 13:00 hrs. on that day. A jeep will be at your disposal to take you to the assembly area, where you will be given additional information.*
> *With kind regards,*
> *A.W.T. Gijsbers,*
> *Chairman*

* * *

I have attended all the Pilgrimages to Holland since the War and participated in all the parades (except the one in 1995), but I think that for me, this one was the most memorable of them all. Some 3,000 Veterans, not only from Canada, but from Britain, the United States and Poland marched or were carried in vehicles from WWII which had been restored by a Dutch Automobile Club called "Keep Them Rolling." Every conceivable type of vehicle was present, from jeeps and carriers to water trucks and heavy recovery vehicles. As deputy commander of the parade, I actually led the Veterans. Fortunately, I was driven in a jeep, otherwise I am not so sure I would have made it to the saluting base. The marchers were greatly assisted by the many bands participating in the parade, including our own Regimental Band.

HH Princess Margriet, accompanied by her husband, took the salute. The Minister of Veterans Affairs, the Honourable Gerald Merrithew; the Burgemeester of Apeldoorn, Mr. Ton Hubers and MGen. George Kitching were among the many notables at the saluting base.

The outpourings of the 300,000 people who lined the route were truly overwhelming. My jeep was soon filled with flowers. One little boy ran out from the crowd and handed me a wooden shoe he had carved. Then an old man gave me a pack of Players cigarettes he had received from our soldiers in 1945. The pack was marked "British Red Cross and St. John." I no longer smoke cigarettes, but the package was a memorable souvenir.

I cannot imagine this happening in any other country in the world. It is a pity that the media in Canada gave so little coverage to this parade and the other events in Holland.

The little boy who handed me a wooden shoe was Pim Bolderman. When I returned to Toronto, I sent him a note.

Dear Pim:

I am the Colonel Frost riding in a jeep in the parade in Apeldoorn on May 6th, to whom you handed a little Dutch wooden shoe which you had carved yourself. It is a wonderful souvenir of my visit to Holland in May 1990, and I shall always treasure it.

Thank you for your generous gift and for remembering the Canadian soldiers who brought freedom to your country 45 years ago.

I enclose a picture of myself taken just after the Liberation in April 1945, when I was a young captain (22 years old) with the Princess Patricia's Canadian Light Infantry.

With my best wishes.

Yours sincerely,

He replied:

Dear Mr. Frost,
   Thank you for your nice letter.
   I have showed your letter at school.
   I am very proud, that I have received a letter from you.
   It was a very nice day in Apeldoorn.
   I enclose a photograph, which was taken by us in Apeldoorn.
   I am 10 years old.
   My teacher has told us much about the war and I hope that there will never be a war.
   With the best wishes and good health.

Yours sincerely,
Pim Bolderman

And so the wonderful love affair between the Dutch and their Canadian Liberators is passed from one generation to another.

Many Dutch newspapers carried the story of the Parade on their front page.

NIEUWE APELDOORNSE COURANT
Monday, May 7, 1990

EMOTIONAL VETERANS' PARADE IN STIFLING HEAT

APELDOORN—Five rows thick along the whole route, both young and old yesterday enjoyed the national parade in Apeldoorn. The temperature was almost too high for the

> *veterans. Thanks to "Keep them Rolling" a large number of them could cover the route by jeep or truck. Standing to accept the parade in the heat were Princess Margriet and her husband, Pieter van Vollenhoven, Minister Ter Beek and the parade commander, General Kitching. The veterans blinked away quite a few tears seeing the enthusiasm of the public. Children distributed flowers and ladies received many hugs. It was almost like 45 years ago.*

In the evening, the Canadian Embassy presented a special concert in commemoration of the Liberation in 1945. This was a performance by the internationally known Orford String Quartet of Toronto of the Music of Alfred Fisher, "Diary of a War Artist," which was inspired by the war art of Alex Colville. The concert was recorded for inclusion in a CBC TV feature to be presented on Remembrance Day, 1990.

At the same time, in the Het Loo Palace, an exhibition was opened by Princess Margriet of paintings by Alex Colville, who was present and guided the Princess.

The events of this wonderful day concluded with dinner for the Veterans and their wives at the "Canadian Club" in Apeldoorn. The PPCLI dance band supplied the music and toward the end of the evening played a song and march composed by a member of the Regiment "Goodbye Wonderful Holland." A "choir," made up of the Burgemeester and members of the Liberation Committee, led the singing.

* * *

May 7th, Monday

On this day, the Veterans gathered at the Groesbeek Canadian Cemetery south of Nijmegen. In bus loads we came from all over Holland, blocking the roads leading to the Cemetery. Some had to walk half a mile to attend the Ceremony.

The Cemetery is marked by a large stone Cross of Sacrifice bearing on its shaft a crusader's sword of bronze. More than 2,300 Canadians are buried here. A Memorial at the entrance to the cemetery contains the names of another 103 Canadians who have no known graves. There are no Patricias buried at Groesbeek. The headstones are laid out in 20 groups of about 120 each, all carefully lined up like soldiers on parade. As I stood at the Cross of Sacrifice and looked down on the serried ranks, I was struck by the awful sacrifice these stones represent. Before me lay the fighting strength of a Brigade.

The Ceremony commenced with a Royal Salute to Princess Margriet followed by an introduction of the principal guests: Mr.

Jacques Gignac, Canadian Ambassador; The Honourable Gerald Merrithew, Minister of Veterans Affairs; His Excellency Mr. A. L. Ter Beek, Dutch Minister of Defence. The PPCLI Band provided the music. After laying of wreaths, the impressive service concluded with the beautiful Dutch National Anthem "Wilhelmus" sung with great enthusiasm, and "O Canada."

Following the Ceremony, the Minister of Veterans Affairs gave a reception at the Hotel Erica in nearby Berg en Dal, where we had an opportunity to meet Princess Margriet and her husband, Pieter van Vollenhoven. They are a charming couple and very popular with the Veterans. The Princess was born in Canada on January 19th, 1943, and as a tiny Princess, in those far-off days, captured our hearts. She still does. Her husband served as a legal officer on the staff of The Netherlands Air Force.

Many mayors and members of their Liberation Committees were also present. As I worked my way through the throng toward the bar, I heard a familiar voice, "Sydney, get a drink for me too." It was my old friend Johannes van Blommestein from Twello.

While we were enjoying our drinks, he asked if I had met the Princess. "No, I haven't, but the crowd is so thick I don't think I have a hope."

"Don't worry about that. I'll go with you. By the way, do you have a copy of your book handy?"

"I think there's one in the car. Why?"

"Would you like to present it to HRH?"

"Well, of course. I'll try to get through this crowd and pick it up."

I soon returned.

"How do you think I should autograph it?"

We settled on an appropriate wording and walked toward the Princess who was surrounded by a crowd of admirers. She immediately spotted Johannes and motioned him to come forward. I followed and had the great pleasure of meeting HRH and her husband, in the presence of Gerry Merrithew and the Canadian Ambassador, Mr. Jacques Gignac. The Princess graciously accepted my book and thanked me for the note I had written on the front page. Immediately photographers appeared and pictures were taken of the event. They rest among my most treasured souvenirs.

Before the Reception was over, I was anxious to meet any Patricias who were present, but it was a real challenge to find them in the crowd. As the guests thinned out, I was happy to spot several old friends and comrades. Some I have already mentioned in connection with other events: Wally Smith, John Moore, Charlie King, Bert Bolton; others whom I had been trying to contact during the week: Elwood Birss, Art Grenier, R. McKay and possibly one or two others. At the conclusion of this chapter, I give a nominal roll of the Patricias who I believe attended the Pilgrimage, including a few I do not recall meeting, but whose names were given to me. For any who were present, but not listed, I apologize. I can only plead I gave it my best Patricia effort.

In the evening, a Farewell Party was held at the Canadian Club, where those Veterans who had been lodged with Dutch families entertained their hosts. It was a very happy occasion, but toward the end some of us became rather nostalgic, realizing this would likely be the last time we would gather in such numbers and see each other again. But no one was going to ruin a good party on that account. The tempo soon picked up, aided by some boisterous antics of both Veterans and members of the Liberation Committee, including an ad hoc choir singing wartime and other ditties.

My memory of the occasion is a little dim, but I can remember being driven home by the Mayor of Voorst.

The Pilgrimage of 1990 was over, but the wonderful memories would always remain. As soon as I returned home, I began writing letters to all the Dutch people who had worked so hard and given so much to make the Pilgrimage such a success: the Mayors, the members of the Liberation Committees, their advisors and staff, and many others. It gave me much pleasure and satisfaction to do this and yet, to be truthful, it was a difficult task not to fall into a rut and say the same thing over and over again. In other words, I endeavoured to recall the kindness and friendship each person had given me.

As in prior chapters, I would now like to quote from four of these letters because they show how I felt then, untrammelled by the passage of time. My letters also give a certain flavour of the events that frankly I find difficult to capture twelve years later. The order in which they are given has no significance.

General A.W.T. Gijsbers
Chairman Liberation '45
Apeldoorn
Dear General Gijsbers:
I have now returned from my strenuous five week trip to Europe. The high point of my trip was of course, the wonderful week I spent in Apeldoorn. As you know, I have attended many Anniversary Celebrations over the years but I believe that 1990 was one of the most memorable and inspiring. The friendship and affection shown by the 300,000 people who lined the route of our parade on May

6th, was overwhelming. I cannot imagine this happening in any other country in the world.

Likewise, the Canadian Veterans have a high regard and affection for the people of Holland and are deeply moved by their friendship and kindness. These close ties, forged in War and strengthened in peace by Pilgrimages to Holland, will never be forgotten by the Veterans, so long as there is one of them left to answer the call.

I want to thank you for the honour you did my Regiment and me, personally, by asking me to act as deputy commander of the Parade on Sunday. Not only did I appreciate leading the parade in a jeep, but without its help I doubt if I would have made it to the saluting base!

I will always have pleasant memories of the functions we attended—the dinner party at Utrecht; the Tattoo (when the band of the PPCLI performed); Ton Huber's dinner party at the Keizerskroon; the concert by the Orford String Quartet, and many happy sessions at the Canadian Club.

I also have a vivid recollection of you singing in the "choir," with a strong voice, "Goodbye Wonderful Holland." Someone observed, I think it was Pieter Beelaerts van Blokland, that I was a better composer than a soldier! But that may not be saying very much!

Sincerely,

Jhr. Drs. P.A.C. Beelaerts van Blokland
Queen's Commissioner
Province of Utrecht
Dear Pieter:

The 45th Anniversary Celebrations have now become history, but their memory will always remain fresh and give me much pleasure.

I have before me the menu of that wonderful dinner at the "Paushuize" on May 1st. I am also looking at the brochure about the "Paushuize" which you kindly gave me. What an elegant place to start the Celebrations!

I have so many delightful memories—your witty speech at the dinner and the plethora of wines from many different countries; your thoughtfulness in having a bottle of liquor in my hotel room along with a note of welcome; lunch with you at the Keizerskroon on May 6th and dinner the same night; your efforts to distract me on the Parade on Sunday as I passed the Saluting base; your joining in the singing of *my song on Monday evening and your leading a "congo line" with a candelabra.*

It seemed that you had the incredible ability of being everywhere at once. I think you should add the word "ubique" to your family motto.

Thank you for giving me the two photos you took at the Saluting Base. I can detect a smile developing on my stern visage, so your efforts were almost successful. I looked for you after the sing-song to thank you for your kindness, but you had sensibly left earlier.

There is so much more I would like to say about my wonderful week in Holland, but it would make another book! May I quite simply express my gratitude to you personally and through you, to all the people of Holland, for your friendship, warmth and your kindness. Thank you for remembering us—we shall never forget you.

Sincerely,

Dr. J.H.J. van Blommestein
Burgemeester van Voorst
Twello
Dear Johannes:

I am now back at my desk after my wonderful Pilgrimage to Holland and my subsequent tour of Germany, Austria, Switzerland, Italy and Sicily.

My week in Holland was the most inspiring and memorable of the many I have made and I have numerous people to thank. Throughout my visit, your helping hand was always present and it was very evident to me that many of the events would not have taken place without your inspiration and hard work. I think of the incredible re-enactment of the crossing of the Ijssel River, on May 2nd, and being driven there by Mr. de Stegge in a Rolls Royce; lunch at Bussloo and an exciting display by parachutists; the moving Remembrance Service at Wilp on May 5th and lunch at de Lathmer, when you presented me with the lovely Delft plate; the joyous parade of floats and happy children celebrating the 45th Anniversary of the Liberation; and the demonstrations and games between the Villages; the Ceremony at the Holten War Cemetery on May 4th, when you grabbed my arm and took me to the area reserved for VIPs; the Ceremony at Groesbeek on May 7th were you again guided me to the reserved seats and later arranged to have me meet HRH Princess Margriet and present her with my book.

And finally, at the Farewell Party on May 7th, in the Canadian Club, at a very late hour, I look up from playing the piano and whom do I see—Johannes van Blommestein! Then to top it off, you take me home to my hotel.

Would you please thank all the members of your staff for the important contribution they made to the events connected with the Celebration of "Victory in Voorst." In particular, I want to thank Colonel Ritse R. Reitsma and Mrs. van Nack for their part in making the events such a success and for the help they gave to me personally.

It is impossible to choose one event that stands out above the others. Certainly, the crossing of the Ijssel River was an enormous undertaking on your part and required detailed planning for months in advance. Just securing the approval of so many government agencies must have been a monumental headache. I had no idea of the size of the project until I joined you at the river.

And then came the biggest surprise of all—your asking me to lead the parade in a jeep!

Another highlight was, of course, the Ceremony at Wilp. To take part in the service in that beautiful old church, in the presence of an overflow audience and young children, was a very emotional experience for me. I tried to express my feelings and my thanks in my address.

Thank you again for the honour and the privilege of addressing the assembly.

Sincerely,

Mr. Evert Gerritsen
Apeldoorn
Dear Evert:

In many ways this Pilgrimage to Holland was, for me, the most memorable of the many I have attended. Certainly it was the most challenging, with every day and night crowded with parades, receptions, memorial services, dinners, etc. But I enjoyed every minute and would be happy to do it all over again—after I've had a chance to catch up on my sleep!

Throughout it all you were a tower of strength, always ready and willing to look after me—arranging plaques on short notice; giving me copies of newspapers and transla-

tions; driving me around town to various functions at the Palace and elsewhere; inviting me to join you at the Canadian Club and making sure that I was introduced to everyone.

I would ask you to thank Ben Johnson for his fine work in organizing the plaques and inscriptions. No task was too much for him and I know he spent a great deal of time on my behalf.

I cannot adequately express my thanks to you in this letter but I want you to know how much I appreciate your kindness.

Sincerely,

PROVISIONAL LIST
PPCLI Veterans Who Attended The Pilgrimage to Holland, May, 1990

C121360	*Pte.*	*C. V. (Carl)*	*Brethour*
H14883	*LCpl.*	*E. N. (Elwood)*	*Birss*
	Lt.	*W. W. (Bert)*	*Bolton*
K85388	*Pte.*	*N. S.*	*Butcher*
		Rudy	*Deutsch*
	Capt.	*C. S.*	*Frost*
M103572	*Pte.*	*A. M. (Art)*	*Grenier*
B103156	*Pte.*	*C. T. (Charlie)*	*King*
H16776	*Sgt.*	*Lloyd*	*Kreamer, MM*
		David	*Larose*
H16693	*Pte.*	*Ray*	*McKay*
K85525	*CSM.*	*J. R.*	*McCullough*
H16760	*LCpl.*	*J. H. (John)*	*Moore*
P22271	*Cpl.*	*D. F. (Don)*	*Parrot*
B68601	*Pte.*	*L. V. (Lloyd)*	*Rains*
P22324	*Lt.*	*W.D.L. (Bill)*	*Roach, DSO*
C78197	*Pte.*	*W. C. (Wally)*	*Smith*

Ranks are given as at the end of WWII

Chapter XVI

APELDOORN—1995

The Veterans left Holland brimming with pride and yet burdened with sadness. Many felt (and I was one of them) that the Dutch people had given of themselves so completely there was nothing left in *"de zolder of de kelder."* There could never be another Pilgrimage like the one in 1990.

How wrong we were. Barely had the last cries of "Thank you Canada, we shall never forget you," drifted away, than our hosts were making plans for a repeat performance in 1995.

The first indications I received that the Dutch people were serious about hosting another Pilgrimage were in May, 1991 when I was honoured with visits by four distinguished citizens of Apeldoorn and their wives: General Gijsbers, Evert Gerritsen, Ton Hubers and Pieter Beelaerts.

On May 11th, General Gijsbers phoned from Holland to say that he and his wife were visiting Canada and would be very pleased to see me. This was followed by similar calls from the others. I was delighted to at last have this opportunity to reciprocate their many kindnesses, and invited them to lunch at my club.

Andrew and Ann Gijsbers were the first to appear. They had just visited Niagara Falls and were staying with friends in Toronto. We had a wonderful chat about the earlier Pilgrimages, like two old veterans reminiscing about past campaigns. Indeed, the General had seen his share of army service. In 1944, he had escaped to England, qualified for a commission and then served in The Netherlands East Indies (now Indonesia) for three years as a Battalion Intelligence Officer and Company Commander. Later in his distinguished career, he commanded the First Netherlands Corps in NATO.

He described some of the preliminary plans being made for 1995. As in the past, he would be in charge of the ceremonies in Apeldoorn.

Next day, Evert Gerritsen and Ton Hubers, with their wives, joined me for lunch. They need no introduction. Evert was the popular friend of Veterans and Ton the Mayor of Apeldoorn. Evert frequently visited Ontario to see his uncle and a cousin who lived in Fergus, and I had the pleasure of meeting them. He always seemed to know what was happening and what was likely to happen, and kept me informed.

A few days later, Pieter Beelaerts phoned to say he and his wife, Dieuwke, had arrived in Toronto after visiting Ottawa and Kingston. Like Gerritsen and Hubers, Pieter Beelaerts is a familiar name in this story. A man of many parts, he is equally at home on his feet giving a witty speech or in a boardroom solving a knotty problem. We recalled his famous dinner in Utrecht and other happy events in 1985 and 1990, and he briefed me on the program for 1995. I was interested to know whether he had visited the Royal Military College in Kingston. "Of course," he said. "That's where you learned to become a soldier." He had even attended a local book store and found a copy of my book.

We now leave our friends from Apeldoorn to record an important occasion which occurred in Twello a few weeks prior to the events just described. On April 29th, 1991, I received a call from Johannes van Blommestein, Mayor of Voorst. He gave me the exciting news that our mutual friend, Col. Ritse Reitsma (known as Bill), was to receive the Order of Orange Nassau the next day. On the spur of the moment, I dictated a note of congratulations for Ritse and wrote Johannes a letter:

April 30, 1991

Dr. J.H.J. van Blommestein
Burgemeester van Voorst
Twello
Dear Johannes:

I am so glad that you let me know about Ritse Reitsma receiving the Order of Orange Nassau. I am well aware of the significance of this Order and I am delighted he has been honoured in this way. He joins a distinguished company which includes your good self.

I hope the random thoughts I gave you on the phone were enough to let you compose a little speech on my behalf. I have written Ritse a note and enclose a copy.

Please do not put off your visit to Canada indefinitely. Time marches on inexorably and old soldiers fade away!

It was a real pleasure to hear your voice again and, for a brief moment, re-live those wonderful times in Holland with you, your family and the wonderful people of Voorst.

Sincerely,

April 30, 1991
TO COLONEL RITSE R. REITSMA
ON THE OCCASION OF HIS
RECEIVING THE ORDER OF ORANGE NASSAU

Hearty congratulations on your well-deserved appointment to this Noble Order. I am delighted that your long and devoted service to your country and your friendship and support for the Canadian Veterans have been recognized in this way.

As one who has had the pleasure of knowing and working with you for many years, I join your many friends in wishing you continued success in all your good works.
Colonel C. Sydney Frost

A few days later, another unexpected pleasure arrived from Twello in the form of a video tape of the Crossing of the Ijssel River, May 2nd, 1990. A further letter to Johannes was the only way I could respond to his kindness:

May 24, 1991

Dear Johannes:

What a pleasant surprise to receive the video tape! I have watched it again and again and it has given me and my family much happiness. It will be a treasured family record of my participation in the 45th Anniversary Pilgrimage to Holland.

Please convey my deep appreciation to Ritse Reitsma and all the others who were connected with this memorable event.

I hope the ceremonies honouring him with the Order of Orange Nassau went well. After speaking with you, I felt that I should have made a supreme effort to attend this special occasion to congratulate him in person.

Again, my thanks for giving me yet another memento of our friendship.
Sincerely,

Still another of my Dutch "constituencies" got in touch with me—Achterveld. Shortly after the Memorial Service held on May 4th, 1990, and the unveiling of a Monument to the Dutch citizens who perished in the War, I received a letter from Mr. Schouten thanking me for the speech I made on that occasion.

He also informed me that Achterveld had decided to convert one of the rooms in the schoolhouse, where the Food Conference was held in

1945, into a Memorial Room commemorating the event and exhibiting photos, plaques and other souvenirs of the War. He had made a brass plaque with an inscription describing the Food Conference, which now hung on the classroom wall. The plaque would be unveiled in May 1995, and he wanted Rudy Deutsch, a fellow Patricia, and me to attend the ceremony. Mr. Schouten kept me abreast of his plans as they developed. On December 12th, 1994, he invited me to open an exhibition of the famous classroom and its valuable display on May 5th, 1995.

* * *

In the meantime, emissaries from Apeldoorn continued to arrive. Evert Gerritsen, who was visiting his sick uncle in Cambridge, kindly took the time to call on me and bring me up to date on the activities planned for 1995. From what he told me, it was obviously going to be a very big event. The Dutch people were opening up their homes and their hearts to Canadians and offering free accommodation and meals for up to twelve days. Several committees in both Holland and Canada were looking after all the arrangements and could accommodate approximately 4,000 Veterans and their spouses. Travel agents right across Canada were offering twelve-day tours at $1,000 per person.

Almost every city and town in Holland was organizing receptions, parades, dinners, displays, memorial services, tours and other events. The Canadian Department of Veterans Affairs and the Legion were also involved.

"That's wonderful," I enthused. "I'll be there but don't forget I'm still a "young fellow" compared to some of the Vets who are in their 80s and 90s."

"Don't worry about that. There'll be doctors, nurses and medical orderlies. Anyway, you veterans are a pretty sturdy bunch. One of them came up with a good slogan—"We'll stay alive 'till '95.""

I immediately made my own tentative plans and reservations and awaited further news from my Dutch friends.

In a few months Evert was back in Canada to see his ailing uncle and paid me a flying visit. Plans for the 1995 Pilgrimage were well advanced. The response from veterans had been overwhelming. Apeldoorn would be the centre of several celebrations including a Tattoo on May 5th and a National Parade on May 7th. A major Service of Remembrance would be held May 8th at Groesbeek Canadian War Cemetery. Evert brought greetings from my friends in Apeldoorn, including Jan Koorenhof, who was a member of the Liberation Committee. He would be visiting Toronto in September and would phone me.

True to his word, Jan Koorenhof phoned me on September 13th. He was in charge of a group of 50 Apeldoorners touring Ontario. They had visited North Bay, Algonquin Park (including canoe trips), Kingston (RMC) and Ottawa. He could see me on October 1st.

We now pause for a musical interlude. In 1985, as a lark, I had composed a song called "Goodbye Wonderful Holland" to be played at the Farewell Party which the Veterans gave their hosts. To my great surprise it caught on and during the evening was sung with great gusto by Veterans and hosts alike.

Again in 1990, as already described, the walls of the Canadian Club reverberated with voices raised in song. A make-shift choir of General Gijsbers, Pieter Beelaerts, Johannes van Blommestein and others sang "Goodbye Wonderful Holland" accompanied by a nondescript piano player.

With such encouraging ratings for my song, I thought I would try my hand at composing another one for the 1995 Pilgrimage. It was a rather ambitious effort because it was a combination song and march, and was entitled "50th Anniversary March." I am not by any means a composer, and I am certainly not able to score a piece, much less write an arrangement for a band. But I am an indifferent piano player so I taped the piece and showed it to Joe Sealy, a talented and well-known musician, composer and transcriber in Toronto. He kindly wrote the score for my piece, played it, and had it taped.

And so, when Jan Koorenhof appeared on October 1st, 1993, I was able to surprise him with the score, words and a cassette of the song. At last I had an opportunity to show my gratitude to the people of Holland in a tangible way. But when it comes to giving surprises, you can't beat the Dutch. Jan responded by presenting me with a beautiful medal from Apeldoorn, commemorating its 1200th Anniversary.

Jan brought me up to date on the forthcoming celebrations. They would far surpass the prior Pilgrimages, both in interest and numbers. He could hardly believe the enthusiasm. The Department of Veterans Affairs were sending a large contingent to Holland, including a band. He had met with two of my "Sicilian" friends, André Petelle and Peter Caisse, in Ottawa, and co-ordinated plans with them. He was certain that my song would be featured at the various parades and tattoos. As we parted, he gave me some welcome news. General Gijsbers would be in Toronto in November and would give me a call.

Another thing about the Dutch is that when they tell you something, you can rely on it. General Gijsbers phoned me on November 19th and we had lunch at the Royal York Hotel the next day. News from the "front" (the 50th Anniversary Celebrations) continued to be most encouraging. Veterans from all over Canada were registering for the 4,000 billets offered by the Dutch people. Twenty-five cities, towns and villages were participating. The list of events was now pretty firm and included twelve days. The highlights were:

> April 27/28/29—Veterans arrive
> May 4—National Remembrance Day, Amsterdam and local ceremonies
> May 5—National Liberation Day, Apeldoorn Tattoo
> May 7—National Parade, Apeldoorn
> May 8—Groesbeek Cemetery
> May 9—Farewell Parties

I then produced my song—the score, words and the cassette, which we played a couple of times. The General is a man of many interests, including music. Indeed, his fine baritone voice could always be heard loud and clear in the impromptu sing-songs that developed during the Farewell Parties. I asked him, "What do you think of it?"

"Sydney, it's fine, but it needs another verse or two."

I appreciated his frank advice and went to work composing two more verses and music. My piano teacher, Joe Sealy, agreed that the new version was an improvement and wrote out the score. On February 10th, 1994, I sent General Gijsbers the revised piece.

> *February 10, 1994*
>
> *Dear Andrew:*
>
> *This past month I have had time to do some thinking about the past year and the things I had done or should have done (mostly the latter). I remembered your saying that you liked the March I had composed for 1995, but that it would be better if there was another verse or two.*
>
> *Well, I took your words to heart and composed a "Chorus" with new words and music. It gives the work more body and I hope you will like it.*
>
> *I enclose the words for the entire song and a score for the music as well as a cassette recording of a piano rendition of the music. The first verse should be sung by the Veterans and the second verse by the Dutch people. The chorus would be sung by both.*

50TH ANNIVERSARY MARCH—1995
Liberation of Holland—1945

Key of F By C. S. Frost

Dear Holland, Holland, noble land,
Where Canada's soldiers sleep,
Their sacrifice you honour still,
Their memory you keep (sung by Veterans)

Chorus

Constancy shall mark our vigil,
Guard our freedom, peace maintain,
That the sacrifice we honour
Was not made in vain. (sung together)

Fifty years have passed away,
Since victory brought us peace,
Oh! May our friendship long endure
And wars forever cease. (sung by Dutch people)

Chorus

Constancy shall mark our vigil,
Guard our freedom, peace maintain,
That the sacrifice we honour
Was not made in vain. (sung together)

Articles now began to appear in the newspapers and the *Legion Magazine* about the great 1995 Pilgrimage to Holland. Travel agents were busy promoting their tours. Prices ranged from $1,100 for a twelve-day trip to Holland, to $3,600 for an eighteen-day tour, including Belgium, France and Germany. (In all cases accommodation and meals in Holland were provided by Dutch hosts free of charge.) It was the opportunity of a lifetime and many Veterans took advantage of it.

I was still not clear about the part being played by the Department of Veterans Affairs but I knew that John Gardam, a retired army colonel, was organizing the role of the Department.

On July 26th, 1994, out of the blue, I received a call from Col. Gardam himself. He quickly filled me in on the recent developments. The Pilgrimage would be 135 strong with representatives from most Regiments, Corps, the Air Force and the Navy. Supporting the Veterans there would be a 100-member Guard of Honour, a Naval Flag Party and the Canadian Forces Central Band. In addition, a 160-strong teen tour band from Burlington would be in attendance.

APELDOORN—1995

It was enough to stir the heart of many an old Veteran and encourage him to return once more to the country he had helped to set free. I frankly admit I was one of them.

The time had now arrived when I had to make detailed plans for my own itinerary. I had already made reservations at the Keizerskroon Hotel in Apeldoorn from April 27th to May 10th and rented an automobile. Unfortunately, I was not in a position to take advantage of the hospitality of the Dutch families who were billeting the Veterans. I realized that I would be heavily involved in the celebrations not just in Apeldoorn, but in my other "constituencies" in Wilp, Twello, Achterveld and Barneveld, as well as attending ceremonies at the Groesbeek and Holten Cemeteries. I thus needed freedom to move about at all hours of the day and night and access to telephone, fax and computer. The facilities at the Keizerskroon suited my requirements exactly.

The next question was what to do and where to go after Holland. I decided that this might well be my last chance to visit Switzerland and France. I had been to Italy in 1994 and all was quiet on that front. I therefore made hotel reservations at St. Goar on the Rhine River south of Koblenz, and at Heilbronn, Germany; at Salzberg, Austria; at Zurich, Interlaken, and Geneva, Switzerland; at Lyon and Paris, France; and finally at Amsterdam and home.

It was now January 1995, and I began to wonder if it would all come together in time for me to catch my plane leaving April 26th. Little did I know that my doubts were well founded.

On February 18th, I received a letter from Johannes van Blommestein enclosing the Program for the Municipality of Voorst and inviting me to attend. Most of the events conflicted with similar ceremonies in Apeldoorn and Achterveld, where I was already committed. This saddened me greatly as Johannes had done so much to establish the PPCLI as the Regiment which had attacked across the Ijssel River and captured Wilp. I resolved to try to squeeze in visits on April 30th to Twello, on May 3rd, the Queen's birthday, to an Airshow at Teuge, and on May 4th at the Holten Cemetery. In a fit of forgiveness I left Wilp to the 48th.

On March 3rd, Evert Gerritsen phoned with incredible news. The citizens of Beekbergen, Oosterhuizen and Lieren were erecting a Monument at Oosterhuizen to the PPCLI who had liberated them in April 1945. The Ceremony would be held April 21st and they wanted me to attend the unveiling and make a speech.

I told Evert that I couldn't possibly make it as I wouldn't arrive in Holland until April 27th.

"Okay," replied Evert, "then we'll hold the Ceremony on April 29th in Beekbergen. And, by the way, a time capsule is being deposited underneath the Monument containing pictures and excerpts about the PPCLI taken from your book. The excerpts have been translated into Dutch. The man behind all this is Gerrit Ham who also designed a plaque for the Monument as well as a medal they are giving to every Veteran. This is one Ceremony you must attend."

I agreed and promised to make a speech, not wanting to disappoint these wonderful people, but with many misgivings as to how I would cope with all the ceremonies.

Time was running out. I immediately set to work trying to compose an appropriate speech. Then, on March 14th, a letter from Gerrit Ham arrived which had been delayed in the mails because the address was not correct.

> *Dear Sir Sydney Frost*
>
> *I've received your address from Mr. K. Huisman, Chief of the Cabinet of Apeldoorn.*
>
> *First I would like to introduce myself. My name is Gerrit Ham. I live in the little village of Beekbergen, that is near to Apeldoorn.*
>
> *I am a member of the Liberation Committee of Beekbergen. They have asked me to investigate who liberated the little village of Oosterhuizen in the area of Klarenbeek. In remembrance of the liberation, there will be a monument unveiled. I have made a remembrance-shield for that monument with the initials PPCLI.*
>
> *Now I've found a book you gave to Evert Gerritsen. That is why I know much more about the PPCLI.*
>
> *The monument with the shield (PPCLI) will be unveiled 21st of April, 1995, by the Mayor of Apeldoorn, in Oosterhuizen at 19:00 hours p.m.*
>
> *On the 29th of April there will be a big remembrance parade in the area of Oosterhuizen, Lieren and Beekbergen. There also will be a fly-past of an old Dakota, a Sherman tank and there are paratroopers. Also, there will be 50 old cars from the Second World War and a V1 flying bomb. We will appreciate it very much if you would be here on April the 21 or April the 29, 1995.*
>
> *We hope that you will let us know if you are able to be with us in April. We want to apologize for advising you of this programme on such short notice.*
>
> *Yours truly,*
Gerrit Ham,
Beekbergen

APELDOORN—1995

This is a draft of the speech I prepared:

Dear Friends:

I am deeply honoured to be asked to speak on this memorable occasion, on behalf of my Regiment, The Princess Patricia's Canadian Light Infantry.

Just a few weeks ago, I received a telephone call from Evert Gerritsen, on behalf of the Mayor of Apeldoorn, inviting me to attend the unveiling of this Memorial to my Regiment. He told me that deposited underneath the Monument was a time capsule containing pictures and an article about the PPCLI translated into Dutch. The man responsible for all these good works was Gerrit Ham.

A few days later, I received a letter from Gerrit himself telling me about this Ceremony and the big Remembrance Parade being organized by the citizens of Beekbergen, Oosterhuizen and Lieren. He graciously asked me to attend.

And so, today, I stand beside this Memorial to my Regiment. I am overawed and deeply grateful for your kindness and generosity in erecting such a unique Monument. It will stand forever as a symbol of the close ties that bind us together.

You have inspired me to make a suggestion how these bonds of mutual friendship and respect can be made even stronger. You have all heard of the idea of twinning cities to promote joint interests in such things as culture, education and government. Amsterdam is twinned with Toronto and The Hague with Ottawa.

My idea is to twin Holland and Canada on the national level! Already there are around a million people in Canada with Dutch blood, and there are untold numbers of Dutch who have Canadian blood in their veins. Thanks to the efforts of Olga Rains, more are turning up every year!

The benefits of such a twinning are enormous—a common currency, one government, one Army and one budget. Then these wonderful Pilgrimages could be financed, at least in part, by Canadians. Of course, we would have to make it retroactive to pay for all the earlier Pilgrimages.

Cities could be renamed to give effect to the new Union. Toronto, often referred to as damn Toronto, could become Torontodam, a much pleasanter name. Ottawa, Ottawadam. Some places could even keep their present names, like South Saskatchewandam and so on.

Don't worry about our countries being divided by a narrow passage of water called the Atlantic. Supersonic planes have cut the time-distance to two or three hours. And don't forget that Newfoundland is closer to Holland than it is to Vancouver.

This idea of a Union of the two countries is not a new one. Many years ago, Canada took the initiative. It declared that a small area in Ottawa was to be considered as Dutch Territory, thereby giving you a chance to create a Canadian Colony. Unfortunately, after Princess Margriet was born, you failed to pursue the matter and a great opportunity to unify the two countries was lost!

Well, it's fun to talk about, and who knows what's in store for us in the new millennium. Whatever happens, I am certain that the respect, love and friendship we have for each other, and so evident here today, will last as long as the Ijssel and Ottawa Rivers flow.

Thank you, thank you dear friends. Now on with the celebrations!

On March 14th, the very day I received the letter from Gerrit Ham, I received a telephone call from Texel, a small island off the northwest tip of Holland. The caller was a Mr. Wilhelm Bakker, who gave me such an explosive story that I believe it should be recorded.

"I got your name from Jan Koorenhof in Apeldoorn who showed me your book. Two weeks after VE Day (May 8th, 1945) a Lt. Gord Grant and 50 men of the PPCLI landed on Texel to stop the fighting that was still going on between Georgian (Russian) troops that had been conscripted into the German Army, and their German officers. I am a Dutch paratrooper and I am going to make a jump next May as a symbolic re-enactment of the landing of the PPCLI during the war.

"The citizens of Texel want a representative from the PPCLI to join me. We will pay for your flight from Canada!!

"A Major Bill Leavey in the Canadian Army knows about this and is doing some more research on the part played by the PPCLI."

Well, I thought, this is a story worthy of a Hollywood film. I had no knowledge of any such escapade by any members of the PPCLI and I had never heard of Texel.

"I'm sorry, Mr. Bakker, but this is all news to me. I will, however, check with Major Leavey in Ottawa but I want you to know that I never was a paratrooper and it's a little late in the game to learn now. I won't be able to join you in your jump."

"Oh, I understand. I didn't mean you had to jump—just attend the ceremony to unveil a monument to the PPCLI."

APELDOORN—1995

It took me a few days to work through the bureaucracy in NDHQ and speak to Maj. Leavey. What he told me only added to the mystery which now took on the proportions of an Agatha Christie novel.

"Yes, Mr. Bakker phoned me some time ago. How he got my name I don't know. Anyway, there is a Col. Gord Grant in NDHQ. He told me he had jumped on Texel two or three years ago with Bakker on a training exercise. He was not a member of the PPCLI during the war.

"Mr. Bakker also phoned Col. Grant and said that a Lt. T. W. Grant, PPCLI, had landed on Texel on May 5th, 1945, with a platoon.

"I checked our files but could not find any record of a Lt. T. W. Grant having been a member of the PPCLI. Nevertheless, I believe the Dutch are going ahead with their plans to erect a monument to the PPCLI on May 5th."

Maj. Leavey added that he had also checked with the Historical Section in Ottawa and they had no record of the PPCLI ever landing on Texel.

To resolve this mystery, I checked my own records of the officers who had served with the PPCLI during the war. The only Lt. Grant is shown as follows:

H16036, Lt. G.W. Grant, joined PPCLI 7 Sep 39, Pte. Cpl.
SOS 20 Mar 43
Rejoined PPCLI as Lt. 25 Nov 44
SOS 23 Jun 45
MID, Bronze Lion (Holland)

I knew Gordon Grant. He was a fine officer and, as indicated, he was awarded a MID and a Dutch decoration, the Bronze Lion. I can personally attest he did not sneak off to Texel with 50 men after the war.

I never did receive an explanation for this "mystery wrapped in an enigma," as Churchill would have called it. Perhaps on my next trip to Holland, I will visit Texel and try to locate the missing Lt. Grant and/or his heirs and next-of-kin.

A week after the "Texel caper," on March 23rd, I received another telephone call that for a moment I feared meant more trouble. It was from a Maj. John Barclay of the 48th Highlanders. Now what? Were they going to re-enact the crossing of the Ijssel River again? My fears were soon put to rest. Pieter Bcclaerts and his wife were visiting Toronto and the 48th were giving a Mess dinner in their honour on April 22nd. Could I join them?

Now that, in a word, is class. The hatchet had been truly buried with honour. However, due to a prior engagement, I could not attend their dinner. I then remembered that Pieter had written me a note at Christmas that he would be visiting Toronto. I immediately wrote Pieter asking him to join me for dinner on April 21st.

APELDOORN—1995

My letter was dated March 24th. Unbeknown to me the fickle finger of fate, otherwise known as Field Marshal Fate, was about to intervene. Nevertheless, I soldiered on and proceeded with my plans.

On April 21st, I picked up Pieter and his wife, Dieuwke, at the University Club and we had dinner at the Granite. Mindful of a very sumptuous and elegant dinner Pieter had hosted in his "Palace" at Utrecht on May 1st, 1990, I was determined to reciprocate his fine selection of wines. It will be recalled that on that occasion he had procured wines from every country the PPCLI had fought over or passed through during the War. My wine list was not quite so impressive but I remember seeing Scotch, Rye, Bloody Marys, Port, Chablis and Ice Wine on the table (not all at the same time). Pieter brought me up to date on the events in Apeldoorn which would commence within the week. As I recall, the Ontario Ice Wine was a winner and we ended up dancing. As we prepared to leave, Pieter took my hand and said, "I have a small gift for you." Whereupon he produced a jewel case, opened it and removed a beautiful set of gold cuff links engraved with the Royal cipher and the motto *Honi Soit Qui Mal y Pense*.

I was stunned. I remember saying something to the effect that I realized this motto was the same as the Order of the Garter (Evil be to him who evil thinks). It was also the motto of our Prince of Wales and The Royal Regiment of Canada, of which Prince Charles was Colonel-in-Chief and I had been the Honorary Colonel.

It was a most generous and appropriate gift and one that I will always treasure.

My wife Margaret was ill and could not be with us. Dieuwke handed me a beautiful book for her—*The Country Flower Companion*.

The fact that my wife was ill on April 21st is of considerable significance in the telling of my story of the Pilgrimage in 1995. In fact, so is the heading of this chapter, which is not called a Pilgrimage but simply Apeldoorn, 1995. Between Major Barclay's telephone call of March 23rd and the dinner on April 21st, I had been struck by lightning, or so it seemed. My wife suddenly became very ill on March 30th and was rushed to hospital.

I am happy to say that she gradually recovered and eventually was restored to full health. There was no question but that I had to cancel my trip. Later, many people asked how I handled the disappointment and frustration after months of planning and preparation. I told them quite frankly that it wasn't easy but concern for my wife put all other matters in the shade. Later, when she got better, I found it helped to think of past experiences and how I had coped with them. I sincerely believe that my training at RMC and in the Army also sustained me. I had learned a great deal about myself and what was important and what was not important in life.

APELDOORN—1995

Probably the most frustrating experience was the paperwork and delays involved in having to cancel airline, hotel and automobile reservations and fighting for refunds. This took several months. Fortunately, I had an excellent travel agent.

It will be recalled that in addition to the reservations for the Pilgrimage in Holland, there were reservations for my *après* Holland trip, through Germany, Austria, Switzerland and France.

But without doubt, the most difficult part was to tell all my friends in Holland who were counting on my presence. I felt very badly about letting them down, but they were all sympathetic and understanding.

To convey some idea of my program in Holland, I give the following list of events:

April 27, Thurs.	—	*Arrive Apeldoorn*
April 29, Sat.	—	*Beekbergen, Oosterhuizen and Lieren—Unveiling Memorial and Parade—Speech*
April 30, Sun.	—	*Queen's Birthday, Twello—Reception*
May 1, Mon.	—	*Voorst—Exhibition*
May 2, Tues.	—	*Voorthuizen—Tattoo—Playing of my March*
May 3, Wed.	—	*Teuge—Air Show*
May 4, Thurs.	—	*National Remembrance Day—Holten Cemetery*
May 5, Fri.	—	*National Liberation Day*
	—	*Achterveld—Opening of Memorial Room in school and Exhibition*
	—	*Apeldoorn Tattoo—Playing of my March*
May 7, Sun.	—	*Apeldoorn National Parade 6,000 Veterans 250,000 Spectators*
May 8, Mon.	—	*VE Day—Groesbeek Cemetery*
May 9, Tues.	—	*Farewell Parties*

At the risk of offending friends whose goodness I may have overlooked, I would now like to mention some of their kind and generous acts.

April 15	—	Klaas Huisman *phoned to express regrets that I would not be there and sent best wishes to Margaret.*
April 20	—	*sent a silk scarf and tie*

APELDOORN—1995

April 24	—	*sent an article and a picture in a newspaper about the Ceremony at Oosterhuizen April 21.*
May 1	—	Johannes van Blommestein *phoned. Ceremonies are just beginning. Will miss my presence.*
May 2	—	General Andrew Gijsbers *phoned (1:00 a.m. Holland). Voorthuizen Tattoo great success. My March played by massed bands—500 musicians. Score presented to Canadian Ambassador. Such a pity I was not present.*
May 5	—	Pieter Beelaerts *phoned (11:45 p.m. Holland). Just back from Apeldoorn Tattoo. Played my March. Great success. I am now known as Liszt! They all missed me.*
May 19	—	General Gijsbers—*sent a full report on the anniversary*
May 20	—	Jan Schouten—*I received from him a large volume on the history of Achterveld, including many excerpts from Once a Patricia.*
June 6	—	Jan Koorenhof *phoned Margaret*
June 6	—	Jan Koorenhof *phoned again (4:00 a.m. Holland). The Apeldoorn Tattoo played my march at the Grand Finale. Sounded great.*
June 20	—	Pipe Major Ross Stewart, *48th Highlanders, phoned to congratulate me on my march which was played in Voorthuizen and Apeldoorn.*
June 29	—	Gerrit Ham *phoned. Ceremony and Parade went well. Lloyd Rains represented PPCLI in my absence.*
July 1	—	Gerrit Ham *sent medal from Beekbergen, Oosterhuizen and Lieren.*
July 12	—	Klaas Huisman *sent Apeldoorn medal.*
July 31	—	Lloyd and Olga Rains *sent letter reporting on Oosterhuizen Ceremony.*
Aug. 10	—	Evert Gerritsen *sent video of bands playing at Voorthuizen.*

As I said earlier, I am sure there are others I should have mentioned. To them, I offer my sincere apologies and I hope they will let me know.

And then the letters from my friends and mine in reply. Again, it is not possible to mention them all. The following are included because they fill in gaps in the above narrative, or give another view of events, or corroborate some unique or special event that may not seem credible. Some repetition of facts is inevitable, but this should not detract from the genuine feelings of appreciation that my letters were intended to convey.

LGEN. A.W.T.G. GIJSBERS
19 May 1995

Dear Sydney,

Peace and quietness have returned after the hectic weeks in April and early May. The last of our Canadian guests flies home today. There is now time to write to you.

The entire period of celebration and commemoration has been a tremendous success. The adjectives to describe it fail me! We were blessed with superb weather all the time the veterans were here, dry and warm and beautiful blue skies; it started raining after the bulk had left.

The parade on May 7th, once again commanded by Maj.Gen. G. Kitching, was happy and emotional at the same time, both for the 7,000 Canadian, British, Polish and Dutch veterans and for the spectators, estimated at 300,000! I hope you have been able to watch the parade on TV; CBC had a live broadcast on all Canadian networks. It was, indeed, a splendid climax of an extremely happy fortnight with our liberators.

Now about your "50th Anniversary March." Enclosed you will find the score, arranged for wind band by a Mr. J. (Sjef) Claessen, a member of a civilian wind band, conducted by Capt. Tom Beekman, also conductor of a military band, to whom I had turned over your tune. On the enclosed tape you will hear the tune as you played it on the piano, followed by the wind band arrangement. This was performed by the Royal Wind Band at Lottum, the civilian band I mentioned above.

I told you on the phone, that your work has been performed at a Tattoo at Voorthuizen on May 2nd; it was announced as the "World Premiere" of the "50th Anniversary March" by Col. Sydney Frost of the PPCLI! The participating bands were the Military Band of the 48th Highlanders of Canada, the Air Command Band (Canada), a British RAF band and the Burlington Teen Tour Band (Canada).

Three days later, on May 5th, it was played again during the Finale of the Royal Apeldoorn Tattoo in the presence of some 10,000 people from our city, including our 750 Canadian veterans and their host families. This time the bands involved were the Johan Willem Friso Kapel (Dutch military band), the Military Band of the 48th Highlanders of Canada, the Air Command Band (Canada), 215 US Army Band (Massachusetts National Guard) and the Burlington Teen Tour Band (Canada). Again, of course, your name was announced as the composer. The Canadian Broadcasting Corporation CBC made a video recording of the Tattoo; you might be able to procure a copy from Mr. David Knapp, Manager Special Projects, at Toronto, tel. (416) 205-7798.

I also enclose a clipping from the Apeldoornse Courant (dated April 11) concerning the unveiling of a monument at the village of Oosterhuizen, liberated by your Battalion on April 16, 1945. It states that you could not be present due to the illness of your wife.

With my kindest regards,
Andrew Gijsbers

July 12, 1995

Mr. K. P. Huisman
Apeldoorn
Dear Klaas:

Your kind letter arrived today and with it a wonderful surprise—the Medal!
You don't know how much this medal means to me and I shall always treasure it. It will be a precious heirloom to be passed on to my children.

I am glad you and Ellen were able to get away and enjoy a nice holiday in Great Britain. I'm not surprised that the City of Apeldoorn is well known there after the incredible parades you have organized and the warmth and affection you have shown to your Allied liberators. Indeed, it is you who should receive a medal for the friendship and generosity you have shown us for so many years.

When you said "the party is over," it brought back memories of a poem written after Queen Victoria's Jubilee, which I learned as a child. The name of the poem is "The Recessional" by Rudyard Kipling. I can't recite the entire work but I remember one stanza:

> The tumult and the shouting dies,
> The captains and the kings depart,
> Still stands thine ancient sacrifice
> An humble and a contrite heart.
>
> Lord God of Hosts be with us yet,
> Lest we forget, lest we forget.

APELDOORN—1995

Whether it is appropriate to recite this verse in connection with our 50th Anniversary I do not know, but I think we all realize how fortunate we are as nations and individuals to have survived a terrible war and to be free.

It is not like me to deliver such a sombre note, but I wanted to share my thoughts with you.

Sincerely,

July 14, 1995

Mr. Gerrit Ham
Beekbergen
Dear Gerrit:

What a surprise! Your wonderful letter arrived today and with it the beautiful medal from Beekbergen, Lieren and Oosterhuizen. How can I ever repay your generosity and kindness.

I have so much to thank you for. Your article about my Regiment, the PPCLI, is simply superb. I was amazed at the amount of your research and, of course, I am very proud you mentioned my book.

Then the monument in Oosterhuizen which was unveiled on April 21st, and for which you designed the plaque honouring the PPCLI. And your thoughtful act of burying a bottle beside the monument containing your article on the PPCLI. I am truly overwhelmed by your deep sense of history.

This monument and your article and the time capsule are so important to me and the PPCLI that I am going to send the Regiment copies of the photo and your article.

I applaud your dedication to the 48th Highlanders of Holland Pipes and Drums, which was responsible for the formation of this unique group. Again your sense of history comes through loud and clear. I have known the 48th many years, as I commanded another Toronto Regiment, The Royal Regiment of Canada, and was its Honorary Colonel for fifteen years. Ross Stewart of the 48th told me about your beautiful medal. He is a fine fellow.

By the way, I was very impressed by the bearing and appearance of your Band in the photo you sent me, especially the military mien of one Gerrit Ham. I'll bet you were a fine soldier in the Garde Regiment Grenadiers.

Sincerely,

August 26, 1995

Jhr. Drs. P.A.C. Beelaerts van Blokland
Queen's Commissioner
Provence of Utrecht
Dear Pieter:

Now that "the tumult and the shouting" of the great 50th Anniversary has died down, I thought it would be an appropriate time to offer my belated thanks for the lovely cuff links. Seeing you and Dieuwke on April 21st and having dinner together did much to ease the pain of missing the Celebrations. Then on May 5th you were kind enough to phone me after the Apeldoorn Tattoo to say that my piece had been played by the massed bands. I can't tell you how much I appreciated your thoughtfulness.

I followed the week-long Celebrations on TV and vicariously experienced the thrills and emotions of the Veterans as they proudly marched through the multitudes of Dutch friends and admirers. Truly, it was a memorable occasion that we will never witness again.

I am very grateful that my own dear friends did not forget me. Besides your wonderful gift, I received a medal from Apeldoorn, another one from Beekbergen and a lovely book about Holland from a lady I only met briefly in 1990. (She handed the book to Pipe Major Ross Stewart to deliver to me in Toronto!)

General Gijsbers kindly sent me the complete score for my march as arranged by J. Claessen and an audio cassette of it being played by the Royal Wind Band at Lottum.

From Evert Gerritsen, that popular friend of Canadian Veterans, I received a video cassette of the Voorthuizen Tattoo which you saw. It was certainly a spectacular event and I must admit that shivers ran up and down my spine when the massed bands played my march.

I should not fail to mention that Klaas Huisman, the Chief of Cabinet of Apeldoorn, thoughtfully sent me a beautiful silk tie and a scarf for my wife, as well as a newspaper clipping describing the unveiling of the monument to the PPCLI in Oosterhuizen which I had been asked to attend. He also sent me the medal I have mentioned.

So you see, though I was not with you in body, I was there very much in spirit. I shall never forget the many kindnesses I received from you and my other Dutch friends.

APELDOORN—1995

Margaret is almost restored to full health and joins me in thanking you and Dieuwke for the delightful book, The Country Flower Companion.

Sincerely,

August 26, 1995

Mr. Jan H. A. Koorenhof
Apeldoorn
Dear Jan:

The Great Anniversary is over and you will now have a chance to relax and bask in the glorious success of the celebration. I am sure that never before has there been such a happy melding of the peoples of two countries as there was during that memorable week in May. Let me congratulate you and your committee on the great work you accomplished.

It was very kind and thoughtful of you to phone first my wife Margaret and then me to describe the Tattoo in Apeldoorn.

Only one event marred the Apeldoorn parade—the insane comments of some of the CBC reporters like Ann (something). She did her best to find something wrong with the event and finally got an old Veteran who complained about not enough vehicles. He shouldn't have been there and Ann should have had the good sense not to ask him such dumb questions. Anyway, I was delighted when she interviewed you and you neatly put her in her place. Good for you!

Though I missed the "Big Fifty," I have not given up my plans to return to Holland and see my many friends. Here's hoping for 1996!

With my best wishes and congratulations again on a job well done.

Sincerely,

September 15, 1995

Dr. J.H.J. van Blommestein
Burgemeester van Voorst
Twello
Dear Johannes:

Now that the excitement of the 50th Anniversary has passed, I thought this would be a good time to write you a note to say how disappointed I was not to attend the Celebrations and see you again. Your telephone call and the many letters I received from my dear friends in Holland have helped me to cope. So has the knowledge that my wife has fully recovered. She feels badly that I had to cancel my trip but we both realize my presence here contributed greatly to her recovery.

I remained glued to the TV the whole week of Celebrations and marched with the Veterans every step of the way. I marvelled at the organization of the many events and the stamina of the Veterans who took part. It was incredible and deserves a special place in the history of our two countries.

I am interested to hear all about the Ceremonies in Voorst especially in Twello and Wilp. I am sure that with you at the helm everything went off perfectly to "The Queen's Taste." I trust you are now having a chance to recuperate from all the excitement.

I have every intention of returning to Holland at the first opportunity, perhaps next year, and I will certainly give you a call.

With my warmest regards to you and Titia.

Sincerely,

September 15, 1995

Mr. J. M. Schouten
Hessenweg 317
Achterveld

Dear Mr. Schouten:

I am writing to thank you for sending me that wonderful book about Achterveld and the War. My last letter was hand written because my wife was still suffering from the effects of her illness and she could not type my letter.

I am naturally very disappointed that I missed all the memorable ceremonies in connection with the 50th Anniversary Celebrations. Your book and the many letters I received from my dear friends in Holland have been a great help.

I am interested to hear all about the Ceremonies in Achterveld. I am sure that with your assistance everything went off perfectly. I trust you are now having a chance to recuperate from all the excitement.

I have every intention of returning to Holland at the first opportunity, perhaps next year, and I will certainly give you a call.

With my warmest regards to you and all the citizens of Achterveld.

Sincerely,

The foregoing seven letters describe the events of the 50th Anniversary in which I was involved, but through no fault of mine, missed. The letters also indicate the main players in this drama with whom I had the privilege of playing a minor part. There are, however, three other actors who appeared only briefly on the stage but deserve recognition.

The first two are Lloyd and Olga Rains, who are well known throughout Holland as the originators of Project Roots, a voluntary agency that has reunited more than 2,500 Canadian Veterans with the War Children they left behind in Europe at the end of WWII.

Olga is a war bride who met Lloyd during the Dutch Liberation in 1945. Lloyd is No. B68601 Pte. L. V. Rains, who joined the PPCLI on February 14, 1945, and was a member of my D Company during the crossing of the Ijssel River and subsequent operations.

The Rains lived in Canada for 50 years and then returned to Holland where they now reside and carry on their work. On April 29th, 1997, Olga was awarded the Cross of Knighthood by Queen Beatrix.

Lloyd and Olga have also been very active in Holland on behalf of the Patricias not only during the Pilgrimages but also in the intervening years. When the "second battle" of the crossing of the Ijssel River erupted, as to which Regiment was involved, the Rains gave their full support to the PPCLI. When the smoke cleared and our claim to the honour had been rightfully restored, the Rains arranged for an additional Memorial to be added to the existing monument on the west bank of the Ijssel which had blandly declared:

With the crossing of the Ijssel River at Gorssel by the Canadian Army on April 12th, 1945, the liberation of western Holland began.

The memorial added by Lloyd and Olga Rains makes it very clear who did the job:

PPCLI
Princess Patricia's Canadian
Light Infantry
First Regiment to cross the Ijssel River
12 April, 1945

Again, in 1995, at Oosterhuizen, where a Monument had been erected in honour of the PPCLI, at the unveiling Lloyd Rains represented the Regiment when I could not attend.

These are just two examples of the devotion of Lloyd and Olga Rains to the Patricias. With that background, I now reproduce a letter from them and my reply.

APELDOORN—1995

Project "ROOTS"
BRINGING PEOPLE TOGETHER
Lloyd and Olga Rains, Haarlem, Holland

July 31, 1995

Col. C. S. Frost
Toronto

Dear Sir:
Hope this finds you and your wife in good health. We hope that Mrs. Frost is doing well. We were so sorry to hear that you were not able to make it to Holland last May.

Enclosed find three photos. They were taken in Oosterhuizen on April 21/95 where a monument was unveiled in Oosterhuizen. Lloyd was invited to say a few words and I was asked to translate. There were some 300 people who came from surrounding villages. It was heart warming and very emotional. The monument was the idea of the villagers to show their gratitude to the PPCLI. Lloyd remembered the village he entered 50 years ago.

After the ceremony, we were driven by Jeep to the church in Beekbergen for a special remembrance service.

I also send you a copy of a newspaper clipping of April 22/95 in Oosterhuizen, Lloyd standing between the little children, each holding a white tulip.

We are living in Holland now and like it very much. On the end of this year we will be married 50 years. We will be coming to Canada to celebrate this with our three children and ten grandchildren on December 24th.

Hopefully you can make it to Holland sometime.
Wishing you both all the best,

Sincerely,
Olga and Lloyd

September 12, 1995

Mr. and Mrs. Lloyd Rains
Dear Olga and Lloyd:
Thank you so much for your kind letter of July 31st and the lovely photos of the monument to the PPCLI. The Regiment is very fortunate that you were there to express our thanks to the villagers of Oosterhuizen for such a unique memorial.

Thank you too for the newspaper clipping showing Lloyd standing between the little children.

I have sent copies of your photos to the Regimental Museum in Calgary where they will remain in perpetuity as a reminder of the kindness of the people of Oosterhuizen and of your participation in the Ceremony.

Did you know that I composed a March in honour of the 50th Anniversary of the Liberation of Holland? It was played at the Tattoo in Voortheuizen on May 2nd by the massed bands of some 500 musicians! Then on May 5th, it was played again by the massed bands at the Grand Finale of the Royal Apeldoorn Tattoo. So you see, even though I was not there in body, I was very much with you in spirit.

I recently received both an audio cassette of the piece being played by the Royal Wind Band at Lottum and a video cassette of the Voorthuizen Tattoo.

I have every intention of returning to Holland at the first opportunity, perhaps next year, and I will certainly give you a call.

Again my belated thanks for your thoughtful letter.
Sincerely,

Throughout my journeys to Sicily, Italy and Holland, I always endeavoured to send reports of my travels to the Regiment, either to the Colonel of the Regiment, or to the Regimental Major, or to the Archives, or sometimes to all three.

In the case of the Oosterhuizen Memorial, I sent my report to the Regimental Major, Major John McComber.

July 17, 1995

Dear Major McComber:

I am writing to report on an event of significance to the Regiment that occurred in Holland during the recent 50th Anniversary Celebrations of the end of WWII.

Following the crossing of the Ijssel River on April 11th, 1945, and the repulse of a counter-attack on the bridgehead at Wilp, the PPCLI pursued the retreating enemy into western Holland. The line of advance passed through three small villages about five miles south of Apeldoorn— Oosterhuizen, Lieren and Beekbergen.

As part of the 50th Anniversary Celebrations, these villages decided to erect a Monument in Oosterhuizen to honour the Canadian soldiers who had liberated them. They also held a parade for the returning Veterans and presented each one with a handsome medal commemorating the event.

APELDOORN—1995

On March 14th of this year, I received a letter from one Gerrit Ham of Beekbergen advising me of the planned ceremonies, asking me to attend the Unveiling of the Monument on April 21st and join the Remembrance Parade on April 29th. I was happy to accept as I was planning to attend the 50th Anniversary Celebrations in nearby Apeldoorn.

Unfortunately, a few days later my wife became ill and I had to cancel my trip. But I kept in touch with my Dutch friends in Apeldoorn and Beekbergen and of course, saw the Anniversary Celebrations on TV. I have never before witnessed anything to equal the outpouring of friendship and affection that our Veterans received from the wonderful Dutch people. My only regret was that I could not be there.

Last week I received a long letter from Gerrit Ham telling me all about the Celebrations and enclosing the medal I would have received! He confirmed that the monument was unveiled on April 21st by the Mayor of Apeldoorn, and on the Monument was a plaque designed by Mr. Ham commemorating the PPCLI, who had liberated the town in 1945.

Mr. Ham has made a lifelong study of the history of the First Canadian Division, and in particular the PPCLI, from its formation in August 1914 to the end of WWII. Based on my book, Once a Patricia, he wrote a short history of the Regiment translated into Dutch, which he encased in a bottle and had buried beneath the Monument in Oosterhuizen— a kind of time capsule to record the history of the PPCLI in perpetuity.

I have, of course, written Mr. Ham thanking him for his remarkable dedication to the Regiment. You may want to ask the Colonel of the Regiment to also send him a note of thanks. His address is:

    Mr. Gerrit Ham
    Engelanderweg 62
    7361 CW Beekbergen
    The Netherlands

I enclose the following material:
1. Copy of Mr. Ham's letter, which I received March 14, 1995.
2. Copy of the history of the PPCLI written by Mr. Ham and deposited in a bottle underneath the Monument in Oosterhuizen.

3. Clipping from an article in the newspaper Apeldoornse Courant, *of April 22nd, describing the Unveiling of the Monument and including a photo showing Lloyd Rains who represented the PPCLI.*
4. *Photo of the Unveiling showing the Mayor of Apeldoorn (wearing his Chain of Office).*
5. *Maps of north-western Holland taken from* Once A Patricia, *showing the advance of the PPCLI. I have added the location of the village of Oosterhuizen.*
6. *Road map of the same area showing the location of the three villages, Oosterhuizen, Lieren and Beekbergen. I have added in yellow the general line of advance of the PPCLI.*

There are now two monuments honouring the memory of the soldiers of the First Division—one at Pachino, in the south-eastern tip of Sicily where the Regiment came ashore on July 10th, 1943, and the other at Oosterhuizen, Holland, a few miles from Achterveld where the Regiment ended its war on May 5th, 1945.

It should be recorded that the Government of Canada played no part in the erection of these monuments that mark the place of the first and the last Patricia to fall in the cause of freedom. These monuments were conceived, raised and paid for by people whom we set free.

Sincerely,

September 12, 1995

Dear Major McComber:

Further to my letter of July 17th, I am writing to report that I have received from Lloyd and Olga Rains three more photos of the Unveiling of the Monument to the PPCLI at Oosterhuizen on April 21st. I enclose copies of these photos. On the back of each one you will find brief descriptions of the events.

You are probably aware that Lloyd Rains served with the Regiment as a private soldier from February 14, 1945, to July 18, 1945. He married a Dutch girl and they divide their time between Canada and Holland. Olga has been very active in tracing down the Canadian fathers of what she calls "Her Liberation Children."

Sincerely

November 2, 1995
C. Sydney Frost, CD, QC, BSc MIL, LLB, LLD
50 Bayview Wood
Toronto, ON M4N 1R7

Dear Col. Frost:
 I have just today received your package of information from Lloyd Rains. It is tremendously interesting to read about how the people of Holland still see our vets, remember our vets, after all this time. I was fortunate to have been able to participate in a number of battlefield tours while on staff at Kingston. I visited Italy and Normandy, and got up to Arnhem on my own. In all cases, I was able to spend many fascinating hours with the vets (from both sides) as they once again "walked the ground" and described the actions in which they had fought.
 Your contributions are most appreciated and constitute very valuable archival material. Increasingly, students and professional researchers are using the archives. I am moving now to obtain the services of a professional (qualified) archivist, to better "put our house in order" and to lay the groundwork in areas such as preservation and a database. While our Sgt. Archives NCOs have done wonders over the years, it is time to get some expert help.

Yours truly
J. McComber
Major

 Earlier in this narrative, I mentioned there were three unsung players in the final Act of the 1995 Liberation Ceremonies. The third person is none other than Pipe Major Ross Stewart, a worthy member of the 48th Highlanders, who rendered me valuable service.
 Ross Stewart and I had been friends for a long time and had not let the Ijssel incident mar our relationship. He had attended every Pilgrimage to Holland and had been instrumental (an appropriate word) in forming the 48th Highlanders of Holland Pipe and Drum Band under Gerrit Ham. If ever there was a typical Pipe Major, it was Ross Stewart, and he was highly respected throughout the Toronto garrison not only for his musical ability but for his soldierly qualities. With these few laudatory remarks on the record, it is now opportune to disclose one small slip in his otherwise exemplary career. He was the person who had the misfortune to slip on the wet marble floor of the Palace in Utrecht when Pieter Beelaerts gave that memorable dinner. But true to

form, he quickly recovered and carried on with fine soldierly bearing. It goes without saying that I had great respect for Ross Stewart.

On June 20th, after the 1995 Pilgrimage, he phoned to say how sorry he was that I could not have been present. My March was played at two tattoos and greatly enjoyed by both the musicians and the spectators. He also informed me that on one of the parades, a fine-looking Dutch lady had handed him a parcel which she asked him to deliver to Colonel Frost.

I immediately asked Ross to lunch and we spent several hours reminiscing about our wonderful "Dutch connection" amid much camaraderie and good humour. First he handed me a copy of the program for the Apeldoorn Tattoo in which nine bands performed: Pipes and Drums of the 48th; Pipes and Drums of the Canadian Legion, Pipes and Drums of the Royal Canadian Regiment, Band of the Dutch Armed Forces, Canadian Air Command Band, 48th Highlanders Military Band, Burlington Teen Tour Band, Band of the Royal Air Force and Royal Dutch Horse Artillery Band. I could now understand the enthusiastic comments I had been receiving from General Gijsbers, Pieter Beelaerts and many others about the performance.

I will not reproduce the entire Program which went to three pages, but I will, with no little pride, produce the Finale:

9. FINALE
Highland Cathedral (Massed Pipe Bands and Massed Bands)
50th Anniversary March 1995—C.S. Frost
Nightfall in Camp—D.A. Pope
Poem (lone piper plays "Flowers of the Forest") (text page 52)
Abide With Me (choir and bands) (text page 52)
O'Canada
Wilhelmus
Reveille sounded by bugles of the 48th Highlanders
Song by the choir: Peace Be With You—A. Snell (text page 52)
Lone Piper: "Mist Covered Mountain"
March off: Voice of the Guns—Alford

I will also admit to momentarily feeling a few pains of regret that I had missed such a spectacular show.

Ross Stewart brought me down to earth by giving me the parcel he had received in Apeldoorn. I opened it and found a lovely book on Holland with many illustrations and scenes in colour. We were both overawed by such a gracious gift and Ross exclaimed, "I never realized you had such devoted fans. Are there others?"

I assured him this was not a case that should be investigated by Olga Rains and her Roots Project, and showed him the note inscribed on the fly leaf of the book.

Apeldoorn, May 5th, 1995

Dear Mr. Frost,

What a pity you could not come to Holland. I did hope to meet you again but I heard your wife is ill. Will you give her this card? I send you a book about Holland and I hope you like it.

We are 50 years free now and we celebrate that in Apeldoorn with many veterans. Thank you for giving me that freedom.

Mr. Stewart will give you this book about Holland which I send to you. I hope you like it.

Many regards,

The book was from a friend of a family I had met during the 1990 Pilgrimage. They lived in a fine home on the outskirts of Wilp, which had been one of the objectives of the PPCLI after crossing the Ijssel. The original house had been destroyed as well as all their cattle, but not for one moment did they bear us any grudge. Their freedom was just recompense for their loss.

This is the letter I wrote my newfound friend:

June 21, 1995

What a beautiful and wonderful surprise I had yesterday! I had lunch with Ross Stewart and he presented me with your lovely book. I was completely overcome. How can I ever thank you enough for your kindness. The book will be a tangible reminder of our mutual feelings of friendship and respect and will become a family heirloom.

Ross told me all about the happy yet emotional events of the Celebrations. Yes, it was a tremendous blow for me to miss it after looking forward to the Anniversary for several years.

My wife has thankfully recovered and I am sure my presence was an important factor. She sends her thanks for your thoughtful card and best wishes.

I wonder if you knew that I composed a special March to commemorate the 50th Anniversary. It was played by the Massed Bands at the Tattoos at Voorthuizen and Apeldoorn.

APELDOORN—1995

>*I enclose copies of the music and words which I have signed.*
>
>*I am confident that I will return to Holland within the next year or two and see you and my many dear friends. The special relationship that exists between the people of Holland and their Canadian Veterans is truly unique. It is a great comfort for all of us to know that our bonds of friendship forged in the chaos of war have endured during the trials of peace. Let us keep in touch.*
>
>*With my best wishes,*
>
> *Sydney Frost*

* * *

On that high note, I was certain that the 50th Anniversary Pilgrimage was over and done and I started to work on my letters of appreciation. But I hadn't counted on other surprises from the indefatigable Ross Stewart.

To understand what follows, it is necessary to give a little background. Each year, in Toronto, the Royal Canadian Military Institute presents a Massed Band Concert in Roy Thomson Hall. It is a spectacular show that provides military, ceremonial and patriotic music, unlike any other concert in Canada.

The purpose is to enhance the image of the Reserve Forces within the community and it is very popular. Bands from the following units take part:

    Governor General's Horse Guards
    The Queen's Own Rifles
    The Royal Regiment of Canada
    The Queen's York Rangers
    The 7th Toronto Artillery Regiment
    The 48th Highlanders
    The Toronto Scottish
    HMCS York
    400 Squadron Air Force Reserve

The show is produced by Murray E. Buckstein of the RCMI; the Principal Director of Music is Major Gino Falconi, of The Royal Regiment of Canada; Mr. Henry Shannon, the well-known radio personality, is the Master of Ceremonies.

The Sixth Annual Concert, for 1995, was being held October 29th. Having Commanded The Royal Regiment of Canada and been its Honorary Colonel, I would have liked to attend the Concert, but could not due to other prior commitments.

On Saturday, October 28th, I received a call from Henry Shannon. "I was so sorry to hear that you missed the 50th Anniversary Celebrations in Holland. I understand you wrote a March that was played at Military Tattoos on at least two occasions."

"So I understand, Henry, but who told you this?"

"Your old friend, Ross Stewart. He says it was a great hit."

"Well, I'll be damned."

"What?"

"I just can't believe what a great guy he is. No wonder he is so respected not only by the 48th, but the whole Garrison."

"That's right. Look, I want the Massed Bands to play your March tomorrow. Ross has given me the arrangement they used in Holland. It looks pretty good. We're having a rehearsal tonight. Can you come?"

"I'll be there. This is one parade I don't want to miss."

That evening I sat with Henry Shannon and the producers of the show, while the bands rehearsed. When my March was played, I involuntarily stood up and so did the others. Then Gino Falconi, the Principal Director of Music, called down from the stage, "Sir, do you mind if we do that once more. I thought I heard a glitch."

I knew darn well there had been no glitches but I readily assented.

As I have indicated, I was not able to attend the actual performance the following night but I didn't mind. The thrill of sitting in Roy Thomson Hall with only a few people and hearing my March played by the Massed Bands was truly a "once in a lifetime."

After the performance, I received many calls congratulating me on the March. Most were from military people who knew me only as a part-time soldier and were a little sceptical that I had any musical talent, let alone being a composer. Apparently Henry Shannon gave me a four-minute introduction and laid it on pretty thick—composer, author, lawyer, soldier. He should have just said soldier and let it go at that!

* * *

I have one last stanza to add to this musical Coda. Mr. Herb Pragnell, a classmate at RMC and a fellow Patricia, had attended the 50th Anniversary in Holland. He was so impressed with the March (again knowing me only as a footslogger) that he asked me to send him the score so that it could be played and sung in his church.

On November 12th, the piece was performed at the Almonte United Church. Herb kindly sent me the program.

50TH ANNIVERSARY MARCH—by C.S. Frost

Dear Holland, Holland noble land where Canada's soldiers sleep
Their sacrifice you honour still their memory you keep.

Chorus:
Constancy shall mark our vigil, Guard our Freedom, Peace maintain
That the sacrifice we Honour was not made in vain.

Fifty years have passed away since victory brought us Peace.
Oh, may our friendship long endure and wars forever cease.

ABOUT THE AUTHOR

Colonel Sydney Frost composed the 50th Anniversary March to commemorate the end of World War II. Holland has close ties to Canada mainly because of the role of the Canadian Army in the liberation of Holland.

The World Premier of the March was performed by massed bands at a military tattoo on May 2nd as part of the 50th Anniversary Celebration in Holland in May 1995. It was performed for the first time in Canada by massed bands at Toronto two weeks ago.

Colonel Frost graduated from Royal Military College, Kingston, in 1942, and was commissioned in the Princess Patricia's Canadian Light Infantry. He served with the Regiment in Italy and northwest Europe and was twice wounded in action.

After the war, he entered Osgoode Hall Law School and since graduation has practised law in Toronto. His military service continued with The Royal Regiment of Canada which he commanded from 1959 to 1962. He subsequently served as Honorary Colonel of the Regiment for a number of years.

It had been a memorable 50th Anniversary. It had also been a remarkable half-century for me personally; from Captain PPCLI, to law student to lawyer, to Colonel was quite enough. If someone wanted to add "author" and "composer" I would take that too. But one thing had remained constant throughout my long journey—I was, am and always will be a Patricia.

PROVISIONAL LIST
*PPCLI Veterans Who Attended the 50th Anniversary
Pilgrimage to Holland
May 1995*

D141397	LCpl. W. (Bill) Adelman
	Lt. W. W. (Bert) Bolton
H57004	Pte. C. W. (Cecil) Buck
M12245	Cpl. J. W. Crossman
	Lt. A. D. (Alan) Fairbairn
M103572	Pte. A. M. (Art) Grenier
	Lt. W. E. (Larry) Harrington, MC
B103156	Pte. C. T. (Charlie) King
	Lt. D. G. (Don) MacCulloch
H16860	LCpl. J. H. (John) Moore
P21426	LCpl. W. T. (Bill) Palfrey
	Lt. H. F. (Herb) Pragnell
B68601	Pte. L. V. (Lloyd) Rains
H17295	Cpl. J. E. (Jack) Slater
	Maj. A. S. (Snuffy) Ennis-Smith
C78197	Pte. W. C. (Wally) Smith

Ranks are given as of end of WWII

Chapter XVII

PILGRIMAGE—2000

WHY 2K
Yours is not to reason why,
It's Y2K, not 2KY
Yours is but to hope and pray
You'll be here when it's Y2K
(With apologies to Alfred, Lord Tennyson and the "Charge of the Light Brigade")

It took some time for both the Dutch and the Veterans to recover from the excitement, emotion and pure physical demands of the great 50th Anniversary. The Veterans were faced with another problem—they were getting old. Most were in their eighties and the "young ones" were pushing that geriatric figure.

While I had not attended the celebrations, I had followed them on television, although the CBC had covered only the main events. My friends in Holland had filled in the missing parts with photos, letters, telephone calls, books, newspaper articles, medals, audio and video cassettes. Indeed, my souvenirs from all the Pilgrimages, began to take on the appearance of the Regimental Archives or a museum.

It wasn't long before further gifts began to arrive. On October 7, 1995, Evert Gerritsen, that popular Ambassador of Apeldoorn, phoned from Holland to say he was arriving on October 13th with a friend. We had lunch at the Granite Club and stopped off at my home to inspect my souvenirs from earlier trips. Evert then presented me with photos of the Monument at Oosterhuizen and copies of the photos, documents and a history of the PPCLI that had been deposited in the time capsule. Before I had a chance to thank him, he delved into his bag and produced a lapel pin from Apeldoorn and a video of the Tattoo.

We returned to my car and were about to drive away when he restrained me and said, "Syd, you've driven me around town so many times that you should take out a licence for a taxi."

Whereupon he led me to the rear of my car and affixed a sticker to the bumper. It said "Apeldoornse Taxi Centrale B.V.5.413.413."

"Now," he grinned, "you can charge me a proper fare."

I realized, of course, that the bumper sticker was from his own taxicab company, and replied, "Only one problem; you'll have to change the telephone number to 489-5844."

For the remainder of 1995, I was kept busy organizing my "Archives," sorting out my photos, writing letters of thanks and reporting to the Colonel of the Regiment on the various events. I actually had to acquire new filing cabinets to store all the material, including my growing library of books, such as the voluminous history of Achterveld.

On November 24th, I received a surprise call from Gerrit Ham to wish me a Merry Christmas. It was he who had organized the erection of the Monument in Oosterhuizen. He asked if I had received the photos and material. I assured him I had and that I had sent them to the PPCLI.

On April 11, 1996, I was delighted to receive a call from Evert Gerritsen. He was visiting a cousin in Guelph who was celebrating an anniversary. Could he pass by for a few moments and deliver greetings from the new Mayor of Apeldoorn? I knew what he meant and I wondered what wonderful gift he had tucked in his bag.

He did not disappoint me. On April 19th, I met his cousin, Harmen Blom, and we had lunch. My friendship with Evert went back many years and we had lots to talk about. Apeldoorn had now hosted three great Pilgrimages, in 1985, 1990 and 1995, and I remarked it was a pity I had missed the biggest, in 1995.

"Yes, that was a shame. But you know I had more fun at the first one in 1985. It was all such a new experience and I got to meet almost everyone. I'll never forget a bunch of us singing songs with Syd Frost at the piano."

It was kind of Evert to put it that way, and, immodestly, I agreed. Evert then dug into his magic bag and handed me a video of Apeldoorn entitled "50 Years of Freedom." He also gave me photos from our last meeting, including one of him affixing the taxicab sticker to the bumper of my car.

A year had now passed since the 1995 Pilgrimage. I was certain that it had been the last one. It could never be repeated. And yet—and yet, I had been wrong about the 1995 Anniversary. Reminiscing with Evert about past glories prompted me to ask, "I wonder if any thought has been given to another Pilgrimage in 2000, but on a very modest scale."

Evert gave his deep chuckle and said, "We were discussing that the other day with the new Mayor. It's a little early to say, but I wouldn't be surprised if we did it again."

It was what I hoped to hear. "If you do, I'll be there this time, no excuses." But I had not reckoned on that Master Disrupter of events—Field Marshal Fate.

On May 12th, 1996, "another country was heard from," as my peripatetic father used to say when a new voice was heard. It was Jan Koorenhof, the long-time organizer of Pilgrimages to Apeldoorn, who was staying in Burlington. The CBC were making a film about the 1995 Pilgrimage, including the Burlington Teen Tour Band which had played in the Apeldoorn Tattoo on May 5th, 1995. Like Evert Gerritsen, he felt that the people of Apeldoorn wanted to have another Pilgrimage. He also gave me the happy news he had been "Knighted by the Queen," i.e., received the Order of Orange Nassau. I was glad his long service to Canada's Veterans had been recognized.

I heard nothing further from Holland until April 5th, 1997, when Gerrit Ham phoned from Beekbergen to bring me up to date. Interest was mounting for another Pilgrimage in 2000. In fact, this year, ceremonies were being held in Apeldoorn and Holten in April and May. Could I attend? It was, of course, impossible, but I was pleased to hear that the Dutch people were thinking of another Pilgrimage. He was writing me a note.

On April 14th, I received this letter:

Beekbergen, April 1, 1997

Dear Sydney:

Here is a letter from Holland again. On the 12th of April, we are going with the band to Holten for the annual remembrance for those who have fallen.

On the 17th of April, I will drive with the Jeep to Apeldoorn. We are remembering the Liberation of Apeldoorn. The Ambassador and Military Attache will be present.

My band has received an invitation from Halifax to perform in a "Taptoe" in 1998.

With this letter I have enclosed a copy of a photo of the Church of Beekbergen that was liberated by you on the 17th of April 1945. In May, we also have a "Taptoe" in Apeldoorn. This will be on the Market Square with several other bands and also a Canadian band.

What is most important to me is that your Canadian soldiers have librated us from the German Army. I will never release myself from those days.

> *In May 1940, my mother told me that there was a war going on and we were attacked by the Germans. I will never forget the days from 1940 'till ... the day I die.*
> *With kind regards,*
>
> *Your friend*
> *Gerrit Ham*

It is letters like this which make a Veteran realize that all the fighting and hardships he endured were not in vain.

Still another "constituency" (my word for a new voice) called to give me a report—LCol. Ritse Reitsma (otherwise known as Bill), who is a familiar figure in this narrative. He had organized all the Pilgrimages to Voorst and had made a legion of friends. Col. Reitsma was visiting Ontario at the invitation of 60 or more Veterans and their wives who had been guests of the Municipality of Voorst in 1995. He mentioned a few towns: Peterborough, Blenheim, Pickering, Scarborough, Orillia and others.

What a wonderful way, I thought, for the Veterans to thank Ritse Reitsma for the immense contribution he had made on their behalf. His country had already acknowledged his service by awarding him the Order of Orange Nassau.

On October 24th, I picked him up at a friend's house in Toronto. We soon started reminiscing about the "good old days," the Pilgrimages in 1985, 1990 and 1995. Ritse exclaimed, "Those were great songs you wrote in 1985 and 1995. What were they called?"

"In 1985, it was "Goodbye Wonderful Holland." The piece in 1995 was actually a March, with words—"50th Anniversary March.""

"Do you still have copies?"

"I'm sure I have, if I can only find them."

I soon located the songs and handed copies to Ritse. I wondered if this had something to do with the year 2000 and asked if Voorst was thinking about another Pilgrimage.

"Not just thinking but actually planning it. However, I've retired and I won't be directly involved."

"Well, that's a great pity. I'm sure Johannes can still count on your help."

"Of course."

"I've just had a thought about those songs for 1985 and 1995. You must be bored with them. How about my trying to compose a new one for 2000?"

"Great idea. Let me know how you make out, and by the way, here is a book on Voorst. On page 35 you'll find a beautiful picture of your favourite church in Wilp."

PILGRIMAGE—2000

I had long ago learned to accept these wonderful gifts with grace, and simply said "Thank you."

Ritse Reitsma had sown a musical seed that was to bloom into not one, but two marches and an anthem. I immediately tried to work up a couple of tunes but pressure of other matters interfered. Some people, in their innocence, believe that writing a song is easy—just a matter of inspiration. Not so. It takes about 90 per cent perspiration and only 10 per cent inspiration.

In November 1997, Evert Gerritsen called but I was not at home, having left for a short holiday in climes warmer than Toronto. When I returned in January 1998, I received a call from Evert's cousin, Harmen Blom, in Fergus. He had a bag full of presents for me that Evert had left with him.

On January 22nd, Harmen joined me for lunch at the Granite Club and a friendship with another fine Dutch family began. His father had emigrated to Canada and, like so many of his countrymen, had worked hard and prospered. In the course of our conversation, I discovered that Harmen knew quite well a cousin of my wife, Robert Crowe, who lived in Guelph and headed a long-established foundry. Later, I met Harmen's wife, Anstice. I had not run across this name before and asked about its derivation.

"It's a Guernsey name," she explained. "Our family came from there and settled near Saskatoon. I was a Ledingham and my father was a member of the National Research Council."

I could scarcely believe my ears. "Ledinghams from Saskatoon? I was brought up in Saskatoon and our fathers knew each other. And something else, my wife's family comes from Guernsey."

It is indeed a small world. Of course, if we go back far enough, we are all related.

But, again, I digress. Returning to my lunch with Harmen Blom at the Granite—he opened his bag and handed me a number of presents: a video showing Deventer in 1945, a video of the Re-crossing of the Ijssel River in 1990, a book about the architecture of Apeldoorn, a silk tie of Apeldoorn, and a painted box bearing the Airborne logo and Allied flags.

The two videos were from Evert Gerritsen and the remaining gifts from Klaas Huisman. I couldn't understand the provenance of the "Airborne" box and wrote Klaas. He told me it was a souvenir of the Market Garden Airborne landings at Nijmegen and Arnhem. It came from the Airborne Museum at Schijndel with a book about the operation and a typical ration—a Mars chocolate bar. I ate the bar but not the box. It safely rests in my library.

Harmen left the best part to be digested with our dessert. Big events

PILGRIMAGE—2000

were being planned for 2000. Evert would be writing me shortly. Harmen and his wife planned to attend.

This was indeed good news and encouraged me to get on with composing my March, but the muse was not at home. It obviously required a further sign of encouragement from Apeldoorn.

The sign was not long in coming. On April 29th, I received a large package of Dutch newspapers from Evert bearing momentous news as well as a medal from the 1995 Anniversary.

Only one problem—the articles in the papers were all in Dutch. It has always been my good fortune to have not only good friends but friends whose knowledge far exceeds my own. One of these was Tom Thomas, whose family was in the Dutch East Indies when WWII broke out. They were all interned and spent four years suffering unspeakable treatment at the hands of the Japanese. Somehow young Tom survived. He eventually made his way to Canada and established a plastics company that became the leader in its field. But he is a man of many parts. He once told me that the first thing he did when he came to Canada was to get season tickets to the Toronto Symphony Orchestra and buy a sailboat. He also speaks Dutch.

On prior occasions, Tom had done a considerable amount of work for me translating articles and books I had received over the years from Holland. From May 1998 until the conclusion of the 2000 Pilgrimage, I called on his services almost continually, not only to translate material but to help me pronounce the difficult (for me) Dutch language. "A friend in need is a friend indeed," or, if I may be pardoned for reverting to Italian, *Chi trova un amico, trova un tesoro* (He who finds a friend finds a treasure).

The following is the essence of the newspaper articles as translated by Tom Thomas:

Liberation Monument for Apeldoorn, to be unveiled on May 7th, 2000.

The march past of the Canadian Veterans in 1995 is still fresh in our memory. It was a memorable event, where more than 16,000 Veterans marched, for the whole world to see.

Apeldoorn was inundated by 300,000 visitors and the "national feeling of freedom" was never felt stronger!

Is Apeldoorn to see another parade like this?

Maybe in the year 2000. After that date, the possibility is slim, as the veterans are aging and their numbers are shrinking.

However, their deeds should never be forgotten and that's why Apeldoorn will get a National Liberation Monument.

PILGRIMAGE—2000

> *The idea of a National Liberation Monument was originated by private citizens, etc., as well as the Liberation Foundation '45 in 1995.*
>
> *This monument should express: Freedom now and in the Future and lasting homage to the Canadian Liberators.*
>
> *Recently the artist, Henk Visch, was chosen to complete this project on the basis of his initial design and proposal.*
>
> *The final design should be ready by January 1999, construction to start in November, 1999.*
>
> *Donations are welcome and can be sent to: ABN-AMRO Bank, Apeldoorn, Acct. No. 5319.45.111.*

Two results ensued from this exciting news:
1. My musical muse suddenly awoke and inspired me to write the first draft of a March for 2000.
2. I was happy to make a generous donation to the cost of the Monument. At last I had a chance to show my appreciation to the citizens of Apeldoorn.

I continued to work on my March, and then a curious thing happened: the theme of a second March came to me almost without effort. I recorded both pieces and called on my music teacher, Joe Sealy, who had transcribed my other pieces. As I have said earlier, he is a well-known Toronto musician with many compositions, concerts and appearances across Canada to his credit. I think he was slightly bemused by my amateur efforts but agreed to write the scores and record the pieces on a cassette.

As I was leaving, I innocently asked, "Joe, when was the last time you played one of your compositions in Roy Thomson Hall?"

"I guess it's been a few years. Why?"

"The Massed Military Bands of Toronto played my 1995 Anniversary March in Roy Thomson Hall, October 29th, 1995." I closed the door before he could give me a sound clap on the back for being so cheeky. (He had been a star football player at university.)

Joe Sealy did a fine job transcribing the pieces and playing and recording them on a cassette. When Evert Gerritsen made his next visit to Toronto, the work was completed.

On November 3rd, Evert arrived in Toronto and gave me a call. At our luncheon with his cousin Harmen (which had now become almost a tradition), I presented him with the cassette along with the score written by Joe Sealy and a note I had written about the pieces, from which I quote:

November 3, 1998

Dear Evert:

You will remember that in 1985 and again in 1995 I composed music in honour of those Anniversaries. Thanks to you, General Gijsbers and others, the March I composed in 1995 was played by the massed bands at the Tattoo.

To mark the year 2000 and the 55th Anniversary of the Liberation, I have composed two pieces—a march entitled Salute to Holland, *another march entitled* Grand March 2000.

I have kept in touch with General Gijsbers and he knows that I have composed these new pieces, but I have not sent them to him.

I have also informed Mr. J. Claessen about the pieces and asked if he would be interested in arranging them for a band, as he did in 1995. He said he would be honoured to do these arrangements. I enclose a copy of his letter to me of December, 1997. There would, of course, be some expense involved, but I would be happy to make a modest contribution.

I have no idea what sort of celebrations you are planning for 2000, but I imagine they will not be as magnificent as the one in 1995—nothing could equal that Anniversary! However, if you feel that my music is worthy, I would be honoured to have it included in your plans.

I enclose the following items in connection with the two pieces:
1. Introduction *to the compositions.*
2. Salute to Holland—*Score for the melody.*
3. Grand March 2000—*Score for the melody.*
4. Cassette *of the pieces being played on the piano, first by Joseph Sealy, a well-known Canadian composer, and secondly by C.S. Frost.*

Please accept these pieces as a small token of my admiration for the people of Holland and my appreciation of the many wonderful things you and so many others have done for me and the Canadian Veterans.

Sincerely,

One week later Evert called around to say goodbye before returning to Holland. His cousin Harmen came with him and brought his charming wife Anstice, whom I was delighted to meet in view of the connections we had established with Saskatoon, where I grew up, and Guernsey, where my wife's relatives lived.

Evert brought me up to date on the forthcoming celebrations in Apeldoorn, now rapidly approaching.

My friend and translator par excellence, Tom Thomas, had kindly joined us and went over some of the material Evert had sent earlier. He was a welcome addition to our little party, helping me with some of the Dutch expressions and clarifying some of my remarks. Altogether, it was a very pleasant occasion and my Dutch friends seemed to enjoy themselves.

The planned Ceremonies for 2000 had now received the attention of the Canadian press and I handed Evert an article in the *Canadian Legion Magazine*.

Before leaving, Evert had his usual surprise for me—a lovely silver medal, struck by the Netherlands Mint, honouring Pieter Beelaerts van Blokland on his retirement from active service to his country. It will be recalled he was Mayor of Apeldoorn in 1985, which office he handled with great wit, charm and efficiency. Later, he became Queen's Commissioner for the Province of Utrecht and served in various other posts. Pieter had thoughtfully asked Evert to present me with this unique medal. It is a constant reminder of a good friend and a great citizen of Holland.

It was now approaching Christmas and I began to receive cards from Holland. Dick Veldhuizen sent greetings from what he termed "the snow white town of Barneveld" and said they were getting ready to receive Canadian Veterans in 2000.

Jan Schouten sent a slightly different weather report from Achterveld. "It is raining almost every day." He was working on their program which would include a band concert and the playing of my marches.

My friend Ati, who had kindly sent me the book on Holland by the hand of Ross Stewart in 1995, wished me well and said that the Veterans would receive a great and warm welcome in 2000. She reported on the Hassinks, who had a farm on the outskirts of Wilp where I had rested after the re-crossing of the Ijssel River in 1990. Forty-five years earlier, it had been one of my Company objectives and had almost been demolished. All the livestock had been killed. Ati reported that Gerard Hassink had now retired and sold all his cows. (A better deal, I thought, than having them blown up.)

The first emissary to call in 1999 was Pieter Beelaerts, who visited me on February 25th. In addition to his other duties, he was President of the National Thank You Canada Committee. He had also taken over the task of reorganizing the City of Hengeld and he had visited the Far East in an official capacity. Pieter advised me that a new Mayor had been appointed in Apeldoorn, Fred de Graaf. He was a younger person

PILGRIMAGE—2000

and very enthusiastic about the Anniversary. Pieter advised me to make my reservations soon, at the Keizerskroon Hotel, as a large delegation from the Department of Veterans Affairs would be staying there. He had an appointment the next day in Ottawa to see George Baker, the Minister of Veterans Affairs, and Art Eggleton, the Minister of Defence.

I took Pieter's advice and registered at the Keizerskroon Hotel. This would give me a chance to meet some of the officials of the DVA and also freedom of action to visit the other communities the PPCLI had liberated. Once again, the Dutch people were opening their homes to Canadian Veterans and supplying lodging and all meals without cost for ten days. It would have been fun to take advantage of this generous offer but, as in the past, I did not want to burden my hosts with my official duties.

The next report on the Millennium Program (as the Anniversary was now called) was a letter of March 2nd from General Andrew Gijsbers, the Head of the Apeldoorn Committee. He had received my two Marches from Evert Gerritsen and had asked out Sef Claessen to arrange these pieces for a band. He warned me that I would probably be the Senior Officer on the big Apeldoorn Parade and gave me an "order" to stay healthy.

He also gave me a challenge I found hard to resist. The slogan for the 1995 Anniversary had been "Stay Alive 'till 95." But he doubted if anyone could come up with a rhyme for the year 2000.

In my reply, I agreed it was difficult to find a rhyming word for 2000. However, I was in the midst of learning computer lingo and Y2K seemed an easier symbol to rhyme than 2000. But I could never remember whether it was Y2K or 2KY. In fact, 2KY seemed more logical to my legal mind. And so it was that I came up with the nonsense rhyme which appears at the commencement of this chapter.

As 1999 came to a close, I realized that I had received a mass of information about the Millennium from many different sources. I have already mentioned some of the people who kept me up to date. But now the media had become interested and each week I received further material from my Web site. My friend, Tom Thomas, a computer expert, also supplied me with information on every event. My library could no longer hold all the paper, which began to encroach on other rooms. And yet, I was still not clear on what duties I would be expected to perform. My doubts were soon to be remedied by further telephone calls and visitors from Holland, but it was obvious that 2000 was going to be another great event.

How do they do it, year after year, I wondered. For that matter, how do the Veterans cope with all this unaccustomed activity? Almost all of us were now in our eighties (except a few "kids" like myself). According to the *Legion Magazine*, Veterans were dying off at a depressing rate of at least 5,000 per year. Would there be anyone left by May 2000?

These black thoughts were banished to the rear by the visit of Ritse Reitsma (otherwise known as Bill) from Twello, on November 12th. While he was no longer in charge of the Celebrations in that city, he knew all about them and gave me a detailed program. He assured me that the Veterans had not "simply faded away." About 3,000 were expected. I would probably be asked to make a speech or two at the Memorial Services and other events. He would get in touch with me as soon as I arrived at my hotel and be available throughout the week if I needed any help.

As he left, he pointed to my tie and with a big smile said, "Where did you get my tie?" He knew very well how I had acquired it. Fifteen years earlier, when I first met him, we had exchanged our Regimental ties in a pub in Wilp. Noticing that he was not wearing mine, I had an easy rejoinder, "You can have it Ritse, but first I want mine back!"

We clasped hands and had a good laugh. No wonder he is so popular with the Veterans. Later I learned he had been made an honorary member of the Legion.

On December 6th, I received more good news, this time from Achterveld. Jan Schouten wrote that on May 9th, they were going to unveil a monument to the PPCLI. A plaque would be affixed with an appropriate inscription. He gave me a draft to consider.

The wording, as finally settled, read as follows:

> *Canadian soldiers from the Princess Patricia's Canadian Light Infantry prevented the destruction of the Parish Church of Achterveld (used as an observation post) on 18 April, 1945.*
> *We thank these soldiers who saved the heart of our village.*
> *May 9, 2000*

In subsequent letters, Mr. Schouten asked me to deliver a speech at the Unveiling and sent me clippings from the local papers.

> *Amersfoortse Krant, December 29, 1999*
> *Unveiling on May 9th*
> *Monument commemorates Canadians*
> *Achterveld—In the centre of Achterveld a third monument will appear to remember WWII. It will be a commemorative plaque in memory of the Canadians who on 18 April*

1945 prevented the Germans from blowing up the Roman Catholic Church.

The two existing monuments were erected in honour of the fallen victims. One monument commemorates 25 civilian victims from Achterveld, the other the slain soldiers of the "Regiment Huzaren." All three monuments are the initiative of the now 71-year-old Jan Schouten, who recorded the history of Achterveld in many books.

Schouten was present in 1945 when on 30 April negotiations took place, about the eventual surrender of Germany.

"I was there and remember," he recalls. "In Wageningen, the surrender was signed at a later date; but in Achterveld everything had been prepared beforehand."

That spring the village was under heavy fire, being situated between the German and Canadian lines. The enemy had used the church tower as an observation post. On 18 April, seven hard-pressed German soldiers tried to destroy the Achterveld tower, however, the Canadians captured them just in the nick of time.

This feat will be recorded on the new monument, in Dutch and English.

The memorial will consist of two plaques with the engraving in a square socle of approximately 1.20 meter high.

The Canadian Colonel C. Sydney Frost has been asked to unveil the monument in Achterveld.

Around Christmas time, I received further telephone calls and information which filled in the gaps in my program. First, I received a letter from Gerrit Ham of Beekbergen about the Parade in that town, Lieren and Oosterhuizen.

Dear Colonel Frost:
Liberation parade 2000
The liberation parade which will be held 29 April 2000, will be organized by "The Liberation Committee Beekbergen, Lieren and Oosterhuizen" in the municipality of Apeldoorn, the Netherlands.

The plans are the same as in 1995, including the same route as previous times.

Many veterans will take part in the parade, accompanied by several bands including "The 48th Highlanders of Holland" and about 130 vehicles from "Keep them Rolling."

PILGRIMAGE—2000

> *We are expecting many spectators along the route to greet the veterans. There will be a beautiful remembrance medal for them just as last time. At the end of the parade there will be a typically Dutch meal of "Boerenkool met worst." There will be music during this meal.*

Gerrit Ham followed that up with a telephone call to say I would be picked up at my hotel in a wartime jeep bearing the PPCLI Tac sign (i.e., code number) 60. Then I would lead the parade of 130 vehicles.

Jan Koorenhof also phoned from Apeldoorn and sent a letter giving the final program for that city. With this latest information, all gaps were pretty well closed and I looked forward to the Millennium Celebrations with great anticipation. All I had to do now was stay healthy, as ordered by General Gijsbers.

January is usually a relatively quiet month after the bacchanalia of Christmas and New Year's. Holland was busy preparing for the Millennium program and I did not expect to hear from them. So I decided to follow General Gijsber's exhortation and get in good shape. Due to pressure of events, I had put off having a cataract in one of my eyes removed and it was now causing some trouble. My eye doctor assured me it was only a minor operation and would not interfere with my trip. It was just a "walk in the park," according to him. I replied, "That's fine, but I hope I don't meet any wild dogs."

I had the operation on January 26th and everything seemed to go smoothly—until that wild dog suddenly pounced. I had a very bad reaction to the medicine, including swelling, shortness of breath and a rash. I was suffering from an allergy to sulpha. This was not the doctor's fault nor mine. He had asked me if I had any allergies and I had said none to my knowledge. When he diagnosed sulpha as the culprit, I could not understand it. During the war I had been injected with gallons of the stuff for my wounds and never had a bad reaction.

So I was quickly taken off sulpha and put on another drug which seemed to be compatible with my peculiar body chemistry. It also produced a quite unexpected side effect. I suddenly felt compelled to write another song about Holland. I had long felt that it was time we recognized the sacrifices and suffering that the Dutch people themselves had endured during the War, and also honoured the friendship and unique bond that existed between our two peoples. The result was a simple anthem.

FREEDOM
(an anthem)
Canada and Holland
Two peoples joined as one
To celebrate their freedom
And peace so dearly won.

Their sacrifice and suffering
In Holocaust and war
We honour and remember
This day and evermore.

I called on Joe Sealy, showed him the words and played the music. Could he transcribe it and have a cassette ready in a few days? The reason for the rush was that I had just received an invitation from the Consul General of The Netherlands, to attend a luncheon being given in Toronto on February 16th, to honour the Mayor of Apeldoorn, Fred de Graaf, and his Chief of Cabinet, Klaas Huisman. Mr. de Graaf was giving an address to The Netherlands Luncheon Club about the upcoming 55th Anniversary Celebrations in Apeldoorn.

It was now February 5th and I wanted to hand my new piece to Mr. de Graaf to take back to Holland.

In the meantime, I phoned Tom Thomas, who was a long-time member of The Netherlands Luncheon Club and knew the President, Mr. Marten Mol, and the members of his Executive Committee. Tom told me a bit about the Club, which was very active in Toronto, and helped me with the pronunciation of Dutch names.

On February 10th, Jan Koorenhof phoned from Apeldoorn to give me the latest developments. I would have a car and driver for the parade in Apeldoorn. Sef Claessen had almost completed arranging my marches. Mr. de Graaf would be very happy to meet me at the luncheon.

On the morning of February 16th (the day of the luncheon for de Graaf), Andrew Gijsbers phoned with further information about the luncheon and the Ceremonies in Apeldoorn. He had just received the complete arrangements of my Marches from Mr. Claessen, and they would be played at the Tattoo. That was exciting news but I was concerned about the cost. I realized it was a long, tedious task and would require substantial financing. Andrew, typically, sloughed it off by saying, "Never mind, you can buy me a drink." I knew it was pointless to object so I undertook to make another donation to the National Canadian Monument in Apeldoorn which he was going to unveil on May 2nd.

I truly appreciated receiving these briefings and I trust they are not perceived as some sort of imposition on my time. Indeed, the contrary is true. Week after week, I imposed on my friends with all kinds of requests and material, to say nothing of my constant importuning in connection with my music. Never once did they cry, "This is too much." Such gracious, understanding people.

The luncheon on February 16th was held at the Royal Ontario Museum with an overflow attendance. I was immediately impressed with Mr. de Graaf and was delighted to meet my friend of many years, Klaas Huisman. His long service as Chief of Cabinet to the mayors of Apeldoorn and as a friend of the Veterans, has already been mentioned, and I was glad he had been given this opportunity to visit Canada. It was also a great pleasure to meet Mr. Marten Mol, the President of the Club; Mr. Kroon, the Consul General; and the members of the Executive Committee.

Tom Thomas was, of course, present and introduced me to many of his friends. I was happily surprised to see my travel agent, as well as two charming ladies from my bank. One of them claimed I was a Canadian fighter pilot in the War and I had crash landed in her garden in Sassenheim.

I'm afraid I had to disabuse her. It was true I was in Sassenheim after the war and attended many enjoyable celebrations there, but I was a member of the PPCLI and the only "crashing" I might have done was to crash one of those parties.

Mr. de Graaf told us about the preparations being made for the Millennium Celebrations in May. Although the numbers might not be as large as in other years, enthusiasm was building to make this another memorable celebration. There was one difference, however, from previous Anniversaries. We all had to acknowledge that the ranks of the "Old Guard," both Dutch and Canadian, were thinning rapidly. If these Anniversaries were to continue, the youth of both countries would have to get involved. In fact, he had sent out a questionnaire to the citizens of Apeldoorn to seek their views. He was proud to say that practically the whole community were in favour and this included 92 per cent of the young people.

Then came the gifts, which seemed to be the *sine qua non* of any meeting between the Dutch people and their Canadian Veterans. Mr. de Graaf presented me with a beautiful silver goblet, a replica of the ones in the Het Loo Palace and engraved with the Royal cipher. A truly magnificent gift. He also gave me an attractive tie with a pattern of little red tulips, and a silver pin for my wife. In return, I handed him my Anthem in recognition of the bond that existed between our two peoples, and a letter for General Gijsbers enclosing the musical score and a recording.

From Klaas Huisman, I received a letter from General Gijsbers, and a lovely book from Johannes van Blommestein on Voorst giving a pictorial history of his municipality, in colour.

The President of the Club, Mr. Marten Mol, gave me a book—*The Dutch Touch in Ontario*. This remarkable volume, which was co-authored by Mr. Mol, presents a vivid picture of the energy and enterprise that have given Dutch-Canadians a solid reputation as hard workers and good citizens.

My library had been augmented by two more valuable books that I would always treasure, not only for their merit, but for the kindness and generosity of their donors.

The luncheon on February 16th was another memorable event which increased (if that were possible) my respect and affection for the Dutch people.

On February 21st, I received from Sef Claessen a tape of my two Marches played by The Royal Wind Band of Lottum. I have to confess it was a tremendous thrill to hear one's compositions played by such a distinguished Band, and I phoned my music teacher, Joe Sealy, to thank him for his help. I couldn't wait to hear them being played at the Tattoo in Apeldoorn on May 5th.

My euphoria, however, was tempered by a sense of impending disaster. For the past week or two, I had been bothered with increasing pain and stiffness in my muscles and general fatigue. I had fought them off with pills and carried on. By March 6th, I was in quite bad shape: difficulty getting out of bed, out of chairs, in and out of cars and climbing stairs. I wrote a detailed report on my condition and attended our family doctor (Dr. X). I emphasized that in six weeks I had to leave on a very strenuous Pilgrimage to Holland and Sicily in connection with 55th Anniversary Ceremonies. As the senior surviving Officer, I would be expected to take part in the parades and make speeches. In my present condition, I could not possibly undertake the journey. In fact, unless she did something pretty quickly, I would cease to be a survivor!

She was not impressed and simply prescribed more pills.

This treatment helped a bit with the pain but made me nauseous, caused itching and did nothing to alleviate the increasing stiffness. Everything ached and I was getting little sleep. I tried to make an appointment on March 13th, but she was out of town. I saw her associate. Of course he knew nothing of my past history and ordered an echocardiogram as well as stronger pills. He also suggested I see a Dermatologist and a Rheumatologist. The buck didn't stop with him. Next day, I phoned a Rheumatologist—no appointments until April.

In desperation, I got in touch with a doctor (Dr. B) who had gone to school with my son. I read him a summary of my condition, reviewed my past history and recent treatment, or more correctly, ill treatment. He immediately diagnosed PMR and recommended a low dosage of Prednisone until I could get an appointment with a Rheumatologist.

To understand this disease and what follows, it is necessary to digress once more. PMR is short for Polymyalgia Rheumatica. It is an insidious disease that causes severe stiffness, aching and pain in one or more areas of the body including neck, shoulders, arms, lower back, hips and thighs. Some people also have joint stiffness and swelling. PMR also causes fatigue, fever and depression.

The most effective treatment for PMR is the drug corticosteriod. Most people receive a derivative of the drug called Prednisone. The response to this treatment is good but the dosage must be reduced gradually, sometimes taking up to two years before it can be safely terminated.

If PMR is not treated, it can develop into temporal arteritis, resulting in loss of vision, a stroke or a heart attack.

It was a classic case of "Catch 22."

On March 20th, I attended Dr. X loaded for bear. The Prednisone prescribed by Dr. B four days earlier had already begun to work and I could drive a car and even shave without too much pain. If only Dr. X had started me on Prednisone two weeks earlier I would likely have been saved all that stiffness and pain. But I still wanted to see a Rheumatologist to confirm Dr. B's diagnosis and get me on a firm regimen of Prednisone. And in the back of my mind lurked the horrible possibility that I was going to miss the 55th Anniversary. My plane left in five weeks.

My appointment with Dr. X on March 20th was so unbelievable and so bizarre that I would not blame anyone for doubting my credibility. For that reason I describe it in detail.

I was shown into an examination room where I waited for 20 minutes. I had brought with me a few souvenirs and medals from my earlier Pilgrimages as well as the beautiful silver goblet and tie from Mr. de Graaf to try to convince Dr. X that this was one Pilgrimage I could not miss. As soon as she entered, I pointed to the souvenirs and tried to explain that it was not I who was important but the people who were counting on my presence. She was not impressed. I said, "If necessary, I'll go in a casket."

Then I began to go through a memo I had given her. After a few minutes, she tossed it aside and said, "I have already given you five minutes."

She left and slammed the door. In eight minutes she returned with her prescription pad in hand. I said, "I don't want any more prescriptions. What I desperately need is for you to tell me what's wrong."

She replied, "I don't know. Doctors aren't magicians. *You may never go on your trip!* Now, you've been here 20 minutes. I have to see other patients."

She threw a prescription for Claritin at me and slammed the door, leaving my memo on her desk.

The next day, March 21st, Dr. X phoned to say that the Rheumatologist could now see me on March 30th.

On March 28th, one of my daughters, who was recovering from chickenpox, attended Dr. X, who told her she could not do anything for me. My daughter replied, "My Dad is the last person to say that to!"

On March 30th, I attended the Rheumatologist, who had known me in 1993 when I had a bad attack of PMR. She had put me on Prednisone for one year and it had been successful. I reminded her of this and gave her the same memo I had shown Dr. X, but which she had declined to read. The memo described my cataract operation in January, the allergic reaction to supha and my consultation with Dr. B.

I asked her point blank, "Could the stress of the operation have triggered a PMR attack?"

"Definitely. Any stress could have triggered it."

She agreed with Dr. B that I had PMR and immediately put me on heavy daily doses of Prednisone which I am still taking, two years later.

The last Act in this absurd tale will now be told.

On April 4th, I phoned Dr. X to report I had PMR. I was taking Prednisone and although still suffering some pain and stiffness, I was going to Holland and Sicily.

"Well," she said, "I've been on an interesting learning curve."

I said, "Well, you can get off it now. You're fired."

Epilogue

A few months later, Dr. X closed her Toronto practice and left for parts unknown.

I was left exhausted, angry and disillusioned but ready to undertake my Pilgrimage to Holland.

Curtain falls on Medical Overture.

* * *

Let us now retrace our steps to February 21st when I received the tape of my Marches from Sef Claessen. For the next five weeks, I battled PMR and doctors until I won both fights. I was wounded but I remained on duty.

PILGRIMAGE—2000

On March 23rd, I had recovered sufficiently to send Gerrit Ham an e-mail asking for details of the parade on April 29th in Beekbergen which I was supposed to lead. The next day Gerrit phoned. I would be picked up at my hotel at 9:00 a.m. by a Mrs. Wil Schuit driving a WWII jeep bearing the PPCLI Tac Sign 60. She would drive me to the head of the parade consisting of 130 military vehicles from WWII, including tanks and several bands. The parade would take about two hours and cover a distance of 10 km through three villages.

Gerrit concluded by saying that my Freedom Anthem had been sung in the local churches and was greatly appreciated.

The Anniversary was only weeks away and the countdown had started. I silently thanked old Field Marshal Fate for getting me this far, but I implored him to get me in shape to leave for Holland on April 26th. The heavy doses of Prednisone had greatly reduced the stiffness and pain but left me quite weak and tired.

I remembered having a similar feeling 56 years earlier when I had a malaria attack while preparing to leave England to rejoin the PPCLI in Italy. I didn't dare report to the Medical Officer as he would have taken me off the draft. So I held on, getting weaker and weaker until the troopship left and I could then report to the Sick Bay for treatment.

More last-minute intelligence arrived. On March 28th, Jan Koorenhof phoned from Apeldoorn. It was going to be another memorable Celebration. Thirty-five hundred Veterans were coming. The Department of Veterans Affairs was sending a large Delegation of Veterans and Officials led by the Minister, George Baker. It was a good thing I had made my reservation at the Keizerskroon Hotel as 45 members of the DVA party were staying there.

General Andrew Gijsbers phoned on March 30th with more news. I was beginning to feel like a general myself, getting all these reports on the eve of the battle. He was happy to tell me that my "nomination" as Parade Commander for May 7th had been approved. I would be picked up and driven to the Saluting Base where I would report to Princess Margriet. My Marches would be played at the Tattoo and I would be presented with the original scores.

On April 18th, Jan Koorenhof phoned again with new duties for me. The Anniversary Committee of Arnhem wanted me to make a speech on April 27th and give a radio interview. I had to decline as my flight arrived in Amsterdam early that morning and I would need at least a day to get over jet lag, to say nothing of my PMR problem.

On April 19th, a new "country" was heard from: a letter from Haarlem where the PPCLI had been stationed briefly, in May 1945, after the German surrender.

Samenwerkingsverband Haarlem
8 April 2000

Dear Colonel Frost,
From Mr. and Mrs. Rains we heard the news that you are coming to Holland and we would like you to know that you are most welcome in our hometown Haarlem, which as we understand is not unfamiliar to you.

You may have heard that this year again on the occasion of the 55th celebration of our liberation quite a program is in preparation for the reception of roughly 3,000 of your fellow countrymen of which we expect about 40 veterans to stay in our region.

This will be in the period from about April 29 until around May 9 next. In this connection please find enclosed our day-to-day program, arranged as a small recognition of the thanks we owe to your comrades-in-arms for the liberation of Holland.

You may note that both Wednesday, May 3, as well as Friday, May 5 and Monday, May 8, have an extra-Haarlem touch and we certainly would be privileged if you could see your way to attend some of these functions.

Hoping to hear from you and—if at all possible—looking forward to having the pleasure of meeting you in person, I am,
Yours faithfully,
"Hans van Ravenzwaaij"

I hardly had time to read through the program but I did and found every function conflicted with one or two other events that I had earlier agreed to attend. It was a pity, but I had to advise Hans that my schedule was already filled.

One of the main events in Apeldoorn was to be the Unveiling of a National Canadian Monument, known as "The Man With Two Hats." I had been very happy to make donations to this worthy project. On April 20th, I received a warm letter of appreciation from Ada Wynston, the Canadian Co-ordinator for the Monument.

April 18, 2000

C. Sydney Frost, Q.C., LL.B., LL.D
Dear Sir:
I wish to thank you most sincerely for the very generous donation toward the Monument, which will be unveiled in Apeldoorn on May 2nd, 2000. This monument is honouring

the Canadian Veterans, such as yourself, who assisted in the liberation of the Netherlands fifty-five years ago, their spouses and other members of their family. It is extremely important the younger generation is made aware of the sacrifices made, be it the loss of life while fighting, or the anxiety of families in Canada waiting for news from the war front.

It is my pleasure to be part of this project, as I too was liberated by the Canadians in 1945. I will always be grateful and participating in a project such as this, shows just a little bit of my gratitude.

I wish you a grand return to the Netherlands and to Italy and please come back safely.
Yours sincerely,
Ada Wynston, R.O.N.

On April 24th, just two days before I was due to leave for Holland, I received from Jan Schouten the final Program for Achterveld.

Dear Sydney,
This will be my last letter before your arrival in Holland. We are honoured that you will participate during the Ceremony. Of course we shall not accept your kind offer to pay for the flowers. As a reminder here is the latest summary of the program:

Tuesday, 9th May 2000
12:45 – 13:15 hrs. — Welcome
14:00 hrs. — Laying a wreath by Mr. M. C. van der Hoog
14:30—15:30 hrs. — Concert by the Johan Willem Friso Kapel — Coffee and drink
16:15 hrs. — Pipers in front. Then next to each other Bailey—Frost—Deutsch. Then the other Canadian War Veterans and other groups

— *While everybody is standing in front of the monument, the pipers will play: "The Lord is my Shepherd." Flame will burn. Boy dressed in kilt will hand over the flowers to Mr. Frost and he will put down these flowers in front of the monument.*
— *Pipers will play. Short speech by Mr. Frost*
— *Hornblower will play "Last Post." Pipers, followed by all other people present, walk to "The Moespot." Here the two local choirs will sing, among others, the hymn from Mr. Frost.*

One of my daughters will try to come to the Ceremony as well. Her English is much better than mine, so she can be our personal interpreter that afternoon. I wish you a good trip!

Best regards,
Jan

The attention I was receiving made me feel like a visiting Head of State instead of an old footslogger in the Infantry. I wished that the incompetent Doctor X could have seen some of the communications I was receiving. She might then have appreciated that I had to go to Holland, "come hell or high water." But on reflection, it probably would not have made any difference. Better she went to hell while I took the water. Actually, I was still taking heavy doses of Prednisone with my water, and hoping I would make that flight to Amsterdam.

Speaking of Heads of State, while I was certainly far removed from that class, I wished I had some of the staff that accompany such distinguished visitors, to handle the voluminous paperwork. It must be remembered that in addition to Holland, I was preparing to travel to Sicily at the conclusion of the Dutch celebrations. I planned to be away one month and arrangements had to be made to handle both my personal and my business affairs. I also had to make travel arrangements, reserve hotels, prepare speeches, send countless letters, e-mail and fax, brush up on my Italian, purchase gifts, arrange for them to be inscribed, and a myriad of other details too numerous to mention.

Actually, the purchase of gifts was the easiest of all to make. In my many contacts with Regimental H.Q. at Edmonton, I had discovered the Kit Shop with its vast store of fascinating Regimental accoutrements. I practically bought out the shop, especially some of the more attractive items. I made a list of people who had done so much for the Regiment and me personally and tried to find an appropriate gift for each one. I won't embarrass my friends by disclosing the list but I will mention some of the items I acquired: hat badges, collar dogs, lapel pins, rhinestone brooches, trophy brass badges, key rings, Regimental plaques (to be suitably engraved), Regimental music cassettes, Regimental ties (both official and "drinking") and the prize gift of all—pewter statuettes of a WWII soldier and a drummer in full dress.

I cleaned out the Kit Shop's stock of rhinestone brooches, Regimental ties and pewter statuettes.

How to transport all these gifts presented a problem. I could hardly rent a Hercules cargo plane, so I bought two of the largest suitcases I could find. I carefully packed the statuettes using my clothing as stuffing. I can report that my precious bundles arrived safely and that PPCLI accoutrements now adorn the libraries, desks, jackets, dresses, necks (ties) and bosoms (brooches) of many a happy Hollander and satisfied Sicilian.

Flight 692 left Toronto at 7:00 p.m., April 26th, 2000, and C. S. Frost was among the passengers. He fell asleep almost immediately and woke up $6^{1}/_{2}$ hours later in Holland at the Schiphol Airport, Amsterdam, 7:45 a.m. April 27th, local time.

I had sensibly planned not to drive from Amsterdam to Apeldoorn as my medication tended to make me drowsy. I took a taxi (300 guilders) and arrived at Keizerskroon Hotel at 9:45 a.m.

After checking in, I wearily made my way to my room, hoping to continue my snoozing for a couple of hours. The moment I opened the door and glanced around the room I realized it would be impossible. My gaze was met by bouquets of beautiful flowers and many notes of welcome asking me to call. Before I had a chance to orient myself, the phone rang. It was Ritse Reitsma whose tie I had "purloined" in 1985. I thought he might be going to press charges.

"Hello, Sydney, a warm welcome to Holland, especially from Voorst and Twello. Johannes also sends his greetings. I am phoning to ask you to open the Canadian Club at Twello tomorrow night, and speak at the Antonius Church in de Vecht on Thursday, May 4th."

"Nice to hear your voice again, Ritse, and thanks for the beautiful flowers. But I have nothing prepared for a speech in your church and I am not a pastor."

"Doesn't matter. You'll think of something. In the meantime, I'll pick you up tomorrow at 7:00 p.m. and drive you to the Club."

There was no point in arguing with Ritse. He was a great friend but he could be, shall I say, a little persistent at times. In truth, I had expected something like this would come up and I had a couple of drafts ready. It was going to be a busy and exhausting ten days, but the important thing was, I had made it on my own initiative, doctors and their damnable pills to the contrary notwithstanding.

I have mentioned that 45 members of the Minister of Veterans Affairs party were staying at the Keizerskroon Hotel. Over the next few days, I met many of them, including the Deputy Minister, Larry Murray, who had been so helpful to me in the "Carmelo incident" when Carmelo Nigro was unintentionally snubbed at the unveiling of the Monument to the Italian soldiers.

Others I met were: Cliff Chadderton, CC, O.Ont, that endurable Veteran who has dedicated his life to helping disabled Veterans; Jean-Guy Chapman, the Project Director of DVA, who gave me timely advice and assistance in connection with the upcoming events; Bob Gardham, the Web site Co-ordinator, who rendered me a special favour, to be described; Mrs. Teresa MacLean, his capable assistant; Dr. Pierre Paquette, whose ready advice on my PMR condition eased my concerns; and Sgt. Raymond (Andy) Anderson, a Patricia, who represented the Aboriginal Veterans.

Both the Senate and the House of Commons were represented, as well as the Legion, Merchant Navy, Nursing Sisters and other Veterans' Associations. Of particular interest to me was the presence of representatives from the Cadet Organizations and Youth Groups. They were well turned out and were a source of inspiration and affection for the Veterans. They were also a great credit to Canada.

I tried to phone all those kind people who had written notes of welcome but soon realized that a good night's sleep was more important. Tomorrow would be a busy day.

April 28th, Friday
Sharp at 11:30, Lex Nordenbus picked me up and drove to the Canadian Club, a large community hall which had been converted to a meeting place for the Veterans. I had not seen Lex since 1985 and it was wonderful to see him again after all these years. At the Club, Jan Koorenhof was awaiting my arrival and introduced me to Mr. J. Scholten, the Manager of the Club, and other officials, some of whom I had known in 1985. I was happy to lighten my gift bag by presenting quite a few items to my friends, which were much appreciated.

In a brief ceremony, the Club was duly declared open by General Andrew Gijsbers, the Head of the Apeldoorn Liberation Committee. I had not seen him since November 20th, 1993, and I was delighted to meet him again. He had taken a great interest in the Marches I had composed for both the 1995 Pilgrimage (which I had missed) and the current one, and had been responsible for financing the cost of having them arranged.

He greeted me warmly and said he was looking forward to hearing my pieces played at the Tattoo on May 5th. In the meantime, could I join him for dinner tomorrow evening. I realized how busy he was and I tactfully tried to demur, but to no avail.

Jan Koorenhof then reviewed the program for the following ten days and I really wondered how those 80-year-old Veterans were going to make it, particularly the National Parade on May 7th. For that matter, I was not too confident about my being able to stay the course.

"Not to worry," smiled Jan, "No one will have to march. You did enough of that during the War. There will be transportation for every

Veteran who needs it—jeeps, vehicles, carriers, water trucks, armoured cars and even tanks. Take your pick. But you're Okay. You'll be picked up by two Dutch Officers, LCol. John Verharen and Maj. Rob Spreeuw, and driven to the Reviewing Stand where you will join Princess Margriet and other dignitaries. You are the Parade Commander, you know."

"Yes, I know and I am very grateful for the honour. I had better start practising my salute."

It was time to leave as I had to get ready to attend the opening of another Canadian Club in Twello, the centre of the celebrations in the Municipality of Voorst. As I drove back to my hotel, I was beginning to get that "Old Dutch Feeling" that I had first experienced on that far-off day in May 1945, and on the Pilgrimages ever since—a feeling of warmth, friendship, even kinship and love for our wonderful Dutch hosts. The entire city of Apeldoorn was likewise in a happy festive mood. Houses and streets were festooned with flowers, ribbons and balloons. Large signs declared: Welcome Canada, Thank you Liberators, We Remember.

Back at the hotel, I quickly spruced myself up in time to meet Ritse Reitsma. On arrival at Twello, I was greeted by the Mayor, Johannes van Blommestein, and the Chairman of the local Liberation Committee, Major-General Messerschmidt, a retired Dutch officer.

As I have often said, the Dutch do things in style. In the centre of the dining room, six tiers of empty champagne glasses had been stacked on a table in the form of a pyramid. The idea behind this was to pour champagne into the lone glass at the top of the pyramid and continue pouring until all the glasses were filled. I had the honour of pouring the first bottle and having a sip from the first glass after the mission had been fulfilled. Whereupon the Club was declared to be officially opened. For my efforts, I received a beautiful medal and a badge of the Municipality of Voorst.

I was able to reciprocate by presenting the Municipality of Voorst with a Regimental Plaque and the Canadian Club with a trophy hat badge. Johannes van Blommestein and Ritse Reitsma and their wives also received appropriate Regimental gifts. The Plaque was engraved as follows:

Presented to the Municipality of Voorst on the 55th Anniversary of the Liberation of Wilp by the soldiers of the PPCLI.

May, 2000

* * *

April 29th, Saturday—Queen's Birthday—Beekbergen, Lieren and Oosterhuizen

This is not the birthday of the ruling Queen Beatrix, nor is it the date of the birthday of former Queen Juliana, in whose honour the day is observed. When Queen Juliana abdicated in 1980, her daughter, Beatrix, promised to celebrate her birthday every year without fail. The proper date was actually April 30th, but as this fell on a Sunday in 2000, the practical Dutch observed it on a Saturday.

This was the day when the three small villages mentioned above held their Liberation Parade. I had been told by Gerrit Ham to be ready at 9:00 a.m. to be picked up by Mrs. Wil Schuit. She appeared promptly at the given hour and drove me to Beekbergen where the parade commenced.

The citizens have never forgotten that the PPCLI liberated these villages in 1945. People lined the streets several rows deep, and gave us a tumultuous welcome. The Veterans were conveyed in WWII vehicles restored by members of the "Keep Them Rolling" organization. This unique collection of vehicles even included a 1942 Chaffee tank, which led the parade followed by my jeep.

The parade took three hours and during the whole time it poured rain. I was soaked to the skin but the rain didn't seem to bother the people, many of whom had taken up strategic positions an hour before the parade started. It was truly an unforgettable demonstration of their love and respect for Canadian Veterans.

Many of the spectators were young children, four and five years old, who bravely stood in the rain waving Canadian flags and crying, "Thank you Canada." Several of these tots (no doubt urged on by their mothers) ran up to my jeep with all sorts of gifts: flowers, cookies, "art work" of their own making, decals, postcards with their name and address asking me to send them a postcard.

Here are two typical letters I sent my young admirers when I arrived home:

June 12, 2000

Jolyn Hendriks and
Carlieke Hendriks
Brummen
The Netherlands
Dear Jolyn, Carlieke:
 Wasn't that a great parade, but it certainly rained buckets. (In Canada we say it rained "cats and dogs").
 You were very brave to stand in the rain all that long time. I hope you didn't get too wet.

PILGRIMAGE—2000

Thank you for remembering Canada's soldiers and thank you for your lovely gift. I am enclosing a postcard from Toronto as a little souvenir of my visit.
I hope we meet again someday.
Sincerely,
P.S. I'm sorry I can't write in the Dutch language. Perhaps your parents understand English.

June 11, 2000

Mr. Thom Schuit
Beekbergen
The Netherlands
Dear Thom:
Bet you thought I had forgotten you. Not at all. I have been very busy since I returned home from my five weeks trip. First to Holland and then to Sicily where I also fought during the War.
I have your beautiful drawing in front of me. It shows a Canadian Maple Leaf in the centre surrounded by a Liberator bomber, a Parachutist and two hearts. You are very artistic.
Do you remember the fun we had at the Farewell Party in the Canadian Club? You speak very good English. Better than my Dutch.
Please give my best wishes to your Mom and Dad and Sister.
As a little souvenir, I enclose a Dutch Guilder note which someone gave me during the War. I also enclose an article about my book Once a Patricia *showing a picture of me as a young man.*
I hope we meet again someday.
Sincerely,

Thom was the son of Mrs. Wil Schuit, who kindly drove me from the Keizerskroon Hotel to Beekbergen. She was an Airline Stewardess with KLM. At the Farewell Party in Apeldoorn, I met her husband, a pilot with KLM, and their two children, a lovely daughter and a lively son, Thom, with whom I had a friendly wrestling match (no contest, he won).

After the parade a Reception was held for all the Veterans and we were served a typical Dutch meal: kale and sausage stew. M'mm, M'mm, good. I had three helpings to restore my circulation. I was happy to see a friend who had come from Apeldoorn, Evert Gerritsen and his grandson.

Someone gave me a hearty slap on the back. "Greetings, Colonel, from the 48th Highlanders." It was that fine soldier and piper, Ross Stewart, who had been playing in the band that marched in the parade. He too was soaked but was undaunted as ever. We clasped hands warmly and I said, "You know, Ross, there's only one thing wrong with you."

He gave me a startled look. "Pray what is that?"

"You should have been a Patricia."

The person behind this Anniversary Celebration in Beekbergen, Lieren and Oosterhuizen, and the one in 1995, was Gerrit Ham. Some years earlier he had formed the 48th Highlanders of Holland Pipe and Drum Band. Despite this connection, he had shown great respect and affection for the PPCLI who had liberated these villages.

I searched through the crowd for a fellow Patricia and found Lloyd Rains and his wife Olga. With them in support, I drew Gerrit Ham aside and made a little speech thanking him for the Parade and all his past kindnesses to the PPCLI, including the Monument at Oosterhuizen and the time capsule buried beneath it. I then presented him with a Regimental figurine, a tie and a plaque on which was inscribed the following:

Presented to Oosterhuizen
On the 55th Anniversary of its Liberation
By the soldiers of the PPCLI
April 29, 2000

Gerrit responded by presenting me with a lovely medal. When I returned home, he sent me numerous photos and articles about the Parade.

Late that afternoon, I was driven back to my hotel and barely had time to peel off my soaking wet clothes and have a hot shower before two Dutch Officers knocked on my door: LCol. John Verharen and Maj. Rob Spreeuw. I had been warned that they might attend to brief me on my duties for the National Parade in Apeldoorn on May 7th. I wasn't sure whether they had come to give me information or to quiz me on my background, so I had brought with me a rough "curriculum vitae" and various attestations about my military career. I realized that as I would be in close contact with Princess Margriet and her husband, it was entirely appropriate that I should be checked out. After all, I was a mere Colonel compared to the illustrious Generals and Brigadiers who had commanded the Parades in the past. Unfortunately (for them), they had all passed away and I was the senior surviving officer available.

I need not have worried about my qualifications or past misdeeds. The two Dutch Officers had been fully briefed about me by General Gijsbers and others. They only wanted to meet me, answer any questions I might have and enjoy a strong cup of coffee.

In the evening, General Andrew Gijsbers himself called round to pick me up and take me to a very posh restaurant, "Echoput," in a secluded spot in a forest. The menu was superb and the wines strictly vintage, but because of my medicine, I had to forgo the latter. Nevertheless, we indulged in reminiscing about our very different Army careers, his as a Corps commander, mine as a junior officer. I was happy to present him with appropriate Regimental gifts for himself and his wife, and the evening ended amid much good humour and camaraderie. It was a refreshing experience to be on such familiar terms with a ranking General and I appreciated it.

It had been quite a day. The program had barely started and I was exhausted. Could I hold on for another nine days? Time would tell.

April 30th, Sunday

The official Program for Sunday called for a day of rest but I was sure that was pure fantasy. At 9:00 a.m., the phone rang. It was Gerard Hassink, the farmer on the outskirts of Wilp whose house we had destroyed during the bombardment preceding the Crossing of the Ijssel River in 1945. Gerard wanted me to join him and his family for lunch at the Bloemink Hotel, quite near my own.

I was delighted to accept. It was ten years since we had first met during the Pilgrimage in 1990, when the Crossing of the River had been re-enacted.

After the parade and reception on May 2nd, 1990, Gerard had kindly invited me and other Veterans to his home to relax on his patio and enjoy some cool drinks. Since then, we had kept in touch and exchanged cards every Christmas.

At the Hotel Bloemink, I was warmly greeted by Gerard, his wife Janny, daughter Ria, and Ati, the fine lady who had given me a lovely book on Holland. We recalled the exciting day in May 1990 when the Dutch Engineers had erected a pontoon bridge for me to re-cross the Ijssel River.

Gerard's memory went back even farther, to April 11th, 1945, when my D Company had made the first crossing. He asked, "You crossed in boats with a funny name, like "Bull"?

"No. They were called "Buffaloes" because they could travel cross-country as well as swim."

Janny then mentioned she had been told that I had composed a hymn in honour of the Dutch people who had suffered so much during the War. She would like to get a copy so that it could be sung in her church. Of course, I would be happy to give her the music. I probably had a copy in my luggage.

Gerard insisted on paying for the meal, including champagne, which I was not supposed to drink, but had a sip to toast our enduring friendship. I was glad I could respond by presenting them some Regimental gifts. Then they took me back to my hotel and left me with a beautiful bouquet of flowers. When I returned home, they sent me a dozen or more photos of the five of us having lunch. From the happy expression on my face, no one would believe I had not been indulging in the champagne.

May 1st, Monday—Reception by Mayor of Apeldoorn
The mayor of Apeldoorn, Mr. de Graaf, and the Town Council received the Veterans in the Orpheus Theatre. Several Veterans were introduced: The oldest man (91), the oldest single lady, the first to enter Apeldoorn (shot down in1941). But the Veterans who received the greatest applause were my good friend Doug Armstrong, PPCLI, and his wife Pauline, a former nurse. They had been married in Holland shortly after the War. Doug was an officer in my company and I had helped to make the arrangements for the wedding. Their bridesmaid, Mrs. De Nooyer, with whom they were staying, was also introduced.

The Master of Ceremonies, Mr. Hans van Willigenburg, a popular radio and TV personality, was quite a wit and conducted some amusing interviews with the Veterans on stage. He asked one old fellow, who was pretty shaky, if he was happy to be here (i.e., in Holland). "Hell no," he responded. I'd rather be with my Dutch hosts having a beer than on this —— stage."

Mr. van Willigenburg tried to elicit some personal information from Doug Armstrong. "Now, Doug, tell everyone where you met Pauline and all about your first date."

Doug was not about to be fazed by this kind of questioning and with true Patricia panache retorted, "There's not much to tell. We met in a London subway station during a bombing attack."

"Hm, sort of an underground romance. But tell me why you *had* to get married in Holland and not wait to go back to Canada."

"Very simple. We didn't *have* to get married anywhere. We were in love."

It brought down the house.

Mayor Fred de Graaf gave a powerful speech, and explained why the traditional pattern of these commemorations had to be changed. The attention had to be centred on young people, just as he had emphasized during his visit to Toronto in February. This new approach would also encourage exchange of information by way of contacts in trade and industry, contacts between Canada and The Netherlands, and between Toronto and Apeldoorn. The Veterans, of course, would never be forgotten. After all, they had laid the groundwork at great personal sacrifice.

At the Reception afterwards, the Veterans received the Apeldoorn medal and a pin, as well as a new CD of the Apeldoorn Anthem sung by the Green Street Boys. The Mayor and I were honoured by receiving the first two copies.

I saw several Patricias in the throng and managed to have a word with them: Charlie King, Rudy Deutsch, Wally Smith, Elwood Birss, David Crook and others.

When I returned to my hotel, several messages were waiting for me: Pieter Beelaerts invited me for lunch next day; Dick Veldhuizen hoped to see me in Achterveld; Sgt. Andy Anderson came around to see how I was making out.

Later that day, I was pleased to have the Mayor, Fred de Graaf, and his Chief of Cabinet, Klaas Huisman, and their wives drop by for a "Happy Hour." I complimented the Mayor on the fine Reception he had given the Veterans that afternoon and how much they had enjoyed it. I took advantage of the occasion to present him with a Regimental plaque inscribed as follows:

Presented to Apeldoorn
In appreciation of the Monument
Erected to Canada's soldiers
On the 55th Anniversary of the Liberation
May 2, 2000

He thanked me with genuine appreciation but I could tell by his quizzical smile he was a bit concerned about the reference to the Monument, which was not to be unveiled until the following day. I quickly explained that there might not be an appropriate occasion next day to hand him the plaque. I thought of misquoting that old Italian proverb—*Meglio tardi che mai*, by saying "Better Early than Never." But I wisely refrained from inflicting such nonsense on the erudite Mayor.

Our little party ended with my presenting my four guests with appropriate Regimental gifts. It had been a very pleasant day, free of any duties, and I was beginning to feel much stronger and hopeful that I would get through the week without any problems. However, past experience had taught me "Not to count chickens—" so I religiously took my pills as ordered.

May 2nd, Tuesday—Unveiling of National Canadian Liberation Monument

This was one of the few events which received some notice in the Canadian Press. Mr. de Graaf had referred to it in his Toronto address and at the Reception on May 1st. The Monument is a statue erected and paid for by the citizens of Apeldoorn and the Province of Gelderland.

It is 4.6 metres high, cast from bronze, and depicts a man standing alongside the road, cheering the arrival of the Liberators. He is waving two hats, but is crying at the same time, tears trickling down from his right eye. (However, the watery tears leave a stain over the length of the statue.) The tiles around the statue proudly display the Maple Leaf. Behind the man are two small walls, one with Canada on it, the other with Nederland. The statue is known as the "Man With two Hats."

I must confess that when I first saw the statue I was not impressed; nor were many other people. However, after hearing a moving address by General Gijsbers I changed my mind. General Gijsbers explained: "By the end of the War, one was lucky to own *one* hat. The two hats represent Canada and the Netherlands, but also the mixed feelings when we were liberated—happiness and sorrow. The statue also pays lasting tribute to the Canadian Liberators."

I began to appreciate the statue and the subtle meaning it conveyed.

Prior to the Ceremony, Pieter Beelaerts had kindly asked me to join him and his wife, Dieuwke, for lunch. He then escorted me to a Reception at de Loohof where Princess Margriet and other dignitaries were assembling for the Ceremony. It was a "by invitation only" affair, and I was glad Pieter was present to introduce me to such a distinguished gathering.

Back at my hotel, Pieter and his wife had a moment to relax and tell me something of their journeys in Asia and his new duties as Mayor of Hengelo. It was a real tonic to see him again and inspired me to carry on.

He gave me a stunning tie with red, gold and blue stripes and the Royal cipher, which he had acquired in the Het Loo Palace. I wear the tie only on special occasions. For once, I could properly reciprocate his kindness with suitable gifts for him and his wife.

May 3rd, Wednesday—Holten Canadian War Cemetery

On this day, I made a private visit to this cemetery where eight Patricias are buried. Their names may be found in my account of my Pilgrimage to Holland in 1990. Holten is about 30 kilometres east of Apeldoorn on the road to Deventer. When I arrived at the Keizerskroon on April 27th, I had hired a car but I had made little use of it. For the events of the past five days, I had been driven and, in any event, I had not yet felt well enough to drive myself. So my car rested in the parking lot.

However, by May 3rd, I was feeling much stronger and decided to make a brief visit to Holten Cemetery by car. I have earlier described the sadness I always experience when I visit this cemetery. These young men, some not yet 20, were struck down in the last weeks or days of the war, after surviving the terrible battles in Italy. I will have much more to say about Holten Cemetery in the account of my visit to Achterveld on May 9th.

I returned to the hotel in time to have lunch with Evert Gerritsen and his wife, Iet. Evert is one of my Dutch friends whom I have labelled "ubiquitous" because he seemed to be everywhere at the same time. He also had advance knowledge of everything and kept me informed. I was pleased to hear that his cousin, Harmen Blom, and his wife, Anstice, had come over from Fergus, Ontario, for the Ceremonies. I would probably have an opportunity to meet them later. Evert also informed me that the newspapers were giving the Anniversary excellent coverage (unlike Canadian media, I muttered to myself). He would hand me copies of all the articles on the last day of the Celebrations. I responded with my usual Regimental gifts, as well as a hat badge for Harmen.

Later that day, Ellen Huisman, wife of Klaas, picked me up at the hotel and we had tea in their lovely home. I had not been feeling too well due to the PMR and I needed a little quiet relaxation. This act of kindness was so typical of Klaas and Ellen Huisman. They must have known I was in poor shape just from my appearance. (How bad I looked I didn't realize until I saw some photos later that week.)

May 4th, Thursday—National Remembrance Day Memorial Service
—De Vecht, Municipality of Voorst

On this day, the Dutch remember their own people who perished during the war. Shortly after I arrived in Holland, Colonel Ritse Reitsma had "persuaded" me to give an address in Antonius Church at de Vecht. This is what I said.

> *Dear Friends:*
> *I am deeply honoured and very pleased to say a few words on this,* Your *National Remembrance Day.*
> *I have returned to Holland many times since the War. The tremendous respect, love and kindness we Veterans receive from the Dutch people is truly overwhelming. I am certain that nothing like it has ever been seen before.*
> *Now, at last, I have an opportunity to recognize the sacrifices and suffering the Dutch people themselves endured*

during the War, and to thank you for honouring Canada's soldiers who gave their lives in the cause of freedom.

So, today I would like to join you in remembering those Dutch people who suffered and died during the Nazi occupation—five years of tyranny and oppression. I am unable to describe what you endured, but I would like to read from an article written by a Dutch girl who tells what it was like. Her name is Olga Rains:

> Starting in September, 1944, the western part of Holland was isolated from the rest of the country. The winter of 1944/45 was the coldest winter of the War. Millions of people were hunting for food and fuel, many of them starving or freezing to death. Sugar beets and ground-up tulip bulbs were the main food. Water was rationed to a trickle. No electricity, no fuel. Most of the trees in the parks were cut down. My parents had to burn the furniture to keep us warm.
>
> The enemy stole everything we owned—radios, coats, blankets, copperware, bicycles and even our dogs. The enemy was losing the war and they took revenge on us. People were lined up on street corners and shot.

I'm sorry, I cannot read any more of these unspeakable crimes. I can only express my admiration for your courage and determination never to give in. You are a very strong people

Now, let me pass to a more pleasant subject—Freedom. Let us be happy and thank God that our mutual struggles and sacrifices were not in vain and that we are together once again to celebrate the glorious Liberation. Let us rejoice too in the strong ties that bind our two peoples.

These feelings are not just confined to the war generation. I can't express how proud and thrilled we are to march in your streets and see so many parents with their young children lining our route and waving Canadian flags.

It is gratifying to know that in future years the Commemorations will be focused on young people. You parents have taught them the meaning of freedom and they have learned it well. The torch has been passed to them and they will hold it high.

It's been fifty-five years since my D Company assaulted across the Ijssel River and drove the enemy out of Wilp. Then, in 1990, the wonderful citizens of Voorst, under the leadership of Johannes van Blommestein, had the Engineers

> *erect a bridge for me to cross the river once more. This time in a jeep instead of a water buffalo! An unforgettable experience.*
>
> *As for the future, who knows what's in store. Whatever happens I am certain that the friendship, love and goodwill that we have for each other, so evident during this Pilgrimage, will last as long as the Ijssel River flows.*
>
> *I hear talk that this is our last Parade. Well, maybe it is. But I can assure the people of Voorst that so long as there is one Veteran alive and well, he will accept your invitation to make another Pilgrimage to the land he helped to set free. And I hope that person is me!*
>
> *In conclusion, I want to express my profound respect and admiration for all the people of Holland. These Pilgrimages are now a unique part of our common heritage and will be marvelled at one hundred years from now. We will not be here, but the children of our grandchildren will be. They will never forget.*
>
> *Thank you and God bless the precious bond that has united us these past fifty-five years.*

It was quite a novel experience for me to speak from a pulpit before an attentive, captive audience. Frankly, I rather enjoyed it, but I am not contemplating taking Holy Orders any time soon.

After the service, we all assembled for lunch at a nearby restaurant in the Teuge Airport. This airport has a special significance for the Dutch because it was here that the Dutch Royal Family first landed on Dutch soil after the War.

This was my last meeting with the wonderful citizens of Voorst, whose friendship I had enjoyed over many years, and it was difficult to leave. Johannes van Blommestein drove me back to Apeldoorn and promised to keep an eye on me for the rest of the Celebrations. I appreciated this kindly gesture as I was still not feeling 100 per cent. In fact, Johannes kept his promise and appeared at all the remaining ceremonies I attended.

As soon as I arrived home, I wrote my friend a note.

> *Dr. J.H.J. van Blommestein*
> *Burgemeester van Voorst*
>
> June 8, 2000
>
> *Dear Johannes:*
>
> *Thank you for giving me the honour of delivering an address at the Memorial Service in Antonius Church at de*

Vecht. I have now spoken in two of your lovely churches and I must say I rather enjoyed standing in the pulpit.

The visit to Teuge Airport was most interesting. I learned that this was the place where the Royal family first landed on Dutch soil after the war. What an emotional experience. I also learned that Glider Captain van Blommestein also touched down from time to time.

Thank you for trying to get in touch with Gerard Burgers. You will be pleased to learn that we finally met at the Farewell Party on May 8th.

You were very kind to include me in the opening Ceremonies at the Canadian Club where I joined you and General Messerschmidt in creating a Niagara Falls with champagne! And I was so happy to see Titia and Ritse and Nan again. Hard to believe ten years have flown by since the last Pilgrimage. Please give them all my fondest greetings.

Thank you too for giving me that attractive album with photos of the Liberation Ceremonies in Voorst. It is really a magnificent record of the many events and I congratulate you on producing it so quickly before the Veterans departed. I realize now how much I missed by my sickness. I think the photos of me confirm that I was not in top shape. I was very impressed with the large yellow folder containing the program and other interesting material.

I am not forgetting the valuable medal and badge. They are very special souvenirs of the Pilgrimage and will always be treasured by my family.

How you and your Committee found the time and energy to do all these things I will never understand. I realize it was a labour of love and you do not expect any reward. But I want you and all the citizens of Voorst to know how much we Veterans appreciate your love, respect, friendship and kindness. We, too, will never forget.

I have so many people to thank. Ritse Reitsma (for persuading me to speak at de Vecht and taking me to the Canadian Club), Hans Muller (for driving me home), Henk Hutten (for driving me to de Vecht), Mr. de Groot (for presenting me with an attractive towel, beautifully wrapped, of Café de Vecht). Heading the list is of course your good self. No matter where I was, you would suddenly appear at my right hand like a "guiding" angel to make sure I was being taken care of and not getting into any trouble. Your *presence was a real comfort to me and I deeply appreciate your thoughtfulness.*

This Pilgrimage may be the end of these great Celebrations, but I prefer to think of it as the end of the beginning. The time has come to hand the torch to the younger generation, who, I am sure, will continue to honour and remember the wonderful ties that have bound us together all these years.

Sincerely,

May 5th, Friday—National Liberation Day Tattoo—Apeldoorn

Another national event, which is held on every Pilgrimage, is a Tattoo (the Dutch call it a Taptoe which perhaps better describes this musical ceremony). Six bands took part:

    Johan Willem Friso Kapel
    Canadian Forces Band
    48th Highlanders of Canada Pipes and Drums
    48th Highlanders of Canada Military Band
    48th Highlanders of Holland Pipes and Drums
    Queen's York Rangers Fife and Drums

In my opinion, the Dutch Band, Johan Willem Friso Kapel, outshone the others in musicianship, marching and smartness, although for sheer spectacle it is hard to beat the 48th Pipes and Drums!

Prior to the Ceremony, which was held in the evening, Sef Claessen and his wife, Corrie, joined me for dinner at the hotel. Sef, it will be remembered, had arranged my music which was to be played at the Tattoo. The purpose of my dinner was to express, in some small way, my appreciation for his work. I also wished to present him with the Drummer Statuette, a CD of the PPCLI Drum Band and other souvenirs. He graciously accepted my gifts and gave me two dozen roses! I had met another kind, generous person. Are all the people from Holland cut from the same cloth? I think so.

I found out that Sef, besides arranging music, taught school and was looking forward to hearing my pieces played at the Tattoo. He had also arranged my March in 1995 which was performed by 500 musicians.

After dinner, we strolled through the beautiful grounds surrounding the Het Loo Palace where the Tattoo was to be performed. Bleachers had been erected and soon thousands of spectators assembled for the show which began at 7:15. It was a beautiful evening and the bands enthralled the people with their music, marching and colourful uniforms. The Canadian Band chose to perform a musical charade and turned themselves into soldiers guarding an airport under attack—or something. I was not amused but the Dutch loved it.

Sef Claessen and I waited, and waited some more, to hear our music. Finally, the announcer called on us to come forward to the podium where the Band Master, the Conductor of the Johan Willem Friso Kapel, awaited us. I had been warned that Claessen would formally hand me the original arrangement. I would then hand it to the Band Master and the Bands would commence playing from music they had already received (and presumably practised).

By this time, the show had been going on for three hours and it was quite dark. Sef and I looked at each other and I said, "I hope the Bands have had time to learn the music. It's as dark as the insides of those bagpipes. They won't be able to read a note." Sef slowly nodded his head.

Sef was handed the original arrangement for the music and we marched out together to the podium. Sef handed the music to me and I passed it to the Band Master. He was about to walk away but I had prepared a little speech which I thought the occasion warranted.

> *Thank you, Sef Claessen, for presenting me with these scores for my Marches and Ballad. You have done a wonderful job of arranging the pieces and converting them from mediocre tunes to proper military music.*
>
> *There is one other person who deserves my heartfelt thanks—General Gijsbers, who generously helped to fund the cost of having the pieces arranged, and was largely responsible for having them included in the program.*
>
> *Thank you for the honour you have bestowed upon me this evening.*

The show was over! The Bands marched off and Sef and I were left speechless! Our music had not been played and the Band Master had walked away with the scores. General Gijsbers was furious (although he maintained an outward calm). He had no idea what had happened and apologized profusely. He would find the answer and let Sef and me know.

Back at the hotel, Sef and his wife, Corrie, had a few drinks to drown our disappointment (I had to settle for a soda). But, like his phlegmatic countrymen—and to his credit—he took it all in stride. I also managed to forget it, as something had occurred that put all other matters in the shade. I had just received a call from my wife in Toronto that our youngest daughter was seriously ill with pneumonia.

My first reaction was, naturally, to catch the next flight home. My daughter suffered from asthma, which combined with pneumonia was cause for grave concern. I immediately got in touch with several specialists in Toronto (including the doctor who had correctly diagnosed my problems) and asked their opinion. In consultation with our family doctor, they felt my daughter's condition was under control and they would advise me immediately of any change. With their assurance, I carried on with my trip, checking every few days how my daughter was progressing. She eventually recovered, but it took a long time, and, of course, she worried about my health.

I am happy to mention a very timely and thoughtful act that gave my daughter and me a much needed boost in morale at a critical time. When Bob Gardham, the DVA Webmaster, heard of my daughter's illness, he sent her an e-mail with a digital photo of me on the Reviewing Stand with Princess Margriet during the May 7th Parade. He wrote that I was fine and feeling well. I shall never forget his kindness.

May 6th, Saturday

On this date, the Department of Veterans Affairs held a Memorial Service at Groesbeek Canadian War Cemetery, where more than 2,300 Canadians are buried. A Memorial at the entrance contains the names of another 103 Canadians who have no known grave. While I was not a member of the Minister's Official Party, I was invited to join them for the Ceremony and Jean-Guy Chapman, the Project Director, offered me a lift. I had to turn him down. It would mean a long drive and considerable walking and standing around, and my PMR had flared up again. I wisely decided to save my strength for the great National Parade the next day and the ceremonies at Achterveld on May 9th.

I had already paid my respects at the Holten Cemetery where the Patricias who were killed in Holland are buried.

Later that day, Evert Gerritsen called on me with the newspaper clippings he had promised. They made quite a bundle. The pictures were great, but the articles I left for my friend Tom Thomas to translate when I arrived home.

May 7th, Sunday—National Parade – Apeldoorn

For many, this was the highlight of the week-long ceremonies. Veterans from all over Holland converged on Apeldoorn to take part in the Parade. Estimates of the numbers vary but probably about 2,500 Veterans took part. Most of them were conveyed in WWII reconditioned vehicles driven by the "Keep Them Rolling" organization.

The enthusiasm of the crowds was overwhelming. Our route through the city was lined with people, some standing 15 ranks deep. Parents and grandparents with their young children waved Canadian flags and gave us the "Thumbs Up" or the "Victory" salute. Shouts of "Thank you Canada," "We shall never forget," filled the air.

In a way, this was the most significant Pilgrimage of them all. Fifty-five years is a very long time and memories do fade. But not in

Apeldoorn. I could hardly believe the enormous crowds that greeted us wherever we went. Some estimates were as high as 250,000. And the pride and enthusiasm of the Veterans themselves was undiminished by the years. Perhaps it was because many of us, both Dutch and Canadians, realized this would be the last Pilgrimage and we all wanted to make it a good one.

As mentioned earlier, General Gijsbers had appointed me Parade Commander. I was picked up at my hotel by two Dutch Officers I had previously met, LCol. Verharen and Maj. Spreeuw, and driven to the forming up place for the parade in the grounds of the Paleis Het Loo. Promptly at 1400 hours the parade moved off with my jeep in the lead. Immediately the crowds started to roar and little children advanced on my jeep bearing flowers and other gifts with letters asking me to write. It was Beekbergen all over again, but on a much larger scale. And thankfully, the weather was beautiful, unlike Beekbergen.

Soon I approached the Saluting Base. The jeep stopped, I got out, stood to attention and saluted Princess Margriet—"Canadian Veterans formed up and ready to march past Your Royal Highness." She then invited me to join her on the dais along with her husband Pieter van Vollenhoven, their son Prince Floris, Mayor de Graaf, General Gijsbers, the Dutch Minister of Defence and our Minister of Defence Art Eggleton.

The Veterans were really magnificent and I felt very proud to be standing there with my Patricia blazer, beret and cap badge. As I say, most were driven in WWII vehicles but quite a number walked. A section of Patricias with a Regimental Banner marched past. I recognized some of them—Doug Armstrong with his wife Pauline, Wally Smith, Charlie King, Lloyd and Olga Rains, Elwood Birss, Rudy Deutsch. They were very smart and everyone was in step and properly dressed. If there had been a prize for the best group I would have awarded it to them (no bias there).

Everyone was in a happy, relaxed, carefree mood, including the members on the Reviewing Stand. Some of the Veterans gave smart salutes but most waved or gave the Victory sign or thumbs up. Some yelled out, "Hi Syd," followed by a friendly rude remark. Others directed their comradely remarks at the Minister: "How are you doing, Art."

Several rolled by in open vehicles singing wartime ditties and drinking what looked like Amstel beer, but I could be mistaken. One old guy stopped the whole parade, danced a jig for the Princess and presented her with roses.

HRH, her husband and all the members of the Reviewing Party accepted all the antics in good humour and encouraged the performers with enthusiastic clapping and waving of hands. It was an unforgettable, spontaneous outburst of mutual love and affection, such as I had never witnessed before as a Reviewing Officer (so-called).

After the parade, Princess Margriet invited a group of us to her home for tea. I hitched a ride with General Gijsbers and we quickly arrived at the Royal residence before the other guests. Met by several uniformed guards, we were ushered into the garden to await HRH. In a few moments she appeared with her husband, Pieter van Vollenhoven, apologized for not meeting us and offered drinks. (Actually we were probably about 15 minutes early.) Until the other guests arrived, the four of us relaxed and talked about the Parade and "the wonderful Canadian Veterans." As mentioned earlier, her husband was a member of the Netherlands Airforce and is very interested in military operations. He and HRH wanted to know how the First Division was moved all the way from Italy to Holland in time to join the battle to help liberate Holland. I was happy to tell them about Operation Goldflake—how the First Canadian Corps was moved in great secrecy from under the very noses of the Germans along the banks of the Senio River, to an embarkation area near Pisa; from there by ship to Marseilles; then by lorry up the Rhone Valley to Belgium; and finally to a concentration area in Holland, all in a space of six weeks. The Germans had not a clue as to the whereabouts of the Canadians until the Patricias assaulted across the Ijssel River in Buffaloes on April 11, 1945. Throughout my narration, I received some helpful comments from General Gijsbers about the logistics of moving troops. After all, he had been a Corps Commander.

Princess Margriet and her husband were obviously thrilled to learn about the operation and asked several questions. They are a charming couple and I am fortunate to have had this brief interlude with them.

I presented Princess Margriet with a rhinestone brooch and Pieter van Vollenhoven with a Regimental cap badge. HRH immediately pinned the brooch to her dress, just as the guests began to arrive.

* * *

As soon as I arrived home, I wrote all the children and even the parents who had given me such lovely gifts. I reproduce only one letter and the reply I received at Christmas.

PILGRIMAGE—2000

June 12, 2000

Fam. Van Polen
Putten
The Netherlands
Dear Friends:

I suppose you thought I had forgotten you. Not at all. I have been very busy since I returned from my wonderful trip to Holland.

Wasn't that a great Parade. You must have been very, very tired standing for such a long time.

Thank you for remembering Canada's soldiers and thank you for your lovely flowers. I am enclosing a postcard from Toronto as a little souvenir of my visit.

I hope we meet again someday.

Sincerely,

December 13, 2000

Dear Mr. Frost,

I suppose you thought we had forgotten you. Not at all. Thank you for the letter. That was very kind of you.

Greetings and best wishes from Holland

Hans, Karin, Marge en Robin v. Polen

* * *

When I returned to my hotel, there were several messages from people who had seen me at the Parade, as spectators or on TV. But one message took precedence—from my sick daughter. I immediately got through and was thankful to hear she was out of the dangerous category and feeling much better.

Another message that caught my attention was one from Dieneke Dirksen-Boot. I thought I knew who it was but I wasn't sure. Was she the youngest daughter of Phil and Helen Boot and the sister of Jean whom I had met in Sassenheim after the War? The moment I spoke to her I knew it was Jean's sister. The spelling of her first name and her married name had thrown me. I always referred to her as "little Dinica," but that was 55 years earlier.

For some years after the war I had kept in touch with the Boots. In 1956 during my first visit to Holland, with my wife, I had visited them and spent an enjoyable evening or two reminiscing about "old times."

Again, during the 1980 Pilgrimage, I had visited Phil and Helen as well as Jean's family in Muiden. In 1986, during my visit to Daimler-Benz in Stuttgart, I managed a quick side trip to Holland, as already described in Chapter XIII. On my next Pilgrimage to Holland in 1989, I tried to contact the family but Phil and Helen had died and Jean was in Greece. After that we lost contact.

So, on May 7th, 2000, it was a pleasant surprise to hear from Dieneke. Jean was in hospital awaiting surgery and could not walk, but Dieneke was fine and hoped to attend Achterveld on May 9th when the new Monument to the PPCLI was to be unveiled.

It had been another memorable but exhausting day. Only two more to go. Could I make it? Of course I could. The good news from my daughter, the inspiring Parade, the encouragement of my friends would see me through.

May 8th, Monday—Farewell Party

Those good Samaritans, Klaas and Ellen Huisman, called for me at my hotel and drove me to the Canadian Club, the large convention hall that had been transformed into a meeting place for the Veterans and their friends. It was my last chance to greet my Patricia comrades and thank my friends in Apeldoorn for all their kindness, not only during this Pilgrimage, but in many cases going back some 15 years.

The place was packed and a non-stop orchestra played tunes new and old to encourage the Veterans to get up and dance. Many did, just to show they had not yet faded away. In this throng, it was difficult to make contact with anyone, but I spoke to a few Patricias, some of whom I had not seen in years: Bill Adelman, H. W. Leonard, T. Crook, Elwood Birss, Charlie King, Doug and Pauline Armstrong and their bridesmaid of 1945.

I was particularly keen to see Jan Koorenhof, who had recently married, and his wife, whom I had not yet met. Jan had been very busy throughout the past week co-ordinating all the activities which he performed with his usual quiet efficiency. After searching the Hall, I finally located Jan but not his wife. I handed him his Regimental gifts, including one for his wife. "Thanks for my lovely presents," he said, "but Eugenie would appreciate your personally presenting hers."

It was a gallant remark and I assured my friend I would be delighted to meet her. With his help my mission was accomplished and I bestowed her pin with much formality in the fashion of a French General.

Many of my other friends were there to say farewell: General Gijsbers, Evert Gerritsen, Fred de Graaf, Pieter Beelaerts, Johannes van Blommestein. It was the best of times and the saddest of times. Wonderful to have this chance to meet friends and talk about Pilgrimages past and present. Sad to realize that such a joyous meeting would never be repeated. But no one was going to spoil a good party on that account and it outlasted many of the participants who decided to call it a day.

I was one of those who decided to call it not only a day but a memorable week. Dear Klaas and Ellen Huisman saw my weary form and kindly drove me to the hotel. On the way, they stopped off to buy me some milk and cakes for my diet. Such friendship is a treasure that cannot be measured in the exchange of gifts.

May 9th, Tuesday—Achterveld—Unveiling Monument to the PPCLI

From a Regimental point of view, my visit to Achterveld was probably the most rewarding. It was here that the Regiment ended the war. It was also the site of the famous Food Truce on April 30, 1945, held in the little schoolhouse right in my D Company area. Many times in this narrative, the historical importance of this small village has been mentioned, but perhaps a quick review would be helpful.

My first visit to Achterveld was in 1956, when I found the old schoolhouse where high-ranking Allied and German officers had met to arrange a truce so that food could be sent to the starving Dutch.

During my visit in 1985, I had the good fortune to meet Jan Schouten who told me he was the "Official Archivist of Achterveld." He also informed me that he had 25 volumes about the War, including the Truce negotiations with Seyss-Inquart in the schoolhouse, the Liberation and "the wonderful PPCLI soldiers." His archives also contained a complete record of the visit by B Company of 2 PPCLI in 1967 when they re-enacted the crossing of the Ijssel River.

During my Pilgrimages in 1986 and 1989, I renewed my acquaintance with Mr. Schouten. Then, in 1990, he invited me to unveil a Memorial commemorating 25 civilians who were killed in the fighting or who died in concentration camps during the War. I gladly accepted and attended a Ceremony in Achterveld on May 4, 1990

We kept in touch and in January 2000 Mr. Schouten informed me that Achterveld was planning to erect a Memorial honouring the soldiers of the PPCLI who prevented the Germans from blowing up their church. Again, I was asked to attend a ceremony to unveil this Memorial and deliver a speech.

On May 9, I participated in a very impressive program that extended over the entire afternoon. The schoolroom where the Truce took place was now a museum and was opened to the public; the famous Dutch Army Band, Johan Willem Friso Kapel, gave a concert; the Seaforth Highlanders of Holland Pipes and Drums performed; a buffet meal and refreshments were served; the Monument was unveiled and the church choir sang a hymn I had composed called "Freedom."

Seven Patricias formed up facing the Monument, including Rudy Deutsch who assisted me in the unveiling. The Ceremony ended with my speech and the Last Post. The seven Patricias were:

    Doug Armstrong
    Elwood Birss
    Rudy Deutsch
    Syd Frost
    Ben Kelter
    Lloyd Rains
    Wally Smith

A plaque on the Monument carried the following inscription:

CANADIAN SOLDIERS FROM THE PRINCESS PATRICIA LIGHT INFANTRY PREVENTED THE DESTRUCTION OF THE PARISH CHURCH OF ACHTERVELD
(used as an observation post)
on 18 April 1945

WE THANK THESE SOLDIERS WHO SAVED THE HEART OF OUR VILLAGE
May 9, 2000

Much to my surprise, I was then presented with a full-size replica of the plaque bearing the above inscription. (Some die-hard Patricia [aren't we all] will notice a glitch in the name of our Regiment, so I must point it out to forestall any slanderous rebuke. But let us remember it is the thought behind this magnanimous act, not the wording, which is important.)

The following is the text of my speech:

Dear Citizens of Achterveld:
I am greatly honoured and very pleased to say a few words on behalf of my Regiment, The Princess Patricia's Canadian Light Infantry, on this memorable occasion—the unveiling of a Monument to the soldiers of my Regiment who prevented the Germans from blowing up the tower of St. Joseph's Church.
What a tragedy it would have been, if this imposing fortress for the Lord, and all its beautiful stained-glass windows, the figures of the Saints, the altars, and all the other adornments, had been reduced to rubble. One is tempted to believe that a force more powerful than the soldiers themselves was protecting your church on that perilous day.

Now there will be three monuments in Achterveld remembering World War II. One Monument honours the fallen soldiers of the Regiment Huzaren. The other Monument commemorates twenty-five civilians who died as a result of fighting in this Village, or were killed by shellfire or mines, or who died in concentration camps. I had the honour of participating in the unveiling of this Monument ten years ago (on May 4th, 1990, to be exact), and now you are so kind as to bring me back once more. This is surely an unique honour for me and I am very grateful.

Achterveld itself is, as you know, a community of tremendous historical importance, far exceeding its modest size. It was the site of the famous Food Truce on April 30, 1945, held in the little schoolhouse right in my D Company area. The Truce Agreement was actually copied by a typewriter owned by the PPCLI. The Regiment also supplied pickets, check posts and guards in the Village, and refreshments in the messes.

Many accounts have been written of this vast relief operation, but I think the one that best describes the events was written by one John Redfern in a dispatch sent May 2nd, 1945. I would like to quote a few lines from his dispatch.

> *Food to save three and a half million Dutch citizens from starvation is lumbering into Holland this morning on 100 Army lorries, along roads which, only 24 hours ago, were crammed with mines or roadblocks, right under the German front-line troops who are doing nothing about it.*
>
> *All this is possible because of a "cease fire" order which now operates in the Grebbe Line, the front 25 miles south of the Zuyder Zee....*
>
> *Then a rendezvous was fixed at Achterveld, a front-line village with a modest school building that deserves to go down in history as the place where, when the free world was quivering over Buchenwald and Belsen, Britons, Dutch and Germans discussed the chances of giving humanity a break.*
>
> *For four hours they discussed the Dutchman's stomach, with an interval in which the visitors wolfed the food served them in one of the schoolrooms.*

And so, my Regiment feels it has a very special and unique bond with Achterveld and its people. This fine

> *Monument raised in honour of the soldiers of the PPCLI not only honours the past but reminds future generations of our common heritage.*
>
> *One other historical fact should be recorded. One thousand miles from Achterveld, near a little village in Sicily called Ispica, another Monument stands to honour the soldiers of the PPCLI and of the First Canadian Division. On July 10th, 1943, they assaulted the beaches of Sicily as part of the famous Eighth Army. The landing marked the beginning of the end of the War and Hitler's Fortress Europa. I had the honour of participating in the dedication of that Monument in Sicily several years ago.*
>
> *Now we have two monuments marking the beginning and the end of the long march of the PPCLI from the rugged beaches of Sicily to the pleasant pastures of Holland. Thank you, thank you, dear citizens of Achterveld, for your thoughtfulness, your kindness and your friendship. We shall never forget you.*
>
> *My remarks would not be complete without mentioning that indomitable keeper of records these past fifty-five years, your famous Archivist—Jan Schouten. Without his persistent hard work I am sure this noble memorial we see today would not exist. Thank you Jan, on behalf of the PPCLI and personally as a dear friend.*

After the Ceremony, I presented Mr. Schouten with some personal gifts and a Regimental Plaque bearing the following inscription:

> *Presented to Achterveld in appreciation of the*
> *Monument erected in honour of the soldiers of the PPCLI*
>   *May 9, 2000*

Further surprises awaited me. In the midst of an inspection of the Museum with Mr. Schouten, in marched a Section of soldiers dressed in authentic WWII Battle Dress with PPCLI and First Division flashes, ammunition boots, web belts, gaiters and shell dressings tucked under the camouflage netting of the helmet. For a moment I thought I was having a hallucination and I was back in WWII!

They are a fine-looking body of men who live in the vicinity of Achterveld. They showed me a copy of our Regimental History and, incredibly, knew almost as much about the Regiment's fighting record in Holland as I used to know! They are known as the PPCLI Re-Enactment Group in Holland and train regularly with the Dutch Active Force.

Later, during the reception, I had a long talk with the leader of this group, Mark Hoedeman, a remarkable young man who had formed the group four years earlier. They put on demonstrations and displays throughout the area and each year, at Christmas, attend candlelight ceremonies at the Holten Cemetery. Mark himself had taken a parachute course and is a qualified jumper.

For a fuller description of the group and its activities, I quote from Mark Hoedeman's letter to me:

Amsterdam, 14th August, 2000
C. Sydney Frost, Q.C., LL.B., LL.D.
Dear Sir:

I started out to form a group of Canadian re-enactors about four years ago, after the decision to do so was made at a town called Bussum. I attended a liberation event there and invited Mr. Lloyd Rains to accompany me on the motorcade which was organized for the occasion. When we arrived at the center of Bussum, I learned from Lloyd several things about our own history and it was from that moment on that I decided to form a P.P.C.L.I. re-enactment group.

At first I was not fully aware of the "honours" of the regiment but during the last couple of years Lloyd told me more and more and I read several books and articles about the Canadian Army and the P.P.C.L.I. in particular. That is why I hope that we are not insulting anybody by re-enacting such a famous regiment, because fame is not what we are after. The decision to choose the P.P.C.L.I. is made first of course because of my friendship with Lloyd and secondly because of P.P.C.L.I.'s achievements, making them one of the best examples of a Canadian unit doing their best to liberate Europe. With this P.P.C.L.I. group we want to honour the memory of all the Canadians and other allies who fought for our freedom and especially of those who gave their lives.

Furthermore, I registered the name of the P.P.C.L.I. in the form of a re-enactment association with the Chamber of Commerce here in Holland, but we leave the association unused. I decided to do this in accordance with Mr. Lloyd Rains in order to protect the name. The association can be activated and then P.P.C.L.I. can be used as the name of our group, but we will only do this when you and/or the Regiment will decide to give us permission to do so.

PILGRIMAGE—2000

> *Some time has passed now since our meeting in Achterveld on the 9th of May and I must say that I'm still not fully down to earth from all our events in that week. Although we could not turn out the whole of the group that day, it was for me the most important event of the week. Being able to meet you and some of the other veterans was very important to me. The fact that you yourself were very pleased with us as a P.P.C.L.I. re-enactment group and complimented us on our appearance was the biggest award I received that week. Of course all of it is a joint venture and, although the others were not able to be present, I carried the compliment to them and told them our group effort is very much being appreciated.*
>
> *For Jacob, Tjarko and me, as representatives of our group, being present at the unveiling of the monument in Achterveld was a great honour and I am proud that you and the other veterans allowed us to do so. I hereby send you some photographs and I hope you like them and show them to family and friends so that they can see that "the boys" are not forgotten in Holland, not even by the younger generation.*
>
> *Maybe some day we'll meet again but for now, thank you for your efforts and your latest visit to Holland. With your consent and that of the other veterans, we will go on with re-enacting and preserving a part of history so dearly paid.*
>
> *All the best to you and your family, with the highest regards,*
> *Mark Hoedeman*

Mark also sent me a book of coloured photographs of the headstones of the eight Patricias buried in Holten Cemetery. I produce a copy of his letter describing the photos and the ceremony held every Christmas Eve.

Amsterdam, 14th August, 2000
Dear Mr. Frost,
  The photographs in this book were taken at the Holten Canadian War Cemetery during an event of remembrance, which is taking place yearly, on Christmas Eve 1998.
  The Cemetery is located near the village of Holten which is 20 kilometres east of the town of Deventer. It is in this cemetery that the great majority of the burials are of

Canadians who died during the last stages of the war in Holland and during the advance of the Canadian 2nd Corps into northern Germany and across the Ems River in April and the first days of May 1945.

The initiative for this remembrance was taken by a Scandinavian lady who lives in Deventer and who introduced this tradition locally. She started this initiative seven years ago. These days it is the organization "Welcome again veterans" who has taken it upon themselves to coordinate this event yearly. For this they contact the local schools and ask the children to take part in the event.

At sunset, the children put a candle on each grave so that eventually the whole cemetery is flooded with candlelight. During the ceremony "Slow Airs" and "Laments" are played on the Bagpipes and drums—these Pipers and Drummers are in close contact with the Royal Winnipeg Rifles and also have the permission of the Regiment to wear the uniform. On one of the photos a large kind of flute is shown, called the "Midwinter horn" on which every performer plays his own tune and melody, which is recognized among the other performers as a kind of signature.

Last year members of our group attended the 7th commemoration of this event together with a Canadian veteran and his wife, Mr. & Mrs. Lloyd Rains, who now live in The Netherlands. Mr. Rains served with the Princess Patricia's Canadian Light Infantry of the 1st Div.

The photos of the graves in this book are the men of the P.P.C.L.I. who died at the end of the war during the liberation of the western part of the Netherlands. We remembered them together with Mr. Lloyd Rains and his wife Olga Rains and put flowers on their graves.

With this we want to symbolize our feelings toward all Canadian Veterans who fought for the freedom of our country.

Yours sincerely,
Mark Hoedeman

These two letters from Mark Hoedeman are, in my opinion, an enduring tribute to the PPCLI and a source of great comfort to the next-of-kin of the young soldiers who gave their lives in the cause of freedom. His efforts and his dedication to the Regiment deserve to be recognized. On my own initiative, I took it upon myself to thank him on behalf of the Regiment. If I have transgressed on the powers that be, I assume full responsibility for my action.

August 28, 2000

Mr. Mark Hoedeman
Amsterdam
Dear Mark:

I was so thrilled to receive your letter and the marvellous photos. I had no idea that every year, on Christmas Eve, the people of Holten honour Canada's dead with a beautiful Candlelight Ceremony. What a wonderful way to demonstrate your love and respect for Canada's Veterans. I am deeply moved.

I can assure you that you are not insulting anybody with your fine Re-Enactor Group. In my opinion, you are doing a great job and are a credit to the Regiment. I have sent copies of your letter and all the photos to the Colonel of the Regiment. (He is actually a retired Major-General and the Senior Officer of the Regiment, next to the Colonel in Chief.) I have also sent your material to an Historian who is writing a new History of the PPCLI, from its beginning up to the present time.

I was very touched with the way you expressed your feelings about the Regiment and described the Candlelight Ceremony. I was also impressed with the professional way in which you presented all the material.

Please thank Mr. Oud for the excellent photo of the group taken after the service in Achterveld. I was glad that you included my old friend Dr. Johannes van Blommestein, Mayor of Voorst. As you know, my final objective after crossing the Ijssel River was Wilp in the Municipality of Voorst. I am sending him a copy of the photo.

As a small token of my appreciation and admiration for the great work you and your Re-Enactors are doing, I am sending by separate mail a copy of my book—Once a Patricia.

I am also enclosing with this letter a copy of the speech I made at the Unveiling of the Memorial at Achterveld on May 9th, as well as a copy of the Freedom Anthem I had composed for the Pilgrimage. I understand that the Anthem was sung by the church choirs but I missed it as I was in the schoolhouse with my old comrades and friends reminiscing about the War.

Again, my heartfelt gratitude for your interest in my Regiment. I shall look forward to receiving news from the Re-Enactors from time to time.

With my best wishes,
C. Sydney Frost

Among the many guests present was the Mayor of Achterveld and Leusden, Dr. C.J.G.M. de Vet. Unfortunately, we had only a few moments to chat but I presented him with a Regimental pin and later wrote him a note.

July 22, 2000

Dr. C.J.G.M. de Vet
Mayor Leusden and Achterveld
The Netherlands
Dear Dr. de Vet:

The wonderful Pilgrimage of the Canadian Veterans to Holland is over but it will never be forgotten. Everywhere I went the citizens were so enthusiastic and friendly. They made us feel like delivering angels!

I was very honoured to be asked to unveil the Memorial to the PPCLI soldiers and deliver an address. This was a very thoughtful and generous act on the part of your Municipality, for which my Regiment will be forever grateful. I can do no better to express our thanks than to enclose a copy of my address. It was quite a surprise to see the PPCLI Re-Enactment Group. They looked very realistic in their World War II battle dress.

It is very gratifying to see how reverently Achterveld keeps alive and honours the memory of Canada's soldiers, especially the PPCLI. I am sure that a great deal of the credit goes to Jan Schouten for maintaining his invaluable archives and for helping to organize the Liberation Committees over the years. You will note that I was happy to mention his hard work in my speech.

I am sorry we did not have more time to chat. So many old comrades and friends came up to reminisce that I was overwhelmed and I missed the Choirs "Sint Ceacilia" and "De Rietzangers" who were singing a hymn I had composed. It was such a pity that I missed it but I am writing to them to apologize. I enclose a copy of the hymn for your records.

With my warmest regards,

Sincerely,
C. S. Frost

c.c. Jan Schouten

To the choirmasters of the two choirs who had spent some time rehearsing my song and then sang it on May 9th, I sent the following note of apology for not having heard them.

July 22, 2000

Mr. G. Wijnands
Mrs. R. van Hattum
c/o Parochiecentrum
Achterveld
Dear Friends:
   It is with considerable embarrassment that I write you this note of apology.
   As you know, I composed the Hymn Freedom which your Choirs, "Sint Ceacilia" and "De Rietzangers," sang on May 9th last in connection with the dedication of the Memorial to the soldiers of the PPCLI.
   After the Ceremony, a number of old comrades and friends approached me in the schoolhouse to reminisce. I got so tied-up with them and a group called the PPCLI Re-Enactors that I completely overlooked your performance of my hymn. It was such a shame that I missed it and I am terribly sorry.
   I hope you will accept my heartfelt apology. The citizens of Achterveld have always been so kind and generous to the Canadian Veterans who liberated them. There is no way we can reciprocate your kindness, but I hope you will accept my little Hymn as a token of our appreciation.
   With my warmest regards,

Sincerely,

c.c. Jan Schouten

Little more need be said about this memorable day. Dick Veldhuizen, the Historian from Barneveld, attended the ceremonies. He kindly gave me a pin, decals and brochures on Barneveld and I responded with Regimental gifts.

Dieneke Dirksen-Boot, as promised, also attended the Unveiling of the Monument and we had time to talk about the exciting days when Holland was set free by the Canadians and the wonderful times we enjoyed with her parents in Sassenheim.

My bag of presents was almost exhausted and so was I. I climbed into my automobile and set my sights for Apeldoorn. I remember little of that sad journey, but I took with me beautiful memories that would last the rest of my life. And, I had made it!

May 9th, Tuesday—Reception by the Minister of Veterans Affairs

Due to my commitment in Achterveld, I was not able to attend this Reception. I had already met the Minister of National Defence, Art Eggleton, who filled in for George Baker at the Saluting Base of the May 7th Parade when the latter was called back to Canada.

The Minister of Veterans Affairs and his party were staying at my hotel, the Keizerskroon, as already mentioned. I thus had an opportunity to meet most of them, including the Deputy Minister, Larry Murray, Cliff Chadderton, various members of the Senate and House of Commons, the Youth Groups and the Cadets.

So ends Phase I of my trip to Europe in May 2000. After a short rest in Amsterdam, I undertook Phase II—Sicily. But that story has already been told.

As in prior Pilgrimages, I have attempted to compose a nominal roll of all Patricias who attended this Pilgrimage, but again I was not too successful, the reason being they were lodged in so many different towns. But even when all the Veterans were brought together, such as for the Parade in Apeldoorn, it was almost impossible to find anyone in the throng. The attached list is therefore only a "best effort." Ranks given are as at the end of WWII.

PROVISIONAL LIST
PPCLI Veterans Who Attended The Pilgrimage to Holland, May, 2000

D141397	LCpl.	W. (Bill)	Adelman
K48659	Lt.	D. A. (Doug)	Armstrong
H14883	LCpl.	E. N. (Elwood)	Birss
H17723	Sgt.	T.	Crook (Note 1)
		Rudy	Deutsch
	Capt.	C. S.	Frost
H18772	Pte.	L. A.	Hammerquist
B8374	Pte.	M. A. (Ben)	Kelter (Note 2)
B103156	Pte.	C. T. (Charlie)	King
M36916	Pte.	H. W.	Leonard (Note 1)
B68601	Pte.	L. V. (Lloyd)	Rains
C78197	Pte.	W. C. (Wally)	Smith
	Sgt.	Raymond (Andy)	Anderson (Note 3)

Ranks are given as at the end of WWII

NOTES

1. Regimental number not confirmed.
2. Ben Kelter is blind and was accompanied by his wife.
3. "Andy" Anderson is Post War. He represented the Aboriginal Veterans.

POSTSCRIPT TO CHAPTER XVII—2000

Someone once said, in connection with a baseball game: "It's not over till it's over." That *bon mot* also applies to the Pilgrimage of 2000. Indeed, I would add a corollary that in the case of this Anniversary, it never will be over. The memories will always remain fresh.

On May 23rd, whilst I was in Sicily, my wife received a call from a newspaper reporter in Holland who had seen that article stating I had no friends in Toronto—they were all in Holland. He wanted to know if that was true and if so, to offer his sympathy.

On June 27th, Jean-Guy Chapman, the efficient Director attached to the Minister's Party, phoned to say he had a photograph of the guests at the Reception given by Princess Margriet on May 7th. I was in the front rank and he was sending me a copy.

On July 18th, Ritse Reitsma and his wife Nan visited me in Toronto and gave me a beautiful Apeldoorn tie bearing the new logo, and a unique photograph he had taken of one of the last working windmills in Holland. Attached to one of the wings was a Canadian flag. Ritse patiently waited until the flag was it its highest point and snapped the photo. It is a remarkable piece of artistry and I am sure should be exhibited.

On October 30th, I received a huge package from Jan Schouten containing 31 original newspaper articles about the ceremonies in Achterveld and elsewhere; also the journal of the Regiment Huzaren, the local Militia Unit which had fought the Germans in Achterveld, a photo album of the Seaforth Highlanders of Holland and a colour photo of the Monument.

On November 10th, General Gijsbers sent me, "as an early Christmas present," a video of the Commemorations at Apeldoorn and Groesbeek Cemetery. This was a thoughtful act, as I had been too ill to attend the Groesbeek Service.

On November 17th, I received another gift from Jan Schouten—a video of the full Program at Achterveld including my speech at the Unveiling of the Monument. On the front of the cassette was a photo of Rudy Deutsch and me in colour.

It finally reached the stage that I was disappointed if the mailman passed by without leaving me a parcel or two. Actually, I was kept happily occupied sorting out all the wonderful articles, letters, photos and other material, as well as drafting letters of thanks for the gifts and the many kindnesses I had received in Holland. The problem (although

POSTSCRIPT TO CHAPTER XVII—2000

that is an ungracious word) was not to allow my letters to lapse into a stereotype form and at the same time to express my honest feelings of appreciation. Here are a few of the many letters I wrote.

June 6, 2000

General A.W.T. Gijsbers
Dear Andrew:

Just a quick note to let you know I arrived home safely May 31st, tired in the extreme, but happy that I was able to attend the Ceremonies despite the injunctions of my ex-Doctor!

May I offer my sincere congratulations on the superb job you did in organizing the Pilgrimage and seeing it through to a successful conclusion. From all sides, Veterans and Citizens, I heard nothing but accolades and approval during the entire week.

Thank you for giving me such personal attention when you were so involved with other matters. At every event you were always ready to guide me to my proper place—at the Reception at the Orpheus Theatre, the Unveiling, the Reception at the Palace, the Tattoo, the National Parade.

There were many highlights—Dinner at "Echoput" was a delightful experience and did much to put me at ease. Our "private audience" with HRH Princess Margriet and her husband in the garden before the other guests arrived was something very special. And, of course, being the Parade Commander was another highlight and a wonderful way to end my military career.

I was very honoured at the Tattoo when you arranged for me to receive the scores for my pieces from Sef Claessen and present them to the Bandmaster.

I believe I mentioned to you that Sef and his wife joined me for dinner prior to the Tattoo. I was happy to present him with some small gifts as a token of my appreciation for the great work he did in arranging the pieces and converting them from mediocre tunes to proper military music. He in turn surprised me by handing me the scores for my Anthem—Freedom. He is really a very fine chap.

I have only touched on some of the highlights and I could say much more. After I have recovered from my malaise, I will write again. Thank you, Andrew, for your kindness and for giving me so many wonderful memories.

Sincerely,

POSTSCRIPT TO CHAPTER XVII—2000

June 9, 2000

Mr. G. J. de Graaf
Dear Fred:

The party is over but for me the memories will always remain. As you know, I have returned to Holland many times since the War, going back to 1956. Each time I am overwhelmed by the tremendous respect, love and enthusiasm we Veterans receive from the people of Holland. I can't express how proud and thrilled we are to parade in your streets and see so many parents with their young children lining our route and waving Canadian flags.

In 1985, our Minister of Veterans Affairs, George Hees, expressed his feelings to HRH, Princess Margriet, when he said, "This is really a love story. The Dutch people make us feel like delivering angels."

That was 1985. But the words of George Hees are as true today as they were fifteen years ago and aptly describe the feelings of the Veterans throughout the week-long Celebrations in Apeldoorn. I am not so sure, however, that we are angels, but there is no doubt it is a love story!

I thought that the Reception in the Orpheus Theatre was one of the best I have attended. Your Master of Ceremonies put on a remarkable performance and you delivered a powerful speech. It is gratifying to know that in future years the Commemorations will be focused on young people. You have taught them the true meaning of freedom and they have learned it well. The torch has been passed to them and they will hold it high.

These Pilgrimages are now a unique part of our common heritage and will be marvelled at one hundred years from now. We will not be here, but the children of our grandchildren will be. They will never forget.

Thank you for including me in the events and presenting me with the lovely medal even though I was a "lone ranger," not attached to any group. Unfortunately, my sickness precluded me from attending every function or hanging on to the bitter end as I used to!

I enclose a nice picture of you escorting Princess Margriet to the Unveiling, which my daughter found on the internet.

Sincerely,

POSTSCRIPT TO CHAPTER XVII—2000

June 9, 2000

Mr. Evert Gerritsen
Dear Eef:

I made it home after a very exhausting trip to Sicily. I suppose I should have cancelled it, but I felt I couldn't let my Italian friends down.

You may not believe me when I say that for me this was the most significant Pilgrimage of them all. After all, fifty-five years is a very long time and memories do fade. But not in Apeldoorn. I could hardly believe the large, enthusiastic crowds that greeted the Veterans wherever we went. And, if I may say so, the pride and enthusiasm of the Veterans themselves was undiminished by the years. Perhaps it was because many of us, both Dutch and Canadians, realized this would be the last Pilgrimage and we all wanted to make it a good one. Well, it was magnificent in every way.

Of course, for me, having missed the Pilgrimage in '95, there was a gap of ten years since my last visit and I really didn't know what to expect. I was afraid that many of my friends would have lost interest or passed on. But I need not have worried. I received so many requests to lead parades, make speeches, give interviews, unveil monuments, attend dinners, that had I been young and healthy, they would have taxed my energies to the limit.

So I had a wonderful time even though due to my illness I was not able to take in all the events. Throughout the whole week there was one person who miraculously seemed to appear at every function and give me encouragement to carry on—my friend, Evert Gerritsen!

At Beekbergen, I saw you standing in the pouring rain as I drove by, and later met your grandson as well as your friend Herman Schaftenaar. At the Reception on May 1, there you were again as well as your son Eddie. On May 2, it was at the Unveiling of the Monument. On May 3, you and Iet joined me for lunch. On May 5, it was at the Tattoo and on May 7 at the Orpheus Theatre after the Parade. Finally, at the farewell party, I was pleasantly surprised when Herman Blom slapped me on the back to say hello.

No wonder that a newspaper reported that I have more friends in Holland than in Canada. That is perfectly true, but someone saw the article and phoned my wife to say he was sorry I had so few friends in Canada!

You were very kind and thoughtful to cut out all those

POSTSCRIPT TO CHAPTER XVII—2000

newspaper articles. I am having a Dutch friend in Toronto go through them and translate the ones of particular interest to the PPCLI. I may even have a few about the 48th Highlanders translated!

Sincerely,

June 9, 2000

Mr. Jan H.A. Koorenhof
Dear Jan:

At last I have a chance to put pen to paper and thank my friends for the wonderful time I had in Holland.

I am only sorry that due to my illness I could not accept all the invitations you so kindly offered me. I hope you will understand.

The attention I received made me feel like a V.I.P.—my old friend Lex Nordenbus picking me up and driving me to the Canadian Club—the Reception at the Orpheus Theatre, when I was seated in the front row and called to the stage to receive a CD of the Green Street Boys—the Unveiling of the Monument, when I was again placed in the front row.

Throughout it all, I detected the fine hand of one Jan Koorenhof behind the scenes, who seemed to have the knack of being everywhere at once and kept the whole thing rolling. Thank you my friend for taking such good care of me and congratulations on an outstanding job of organizing and executing the Liberation Ceremonies.

Sincerely,

As mentioned earlier, I regularly sent reports at the conclusion of each Pilgrimage to the Colonel of the Regiment who, up to June 2000, was MGen. D. W. Hewson, CMM, CD. I also sent reports to his successor General A.J.G.D. de Chastelain, OC, CMM, CH, CD.

* * *

My flight left Schiphol Airport, Amsterdam, on May 14th at 9:05 a.m. As the aircraft gained altitude, I glanced out the window to say a final goodbye to this wonderful land and its people. It was a bright, sunny day and the features stood out in proud relief—quaint Dutch homes and barns, tidy farmyards, verdant pastures, row upon row of tulips of every colour and hue. Even a lazy windmill waved its arms at me in solemn goodbye.

A great sadness overcame me. Would I ever come back again? I found myself softly humming a tune composed by a Canadian soldier:

POSTSCRIPT TO CHAPTER XVII—2000

Never, never again
Will that magic return
When we met in the springtime
And the world was at peace.

The fighting and starving were over
At last we could love and be loved
We pledged to each other
A new life together
And waited for the dawn.

The convoy came in the morning
And took me away from your arms
I'll never forget
But this I know
We'll never meet again.

Never, never again
Will that magic return
When we met in the springtime
And the world was at peace.

It was supposed to be a ballad about a Canadian soldier in Holland, in May 1945, just after the end of the war, and about the liberation of the Dutch people who had suffered terribly under the German occupation. Many had starved to death.

The Canadian soldier had fought with the First Division all through the Italian campaign. Near the end of the war, the Division was transferred to Holland and took part in the liberation of that country.

He fell in love with a Dutch girl and planned to marry. But his Division was sent to England and then home to Canada. He never returned.

I now have a confession to make. I was the soldier who had composed the ballad. When I was working on the two Marches for the Anniversary, the tune came to me and later the words. But I will frankly admit it was not a hit. The music was not bad but many people took exception to the words. The Veterans didn't like them because they belied the perceived image of myself and them as tough old Veterans with nary an ounce of romance in our tired old bones.

The Dutch people didn't like them because they were so melancholy. They reminded them of the terrible hardships they had endured.

My wife didn't like them because, so she said, everyone would assume I was writing about myself, and had left behind more than a lover. And anyway, who was she?

The force of these arguments soon persuaded me to abandon the piece. My reputation, as a composer, would have to rest on my Military Marches and other songs.

The aircraft continued to gain height and was soon over the Alps. A new country and a fresh adventure beckoned. My feeling of sadness faded. My spirits began to soar. Why had I thought I would never return to the country and people I loved so much? I remembered having that same kind of feeling after other Pilgrimages and each time I had returned.

I began to hum another tune I had learned in 1985:

Goodbye wonderful Holland
We do remember you too
Your friendship, warmth and your kindness
Make this a tearful adieu.

Oh, keep your home fires burning
In polder, town and farms
We'll soon return to you see you again
And hold you in our arms.

EPILOGUE I
TO CHAPTER XV

THE MISSING GERMANS
1945

It will be remembered that the re-enactment of the crossing of the Ijssel River was witnessed by thousands of spectators and given wide publicity in Dutch TV, radio and press. As a result, I had the pleasure of meeting many Dutch people during my visit and later receiving letters and photographs at my home in Toronto.

One person I met was Huub van Sabben. We had only a few moments to chat but he told me such an incredible, complex tale that it deserves a special section in my book.

Mr. van Sabben had been retained by the German or Dutch Government (I am not sure which one) to find the remains of hundreds of Germans who were allegedly killed in and around the Municipality of Voorst near the end of the War. He had made a careful study of the original crossing of the Ijssel River (code-named Cannonshot), on April 11th, 1945, and subsequent operations. He had found some German remains, mostly buried in the dykes of the river, and he showed me photographs. I am not going to describe them except to say it gave me a rather eerie feeling to meet the remains of an enemy I had fought against 45 years earlier.

Mr. van Sabben had also read my book and was fully acquainted with the role of my D Company in these operations. There were still many Germans unaccounted for, in the order of two or three hundred, and he wondered if I could help by sending him maps, orders and other materials I might still have in my possession. I was happy to oblige, and as soon as I returned home I sent him a letter.

June 19, 1990

Dear Mr. van Sabben:

As promised, I am writing a note to thank you for giving me the photos of the crossing of the Ijssel River on May 2nd. They are really excellent and will be valuable mementoes of this memorable and emotional event.

I am sorry we did not have more time to discuss the difficult task you have of locating the remains of German soldiers. I enclose a rather poor photocopy of my actual battle map showing the route my D Company took in the attack across the Ijssel and the subsequent capture of Wilp. I also enclose a photocopy of a map taken from Colonel Stacey's

EPILOGUE I TO CHAPTER XV

book, The Victory Campaign. *It is map No. 13 and shows in green the route taken by the PPCLI from its concentration area in Germany (after its arrival from Italy) to its final position in Achterveld.*

Your pictures of what you have found in the course of your work I found quite fascinating, and I have been telling my military friends, who are very interested.

I enjoyed our meeting and I look forward to hearing from you.

Yours Sincerely,

His reply gave me quite a shock.

Deventer
August 18, 1990

Dear Mr. Frost,

Thank you very much for your letter of June 19th, and for the photocopies of the maps.

In the search for the "disappeared Germans" I haven't made any progress. We've checked and re-checked all available information without success. In short I'll give you the known facts.

1. From an eye-witness, a former member of the Dutch Underground, who was attached to an Intelligence Section of Cdn. 7 Bde (Brig. Gibson), and who came over from the other side of the river to search for the leader of the Underground in Twello, I received the information, that when they came over the bridge in the afternoon of Friday, 13th April 1945, he saw near "WINNIPEG" German POWs collecting the bodies of their dead comrades in that area. He counted 20+ of them. In the Twello archive is a map which shows the places where bodies of Germans were recovered when the war was over. In the whole of the Voorst municipality 98 of them were found, none of them in the vicinity of "Winnipeg."

2. The Intelligence Section (under the late Sgt. Percy Weissman) went shortly afterwards to the Appense Woods, which your Coy helped to clear. They arrived there shortly after the fighting was done. On a path in those woods they spoke to a Canadian Captain. Here they saw how the bodies of killed Germans

> *were collected. These bodies were laid alongside that path in a large row, many of them on top of each other. In some places that row was three to five bodies high. He guessed he saw 150 to 200 dead Germans. On the Twello map there are five marks, all in the vicinity of the crossroads.*
>
> *A very clear view of what happened there is given in the War Diary of the Headquarters Saskatoon Light Infantry.*
> *"13 April 1945: Major Clough was in the BHQ for supper and reported everything going well with Lieut. Gowan's platoon having a particularly good shoot—killing about 50 Jerries with direct fire."*
> *The War Diary of B-Coy Saskatoons:*
> *"13 April 1945: ... at 1430 PPCLI sent out two carrier patrols to clear woods at map reference 8800. These patrols were led by a Wasp, followed by 2 MMG carriers. They both advanced 1.5 miles to the western edge of the woods, where they caught over 100 enemy fleeing across an open field at 876004. Both guns opened up at 200 yds range with great effect. We suffered no casualties."*
> *Maybe you can give some information about how to continue. Any names, addresses or whatever will be of the greatest help.*
> *I look forward to hear from you.*
>
> *Yours sincerely,*
Huub van Sabben

On first reading of his letter I was thankful our side had won the war, otherwise I might have ended up in the dock in a German War Crimes trial in Ottawa for causing a needless massacre. On second thought, I wanted to get my hands on that member of the Dutch Underground and the Intelligence Section which had counted 200 dead Germans in my D Company area. On a more rational third thought, I decided I had nothing to worry about and I wrote a sensible answer to these wild claims.

October 23, 1990

> *Dear Mr. van Sabben:*
> *Thank you very much for the pictures you "liberated" from Mr. Burgers, as well as the pictures you obtained from a local newspaper. I am at loss to express my appreciation for your kindness.*

EPILOGUE I TO CHAPTER XV

I have been doing some snooping around to see if I could find leads that would help you locate the "disappeared Germans." So far, I have not much to report but I offer the following suggestions:

1. *I don't think you will get much information from the members of the PPCLI because we were so busy fighting that we had no time to bury and record dead Germans. Also, we were constantly on the move. You refer to the area code-named "Winnipeg." This objective was captured by C Company under a Major Jones, who was a personal friend and might have shed some light on the 20+ bodies at Winnipeg, but unfortunately he passed away many years ago.*
2. *You also mentioned 150 to 200 dead Germans piled up in the Appense Woods which my D Company helped to clear. I really find it hard to believe that so many Germans were killed in that area. I can assure you that my Company did not have any such luck, or we would all have received medals. I do recall that our Carrier Platoon, under a Capt. W.N.J. Stutt, who were firing medium machine guns, had some pretty good shoots. However, I am certain that the platoon could not have cut down anything like the numbers suggested because I would certainly have heard about it!*
3. The Saskatoon Light Infantry. *You also mention this Battalion in your letter. I worked closely with them during the War and knew a number of their officers (including their Commanding Officers, Scott Dudley and Alan Embury), as I had grown up in Saskatoon. I am sure that most of them have long since passed away but you might be able to contact any survivors by writing the Mayor of Saskatoon, Saskatchewan, and asking his help. You could mention that I lived there 1930-1938 when my father was manager of The Bank of Nova Scotia and that I served in the PPCLI and suggested that you write to him.*
4. *I have been in touch with the Directorate of History in Ottawa who in turn made enquiries in our Archives. They advise they have no records of German dead but they suggest you write to the Head Office of the Commonwealth War Graves Commission, as follows:*
    2 Marlow Road
    Maidenhead
    Berkshire SL6 7DX England

EPILOGUE I TO CHAPTER XV

    5. *It occurs to me that the Canadian Embassy in The Hague might be of some help. Their address is:*
Sophialaan 7
P.P. Box 30820
2500 GV The Hague

Now that Germany is one, I suppose there will be a renewed interest in your work.
I will continue to keep my eyes and ears open and my nose to the ground in the hope of turning up some useful information for you. In the meantime, let's keep in touch.

Yours sincerely,

While I was awaiting Mr. van Sabben's response to my letter, I received a jolt from another quarter, a Mr. Boesveld from Twello. Like Mr. van Sabben he knew a great deal about the War and had read the *Official History of the Campaign in Northwest Europe* by C. P. Stacey, and *Once a Patricia*. His interest was not in locating the remains of German soldiers, but in commenting on my account of the fighting in Holland. However, he made a statement about graves of Germans at the crossroads in the Appense Woods which corroborated the Twello map mentioned in paragraph 2 of Mr. van Sabben's letter—"At the road junction at Appense Bossen (Woods) about 5 Germans were buried."

This was considerably less than the 200 bodies that a member of the Dutch Underground had allegedly seen, and I was greatly relieved

Mr. Boesveld also made another comment that I appreciated—that the Patricias were the first to cross the Ijssel River, not the 48th Highlanders. The following is an extract from his letter.

Twello, Dec. 4, 1990.

Sir,
From a person fully unknown to you, may you receive the best wishes for Christmas.
In the meantime, I enclose some postcards of Klarenbeek. I think it is not unknown to you. You see: the local windmill; the RK church and a piece of the "Appense Bossen," still a sand road as it was in 1945.

Reading your book "Once a Patricia," I had to try to contact you, the writer. From Mr. Burgers at Twello, I received the address and I am hopeful you are not disturbed about it. My English is not what it should be, sorry for this.

EPILOGUE I TO CHAPTER XV

>   *Your book makes it clear that the first who crossed the River Ijssel (Cannonshot) were the Patricias. From years back, when I was still a customs officer, I have been interested in that operation and I know the facts about the fight at Wilp, but it was of no interest to local historians.*
>
>   *Then came 1985 and the 48th Highlanders were celebrated, with pipes and bags, as the "Liberators." A monument at the crossing-place (which is rather the wrong place), was erected; another plate was fixed on the church wall at Wilp, with the remembrance to 48th Highlanders. The stone at the crossing-place bears the wrong date—12 April 1945!*
>
>   *When I said to local officials that it was wrong, the answer was that I did not know anything about it.*
>
>   *Then I went my own way and once more I visited Holten, the Canadian Grave Field and took photos of the stones of the "Pats," who died on 11th of April 1945. In May 1990, I gave some of these photos to Mr. Reitsma, to hand them over to you.*

For the remainder of his long letter (four closely spaced pages), Mr. Boesveld made some very informed comments on certain statements in my book, some of which I would have been happy to have included in the original text. He also asked for more information on a number of tactical and logistical matters, such as: the exact point where the PPCLI contacted the 49th British Division; where, exactly, did the Patricias concentrate after a night march through the woods—was it Beekbergen; what troops formed the bridgehead; did I have any idea who was the Bridge Construction Unit; did I know anything about the Grave-Company of the Canadian troops; did I have any air photos; and so on.

To properly answer all his questions would have filled another book.

Mr. Boesveld concluded his letter with a very informative account of the last day of the War for him and his family and a very touching description of the day the Germans "took his land."

>   *WHAT DID I SEE ON 14/15 APRIL, 1945*
>
>   *My parents' house is about 3 km south of the village of Klarenbeek. During the night of 14/15 April 1945, when we lived in the cellar, many Germans troops passed by to reach the canal Apeldoorn-Dieren; in the morning they blew the bridge.*
>
>   *At 1400 hours there passed a couple of German paratroops; they had been digging in during the night and morning in the neighbourhood.*

EPILOGUE I TO CHAPTER XV

At about 1500 hours three German soldiers entered our farm. They belonged to the SS-Polizei-Regiment, one of the most feared units in occupied Holland. They took off their winter clothes and sat down in mother's kitchen, wanting some food.

After that, they said to my parents that they wanted to wait for the night. Later on, it was clear that they liked to wait for the Canadians, to surrender. (A most unexpected statement by a Polizei member !!) My father asked them for their papers (paybook, etc.) which they handed over. Rather also unexpected; a German policeman giving his papers!

About 1900 hours Canadian troops came in the neighbourhood and my uncle asked them to come and take prisoner the unwanted Germans. Then a bren-gun-carrier came forward with a Vickers (Saskatoon?) and also about a platoon of infantry. The Germans were sent out of the kitchen as soon as the Canadians soldiers entered. One (called Karl Knott, from Duisburg) tried to escape but a Canadian soldier knocked him down. In the meantime, in the backyard, the other Germans were stripped of their watches; one of them was wearing three around his wrist. When all was over, two were placed on the carrier and Karl had to run in front of the vehicle.

Silence returned; for us the war was over.

WHEN THE GERMANS CAME
On 10 May 1940, I was a 10 year old boy. That first day that the Germans took our land, my father was killed in action as a full-corporal with The Royal Horse Artillery.

My mother became suddenly a widow and had to run a farm, only with the help of my grandfather, who died within six weeks. My mother remarried at the end of 1943.

During the war, she took in all kinds of "divers," amongst them two escaped Russians, P.O.W. She never got an award, she never asked for it, but she took the risk of life.

May this be the end for the moment.

Yours sincerely
P. Boesveld

How does one reply to such an informed, thoughtful letter, especially during a holiday in Florida! Furthermore, it wasn't the only letter I had received. Besides Mr. van Sabben's correspondence, several letters arrived from other Dutch people who had a keen interest in the

EPILOGUE I TO CHAPTER XV

war and were very knowledgeable about the part played by the Patricias. This may be difficult to believe, but it is true. In all the towns and villages that were liberated by Canadian soldiers, the local citizens have made it almost a solemn duty to study the campaign which brought them freedom.

In the case of Mr. Boesveld, I am ashamed to say I could not, at that point, give him the reply he deserved. However, I did my best.

Longboat Key, Florida
January 13, 1991

Dear Mr. Boesveld:

What a nice surprise to receive your letter of December 4th! It came with the Christmas mail and was forwarded to me here in Florida where I am enjoying a holiday. Hence the delay in sending you a reply.

You are certainly a serious student of military history, particularly the part played by the Canadians in Holland, and you ask some very interesting and pertinent questions. But I cannot be of much help right now. First of all, my own sources and references on which my book is based are at my home in Toronto. Secondly, my records would not have the details you require and I am not sure where I could find the answers. Neither is my memory of things that happened forty-five years ago equal to the task!

I have taken the liberty of forwarding a copy of your letter to a friend of mine in Holland, a Mr. van Sabben, who is also very interested in the Canadian operation in Holland, particularly the possible location of German graves. His address is the following:

Mr. Huub van Sabben
Bastion 24
7411 D. B.
Deventer, Netherlands

You are probably right about the girl in the Underground. She spoke only a few words of English and I may have misunderstood her.

I am sorry I cannot be of more help at this time. However when I return to Toronto I will try to find the time to do some more research but it will not be for several weeks. In the meantime, perhaps you will contact Mr. van Sabben.

It was sad to learn that you lost your father in the war. That terrible conflict seems to have touched almost everyone who lived during those days. And now we are faced with

> *another madman who wants to bring us all to the brink of another Armageddon. It has been truly said that—"Plus ça change, plus c'est la même chose"!*
> *With my best wishes for a Happy New Year.*
> Yours sincerely,

I also owed Mr. van Sabben a letter:

> Longboat Key, Florida
January 13, 1991
>
> *Dear Mr. van Sabben:*
> *Thank you very much for your nice Christmas card. I trust we will have a Happy New Year, but with Saddam Hussein on the rampage, 1991 may be a very difficult and unhappy time.*
> *I have recently received a letter from a gentleman in Twello who has read my book and appears to know a great deal about the Canadian assault across the Ijssel River and "Operation Cannonshot." His name and address are:*
> > *Mr. P. Boesveld*
> > *Groen v Prinstererstraat 15*
> > *7391 KS Twello*
>
> *I enclose a copy of his letter dated December 4th.*
> *I thought his comments would interest you, particularly his statement that "At the Road junction at Appense Bossen, known as Groen-Allee, about 5 Germans are buried."*
> *I advised Mr. Boesveld to get in touch with you in the hope that you both might gain some useful information that would be to your mutual benefit.*
> *With my warmest regards.*
> Yours sincerely,

In the meantime, Mr. van Sabben had sent me another letter wherein he disclosed that he had undertaken another matter – the identification of an Australian pilot who was murdered by the German SS.

> Deventer, 10 December 1991
>
> *Dear Mr. Frost:*
> *Thank you for your beautiful card of the trapped whales.*
> *I've been very busy the past few months, but unfortunately I didn't succeed in finding the disappeared Germans we were looking for. So be it. I wrote a report on this matter to the burgomaster of Voorst.*

EPILOGUE I TO CHAPTER XV

In Voorst are enormous stocks of ammunition hidden in the ground and in some of the waters. The removal of these items cost a huge amount of money. In Holland every burgomaster has to pay a percentage of the costs.

Another interesting matter which I have undertaken is the identification of an Allied pilot who was killed in the village of Klarenbeek in 1944. This "Aussie" was murdered by the SS, and after the war buried as an unknown soldier. I have good hope to give this poor fellow his name back. Concerning this case, I wrote reports to the British and Australian authorities who are now researching in their countries.

Yours sincerely,
Huub van Sabben

My last communication from Huub van Sabben was a letter of January 15th, 1993, in which he confirmed that the problem of the alleged massacre of Germans had been resolved by a visiting Patricia, Dick Hughes!

The sad case of the murdered Aussie pilot remained outstanding and would probably never be solved.

Huub had, however, come across another case of a missing P.O.W., a Canadian, No. 18293, Pte. Stanley E. Cuppes. This is Huub's letter to me:

Deventer
15 January 1993

Dear Mr. Frost:

A few weeks ago, we received a phone call from a farmer in Wilp, Mr. Diks, who had a Canadian visitor. It turned out to be Dick Hughes who was with BCoy in Wilp. We showed him our videotape with the Canadian newsreels about Zutphen, Deventer and Wilp. He knew a lot of people on this film and a lot of places shown.

I believe he solved our little problem concerning the clearance of the Appensche Woods, and the killing of those large numbers of Germans on Friday the 13th, April, 1945. He pointed out that his "group" reached their objective at the crossroads and that they saw many, many Germans running like madmen on the road to Klarenbeek. Their intention was to go after them but the presence of a German tank or SP gun on the side of this road, some distance away, which was covering their retreat, prevented

EPILOGUE I TO CHAPTER XV

them from doing so. One or two carriers from the Saskatoons, armed with Vickers guns, were called forward and they opened fire from a great distance (1,500 to 2,000 yards). Through binoculars they could see that many were hit.

About my enquiry concerning the Aussie pilot who is missing from Klarenbeek, I'm a bit disappointed. The British will do nothing about it, although he flew in a RAF-Squadron. I feel that they just don't care. So it is all up to myself to prove this case, or the findings of the Australian authorities. Maybe you can help me?

I recently found out that the Germans, on the farm where P/O Bell was held after being shot down on 9 September 1994, had a Canadian POW, who they had brought from France on their retreat.

His name was Private Stanley E. Cuppes (18293) 7 Field Coy, Royal Canadian Engineers. He was POW near Rouen, France, at the end of August 1944.

Is there any way to trace this man? Do you have any suggestions who I can write to? Letters to the Min. of Veterans Affairs remain unanswered. He is my last hope, because many of the Germans involved (from the SS-Div. Hohenstaufen) were not to be found by the Allied War Crimes Investigation teams from 1945 till 1948 (the year this case was closed). Investigations in Germany were also negative. One of the persons who was on that farm died a few years ago.

I'd be very pleased if you can help me. In the meantime I wish you and your family all the best in good health and I hope to meet again in Holland.

Yours sincerely,
Huub van Sabben

Again, I was faced with a problem I could not solve and I felt very badly that I could not help my friend. He had written the Minister of Veterans Affairs but received no reply. In retrospect, I should have written the Minister myself or the Commonwealth War Graves Commission. As I intimate in my reply to Huub, there were a thousand reasons why I had not written sooner and a thousand more why I could not, at that point, spare the time to follow up the matter. This is my letter.

EPILOGUE I TO CHAPTER XV

March 25, 1993

Dear Mr. van Sabben:

I am sorry it has taken me so long to reply to your letter of January 15th. There are a thousand reasons why I have not written sooner but I am not going to waste your time explaining them.

First, let me thank you for sending the five excellent photos of Holten Canadian War Cemetery. The idea of placing lighted candles on the graves is indeed a wonderful thought. I have shown the photos to several veterans and they were deeply moved.

I do not remember Dick Hughes but I am glad he helped to solve the problem of the Appensche Woods. I knew it couldn't possibly be my D Coy who killed so many Germans and always thought it was due to the good shooting of the Saskatoon Light Infantry.

I looked up my Regimental Records of the PPCLI and found that one R.B. Hughes No. M36553 joined the PPCLI on May 25, 1944, in Italy and was struck off strength as a corporal on June 15th, 1945. Whether this is the same person as your friend I do not know.

With regard to the Australian pilot, I am sorry to say that your experience with the British is becoming all too common with government authorities now that the War has been over for 48 years. I am afraid that our government will be of no help in tracing either P/O Bell or Stanley E. Cuppes.

Thank you for your best wishes. As I mentioned in my Christmas card, I am planning to attend the "Final Pilgrimage" to Holland in 1995 and will certainly make a point of looking you up.

With my kindest regards to you and your family.

Yours sincerely,

Not only did I fail to help my friend to trace the missing soldier, but I also defaulted in my plans to see him in 1995. A higher obligation had to take precedence.

I am pleased to report that Huub understood my failure and default and we became close pen pals. Each Christmas we exchanged cards. Finally, on the great 2000 Pilgrimage, we met again, after a lapse of ten years. All my transgressions were forgiven, but I believe that the fact I was the Parade Commander and was escorted by a beautiful Mountie (female, of course) may have had something to do with it. In any event, he wrote on his Christmas card:

EPILOGUE I TO CHAPTER XV

So good those few happy moments at the Apeldoorn Parade. And how that Mountie looked! Great! Hope we meet again someday. Good health!!

We continued to send each other Christmas cards. Huub always mentioned the Apeldoorn Parade and expressed the hope we would meet again.

I felt the same way, but deep down I realized the chances were slim and getting slimmer each year. I wondered too if Huub had been successful in his quest to identify the Aussie pilot and "give the poor fellow his name back."

On October 24th, 2003, my doubts were resolved. On that day I received a telephone call from Holland. "Hello, is that you, Syd? This is Huub van Sabben, I am coming to Canada next month to visit a friend who lives in Kincardine. Can I see you?"

The thrill of hearing from my friend can easily be imagined. We soon settled on a date and he gave me some incredible news: He had identified the Aussie pilot, and his remains had been re-interred with due ceremony in the presence of relatives from Australia.

The date of our meeting was November 13th, at one o'clock, for lunch at The Granite Club, to be followed by a quick visit to my apartment to view my "Dutch Memorabilia" acquired over the past fifty years. But I had forgotten about that "Master Disrupter of Events"— Field Marshall Fate.

On November 13th at 9:00 a.m., Huub phoned from Kincardine to say he would not be able to see me. A severe winter storm with gale-force winds, hail pellets and heavy snow had hit the area. Power lines were down and some highways were closed. (Kincardine is a small town on the east shore of Lake Huron, south of the Bruce Peninsula.)

This was crushing news for both of us, but Huub said that if the storm abated he would try to drive to Toronto, as he had to catch his plane at seven o'clock that evening. But there would not be time to visit me.

At three o'clock my phone rang. It was the concierge. "There is a Mr. Sabben here to see you."

Somehow my friend had bested the elements and we had a joyous reunion. He was accompanied by his wife, Henriette, and a Mr. Jan Koster, who had been a Resistance Fighter in the Dutch Underground. Now 85 years old, this doughty warrior had been recognized by the Kincardine Branch of the Canadian Legion and made an Honorary Member. During WWII he had been attached to the Intelligence Section of the 7th Canadian Infantry Brigade that had crossed the Ijssel River on 13th April, 1945, two days after my D Company had assaulted across the river. He was also the person who had counted all those dead Germans!

There was no point in spoiling our happy meeting by dredging up that episode and so we spoke of other matters. Huub gave me a full report of his success in identifying the Aussie pilot. For years he had corresponded with the Australian and British Governments but they had no records of the missing airman. Then Huub had an inspiration. The remains of the pilot had been clothed in the uniform of a Sergeant in the RAF. Huub's queries had always referred to a Sgt. Bell.

Huub renewed his search, this time giving the airman an officer's rank. Incredibly, the missing pilot was identified! Unknown to him, he had been promoted to officer just before his death. Apparently, both the British and Australian Governments keep separate lists for Officers and NCOs!

It was time for my friend to leave for the airport. As we were saying goodbye, he reached in his bag and produced two lovely Delft plates, one for me and one for my wife. They now rest among my souvenirs of wonderful Holland—tangible reminders of Huub Sabben who has done so much for the airmen and soldiers who liberated his country.

Once again I was overwhelmed by the friendship, warmth and kindness of another Dutch friend. Impulsively, I guided him, his wife and Jan to the piano, sat down, and began to play that beautiful Dutch Anthem, "Wilhelmus," followed by "Goodbye Wonderful Holland." The enthusiastic singing drowned out any false chords of the piano player.

EPILOGUE II
TO CHAPTER XVI

TEXEL AND THE GEORGIANS (RUSSIANS)
1945

It will be remembered that in March 1995, I became involved in what I termed an "Agatha Christie" mystery. I received a call from a Mr. Wilhelm Bakker of Texel, a small island off the northwest tip of Holland, asking me to attend a symbolic re-enactment of the landing of the PPCLI on his Island at the end of the War. He even intimated that I might join him in a parachute jump! He claimed that a Lt. Gord Grant of the PPCLI and 50 men had landed on Texel on or about May 22nd, 1945, and stopped the fighting between Georgian troops who had been conscripted into the German Army, and their German officers.

This was all news to me. I had never heard of the Texel incident and I was certain that Lt. Grant, whom I knew, and 50 of his men had not taken part in any such escapade in May 1945.

We were too busy rounding up Germans in Bloemendaal, where we were billeted, and in the adjoining coastal area.

To be certain that I had not been drinking too much Bols gin at the time, I checked with NDHQ in Ottawa and they had no record of the PPCLI ever landing on Texel. Neither did the Historical Section.

In all conscience, I could not accept Mr. Bakker's kind offer to represent the PPCLI at the forthcoming re-enactment (even though he had offered to pay for my flight!).

I let the matter drop until May 4th, 2002, when I happened to be browsing through an issue of the *Nederlandse Courant*, a Dutch Canadian Bi-Weekly newspaper, and read this article:

De Nederlandse Courant
May 04, 2002, Volume 48 Issue 09

Back to Texel after 55 years:

TREMENDOUS WELCOME FOR
RETURNING LIBERATORS
By Ger Graaskamp
On May 5, 1945, the German armies in The Netherlands surrendered and officially the war ended at that time. On Texel however the fighting lasted until May 20th, when about 100 members of the First Canadian Survey Regiment,

EPILOGUE II TO CHAPTER XVI

Royal Canadian Artillery sailed to Texel, disarmed the Germans and sent them to the mainland as prisoners of war. That was the last military action by Canadian troops in The Netherlands.

The cause of the extended war on Texel was a group of Georgian (Russian) soldiers, formerly taken prisoners of war by the Germans. The treatment they had received from the Germans had been horrible; they had been treated as if they were animals.

In February 1945 about 800 of them came to Texel after the Germans had persuaded them to switch sides. They had little choice. They put on German uniforms but they kept on hating their oppressors. On April 5th, they rebelled and attacked the German troops killing a large number of them. The Germans however were too strong even though the Dutch population was on the side of the Georgians and helped them wherever they could at great danger to themselves.

The Germans took no prisoners, they killed their enemies on the spot where they caught them. About 800 Germans, 565 Georgians and 117 civilians lost their lives during the fighting.

When on May 5 the Germans put down their arms in the rest of Holland those on Texel refused to disarm; they knew they would have been set upon by the civilian population and the remaining 225 Georgians. There was a lot of tension which only disappeared on May 20 with the arrival of the Canadians.

One of the Canadian soldiers involved in the action on Texel was Andre Bernier from London. He and his Canadian comrades left Texel after less than two weeks and he kept wondering ever since what happened to Texel during the last few months of the war.

About 5 years ago he wrote to us asking for information about what happened on Texel. We published his letter and he got a lot of information from several of our readers. Since leaving Texel he always had a wish to sometime go back to that island and what he found out strengthened that wish. Finally he got his wish. He and other surviving members from his regiment were invited to Texel to attend the 55th anniversary celebrations of Texel during May of 2000.

In 1945 there were about 100 men who had a share in the liberation of Texel but Mr. Bernier could find only two other

EPILOGUE II TO CHAPTER XVI

> survivors, Alex Rezanowich from London and Phil Levine from Calgary.
> So, after 55 years, the three Canadians returned to Texel. There they received a tremendous welcome; literally everybody did their utmost to make their visit a memorable one. Going by Mr. Bernier's reaction, "We were treated as if we were royalty," they succeeded.

This was incredible news indeed. I lost no time getting in touch with Andre Bernier, through the office of the *Nederlandse Courant*. He was very happy to hear of my interest in Texel and the Georgians and confirmed the report I had read in the paper. He had made a lifetime hobby of gathering information, material and pictures of the part played by his First Canadian Survey Regiment in the liberation and occupation of Texel. The operation began on May 20th, 1945, and was the last action of the Canadian Army in WWII.

Understandably, he was very proud of what his Regiment had accomplished in this "Unknown War" and said he would be happy to send me copies of some of his papers.

By sheer coincidence, a few weeks before making contact with Mr. Bernier, I had received the latest issue of *The Patrician*, the annual Journal of the PPCLI. I had only time to skim through my copy, but I suddenly recalled seeing a short article in the Archives Section about Texel. After my talk with Mr. Bernier. I quickly re-read the article, which had now assumed a new importance.

The Patrician 2001

> Scottish researcher Alan Newark has asked that anyone who remembers the Texel (Tessel)—Georgian incident in Holland in 1945, please e-mail him with their recollections.
> In April 1945, 600 Georgians rose against the German garrison on the NW Holland Island of Tessel killing some 1,800 Germans and wounding 200 others. On 17 June 1945, Lt. F.E. Mooney of the PPCLI with a small party of soldiers escorted the 250 survivors from Texel to Den Helder and over the causeway into northern Holland. Lt Col Tweedsmuir accompanied the party.

Had the missing link to the PPCLI that I had searched for in vain in 1995 been found? I couldn't remember any Lt. Mooney having been with the Regiment. So I checked my records and discovered that No. L9949, Lt. F. E. Mooney, had joined the Patricias on 28 May 1945 and been SOS 18 July 1945. Then I remembered that during this period a

EPILOGUE II TO CHAPTER XVI

great change of personnel had taken place. Most of the "Old Guard" officers left for new postings with the Army of Occupation in Germany or with the Far East Force. Their places were taken by officers from other units. This would explain why I had not met Lt. Mooney. Furthermore, each Rifle Company was billeted in a separate area.

I immediately sent the article in *The Patrician* to Andre Bernier and he responded with a mass of information and pictures about his original occupation of Texel on May 20th, 1945, and his return to the Island in May 2000. One of the most revealing documents was a copy of a letter written by LCol. Tweedsmuir on June 16th, 1945, on behalf of the Commander of First Canadian Corps, LGen. Foulkes.

HEADQUARTERS 1ST CANADIAN CORPS
16 Jun 45
In The Field
TO WHOM IT MAY CONCERN:
ACTION OF SOVIET TPS ON TEXEL ISLAND

In connection with the movement of 226 SOVIET soldiers from TEXEL ISLAND to the RUSSIAN camp near WILHELMSHAVEN, it is desired to bring to the attention of the SOVIET HIGH COMMAND the assistance received by Canadian tps from this group from the 6 Apr 45 to the capitulation.

When on 6 Apr 45, this group was ordered to fight the English, they rose up against the Germans. The 700 GEORGIANS fought 4,000 Germans for three days. The Germans then bombarded the Island from DEN HELDER with heavy weapons, resulting in much damage being done to buildings and considerable casualties to civilians. The Germans then landed tanks, mortars and heavy weapons, and the SOVIET group withdrew to prepare defensive positions from which they withstood every German onslaught for over a month, when, with ammunition gone, their Commander ordered them to break out in small groups and carry on the fight as partisans.

This lasted until 21 May 45, when Canadian troops landed on the Island. The SOVIET tps then assisted the Canadians to round up and disarm the remaining Germans, and were permitted to retain weapons for their protection.

During the course of the above engagements, the Soviet Gp sustained casualties amounting to 470 killed, 13 seriously wounded, and 40 others wounded. The German casualties are estimated at about 2347. It is significant to note

EPILOGUE II TO CHAPTER XVI

that the enemy capitulated, the Soviet group sustained about 200 casualties when assisting to round up the enemy tps. These are included in the casualty figures given above.

It is felt that the assistance rendered to the Allied Cause generally, and to the 1st Canadian Corps in particular, by this group was of inestimable value. The great courage displayed against overwhelming odds when ordered to fight against the Allies, and the determined will to resist to the last, despite their desperate position at that time, is to be highly commended.

Since the cessation of hostilities this group has remained on the Island pending arrangements for their return, and has displayed a spirit of discipline and behaviour which would be a credit to any corps. An excellent spirit of cooperation with Canadian HQ has pervaded in all dealings with us and in spite of the fact that it is their misfortune to have to wear the despised uniform of the enemy, we feel that they are entitled to all the honours of a brave and dauntless Ally.

I have the honour to be, sir,
Tweedsmuir, Lt-Col
For (C. Foulkes) Lt.Gen
Comd 1 Cdn Corps

Andre Bernier's letter to me sheds some light on the involvement of the Patricias in this Operation.

Dear Mr. Frost, Q.C.,

I am going to try and answer your letter to the best of my knowledge, and your request about the final weeks of the liberation of Texel Island.

Perhaps there is a little confusion about the dates of the soldiers of the PPCLI going over to Texel. On the 20th of May 1945, it was our boys, (including myself) of the First Canadian Survey Regiment, RCA, who went to Texel, so as to disarm and remove all the Germans from Texel. That part of the mission took no more than 10 days. After completing our work with the Germans, and having them all on the mainland at Den Helder, the First Canadian Corps sent a certain group of Canadian soldiers, along with supplies, such as food and fuel. Life was pretty hard on Texel for several weeks.

The letter of Lt.Col Tweedsmuir, dated the 16th of June 1945, was sent nearly a full month after the arrival on Texel of the First Cdn. Survey Regt. And, at that time, perhaps some of the PPCLI soldiers were involved in assisting the Texel population, and also in helping to transport what was left of the Georgians on Texel. Our job was to take care of the Germans, and later other troops came to the Island of Texel so as to help the Georgians.

You can see for yourself, Mr. Frost, that the Georgians were of great help to our boys upon landing on Texel. We had some of the Georgians help us by showing where the Germans were. One big job was to find the mine fields.

By what I can read on the small "Patrician clipping" you sent me, it is very possible that on the 17 June 1945, Lt. F.E. Mooney of the PPCLI with a small party of soldiers escorted the Georgian survivors from Texel to Den Helder. They were our allies, and they had to be repatriated to their own country. Most of them were very well received when they got back home. Since the end of the war, many Georgians who were on Texel, returned as tourists. The people of Texel received them always as heroes, just as they do for the Canadians. But unfortunately, as you can see by the many papers I am sending you, only three of us from the 1st Cdn. Survey Regt., have managed to return to Texel, and it was 55 years after we had liberated the Island of Texel.

To tell you the truth Mr. Frost, why I went all out to find what was written about the final liberation of Texel, was because in most cases they write the names of Infantry Regiments and never anything good is said about the Artillery Regiments. In this case, Texel was liberated by the First Canadian Survey Regiment, RCA. I really am happy that finally an Artillery Regiment was named for completing that mission.

* * *

My final act in trying to solve the mystery of Texel Island was to get in touch with the Curator of the PPCLI Archives, a step I should have taken seven years earlier when I received that strange call from Mr. Bakker.

The Archives held a wealth of material on Texel and have been in active correspondence with Alan Newart, a researcher living in Scotland, who is writing a book on the Texel Operation. The Archives sent me copies of this correspondence as well as photos taken of the Germans and Georgians as they were being removed from the Island and transported to Den Helder.

EPILOGUE II TO CHAPTER XVI

Included in the material was a copy of the entry in the PPCLI War Diary for June 17th, 1945.

> *PPCLI WAR DIARY*
> *BLOEMENDAAL, HOLLAND*
> *17 JUN 45*
> *Weather—A perfect summer day.*
> *A large party of Russians, taken from the Island of Tessel of northwest HOLLAND, was escorted by a party i/c of Lt F.E. MOONEY, to DEN HELDER and over the causeway into northern HOLLAND. They numbered around 250 and are the survivors of some 600 (members of the TODT Organization), who, at the conclusion of the war, rose in arms against the garrison of 2700 Germans. The final census of TESSEL revealed 250 Russians, 500 German PW and 200 German wounded. The remaining 1800 Germans were killed.*
> *The party was accompanied by Lt.Col Lord Tweedsmuir, who is to make clear to the Russian authorities what a valuable job they have done and to recommend clemency for their former collaboration with the enemy.*
> *Church services were held in the old Patricia Club at 0915 hrs and 1000 hrs.*

The Archives also gave some information about the long perilous journey of the Texel Georgians to their homeland and the mixed receptions they received—fascinating reading but beyond the scope of this book.

While much of the original mystery surrounding the participation of the PPCLI in the events described has now been solved, there still remain some grey areas and some unanswered questions:

1. When did the Patricias actually land on Texel and how long did they stay?
2. Did they bring supplies of food and fuel for the local population and help them restore order?
3. Were the Georgians made to march across the causeway to their final destination, like the Germans, or were they transported in lorries? Some of the photos in the Archives show the Georgians beside long lines of army vehicles.
4. What was the final destination of the PPCLI? Some of the correspondence in the Archives suggests that it may have been Wilhelmshaven or Oldenburg.
5. How were the PPCLI conveyed?

6. Did the PPCLI and/or LCol. Tweedsmuir make contact with the Russian representatives who ultimately took charge of the Georgians?
7. How long were the PPCLI group with the Georgians and when and where did they return to the Regiment?
8. And why were the PPCLI (and in particular Lt. Mooney) chosen for this difficult but important task?
9. Did Lt. Mooney speak Russian? (Soon after he returned he was SOS.)
10. Is there a nominal roll of the Group?
11. Are any still living?

EPILOGUE III
TO CHAPTER XVII

THE MAN WITH TWO HATS
THE OTTAWA MONUMENT
MAY 11TH, 2002

One of the highlights of the Pilgrimage in 2000 was the unveiling of the National Canadian Liberation Monument in Apeldoorn on May 2nd, as described in Chapter XVII. The statue became known as "The Man with Two Hats."

On that occasion, General Gijsbers, Chairman of the Foundation Liberation 1945, expressed the hope that a similar monument would be erected in Ottawa. On May 11th, 2002, his desire was fulfilled. In the presence of distinguished representatives from Holland and Canada, HRH Princess Margriet unveiled another statue, identical to the one in Apeldoorn.

The hour-long Ceremony began with a powerful speech by General Gijsbers in which he reviewed the role of the Canadian Army in liberating the people of Holland after five years of persecution, fear, murder and starvation. He then described the tremendous gratitude and joy of the Dutch people and their desire to erect this monument as a lasting tribute to their Canadian Liberators.

The Canadian Minister of Veterans Affairs, Dr. Rey Pagtakhan, thanked Princess Margriet for her continuing interest in Canada's Veterans.

He reminded the assembly that HRH was born during the War in a hospital not far from the site of the Monument. "She's our Princess too," a very young member of a youth group at the Ceremony had told him. "She was born in Canada."

The Ceremony concluded with a very thoughtful and moving "Dutch Touch"—the Christening of the "Canadian Liberation Tulip." Pieter Beelaerts van Blokland, former Mayor of Apeldoorn, Queen's Commissioner for the Province of Utrecht and President of the National Committee "Thank you Canada," delivered an inspiring address, as he has so often done in the course of his distinguished career. "Citizens of Canada," he declared, "Words fail to express my sentiments on this occasion. We Dutch people do remember the sacrifices of your young soldiers. We will never forget."

Referring to the new tulip, he said it was a symbol of love as well as of freedom and democracy. And like our soldiers, it came from a sturdy breed. Princess Margriet herself was named after a flower that

Queen Wilhelmina had chosen as a symbol of resistance against tyranny.

Then HRH came forward and "christened" a bed of the new tulips with a bottle of champagne!

In the course of the proceedings, three persons received special commendation for the time and effort they had devoted to the project. The name Jan Koorenhof often appears in these pages. For three years he served as Chairman of the committee responsible for erecting the Monument.

The name Jean-Guy Chapman is also a familiar one in connection with the 2000 Pilgrimage. As a member of the Department of Veterans Affairs, he was the Project Director and contributed much to the success of that Pilgrimage. He also served as a member of the Canadian Committee that made the arrangements for the erection of the Monument in Ottawa.

Mrs. Ada Wynston, of Toronto, was also a member of the Canadian Committee. For many years she has devoted her time and energy on behalf of Canadian Veterans and the Pilgrimages. She was born in Holland and has never forgotten how Canada's soldiers liberated her country and put an end to the horrors of the Holocaust.

It will be observed that unlike the preceding chapters of the book, this account of the Ottawa Unveiling is given on a rather impersonal basis. The reason is I was not present. I had been a keen supporter of the project and was looking forward to attending the Ceremony. But that indefatigable "spoiler of plans," my bête noire, Field Marshal Fate, intervened and laid me low with a PMR attack and other ailments. However, I watched the whole ceremony on TV. The CBC put on a fine show with commentary by that durable historian, Jack Granatstein, and flashbacks to the 1995 Pilgrimage. Fortunately, my son-in-law taped the program and it is another treasured souvenir of my "Dutch Connection."

But if the CBC excelled themselves, the Canadian Press were a disgrace and embarrassed the Dutch people and Canada. Not a line appeared in Canadian newspapers except in Quebec, where a full account appeared in the Gazette and one other paper. And yet the press had been duly informed of the Ceremony and many press photographers were present.

In my view, the Ceremony was another historic occasion in the ever-growing friendship and love that the people of Holland have for Canadian Veterans and for Canada itself. If any further evidence of this cherished bond between our countries is needed, I can do no better than quote the speech of General Gijsbers given at the Ceremony.

EPILOGUE III TO CHAPTER XVII

*ADDRESS ON THE OCCASION OF THE UNVEILING OF THE NATIONAL CANADIAN LIBERATION MONUMENT AT OTTAWA, 11 MAY 2002.
By LtGen RNLA (ret) A.W.T. Gijsbers, Chairman of the Foundation Liberation '45 at Apeldoorn, Netherlands*

Your Royal Highness, Mr. Pieter van Vollenhoven, Excellencies, Ladies and Gentlemen,

Two years ago, on May 2nd 2000, H.R.H. Princess Margriet of the Netherlands unveiled the National Canadian Liberation Monument at Apeldoorn, the Netherlands. The ceremony was attended by a great number of Canadian and Dutch authorities, many of whom are here today, and by numerous Canadian veterans of World War II. In my speech on that occasion, I referred to our intention to emphasise the importance of the bonds between Canada and the Netherlands by erecting the same monument in Ottawa, but I also added that the prospects at that time were not bright because of the lack of financial means. However—so I said—"We keep trying! I firmly believe in miracles!"

Today the miracle has happened. In a moment H.R.H. will unveil the counterpart of our Dutch monument here in Ottawa.

In World War II Canadian commanders were not quite happy with the role attributed to them by the Supreme Allied Commander General Eisenhower. Canadian formations were to operate on the left flank of the allied advance. Their task was NOT to break through to the heart of Germany, but to clear the ports of France, Belgium and the Netherlands, where the retreating German armies had left pockets of stubborn resistance. Of course, the good aspect of this is that your troops thus became the liberators of a large part of the Netherlands.

In October and November 1944, Canadian units were engaged in fierce battles in the provinces of Noord Brabant and Zeeland, often suffering severe losses. A very sad example is "Black Friday," Friday 13 October 1944, when the Canadian Black Watch Regiment had 180 casualties on a total strength of about 800 men.

Later, in the spring of 1945, after having cleared the German Reichswald, the Canadian II Corps crossed the Rhine and advanced towards the northern provinces of Groningen and Friesland, followed by the I Corps, which

EPILOGUE III TO CHAPTER XVII

advanced through the province of Gelderland to the line Amersfoort—Wageningen, and after the German capitulation on 5 May to the western part of the Netherlands.

In this way, apart from the southeastern region, practically the whole of our country was liberated by Canadian forces. Almost 6000 Canadian soldiers gave their lives in these operations; they lie buried in three cemeteries in the Netherlands. Many Canadian units continued to stay until the spring of 1946. They assisted the Dutch government in the reconstruction of roads and bridges, in clearing minefields, in collecting German equipment, and even in the harvest in the summer of 1945. During this entire period the Headquarters of the First Canadian Army were located in the town of Apeldoorn.

Liberation after five years of occupation, five years of food scarcity and hunger, five years of oppression and fear, five years of persecution and the murder of 100,000 Jews and many other Dutchmen, five years of reluctant resignation and determined resistance—that liberation caused a tremendous wave of joy among the Dutch people. The important role of the Canadian forces in the liberation also prompted intense feelings of gratitude towards them.

Joy and gratitude: these emotions have been active ever since 1945. In the latest decades, as the war generation had the time to look back and reflect, these feelings only have increased in intensity.

In 1980, '85, '90, '95 and again in 2000, we have been able to express our feelings by receiving Canadian veterans in our homes and by cheering them during their parades and march pasts. Hundreds of thousands of Dutchmen of all ages applauded when Canadian veterans marched through the streets of Apeldoorn, and you, Your Royal Highness, took their salute.

But, we also became aware of the fact that the number of active veterans decreases steadily and that the time had come to express our feelings of joy and gratitude in another, a permanent way, in a monument.

Initiatives to that effect, both with the Foundation Liberation '45 and among private citizens, led to the formation of a Committee for the National Canadian Liberation Monument, a committee which worked extremely hard for three years under the inspiring leadership of Mr. Jan Koorenhof. A sculptor was selected, Mr. Henk Visch, whose design, popularly known as "The Man with the Two

EPILOGUE III TO CHAPTER XVII

Hats," was admired by all concerned. I trust that shortly, having seen it, you will share their admiration. The monument was placed at a very prominent location in Apeldoorn.

The attractiveness of a piece of art is, of course, that one may have his own interpretation and his own feelings about it. Undoubtedly the viewers will experience a sort of mystery, when they reflect upon the significance of this monument.

Seeing it, you will recognise a somewhat mysterious figure. From a distance he shows an abundance of joy; on closer approach, however, he reflects meditation and melancholy.

The figure waves two hats—a mystery in itself! At the end of the war one was lucky to have preserved one's own hat; the chances were that it already had been traded for food; where then did you get a second one? For me the two hats symbolize a number of dualities:

- *our two countries, Canada and the Netherlands;*
- *the transition from war to peace;*
- *feelings of joy, coupled with sadness about the loss of friends or relatives;*
- *loneliness and friendship, always present, but accentuated during an enemy occupation, due to the uncertainty about your environment;*
- *the cheers for our liberators and the farewell to those who did not live to see freedom;*
- *exuberance versus modesty in showing one's sentiments;*
- *gratitude for what has been achieved and concern about the way ahead;*
- *the past and the future, and in connection with that: memory and hope.*

Speaking about future and hope: the active participation of young people in our commemorations and their great interest in this monument demonstrates that we can safely hand over the torch of freedom and democracy to them. As at Apeldoorn in the year 2000 young people are present at this ceremony and are playing an active role in it. Together with Canadian students, two youngsters from the Royal Schools Community at Apeldoorn, who have adopted the monument in their home town, will recite some poems about liberation and freedom.

EPILOGUE III TO CHAPTER XVII

The Foundation Liberation '45 and the Committee for the National Canadian Liberation Monument sincerely want to express their gratefulness for a great number of agencies and persons, who made this miracle happen.

We thank the Royal Netherlands Air Force for providing transport facilities. The arrangements here in Ottawa were performed by two Canadian members of our committee, Mr. Jean-Guy Chapman and Mrs. Ada Wynston. Also great assistance was given by the Canadian Ministry of Veterans Affairs and the National Capital Commission, in close co-operation with the Dutch Embassy.

The Canadian-Dutch contractor firm Westeinde literally prepared the ground for the monument.

Thank you all for your invaluable support!

We now have two identical monuments, one at Apeldoorn in the Netherlands, one here at Ottawa in Canada, waving their hats at each other across the ocean. Another form of duality! Although, I prefer to think of the two statues as one monument, consisting of two identical parts, only separated by a stretch of water between them.

I sincerely wish that this one monument will remind present and future generations of our common history and of the bright prospect of peace and prosperity in both our countries.

EPILOGUE IV
TO CHAPTER XVII

BEEKBERGEN, OOSTERHUIZEN, LIEREN
THE LIEREN MONUMENT
APRIL 17TH, 2002

In March 1995, a few weeks before I was due to leave Toronto for the Pilgrimage, I received a letter from one Gerrit Ham of Beekbergen informing me that his town and two nearby villages, Oosterhuizen and Lieren, were holding a parade on April 29th. On the same day Oosterhuizen would unveil a Monument to the PPCLI. Could I attend both ceremonies and make a speech. I was honoured to accept and prepared an address.

However, fate intervened with a heavy hand. My wife became very ill and I had to cancel my trip.

In 2000, during the Pilgrimage held that year, the good citizens of these three villages held another parade on April 29th. This time I was not denied the honour and pleasure of attending the parade. The citizens gave the Veterans a tumultuous welcome and lined the streets in their thousands even though it poured rain the whole time.

Gerrit Ham and I kept in touch both by telephone and letter. On April 11th, 2001, he telephoned me to offer his best wishes on the 56th Anniversary of the crossing of the Ijssel River in 1945! He informed me that on April 17th, Beekbergen, Oosterhuizen and Lieren were holding another ceremony in honour of Canada's Veterans who had liberated them in 1945. The event had now become an annual celebration and he would send me photos.

When the pictures arrived I could scarcely believe them. Once again the people had assembled around the Monument they had erected in 1995. This time, however, the ceremony was conducted mainly by the children, who recited poems and played guitars before a large gathering of admiring parents, in the pouring rain.

True to his word, Gerrit Ham, in early 2002, informed me that the ceremony would be repeated on April 16th in Oosterhuizen. He then added, "I really wish you could attend because we have a big surprise for you. The next day Lieren is unveiling another monument to the PPCLI!"

It was indeed a huge surprise and for a moment words failed me. I had to tell Gerrit that I had been ill and could not possibly attend the Ceremony. I felt very badly that once again I had let my friend down but I believe he understood, and wished me well.

EPILOGUE IV TO CHAPTER XVII

After the two ceremonies, Gerrit sent me letters and pictures showing the new Monument in Lieren. It is set in a beautiful park. A large bronze plaque is inscribed:

Princess Patricia's Canadian Light Infantry
17–04–1945
2nd Brigade 1st Division
Thank You Liberators
Lieren

The date, April 17th, 1945, is the date the PPCLI liberated Lieren.

I was pleased to see that Lloyd and Olga Rains (whom I have often mentioned in this narrative) had attended the unveiling of the Monument on behalf of the PPCLI.

With this noble and generous act of the people of Lieren, the long story of my love affair with Holland ends. However, the memories will never fade. Nor will the people of Holland ever forget the PPCLI. Their record is enshrined in no less than five Memorials in Holland—one on either bank of the Ijssel River, another in Achterveld, another in Oosterhuizen and one more in Lieren. Encased in time capsules in Oosterhuizen and Lieren monuments is a history of the PPCLI in Holland, translated into Dutch.

ONCE A PATRICIA—ALWAYS A PATRICIA

EPILOGUE IV TO CHAPTER XVII

AMBASSADE VAN HET KONINKRIJK DER
NEDERLANDEN
Royal Netherlands Embassy
Defence Attache
350 Albert Street, Ste. 2020
Ottawa, ON K1R 1A4

Mr. C.S. Frost
PH4—3800 Yonge Street
Toronto, ON
M4N 3P7

Date	June 2002	Contact	Mrs. P.J.G.A. van Bragt
Our ref.	3.5	Tel.	(613) 237 5030 ext 233
Re	Medal	Fax	(613) 237 6471

Dear Mr. Frost,

On the occasion of the 50th and 55th anniversary of the liberation of Holland, the Netherlands offered a "Thank you Canada" anniversary medal to the Veterans who came to Holland to celebrate this memorable occasion.

To honour the equally important contribution of those veterans, who were unable to attend the festivities in the Netherlands, The National Dutch Committee "Thank You Canada" has minted a medal called "Medal of Remembrance in relation to the liberation of Holland."

I understand you are eligible to receive this medal as you participated in the liberation of the Netherlands. I am very pleased, therefore, on behalf of my country to offer you this commemorative medal as a token of the appreciation and gratitude of the Dutch people for your wartime efforts.

In the hope that you may enjoy the medal for many more years to come, I remain,

Yours sincerely,

Lieutenant-Colonel Leo van den Heuvel
Defence Attache
Kingdom of the Netherlands

44. *The Regiment prepares to load into Buffaloes to cross the Ijssel River—Holland. April 11, 1945.*
Public Archives of Canada PA-140693

45. *Men of Lt. Bob Huestis' Platoon, laden down with equipment, crowd into their Buffalo. Bob at the front of the Buffalo facing camera.*
Public Archives of Canada PA-133332

46. *Memorial to the soldiers who crossed the Ijssel river, 11 April 1945, erected by the Municipality of Gorssel, 1985.*

47. *Author stands near east bank of the Ijssel River where his Company crossed in 1945. He is being interviewed by a local TV station. 1985.*

48. *Mayors of Municipalities on east and west sides of the Ijssel River join hands to signify their mutual feelings of respect and friendship, after the Re-enactment of the Crossing of the Ijssel River—1990.*

49. *Final objective of D Company after crossing the Ijssel River 1945—a group of houses on the outskirts of Wilp code-name Winchester. Animals peacefully graze where their ancestors were killed by shellfire. 1985.*

50. *Author explains to Mayor van Blommestein and LCol. Reitsma that the PPCLI, not the 48th Highlanderes were the first to cross the Ijssel River—1985.*

Parade, Beekbergen—Lieren—Oosterhuizen. 29 April 2000

51. *One of the trucks that entered the parade. (School Oosterhuizen)*

52. *Raining ... "the Canadians called it "liquid sunshine."*

The Oosterhuizen Monument to the PPCLI. 21 April 1995.

53.

54.

The Lieren Monument to the PPCLI. 17 April 2002

55.

56.

The Achterveld Monument to the PPCLI. 9 May 2000.

57.

58. Final platoon position on the outskirts of Achterveld, just before the surrender. Due to the low-lying land the position is constructed above ground. A slit trench would soon fill with water.

59. German officers on their way to the Food Truce in Achterveld. 30 April, 1945.

60. On 18 April 1945, a PPCLI carrier patrol entered Achterveld and captured seven prisoners who were about to dynamite a church tower in the village.

This photo was taken by a priest and shows the crew of one of the carriers and jubilant Dutch villagers. A German prisoner is visible in the middle of the photo.

61. Schoolhouse in D Company area in Achterveld where the Food Truce was signed and the War ended for the Patricias. 1956.

Groesbeek Canadian War Cemetery—7 May 1980.

62. *Two thousand veterans honour more than 7000 Canadians who died in Belgium and Holland. Queen Beatrix laid the first wreath followed by the Hon. Donald MacDonald.*

63.

64. *Keukenhof Gardens. 6 May, 1980.*

Holten Cemetery. Christmas Eve, 1998.

65.

66.

Holten Cemetery. May 1990.

67. *Johannes van Blommestein and LCol. Ritse Reitsma, Chairman Liberation Committee.*

68. *Gerald Merrithew, Minister of Veterans Affairs, Johannes van Blommestein, Mayor of Voorst.*

69. *Veterans in vintage vehicles from the War re-enact entry of Canadian Corps into Amsterdam. May, 1945. Leading vehicle is a DUKW (amphibious truck). More Canadian flags line the route than would be seen at any parade in Canada—1980.*

70. *The author waves at the crowd from a 15 cwt truck crammed with veterans and children. Bert Bolton on the left—1980.*

71. *Amsterdam. May 1980. Award of Plaque—35th Anniversary of Liberation*

72. *Dinner held by the Mayor of Apeldoorn, Dr. Pieter Beelaerts van Blokland, in honour of the visit of 1,500 veterans of the 1st Canadian Division to his city, May, 1985. Author presented the Mayor with his blazer crest and cap badge.*

73. *Dinner given by Pieter Beelaerts van Blokland, as Queen's Commissioner for the province of Utrecht in honour of the Veterans. 1 May 1990. Author presents him with a PPCLI plaque.*

74. *General Andrew Gijsbers at the dinner. 1 May 1990.*

Apeldoorn National Liberation Parade. 6 May 1990.

75. *Author leads the parade through the city.*

76. *Author presents a copy of his book, "Once a Patricia" to her Royal Highness Princess Margriet, 7 May 1990, in the presence of the Canadian Ambassador, Mr. Jacques Gignac; Mr. Johannes van Bloomestein, Mayor of Voorst; and Gerald Merrithew, Minister of Veterans Affairs, at the Hotel Erica, Berg en Dal.*

Apeldoorn National Liberation Parade. 7 May 2000.

77. *Author leads the parade to the reviewing stand.*

78. *Author and Minister of Defence, Art Eggleton on the Reviewing Stand at Apeldoorn.*

79. *Dutch Minister of Defence, Mayor de Graaf, Princess Margriet, her husband Pieter van Vollenhoven, their son Prince Floris, our Minister of Defence Art Eggleton, Col. Sydney Frost.*

80. *PPCLI contingent including Elwood Birss, Wally Smith, Doug Armstrong and his wife march past.*

81. *Reception by HRH Princess Margriet for Minister's party, Veterans Affairs. 7 May 2000.*
Front Row: Bill Barclay, Legion 1st Vice-President; Cliff Chadderton; HRH, Pieter van Vollenhoven; the author, are 1st, 3rd, 6th, 7th and 9th from left.
Rear Row: Jean-Guy Chapman, Larry Murray, Deputy Minister, LGen. Andrew Gijsbers, Jan Koorenhof, Prince Floris, Mayor de Graaf, are 5th, 8th, 11th, 16th, 17th, 18th from left.

82. The "Man with Two Hats" — Apeldoorn, May 2, 2000.

Re-enactment of the Crossing of the Ijssel River. 2 May 1990.

83. Author leads the parade across the bridge.

84.

85. *Author thanks Jim van Notten, Mayor of Gorssel, for the re-enactment of the Crossing of the River.*

86. Author addresses the spectators.

87. "Padre Frost" delivers an address in Antonius Church, De Vecht, 4 May, 2000.

Ottawa, unveiling Monument—"The Man with Two Hats." 11 May 2002.

88.

89.

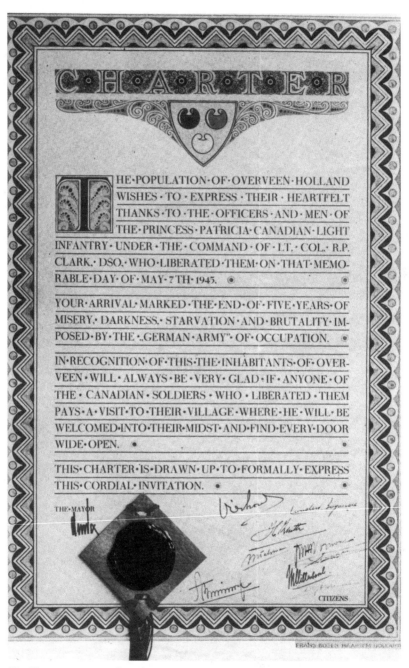

90. *Charter presented to the Regiment by the citizens of Overveen. May 7, 1945.*

Zandvoort
German bunkers in the dunes, 1985.

91.

92.

CYPRUS—1971
Preface to Cyprus

"First Battalion, PPCLI will fire a feu de joie in honour of Canada's National Day—Commence firing."

Immediately, 125 rifles begin to fire, one after the other, in rapid succession, down the first rank of soldiers and back the second rank, like a long wave of staccato notes, punctuated by the music of the Band playing the National Anthem.

This is not the traditional Canada Day Ceremony observed by the Battalion at its home station in Calgary; the Band does not belong to the PPCLI.

The date is July 1st, 1971, and the place is far removed from Calgary—Cyprus. The Band is part of The Royal Regiment of Canada stationed in Toronto, which has been flown to Cyprus to be attached to the 1st Battalion PPCLI serving on peacekeeping duties with the United Nations Force.

I am present at the Ceremony as the Honorary Lieutenant-Colonel of The Royal Regiment of Canada.

At the conclusion of the Parade, I am asked to address the troops. I begin by saying:

> *This is my first visit to the PPCLI since I retired from the Regiment twenty-five years ago, this very month. At that time, we were stationed at Camp Shilo, Manitoba. General Ware was our Commanding Officer. Some of the officers were: Maj. Schelderup, DSO, MC, Maj. Potts, DSO, Capt. Stutt, Capt. Robbins, Lt. Moncrief.*
>
> *Little did I realize that twenty-five years later I would return and bring a band with me to celebrate the occasion with true Patricia Panache!*

How I came to be Honorary Lieutenant-Colonel of The Royal Regiment of Canada requires a word of explanation. With many misgivings and not a few forebodings, I left my Patricias in 1946 and began a new career as a law student at Osgoode Hall, Toronto. I will not say that the experience was stressful, a word that is so popular today in describing all manner of pains and frustrations one experiences in his daily life. Perhaps a better word would be "shattering."

Forcing myself to study after an absence of four years from university was bad enough. But it was the lack of camaraderie of my brother officers and the support of my men that I missed the most and yearned for. My father sensed my loneliness and longing and suggested that I join The Royal Regiment of Canada, in which he had served with the Reserve Battalion in Toronto during the war.

I promptly paraded myself before the Commanding Officer and gave him a brief résumé of my service with the Patricias, including the fact I had been acting Second-in-Command at the end of the war. "Well," he said, "that's fine but I have no vacancies for Majors or Captains, but I could take you on as a Lieutenant and see how you make out." And then, with just a hint of a smile, "You know, in the Royals, we consider a Lieutenant is about the equivalent of a Major in any other unit."

And so I reverted and became a Lieutenant all over again.

I had no regrets. I had found a home that would nourish my desperate need to continue soldiering and the comradeship that had been my life for the previous six years. I was soon promoted to Captain, took the Command and Staff Course, became a Major and then, in 1959, Commanding Officer of the Regiment. After my retirement in 1962, I remained closely in touch with Regimental affairs and in 1967, I was appointed Honorary Lieutenant-Colonel.

And so it was, that on July 1st, 1971, I was present with the band of The Royal Regiment of Canada at the Canada Day Ceremony observed by the First Battalion PPCLI in Cyprus.

How the band became involved with this Ceremony is a story that has never been told but should be. It demonstrates once again how Canada's Militia has been jerked about by the Department of National Defence. I make no apology for departing from my story about the Patricias. As will be explained, the event is relevant to my tale.

Chapter XVIII

CYPRUS—1971

On April 14, 1971, Mobile Command (FMC) at St. Lambert, Quebec, advised Central Militia Area (CMA) in Oakville that FMC required a Militia Brass Band to attend Cyprus, June 23rd to July 7th, to take part in Canada Day Celebrations by the PPCLI. FMC could not provide pay.

BGen. Bruce Legge, Commander of CMA, agreed that CMA would provide pay and had his Chief of Staff, Colonel Steve Andrunyk, ask LCol. Peter Fairclough, Commanding Officer of The Royal Regiment of Canada (RRegtC), if his Regiment could supply a band. LCol. Fairclough stated he could not give a firm commitment until he had contacted all the members of the Band and they had made arrangements with their employers and families. The previous year he had received a similar request to send the Band to New York. At the last minute the trip was cancelled and this caused serious repercussions within the Band, their families and employers.

On April 19th, LCol. Fairclough gave a firm commitment to Col. Andrunyk and this was passed on to CMA and Mobile Command.

Canadian Forces Headquarters in Ottawa then sent the following message to Cyprus:

> *Please be advised that every effort has been made to obtain services of a Canadian Forces Regular Band to assist in Cyprus Day celebrations 12 Jun to 7 Jul 71.*
>
> *Your situation completely understood. However reduction in number of bands has created predicament when demand far exceeds supply. Regret all Canadian Forces Regular Brass Bands are committed during period.*

CYPRUS—1971

> *We are happy to advise that a Reserve Force Band—The Royal Regiment of Canada consisting of one officer plus thirty-five other ranks can be made available.*

On May 14th, CMA re-confirmed to LCol. Fairclough that the Cyprus trip was "on."

This was happy news indeed. For the past month LCol. Fairclough and the members of the Band had spent countless hours getting ready to proceed to Cyprus—vaccinations, medicals, issue of identity discs, new uniforms, rehearsals and the consent of the Musicians' Association.

On May 27th, Col. Andrunyk informed me that in view of the fact that I had served in the PPCLI during the war, I had been authorized to accompany the Band. I was thrilled and proceeded at once to make myself ready for this nostalgic return to the Patricias. I suppose you could even say it was a unique event because I was really wearing two hats. One for each Regiment.

The blow fell on June 8th. I was informed by Col. Andrunyk of CMA that the trip was "off." It had been turned down by the Chief of the Defence Staff (CDS) on the advice of LGen. Turcot, head of Mobile Command. However, the Army would try to compensate the Band for all the inconvenience it had suffered by sending them in the fall!

I was stunned. This was like telling a condemned man he would be shot instead of hanged.

The ball had suddenly landed in my lap. As Honorary Lieutenant-Colonel, it was my clear duty to do all I could to get the operation back on the rails. But I was wearing two hats. It was also my duty not to let down my Patricias who were counting on having the Band.

I do not accept defeat easily. In fact, I do not accept it at all.

My first call was to Col. Allan Neal, the Commander of Toronto Milita District, and a former Commanding Officer of the Royals. Like me, he was horrified and agreed to send a letter to BGen. Legge, Commander of CMA.

My next call was to Bruce Legge himself. Not only was he a close friend of many years, but he was an outstanding Militia soldier and a strong advocate on behalf of the Militia. My first question was why in hell had the CDS turned down the trip. BGen. Legge was also appalled at the enormity of the decision and agreed to fight it. He thought it was lack of air transport that had caused the problem. Probably the space allotted to the Band had been taken by members of the Regular Force. My short reply was, "What is so G.D. sacred about 37 Regulars. Tell them to take the next bus."

CYPRUS—1971

The next person to receive a blast was MGen. Bill Howard, senior Militia Officer, in Calgary. He too appreciated the stupidity of the staff and undertook to do something about it. He had already spoken to LGen. Mike Dare, Vice-Chief of the Defence Staff, who was sympathetic. "Sympathetic?" I cried. "For Chrisake I don't need sympathy, I need action." I gave him until the next day to sort the matter out or I would take it to the Minister.

I then phoned my classmate from RMC, BGen. George Brown, Chief of Staff to LGen. Turcot at Mobile Command, hoping to get some insight into the mindset of his Commander. George agreed the decision was tough on the Band who had gone to such trouble preparing for the trip, but there was nothing he could do. His hands were tied.

It was obvious that some drastic action had to be taken—forthwith. I suddenly remembered that one of my clients was Swiss Air. I phoned the Manager of the Toronto office and explained the problem. I needed return tickets for 37 soldiers from Toronto to Nicosia. How much? The best he could do was $16,000. I asked him to have a talk with his Head Office in Montreal and get a better rate.

I had now turned myself into a fund raiser for the Department of National Defence. It was not a new role. Some years earlier when I was Commanding Officer, the Army had failed to honour its commitment to pay my soldiers for special duty, to the tune of $4,000. I personally paid the troops and threatened to sue. Eventually I was repaid, but just the principal—no interest.

Not being in a position to come up with $16,000 on such short notice, I approached the Mayor of Toronto, Bill Dennison, and reminded him that his predecessor, Nate Phillips, had given the Royals the Freedom of the City. I hinted that in order to ensure the availability of the Band for ceremonial functions for the City, the Royals needed a grant. The Mayor offered $2,000 and suggested I contact the Chairman of Metro. I did and received a prompt refusal.

I then received a call from Swiss Air in Montreal. They had done some number crunching and could now offer a round trip for $14,000 instead of $16,000. Taking into account the grant from the city, I still needed $12,000.

It was time to speak to the Minister.

Being a realist, I realized that the Minister had no doubt been informed of the situation and would make himself "unavailable." But this did not deter me.

An Honorary Lieutenant-Colonel is really in an anomalous position. In some things he is strictly a civilian masquerading as an officer. He is not paid one cent. In fact, he is expected to be ready at all times to give monetary support to the Regiment. Thus, he is not bound to honour the time-honoured chain of command and can insert himself into it at any point. I have already described how I freely spoke my mind to various generals without first going to their staff officers.

However, approaching the Minister himself has political ramifications, and while acceptable is only done in the most serious cases. In my opinion, the Royals Band versus Mobile Command was one of those cases. As I feared, the Minister was busy, but his secretary, Mr. McWhinney, came on the line. For a full twenty minutes I gave him my case by chapter and verse and ended by saying "We want only one thing. That the Army live up to its commitments."

Mr. McWhinney heard me out and thanked me for my presentation. He would inform the Minister and let me know shortly.

That was in the morning of June 10th. That afternoon, Mr. McWhinney phoned. The Minister agreed with my submission. The Band would fly to Cyprus.

The first person I phoned was, of course, LCol. Peter Fairclough, the Commanding Officer of The Royal Regiment of Canada.

The second person was my Commanding Officer when I retired from the PPCLI, who was now the Colonel of the Regiment—MGen. Cammie Ware, DSO.

The band was ecstatic but mindful they had barely 12 days to make final arrangements. There was no doubt they would be ready. That was their motto—Ready Aye Ready.

I would be ready too. I could hardly wait to rejoin my Patricias. I had been away too long.

When word got out that I had bested high brass in the Army, congratulations flowed from many quarters, including Central Militia Area and Toronto Militia District, both from Regular and Reserve Officers. Those who had been on earlier tours to Cyprus offered advice and assistance. Maj. Don Creighton handed me a popular book about Cyprus, *Bitter Lemons* by Lawrence Durrell, and a Greek Phrase Book.

My RMC classmate, LCol. Alf Robbins, PPCLI, and the Senior Staff Officer at CMA apologized for not being able to render much help. He was privy to most of the action that I have described but because of his position on the staff, he felt he could not inform me of confidential matters known only by his senior officers.

Actually I didn't need his help in dealing with CMA because I knew BGen. Legge and Col. Andrunyk so well and trusted them. They did all they could.

However, after the Band had returned from Cyprus, Alf Robbins gave me a memo containing extracts from the files at CMA pertinent to the case. My story is based, in part, on these extracts.

Alf Robbins also sent me a bon voyage card which read, "Have a nice trip—relax, don't worry about a thing—we can screw things up just as nicely without you."

Perhaps the most telling missile hurled at the high brass and their staff in Mobile Command and Canadian Forces Headquarters was a letter sent by Col. Allan Neal, Commander TMD, to BGen. Bruce Legge, Commander CMA, for forwarding to Higher Authority. Col. Neal describes the callous attitude of the staff with such force that it is a wonder he wasn't fired on the spot. His letter deserves to be reproduced.

Colonel A. E. Neal CD
Commander
Toronto Militia District
Moss Park Armoury
130 Queen Street East
Toronto 227, Ontario

June 8, 1971.

Brigadier-General B. J. Legge ED QC
Commander
Central Militia Area
Ortona Barracks
Oakville

Dear General Legge,

Having been made aware of the imminent cancellation of the scheduled trip to Cyprus of the Brass and Reed Band of The Royal Regiment of Canada during the latter part of this month—I must add my share of protest.

There is little being done today to encourage anybody to be a militiaman. All the effort is put into constraints—pay, equipment, training facilities—you name it. This latest piece of blundering is merely another nail in the coffin.

How anyone could have thought up a scheme such as this without ensuring transport capability is beyond me. If I did something like this, just once, in my private business, I would be a statistic on Spadina Avenue. This fellow will no doubt be promoted.

The morale of the Militia is still high in spite of the (by now) accustomed heavy footed—clod-hopping, bureau-

cratic superstructure that can pull tricks such as this latest effort. I am sincere in my belief that if the Staff Officer responsible for this gem, had any notion that the Militia consisted of people, he could not have conceived of a better way to frustrate, demoralize and otherwise confound them, if he spent the rest of his career at it.

Trusting that you will forward these sentiments (if not words) on to the appropriate authority—I remain, sir, most respectfully

*Yours sincerely,
Allan E. Neal, Colonel*

The Mayor of Toronto, William Dennison, with whom the Royals enjoyed a close relationship, offered his best wishes on the trip and handed me two sets of gold cuff links engraved with the City crest: one set for LCol. W.E.J. Hutchinson, Commanding Officer of PPCLI, the other for the Acting Mayor of Nicosia, Cyprus. The letters from Mayor Dennison are reproduced below.

*William Dennison
Mayor
June 21, 1971.*

*Lieutenant-Colonel W.E.J. Hutchinson,
C. O. 1—P.P.C.L.I.,
Cyprus.*

Dear Colonel Hutchinson:

As Mayor of the City of Toronto it gives me much pleasure, through the co-operation of Colonel C. S. Frost— Honorary Lieutenant-Colonel of The Royal Regiment of Canada—to send most cordial Civic Greetings to you and to present you with a set of City of Toronto cuff links.

I am certain that the links will serve as a lasting memento of Colonel Frost's visit to Cyprus,

*Sincerely yours,
"W. Dennison"
Mayor*

CYPRUS—1971

> *William Dennison*
> *Mayor*
>
> *June 21, 1971.*
>
> *Christoforos Kythreotis, Esq.,*
> *Acting Mayor of the City of Nicosia*
>   *And District Commissioner,*
> *Nicosia, Cyprus.*
>
> *Dear Mr. Kythreotis:*
>
> *As Mayor of the City of Toronto it gives me much pleasure, through the co-operation of Colonel C. S. Frost—Honorary Lieutenant-Colonel of The Royal Regiment of Canada—to send most cordial Civic Greetings to you and to present you with a set of City of Toronto cuff links.*
>
> *To you and the citizens of Nicosia I send best wishes for future prosperity.*
>
> > *Sincerely yours,*
> > *"W. Dennison"*
>
> > *Mayor*

In addition to the two hats I was already wearing for the Royals and the Patricias, I was now in possession of a third one on behalf of the City of Toronto. It was going to be an interesting tour!

At Fort York Armoury, Toronto (the headquarters of the Royals), the Commanding Officer, Adjutant, Quartermaster and Director of Music worked long hours to outfit the Band for their tour. Excitement mounted as the Bandsmen were issued new uniforms, shirts, boots and all the other items necessary to send them on their way. I thought back to WWII and the preparations for the landing of the Patricias in Sicily. Now 28 years later, I was preparing to land on another island in the Mediterranean—Cyprus, but in rather different circumstances, to be sure.

While the Band was not going off to war, they were joining a United Nations Peacekeeping Force, on very short notice and with no prior experience to guide them. It was a very large task for a Reserve Unit. An extract from the Movement Order gives an idea of the administrative problems.

CYPRUS—1971

THE ROYAL REGIMENT OF CANADA

REGIMENTAL BAND
MOVEMENT INSTRUCTIONS

1. THE R REGT C BAND WILL MOVE TO CYPRUS 22 JUN 71 RETURNING 7 JUL 71

2. TIMINGS

   7 JUN 71   FULL BAND REHEARSAL, TURN IN SCARLET, ISSUE TW'S (TROPICAL WORSTED UNIFORM)
  21 JUN 71   FULL BAND DRILL, TURN IN INSTRUMENTS
  22 JUN 71   1300 HRS REPORT TO FORT YORK ARMOURY
                  1330 HRS BUS LEAVES FOR TRENTON
                  1700 HRS FLIGHT 753 LEAVES FOR CYPRUS
   7 JUL 71   2330 HRS FLIGHT 754 ARRIVES TRENTON FROM CYPRUS
   8 JUL 71   0200 HRS APPROX ARRIVAL OF BUS TO TORONTO

3. DRESS

   a. ALL PERS WILL BRING THE FOLLOWING:

REGIMENTAL FORAGE CAPS	ARMY SOCKS
TW'S	BOOTS BLACK
2 SHIRTS COTTON KHAKI	ARMLET WITH RANK AND MOBILE COMMAND PATCH
TIE O.D.	CIVILIAN CLOTHES BLACK SHOES PLAIN
TROUSERS FSOD	TOILET GEAR AND TOWEL
BELT 03 (51)	BATHING SUIT (OPTIONAL)
BLACK SOCKS	

>   *b. DRESS WHILE TRAVELING WILL BE:*
>   *REGIMENTAL CAP, FORAGE SHIRT, TIE, TW'S,*
>   *ARMY SOCKS AND BOOTS*
>
> *4. ADMINISTRATION*
>   *a. ALL PERS WILL HAND IN VACCINATION BOOKS TO CAPT MON 21 JUN*
>   *b. IDENTITY DISCS AND CARDS WILL BE HANDED OUT 22 JUN 71*
>   *c. A PAY PARADE WILL <u>PROBABLY</u> BE HELD IN CYPRUS BEFORE RETURNING TO CANADA <u>BUT</u> FUNDS WILL BE RETAINED TO COVER ANY LOSSES OR DAMAGE TO CLOTHING OR EQUIPMENT. THE BAND WILL BE RESPONSIBLE TO PAY FOR ANY DAMAGE TO BARRACKS OR OTHER DND PROPERTY.*
>
> *5. DISCIPLINE*
> *NO PERS WILL BUY ANY DUTY FREE GOODS FOR RESALE OR AS GIFTS FOR ANYONE OUTSIDE THE BASE AREA. PENALTY FOR ILLEGAL PROCUREMENT MAY BE UP TO 5 YEARS IN JAIL AND DISHONOURABLE DISCHARGE.*
>
> ***REMEMBER*** *YOU ARE REPRESENTING CANADA AND THE ROYAL REGIMENT, ACT ACCORDINGLY*

Finally, the big day arrived—June 22. The Royals had lived up to their motto and were "Ready Aye Ready" at precisely 1:30 p.m., but no sign of the bus to take the Band to Trenton where the aircraft was due to leave at 5:00 p.m. After frantic telephone calls to TMD and CMA and any place else that could supply a vehicle, one arrived an hour late. Further calls were made to Trenton to hold the plane. The thought now passed through my mind that certain things in the Army had not changed in the past 25 years, such as the maxim—"Hurry up and wait."

The Band left Trenton, by service air, at 7:30 p.m. and arrived in Gatwick, at 6:45 a.m., June 23. The flight had taken only $6 1/4$ hours. The aircraft departed Gatwick at 9:00 a.m. and touched down in Nicosia at 3:30 p.m.

We were met by the Commanding Officer of PPCLI, LCol. Bill Hutchinson, and his Adjutant, Capt. Chris Smith, and whisked away to our quarters.

I was home at last.

The rest of that day was taken up with administration—allotting quarters, sorting out equipment, band instruments and music, and feeding a very hungry Band. To my great surprise I was put up at the Ledra Palace Hotel, the finest hostelry in town. Again images of my landing in Sicily flirted with my mind until I firmly ordered them out of my thoughts. Sicily and Cyprus have absolutely nothing in common—except a searing heat of 120 degrees.

The Band had hoped to have a day or two in which to relax and become acclimatized to the heat and rigours of active service. No such luck. They were in the Army now, in particular, PPCLI, and its RSM couldn't wait to get them out on the tarmac of the airport for a little drill. While the Band was receiving this friendly instruction, I was being briefed by LCol. Hutchinson on the tasks of PPCLI, its deployment along the Green Line in Nicosia, the geopolitical background and the economy.

LCol. Hutchinson is a fine officer and possessed a very detailed knowledge of Cyprus and its problems. I learned that the Green Line was an imaginary line separating the Greek Cypriots and the Turkish Cypriots. Nicosia was the most sensitive area because in some places there were only a few feet between the two factions. Each side hated the others' innards, mothers and forebears, and it wouldn't take much to ignite the war again.

I also learned that Cyprus is a beautiful island with mountain ranges along the northern coast (Kyrenia Mountains) and in the west central region (Troödos Mountains). The Troödos range is covered with forests and vineyards and is crowned by a peak 6,401 feet above sea level called Mt. Olympus, in imitation of the famous mountain in Greece. The island is blessed with long stretches of sandy beaches, and in quieter times was a favourite vacation spot for Europeans, especially English tourists.

LCol. Hutchinson guided me to one of the observation towers from which I could observe how the Green Line meandered through the city, with Greek and Turkish Cypriots glaring at each other from sandbagged defensive positions in houses on either side. It was unreal, and I banished forever all thoughts of trying to compare this kind of war with my own.

During the next few days, while the Band rehearsed their drill and music, I had further sessions with LCol. Hutchinson and met some of his officers. It was quite a shock to find that not one of them had been in my war and they were so young. But they certainly knew their tasks and were kind enough not to embarrass me with queries about why I was there, such as, "And what instrument do you play, Sir?"

The truth of the matter was that I was there because I had served with the Patricias.

CYPRUS—1971

I don't know what the young officers thought about me. In the first place, like the Band, I was dressed in the old khaki summer drill uniform known as tropical worsteds or "tee dubs," with a Guard's type hat as worn by the Royals. This hardy, serviceable uniform had recently been outlawed by the meddlesome Paul Hellyer, Minister of National Defence. Mr. Trudeau had integrated the Navy, Army and Airforce and decreed they should all wear the same green uniform. The Regular Force had been "greenwashed," but the new uniform had not yet trickled down to the Militia.

The question on many an old soldier's mind was—Why green? Khaki colour was synonymous with Army and had been for 100 years. Civilians like Paul Hellyer could never understand the dynamics of morale or what gives a soldier pride in his Regiment or Corps. It is not because he is dressed the same as the Navy or the Airforce. It is because he is different. It's called *esprit de corps*. Perhaps Mr. Hellyer, in his ignorance of military tradition, unwittingly chose green because that effectively described his lack of knowledge.

I will admit that I could have secured a green uniform but I was damned if I was going to submit to the whims of the Minister. As an Honorary Lieutenant-Colonel, I could get away with it.

I don't think the officers wasted any time pondering my apparent disrespect for the green uniform. They were much too busy with their tasks along the Green Line. This meant there was little opportunity for me to get to know them and enjoy their camaraderie. Also, my contact with them was limited because my arrangement with Ledra Palace Hotel included room and board, so I took quite a few of my meals in the first class dining room. It seemed a shame to pass up this "perk" paid for by DND and I was not depriving the officers of a portion of their Army rations.

LCol. Bill Hutchinson had his hands full with his UN duties and the upcoming Canada Day Ceremonies. He showed me the Program and I was certainly impressed. It seemed to me to be an immense undertaking in the middle of his peacekeeping duties and I wondered how it would all work out. I was particularly concerned about whether my Band would measure up to the high standards of the Patricias.

I need not have worried. As I have intimated, LCol. Hutchinson was a true professional. Had I known about his previous career, I would have had no doubts. In 1961, he had been the Service Representative for the visit of President Kennedy to Ottawa and was charged with making all the military arrangements. A little Canada Day Ceremony was duck soup for him. I only found out about the Kennedy visit many years later when LCol. Hutchinson wrote an article in *NUVO Magazine* about State Visits to Canada. He covered the Kennedy visit as well as describing his participation in the Royal Visit of the Queen in 1984.

Despite his many duties, LCol. Bill Hutchinson found time to take good care of me. I was given a staff car and driver and told to tour the Island while he prepared for July 1st. I took him at his word and spent several days exploring the mountain ranges and the beautiful beaches and facilities at Kyrenia, Famagusta and other popular resorts.

On one occasion, Colonel Bill was able to join me for dinner. I had just spent a marvellous day touring the Island and swimming in the warm, clear waters of the Mediterranean. After a fine meal and copious libations, I became a bit nostalgic and said to the good Colonel, "You know Bill, this is the life. I should never have left the Patricias".

He did not seem to share my sentiments, but I continued after a few more glasses of wine. "I'd love to spend a few weeks on this Island, perhaps even a month or two. Suppose I took over from you, as CO, and you could go on leave. What do you think?"

Bill Hutchinson was not amused and, being on duty at all times, had not shared my over-indulgence in wine. "Syd, what I think you should do is visit Beirut for a few days until the Ceremony on July 1st. Your Band is coming along nicely and your Admin. Officer—what's his name? Oh yes, Peter Marani—is doing a fine job. I'll make all the arrangements."

Well, it was an offer I couldn't refuse and I left the next day for Beirut. When Peter Marani heard the news he wanted to come too. "Look, Sir, the Band have worked hard and are fit and ready for the Ceremony. Capt. Robbins is familiar with the music and the drill. After all, he used to be Regular Force. CSM Cavanagh can look after the administration while I'm away. Besides, you'll need an ADC to take care of you."

Peter was, in fact, practically a professional ADC whose "clients" included the LGovernor, General Simonds and others. His father had been a CO of the Royals. He deserved a holiday from the holiday he had been enjoying. I agreed to his earnest request.

We left Nicosia Airport on June 26, courtesy Middle East Airlines Airliban, and soon arrived at Beirut, a distance of only 155 miles according to our briefing book. I had no idea what we would find. As we flew over the city I was surprised to see tall, modern office and apartment buildings, all dazzling white in the intense sunlight. But, in the suburbs, the scene changed to slums—flat-roofed cinderblock buildings, unpaved roads and narrow alleys.

I had been told that Lebanon was known as the "Switzerland of the Middle East," and Beirut the "Paris of the Middle East." The open, tolerant atmosphere of the country attracted artistic, intellectual and political exiles as well as bankers, merchants and businessmen. Lebanon was the crossroads between the European West and the Arab Middle East.

The country had had its share of the civil unrest that was endemic to the Middle East, but none of this was evident as the aircraft touched down at the modern airport.

In the short time available, I decided to confine my perambulations to two cities, Beirut and Baalbek, and Mount Lebanon in between. Actually, Mount Lebanon is a mountain range that runs the length of the country. My Aide, Peter Marani, was keen to limit our wanderings to Beirut itself and not bother with a long, hot bus ride to Baalbek. But when I told him about the ancient Roman ruins there, which surpass even those in Rome, and the opportunity to shop in its colourful bazaars, as well as a chance to ride a camel or two, he surrendered.

From Beirut on the coast, the road climbed the Lebanon Mountains whose towering peaks reach up to 10,000 feet above sea level. We passed through forests of cedars which had supplied timbers for King Solomon's Temple, then down to the Biqa Valley and the fertile plain that provides the country's grain and vegetables. The area reminded me a bit of the market gardens north of Toronto around Bradford and Holland Landing, but on a much larger scale.

Soon we could see the majestic Roman ruins and the tall minarets and mosques of the city. I turned to Peter and said, "Looks like a Walt Disney Theme Park," but still Peter was not impressed. "I'd rather be in some of those fancy restaurants and night clubs in Beirut."

As we approached the outskirts of the city, I began to think Peter was right. There were no tall, modern buildings with gleaming glass facades as in Beirut, only mud or brick slum dwellings interspersed with food stalls, bazaars, sandwich counters, barber shops, workshops and heaven knows what else. Hordes of harried pedestrians clogged the narrow alleyways, vying for a right-of-way with rickety pick-up trucks and hand-pulled wagons. The people were dressed in traditional flowing robes with the head covered either by a scarf or typical Arab headdress. Soon Peter was haggling in the market and I followed suit. It was fun but it was exhausting.

Finally, we dragged ourselves away to an open space and I tried to make an appreciation of the situation. It would soon be dark and I wanted to investigate the Roman ruins that dominated the city. We joined a group of American tourists and with them marvelled at the genius of the ancient builders. Probably the most impressive structure was the Temple of Jupiter. Some of the marble blocks measured 21 x 14 x 11 feet. Each 63-foot column consisted of three blocks. "How on earth did they do it?" exclaimed one of the group.

We were informed that in 1759 the temple and all the other buildings were destroyed by an earthquake, but I was quick to point out that what was left was still pretty impressive. No modern structure would have survived such a force.

Peter suddenly remembered he wanted to ride a camel, or at least have a picture taken of him and a hump-backed friend. There were none in town but our bus driver said we would probably see one on the way back to Beirut. He warned us, however, there are no deserts in Lebanon and he could not supply us with the usual sand dunes associated with camels.

Luck was with us and we found our camel at a roadside gas pump, but it was strictly a "tourist camel" for taking pictures. It had probably once been a real camel but its days as a beast of burden were long gone and it only wanted to kneel down in the shade. I refused to mount the animal but Peter did, and with the aid of the owner, coaxed it to its feet long enough for me to take a picture of a modern-day Lawrence of Arabia. Peter, of course, had outfitted himself with the traditional Arab costume and headgear supplied by the owner.

On the way home, I received an interesting reminder of my days in Italy. In August 1944, a troopship of the Orient Line brought me back to Italy from England where I had been recuperating from wounds received the year before. The name of the ship was *Orontes*. It was a peculiar name and I have always wondered where it came from. Thanks to my excursion to Baalbek, I believe I have found the source.

As the bus careened along the road back to Beirut, I noticed a sign "Orontes" on a bridge we were crossing. I asked the driver if that was the name of the river. Yes, it was. The Orontes River is one of the few rivers in Lebanon. It begins in the northern part of the Biqa Plain we were traversing and flows into Syria. Would I like to make a little detour and follow the river to the border? I thanked the driver but I didn't take up his kind offer. I just wanted to get back to civilization and Beirut and that nice, clean hotel.

Next day, June 27th, I strolled through the fashionable avenues of Beirut and poked my nose into some of the elegant shops. Not having a letter of credit with me, I merely admired the costly merchandise and left it for the stylishly-dressed passers-by. I purposely avoided the many fine buildings housing banking and financial institutions so as not to be tempted to splurge my life savings.

As mentioned earlier, Beirut is a centre of culture and education. The Lebanese value education very highly and have some of the finest institutions in the Arab world. The American University attracts students from many lands. I felt that such a unique university deserved at least a passing visit and spent an hour or two admiring its facilities.

That evening, I joined Peter for a tour of the night spots of the city. Beirut, like all other cosmopolitan centres, boasts of its low as well as its high life. We were not disappointed. The concierge of our hotel recommended a dinner-theatre palace which he described as having the most exotic, elegant, live theatre and dining experience in the world. I had not yet had such a vast experience but I will say that up to that point it was the most incredible showplace I had ever seen.

The "Palace" was as huge as an indoor football stadium, with hundreds of tables arranged around a vast stage. The dinner, while ample and served by a bevy of beautiful women scantily clothed, took second place to a steady and overpowering flow of wine, spirits and liqueurs of all kinds. By the time the show arrived, Peter and I had already agreed that the concierge had been right.

I do not have a clear memory of that show but I will never forget the impression it made. Never before or since have I seen such a galaxy of gorgeous girls singing and dancing in one set after another for two or three hours. I can't remember how many female performers were on the stage at one time but I believe I was told 500 or more. Throughout the program, girls would arrive by boat, by canoe, by camel, by balloon and by vehicles. The show culminated in a life-size naval battle in ancient warships on a body of water that suddenly replaced the stage. What became of all those girls I do not know but I have a few ideas.

Peter and I left Beirut the next morning, June 18th, well satisfied that we had fulfilled our mandate of making a quick reconnaissance of Lebanon. I resolved to return the first chance I had.

Alas, the opportunity was denied me. Within a few years that beautiful cosmopolitan city of culture and delight was engulfed in a civil war that nearly destroyed it. Lebanon became a post-apocalyptic society where the only law and order came out of the barrel of a gun.

I was glad to get back to Nicosia and see how my Band was making out under the aegis of the Patricias. They were doing just fine. In the two days I had been away, they had worked very hard to prepare for the July 1st Ceremonies, and I could see that a good rapport had developed between the two groups. The PPCLI RSM was perhaps a little tough but that's the way RSMs are supposed to act.

LCol. Bill Hutchinson went over the Ceremonies with me and gave me a copy of the programs for the two main events—"A Stampede Breakfast" and the Feu de Joie and Retreat Ceremony in the evening. I thought it was a pretty ambitious undertaking for a Militia Band but Colonel Hutchinson assured me they could manage.

As this was the first time a Militia Band had performed with a UN contingent on peacekeeping duties, the programs are unique and should be placed on the record. Here they are:

CANADA DAY
1 JULY 1971
CYPRUS

A FEU de JOIE on CANADA'S NATIONAL DAY
by
FIRST BATTALION
PRINCESS PATRICIA'S CANADIAN
LIGHT INFANTRY
UNITED NATIONS FORCE CYPRUS
PROGRAMME OF EVENTS

1815 hrs—Musical Prelude
1830 hrs—Battalion Marches on
1845 hrs—Arrival of the Reviewing Officer —
   Major General D. Prem Chand, PVSM

  General Salute
  Inspection by the Reviewing Officer
  Presentation of UNFICYP Medals
  March Past in Quick Time
  Battalion Fires a Feu de Joie
  The Band Beats Retreat
  Address by the Reviewing Officer
  The Battalion Marches Off

NOTE

Spectators are requested to stand when:
  The Reviewing Officer arrives.
  When the troops march past.
  During the Canadian National Anthem.

It is the custom for all ranks to salute and ladies to curtsey when the Colours pass encased.

CYPRUS—1971

MUSICAL PROGRAMME

Parade Prelude — A selection of Military Marches

March on of the Battalion —"Thin Red Line"

During the Inspection —   "Lili Marlene"
*   "Scipio"*

March Past — PPCLI Regimental March—a Medley of
*   "Has Anyone Seen The Colonel"*
*   "Tipperary" and*
*   "Madamoiselle From Armentieres"*

Feu de Joie —   "National Anthems of Canada"

Beating Retreat —   "Viscount Nelson" and
*   "By Land and Sea"*

Sunset — "Orchestrated Sunset Hymn"

March Off — "Maple Leaf Forever"—*the First Battalion March*
            "British Grenadiers—Here's to the Maiden"—*Regimental March of The Royal Regiment of Canada*

The Regimental Band of The Royal Regiment of Canada— Canadian Forces Militia, conducted by Capt. E. J. Robbins, appears with the permission of LCol. P. Fairclough CD, Commanding Officer and the co-operation of Canadian Forces Headquarters.

CANADA DAY
1 JULY 1971

STAMPEDE BREAKFAST
PRESENTED BY
THE CANADIAN CONTINGENT
PROGRAMME

0700	—	*GATES OPEN—SALOON OPEN*
0715—0845	—	*BREAKFAST AVAILABLE FROM THE "CHUCKWAGONS"*
	—	*WESTERN MUSIC BY THE ROYAL REGIMENT OF CANADA*
	—	*GUESTS ARE INVITED TO VISIT THE JAIL, THE SALOON, THE BLACKSMITH AND THE TELEGRAPH OFFICE*
0750	—	*PRESENTATION OF WHITE STETSONS*
0800	—	*MARCH ON OF COMPETITORS FOR "RODEO" EVENTS*
0805	—	*GREASED PIG CATCHING*
0820	—	*DONKEY RACE*
0830	—	*BARREL RACE*
0835	—	*PRESENTATION OF PRIZES*
	—	*SQUARE DANCING IN THE GYMNASIUM; GUESTS ARE INVITED TO JOIN IN AFTER THE FIRST DANCE*
0900	—	*THE NATIONAL ANTHEM BY THE ROYAL REGIMENT OF CANADA BAND*

FOR CHILDREN RIDES ON THE DONKEYS OR WITH THE HORSEMEN ARE AVAILABLE. SEE THE "OLD PROSPECTOR" FOR A DONKEY RIDE OR ANY OF THE RIDERS FOR A RIDE ON HORSEBACK.

DRINKS ARE "ON THE HOUSE" AT THE SALOON ANYTIME

In addition to these two main events, the Band played on several other occasions including impromptu sessions with the troops, as will be described.

The purpose of these parades and ceremonies was not simply to give the troops something to do or to refresh their military skills on the parade ground. The purpose was to "show the flag," not only to the other UN contingents but to the Cypriot people, of both Greek and Turkish origin, and to extend the hand of friendship to these communities. The events were also meant to demonstrate that the UN, and Canada in particular, were not there as occupiers of their lands but as friends to help them return to normal conditions and prevent any further bloodshed.

The "Western Flavour" to the celebrations was due, of course, to the fact that Calgary was the home base of 1 PPCLI and the Patricias had since WW1 been considered a western unit. Indeed, this had been one of the reasons I had joined the Patricias after RMC. I liked their friendly, outgoing nature and great family spirit.

It was now late in the afternoon of June 28th and only two more days to go. Colonel Hutchinson completed briefing me on the program and excused himself as he had to meet MGen. Cammie Ware and Mrs. Ware, who were arriving that evening. This was wonderful news. I had been Cammie Ware's Scout Officer in Italy and, like all Patricias, had a great respect and affection for him.

On June 30, final rehearsals were held and all was in readiness for the big day. The UN Force newspaper, *Blue Beret*, published this account of the forthcoming events:

CANADA DAY

Five hundred guests, representing the two Cypriot communities, the eight countries on duty with the United Nations in Cyprus, personal friends and special guests are expected to fill Wolseley compound to celebrate Canada Day on 1st July.

In western Canada, the home of the 1st Battalion, Princess Patricia's Canadian Light Infantry, Calgary, wears a ten gallon hat and extends a big friendly handshake to the visitor. For westerners, hospitality is their proudest asset, and the hallmark of Calgary's world famous Stampede.

Extending a friendly hand to visitors here in Cyprus will be the official host and senior Canadian military representative with the United Nations, Brigadier General E.M.D. Leslie. Representing Canada's Diplomatic Corps will be Miss Elizabeth Way, second secretary to the Canadian Ambassador in Israel, combining with the Contingent Commander, Lieutenant Colonel W.E.J. Hutchinson. The day will blast off with a Stampede Breakfast—western style.

> *Guests will return again at 1830 hrs to see one hundred and twenty-five soldiers accompanied by the thirty-six piece band of The Royal Regiment of Canada parade at Camp UNFICYP receive their UN medals. The sunset ceremony will be concluded with a Feu de Joie.*
>
> *Following the parade at 2100 hrs, invited guests will return to individual receptions at the military messes in the Canadian Contingent.*

All the time and energy that had been spent by 1 PPCLI in preparing for the Canada Day Celebrations, and all the work and frustrations in getting the Band to Cyprus, found abundant justification when the last notes of the Retreat had been sounded and the Battalion marched off the parade ground. The day had been an outstanding success. Time and time again the many spectators applauded the troops and congratulations poured in from every quarter. Best of all, the parade had engendered new feelings of friendship and respect by the citizens of Nicosia for Canada and its PPCLI contingent.

The official history of The Royal Regiment of Canada, Battle Royal, describes the important contribution made by the Band:

> *In June 1971, the regimental Band, accompanied by Lieutenant-Colonel Frost and Captain Peter Marani, visited Cyprus for two weeks to take part in the Canada Day Celebrations observed by the Canadian contingent of the United Nations Force. The Band left Trenton on 22 June by a service air flight and arrived in Nicosia on 23 June, where it was attached to the 1st Battalion Princess Patricia's Canadian Light Infantry under the command of Lieutenant-Colonel W.E.J. Hutchinson. The Band was given one week to rehearse with the PPCLI and become acclimatized to the extreme heat, which on occasion rose to 120 degrees. The rehearsals took place in the mornings and evenings, and the afternoons were spent enjoying a siesta or visiting the beautiful beaches at Kyrenia and Famagusta.*
>
> *The Canada Day Celebrations on 1 July began with a section of the Band in western attire playing at a barbecue style breakfast held by the PPCLI. At noon the full Band played for a luncheon held at the headquarters Officers' Mess of the United Nations Force. In the evening the Canada Day parade was held at the Nicosia airport in the presence of representatives from all the contingents of the United Nations Force and a large gathering of the local cit-*

izens. The PPCLI fired a feu de joie in honour of Canada Day, and the Band performed a sunset ceremony.

In addition to these official duties with the PPCLI, the Band also played at a children's hospital in Kyrenia that was being maintained by a group of Canadian churches and service clubs. The Band taped a one-half hour programme at the Cyprus broadcasting studios in Nicosia for the BBC Network and played at the Carlsberg Festival as well as at other impromptu sessions with the troops.

Throughout their two-week stay in Cyprus, the Band performed their duties as musicians and soldiers in a faultless manner and received many compliments from the PPCLI and the other contingents with the United Nations Force. Much of the success of the visit was due to the high standards set by the Director of Music, Captain Ted Robbins, Drum Major Ron Scott and Master Warrant Officer Bill Cavanagh.

Lieutenant-Colonel Frost paid an official visit to Mr. C. Kythreotis, the acting mayor of Nicosia, and on behalf of Mr. William Dennison, the mayor of Toronto, tendered civic greetings from the city and presented Mr. Kythreotis with a set of City of Toronto cuff-links.

The Band returned to Toronto on 8 July after making a brief stop-over at the Canadian Forces Base at Lahr, Germany.[1]

My own feelings of pride in seeing my two Regiments perform together so magnificently are better imagined than described. Suffice it to say, it was one of the most memorable events in my thirty-six years of service.

I thanked Bill Hutchinson (we had been on a first name basis from day one) for all he had done to make this day such a success. It had been a tour de force in every respect. As a token of my gratitude, I presented him with the gold cuff links I had received from the Mayor of Toronto so long ago (so it seemed at the time). He congratulated me on the performance of the Band and said, "Well done, Syd. You have earned a weekend pass. I suggest you visit Athens. I'll make the arrangements!"

No sooner said than done. I was on my way next day, July 2, via Olympic Airways. But in my haste, I almost overlooked observing a date as important as the Canada Day Celebrations, if not more so. It was my 23rd Wedding Anniversary! Before leaving Nicosia I sent a wire to my wife.

CYPRUS—1971

July 1
We are about to go on our big parade at 6:00 p.m. this evening. Temperature today at least 105 degrees. Cammie Ware arrived and staying in my hotel—Ledra Palace. Tomorrow I'm off to Athens for a weekend leave! What an Army! Happy Anniversary.

Love,

After all the good work Peter Marani had done in looking after the administration of the Band, I couldn't leave him behind. So he came aboard Flight OA332 leaving Nicosia at 9:05 a.m. bound for Athens, a distance of 576 miles. This was a longer hop than our flight to Beirut and I wondered whether the airline would feed us. The answer came shortly after take off. Suddenly little gas burners were produced by some of the passengers, who placed them in the aisles and proceeded to cook breakfast! My only thought was: If the plane blows up, no one will believe it was not hit by anti-aircraft fire and the Middle East wars will start up all over again, and incidentally, it's not much of an Anniversary present for my wife.

Thankfully, there was no explosion and we landed safely in Athens at 10:30 a.m. I made a note not to travel Olympic Airways at or close to meal time.

The first question on landing was to find a decent hotel. I had tried to make reservations but nothing was available except a day room at the Grande Bretagne, a hostelry of great repute but beginning to show its age. Luckily, a room became available at the posh Hilton Hotel and we quickly transferred. Again, time was of the essence and we had already wasted most of day one.

Athens. Fountainhead of western culture and democracy, declared the guidebook. That much I knew; also, something about the Acropolis, the Parthenon and Lord Elgin's Marbles. The last item baffled me. I wasn't sure whether he had lost them, found them or stolen them. Peter was slightly more *au fait* with the wonders of Athens but wisely suggested we get a guide, which we did.

The *Acropolis* is the highest point in the city. Indeed, that is the meaning of the word. From its marble ruins one can observe a bright and busy new Athens with broad avenues and glass-faced office buildings. Our guide informed us that the Acropolis stands as an enduring monument to the Glory of Greece. That phrase struck a familiar note and I was tempted to correct him. He had prudently substituted "of" for "that was," but I remained silent.

The area was littered with marble boulders of all sizes, as if a giant explosion had blown apart some of the ancient buildings. My guess proved to be correct. We picked our way through these stones and came to the *Parthenon*, which the guide told us meant "Virgins' Place." As anyone who has read my earlier book knows, this name gave me trouble. In school, I always confused it with the Roman Pantheon until during the War I visited Rome. The moment I saw it the light went on. Pantheon and Roman are alike. "Pan" rhymes with "man."

By process of elimination, Parthenon must be in Athens, and so it was. The guide added a little history. It was built between 447 and 432 B.C. under the rule of Pericles. It had served as a Christian church and a mosque. In 1687, it was used as a powder magazine by the Turks. In an attack by the Venetians, it exploded and the entire centre portion was destroyed.

The Acropolis is ringed by other landmarks of the ancient city: a well-preserved Doric Temple, the Temple of Zeus, the Theatre of Dionysus and the Royal Palace and Gardens.

This was about all Peter and I could take and we returned to our hotel to recoup our strength for the evening's activities. Next day I was keen to visit the Royal Palace and Gardens which we had briefly observed the day before. On approaching the area I thought I heard the unmistakeable whine of bagpipes. My suspicions were confirmed when I arrived at the Palace gates. There stood two sentries in kilts working their bagpipes as if their life depended on it. Déjà vu! The 48th Highlanders had upstaged me again.

My fears were unfounded. The 48th Highlanders are not the only people in the world who have bagpipes. The Greeks had them first.

The remainder of my time in Athens was devoted to a repeat visitation to the Acropolis to examine the monuments I had missed, including the famous Elgin Marbles, which I learned are only replicas. The originals now rest in the British Museum, much to the annoyance of the Greek Government. And so ended a fascinating tour of the cradle of democracy.

No dancing girls this trip, as I had encountered in Beirut. Peter and I had a quiet dinner in the hotel with liberal lashings of Greek wine, strange spirits and liqueurs with peculiar names like Ouzo. I became quite philosophical and mused about my good fortune in having had the opportunity to visit the two great cultural centres of the ancient world, Rome and Athens. The first, courtesy of His Majesty King George VI and the second, courtesy of his daughter Elizabeth. And, more important, how lucky I had been to survive the first so that I could visit the second.

There is little more to tell. We returned to Nicosia July 4th (no burners in the aircraft this time) and found that the members of the Band had been following our example by visiting various cities within easy reach of Cyprus. For many it had been the trip of a lifetime and they were glad to return home. I had a happy hour or two with Bill Hutchinson and we exchanged thanks and congratulations for the parts each of us had played. I apologized for suggesting to him at one of our first meetings that I take command of his battalion while he went on leave. He brushed it off with a good-natured laugh. "Truth is I was afraid you would enjoy it so much you would never leave."

The greatest pleasure of all was to spend several hours with MGen. Cammie Ware, reminiscing about our wartime experiences. His great ability had been recognized and he had held many responsible appointments in the Army. He was retired but was now Colonel of the Regiment, a position of high honour and distinction. Due to my taking up a career in law after the War, joining The Royal Regiment of Canada and finally becoming its Commanding Officer and Honorary Lieutenant-Colonel, I had little time for other pursuits and had lost contact with General Ware. We soon renewed our friendship which I am happy to say continued until his recent passing—an outstanding soldier, a real gentleman and a true Patricia.

The Royals Band left Cyprus on July 7th Service Air. After brief stopovers at Düsseldorf and Lahr, we arrived at Trenton at 2:30 a.m. July 8th and were bussed to the Fort York Armoury, Toronto.

I reported to Mayor Dennison that I had duly presented the City's gold cuff links to LCol. Bill Hutchinson and the Acting Mayor of Nicosia.

So far as I know, nothing appeared in the Toronto papers or anywhere else about this extraordinary trip to Cyprus. The various Headquarters involved in the tour quickly closed their files and it was soon forgotten, except by the grateful Band. No mementos exist save one. I am the proud possessor of a set of gold cuff links of the City of Toronto presented to me by the Mayor in recognition of the several "hats" I wore in connection with the trip.

I also take pride in the knowledge that I had not failed to uphold the mottoes and sayings of my two Regiments:

Once a Patricia, Always a Patricia
Ready Aye Ready
Ich Dien (I serve)

EPILOGUE

One of the young officers serving with the PPCLI in Cyprus during my visit was Capt. Lew MacKenzie. He was the "OPS Officer," responsible for the operations of the Battalion. Even at that stage of his career he had developed a reputation as a keen officer and was showing the aggressive style of leadership that would bring him fame as Canada's ultimate Peacekeeper.

We got to know each other in 1988 when he was the Commander of the Combat Training Centre in Oromocto, New Brunswick. He had read my book, *Once a Patricia*, and wanted a copy for a mutual friend of ours.

We met at the 75th Anniversary of the PPCLI in Calgary, in 1989, and have kept in touch ever since.

When I was writing this book, I sent him a draft of the chapter on Cyprus for his comments. I told him I was certain he was with the Battalion when I visited it in 1971, but frankly, I could not remember meeting him.

Lew is seldom at a loss for words. "Funny thing is, Syd, I can't remember seeing you. From reading your draft chapter, I get the impression you spent most of your time in Beirut and Athens while I was running the Battalion."

One must get up awfully early to get a jump on Lew MacKenzie.

93. Trenton – 22 June 1971 – Royal Regiment Band prepares to board aircraft.

94. Nicosia Mosque – Author with PPCLI Guide.

95. *Nicosia – Turkish Quarter.*

96. *Nicosia – Observation Tower – PPCLI officers indicate Greek and Turkish positions on the "Green Line."*

BAALBEK
Roman Ruins – More impressive than the forum in Rome itself.

97. *Baalbek – Author and Capt. Peter Marani.*

98. *Baalbek*

99. Baalbek

100. Baalbek

101. *Modern-day Lawrence beside his "Fort."*

102. *Ancient Arab ruins.*

103. Bedouin encampment, enroute to Baalbek.

104. Beirut

105. Beirut

106. Athens – Guard at Royal Palace wearing traditional costume.

107. Athens – The Acropolis crowned by the Parthenon.

108. Athens – Lord Elgin's marbles. (Author wasn't sure whether he had lost them, found them or stolen them.)

109. Band of The Royal Regiment of Canada

110. PPCLI prepare to fire a Feu de Joie — Canada, Day, 1 July 1971.

111. *Drum Major Scott*

112. *March Past*

113. Arrivederci Cyprus!

LIST OF MAPS

1. The Sicilian Operations, July 10th–September 3rd, 1943   2
2. Southern Italy   126
3. Northern Italy   127
4. Advance to the Foggia Plain, 1943   128
5. Advance on Campobasso, October, 1943   129
6. The Gothic Line and San Fortunato   130
7. Five Months in the Romagna   131
8. Canadian Cemeteries and Memorials in Italy and Sicily   132, 503
9. North-Western Europe (Holland)   232

CHAPTER NOTES

ITALY

Chapter IX—Pilgrimage—1989
1. LCol. G. W. Nicholson, *The Canadians in Italy*, 1943-1945: Volume II (Ottawa: Queen's Printer, 1956), 562
2. Ibid, 563
3. G. R. Stevens, *Princess Patricia's Canadian Light Infantry*: Volume Three (Griesbach, Alberta: The Historical Committee of the Regiment, 1958), 196
4. Nicholson, *The Canadians in Italy*, 328
5. ———, 328
6. ———, 327
7. Mark Zuehlke, *The Liri Valley* (Stoddart Publishing Co. Limited, 2001), 293
8. David J. Bercuson, *The Patricias* (Stoddart Publishing Co. Limited, 2001), 223
9. Colin McDougall, *Execution* (The MacMillan Company of Canada Limited, 1958), 113
10. Stevens, *Princess Patricia's Canadian Light Infantry*, 160

Chapter X—Pilgrimage—1991
1. LCol. G. W. Nicholson, *The Canadians in Italy*, 1943-1945: Volume II (Ottawa: Queen's Printer, 1956), 329
2. Ibid, 328
3. Ibid, 328
4. Mark Zuehlke, *Ortona* (Stoddart Publishing Co. Limited, 1999), 189

Chapter XI—Pilgrimage—1994
 1. G. R. Stevens, *Princess Patricia's Canadian Light Infantry*: Volume Three (Griesbach, Alberta: The Historical Committee of the Regiment, 1958), 197
 2. LCol. G. W. Nicholson, *The Canadians in Italy*, 1943-1945: Volume II (Ottawa: Queen's Printer, 1956), 590
 3. Stevens, *Princess Patricia's Canadian Light Infantry*, 211
 4. Nicholson, *The Canadians in Italy*, 625
 5. Stevens, *Princess Patricia's Canadian Light Infantry*, 214
 6. Ibid, 216
 7. Ibid, 216

HOLLAND

Preface to the Pilgrimages, Holland 1945, 1985
 1. G. R. Stevens, *Princess Patricia's Canadian Light Infantry*: Volume Three (Griesbach, Alberta: The Historical Committee of the Regiment, 1958), 236
 2. Ibid, 240
 3. Ibid, 240
 4. Col. C. P. Stacey, *The Victory Campaign, The Operations in North-West Europe, 1944-1945*: Volume III (Ottawa: Queen's Printer, 1960), 608
 5. Ibid, 609
 6. Ibid, 583
 7. John Redfern, *First Full Story of the Holland Food Truce*

Chapter XIII—Germany-Holland, 1986
 1. G. R. Stevens, *Princess Patricia's Canadian Light Infantry*: Volume Three (Griesbach, Alberta: The Historical Committee of the Regiment, 1958), 246
 2. C. S. Frost, *Once a Patricia* (Vanwell Publishing Limited, 1988), 488

CYPRUS

Chapter XVIII—Cyprus—1971
 1. LCol. D. J. Goodspeed, *Battle Royal, A History of The Royal Regiment of Canada*, Second Edition (The Royal Regiment of Canada Association, 1979), 725

LIST OF PHOTOGRAPHS

	Photo #
SICILY	
Pachino	1
Modica	2
The Beaches	3, 4
Road to Nissoria	5
PPCLI in action near Valguarnera, 20 July 1943	6
Road to Ispica	7
Mount Etna, 1997	8
Agira Cemetery	9, 10
Ispica Monument to the landing of 1st Canadian Division, Sicily, 10 July, 1943	11
Unveiling ceremony, 22 September 1991	12
Carmelo and author after the ceremony	13
Author with two Patricias, John Clarke and Captain Kurt Fredrickson	14
Ispica Monuments to Canadians and Italians, 8 December 2000	15
ITALY	
Mine clearing, July 1943	16
Lagopesole	17
San Fortunato	18-21
Bovey	22, 23
Marecchia River	24
Savio River	25
Lamone River	26, 27
Palazzo San Giacomo	28, 29

	Photo #
Senio River winter line, Jan, Feb, 1945	30-32
Rimini, Grand Hotel, 1997	33
Republic of San Marino	34

CEMETERIES

Cassino	35-37
Moro River	38
Gradara	39, 40
Coriano Ridge	41-43

HOLLAND

Ijssel River, Wilp. 11 April 1945	44-50
Parade Beekbergen, Lieren, Oosterhuizen 29 April 2000	51, 52
Oosterhuizen monument to PPCLI 21 April 1995	53, 54
Lieren Monument to PPCLI, 17 April 2002	55, 56
Achterveld monument to PPCLI, 9 May 2000	57
Achterveld, 1945	58-60
Achterveld schoolhouse, 1956	61
Groesbeek cemetery, 1980	62, 63
Keukenhof gardens, 1980	64
Holten cemetery	65-68
Amsterdam, 35th anniversary of Liberation May 1980	
— Parade	69, 70
— Award of plaque	71
Apeldoorn, May 1985, dinner honouring Veterans	72
Utrecht, May 1990, dinner honouring Veterans	73, 74
Apeldoorn 1990 – 45th anniversary	
— Parade	75
— Presentation to HRH Princess Margriet	76
Apeldoorn 2000 – 55th anniversary	
— Parade	77-80
— Reception by HRH Princess Margriet	81
— Monument – Man with Two Hats	82
Ijssel River, Reenactment of Crossing, 2 May 1990	83-86
Antonius Church, De Vecht, 2000	87
Ottawa, 11 May 2002, Unveiling monument, Man with Two Hats	88-89
Overveen, Charter presented to PPCLI 7 May 1945	90
Zandvoort, German bunkers, 1985	91, 92

	Photo #
CYPRUS	
Departure, 22 June 1971	93
Nicosia	94-96
Baalbek	97-101
Ancient Arab Ruins	102
Bedouin Encampment	103
Beirut	104, 105
Athens, Greece	106-108
PPCLI Feu de Joie—Canada Day, 1 July 1971	109-112
Arrivederci Cyprus!	113

PHOTO CREDITS

SICILY, ITALY
DND, Public Archives of Canada - **1, 2, 3, 4, 5, 6, 7**
Mayor of Ispica - **11, 12, 15**
Canadian Army Overseas Photo - **16**
Rimini Grand Hotel Postcard - **33**
Jim Reid - **43**

HOLLAND
DND, Public Archives of Canada - **44, 45**
Gerrit Ham - **51-56**
Rudy Deutsch - **58, 59**
Jan Boersen - **60**
Jan M. Schouten - **57**
Kodak Nederland B.V. - **64, 69, 71**
André Petelle - **68, 75, 76**
Patrick Courage - **67**
Mark Hoedeman - **65, 66**
John Moore - **70**
Pieter Beelaerts van Blokland - **72, 73**
Olga Rains - **77, 80**
Bob Gardham, Veterans Affairs Canada - **78, 81, 88, 89**
Wysiwg://thepage.3//http://www.fortunec - **79**
Ati Derkse – den Boer - **86, 87**
Program of the Unveiling of the Monument, Man with Two Hats, Apeldoorn - **82**
G. J. Burgers - **83, 84**
Huub van Sabben - **85**

Note: Photos not listed above were taken by the author or by persons unknown

ARMY RANKS

Field Marshal	not abbreviated
General	Gen.
Lieutenant General	LGen.
Major General	MGen.
Brigadier General	BGen.
Brigadier	Brig.
Colonel	Col.
Lieutenant Colonel	LCol.
Major	Maj.
Captain	Capt.
Lieutenant	Lt.
Second Lieutenant	2Lt.
Temporary Second Lieutenant	Temp 2Lt.
Regimental Sergeant Major	RSM
Company Sergeant Major	CSM
Company Quartermaster Sergeant	CQMS
Lance Sergeant	LSgt.
Sergeant	Sgt.
Lance Corporal	LCpl.
Private	Pte.

MUSICAL SCORES

1985   Goodbye Wonderful Holland
1995   50th Anniversary March
2000   Salute to Holland
           Grand March 2000
           Never Again—A ballad
           Freedom—An anthem

GOODBYE WONDERFUL HOLLAND

By C. S. Frost, May 1985

Goodbye wonderful Holland
We do remember you too
Your friendship, warmth and your kindness
Make this a tearful adieu.

Oh, keep your home fires burning
In polder, town and farms
We'll soon return to see you again
And hold you in our arms.

50TH ANNIVERSARY MARCH – 1995

Liberation of Holland – 1945

Key of F   *By C. S. Frost*

Dear Holland, Holland, noble land,   *(Sung by Veterans)*
Where Canada's soldiers sleep,
Their sacrifice you honour still,
Their memory you keep.

CHORUS
Constancy shall mark our vigil,   *(Sung together)*
Guard our freedom, peace maintain,
That the sacrifice we honour
Was not made in vain.

Fifty years have passed away,   *(Sung by Dutch people)*
Since victory brought us peace,
Oh! May our friendship long endure
And wars forever cease.

CHORUS
Constancy shall mark our vigil,   *(Sung together)*
Guard our freedom, peace maintain,
That the sacrifice we honour
Was not made in vain.

"Grand March 2000" — music by: Sydney Frost.

Introduction to

NEVER AGAIN – 2000

This is the ballad of a Canadian soldier in Holland, in May 1945 just after the end of the War, and the liberation of the Dutch people who had suffered terribly under the German occupation. Many had starved to death.

The Canadian soldier had fought with the first division all through the Italian campaign. Near the end of the War, the division was transferred to Holland and took part in the liberation of that country.

He fell in love with a Dutch girl and planned to marry. But his division was sent to England and then home to Canada. He never returned.

NEVER AGAIN – 2000

A ballad - Key of C   *Words and Music by C. Sydney Frost*

Never, never again
Will that magic return
When we met in the springtime
And the world was at peace.

The fighting and starving were over
At last we could love and be loved
We pledged to each other
A new life together
And waited for the dawn.

The convoy came in the morning
And took me away from your arms
I'll never forget
But this I know
We'll never meet again.

Never, never again
Will that magic return
When we met in the springtime
And the world was at peace.

Princess Patricia's Canadian Light Infantry

THE ROLL OF HONOUR WORLD WAR TWO

(With place of burial)

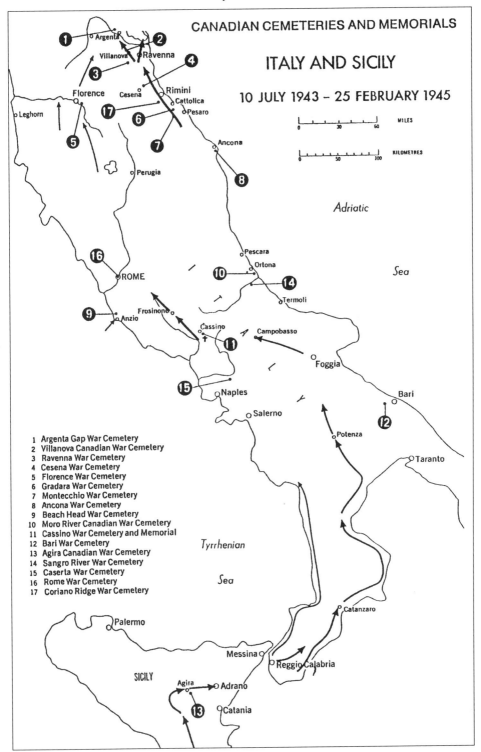

THE ROLL OF HONOUR—WORLD WAR TWO

REGIMENTAL CASUALTY LIST —PPCLI—WWII—ITALY

ITALY

AGIRA CANADIAN WAR CEMETERY, SICILY

Commonwealth War Dead, 1939-1945
ANDROS, Lance Corporal, JACK ALBERT, K/63095. "C" Coy. Princess Patricia's Canadian Light Infantry, R.C.I.C., 22nd July, 1943. Age 23. Son of John Hewitt Andros and Frances Victoria Andros, of Vanderhoof, British Columbia. B, A, 135.

BOULTON, Private, WILBERT ROY, H/95593. Princess Patricia's Canadian Light Infantry, R.C.I.C., 23rd July 1943. Age 24. Son of Albert and Harriet Cora Boulton, of Morden, Manitoba. B, H, 249.

BROWN, Private, ALBERT, H/101378. Princess Patricia's Canadian Light Infantry, R.C.I.C., 23rd July, 1943. Age 27. Son of Paul and Anne Brown, of Balmoral, Manitoba. B, B, 147

BROWN, Private, GEORGE DONALD, H/16583. Princess Patricia's Canadian Light Infantry, R.C.I.C., 25th July 1943. Age 31. Son of Donald and Ida Brown. B, A, 128.

BUCK, Sergeant, JOHN, K/85325. Princess Patricia's Canadian Light Infantry, R.C.I.C. 2nd August 1943. Age 27. Son of James C. and Margaret Buck, of Vancouver, British Columbia. D, D, 439.

CAMELON, Private, WILMER, H/16455. Princess Patricia's Canadian Light Infantry, R.C.I.C. 22nd July 1943. D, G, 482.

COUSINS, Private, SIDNEY JOHN, H/16736, Princess Patricia's Canadian Light Infantry, R.C.I.C., 22nd July 1943, Age 23, Son of William J. and Mabel E. Cousins, of Bagot, Manitoba. B, A, 140.

CURRIE, Lance Corporal, CECIL HARVEY, H/16591, Princess Patricia's Canadian Light Infantry, R.C.I.C. 22nd July 1943, Age 23, B, H, 247.

DE BALINHARD, Lieutenant, JOHN STEWART CARNEGIE, Princess Patricia's Canadian Light Infantry, R.C.I.C., 28th July 1943. Age 33. Son of John and Jessie de Balinhard, of Yorkton, Saskatchewan; husband of Iris Alice de Balinhard, of Yorkton, A, E, 66.

DOBSON, Corporal, HUGH WINSTON, K/85330. Princess Patricia's Canadian Light Infantry, R.C.I.C.. 26th July 1943. Age 29. Son of Melvin and Anna Dobson, of Wainwright, Alberta. C, E, 330.

THE ROLL OF HONOUR—WORLD WAR TWO

EGERTON, Private, LOUIS MARTIN, P/21464. Princess Patricia's Canadian Light Infantry, R.C.I.C.. 23rd July 1943, B, B, 153.

GARNEAU, Private, DANIEL, H/103249. Princess Patricia's Canadian Light Infantry, R.C.I.C.. 22nd July 1943. Age 22. Son of Francis and Mary Garneau, of Dinorwic, Ontario. B, F, 218.

GILL, Corporal, BASIL ERIC, K/42051. Princess Patricia's Canadian Light Infantry, R.C.I.C.. 22nd July 1943. Age 23. Son of Eric E. and Dorothy M. Gill, of Armstrong, British Columbia. B, B, 146.

GOSSELIN, Private, ALBERT JOHN CHARLES, H/101406. Princess Patricia's Canadian Light Infantry, R.C.I.C.. 22nd July 1943, C, E, 327.

HARRISON, Private, ROY, U/1606. Princess Patricia's Canadian Light Infantry, R.C.I.C. 5th August 1943. Age 23. Husband of Dorothy Harrison, of Leeds, Yorkshire, England. D, A, 385.

HILL, Lance Corporal, HAROLD JOSEPH EMIL, H/16741. Princess Patricia's Canadian Light Infantry, R.C.I.C. 26 July 1943. Age 26. Son of Walter and Katherine Hill. D, E, 441.

HORN, Lieutenant, JOHN ARCY, Princess Patricia's Canadian Light Infantry, R.C.I.C. 7th August 1943. Age 26. Son of David Horn, and of Eva Horn, of Finchley, Middlesex, England. B, C, 167.

JOHNSON, Private, WILLIAM, M/31507. Princess Patricia's Canadian Light Infantry, R.C.I.C. 23rd July 1943. A, A, 9.

KLASSEN, Private, DIETRICH VICTOR, H/17884. "C" Coy. Princess Patricia's Canadian Light Infantry, R.C.I.C. 23 July 1943. Age 20. Son of George and Anna Klassen, of Rivers, Manitoba, C, G, 354.

McFEE, Private, SAMUEL, H/16824. Princess Patricia's Canadian Light Infantry, R.C.I.C. 22nd July 1943. B, A, 132.

McKAY, Lance Corporal, EUGENE JOSEPH, H/16895. Princess Patricia's Canadian Light Infantry, R.C.I.C. 22nd July 1943, B, A, 134.

NICOL, Private, JAMES, K/66089. Princess Patricia's Canadian Light Infantry, R.C.I.C. 22nd July 1943. Age 32. Son of Robert B and Ann Nicol, of Vancouver, British Columbia, B, D, 178.

ODDY, Private, HERBERT, H/17792. Princess Patricia's Canadian Light Infantry, R.C.I.C. 27th July 1943. Age 21. Son of Jane Oddy, of Thornhill, Manitoba. C.E. 317.

PEARSON, Lance Corporal, THOMAS, H/17051. Princess Patricia's Canadian Light Infantry, R.C.I.C. 22nd July 1943. C, E, 328.

THE ROLL OF HONOUR—WORLD WAR TWO

POULAIN, Private, ADOLPHE LOUIS, K/85284. Princess Patricia's Canadian Light Infantry, R.C.I.C. 23rd July 1943. Age 22, Son of Lewis and Martha Elliot Poulain, C, G, 357.

SCHOLEY, Private, JOHN RICHARD, P/22256. Princess Patricia's Canadian Light Infantry, R.C.I.C. 22nd July 1943. Age 25. Son of William Arthur and Clarice May Scholey, of Winnipeg, Manitoba. B, F, 217.

SINCLAIR, Private, DONALD, H/16214. Princess Patricia's Canadian Light Infantry, R.C.I.C. 22nd July 1943. A, H, 126.

STEVENS, Company Quartermaster Sergeant, JOHN FRANK, K/85262. Princess Patricia's Canadian Light Infantry, R.C.I.C. 12th July 1943. Son of John Slade Stevens and Mary Stevens, of Victoria, British Columbia. A, A, 1.

VERMETTE, Private, RENE, H/17742. Princess Patricia's Canadian Light Infantry, R.C.I.C. 31st August 1943. Age 24. Son of Joachim and Marie Vermette, of St. Germain, Manitoba. A, E, 69.

ANCONA WAR CEMETERY

Commonwealth War Dead, 1939-1945

BIRCH, Private, RONALD, K/57272. Princess Patricia's Canadian Light Infantry, R.C.I.C. 27th September 1944. Son of George and May E. Birch; husband of Elizabeth Edith Mary Birch, of Victoria, Vancouver Island, British Columbia, Canada I,C, 17.

COUSENS, Private, JOHN, D/137893. Princess Patricia's Canadian Light Infantry, R.C.I.C. 4th September 1944. Age 33. Son of Samuel and Lilly A. Cousens, of Bolton Centre, Province of Quebec, Canada. I. C. 15.

RAY, Private, KENNETH REGINALD, H/16498. Princess Patricia's Canadian Light Infantry, R.C.I.C. 11th September 1944. Age 25. Son of Tom and Eva Pearl Ray, of St. James, Winnipeg, Manitoba, Canada. I. D. 1.

REID, Private, JAMES HOWARD, M/17457. Princess Patricia's Canadian Light Infantry, R.C.I.C. 17th September 1944. Age 33. Son of William and Elizabeth Reid; husband of Sadie M. Reid, of Grimshaw, Alberta, Canada. I. H. 13.

WEIDENHAMER, Lance Corporal, HUBERT CLAYTON, H/1406. Princess Patricia's Canadian Light Infantry, R.C.I.C. 23rd November 1944. Age 21. Son of Roy and Nellie Weidenhamer, of Dand, Manitoba, Canada, I. A. 3.

ARGENTA GAP WAR CEMETERY

Commonwealth War Dead, 1939-1945
GOODBURN, Sergeant, WILFRED, H/17155. Princess Patricia's Canadian Light Infantry, R.C.I.C. 16th February 1945. Age 23. Son of John and G. Margaret Goodburn, of Napinka, Manitoba, Canada. IV, D, 1.

STRACHAN, Private, ROBERT JOHN, K/16073. Princess Patricia's Canadian Light Infantry, R.C.I.C. 22nd December 1944. Husband of Henrietta B. Strachan. IV, G, 20.

ASSISI WAR CEMETERY

Commonwealth War Dead, 1939-1945
RATHERT, Private, HERBERT DONALD, H/103768. Princess Patricia's Canadian Light Infantry, R.C.I.C. 4th March 1945. Age 24. Son of Henry and Louise Rathert, of Starbuck, Manitoba, Canada. V, G, 4.

BARI WAR CEMETERY

Commonwealth War Dead, 1939-1945
BRADSHAW, Lance Corporal, FRANK VAUGHEN, M/11050. Princess Patricia's Canadian Light Infantry, R.C.I.C. 28th December 1943. Age 26. Son of Nellie Bradshaw, of Macleod, Alberta, Canada. III. D. 2.

CALDER, Private, CLIFFORD ALLAN, H/6599. 1 Princess Patricia's Canadian Light Infantry, R.C.I.C..9th October 1943. Age 23. Son of William and Blanche Calder; husband of Myrtle Calder, of Winnipeg, Manitoba, Canada, III. B. 11.

DODD, Private, CHARLES, H/103756. Princess Patricia's Canadian Light Infantry, R.C.I.C. 11th May 1944. Age 21. Son of Margaret Alice Dodd, of Ekhart, Manitoba, Canada. III. E. 12.

GRAHAM, Corporal, COLVILLE CHARLES,K/85361. Princess Patricia's Canadian Light Infantry, R.C.I.C. 23rd September 1943. Age 41. Son of Thomas and Ellen Graham, of Comox, British Columbia, Canada; husband of Maudie Graham. XV. C. 37.

LUDWIG, Private, ERIC GUNWAR, K/48052. Princess Patricia's Canadian Light Infantry, R.C.I.C. 31st March 1944. III. E. 11.

VICKERY, Private, WILLIAM GEORGE, C/80163. Princess Patricia's Canadian Light Infantry, R.C.I.C. 13th October 1943. Age 23. Son of Norman and Honor Vickery; husband of pearl Vickery, of Prescott, Ontario, Canada. III. B. 25.

THE ROLL OF HONOUR—WORLD WAR TWO

BEACH HEAD WAR CEMETERY, ANZIO

Commonwealth War Dead, 1939-1945
BROPHY, Captain, JOHN PURCELL, Princess Patricia's Canadian Light Infantry, R.C.I.C. 13th June 1944. Age 36. Son of Arthur and Agnes Brophy; husband of Vivien Brophy, of Toronto, Ontario, Canada. XVII. D. 5.

BOLSENA WAR CEMETERY

Commonwealth War Dead, 1939-1945
GATTINGER, Private, Jacob PHILIP, L/104951. Princess Patricia's Canadian Light Infantry, R.C.I.C. 23rd May 1944. Age 23. Son of Frank and Katherine Gattinger, of Bateman, Saskatchewan, Canada. IV, A, 2.

CASERTA WAR CEMETERY

Commonwealth War Dead, 1939-1945
McKAY, Private, WILFRED LAWRENCE, K/85206. Princess Patricia's Canadian Light Infantry, R.C.I.C. 10th May 1944. VII, D, 1.

PALMER, Private, LEONARD, K/85329. Princess Patricia's Canadian Light Infantry, R.C.I.C. 10th May 1944. Age 24. Son of Phillip and Mary Elizabeth Palmer; husband of Marjorie Joan Palmer, of Tillsonburg, Ontario, Canada. VII, D, 7.

CASSINO MEMORIAL

Commonwealth War Dead, 1939-1945
FALARDEAU, Private, ARTHUR MARTIN, H/9514. Princess Patricia's Canadian Light Infantry, R.C.I.C. 23 May 1944. Son of Osias and Orilda Falardeau, of Flin Flon, Manitoba, Canada, Panel 14.

HANISHEWSKI, Private, JOSEPH EDWARD, H/17798. Princess Patricia's Canadian Light Infantry, R.C.I.C. 24th July 1943. Panel 14.

LARUE, Private, ROBERT LOUIS, K/51631. Princess Patricia's Canadian Light Infantry, R.C.I.C. 20th October 1944. Age 20. Son of Antoine and Mary Larue, of Kamloops, British Columbia, Canada. Panel 14.

PARKER, Private, EARL CLIFFORD, A/107269. Princess Patricia's Canadian Light Infantry, R.C.I.C. 21st September 1944. Age 24. Son of Mr. And Mrs. Adam Parker; husband of Marian C. Parker, of Woodstock. Ontario, Canada, Panel 14.

ZEGLINSKI, Private, PHILLIP, H/102269. Princess Patricia's Canadian Light Infantry, R.C.I.C. 27th May 1944. Panel 14.

CASSINO WAR CEMETERY

Commonwealth War Dead, 1939-1945

AMOS, Lance Corporal, GEORGE, H/2957. "A" Coy. Princess Patricia's Canadian Light Infantry, R.C.I.C. 23rd May 1944. Age 31. Son of Frederick and Elizabeth Brown Amos; husband of Winifred Phyllis Amos, of Carnduff, Saskatchewan, Canada. IX .B 4.

ARGUE, Lance Corporal, REGINALD GLEN, H/17103. Princess Patricia's Canadian Light Infantry, R.C.I.C. 23rd May 1944. Age 24. Son of Robert Herbert and Ethel May Argue, of Brandon, Manitoba, Canada. IX. B. 7.

BANGLE, Lance Corporal, CLARENCE FRANCIS, H/17778. Princess Patricia's Canadian Light Infantry, R.C.I.C. 23rd May 1944. Age 21. Son of Rexford Esmond Bangle, and of Mary Josephine Bangle, of Walkerburn, Manitoba, Canada. IX. A. 18.

BEITZ, Private, FREDERICK, H/104105. Princess Patricia's Canadian Light Infantry, R.C.I.C. 24th May 1944. Age 22. Son of Reinhardt and Susan Beitz, of Winnipeg, Manitoba, Canada. XIII. F. 11.

BENNETT, Private, RUBEN RAY, H/8957. Princess Patricia's Canadian Light Infantry, R.C.I.C. 23rd May 1944. Son of Chester and Martha Bennett, of McCreary, Manitoba, Canada. IX. A. 16.

BOTHAM, Private, CHARLES R. L/105832. Princess Patricia's Canadian Light Infantry, R.C.I.C. 23rd May 1944. Age 21. Son of Robert Samuel and Doris Lillian Botham, of Plato, Saskatchewan, Canada. IX. A. 11.

BROWN, Private, WALLACE, D/141500. Princess Patricia's Canadian Light Infantry, R.C.I.C. 23rd May 1944. IX. A. 10.

BUTTERFIELD, Private, ROSS, K/85326. Princess Patricia's Canadian Light Infantry, R.C.I.C. 23rd May 1944. IX. C. 16.

CHARNEY, Private, PETER, H/16285. Princess Patricia's Canadian Light Infantry, R.C.I.C. 23rd May 1944. Age 27. Son of Peter and Magda Charney; husband of Winnifred Peggy Charney, of Vancouver, British Columbia, Canada. IX. A. 22.

CHILD, Corporal, PETER, K/69512. "D" Coy. Princess Patricia's Canadian Light Infantry, R.C.I.C. 23rd May 1944. Age 26. Son of Harry and Augusta Child; husband of Josephine Anne Child (nee Stopforth), of Vancouver, British Columbia, Canada. IX. B. 18.

CHRISTIE, Sergeant, CHARLES E. K/85350. Princess Patricia's Canadian Light Infantry, R.C.I.C. 23rd May 1944. Age 41. Son of

Albert E. And Mary L. Christier, of Victoria, British Columbia, Canada. B.S.A. (University of Toronto). IX. A. 3.

CLARK, Private, ARCHIE, C/102064. Princess Patricia's Canadian Light Infantry, R.C.I.C. 23rd May 1944. Age 21. Son of Ambrose and Charlotte Clark, of Ottawa, Ontario, Canada. IX. A. 5.

CLARK, Private, ALBERT G., H/3523. "B" Coy. Princess Patricia's Canadian Light Infantry, R.C.I.C. 23rd May 1944. Age 34, Son of Mr. and Mrs. George Clark; husband of Joan Peggy Clark, of Hounslow, Middlesex, IX. B. 16.

CRABTREE, Lieutenant, JOHN COLLINS, Princess Patricia's Canadian Light Infantry, R.C.I.C. 23rd May 1944. Age 24. Son of George William and Margaret Crabtree, of Regina, Saskatchewan, Canada. IX. B. 12.

DAVIDSON, Warrant Officer Class II (C.S.M.), WILLIAM DAVID, M M, P/21454. Princess Patricia's Canadian Light Infantry, R.C.I.C. 25th May 1944. Son of William Davidson, and of Emily Kate Netterville Davidson, of Denton, Texas, U.S.A. IX. C. 15.

DUNCAN, Corporal, SYDNEY CHARLES, H/16630. Princess Patricia's Canadian Light Infantry, R.C.I.C. 23rd May 1944. Age 23. Son of Percival and Emily Duncan, of Winnipeg, Manitoba, Canada; husband of Joan Duncan, of Winnipeg. IX. C. 3.

EHINGER, Private, FREDRICK, H/16611. Princess Patricia's Canadian Light Infantry, R.C.I.C. 23rd May 1944. IX B. 15.

FIDIADIS, Corporal, PETER, D/157549. Princess Patricia's Canadian Light Infantry, R.C.I.C. 23rd May 1944. Age 26. Son of George and Albertine Fidiadis, of Montreal, Province of Quebec, Canada. IX. B. 14.

FOULSHAM, Private, ARTHUR, B/127859. Princess Patricia's Canadian Light Infantry, R.C.I.C. 23rd May 1944. Age 26. Son of Frank and Eileen Foulsham, of Mackayville, Province of Quebec, Canada. IX. A. 14.

GRIMSHAW, Sergeant, WILFRED, K/85412. "C" Coy. Princess Patricia's Canadian Light Infantry, R.C.I.C. 23rd May 1944. Age 38. Son of Beesley and Hannah Grimshaw, of Barrowford, Lancashire. IX. A. 6.

GROVES, Private, GORDON, H/100742. Princess Patricia's Canadian Light Infantry, R.C.I.C. 23rd May 1944. Age 20. Son of Henry and Lillian Groves, of Dominion City, Manitoba, Canada. IX. B. 3.

HAIGHT, Private, CLIFFORD RAY, C/78083. Princess Patricia's Canadian Light Infantry, R.C.I.C. 23rd May 1944. Age 29. Son of Percy and Effie Haight; husband of Frances Margaret Haight, of Sunderland, Ontario, Canada. IX. A. 19.

HAYWARD, Private, WILLIAM ALEXANDER, L/104308. Princess Patricia's Canadian Light Infantry, R.C.I.C. 30th May 1944. Age 31. Son of John David and Nettie Douglas Hayward, of Morris, Manitoba, Canada. V. K. 7.

HEPPELL, Lieutenant, JOHN ROY, Mentioned in Despatches, Princess Patricia's Canadian Light Infantry, R.C.I.C. 23rd May 1944. Age 32. Son of John Rae McKay Heppell and Eleanor May Heppell, of Calgary, Alberta, Canada; husband of Lilian Heppell, of Calgary. IX. B. 8.

HURFORD, Private, GLYNN LLOYD, K/48930. Princess Patricia's Canadian Light Infantry, R.C.I.C. 23rd May 1944. IX. A. 17.

HUTCHINSON, Corporal, JOHN, K/85212. Princess Patricia's Canadian Light Infantry, R.C.I.C. 23rd May 1944. IX. C. 8.

KOLCUN, Private, PETER, H/103967. Princess Patricia's Canadian Light Infantry, R.C.I.C. 23rd May 1944. Age 23. Son of Nick and Cassie Kolcun, of Gilbert Plains, Manitoba, Canada, IX. B. 10.

KRYSOWARY, Private, SAM, H/17829. Princess Patricia's Canadian Light Infantry, R.C.I.C. 23rd May 1944. Age 29. Son of Steve Krysowaty and of Sofie Krysowaty (nee Sicharska); husband of Mary Margaret Krysowaty, of Shoal Lake, Manitoba, Canada. IX. B. 13.

KUCY, Private, LEO FRANK, M/107304. Princess Patricia's Canadian Light Infantry, R.C.I.C. 23rd May 1944. Age 31. Son of Frank and Rosie Kucy, of St. Michael, Alberta, Canada. IX. B. 11.

LONGNEY, Private, LEONARD VICTOR, H/103457. Princess Patricia's Canadian Light Infantry, R.C.I.C. 13th June 1944. Age 21. Son of William Henry and Jane Mabel Longney, of Thornhill, Manitoba. Canada. XIII. F. 4.

LORD, Lance Sergeant, CHARLES GRAINGER, K/37020. "A" Coy. Princess Patricia's Canadian Light Infantry, R.C.I.C. 23rd May 1944. Age 23. Son of Charles and Grace Graham Lord, of Provincial Cannery, British Columbia. Canada. IX. A. 12.

LOW, Private, DUNCAN MCGREGOR, K/69326. Princess Patricia's Canadian Light Infantry, R.C.I.C. 23rd May 1944. IX. A. 23.

MANNESS, Corporal, LESLIE CHARLES, H/16783. Princess Patricia's Canadian Light Infantry, R.C.I.C. 23rd May 1944. IX. C. 1.

MARKS, Private, MAURICE HERMAN, K/50142. Princess Patricia's Canadian Light Infantry, R.C.I.C. 30th May 1944. Age 30. Son of John Woolley Marks and Elizabeth Ann Marks; husband of Jean Elizabeth Marks, of High River, Alberta, Canada. V. K. 8.

MARQUETTE, Private, ROLAND MARTIN, K/69614. Princess Patricia's Canadian Light Infantry, R.C.I.C. 23rd May 1944. Age 20. Son of Lorette Marquette, of Victoria, British Columbia, Canada. IX. A. 8.

MARTY, Private, FERNIEL, M/59202. Princess Patricia's Canadian Light Infantry, R.C.I.C. 23rd May 1944. IX. C. 5.

MAYNARD, Private, PERCY, H/17726. Princess Patricia's Canadian Light Infantry, R.C.I.C. 23rd May 1944. Age 33. Son of Henry and Cecilia Maynard; husband of Irene Tawse Maynard, of Edmonton, Alberta, Canada. IX. B. 2.

MILLER, Private, ORTAN EARL, B/127785. Princess Patricia's Canadian Light Infantry, R.C.I.C. 23rd May 1944. Age 23. Son of Hugh and Agnes Miller, of Brantford, Ontario, Canada. IX. B. 19.

MONSON, Private, HAROLD ROSCOE, M/106810. Princess Patricia's Canadian Light Infantry, R.C.I.C. 23rd May 1944. Age 24. Son of Ludvik Peter Monson, and of Clara Woodstrom Monson, of Linaria, Alberta, Canada. IX. B. 6.

MOORE, Warrant Officer Class II (C.S.M.), GEORGE SYLVESTER, K/85300. Princess Patricia's Canadian Light Infantry, R.C.I.C. 23rd May 1944. Age 25. Son of Sylvester T. and Leah Moore, of Belle Ewart, Ontario, Canada. IX. B. 9.

MOWATT, Private, WILLIAM, H/9301. Princess Patricia's Canadian Light Infantry, R.C.I.C. 23rd May 1944. Age 36. Son of James G. and Charlotte Brown Mowatt, of Laurencekirk, Kincardineshire. IX. C. 4.

McAuley, Private, RAYMOND HERBERT, H/17352. Princess Patricia's Canadian Light Infantry, R.C.I.C. 23rd May 1944. IX. C. 2.

McGOWAN, Lance Corporal, JOHN FRANCIS, B/105116. Princess Patricia's Canadian Light Infantry, R.C.I.C. 20th May 1944. Age 25. Son of William and Evelyn Long McGowan, of Toronto, Ontairo, Canada. IX. B. 22.

McKEE, Sergeant, WILLIAM GEORGE, C/80113. Princess Patricia's Canadian Light Infantry, R.C.I.C. 6th October 1943. Age 21. Son of William and Charlotte E. McKee, of Lansdowne, Ontario, Canada. V. G. 1.

McLEAN, Private, PAUL, H/10373. Princess Patricia's Canadian Light Infantry, R.C.I.C. 25th May 1944. Age 27. Son of Peter and Anne McLean, of Newdale, Manitoba, Canada. IX. C. 13.

McRAE, Private, ALBERT HORACE, B/134571. Princess Patricia's Canadian Light Infantry, R.C.I.C. 23rd May 1944. IX. B. 1.

NELSON, Private, HARVEY THOMAS, M/105961. Princess Patricia's Canadian Light Infantry, R.C.I.C. 23rd May 1944. Age 21. Son of Albert L. and Mary N. V. Nelson, of Heinsburg, Alberta, Canada. IX. C. 12.

NELSON, Private, LEONARD, K/40812. Princess Patricia's Canadian Light Infantry, R.C.I.C. 23rd May 1944. Age 23. Son of Charles A. and Celia Nelson, of Bridal Falls, British Columbia, Canada. IV. C. 23.

NIXON, Lance Corporal, HARRY COTIGAN, B/127687. Princess Patricia's Canadian Light Infantry, R.C.I.C. 23rd May 1944. Age 26. Son of George and Annie Nixon; husband of Audrey Lillian Nixon, of Scarboro Bluffs, Ontario, Canada. IX. C. 4.

O'KEEFE, Corporal, DONALD PATRICK, H/16794. Princess Patricia's Canadian Light Infantry, R.C.I.C. 23rd May 1944. Age 25. Son of Charles and Ella Mildred O'Keefe, of West Fort William, Ontario, Canada. IX. C. 10.

OSLUND, Private, JOHN ERIC, K/40814. Princess Patricia's Canadian Light Infantry, R.C.I.C. 23rd May 1944. IX. A. 7.

PEARSON, Private, LEVI GLEN, K/49326. Princess Patricia's Canadian Light Infantry, R.C.I.C. 23rd May 1944. Age 30. Son of David H. and Catherine Pearson, of New Westminster, British Columbia, Canada. IX. C. 9.

PETERS, Private, LAWRENCWE ROBERT, B/46890. Princess Patricia's Canadian Light Infantry, R.C.I.C. 23rd May 1944. Age 21. Son of Helena Peters, of Welland, Ontario, Canada. IX. A. 2.

QUARTLY, Private, GEORGE CLIFFORD, M/105756. Princess Patricia's Canadian Light Infantry, R.C.I.C. 23rd May 1944. Age 21. Son of John and Florence Quartly, of Innisfail, Alberta, Canada. IX. A. 20.

REID, Private, ROBERT FRANCIS, L/106103. Princess Patricia's Canadian Light Infantry, R.C.I.C. 20th May 1944. Age 22. Son of Olive M. Reid, of Moose Jaw, Saskatchewan, Canada. IX. B. 17.

ROUTH, Corporal, PATRICK ALBERT DARNLEY, K/85370. Princess Patricia's Canadian Light Infantry, R.C.I.C. 23rd May 1944.

Age 24. Son of Albert and Cherrie Meredith Routh, of Vancouver, British Columbia. Canada. IX. B. 5.

SHARP, Private, HARVEY RICHARD, H/9208. Princess Patricia's Canadian Light Infantry, R.C.I.C. 30th May 1944. Age 21. Son of Richard and Mary Jane Sharp, of Portage-la-Prairie, Manitoba, Canada. V. K. 9.

SHEA, Lieutenant, CECIL NELSON, Princess Patricia's Canadian Light Infantry, R.C.I.C. 23rd May 1944. Age 28. Son of Nelson T. and Leita G. Shea, of Deseronto, Ontario, Canada; husband of Mary Shea. IX. A. 4.

SKINNER, Lance Corporal, ALLAN REA, H/17059. Princess Patricia's Canadian Light Infantry, R.C.I.C. 20th May 1944. Husband of Joan Irene Skinner, of Reading, Berkshire. IX. B. 23.

SLEMMON, Private, MOMRTON, H/63685. Princess Patricia's Canadian Light Infantry, R.C.I.C. 23rd May 1944. Age 25. Son of William and Della Slemmon, of Grandview, Manitoba, Canada. IX. A. 9.

SMALLPIECE, Private, ERNEST VICTOR, H/16108. Princess Patricia's Canadian Light Infantry, R.C.I.C. 23rd May 1944. Age 23. Son of Arthur and Ellen Smallpiece; husband of Dorothy Smallpiece, of Winnipeg, Manitoba, Canada. IX. B. 21.

STEELE, Private, JAMES HERBERT, H/16268. Princess Patricia's Canadian Light Infantry, R.C.I.C. 17th May 1944. IX. J. 13.

TAYLOR, Private, SHERMAN, H/102132. Princess Patricia's Canadian Light Infantry, R.C.I.C. 23rd May 1944. Age 19. Son of John Wilson Taylor and Eva Mills Lee Taylor, of Bethesda, Maryland, U.S.A. IX. C. 11.

TOD, Private, JAMES ALEXANDER, H/17112. Princess Patricia's Canadian Light Infantry, R.C.I.C. 23rd May 1944. Age 30. Husband of Anne E. Tod, of Winnipeg, Manitoba, Canada. IX. C. 6.

TUCKER, Lance Corporal, CONRAD, K/37268. Princess Patricia's Canadian Light Infantry, R.C.I.C. 23rd May 1944. Age 24. Son of Michael and Annabella Tucker, of Vancouver, British Columbia, Canada. IX. A. 1.

UNROW, Private, EDWARD NELSON, H/41036. Princess Patricia's Canadian Light Infantry, R.C.I.C. 23rd May 1944. IX. A. 21.

URQUHART, Private, LEONARD, E/106604. Princess Patricia's Canadian Light Infantry, R.C.I.C. 23rd May 1944. Age 23. Son of William and Christina Urquhart, of Barachois West, Gaspe Co., Province of Quebec, Canada. IX. A. 13.

VINETTE, Private, GABRIEL, H/8249. Princess Patricia's Canadian Light Infantry, R.C.I.C. 20th May 1944. Age 24. Son of Philibert and Alma Vinette, of St. Boniface, Manitoba, Canada. IX. B. 20.

WARRINGTON, Private, ROBERT JAMES, M/30908. Princess Patricia's Canadian Light Infantry, R.C.I.C. 23rd May 1944. Age 30. Son of Arthur Henry Warrington and of Mary Elizabeth Warrington (nee Boudriau); husband of Winnifred Nora Warrington, of New Westminster, British Columbia, Canada. IX. A. 15.

WATSON, Private, GEORGE RONALD, H/103598. Princess Patricia's Canadian Light Infantry, R.C.I.C. 23rd May 1944. Age 21. Son of George Alfred and Isabell Gertrude Watson, of Argyle, Manitoba, Canada. IX. C. 14.

CESENA WAR CEMETERY

Commonwealth War Dead, 1939-1945
DAVIS, Private, WESLEY THOMAS, D/157580. Princess Patricia's Canadian Light Infantry, R.C.I.C. 20th October 1944. Age 25. C.I.C. Son of William and Sarah Davis, of Arundel, Province of Quebec, Canada. III, E, 16.

EASTLAND, Private, JACK, H/92438. Princess Patricia's Canadian Light Infantry, R.C.I.C. 20th December 1944. IV, C, 5.

GENAILLE, Private, LOUIS, H/92488. Princess Patricia's Canadian Light Infantry, R.C.I.C. 27th December 1944, IV, C, 8.

LAMKE, Private, NORMAN EDWARD, H/105047. Princess Patricia's Canadian Light Infantry, R.C.I.C. 2oth October 1944. Age 21. Son of George Lenard and Alice Emely Lamke, of Fort William, Ontario, Canada. III, E, 15.

LOWSON, Sergeant, CLIFFORD JAMES, K/85277. Princess Patricia's Canadian Light Infantry, R.C.I.C. 23rd October 1944. Age 34. Son of William James Lowson and Maude Lowson; husband of Wilda E. Lowson, of Canoe, British Columbia, Canada. IV, H, 5.

McLEOD, Corporal, ALASTAIR DUNCAN, B/11345. Princess Patricia's Canadian Light Infantry (Eastern Ontario Regt.). 20th October 1944. Age 21. Son of Thomas R. and Isabelle McLeod, of Owen Sound, Ontario, Canada. III, E, 13.

NILE, Sergeant, JACK, H/17036. Princess Patricia's Canadian Light Infantry, R.C.I.C. 22nd October 1944. Age 25. Son of Edwin and Lilie Nile, of Winnipeg, Manitoba, Canada; husband of Gudrun Helen Nile, of Winnipeg, III, F, 2.

THE ROLL OF HONOUR—WORLD WAR TWO

PULFORD, Private, ALBERT, B/144560. Princess Patricia's Canadian Light Infantry, R.C.I.C. 20th October 1944. Age 28. Son of James and Martha H. Pulford; husband of Irene Pulford (nee Dobson), of Scarboro, Ontario, Canada. III, E, 14.

ROBINSON, Private, HARVEY, L/64699. Princess Patricia's Canadian Light Infantry, R.C.I.C. 6th November 1944. Age 21. Son of Bertram Russell Robinson and Edna Ruth Robinson, of Weyburn, Saskatchewan, Canada. III, D, 9.

ROTH, Private, HENRY, M/60373. Princess Patricia's Canadian Light Infantry, R.C.I.C. 21st October 1944. Son of John J. and Caroline Roth, of Irvine, Alberta, Canada. III, F, 1.

YOUNGREN, Private, JULIUS ALLAN, K/1759. Princess Patricia's Canadian Light Infantry, R.C.I.C. 20th October 1944. Age 26. Son of Allan and Arleen Youngren; husband of Marjorie Bevan Youngren, of Vancouver, British Columbia, Canada. III, F, 3.

CORIANO RIDGE WAR CEMETERY

Commonwealth War Dead, 1939-1945

BADLECK, Private, HENRY, B/68456. Princess Patricia's Canadian Light Infantry, R.C.I.C. 27th October 1944. Age 27. Son of Albert and Aniela Badleck, of Landrienne, Province of Quebec, Canada, XIII, D, 8.

BAKER, Private, LOUIS, C/77083. Princess Patricia's Canadian Light Infantry, R.C.I.C. 18th September 1944, XIII, E, 6.

BEATON, Private, BILL GERALD, C/121240. Princess Patricia's Canadian Light Infantry, R.C.I.C. 20th September 1944. Age 20. Son of John Lawrence Beaton and Margaret Mary Beaton, of Brockville, Ontario, Canada. XIII. F. 11.

BJORNSON, Private, JOEL THEODORE, K/85316. Princess Patricia's Canadian Light Infantry, R.C.I.C. 18th September 1944. Age 25. Son of Herman and Freda Bjornson, of Winnipeg, Manitoba, Canada. XIII, E, 7.

BURTON, Captain, LLOYD GRAYDON, Princess Patricia's Canadian Light Infantry, R.C.I.C. 17th September 1944. Age 24. Son of Francis and Eugenie Victoria Burton, of Portage la Prairie, Manitoba, Canada; husband of Avril Marie Burton. XIII, E, 8.

COLLINS, Private, ALBERT CLARE, H/64824. Princess Patricia's Canadian Light Infantry, R.C.I.C. 18th September 1944. Age 21. Son of Albert Arthur and Margaret Jane Collins, of Brandon, Manitoba, Canada. XIII, E, 10.

CORKETT, Captain, GEORGE RICHARD, Princess Patricia's Canadian Light Infantry, R.C.I.C. 22nd September 1944. Age 28. Son of Lt.-Col. Cecil Mansfield Corkett and Madeline Grace Corkett; husband of Aileen Maud Darracott Corkett, XIII, G, 11.

DOOL, Private, JOH, B/134365. Princess Patricia's Canadian Light Infantry, R.C.I.C. 20th September 1944. Age 20. Son of Archibald and Lucy Dool, of North Bay, Ontario, Canada. XIII, F, 5.

DURR, Private, JOHN, M/53871. Princess Patricia's Canadian Light Infantry, R.C.I.C. 20th September 1944. Age 19. Son of Christian and Johanna Durr; husband of Catherine Durr, of Hope, British Columbia, Canada. XIII, G, 9.

GERASSIMOU, Private, CONSTANTIN, H/94590. Princess Patricia's Canadian Light Infantry, R.C.I.C. 20th September 1944. XIII, D, 6.

GRIFFIN, Private, MICHAEL, H/8547. Princess Patricia's Canadian Light Infantry, R.C.I.C. 18th September 1944. Age 37. Son of John and Ellen Griffin, of Quilty, Co. Clare, Irish Republic. XIII, F, 10.

GRIFFITHS, Private, JAMES, A/106497. Princess Patricia's Canadian Light Infantry, R.C.I.C. 20th September 1944. Age 18. Son of George H. and Isabel M. Griffiths, of London, Ontario, Canada. XIII, E, 2.

HARFORD, Private, WILFRED JOSEPH JOE, H/3215. Princess Patricia's Canadian Light Infantry, R.C.I.C. 17th September 1944. Age 23. Son of Wilfred and Amy Harford, of St. James, Manitoba, Canada. XIII, E, 4.

HILL, Private, ALLENBY EDWARD, M/104932. Princess Patricia's Canadian Light Infantry, R.C.I.C. 17th September 1944. XIII, F, 4.

JACOBS, Private, CARLTON GUY, D/140001. Princess Patricia's Canadian Light Infantry, R.C.I.C. 16th September 1944. Age 24. Son of Owen E. and Mabel M. Jacobs, of Glen Sutton, Quebec City, Canada. XIII, G, 8.

JONES, Private, RONALD, G/17671. Princess Patricia's Canadian Light Infantry, R.C.I.C. 20th September 1944. Son of Frank L. and Bessie Foster Jones; husband of Gretchen M. Jones, of Perth, Victoria Co., New Brunswick, Canada. XIII, F, 1.

KYLER, Private, ROBERT, L/105431. Princess Patricia's Canadian Light Infantry, R.C.I.C. 20th September 1944. Age 20. Son of Emmett William and Cora Bele Kyler, of Silver Park, Saskatchewan, Canada. XIII, F, 9.

MENCINI, Private, LOUIS, H/16705. Princess Patricia's Canadian Light Infantry, R.C.I.C. 20th September 1944. Age 31. Son of Dominico Mencini and of Josephine Mencini (nee Deloli). XIII, D, 12.

MILLIKEN, Private, JOHN, H/853.1, Princess Patricia's Canadian Light Infantry, R.C.I.C. 22 September 1944. Son of John and Agnes Milliken, of Winnipeg, Manitoba, Canada. XIII, G, 7.

MILNE, Private, ERNEST, H/36890. Princess Patricia's Canadian Light Infantry, R.C.I.C. 20th September 1944. Son of Harry and Elizabeth Milne; husband of Pauline Milne, of Fort William, Ontario, Canada. XIII, E, 12.

MacNEIL, Lieutenant, WILLIAM JOHN, Princess Patricia's Canadian Light Infantry, R.C.I.C. 20th September 1944. XIII, G, 5.

McGEE, Private, EMERSON, M/105758. Princess Patricia's Canadian Light Infantry, R.C.I.C. 20th September 1944. XIII, F, 8.

NICHOLSON, Private, KEITH, K/85425. Princess Patricia's Canadian Light Infantry, R.C.I.C. 22nd December 1944. Age 27. Son of Colin and May Nicholson, of Squamish, British Columbia, Canada. XIII, D, 9.

NORGANG, Private, JOSEPH, L/28052. Princess Patricia's Canadian Light Infantry, R.C.I.C. 16th September 1944. Age 25. Son of Adam and Helen Norgang, of Cupar, Saskatchewan, Canada. XIII, G, 4.

PARRISH, Private, JOH, L/107356. Princess Patricia's Canadian Light Infantry, R.C.I.C. 18th September 1944. Age 19. Son of Samuel and Christina J. Parrish, of Battleford, Saskatchewan, Canada. XIII, D, 7.

PASOWYSTY, Private, PETER, H/101254. Princess Patricia's Canadian Light Infantry, R.C.I.C. 20th September 1944. XIII, E, 9.

PAULSON, Private, EDWIN, H/90005. Princess Patricia's Canadian Light Infantry, R.C.I.C. 17th September 1944. Age 21. Son of Peter C. and Hannah N. Paulson, of Bowsman River, Manitoba, Canada. XIII, G, 12.

PEREPELITZ, Private, FRED, L/105946. Princess Patricia's Canadian Light Infantry, R.C.I.C. 19th September 1944. Age 24. Son of George and Mary Perepelitz, of Preeceville, Saskatchewan, Canada. XIII, F, 6.

PIETRASZ, Private, ANTONI, D/139410. Princess Patricia's Canadian Light Infantry, R.C.I.C. 27th August 1944. Age 23. Son of Nick and Tekla Pietrasz, of Bourlamaque, Province of Quebec, Canada. XIII, B, 4.

THE ROLL OF HONOUR—WORLD WAR TWO

PULIN, Private, EUGEN, L/847. Princess Patricia's Canadian Light Infantry, R.C.I.C. 17th September 1944. XIII, F, 12.

PRETTY, Private, NORMAN LESLIE, M/106210. Princess Patricia's Canadian Light Infantry, R.C.I.C. 17th September 1944. Age 33. Son of Daniel and Mabel Irene Pretty, of Edmonton, Alberta, Canada. XIII, G, 2.

PUGH, Private, GORDON, H/195479. Princess Patricia's Canadian Light Infantry, R.C.I.C. 22nd September 1944. Age 23. Son of Samuel Noble Pugh and Ada Mary Pugh, of Fort William, Ontario, Canada. XIII, G, 3.

REES, Private, HENRY CAVENDISH, K/42999. Princess Patricia's Canadian Light Infantry, R.C.I.C. 19th September 1944. Age 23. Son of Charles Gerald and Dorothy Winifred Rees; husband of Winnifred Ruby Rees, of Armstrong, British Columbia, Canada. XIII, E, 11.

RIES, Private, EMIL, L/105210. Princess Patricia's Canadian Light Infantry, R.C.I.C. 18th September 1944. XIII, G, 6.

SADDLEMAN, Private, ALBERT JOSEPH, K/49420. Princess Patricia's Canadian Light Infantry, R.C.I.C. 17th September 1944. Age 34. Son of Maria Saddleman; husband of Della Saddleman, of Vernon, British Columbia, Canada. XIII, G, 10.

SEMAN, Private, METRO, H/1704. Princess Patricia's Canadian Light Infantry, R.C.I.C. 20th September 1944. Son of Fred Seman, and of Katie Seman (nee Kosh), of Brooklands, Manitoba, Canada. XIII, F, 7.

SHERB, Private, CHARLES, H/18204. Princess Patricia's Canadian Light Infantry, R.C.I.C. 20th September 1944. Age 20. Son of Joseph Francis and Lena Sherb, of Brandon, Manitoba, Canada. XIII, C, 11.

STEINKE, Private, WILLIAM, H/89123. Princess Patricia's Canadian Light Infantry, R.C.I.C. 21st December 1944. Age 29. Son of August and Matilda Steinke; husband of Iris Lillian Winnifred Steinke, of Banff, Alberta, Canada. XIII, D, 11.

STEPHENSON, Lance Corporal, FREDERICK GEORGE, H/16313. Princess Patricia's Canadian Light Infantry, R.C.I.C. 20th September 1944. Age 22. Son of Frederick George and Georgina Dent Stephenson, of Souris, Manitoba, Canada. XIII, F, 3.

THACKER, Lance Corporal, HUBERT, K/49050. Princess Patricia's Canadian Light Infantry, R.C.I.C. 17th September 1944. Age 21. Son of William and Emily E. Thacker, of New Westminster, British Columbia, Canada. XIII, E, 5.

THE ROLL OF HONOUR—WORLD WAR TWO

THOMPSON, Lance Corporal, LAVERN, H/17166. Princess Patricia's Canadian Light Infantry, R.C.I.C. 21st December 1944. Age 24. Son of Bertram Reginald and Mabel Ida Thompson; husband of Sarah Elizabeth Thompson, of Winnipegosis, Manitoba, Canada. XIII, D, 10.

THORNE, Private, CLIFFORD, H/18007. Princess Patricia's Canadian Light Infantry, R.C.I.C. 20th September 1944. XIII, C, 12.

UMPHERVILLE, Private, JERRY, L/106905. Princess Patricia's Canadian Light Infantry, R.C.I.C. 17th September 1944. XIII, F, 2.

WHITLAM, Private, RAYMOND DELMAR, M/31656. Princess Patricia's Canadian Light Infantry, R.C.I.C. 20th September 1944. XIII, E, 3.

WOOD, Sergeant, ALVIN STEWART, K/85365. Princess Patricia's Canadian Light Infantry, R.C.I.C. 17th September 1944. XIII, E, 1.

WYNNE, Lance Corporal, CHARLES, H/17422. Princess Patricia's Canadian Light Infantry, R.C.I.C. 20th September 1944. Son of Charles and Martha Wynne; husband of Dorothy Irene Wynne, of Fort Garry, Manitoba, Canada, XIII, G, 1.

FLORENCE WAR CEMETERY

Commonwealth War Dead, 1939-1945
BLACK, Private, DOUGLAS ALEXANDER, H/17223. Princess Patricia's Canadian Light Infantry, R.C.I.C. 8th August 1944. Age 32. Son of Hugh Allen Black and Agnes Marion Black, of Vancouver, British Columber, Canada. VI. A. 5.

CORMIER, Private, OMER, H/16449. Princess Patricia's Canadian Light Infantry, R.C.I.C. 8th August 1944. VI. A. 14.

FRANCIS, Private, LINDSAY, H/103294. Princess Patricia's Canadian Light Infantry, R.C.I.C. 7th August 1944. Age 31. Son of Harry and Elizabeth Francis, of Norgate, Manitoba, Canada. VI. A. 7.

PROULX, Private, AUGUSTUS, C/81054. Princess Patricia's Canadian Light Infantry, R.C.I.C. 7th August 1944. Age 33. Son of Napoleon and Eliza Proulx; husband of Aurore Proulx, of St. Catharines, Ontario, Canada. VI. B. 2.

GRADARA WAR CEMETERY

Commonwealth War Dead, 1939-1945
DENMAN, Corporal, WILLIAM, K/85207. Princess Patricia's Canadian Light Infantry, R.C.I.C. 2nd September 1944. Age 25. Son of

William George and Kathleen Alberta Denman, of Marigold, Victoria, British Columbia, Canada. I, H, 19.

DURANT, Private, DWIGHT, C/121493. Princess Patricia's Canadian Light Infantry, R.C.I.C. 21st September 1944. II, G, 73.

KRAMER, Private, LESLIE EVAN, B/46993. Princess Patricia's Canadian Light Infantry, R.C.I.C. 22nd September 1944. Age 21. Son of Henry and Grace Kramer, of Port Colborne, Ontario, Canada. II, G, 72.

RENZ, Private, ALBERT, M/36953. Princess Patricia's Canadian Light Infantry, R.C.I.C. 20th September 1944. Age 31. Son of Fred Renz, and of Mathilda Renz, of Chilliwack, British Columbia, Canada. II, G, 71.

TURNBULL, Private, WILLIAM, K/43059. Princess Patricia's Canadian Light Infantry, R.C.I.C. 18th September 1944. Age 20. Son of Harvey and Mary Lavina Turnbull, of White Rock, British Columbia, Canada. II, G, 74.

MONTECCHIO WAR CEMETERY

Commonwealth War Dead, 1939-1945
CORNWALL, Private, RONALD, K/85368. Princess Patricia's Canadian Light Infantry, R.C.I.C. 1st September 1944. Age 28. Son of Fitzallan Victor and Mabel Garnett Cornwall, of Victoria, British Columbia, Canada. III. E. 5.

CORY, Private, WILLIS, H/17010. Princess Patricia's Canadian Light Infantry, R.C.I.C. 31st August 1944. Age 41. Son of William and Ann Cory; husband of Annie Louise Cory, of Winnipeg, Manitoba, Canada. IV. H. 9.

PPCLI – SECONDARY REGIMENT CASUALTY—WWII—ITALY

ITALY

MONTECCHIO WAR CEMETERY

Commonwealth War Dead, 1939-1945
EATON, Chaplain 4th Class, The Revd. KENELM EDWIN, Canadian Chaplains Service attd. Princess Patricia's Canadian Light Infantry, R.C.I.C. 31st August 1944. Age 30. Son of Lt.-Col. Edwin Kenelm Eaton (formerly of The Royal Canadian Regt.), and Edit Marguerite Eaton; husband of Marie Saunders Eaton. Rector of St. Peter's Church, Eastern Passage, Nova Scotia; B.Sc. (Dalhousie University, Halifax); L. Th. (King's College, Halifax). III. H. 15.

ELEFSON, Private, GEORGE, L/105642. Princess Patricia's Canadian Light Infantry, R.C.I.C. 27th August 1944. Age 31. Son of Henry and Olena Elefson, of Ordale, Saskatchewan, Canada. III. C. 7.

ELLIS, Private, ALBERT DAVID, K/49004. Princess Patricia's Canadian Light Infantry, R.C.I.C. 27th August 1944. Age 20. Son of George Frances and Cora Olive Ellis, of Vancouver, British Columbia, Canada. III. C. 8.

GRAVELLE, Private, THOMAS CENA, B/143163. Princess Patricia's Canadian Light Infantry, R.C.I.C. 27th August 1944. Age 22. Son of Charles and Rosanne Compeau Gravelle, of Toronto, Ontario, Canada. III. C. 6.

HICKEY, Lance Sergeant, WALTER HEPBURN, H/16682. Princess Patricia's Canadian Light Infantry, R.C.I.C. 31st August 1944. Age 27. Son of George Edward and Esther Louise Hickey, of Winnipeg, Manitoba, Canada. IV. H. 10.

MILLER, Private, EDMOND RONAYNE, K/65739. Princess Patricia's Canadian Light Infantry, R.C.I.C. 27th August 1944. Age 31. Son of William Morgan Miller and Teresa Miller, of Pemberton, British Columbia, Canada. III. C. 5.

O'CONNOR, Corporal, LEO, E/52887. Princess Patricia's Canadian Light Infantry, R.C.I.C. 27th August 1944. Age 26. Son of Richard and Rose O'Connor, of Marmora, Ontario, Canada. III. C. 3.

SAUNDERS, Corporal, JOHN, H/17213. Princess Patricia's Canadian Light Infantry, R.C.I.C. 27th August 1944. III. C. 4.

SEIVEWRIGHT, Private, JOHN, H/3568. Princess Patricia's Canadian Light Infantry, R.C.I.C. 1st September 1944. Age 25. Son of John Seivewright, and of Maud Edith Seivewright, of North Vancouver, British Columbia, Canada. His brother, Stanley C. Seivewright, also fell. III. F. 5.

MORO RIVER CANADIAN WAR CEMETERY

Commonwealth War Dead, 1939-1945

ANDERSON, Private, VERNON, H/17897. Princess Patricia's Canadian Light Infantry, R.C.I.C. 14th December 1944. Age 19. Son of Joseph T. and Mary E. Anderson, of Fuller's P.O., Manitoba. IX. D. 4.

BAKER, Private, ARTHUR JOHN, B/127621. Princess Patricia's Canadian Light Infantry, R.C.I.C. 6th April 1944. Age 24. Son of Albert and Mary L. Baker, of Owen Sound, Ontario. VI. F. 11.

BARNES, Private, EARL, H/65994. Princess Patricia's Canadian Light Infantry, R.C.I.C. 13th October 1943. Age 23. Son of Horace Henry and Helena Morinda Barnes, of Medora, Manitoba. IV. H. 13.

BAZZLO, Private, MIKE, H/16621. Princess Patricia's Canadian Light Infantry, R.C.I.C. 8th December 1943. XI. A. 4.

BERNATH, Private, FRANK, H/9616. Princess Patricia's Canadian Light Infantry, R.C.I.C. 29th March 1944. Age 23. Son of John and Mary Bernath, of Stratton, Ontario. VI. F. 10.

BRAIN, Major, DONALD, Princess Patricia's Canadian Light Infantry, R.C.I.C. 10th December 1943. X. E. 10.

CARTER, Sergeant, ROBERT, K/85289. Princess Patricia's Canadian Light Infantry, R.C.I.C. 17th October 1943. Age 23. Son of James and Minnie Carter, of Victoria, British Columbia; husband of Ann Carter, of Victoria. VIII. H. 7.

CASSELLS, Private, JAMES ALTON, H/103870. Princess Patricia's Canadian Light Infantry, R.C.I.C. 15th December 1943. VII. E. 14.

CLARKE, Private, NORMAN FREDERICK, K/65913. Princess Patricia's Canadian Light Infantry, R.C.I.C. 15th December 1943. Age 31. Son of Frederick J. and Louisa Clarke, of Vancouver, British Columbia. VII. E. 16.

CLIFTON, Private, ARTHURE, H/16360. Princess Patricia's Canadian Light Infantry, R.C.I.C. 15th December 1943. XI. A. 12.

COWIE, Private, ROBERT, H/17169. Princess Patricia's Canadian Light Infantry, R.C.I.C. 13th December 1943. Age 27. Son of George and Annie Cowie; husband of Phyllis Dorothy Cowie, of Peacehaven, Sussex, England, X. D. 16.

CRANE, Private, GORDON, H/17224. Princess Patricia's Canadian Light Infantry, R.C.I.C. 24th January 1944. Age 23. Son of Thomas and Maude Crane, of Portage La Prairie, Manitoba. V. E. 10.

CRASSMAN, Private, ANDREW LOUIS, K/85285. Princess Patricia's Canadian Light Infantry, R.C.I.C. 17th January 1944. VII. D. 6.

DANIEL, Lance Corporal, GEORGE BURWASH, B/93527. Princess Patricia's Canadian Light Infantry, R.C.I.C. 16th April 1944. Age 31. Son of Roy L. and Hester H. Daniel; husband of Eveline M. Daniel, of Toronto, Ontario. IV. A. 4.

DRIEDGER, Private, JOHN HENRY, H/21112. Princess Patricia's Canadian Light Infantry, R.C.I.C. 7th December 1943. II. F. 10.

THE ROLL OF HONOUR—WORLD WAR TWO

ELLIS, Lance Sergeant, EDWARD HAROLD, K/37018. Princess Patricia's Canadian Light Infantry, R.C.I.C. 17th January 1944. Age 30. Son of George Frances Ellis and Cora Olive Ellis, of Vancouver, British Columbia. VII. D. 4.

FUREY, Lance Corporal, PATRICK, H/17773. Princess Patricia's Canadian Light Infantry, R.C.I.C. 12th December 1943. Age 21. Son of James and Kate Furey, of Carberry, Manitoba. VII. E. 13.

GAYOWAY, Private, MICHAEL, H/17785. Princess Patricia's Canadian Light Infantry, R.C.I.C. 4th December 1943. Age 23. Son of Michael and Louise Gayoway, of Winnipeg, Manitoba. X. B. 11.

GENSORICK, Private, FRANK, H/16225. Princess Patricia's Canadian Light Infantry, R.C.I.C. 6th December 1943. IX. F. 5.

GREEN, Private, BURTON, K/46750. Princess Patricia's Canadian Light Infantry, R.C.I.C. 13th October 1943. IV. H. 14.

HAYES, Private, JOHN, U/1527. Princess Patricia's Canadian Light Infantry, R.C.I.C. 13th December 1943. IX. D. 3.

HOSSAY, Private, JOHN, U/1527. Princess Patricia's Canadian Light Infantry, R.C.I.C. 14th December 1943. Age 23. Son of Jean and Marie Hossay; husband of Betty Hossay, of Tottenham, Middlesex, Angland. II. D. 6.

HUNT, Captain, JOHN BLAIR. Princess Patricia's Canadian Light Infantry, R.C.I.C. 14th December 1943. Husband of Barbara Campbell Hunt, of London, Ontario. IX. D. 9.

HUTSON, Private, DONALD, E/52872. Princess Patricia's Canadian Light Infantry, R.C.I.C. 21st December 1943. Age 28. Son of Walter and Susannah Hutson, of Kingston, Ontario. VII. C. 2.

JACKSON, Lance Corporal, STEPHEN, K/85394. Princess Patricia's Canadian Light Infantry, R.C.I.C. 6th December 1943. Age 21. Foster-son of David and Ellen Mary Jackson, of Sidney, British Columbia. II. F. 12.

JANKULAK, Private, LAWRENCE JOSEPH, M/103555. Princess Patricia's Canadian Light Infantry, R.C.I.C. 28th December 1943. Age 21. Son of John and Anna Jankulak, of Coleman, Alberta. I. G. 4.

JOHNS, Private, ROY ERNEST, H/16364. Princess Patricia's Canadian Light Infantry, R.C.I.C. 20th December 1943. Son of Aaron D. and Mary Jane Johns; husband of Vera Johns, of Windsor, Ontario. III. F. 11.

THE ROLL OF HONOUR—WORLD WAR TWO

JOYAL, Private, JOSEPH ARTHUR JOHN, H/17136. Princess Patricia's Canadian Light Infantry, R.C.I.C. 14th December 1943. V. F. 11.

KENNARD, Private, JOHN, H/16964. Princess Patricia's Canadian Light Infantry, R.C.I.C. 12th December 1943. Age 29. Son of John and Elizabeth Kennard, of Cupar, Saskatchewan. VII. F. 10.

KOTCHOREK, Private, ROBERT BERNARD, H/17002. Princess Patricia's Canadian Light Infantry, R.C.I.C. 1st April 1944. Age 24. Son of August and Hilda Kotchorek, of Lansen, Saskatchewan. VI. E. 4

KRASNY, Corporal, WALTER, H/3025. Princess Patricia's Canadian Light Infantry, R.C.I.C. 25th January 1944, V. E. 11.

LEGUEE, Sergeant, FREDERICK JOSEPH, H/16567. Princess Patricia's Canadian Light Infantry, R.C.I.C. 1st January 1944. Age 25. Son of George Auan Leguee and Bernadette Leguee, of Winnipeg, Manitoba. V. H. 5.

LEWIS, Private, DEAN EDWARD, H/103190. Princess Patricia's Canadian Light Infantry, R.C.I.C. 13th December 1943. Age 21. Son of Evan and Catherine Lewis, of Medora, Manitoba. VII. E. 15.

LOW, Private, CHRISTOPHER, B/127792. Princess Patricia's Canadian Light Infantry, R.C.I.C. 14th December 1943. Age 27. Son of James and Elizabeth Low, of Toronto, Ontario. VII. E. 11.

MADIGAN, Private, CHARLES LAWRENCE, H/87682. Princess Patricia's Canadian Light Infantry, R.C.I.C. 11th December 1943. IX. D. 2.

MILNE, Private, ARTHUR LANG, H/16037. "D" Coy. Princess Patricia's Canadian Light Infantry, R.C.I.C. 11th December 1943. Age 33. Son of George Milne, and of Agnes Milne, of Winnipeg, Manitoba. I. E. 9.

MORRIS, Private, CLIFFORD ERNEST, K/69648. Princess Patricia's Canadian Light Infantry, R.C.I.C. 6th December 1943. Age 20. Son of Ernest Arthur and Alice Hope Morris, of Rossland, British Columbia. IX. F. 3.

MUIR, Private, JOHN, H/17400. Princess Patricia's Canadian Light Infantry, R.C.I.C. 16th December 1943. X. D. 11.

MUNRO, Lieutenant, CAMPBELL STUART, Princess Patricia's Canadian Light Infantry, R.C.I.C. 16th December 1943. X. D. 11.

MURRAY, Private, CYRIL, H/70151. Princess Patricia's Canadian Light Infantry, R.C.I.C. 7th December 1943. IX. F. 6.

McIVOR, Private, WILLIAM, H/17182. Princess Patricia's Canadian Light Infantry, R.C.I.C. 22nd February 1944. IX. A. 12.

McQUITTY, Private, LEWIS, K/85395. Princess Patricia's Canadian Light Infantry, R.C.I.C. 22nd March 1944. Age 25. Son of William Gilmour McQuitty and Ethel Gertrude McQuitty; husband of Marion Steele Whitelaw McQuitty, of Vancouver, British Columbia. VI. D. 5.

NELSON, Private, LESLIE WILLIAM, H/17786. "D" Coy. Princess Patricia's Canadian Light Infantry, R.C.I.C. 17th January 1944. Age 22. Son of Joshua and Edith Nelson, of Winnipeg, Manitoba; husband of Emily Nelson, of Winnipeg. VII. D. 3.

NICHOLSON, Private, ALBERT HOLMSTIEN, L/154182. Princess Patricia's Canadian Light Infantry, R.C.I.C. 1st January 1944. Age 26. Son of Norman and Ninna Nicholson, of McLaren, Saskatchewan. IX. F. 2.

PARMETER, Lance Corporal, BENJAMIN HAROLD, H/16410. Princess Patricia's Canadian Light Infantry, R.C.I.C. 20th February 1944. Age 26. Son of Wally and Helen Parmeter; husband of Evelyn Parmeter. IX. C. 3.

PINKERTON, Private, LEWIS ST CLAIR, H/16278. Princess Patricia's Canadian Light Infantry, R.C.I.C. 2nd March 1945. Age 36. Son of Frederick and Alice Pinkerton, of Port Arthur, Ontario. XI. H. 7.

POTTER, Private, JOHN EDWIN, K/73960. Princess Patricia's Canadian Light Infantry, R.C.I.C. 16th March 1944. Age 24. Son of Alexander and Maude Potter, of Kitscoty, Alberta. VI. D. 7.

PRESCOTT, Private, Sydney, C/100819. Princess Patricia's Canadian Light Infantry, R.C.I.C. 13th December 1943. Age 22. Son of John Prescott, and of Elizabeth Prescott, of Beachburg, Ontario. V.C. 15.

PRIOR, Sergeant, GEORGE, H/16780. Princess Patricia's Canadian Light Infantry, R.C.I.C. 14th December 1943. Age 29. Husband of Marjorie Gwendoline Mabel Prior, of Hampden Park, Sussex, England. IX. D. 8.

RENAUD, Private, HALFDEN, H/17728. Princess Patricia's Canadian Light Infantry, R.C.I.C. 15th December 1943. Age 24. Son of Emile Joseph and Gudlang Jonina Renaud, of Riverton, Manitoba. VII. E. 9.

RUDKO, Private, HENRY, H/16124. Princess Patricia's Canadian Light Infantry, R.C.I.C. 30th January 1944. VII. H. 12.

THE ROLL OF HONOUR—WORLD WAR TWO

SAUNDERS, Private, WILLIAM GEORGE, H/17763. Princess Patricia's Canadian Light Infantry, R.C.I.C. 1st – 31st December 1943. Age 20. Son of George and v Alexandria Saunders, of St. James, Manitoba. V.C. 16.

SCOTT, Private, WILLIAM CAMPBELL, K/85420. Princess Patricia's Canadian Light Infantry, R.C.I.C. 15th December 1943. Age 22. Son of Mr. And Mrs. Thomas Scott, of Victoria, British Columbia. VII. E. 12.

SERHON, Private, DAN, H/17025. Princess Patricia's Canadian Light Infantry, R.C.I.C. 24th January 1944. Age 21. Son of Joseph and Tokla Serhon, of Rama, Saskatchewan. II. F. 13.

SHANAS, Private, BEN, H/16497. Princess Patricia's Canadian Light Infantry, R.C.I.C. 7th December 1943. Son of Isaac Jacob and Dorothy Shanas, of Winnipeg, Manitoba. IX. F. 7.

SLOAN, Private, DEMPSEY, H/16207. Princess Patricia's Canadian Light Infantry, R.C.I.C. 14th December 1943. Age 20. Son of Allan and Agnes Sloan, of Winnipeg, Manitoba. IX. D. 6.

ST DENIS, Corporal, MEREDITH, C/79325. Princess Patricia's Canadian Light Infantry, R.C.I.C. 6th December 1943. Age 26. Son of Albert and Catherine St. Denis, of West Toronto, Ontario. IX F. 4.

TALBOT, Private, JOHN, H/17133. Princess Patricia's Canadian Light Infantry, R.C.I.C. 16th October 1943. Age 21. Son of John and Annie Talbot, of St. James, Manitoba. VIII. H. 10.

TARALSON, Private, HALVOR, M/105953. Princess Patricia's Canadian Light Infantry, R.C.I.C. 15th March 1944. Age 20. Son of Halvor and Tone Taralson, of Franchere, Alberta. XI. E. 9.

THEBERGE, Private, LEON, M/106717. Princess Patricia's Canadian Light Infantry, R.C.I.C. 29th December 1943. XI. G. 4.

TREWOLLA, Private, WARREN HENRY, B/127753. Princess Patricia's Canadian Light Infantry, R.C.I.C. 17th January 1944. Age 23. Son of Francis W. and Ada L. Trewolla, of Hamilton, Ontario; grandson of Alice Trewolla, of Hamilton. VII. D. 5.

TURCOTTE, Corporal, ROBERT, K/85288. Princess Patricia's Canadian Light Infantry, R.C.I.C. 6th December 1943. X. C. 7.

TURNBULL, Private, HIGH DAVID, K/57691. Princess Patricia's Canadian Light Infantry, R.C.I.C. 29th December 1943. Age 23. Son of Robert Ernest and Muriel Hope Turnbull, of Comox, British Columbia. VI. B. 15.

WEARMOUTH, Private, ERNEST JOHN, K/50605. Princess Patricia's Canadian Light Infantry, R.C.I.C. 20th March 1944. Age 20. Son of Herbert Farrow Wearmouth and Margaret Ella Wearmouth, of Sidney, British Columbia. VIII. G. 15.

WHITTAKER, Corporal, CHARLES. H/16191. "B" Coy. Princess Patricia's Canadian Light Infantry, R.C.I.C. 18th December 1943. Age 31. Son of Harry and Lillian Maude Whittaker; husband of Helena Whittaker, of St. Paul, Minnesota, U.S.A. IX. D. 1.

NAPLES WAR CEMETERY

Commonwealth War Dead, 1939-1945
GREEN, Captain, ELMES PATRICK TREVELYAN, Princess Patricia's Canadian Light Infantry, R.C.I.C., formerly Queen's Own Rifles of Canada, R.C.I.C. 1st May 1944. Age 30. Son of Walter H. and Millicent Henderson Green, of Toronto, Ontario, Canada. II. B. 13.

PADUA WAR CEMETERY

Commonwealth War Dead, 1939-1945
McCourt, Private, JAMES HILL, L/26469. Princess Patricia's Canadian Light Infantry, R.C.I.C. 3rd February 1945. V. C. 1.

RAVENNA WAR CEMETERY

Commonwealth War Dead, 1939-1945
ALLAN, Lieutenant, VAUGHAN STUART< Princess Patricia's Canadian Light Infantry, R.C.I.C. 15th December 1944. Age 22. Son of William Alexander Vaughan Allan and Violet Stuart Allan, of Edmonton, Alberta, Canada. VI. D. 10.

ARBOUR, Sergeant, ELWIN GLEN, H/16217. Princess Patricia's Canadian Light Infantry, R.C.I.C. 20th December 1944. Age 29. Son of Harry and Elizabeth Jane Arbour. VI. D. 30.

ARCHER, Corporal, JAMES F., A/82052. Princess Patricia's Canadian Light Infantry, R.C.I.C. 3rd February 1945. VI. F. 1.

BLAIR, Private, REGINALD ROY, H/16196. Princess Patricia's Canadian Light Infantry, R.C.I.C. 20th December 1944. Age 20. Son of James Johnston Blair and Flora Blair, of Georgetown, Ontario, Canada; husband of Nancy Frederica Blair, of Lancing, Sussex. VI. D. 22.

CARLETON, Lance Corporal, GLEN IRA, L/104893. Princess Patricia's Canadian Light Infantry, R.C.I.C. 3rd February 1945. VI. F. 5.

THE ROLL OF HONOUR—WORLD WAR TWO

CHERRY, Private, WILLIAM H., H/101104. Princess Patricia's Canadian Light Infantry, R.C.I.C. 10th December 1944. Age 20. Son of William Cherry, and of Sarah Cherry, of Wellwood, Manitoba, Canada. VI. D. 12.

CLARK, Private, ROBERT G., L/104788. Princess Patricia's Canadian Light Infantry, R.C.I.C. 20th December 1944. Age 31. Son of James and Mary Clark; husband of Bertha Alice Clark, of Chelan, Saskatchewan, Canada. VI. D. 21.

CLEUNION, Private, LUCIEN JOHN, H/18177. Princess Patricia's Canadian Light Infantry, R.C.I.C. 4th January 1945. Son of Mrs. M. Cleunion, of Winnipeg, Manitoba, Canada. VI. D. 13.

CONNOLLY, Private, JOHN E., M/31473. Princess Patricia's Canadian Light Infantry, R.C.I.C. 20th December 1944. Age 21. Son of Edward William and Rubena Elizabeth Connolly, of New Westminster. British Columbia, Canada. VI. F. 10.

COX, Private, WILLIAM JAMES, A/105806. Princess Patricia's Canadian Light Infantry, R.C.I.C. 15th December 1944. Age 21. Son of James and Martha Jane Cox, of Hespeler, Ontario, Canada. VI. F. 18.

DEARLE, Private, ROBERT H., H/8810. Princess Patricia's Canadian Light Infantry, R.C.I.C. 12th February 1945. Age 21. Son of Robert H. and Charlotte May Dearle, of St. James, Manitoba, Canada. VI. D. 16.

DELL, Private, JACK STEWART, B/100086. Princess Patricia's Canadian Light Infantry, R.C.I.C. 20th December 1944. Age 25. Son of Alice Dell of Hamilton, Ontario, Canada. VI. F. 22.

FENNELL, Private, WILLIAM JAMES, K/70177. Princess Patricia's Canadian Light Infantry, R.C.I.C. 17th January 1945. VI. F. 4.

FLEMING, Lance Corporal, HAROLD JAMES, K/62230. Princess Patricia's Canadian Light Infantry, R.C.I.C. 20th December 1944. VI. F. 11.

GARRITTY, Lieutenant, MERVYN EDWARD, Princess Patricia's Canadian Light Infantry, R.C.I.C. 20th December 1944. Age 30. Son of Edward Joseph and Ellen Theresa Garritty; husband of Helen J. Garritty, of Ottawa, Ontario, Canada. VI. D. 20.

GATES, Corporal, JOHN, K/85278. Princess Patricia's Canadian Light Infantry, R.C.I.C. 22nd December 1944. VI. F. 9.

GROOMES, Lieutenant, WILLIAM ANTHONY, Princess Patricia's Canadian Light Infantry, R.C.I.C. 4th January 1945. Age 27. Son of William Stanton Groomes, and of Stella Groomes, of Vancouver, British Columbia, Canada. VI. D. 29.

THE ROLL OF HONOUR—WORLD WAR TWO

HOWARD, Sergeant, WILLIAM ROSS, M M, K/42053. Princess Patricia's Canadian Light Infantry, R.C.I.C. 4th January 1945. Age 22. Son of Ross and Mary Howard; husband of Ethel J. Howard, of Victoria, British Columbia, Canada. VI. D. 14.

JOHNSON, Private, OSCAR E., L/103914. Princess Patricia's Canadian Light Infantry, R.C.I.C. 4th January 1945. Age 22. Son of Theodore and Jenny Johnson, of Cloverdale, British Columbia, Canada. VI. D. 28.

LANDRY, Private, STANLEY JOSEPH, L/106133. Princess Patricia's Canadian Light Infantry, R.C.I.C. 15th December 1944. Age 22. Son of Darnas and Virginia Landry, of Meadow Lake, Saskatchewan, Canada. VI. D. 23.

LOREE, Private, BERNARD W., M/31560. Princess Patricia's Canadian Light Infantry, R.C.I.C. 19th December 1944. Age 22. Son of W. W. and Mary A. Loree, of Edmonton, Alberta, Canada. V.C. 18.

MAXWELL, Private, SHIRLY ROY, M/12008. Princess Patricia's Canadian Light Infantry, R.C.I.C. 3rd February 1945. Age 27. Son of Roy W. and Ruby M. Maxwell, of Claresholme, Alberta, Canada. VI. D. 27.

MUSQUASH, Private, PETER, H/70619. Princess Patricia's Canadian Light Infantry, R.C.I.C. 12th January 1945. Age 25. Son of Ambrose and Charlotte Musquash, of Nipigon, Ontario, Canada; husband of Frances Musquash, of Nipigon. VI. F. 3.

NORTH, Private, JEAN ANDRE, K/1758. Princess Patricia's Canadian Light Infantry, R.C.I.C. 3rd February 1945. Age 31. Son of Amelie Marie North; husband of Anne Teresa Marilyn North, of Vancouver, British Columbia, Canada. VI. D. 26.

PAVELICK, Private, ANTHONY, B/103190. Princess Patricia's Canadian Light Infantry, R.C.I.C. 3rd February 1945. Age 31. Son of Roko and Mara A. Pavelick, of Henaston, Saskatchewan, Canada. VI. D. 25.

PEARCE, Private, ROY FRANK, A/115074. Princess Patricia's Canadian Light Infantry, R.C.I.C. 23rd February 1945. Age 27. Son of Charles Bond Pearce and Gladys Elizabeth Pearce, of Stratford, Ontario, Canada; husband of Berenice Elizabeth Pearce, of Stratford. VI. F. 8.

PENNER, Private, FRANK, L/103004. Princess Patricia's Canadian Light Infantry, R.C.I.C. 15th December 1944. Age 22. Son of David and Helen Penner, of Wymark, Saskatchewan, Canada. VI. D. 24.

PRINCE, Private, HERBERT, K/65257. Princess Patricia's Canadian Light Infantry, R.C.I.C. 3rd February 1945. VI. D. 18.

REBBECK, Private, ALFRED J., L/104524. Princess Patricia's Canadian Light Infantry, R.C.I.C. 21st September 1944. Age 29. Son of Ernest Henry and Elizabeth Rebbeck, of South Fork, Saskatchewan, Canada. VI. A. 16.

SOWBERRY, Private, JOSEPH M., H/204123. Princess Patricia's Canadian Light Infantry, R.C.I.C. 20th December 1944. Age 23. Son of Joseph and Agatha Sowerby, of Winnipeg, Manitoba, Canada; husband of Laura Mary Gabrielle Sowerby, of Winnipeg. VI. D. 11.

STEFANSON, Private, GISLI SIGURDUR, H/9155. Princess Patricia's Canadian Light Infantry, R.C.I.C. 23rd February 1945. Age 34. Son of Stefan Gul Stefanson and Rannveig Stefanson, of Selkirk, Manitoba, Canada. VI. F. 7.

STINSON, Private, JOHN GORDON WISHART, K/63206. Princess Patricia's Canadian Light Infantry, R.C.I.C. 12th January 1945. Age 20. Son of Hugh H. and Effie I. Stinson, of New Westminster, British Columbia, Canada. VI. F. 2.

TARNAUSKY, Private, JOHN JOESPH, H/10044. Princess Patricia's Canadian Light Infantry, R.C.I.C. 16th December 1944. VI. F. 20.

WALLER, Sergeant, MAURICE FETHERSTON, K/85268. Princess Patricia's Canadian Light Infantry, R.C.I.C. 16th December 1944. Age 26. Son of Jessie Waller, of Victoria, British Columbia, Canada. VI. F. 19.

WIEBE, Private, PETER DONALD, H/3582. Princess Patricia's Canadian Light Infantry, R.C.I.C. 20th December 1944. Age 31. Son of Mr. And Mrs. John Wiebe; husband of Irene Wiebe, of St. Boniface, Manitoba, Canada. VI. F. 21.

WRIGHT, Private, RONALD HARRY, L/103143. Princess Patricia's Canadian Light Infantry, R.C.I.C. 20th December 1944. Age 27. Son of Harry and Jane Wright, of New Westminster, British Columbia, Canada. VI. F. 12.

ZENTNER, Private, WILLIAM JOHN, L/101208. Princess Patricia's Canadian Light Infantry, R.C.I.C. 8th February 1945. Age 27. Son of John and Margaret Zentner, of Langenburg, Saskatchewan, Canada. VI. D. 17.

CASUALTY LISTING REPORT FOR P.P.C.L.I.—NETHERLANDS—WORLD WAR II

NETHERLANDS

BLOEMENDAAL (ST. ADELBERTUS) ROMAN CATHOLIC CHURCH—Noord-Holland

Commonwealth War Dead, 1939-1945
DONOHUE, Private, ALEX JOSEPH, F/4007. Princess Patricia's Canadian Light Infantry, R.C.I.C. 11th May 1945. Grave 17.

HOLTEN CANADIAN WAR CEMETERY—Overijssel

Commonwealth War Dead, 1939-1945
BROWN, Private, EDWARD HECTOR, H/60603. Princess Patricia's Canadian Light Infantry, R.C.I.C. 22nd April 1945. Age 22. Son of William E. and Alice M. Brown, of Petersfield, Manitoba. II. C. 9.

GOSSELIN, Private, ROMEO, H/2691. Princess Patricia's Canadian Light Infantry, R.C.I.C. 12th April 1945. Age 24. Son of Philippe and Cora Gosselin, of Winnipeg, Manitoba. II. C. 11.

GRAHAM, Private, JOHN JAMES, L/107406. Princess Patricia's Canadian Light Infantry, R.C.I.C. 15th July 1945. Age 31. Son of James and Sarah Ann Graham, of Leroy, Saskatchewan; husband of Gwendolyne Graham, of Leroy, X. F. 11.

HUDSON, Private, MITCHELL, H/204125. Princess Patricia's Canadian Light Infantry, R.C.I.C. 22nd April 1945. I.D. 10.

ILASEVICH, Corporal, HARRY, H/17855. Princess Patricia's Canadian Light Infantry, R.C.I.C. 12th April 1945. Age 21. Son of Michael Ilasevich, and of Lena Ilasevich, of Sadlow, Manitoba. III. A. 6.

PURVIS, Private, JACK WILLIAM, H/18598. Princess Patricia's Canadian Light Infantry, R.C.I.C. 11th April 1945. Age 19. Son of Louise C. Purvis, of St. James, Manitoba. II. H. 12.

SLYZUK, Private, JOHN, H/204139. Princess Patricia's Canadian Light Infantry, R.C.I.C. 11th April 1945. Age 30. Son of Nicholas and Pearl Slyzuk, of Ashville, Manitoba. I. D. 8.

WRIGHT, Sergeant, JAMES DUNCAN, H/16782. Princess Patricia's Canadian Light Infantry, R.C.I.C. 15th June 1945. X. F. 1.

INDEX

A

Achterveld 250-253, 255-258, 266, 273, 281-282, 297, 302, 308-309, 315, 320, 329, 336, 338-339, 348, 358, 360, 366, 370-374, 376, 378-381, 383, 391, 419, 427-429
Agosta, Gaetano, Enza, Sam, Eleonora 69, 86
Alberona 156, 207
Alexander, Field Marshal Harold 174, 182, 207
Allan, Lt. V. S. (Vaughan) 180
Amalfi Drive 141, 142, 206
Amore, Giombattista, Dr. 61, 63, 74, 76, 78-80, 86, 106
Amsterdam 252, 256, 258, 259, 263, 264, 268, 350, 387
Ancona 133-134, 137, 209, 211
Anderson, Sgt. Andy 351, 358, 382
Andrunyk, Col. Steve 450
Apeldoorn 239-242, 244, 246-248, 254-256, 258-259, 266, 272-274, 276, 278-279, 285-288, 290, 293, 295-330, 332-334, 336-337, 339-343, 346-347, 350-352, 354-355, 357-359, 362, 364, 366-367, 370, 380-381, 383, 385-386, 395, 402, 412, 414-417, 434, 436-437
Aprile, Dr. Michelangelo 76, 78, 79, 106
Aquino 145, 151, 205
Armstrong, Lt. Doug and Pauline 357, 367, 370, 372, 382
Arno River 167, 211
Aspromonte Range 154, 207
Associazione Centro d'Incontro Anziani 14, 37, 39-40, 44, 47, 49, 52, 56, 60, 61, 66, 74, 91, 104, 107, 110
Athens 479-480
Ausa River 134, 210
Avellino 141-142, 180, 206
Avveduto, Giovanni, Carmela 71, 72, 85

B

Baak 233
Baalbek 460, 461
Baker, George 88-91, 337, 346, 381
Bakker, Wilhelm 305, 404
Barneveld 244, 250, 253, 255, 257-258, 260, 263-266, 281, 302, 336, 380
Basingstoke Plastic Surgery Hospital 187
Beamish, Capt. L.G. 120
Beaumont Hamel 151
Beardmore, Lt. Harvey 236-239, 249
Beekbergen 249, 253, 302-304, 308-309, 312-313, 317-320, 330, 339, 346, 353-355, 367, 386, 395, 418, 424
Beirut 461, 463, 464
Bellisario, Mayor Quinto 14, 31
Berchtesgaden 268, 270, 271
Berg en Dal 289
Bernier, André 406-410
Biferno River 159-160
Bilthoven 260
Blaskowitz, General 251-252
Bloemendaal 258-259, 261, 280, 404, 410
Bloemendaal Church 280
Blom, Harmen 329, 332, 360
Boesveld, P. 394-398
Bogert, MGen Pat 41, 44, 63
Boisschot 232-233
Bologna 177, 182, 203
Bolton, Lt. Bert 237, 244, 245, 246, 247, 281, 289, 294, 327
Boot, Jean 261, 369, 370
Brain, Maj. Don 155, 165, 166
Brown, Capt. G. (George) 181, 450
Buckstein, Murray E. 324
Buffaloes 234-235, 242-243, 356, 368, 421
Burgers, Gerard 278, 285, 363
Burton, Capt. L. G. 135

INDEX

Bussloo 244, 249, 253, 277, 292
Busso 161, 164

C
Caissie, Peter 14, 17, 23, 25, 48, 54, 60, 63, 273, 299
Campbell, Dr. Hoyle 187
Campobasso 134, 150, 153, 156, 158, 161, 163, 207
Canadian Club 241, 278-279, 288, 290-291, 293-294, 299, 350-352, 354, 363, 370, 387
Cannonshot (code name) 234, 390, 395, 398
Cape Passero 23
Carey, Lt. Rex M.C. 133
Carter, Sgt. Robert 158
Casa Berardi 164
Cassino 141-144, 146-147, 158, 163, 205, 211, 226
Castello di Lagopesole 155, 169, 172, 207, 217
Catania 4, 9, 12, 18, 21, 26, 40, 42-43, 63, 79, 101, 103, 153, 161
Catanzaro 154, 155
Cattolica 134, 137, 166, 180, 193, 197, 210
Cava d'Ispica 24, 78, 79, 80, 106, 113
Cavanagh MWO, 468
Cemeteries
  Agira 10-12, 18-19, 21-22, 36, 42, 74, 121-122
  Ancona 51, 73, 133, 135, 138, 209, 211
  Argenta Gap 201-202
  Cassino 152, 153, 205, 226, 227
  Cesena 51, 201
  Coriano Ridge 51, 134, 135, 137, 229, 230
  Florence 51, 211
  Gradara 51, 134, 137, 228
  Groesbeek 288, 298, 300, 308, 366, 430
  Holten 279, 280, 281, 292, 308, 359, 360, 375, 376, 395, 401, 431

Montecchio 51, 134, 137
Moro River 50, 166, 207, 228
Ravenna 201
Centoscale 28, 79, 106-109, 113
Central Militia Area 448
Centro di Cultura Popolare 14, 31, 37, 44, 48, 54, 56, 71-72, 74, 78, 109
Centro Geriatrico 76-77
Cercemaggiore 156, 207
Cesena 201
Cesenatico 180
Chadderton, Cliff 64, 281, 350
Chambers, Capt. Egan 185, 236
Chapman, Jean-Guy 350, 366, 383, 413, 417, 439
Charter of Thanks 259
Chastelain, Gen. John de 387
CHIN 14, 28, 30
Chuckle (Operation) 177, 270
Cittanova 154
Claessen, Sef 310, 313, 335, 337, 341, 343, 345, 364-365, 384
Clark, Lt. Knobby 165
Clark, LCol. R. P. "Slug" 134, 175-177, 198, 213, 233, 249, 261
Clark, Gen. Mark 140
Clarke, John 41, 48, 124
Cleve 233
Coleman, BGen. Rowan 5, 185
Commonwealth War Graves Commission 4, 12, 19, 20, 22, 42
Corkett, Capt. George 135, 150, 230
Corleone 84, 113
Corriere Canadese 14, 28-31, 112, 116
Countess Mountbatten of Burma 133
Crabtree, Lt. J.C. 152
Crofton, LCol. P. D. 134, 165, 187

D
Dachau 268-270
Dare, MGen Mike 450
Decorata 156, 161, 185, 207
Dennison, Mayor Bill 450, 453, 454, 468, 470

534

INDEX

Derkse - Den Boer, Ati 336, 356
Deutsch, Rudy 281, 283, 294, 358, 367, 372, 382, 383
De Vecht Antonius Church 360, 362
Dieren 249
Dirksen - Boot, Dieneke 369, 370, 380
Dutch Liberation Committee 241

E

Eagle's Nest (The) 270-271
Eaton, Hon. Capt. Ken 134
Eggleton, Art, Min. of Defence 367
Elba, Isola d' 167
Embree, Capt. Don 285
Epp, Reg 58

F

Fairclough, LCol. Peter 448, 449, 451, 464
Fairfield, Maj. G. D. 251
Falconi, Maj. Gino 324, 325
Fazzino, Biaggio 157-158
Festino, Mazzotti and Paolina 139, 140
Festung Europa 13, 23
First Canadian Corps 142, 184, 232, 368, 407-408
First Division 164, 232, 275, 320, 368, 374, 388
Fisher, Alfred 288
Fiumicino 168, 174
Florence 140, 143, 167, 199, 203, 205, 211, 212
Foggia 156
Foglia River 134
Fosso Munio 141, 180, 182
Foulkes, LGen. Charles 251, 252, 407
Fredrickson, Capt. Kurt 41, 48, 124
Frezenberg 7-8
Frosinone 163, 205
Frosolone 134, 150, 158, 160, 162-164, 207
Frost, Sr. Maj. C.S. 151
Frost, Maj. R.J. 151

G

Gardam, Col. John 301
Gardham, Bob 351, 366
Gault, Colonel Hammie 4, 43, 83, 104
Gennaro, Frank and family 14, 27, 32-33, 36, 55
George, LCol. Mike 67, 266
Georgians *see* Texel
Gerritsen, Evert 255, 266, 272, 274, 279, 293, 295-296, 298, 302-304, 309, 313, 328-330, 332, 334-337, 354, 360, 366, 370, 386
Gietelo 249, 253
Gignac, Jacques, 289, 436
Gijsbers, General Andrew 274, 279, 285-286, 290, 295, 299-300, 309-311, 313, 322, 335, 337, 340-343, 346, 351, 356, 359, 365, 367-368, 370, 383-384, 412-414, 435, 439
Goldflake (Operation) 232, 368
Goodburn, Sgt. W. 191-192, 194-195, 197, 202
Gorssel 233, 243-244, 276-277, 285, 316, 421, 441
Gothic Line 134-137, 173, 199, 207, 209-210
Graaf, Fred de 336, 341, 342, 344, 357, 358, 359, 367, 370, 385
Gradanti-Fronte family 35, 44, 48
Graham, BGen. Stuart 187
Granarolo 183-184
Granatstein, Jack 55, 413
Grand Hotel 133, 140, 166, 172, 225
Grant, Col. Gord 306
Groomes, Lt. W.A. 183, 201
Gugliotta, Mayor (Doctor) Rosario 89-91, 95, 97, 102, 104, 105, 107, 109, 110, 112, 113
Guingand, MGen. Freddy de 251

H

Haarlem 317, 346, 347
Ham, Gerrit 303-305, 309, 312, 319, 321, 329-331, 339-340, 346, 353, 355, 418

535

INDEX

Hamer, Dr. de Witt 259
Hamer, Mimi 260
Hanberry, LSgt. 236
Hannivort, Dr. Henk 242-244, 246-248, 255, 334, 363, 415
Harrington, Lt. W. E. 181, 327
Harskamp 250
Hassink, Gerard 336, 356
Hayes, Jim 56, 57
Hees, George 259, 262, 385
Hellyer, Paul 458
Heppell, Lt. J.R. 152
Het Loo Palace 285, 288, 342
Hewson, MGen. Bill 92-98, 101, 109, 387
Hitler Adolf 142, 268, 270, 271
Hitler Line 136, 141-144, 146, 150-152, 158, 167, 185, 190, 203, 205, 207
Hoedeman, Mark 375-378
Horn, Lt. d'Arcy 22
Horton, Lt. J. H. 183
Hotel Bloemink 356
Hotel Keizerskroon 274, 291, 302, 337, 346, 350, 354, 359
Hotel Progresso 208-209
Hotel Sydney 209
Howard, MGen. Bill 450
Hubers, Ton 266, 272, 279, 286, 291, 295-296
Huestis, Lt. R.S. (Bob) 181
Huisman, Klaas 255, 274, 279, 308-309, 311, 313, 332, 341-343, 358, 370, 371
Hunt, Capt. J.B. 165
Hutchins, Muriel 192, 195
Hutchinson, LCol. W.E. J. (Bill) 453, 456, 457, 458, 459, 462, 466, 467, 468, 471

I

Iabichella, Friar Pietro 45, 110
Ijssel River 214, 233-234, 239-243, 248-250, 252-254, 257-258, 266-267, 273, 276, 280, 283-285, 292-293, 297, 302, 306, 316, 318, 332, 336, 356, 361-362, 368, 371, 378, 390, 394, 398, 402, 418-419, 421-423, 440
Ispica 1, 5, 6, 14, 18, 23-25, 28, 31, 33, 35-41, 44-48, 51, 52, 55, 56, 59, 60, 63, 64, 67, 69, 74, 75-78, 95, 104-109, 113, 114, 116, 117

J

Jessi 180
Johan Willem Friso Kapel 310, 348, 364, 371

K

"Keep Them Rolling" 286, 288, 339, 353, 366
Kesselring, Field Marshal 136, 142, 165
Kinsman, Jeremy 88-91
Kitching, MGen. George 288
Klarenbeek 249, 303
Kohl, Dr. Helmut 253
Koorenhof, Jan 240, 254, 279, 298-299, 305, 309, 314, 330, 340-341, 346, 351, 370, 387, 413, 415, 439
Kroon, Consul General 342

L

La Rocca 152, 157-159, 207
Labree, C. W. 263-265, 281
Lady Nelson 186
Lamone River 140, 166, 177-179, 190, 200, 222-223
Lauretta, Antonino 14, 31, 37, 44, 48, 54, 71-74, 78, 109, 205
Leavey, Maj. 306
Lebanon 459, 461, 462
Ledra Palace Hotel 457, 458, 469
Leese, General Sir Oliver 135
Legge, BGen. Bruce 448, 452
Leghorn. *See* Livorno

Legion Magazine 192, 301, 336, 338
Leonforte 5
Leusden 379
Lieren 249, 253, 302-304, 308-309, 312, 318, 320, 339, 353, 355, 418-419, 424, 426
Liri Valley 136, 142-143, 146, 152, 164, 190, 207
Livorno 214-215
Lombardi, Johnny 14, 28, 30-31, 62, 71
Lucca 212-213
Lugo 202-203

M

MacAulay, Lawrence 60, 98
Machine Gun Platoon 173-174, 176, 178, 191
MacKenzie, MGen. Lewis 189, 472
MacKenzie, LCol. D.A. 243
MacNeil, Lt. J.W. 135
Malta Conference 231
Maniscola 14, 30-31
Marani, Capt. Peter 459, 460, 467, 469, 475
Marecchia River 134-135, 137-139, 173, 210, 221
Marza 1, 29, 38, 44-49, 61, 63, 90-91, 105, 110, 111
Maucieri, Carmela 14, 39-40, 44-45, 47, 61
McAndrew, Dr. Bill 11, 23
McComber, Major 318, 320-321
McCowan, Norm 60, 64, 65
McCreery, LGen. 176
McDougall, Maj. Colin 143, 164, 185
McKinnon, Lt. A. B. 183, 184, 235, 239
McNeil, LCol. Jock 56-58
Mercedes-Benz 154, 156, 169, 172-173, 179, 203, 210-211, 253, 256
Merrithew, Honourable Gerald 11-21, 31-33, 35-37, 42, 44-45, 47-48, 51-54, 98, 273, 280, 286, 289, 432
Messerschmidt, MGen. 352, 363

Metauro River 134, 173, 210
Milko, C.S.M. 235
Mines 161, 216
Mobile Command 448
Modica 23, 45, 63, 79, 90, 92, 118
Mol, Marten 341-343
Monaca, Francesco 24, 61
Monaco, Mayor Giuseppe 14, 24-25, 27-28, 31, 61
Montone River 140, 166, 177-178, 182
Mooney, Lt. F. E. 406
Moore, Cpl. John 65, 244, 245, 246, 281, 289, 294, 327
Moro River 164, 166, 186, 207, 228
Mount Etna 4, 5, 21, 43, 82, 84, 103, 104, 113, 121
Mount Seggio 5, 21-22, 82
Mount Vesuvio 205
Mowat, Farley 188
Mulherin, LCol. Willie 187
Munro, Lt. Don 88, 93
Murdy, Pte. Mel 185, 195-199
Murray, Vice-Admiral Larry 88, 94-99, 350

N

Napoleon 167, 212, 271
Naviglio Canal 141, 166, 180-184, 190, 223
Neal, Col. Allan 449, 452, 453
Nederlandse Courant 404, 406
Nicholson, LCol. G.W.L. 135, 164, 252
Nicholson, Lt. G.D.M. 182
Nicosia 456, 459, 462, 467
Nigro, Carmelo and family 14, 27-28, 32-40, 44-47, 49-50, 54-56, 60-63, 66, 69-70, 74-77, 79-80, 86-89, 90-102, 104-112, 114-117, 123, 179, 203, 207, 209, 214, 350
Noordwijk 259-260
Noordwijkerhout 259
Nordenbus, Lex 351, 387
Nuremberg 268

INDEX

O

Oosterhuizen 249, 253, 302-304, 308-309, 311-313, 316-320, 328-329, 339, 353, 355, 418-419, 424-425
Oriano, Emanuele 116
Orontes 461
Ortona 136, 164-166, 190, 207
Orvieto 203
Osteria Nuova 134
Overveen 259, 261-262, 444

P

Pachino 1, 12, 14, 17, 18, 22, 30, 33, 34, 35, 36, 37, 39, 44, 45, 46, 47, 48, 51, 52, 54, 55, 56, 60, 64, 67, 69, 74, 95, 113, 114, 117, 118, 122
Pagtakhan, Dr. Rey 412
Palazzo San Giacomo 178-179, 190, 200, 222-223
Patrician (The) 406-407
Perugia 180, 199
Petelle, André 14, 32, 36, 48, 54, 59-60, 63-64, 273, 299
Piat bomb 238
Pisa 200, 204, 211-214, 233, 368
PMR 60, 64, 344-346, 351, 360, 366, 413
Pompei 205
Ponte di Tiberio 140
Ponte Vecchio 167, 211, 212
Pontesieve 199
Potenza 154-155, 169-172, 203, 207
Pieve Sestina 175
Potts, Maj. R. W. (Sam) 181, 187, 446
PPCLI Re-Enactment Group 374-379
Pragnell, Lt. Herb 325
Prince Bernhard 240, 251-252, 256
Prince Floris 367
Princess Margriet 259, 286, 288-289, 293, 305, 346, 352, 355, 359, 366-368, 383-385, 412, 414, 436, 438-439

Project Roots 316
Puglisi, Salvatore 91-92

Q

Queen Beatrix 353
Queen Juliana 353
Queen Wilhelmina 251, 413

R

Rains, Lloyd V. 309, 316-317, 320-321, 355, 367, 372, 375, 377, 382
Rains, Olga 304, 309, 316-317, 320, 323, 328, 355, 361, 367, 377, 419
Ravenna 180, 201-202
Reggio di Calabria 141, 154-155, 158, 169, 206
Regiments
    Seaforth Highlanders of Canada 175, 181, 234, 371, 383
    Loyal Edmonton Regiment 175, 181, 185, 249
    The Royal Canadian Regiment 165, 166, 178, 248, 322
    The Hastings and Prince Edward Regiment 178
    48th Highlanders of Canada 239-241, 243-244, 248, 253-254, 257-258, 266, 275, 277, 306, 309-310, 312, 321-322, 324, 339, 355, 364, 387, 394-395
    Royal 22nd Regiment 164, 475, 483, 484, 485
    Princess Louise Dragoon Guards 54-58
    The Royal Regiment of Canada 307, 312, 324, 326, 446-471, 473, 481, 482
    The Royal Newfoundland Regiment 152, 233
Reichwald Forest 233
Reid, James M. 8, 86, 88-91, 93-94, 230
Reitsma, LCol. Ritse R. 245-247, 254, 293, 296-297, 331-332, 338, 350, 352, 360, 363, 383, 423, 432
Richards, Dr. Jerry 185
Riccione 176, 177, 178

INDEX

Rimini 50-51, 73, 133, 138-140, 166, 168-169, 172-173, 193, 204, 207, 209-210, 225
Roach, Lt. W. D. L. (Bill) 181, 182, 185, 277
Robinson, Capt. A.G. 175, 185
Robbins, LCol. Alf 451
Robbins, Capt. E.J. 464, 468
Romagna 140, 141, 153, 166, 168, 169, 173, 182, 190, 191, 198, 200, 204, 207
Rome 136, 140-143, 152-154, 163, 165, 167-168, 171-173, 203, 205, 207, 211
Royal Canadian Military Institute 56, 65, 66, 324
Royal Military College 63, 81
Russi 191

S

Salerno 141, 170, 172, 203, 206
Salvatore, Ferlisi 14, 61, 62, 74, 76, 78
San Benedetto 199, 204, 207-209
San Elena 160, 163
San Fortunato 134-138, 140, 150-151, 162, 165, 173, 190, 210, 218
San Marino 204, 209-211, 226, 271
Sassenheim 260, 261, 262, 342, 380
Savio River 174-176, 178, 201, 221
Scholten, J. 351
Schouten, Jan 256-257, 266, 273, 281, 282, 297-298, 309, 315, 336, 338-339, 348, 371, 374, 379-380, 383
Schuit, Thom and Wil 354
Scifo, Enzo and Rosy 45
Scott, Drum Maj. Ron 468
Sealy, Joe 299-300, 334, 341, 343
Sebastiano, Mayor Lupo 14, 44, 54, 74, 117
Semprini, Gabriele and Renzi 137-138
Senio 141, 166, 169, 177, 183-184, 190-191, 193, 199-203, 207-208, 213, 224-225, 232, 234, 368
Seyss-Inquart 250-251, 256, 371

Shannon, Henry 324-325
Shea, Lt. Cecil 152, 158
Simpson, Jim 146, 150
Simpson, R. 18-19, 21-22
Sint Ceacilia and de Rietzangers choirs 379, 380
Smith, Pte. W.C. (Wally) 277, 294, 327, 358, 367, 372, 382
Smith, Pte. E.A. (Smoky) 41, 44, 49, 63, 123, 175, 176
Smith, LGen. Bedell 251
Sorrento 141-142, 180, 206
Spataro, Sebastian and family 14, 36, 54-56, 69, 86, 88, 101, 109, 110, 117
Spinete 159-162
Spreeuw, Maj. Rob 352, 355, 367
Stacey, C.P. 252, 390
Stevens, LCol. G.R. 144, 145, 164, 252
Stevens, CQMS J.F. 22
Stewart, Pipe Major Ross 309, 312-313, 321-325, 336, 355
Strait of Messina 141, 154, 169, 193, 206
Stress 188-190
Stromboli 83, 84, 113
Sugar Beach (code name) 23
Sykes, Pte. 239

T

Taormina 4, 5, 18, 22, 23, 25, 38, 43, 50, 57, 60, 61, 62, 73, 74, 75, 79, 81, 82, 101, 102, 103, 104, 108, 113
Teatro Greco-Romano 113
Termoli 164, 207
Texel 305-306, 404-411
Teuge, Airport 278, 362, 363
The Man With Two Hats (Apeldoorn) 347, 358, 412
The Man with Two Hats (Ottawa) 412-416
Thomas, Tom 333, 336, 337, 341, 342
Tomasi, Mayor Dr. Carmelo 14, 44, 60-61

INDEX

Tortorici, General 110
Triquet, Capt. Paul 164-165
Turcott, LGen. 452
Tweedsmuir, Lord 406, 407, 408, 410, 411

U

United States Naval Air Facility 39, 48, 64, 111

V

Valguarnera 119
van Blokland, Pieter Beelaerts 242, 248, 255, 266, 273-275, 291, 295-296, 299, 306, 309, 314, 321-322, 336, 358-359, 370, 412, 434-435
van Blommestein, Dr. Johannes 244, 249, 253-254, 267, 272, 276-277, 283-285, 289, 292-293, 296, 299, 302, 309, 314, 343, 352, 361-363, 370, 378, 423, 432
van der Zanden 260
van Notten, Jim 276, 285, 441
van Sabben, Huub 390-394, 398-403
van Vollenhoven, Pieter 288-289, 367-368, 414, 438-439
van Willigenburg, Hans 357
VE Day 252, 258, 305, 308
Veldhuizen 257-258, 260, 263-264, 336, 358, 380
Venice 7
Verharen, LCol. John 352, 355, 367
Vet, Dr. C.J.G.M. 379
Via Emilia 139, 174
Vienna 269
Villa Rogatti 150, 164-166, 207
Villanova 201-202
Vincenzo, Capt. Piccitto 90, 104, 105
Vino Ridge 164, 165, 166, 207
Vokes, MGen. Chris 164

Voorst , Municipality of 242-246, 248-249, 253-254, 267, 272-273, 276-277, 283-285, 290, 292-293, 296, 302, 308, 314-315, 331, 343, 350, 352, 360-363, 378, 390-391, 398-399, 432, 436

W

Wageningen 252, 273, 339, 415
Walpole, Horace 82
Wannop, Sister Eva 187-188
Ware, MGen. Cammie 65, 143-144, 146, 160, 165-166, 187, 197, 451, 466, 469, 471
Watson, Maj. W. DeN (Bucko) 144, 145, 146, 165, 187
Williams, LCol. Jeff 163, 207
Wilp 234, 236, 239-248, 253-254, 257, 266-267, 275-277, 283-285, 292-293, 302, 315, 318, 323, 331, 336, 338, 352, 356, 361, 378, 390, 395, 399, 423
Worobetz, Capt. Steve 180, 184, 190
Wynston, Ada 347, 348, 413, 417

Z

Zandvoort 260, 445
Zuehlke, Mark 137, 143, 164

540

ABOUT THE AUTHOR

Charles Sydney Frost attended the Royal Military College of Canada. Upon graduation in 1942 he was commissioned into the PPCLI and served with the regiment in Europe. By 1945 he was acting second-in-command of the battalion. He was twice wounded in action.

After the war he entered Osgoode Hall Law School, then, following graduation in 1949, he practised law in Toronto. He was appointed Queen's Counsel in 1960.

His military service continued in the Royal Regiment of Canada which he commanded from 1959 to 1962. He subsequently served as Honorary Lieutenant Colonel and Honorary Colonel for 15 years.

He served as president of the RMC Club of Canada for the year 1971-1972. He was also a member of the Canadian Military Colleges Advisory Board to the Minister of National Defence, 1975-1978, and was Chairman of the Sub-Committee responsible for RMC affairs. He received an honorary Doctorate of Laws from RMC in 1976.

Colonel Frost was awarded the Canadian Forces decoration and two bars, the Canadian Silver Jubilee Medal, 1977, and the Commemorative Medal for 125th Anniversary of Canadian Confederation, 1992. Since 1978 he has been a member of the Senate of the PPCLI.

Author
Once a Patricia, 1988
A Life Worthwhile, 1994

Quebec, Canada
2004